beginning
with C

beginning
with C

Ron House

I(T)P Thomas Nelson Australia is an International Thomson Publishing company

First published in Australia in 1994 by Thomas Nelson Australia.Simultaneously published by
PWS Publishing Company, a Division of Wadsworth, Inc
20 Park Plaza, Boston, Massachusetts 02116-4324

10 9 8 7 6 5 4 3 2
99 98 97 96 95 94
Copyright © Ron House 1994

National Library of Australia
Cataloguing -in- Publication data:

House, Ron.
   Beginning with C: an introduction to professional
   programming.
   Bibliography.
   Includes index.
   ISBN 0 17 008821 9.

   1. C (Computer program language). I. Title.
005.133

Library of Congress
Cataloguing-in-Publication data:

House, Ron (Ronald)
   Beginning with C; an introduction to professional programming
   by Ron House.
       p.   cm.
   Includes index.
   ISBN 0-534-94122-2

   1. C (Computer program language) 1. Title
QA76.73.C15H68 1993
005.13'3--dc20

Designed by Cristina Neri
Cover design by Grant Slaney, The Modern Art Production Group
Printed by McPherson's Printing Group

Nelson Australia Pty Limited ACN 004 603 454 (incorporated in Victoria) trading as Thomas Nelson Australia.

The I(T)P trademark is used under licence.

Within the publishing process Thomas Nelson Australia uses resources, technology and suppliers that are as environmentally friendly as possible.

Preface

To the Student

Welcome to the world of programming. If you have used a computer for any purpose, such as word processing or even games, but have never programmed one before, then this book is for you. Its aim is to explain as clearly and simply as possible what computer programming is and how to do it well. The C language is used, as C has become one of the most widely used computer languages in the world.

Why should you use this book? As studying a book is a big investment of time, I owe you an answer to that question at the outset.

In the first place I have adopted a presentation which is geared to the problems that I have seen troubling most beginners. Next, the accuracy of the material has been checked thoroughly. Every single program, every single line and statement of C code has been compiled and run under compilers conforming to the C standard adopted by ANSI (American National Standards Institute) and ISO (International Standards Organisation). (The ANSI and ISO standards are identical in substance.) In my investigations while writing, I was surprised to find that many authors apparently do not take this simple precaution against publishing incorrect information. Also, the ISO/ANSI C standard was consulted extensively at all stages during the preparation of the text in order that the information presented should be as accurate as possible.

Many readers will later wish to study object-oriented programming using the C++ language, so this text teaches C in a way that is **completely compatible with C++**. All program listings have been compiled and run using a C++ compiler. You can therefore use a C++ compiler while studying C with this text.

You may also be sure that the text is designed to help you develop professional programming skills rather than merely learn the rules of the C programming language. There are many issues of importance in advanced computing studies which are beyond the scope of this book, such as program verification and object-oriented programming. Nevertheless, the approach here was planned so that, when you do move on, you will have had a sound preparation for your study of advanced material. In other words, you should not have to unlearn material later on. In this regard, there is just one caveat: the primary purpose of this book is to help you develop good programming skills; it is *not* intended to turn you into a C Guru (that is, a person who knows every minute detail of the C language). Therefore, in many places during the presentation, I have skipped over or simplified various complications in C that do not relate to fundamental programming skills. To become a C or C++ expert, you will need to do further study after finishing this text.

Lastly, I have tried to make your learning as convenient and pleasant as possible. New technical terms are mentioned first in *italics*, and a glossary of terms is provided.

Descriptions of nearly all of the C library functions are included. A selection of questions accompany each chapter, with answers to those in the Self-test Exercises included in Appendix A, so that you can study either on your own or with an instructor. But in the end, no matter what an author may think, the judgement that matters is the reader's. I hope your judgement will be that you are glad you used this book. Best wishes in your studies.

To the Instructor

This text is intended, first and foremost, to give insights and teach skills relevant to sound professional programming. The C language is the vehicle for teaching these skills. This means two things: first, the book is not an exhaustive treatise on the C language: many low-level or complex aspects of C are simplified or omitted. Second, this book is not laid out like a C language manual; rather, the arrangement is according to important programming concepts. Thus it may be that a single language feature is addressed in several places, or that a certain concept relates to more than one language feature. For example, the chapter on looping focuses on the looping concept and its two main variants, pretest and posttest loops, some common looping styles, and (optionally) loop correctness verification. The C looping statements are discussed in this context. Other language features, such as comparison operators and macros, are also introduced with a focus on their relationship to looping.

While I believe this presentation provides an excellent learning path, it requires backup for situations where a student needs to check up on a specific language feature. Accordingly, the Appendices provide extensive indexing, both alphabetically and by language feature. Also, syntax rules and library function descriptions are supplied.

There has been considerable discussion about whether C is a suitable language for beginners. I too agonised over the issue when my university chose C for its first-year classes. However, while teaching beginning students and planning and writing this book, I became convinced that not only is C suitable, it is actually one of the most suitable languages. Let me explain.

I have noticed that many students learn programming by a process of "pattern matching". That is, they write programs by imitating similar programs found in books or written by the instructor, rather than by understanding what is going on. Languages that hide the tricky bits, such as Pascal, allow students to progress quite far by slavishly replicating without understanding. In C, one must properly understand concepts in order to write significant programs. This is C's biggest advantage! A conceptual misunderstanding cannot go unnoticed as it gives rise quite soon to faulty programs, allowing the instructor to rectify the student's problem.

I have adopted a strategy throughout of giving advance information that the student does not need to apply at that particular time. Thus Chapter 3 introduces addresses (pointers), but all the students are asked to practice is writing simple programs with assignments, printf, etc. By the time the students are asked to deal fully with pointers, they will have had many opportunities to see them in action and grow familiar with them.

The usual techniques such as top-down programming are, of course, covered, but there are many advanced topics which beginners do not have the grounding to fully appreciate, or which go beyond the scope of a first course. These include abstract data types and object-oriented programming, program correctness proofs, and advanced system and program design skills. Throughout I have tried to incorporate simplified advice and examples based on these advanced methods. I hope that students will thereby be prepared to engage in further study much faster and less painfully than if these ideas were to be introduced in their full complexity without prior preparation. However, this does mean that to prevent information overload, various subtleties are overlooked. For example, coverage of pointers and arrays is simplified. Thus pointers are referred to as addresses, but in fact an address is a machine feature whereas a pointer is a semantically-laden language feature which compilers may or may not implement as a simple address. Those aspects of arrays that are idiosyncracies of C and C++ are also simplified in the main text. Ultra-fine detail certainly has its place, but not, I feel, in a book for beginners for whom mastering the basic idea is work enough. For a second example, some program listings are not written to full "industrial strength" standards because to do so would introduce unwanted complications. The language Pascal did not even permit robust programming in many cases, so most introductory standard Pascal texts virtually overlook the entire issue. By using C, this text can introduce the students to the concept and provide some easy illustrations, while leaving the full development to later courses.

The text is completely compatible with the use of C++ compilers, so students can progress to an object-oriented C++ course using the same software. I felt that this was much more important than retaining full compatibility with the old Kernighan and Ritchie C (although its main features are explained): all popular PC C compilers are now ANSI/ISO compatible, and on Unix a free ANSI compiler is readily available.

To assist with course planning, the final six chapters are substantially independent, giving you significant flexibility in choosing and arranging material to suit the student audience and course goals. Nevertheless, Chapter 14 should be studied before Chapter 19.

Finally, in spite of its goal as a beginner's text, this book does in fact contain virtually all of the C language: most features not mentioned in the main chapters are covered in the Appendices.

Acknowledgments

I wish to specially thank my wife Gitie for her exhaustive and thoughtful criticism of the manuscript and her unflagging support and encouragement throughout its development. Also, thanks to my friends and my colleagues at the University of Southern Queensland for their interest and support.

Ron House
Toowoomba, Australia.

Table of Contents

Preface   *v*

Acknowledgments   *viii*

1 Background and overview   **1**
   1.1   The basic operations of a computer   2
   1.2   Controlling the computer: programs   3
         1.2.1   Why write programs?   4
         1.2.2   Machine language programs   4
         1.2.3   Programming languages   5
         1.2.4   Using a compiler   7
   1.3   Algorithms   7
   1.4   The program development process   8
   1.5   Documentation   9
   1.6   Summary   10
   1.7   Self-test exercises   11
   1.8   Test questions   12

2 Developing programs: calling functions   **15**
   2.1   Overview: why we structure computer programs   16
   2.2   C functions and programs   18
         2.2.1   The function main   19
         2.2.2   Calling functions   19
         2.2.3   The standard C function library   21
         2.2.4   Writing void functions   22
         2.2.5   Frequently-asked questions about functions   24
         2.2.6   Structuring the program with functions   26
   2.3   Comments   27
         2.3.1 Documenting functions; preconditions and postconditions   28
   2.4   Function declarations   29
   2.5   Example: Printing name tags   29
   2.6   Some formalities (syntax)   33
   2.7   Summary   34
   2.8   Self-test exercises   35
   2.9   Test questions   36

3 Data   39

3.1   Data types   40
3.2   Constants, variables and expressions   41
     3.2.1   String literals   43
     3.2.2   Constants: integers and characters   45
3.3   `char` and `int` variables; `char` arrays   47
3.4   `printf` facilities for data output   49
3.5   Example: Name tags with seat numbers   51
3.6   Expressions   55
     3.6.1   Operators   55
     3.6.2   Function results   57
3.7   Other data types   57
     3.7.1   Floating point data: `float` and `double`   57
     3.7.2   The type `long`   60
3.8   Summary   61
3.9   Self-test exercises   62
3.10   Test questions   64

4 Repetition   67

4.1   Introduction   68
4.2   Types of loops   68
4.3   Writing loops in C   69
     4.3.1   The `while` loop   69
     4.3.2   The `for` loop   72
     4.3.3   The `do...while` loop   73
4.4   More C operators   75
     4.4.1   Comparison operators   75
     4.4.2   Operator precedence   75
4.5   Example: Computing products and sums   76
4.6   Creating quality programs: giving names to constants (`#define`); the preprocessor   79
4.7   Program verification: correctness of a loop (optional)   82
4.8   Short examples   86
4.9   Summary   88
4.10   Self-test exercises   89
4.11   Test questions   91

5 Input: obtaining data from outside the program   97

5.1   Introduction—how input happens   98
5.2   Input in C programs   99
     5.2.1   Using the `scanf` library function to read `int`s   99
     5.2.2   Reading other numeric data types   101
     5.2.3   Reading `char`s, whitespace   101
     5.2.4   Some important warnings   103

5.3		Inputting and outputting strings	104
	5.3.1	Inputting words with scanf	104
	5.3.2	Inputting lines with gets	106
5.4		Programming examples and some useful techniques	107
	5.4.1	Example: Rearranging names	107
	5.4.2	Example: Processing until a certain event happens	109
	5.4.3	Short example: Skipping incorrect input	112
	5.4.4	The scanf function return	113
	5.4.5	Example: Report of purchases and sales	115
5.5		Input and output redirection	119
5.6		Summary	120
5.7		Self-test exercises	121
5.8		Test questions	123

6   Making choices: the conditional statements if and switch   129

6.1		Conditional statements	130
6.2		if: C's main selection statement	131
	6.2.1	Simple if statements	131
	6.2.2	A remark about program layout rules	133
	6.2.3	Multiple-test conditionals	134
6.3		Logical expressions	136
	6.3.1	More logical operators	137
	6.3.2	Reasoning about logical expressions	138
6.4		The switch statement	140
	6.4.1	Example: Telephone charges	141
6.5		The string comparison functions	146
6.6		Structured programming	148
6.7		Summary	148
6.8		Self-test exercises	149
6.9		Test questions	150

7   Writing functions with arguments and results   155

7.1		Introduction	156
7.2		Writing functions with simple arguments	156
7.3		Writing functions with array arguments	162
7.4		Example	165
7.5		Writing functions that return results	167
	7.5.1	A larger example of a function returning a result	169
7.6		Using return	171
	7.6.1	Using return inside main: program exit status	172
7.7		Old-style function definitions and declarations	172
7.8		Function libraries	173
7.9		A brief stock-take	174
7.10		Summary	174

7.11 Self-test exercises   176
7.12 Test questions   178

8 Top-down programming: choosing the program structure   183
8.1   Top-down programming   184
8.2   Designing a good program structure   185
8.3   Example: A simple calculator   186
8.4   Example: Printing a month in a calendar   193
8.5   Object-oriented programming   203
8.6   Program debugging   203
8.7   Summary   206
8.8   Self-test exercises   206
8.9   Test questions   207

9 Arrays   211
9.1   Introduction   212
9.2   Storing numeric data   213
9.3   Using array elements to represent categories   217
9.4   Searching and sorting   220
9.5   Multi-dimensional arrays; initialization   224
      9.5.1 Initialization during declaration   226
      9.5.2 Example: Matrix multiplication   228
9.6   Summary   231
9.7   Self-test exercises   232
9.8   Test questions   233

10 Text files   239
10.1 Storing data in files; text and binary file types   240
10.2 Overview of file processing in C   240
10.3 File output   241
10.4 File input   245
      10.4.1 End of file (EOF)   250
10.5 Predefined FILE pointer names   257
10.6 Example: File merge   258
10.7 Data conversion functions (optional)   265
10.8 A warning   266
10.9 Summary   267
10.10 Self-test exercises   268
10.11 Test questions   269

11 Structuring data   273
11.1 Introduction   274
11.2 Creating new data types (typedef)   274
11.3 Creating structures (struct)   276
11.4 Example: Sorting employee records   280

11.5	Example: Vectors	285
11.6	Summary	294
11.7	Self-test exercises	295
11.8	Test questions	295

12 Memory addresses: pointers — **299**

12.1	Introduction to pointers	300
12.2	Important example: Modifying function arguments	302
12.3	Pointers, arrays, and pointer arithmetic	305
	12.3.1 Pointer arithmetic	306
	12.3.2 Library string and memory functions	308
12.4	Pointers and structures	312
12.5	Summary	317
12.6	Self-test exercises	318
12.7	Test questions	319

13 Advanced programming with pointers — **323**

13.1	Dynamic memory allocation	324
13.2	Creating linked data structures	331
13.3	Processing command-line arguments	341
13.4	Pointers to functions	343
13.5	'Complicated' C declarations	346
13.6	Summary	348
13.7	Self-test exercises	349
13.8	Test questions	350

14 Recursion — **355**

14.1	Introduction	356
14.2	Example: Parsing arithmetic expressions	356
14.3	Designing recursive algorithms: what works and what doesn't	359
	14.3.1 Some general principles for writing correct recursive functions	364
	14.3.2 Some pitfalls	368
14.4	Example: Matchstick puzzle	371
14.5	Summary	378
14.6	Self-test exercises	379
14.7	Test questions	379

15 Data structures and abstract data types — **383**

15.1	Introduction	384
15.2	Example: The stack as an abstract data type	385
	15.2.1 Array-based stack implementation	389
	15.2.2 Stack implementation using a linked list	391
15.3	Key issues concerning abstract data types	393
15.4	Summary	395

15.5   Self-test exercises   395
15.6   Test questions   396

16 Further issues concerning numeric computation   397

16.1   Introduction   398
16.2   Integral data types   398
        16.2.1 Choosing the right integral type   400
        16.2.2 Integral constants   401
16.3   Floating-point data types   402
        16.3.1 Floating-point constants   404
16.4   Additional `printf` and `scanf` formatting features   404
        16.4.1 `printf`, `fprintf`, and `sprintf`   404
        16.4.2 `scanf`, `fscanf`, and `sscanf` formats   405
16.5   Mixing types in expressions   406
16.6   Overflow, underflow, and accuracy   408
16.7   Representing money   411
16.8   Summary   412
16.9   Self-test exercises   412
16.10   Test questions   413

17 Random-access and binary input-output   415

17.1   Introduction   416
17.2   Binary input-output and binary files   416
17.3   Random-access to files   422
17.4   Additional file manipulation functions   436
        17.4.1 `ftell` and `fseek`   436
        17.4.2 `fflush`   437
        17.4.3 `setvbuf`   438
17.5   Summary   439
17.6   Self-test exercises   439
17.7   Test questions   440

18 Scoping and linkage rules, storage duration, source file management, `const` parameters   443

18.1   Introduction   444
18.2   Scope   444
18.3   Linkage   447
18.4   Storage duration   449
18.5   Additional preprocessor features   450
        18.5.1 Conditional compilation   450
        18.5.2 Writing reliable header (`.h`) files   454
        18.5.3 (Optional) Parameterized macros   455
18.6   The `const` attribute   460
18.7   Summary   461
18.8   Self-test exercises   462
18.9   Test questions   463

19 Efficiency, searching and sorting   465

19.1	Introduction	466
19.2	Algorithm efficiency	466
19.3	Searching	466
	19.3.1 Example: Binary search	468
	19.3.2 Using the bsearch standard library function	470
	19.3.3 Writing your own version of bsearch (optional)	473
19.4	Sorting	475
	19.4.1 Example: Quick sort	476
	19.4.2 Using the library qsort function	478
19.5	Conclusion	480
19.6	Summary	480
19.7	Self-test exercises	481
19.8	Test questions	481

Appendix A: Answers to self-test exercises   483

Appendix B: Sample sessions   491

B.1	Compiling C programs under Unix	491
B.2	Compiling C programs under DOS	493

Appendix C: Additional C language features   497

C.1	Additional statement types	497
	C.1.1 goto statements and labels	497
	C.1.2 break statements in loops	497
	C.1.3 continue statements	498
	C.1.4 Empty statements	498
C.2	Additional features in declarations	499
	C.2.1 The auto and register storage class specifiers	499
	C.2.2 Unions	500
	C.2.3 Bit-fields	500
	C.2.4 Enumeration (enum) specifiers	500
	C.2.5 The volatile type qualifier	501
	C.2.6 Functions with a variable number of parameters	501
C.3	Additional operators	503
	C.3.1 Bitwise operators (~, >>, <<, &, |, and ^)	503
	C.3.2 The conditional (? :) operator	503
	C.3.3 Priority of all operators, and sequence points	504
C.4	Miscellaneous features	505
	C.4.1 Multibyte characters	505
	C.4.2 Trigraph sequences	506
	C.4.3 Further preprocessor features	506
C.5	Rvalues, lvalues, arrays and pointers	507

Appendix D: Descriptions of frequently-used standard library functions and macros 509

D.1	Common definitions (include `<stddef.h>`)	509
D.2	Character handling (include `<ctype.h>`)	509
D.3	Mathematics (include `<math.h>`)	510
D.4	Nonlocal jumps (include `<setjmp.h>`)	512
D.5	Variable arguments (include `<stdarg.h>`)	512
D.6	Input/output (include `<stdio.h>`)	512
D.7	String conversion functions (include `<stdlib.h>`)	516
D.8	Random number functions (include `<stlib.h>`)	517
D.9	Memory allocation functions (include `<stlib.h>`)	517
D.10	Communication with the environment (include `<stlib.h>`)	517
D.11	Searching and sorting utilities (include `<stlib.h>`)	518
D.12	Integer arithmetic functions (include `<stlib.h>`)	518
D.13	String handling (include `<string.h>`)	519
D.14	Date and time (include `<time.h>`)	520
D.15	Diagnostics (include `<assert.h>`)	523

Appendix E: Program layout rules used in example programs 525

Appendix F: C syntax summary 529

F.1	Lexical grammar ('building blocks' of the language)	529
	F.1.1 Keywords	529
	F.1.2 Identifiers	530
	F.1.3 Constants	530
	F.1.4 String literals	531
	F.1.5 Operators	531
	F.1.6 Punctuators	531
	F.1.7 Header names	532
F.2	Phrase structure grammar	532
	F.2.1 Expressions	532
	F.2.2 Declarations	533
	F.2.3 Statements	535
	F.2.4 External definitions	535
F.3	Preprocessing directives	536

Appendix G: ASCII codes 539

Glossary 541

Bibliography 553

Index by topic and language feature 555

Alphabetic index 561

1

Background and overview

Objectives

Understand the most fundamental actions a computer can perform:
— input
— processing
— output.

Appreciate the nature and purpose of computer programs:
— programming languages
— algorithms
— machine language.

Investigate why and when we need to write programs to control a computer.

Preview the way programs are developed.

Be aware of the possibilities for errors, or 'bugs', in computer programs.

Understand the importance of good documentation:
— comments.

1.1 THE BASIC OPERATIONS OF A COMPUTER

Computers have become important tools in the modern world. We can use them at home for games, education, personal accounting, storing cooking recipes, and so on. In business they can store databases of stock, customers, suppliers, staff, etc. They work out business financial planning and do word processing. In industry they control machines and robots, monitor manufacturing plants, and compute solutions to complex technical problems. In science and universities they solve mathematical problems, control experiments, guide telescopes, and sometimes even predict the weather.

To solve these complex problems, a computer performs many simpler actions which can be grouped under three categories: *input*, *processing*, and *output*. Input is the obtaining of data from outside the computer. Processing is performing operations on data, such as arithmetic, logical tests, and rearranging data. Output is the sending of data from the computer to the outside world. Here are some examples of these three operations.

Word processing

The computer must read documents from files, accept commands and text from the keyboard (input), arrange text and diagrams (processing), and display the document on the screen and print it on paper (output).

A computer-generated bill

Suppose we have just received the electricity account. To produce the bill, a clerk typed the meter readings and the account number into the computer (input), the computer checked its database (more input) to see what the readings were last time the meter was read, and worked out the electricity usage since then (processing). Finally, an invoice was printed (output) and a record of the invoice was added to the database for future reference.

A robot

Suppose an assembly-line robot has to put a bolt in a particular hole. Data from sensors (input) tell the controlling computer where the hole is located. The computer calculates the movements needed by the arm (processing), and then sends instructions to the motors controlling the robot's arms (output). This sort of operation has heavy processing requirements. For example, the computer must decide the meaning of various readings from sensors, and determine how to move an arm so that the rivet is taken to the right place.

We can visualize a computer as a machine that transforms data into a more useful form by performing input, processing, and output operations.

1.2 CONTROLLING THE COMPUTER: PROGRAMS

You do not have to understand electronics to appreciate how computers are controlled; just a few points are important. A computer contains a *processor* and *memory*. The processor loads instructions from the memory and carries out the actions they specify. The memory stores both the instructions describing the required processing, and the data being operated on. The memory is sometimes called *main memory*, or *main storage*. Some instructions perform input, obtaining data from external devices and storing it in memory. Some perform output, which sends data to an external device. Some order the processor to perform arithmetic, some tell it to perform logical tests such as comparing two data items, while other instructions tell it how to decide what to do next. This last point is crucial: to be a computer, the computer itself must be able to make decisions about which actions to perform, without the need for human intervention.

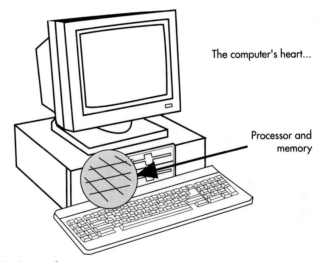

The computer's heart...

Processor and memory

Figure 1.1   The heart of a computer

So what is *programming* all about? Simply put, it is devising the instructions that control the processor. A complete list of instructions to perform a job is called a *program*. Systems of programs are often called *software* or *software packages*.

Many people have some experience writing simple programs. There is a big difference, though, between programming for ourselves and writing systems that will be relied upon in a business, scientific or industrial setting. Writing commercial-quality software requires discipline and planning in order to build quality into the system from the outset. By quality we mean that the software should perform reliably, it should be robust, and it should be easily maintainable. Reliable programs, basically, are correct; given valid input, they produce correct output. A robust program is resilient against unexpected happenings such as incorrect input or missing data files. It is easily maintainable if it is straightforward to modify to cater for changed circumstances.

For example, suppose a company uses a program to produce reports for tax purposes. If the reports are wrong, the company might be fined heavily for filing incorrect returns, and if a fault is found, the company will be without useful software until the programmer can correct the problem. Thus software should be reliable and robust from the outset. But a year seldom goes by in which tax rules remain unaltered. If the program is unclear or inflexible, the programmer cannot readily make the necessary changes, and extra expense will be incurred. Thus programs must be clear, simple, and properly documented.

These requirements demand sound programming methods and planning. The size and complexity of a system make a big difference to the way it should be organized. Consider the difference between mail delivery in a country district and in a big city. In a city, addresses in a street are always numbered to assist in mail delivery. In many country districts this is not done due to the cost, as the deliverer knows where everyone lives anyway. In a city, without street numbers the mail service would be a shambles. The same is true of computers. Software systems in industry may be very large indeed, and good programming techniques such as those discussed in this text are necessary to write them properly.

1.2.1   Why write programs?

We all know that writing programs can be avoided by using standard software such as spreadsheets and word processors. However, such software has been designed to solve certain types of problems. When a problem involves unusual or specialized requirements, a program must usually be written to handle it. For example, complex scientific and mathematical problems often require specially written programs. *Systems analysis* is the study of the operation of an organization to determine the best way to handle its needs. A *systems analyst* may recommend using standard packages, writing special-purpose software, or even using manual methods, depending on the problems involved.

Programming an application can often be expedited by using commercially available libraries of C *functions* that perform complex tasks such as graphics, statistics, and database operations. These functions can be called into operation whenever they are needed in a C program.

1.2.2   Machine language programs

The memory of most digital computers consists of a series of *memory locations*, each of which can store a number. Although people usually write numbers in a *decimal* code (using ten symbols, 0 to 9), computers are usually built to store numbers in *binary* (which uses only two symbols, 0 and 1). This is done because it is easier to build electronic components that work with binary numbers. Binary numbers use powers of *two* just as decimal ones use powers of *ten*: in decimal, 1 means one unit, 10 means one lot of ten, 100 means ten squared, 1000 means ten cubed, and so on. Similarly, in binary, 1 means one unit, 10 means one lot of two, 100 means two squared, 1000 means two cubed, etc. So, for example, 1011 in binary is two cubed (i.e. 8) plus two plus one, totalling 11 in decimal.

Some important terms are *bit*, *byte* and *word*. A *bit* is a single *binary digit*, either 0 or 1. A collection of (usually) eight bits is called a *byte*. Many computers group two, four, or more bytes together in a *word*. The electronics are designed so that the computer can efficiently manipulate the bytes and words which make up the memory. For example, in a computer with sixteen-bit words, we could view the structure of a word containing the binary number 10110100011011 (which is 11,547 in decimal) as follows:

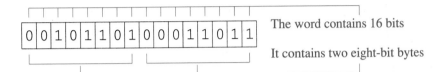

The word contains 16 bits

It contains two eight-bit bytes

Each byte or word (depending on the type of computer) has an *address*, which is a unique number allowing that particular place in the memory to be located easily. The processor's electronics allow it to use or alter the value stored at the location any given address refers to. For example the word pictured above might be located at address 40,462. Do not confuse the value stored at a location (that is, its *contents* — 11,547 in the above example) with its address.

The computer's instructions are binary numbers stored in memory. The electronics are built to act correctly when the processor receives the various numeric instruction codes. For example, if the binary code 101 had been assigned by the computer manufacturer to mean ADD, then when the computer executes code 101, the addition circuits operate. The values being added are called *data*. These are also numbers. Whether a particular value is an instruction or a data item depends on how it is used. We can, of course, have such things as names and other non-numeric data, but these too are encoded as numeric values.

A sequence of numeric codes to make a computer perform a particular task is called a *machine language program*. When a program is running on a computer, we say it is being *executed* by the computer, so machine language programs are often called *executables*. In the early days of computing, all programs were laboriously written in machine language.

1.2.3 Programming languages

Assemblers were among the earliest programming aids. They allowed the use of *mnemonics* instead of the numeric codes. For example, one could write the mnemonic ADD instead of its machine-language equivalent. Although better than machine language programming, this is still difficult, and programs can only be executed on the particular type of computer for which they were written. Machine and assembly languages are called low-level languages.

Modern *high-level languages* such as Pascal and C are designed to focus on the problem to be solved rather than on the details of how the computer works. Also they are *portable*: one can use a program written for one type of computer on another with few, or no, alterations. C is especially good for writing portable programs, but it is unusual in that it has both high-level and low-level features. This book is concerned only with the use of C as a high-level language.

Before a program can be executed, it must be translated into machine language with a program called a *compiler*. A C compiler will input a C program (that is, the C program is the compiler's input data) and translate it into machine code. A separate compiler is needed for each language/machine combination. In your study of C, therefore, you will need to use a compiler specifically written to compile C into the machine code of the computer you intend to use.

There is a second way to execute high-level language programs, using a program called an *interpreter*. Most C implementations use compilers rather than interpreters.

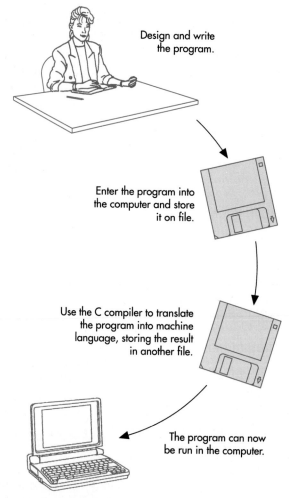

Design and write
the program.

Enter the program into
the computer and store
it on file.

Use the C compiler to translate
the program into machine
language, storing the result
in another file.

The program can now
be run in the computer.

Figure 1.2 Creating a working program

1.2.4 Using a compiler

Once we have written a program, we must enter it into the computer with a *text editor*. It will be kept on a semi-permanent storage device, usually a magnetic disk. Disks and similar devices are known as *secondary storage* to distinguish them from the main memory, or primary store. Programs and other data in secondary storage are stored in *files*. You should be familiar with files already from your previous experience with computers.

When the program has been entered and stored in a file, we must *compile* it with a C compiler to create a machine code translation. The created code is not directly usable until a further step called *linking* is done by a program called a *linker*. Linking is needed because all C programs make use of standard machine code modules called *library functions* which are supplied with the C compiler. The linker adds these to create the complete working program. Some systems do this when compiling or when the program is loaded for execution, so it might be that no specific linkage step is required. (Your instructor or, if you are on your own, your C compiler manual, will have more information about this.) Appendix B shows some examples of compiling and running programs using some popular compilers. Once we have the machine language program (also stored in a file) we can run it in the same way we ran the compiler.

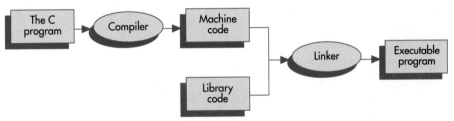

Figure 1.3   Steps in creating an executable program

1.3 ALGORITHMS

There is another important ingredient in a computer program. With high-level languages like C, you can easily write instructions telling the computer what to do. But it turns out to be a significant problem deciding just what it is you really do want it to do. Because computers are machines, they must be given precise instructions. A car, for instance, will not stop just because we yell out "STOP!" We have to give it the right instruction: we must put our foot on the brake pedal. Similarly, a computer will not work out a tax return just by being told "WORK OUT MY TAX RETURN!" It must be given precise instructions telling it every step it must perform to accomplish the task.

Learning to program, therefore, involves a lot more than just learning how to write C instructions. We must also learn how to compose our thoughts so that we know which C commands to give the computer to do the required job. A series of precise instructions (in any language) stating how to perform a task in a finite number of steps is called an *algorithm*. A computer program is a set of instructions in a language such as C which embodies an algorithm for solving some problem. The word 'program' is sometimes used to refer to the machine code version, and sometimes to the C version. People often refer to the high-level language version as source code.

To make programs robust, reliable, and maintainable, as discussed in Section 1.2, the algorithms on which they are based should be **correct**, **complete**, and **clear**. The importance of correctness is obvious. Completeness means writing programs that can handle all situations that might arise. Clarity ensures that correctness and completeness can be more easily obtained, and so that programs can be understood and modified long after they have been written.

There are other factors to be considered, such as efficiency. Although programs should not be needlessly **in**efficient, many programmers wrongly sacrifice clarity, completeness, and even correctness in a misguided search for speed. Provided a suitable algorithm is used, it is seldom necessary to go to extreme lengths in search of efficiency.

1.4   THE PROGRAM DEVELOPMENT PROCESS

Once we have decided on the function to be performed, we are ready to develop a suitable program.

An important ingredient in developing a program is the algorithm, explained earlier. Much of the skill of programming is devising good algorithms. If they are correctly written in a programming language such as C and compiled, then we have a program to solve our problem. The program must be tested to ensure that it works as expected. If not, we say it has a bug, which means that we made an error in programming; even though the computer is faithfully performing the program's instructions, it is not doing the right thing because the instructions themselves are incorrect. For example, if we wish to add some numbers and we accidentally give a 'subtract' command instead of an 'add' command, then our program has a bug. The error(s) must be found and the program must be corrected, recompiled, and tested again. We often find ourselves going around what is sometimes called the edit–test–debug cycle, as shown in Figure 1.4.

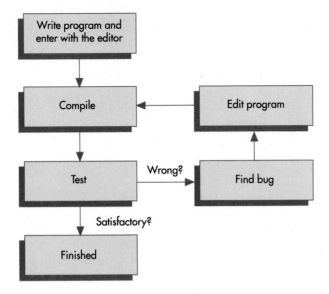

Figure 1.4 The edit–test–debug cycle

Sometimes we will not even get as far as the testing phase: the compiler can reject the program because we have broken the rules of the language (C in our case). When our program is grammatically incorrect, we say it has *syntax errors*. We must edit the program to correct these before the compiler will produce a machine-language program.

Programmers probably spend more time looking for errors than writing the program in the first place. Errors can have serious consequences, so:

- we should follow disciplines when writing programs to minimize the number of errors
- nevertheless, we cannot put a program into serious use as soon as we finish it. Programs should be extensively tested under true operating conditions
- as we find bugs, we should investigate their cause and correct the program. This means we should look for the true cause of the trouble. Some programmers try to fix bugs by tinkering in the hope that the bug will go away; often it does, but only because additional bugs have masked the effect. This gives rise to unreliable programs that may suddenly malfunction months or years after they were thought to be correct. It is wise never to make a change until you are sure you know why it will rectify the problem.

1.5   DOCUMENTATION

There are two kinds of documentation: *user documentation* and *internal documentation*. User documentation includes things like the manuals which explain how to use the software and what it does. It is intended for users of the software. Although it is very important, it is not the subject of this book.

Internal documentation, on the other hand, is intended to explain the software to other programmers who might have to alter it or correct bugs. One of the commonest ways to write this sort of documentation is to include *comments* in programs. These are explanations intended for human readers; they are ignored by the compiler, and therefore have no effect on the behavior of a program.

There are many opinions about what should be put in comments. About the only thing everyone agrees on is that comments are a good idea. We will be looking at some commenting principles which assist in making comments genuinely helpful, instead of being there for their own sake. Remember, we can not be sure we have a correct program unless we know what the correct behavior should be. Thus we must write accurate, precise specifications for programs and clear, complete and precise documentation.

We shall write documentation in this text entirely in the form of program comments combined with clear programs. When creating much larger systems than we shall consider here (such as the ones needed in commerce and industry), it is often not possible or desirable to write all the documentation of the algorithm as comments within the program. For example, diagrams will be needed showing how various modules of the software and the data are related, and in many scientific and technical programs mathematical derivations and diagrams will be needed to explain why calculations in the program are correct. Unfortunately many programmers allow such documents to become outdated as changes occur due to bug fixes, changes in the specifications, or enhancements that add new features. This is a serious oversight, as the system becomes muddled and confusing to future programmers who are not aware of the carelessness of their predecessors. If such documents are used, therefore, they should be scrupulously maintained to accurately describe the program at all times.

1.6 SUMMARY

- Computers are *information processors*: they *input* data, *process* it (perform calculations, rearrange, select important facts), and *output* results.
- Computers contain a *processor* and *memory*.
  - The *memory* consists of a series of *memory locations* which can store both *data* and *programs*.
  - Memory locations are *bytes* or *words*, each of which is composed of a certain number of *bits*.
- The *programs* controlling a computer are called *software*, and must be in a special code called *machine language*.
- *Assembly languages* were invented to ease the burden of writing machine language programs, but they still have many of the disadvantages of machine language, such as being tied to particular makes and models of computer.
- Programmers usually prefer to use *high-level languages*; that is, languages more suited to human needs.
  - High-level languages are much more *portable* than either assembly or machine language.

- High-level language programs must be *compiled* (i.e. translated) into machine language by a *compiler* before they can be *run* (i.e. control the computer).
- C is a high-level language.
- One must know precisely the *algorithm* needed to do a job in order to write a program.
  - We must make sure our algorithms are *correct, complete, clear* and where compatible with these other goals, *efficient*.
- The goal in writing correct, complete, and clear software is to make programs *reliable, robust*, and *maintainable*.
- The process for developing a program is:
  - design the algorithm and write the program
  - enter it into the computer with a *text editor*
  - *compile* and *link* the program to produce an *executable* version
  - run and test this executable version
  - fix the *bugs* and edit, recompile, and test again.
- The software must be properly *documented*, both for the *users* and the programmers.

1.7 SELF-TEST EXERCISES

For each question, select the most appropriate answer from the alternatives given. Solutions are given in Appendix A.

1 In computing terminology, a bit is:
  - a a part of a computing circuit
  - b a yes/no question
  - c a binary digit
  - d a group of bytes, usually eight.

2 The smallest amount of information possible is called a:
  - a fact
  - b byte
  - c bit
  - d word.

3 Portable programs are programs which:
  - a can be run on many different computers of the same kind
  - b can be made to work on many different kinds of computers very easily
  - c can be compiled by compilers for many different computer languages
  - d can be written in either machine or assembly language.

4 A text editor most closely resembles:
  - a a typewriter
  - b a spreadsheet
  - c a compiler
  - d a word processor.

5 The correct order of steps to get a program to work on a computer is:
   a   compile, edit, link, run
   b   compile, link, edit, run
   c   edit, link, compile, run
   d   edit, compile, link, run
   e   link, edit, compile, run.

6 If a program contains a bug, then:
   a   it might malfunction
   b   it will refuse to operate
   c   it must be run twice as often to get good results
   d   it will not contain any other bugs, until the first one is removed.

7 If a program has good user documentation:
   a   we can be sure it contains no bugs
   b   it will be portable
   c   it will be easy to maintain
   d   none of the above.

1.8 TEST QUESTIONS

For each question, select the most appropriate answer from the alternatives given.

1 In computing terminology, a byte is:
   a   a part of a computing circuit
   b   a yes/no question
   c   a binary digit
   d   a group of bits, usually eight.

2 A computer is capable of directly executing programs written in:
   a   machine language
   b   assembly language
   c   high-level language
   d   all of the above.

3 One big problem with machine language is:
   a   it uses a lot of computer memory
   b   it is inefficient
   c   it is hard to write
   d   it does not work on modern computers.

4 The program that allows you to type a C program into the computer and store it in a
   file is called:
   a   an editor
   b   an algorithm
   c   a linker
   d   a compiler.

5 A C program is incapable of directly executing on a computer unless it is:
  a   correct
  b   documented
  c   written in a high-level language
  d   compiled into machine code.

6 A bug:
  a   is a mistake in a program
  b   must only be included in a correct program
  c   causes a program to produce extra output
  d   causes a program to fail while being edited.

7 Documentation:
  a   is written to assist the user
  b   is written to assist the programmer
  c   both of the above
  d   none of the above.

2

Developing programs: calling functions

Objectives

Appreciate the importance of designing properly structured computer programs.

C topics. See how functions help us obtain well-structured C programs:

— what is a C function?

— the function `main`

— calling functions

— standard C library functions: introducing `printf`, `#include` and library headers

— writing `void` functions — function definitions and declarations

— comments, preconditions and postconditions

— identifiers and keywords.

2.1 OVERVIEW: WHY WE STRUCTURE COMPUTER PROGRAMS

Most readers will be keen to start some actual programming. We shall do that very shortly, but due to the size and complexity of serious professional programs, there is one more preliminary we must discuss: structure.

We all know the difficulty of thinking about many things at once. Nevertheless in daily life we routinely deal with very complex structures. For instance most towns and cities have thousands or millions of residences, yet we do not get lost finding our way home. One technique for managing complexity is to group concepts and facts in *hierarchies*. In finding an office in a city, we think first about finding the right suburb or district, then about locating the street we require, and finally about the address of our destination within the street. To find an office in a building, we first think about getting to the right floor, and then the right office. In doing this we have located one particular office among millions, yet we do not have a knowledge of the relative positions of millions of offices. We solved the problem by making use of hierarchies.

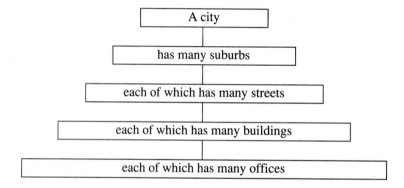

We always deal with only **one level** in the hierarchy at a time. Thus, having found our suburb, we forget about the difficulties we had finding the suburb. We can summarize these principles as follows.

> 1 *Complex systems must be structured.*
> 2 *We should only worry about one level of the structure at a time.*

Similar considerations arise in designing programs. Suppose we wish to solve a problem needing ten programming commands. We might simply puzzle out the ten commands, and write a program looking something like this:

```
command 1
command 2
command 3
command 4
command 5
command 6
command 7
command 8
command 9
command 10
```

Note: this is not a real program – each line stands for whatever C code is actually needed.

We might just muddle through — **if** our program only needs ten or so commands. But serious programs often need thousands, even hundreds of thousands, of commands. In a 100,000-line program with no structure, finding an error would be as hard as finding a building in a strange city with no street names and no road map. The program must be structured hierarchically. For example, the program might be a word processor. We should think of the various major tasks a word processor does, such as text editing, arranging, and printing. Each of these tasks would have a number of subtasks. For example the text editing phase would have to display text on the screen, allow insertion, deletion, replacement, searching for words, etc. We continue in this way until we arrive at tasks so simple that we can easily see how to solve them without further ado. Proceeding in this way is called *top-down design*. The program's overall structure will therefore be a hierarchy:

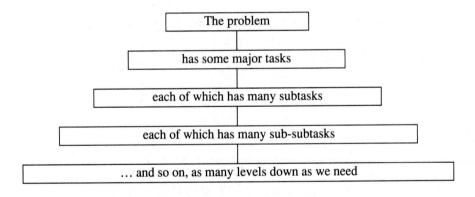

Of course not just any structure will do. If the town planners decided to make each suburb 20 miles long and 6 inches wide, the suburbs would not be capable of any sensible division into streets. Similarly, in programming there are both good and bad ways to structure any given program.

2.2   C FUNCTIONS AND PROGRAMS

We shall commence by looking at the C feature which allows us to implement hierarchies — functions. A function is a list of instructions describing how to perform some task. Every function has a name. When we want the computer to execute a function, we must refer to the appropriate function by name. A command to execute a function is called a function *call*.

There are well-known analogies to C's functions in everyday life, namely all sorts of lists of instructions such as recipes, sewing instructions, appliance handbooks, and repair manuals. For example, a recipe might read as follows:

How to *make some lime pickle*
Boil 2 lb limes for 1 minute to soften the peel.
Squeeze the juice and cut the peel in strips.
Add 6 oz sugar, 6 oz salt, 1 oz chilli powder, and 1 oz garam masala.
Place in jar and cover with muslin cloth.
Sun for 10 days.
Seal and keep in cool dark place.

To get a friend to make some lime pickle, we might say, "Would you please *make some lime pickle.*" By naming the recipe in this way (in programming terms, by calling the 'lime pickle' function), our friend knows which instructions to follow. All sorts of things in daily life work like this. Here are some more examples:
– how to change a car tire
– how to fill out a tax form
– how to get to the theater (road directions)
– how to differentiate a mathematical function
– how to do double-entry bookkeeping.

C functions are lists of instructions written according to the rules of the C language instead of in English. A complete program contains a hierarchical collection of functions which work together to perform the required programming task. Any task can be divided into functions in this manner. One function must be called main; this is the function at the top of the hierarchy. When a C program executes, it always starts by executing main. Functions with other names are executed if main directly or indirectly calls them. For example, if our program contains functions edit and delete, main might call both edit and delete, or perhaps main calls edit and then edit calls delete. But unless edit and delete are called somehow, the instructions they contain will not be executed.

2.2.1 *The function* main

Here is the simplest possible C program. It has a main function, but does absolutely nothing.

```
main() {
}
```

The braces ({ }) mark where we can place the list of commands to be performed. Commands in computing are called *statements*. C compilers do not care how the program is laid out on the page. For example, the following represents exactly the same C program:

```
main (
){   }
```

The difference between these two listings consists solely of *whitespace*; that is, characters that need no actual ink in a printed listing. The commonest whitespace characters are spaces and newlines. C allows almost complete freedom in using whitespace: wherever any whitespace is permitted, any amount of it is also permitted — with one exception, described in Section 2.2.3.

We must not split a word in two, or run two words together. For example, we cannot write main as ma in or as m ain.

We are now ready to make main do some useful work.

2.2.2 Calling functions

C functions can call other functions, which in turn can call others, and so on as many times as necessary. To illustrate, let us write a program which displays a message on the computer screen or terminal. We shall use a function called printf from the C *library*, which is a collection of useful functions that the writers of the C compiler provide for our use as part of the system. printf outputs information generated by the program. Here is a simple program which calls printf.

Listing 2-1 (*see compiler note on page 38*)

```
#include <stdio.h>

main() {
    printf("The start of my successful career.\n");
}
```

The first line (#include <stdio.h>) allows the program to use printf, as will be explained in Section 2.2.3. The main function calls the printf function to output the message written in quotes. It will show the message

```
The start of my successful career.
```

on the computer display. Character sequences such as this quoted message are called *strings*. The \n in the string causes printf to output a newline character which makes the output on the screen advance to a fresh line.

Functions are C's way of allowing us to simplify programs using hierarchies. For example, the printf function used above is very complex, but because someone else has already written it, all we need to remember is how to call it.

Just as we can have more than one instruction in recipes, and so on, so we can include more than one statement in a C function. Here is a slightly more complicated program.

Listing 2-2

```
#include <stdio.h>

main() {
    printf("The start of my successful career\n");
    printf("as a master programmer!\n");
}
```

This main function calls printf twice. It will display the message

```
The start of my successful career
as a master programmer!
```

Each printf call starts with the function name ('printf'), has some information in parentheses, and ends with a semicolon. (C requires statements to end with semicolons to simplify the compiler's task when translating the program; there are some exceptions to this rule.) Let us examine one of the printf function calls more closely.

```
printf ( "The start of my successful career\n" );
```

The name of the function we wish to call.

A semicolon marks the end of the statement, much like a full stop in English.

*Parentheses marking the function arguments (see below). Whenever we call a function in C, we **must** put a pair of parentheses after its name; this is how C knows we are making a function call.*

The *arguments* contain information needed to perform the printf call. Arguments are very familiar in daily life. In the lime pickle recipe, we are told to boil **limes**. Yet we have probably never been told specifically how to boil limes. We learnt how to boil things in general, and we apply that general knowledge to limes in particular. The same applies in C. The writers of printf dealt with the problem of how to print things in general, and whenever we call it, we must tell it which particular thing it should print. printf is powerful, and we shall return to it several times in the following chapters to learn more about it.

2.2.3   The standard C function library

Since there are at least 140 functions in the library, they are divided into categories for clarity. Thus `printf` is in a category concerned with input and output. We should warn the compiler that we want to use functions in a category by telling it to read a special *header* containing definitions of the functions and other items in that category. We do this with the `#include` command, as shown in the previous two program listings. `printf` and the other input-output functions are defined in a header called `stdio.h`.

Always include the appropriate headers for the functions called in the program. C manuals provide full descriptions of the functions in the library, including the names of the appropriate headers. Appendix D briefly describes most standard library functions.

Whenever we use a `#include` statement the compiler reads the specified header, which is usually stored in a file. This is done by a special part of the C compiler called the *preprocessor*. Commands to the preprocessor are called *directives*. All directives start with #, and are exceptions to C's normally very permissive layout rules. Some old compilers insist that # should be in column 1. You may put spaces between # and `include`, but you must keep the entire directive together on one logical line by itself. The following are illegal directives:

```
#include
    <stdio.h>
```

and

```
#include <stdio.h> main() {
```

Example: Using a C library function

We shall now write another program to practice looking up the function descriptions. Our program will change the name of a file on the computer's disk. We shall assume that the current name of the file is 'rabbit' and that we wish to change this to 'zebra'. There is a library function to rename files called `rename`, listed in Appendix D. If we consult that description, we find that the function definition is given as:

```
int rename(const char * oldname, const char * newname);
```

You will not yet understand all the details of this definition, but note that rename has two arguments which are called `oldname` and `newname`. Those words allow the function description to be written in a concise form. We are not restricted, though, in the names we pass as arguments to `rename`. The description in Appendix D says:

> Renames `oldname` to `newname`. On some computers, any existing file `newname` will be overwritten; on others an existing `newname` file prevents the renaming operation from occurring, and `oldname` is not renamed.

The other thing we must check is the required header file. The description is under the heading **Input/Output <stdio.h>**, which tells us that `<stdio.h>` is the required header. Now we can write our program:

Listing 2-3

```
#include <stdio.h>

main() {
    rename("rabbit", "zebra");
}
```

Try out this program on your computer. You will need to create a file called 'rabbit' before running the program. You may do this with the same editor you use to enter your C programs. It doesn't matter what you put in the file; a simple message such as "This is the rabbit file" will do. After you run the program, you will find that the file 'rabbit' has disappeared, and a file called 'zebra' has appeared. Using the editor again to edit zebra, you will see that it is the same file you originally called 'rabbit'.

2.2.4 Writing void functions

An important type of C function is the void function. The word void is C terminology for a function whose only purpose is to carry out certain instructions. There is one other thing functions can do (return *results*), which will be discussed in Chapter 3.

For example, let us write a function to display a triangle of asterisks. This is an unimportant problem, but it allows the main principles to stand out. The obvious name for this function is triangle. It could be written as follows:

```
void triangle(void) {
    printf("  *\n ***\n*****\n");
}
```

This is called the function *definition*. The various parts of the first line of the function all serve useful purposes.

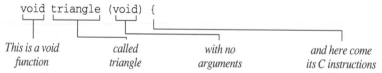

| This is a void function | called triangle | with no arguments | and here come its C instructions |

The two uses of the word void mean two different things. The first one makes triangle a void function. The second one tells the C compiler that triangle has no arguments (unlike printf, which does have arguments). That second void helps the compiler warn us if we make a mistake in calling a function. We can write this second void in the parentheses when writing main functions, but it is less critical because of the special way main is used. The first void should **not** be used when writing main, because main is not a void function.

On the last line, the closing brace (}) means "That's the end of the function." Now suppose we want to use this function to print this message:

```
Wait for it folks...
   *
  ***
 *****
That's all folks!
```

Three things are involved here. First the "Wait for it..." message, then the triangle, then the "That's all..." message. A program to do that must issue appropriate commands to perform those tasks in that order. Such a program is shown in Listing 2-4.

Listing 2-4

```c
/* A program to print a triangle */

#include <stdio.h>

void triangle(void) {
    printf("  *\n ***\n*****\n");
}

main() {
    printf("Wait for it folks...\n");
    triangle();
    printf("That's all folks!\n");
}
```

The first line in the program

```c
/* A program to print a triangle */
```

is a comment for human readers; the compiler ignores it (see Section 2.3).

The call to the function is the line

```c
triangle();
```

in `main`. The parentheses contain nothing, unlike the parentheses for `printf` calls. This is because our function has no arguments, but `printf` does. **We must include the parentheses, even if they are empty**, as this is how the compiler knows we wish to call the function. The first instruction in the program listing (reading down from the top of the listing) is

```c
printf("  *\n ***\n*****\n");
```

but that is **not** the first statement executed when the program runs, as we can see from the printout given earlier. The first statement executed is

```c
printf("Wait for it folks...\n");
```

This is because **the first function executed is always main,** irrespective of the order in which functions are listed in the program. Other functions are only executed if they are called. In Listing 2-4, the second command in main calls triangle, so triangle is executed then, and at no other time. Of course, if you call a function twice (or more) it happens twice (or more). You are in charge: what you write in your program dictates what happens. Here are the statements in the order they are executed; the statement inside triangle is shown indented.

```
printf("Wait for it folks...\n");
triangle();  /* (This call causes the following line to execute.) */
    printf(" *\n ***\n*****\n");
printf("That's all folks!\n");
```

2.2.5   Frequently-asked questions about functions

Questions often asked about functions include:

a   Can I call a function more than once?
b   Can one function contain calls to another?
c   Can a function contain more than one statement?
d   Can a function contain calls to itself?

In C, most things that make logical sense are allowable; almost everything **can** be done, but the point is, do you **want** it to be done? The answer to every one of the above questions is "**yes**". Regarding question (d), a function which calls itself is called *recursive*. Writing recursive functions is not hard, but it requires care. We shall examine recursive functions in Chapter 14. Listings 2-5a and 2-5b show short programs illustrating (a) to (c) above.

Listing 2-5a

```
/* A program to print four triangles */

#include <stdio.h>

void triangle(void) {
    printf(" *\n ***\n*****\n");
}

main() {
    printf("Wait for it folks...\n");
    triangle();
    printf("And again:\n");
    triangle();
    printf("And again and again:\n");
    triangle();
    triangle();
    printf("That's all folks!\n");
}
```

Sample run

```
Wait for it folks...
   *
  ***
 *****
And again:
   *
  ***
 *****
And again and again:
   *
  ***
 *****
   *
  ***
 *****
That's all folks!
```

Listing 2-5b

```c
/* A program to demonstrate calling one function from another */

#include <stdio.h>

void triangle(void) {
    printf("   *\n ***\n*****\n");
}

void another_func(void) {
    printf("Inside another_func\n");
    triangle();
    printf("Leaving another_func\n");
}

main() {
    printf("Wait for a triangle folks...\n");
    triangle();        /* Call to triangle directly from main */
    printf("Calling another_func:\n");
    another_func();  /* Call to triangle via another_func */
    printf("That's all folks!\n");
}
```

Sample run

```
Wait for a triangle folks...
  *
 ***
*****
Calling another_func:
Inside another_func
  *
 ***
*****
Leaving another_func
That's all folks!
```

2.2.6 Structuring the program with functions

C allows us to put whatever statements we please in a function, but for our own benefit we should **never** violate the following rule.

> *Always make sure that each function serves a single, well-defined purpose.*

For example, the function `triangle` had a very specific job to do: display a triangle. We might have written a function which displayed two lines of the three in the triangle, leaving it to `main` to display the third line. But such a function would violate the rule of having a single task per function, as it would only do part of a task. Another way to violate the rule would be to write a function that does two unrelated jobs. Maybe we could get our program to work in spite of this; all that matters as far as the computer is concerned is getting the right instructions in the right order. But every time we break this rule we make our own life harder. In industry, programs often need to be modified to keep up with changing requirements, so the simpler it is, the easier it will be to understand and modify correctly.

How do we know whether we have obeyed the rule? One test is: **Can you find clear, explanatory names for functions?** If so, chances are you have chosen a reasonable division of labor between functions. We called our function 'triangle' (although 'display_triangle' might have been clearer). But what would we call a function that only displayed two lines of the triangle? 'Part_triangle'? Not really, because it is far too vague. How about 'display_first_two_lines_of_triangle'? Perhaps, although we might be aghast at the prospect of having to type that name every time we wanted to call the function. Such a dilemma is a sure sign that we have gone wrong somewhere.

Another good practice is to give `void` functions verbs as names: 'do this', 'do that', because we are instructing the computer to execute the statements in the function. Although this may seem a minor matter, it all helps the program to read properly, which aids understanding. Finally, pay attention to whether a function processes one thing or more than one. A function that processes a series of items might be called `process_items`, whereas one that processes a single item might be called `process_item`. That 's' makes all the difference to the clarity of the program.

2.3 COMMENTS

Comments are remarks in a program intended for human readers, providing internal documentation as discussed in Section 1.5. They start with the sequence /*, and end with the sequence */. The contents of comments are ignored by the compiler. Every program and function should start with a comment saying what that program or function does. For example, Listing 2-3 would be vastly improved by a comment, as in Listing 2-6.

Listing 2-6

```
/* Program to rename the file called "rabbit" to "zebra".
   Author: Ron House, 11 July 1990.
   Requirements: There should be a file called "rabbit".
                 There should NOT be a file "zebra".
*/

#include <stdio.h>

main() {
    rename("rabbit", "zebra" );
}
```

When the compiler sees a comment, it replaces it with a single blank before analyzing the meaning of whatever remains. Thus,

```
prin/*This ain't gonna work!*/tf("Hi folks\n");
```

really means

```
prin tf("Hi folks\n");
```

which is incorrect because it splits the name `printf`.

> **Beware the unterminated comment.** It is very easy to inadvertently forget to end a comment with */, or to accidentally type it as * / (wrong), or as /*. In such cases the compiler will swallow up parts of the program as comments until it finds a correct termination. This can cause seemingly inexplicable behavior and waste a lot of time, so check comment endings carefully.

2.3.1 Documenting functions; preconditions and postconditions

The header comment in Listing 2-6 answers two questions for the reader: first, "What task will the program or function do for us?" and second, "What requirements must be met before running this program or calling this function?" There are special terms for such comments: a *precondition* is a specification of some condition which must be met in order for a piece of code to work properly. If the precondition is met, the *postcondition* describes the effect the code is guaranteed to produce. Thus in the above, if we have a file called 'rabbit' but not one called 'zebra' (the precondition) then we are guaranteed that 'rabbit' will be renamed to 'zebra' (the postcondition). Any piece of program can have preconditions and postconditions: a complete program, a function, or even just a single statement.

When reading a large program or function, we first need a short and clear comment stating what it does — perhaps only one line long. This helps a reader locate sections of interest and get a feel for how the program is designed. But this is not enough. Many errors in large systems are caused by misunderstanding, perhaps only slightly, the task performed by some particular piece of code. The preconditions and postconditions are designed to state precisely the effect of executing a piece of code. This is not the same as explaining how the code does its job; additional comments may be needed to clarify that.

When calling a function, check carefully that all the requirements mentioned in the precondition are satisfied at the point of call. After the call completes, you can assume that the things which are mentioned in the postcondition actually are so. For example, consider the simple function `triangle` given earlier. The postcondition for `triangle` is clearly that a three-line triangle of asterisks is printed. But how about the precondition? Will `triangle` **always** print such a triangle? Consider:

```
printf("Hello folks!");
triangle();
```

These print

```
Hello folks!  *
  ***
*****
```

and we don't have a triangle. The precondition therefore is that the latest line of output should be empty when the function is called, as characters on the line disrupt the position of the first asterisk. Thus the opening comment for function `triangle` should include something like this:

```
/* triangle: prints a three-line triangle of asterisks.
   On entry, output must be at the start of a new line. */
```

The preconditions and postconditions are the basis of a precise mathematical method, called *program verification*, for proving the correctness of programs. In such work they are usually stated in mathematical form rather than in English.

2.4 FUNCTION DECLARATIONS

In Listing 2-5b, the `main` function definition, which we wrote **first**, is listed **last**. In fact to read the functions in the order they are called, we more or less have to read the program from the end backwards. It would be much better to place `main` first, then the functions `main` calls, then the ones they call in turn, and so on. But we run into a problem: it is highly desirable (and in C++, compulsory) that the compiler knows what sort of function we are calling **before** we call it, and this seems to compel us to use the inverted function order of Listing 2-5b.

This difficulty is circumvented by a facility called a function *declaration*. For example,

```
void triangle(void);
```

is a function declaration for `triangle`. It is essentially just the first line of the function, without the actual code that defines what the function does. In a function declaration, the '{...}' part of the function definition is replaced with a single semicolon. By writing a function **declaration** first, the compiler knows exactly what sort of function `triangle` is when it is called. The actual function **definition** (where we say what `triangle` does) can follow any time later, so we can re-order the program in the clearest and most logical way. We shall use function declarations in the example that follows.

2.5 EXAMPLE: PRINTING NAME TAGS

Our task is to produce name tags in this form:

```
**************************************************
**************************************************
**                                              **
**                  John Smith                   **
**                                              **
**************************************************
**************************************************
```

We want tags for John Smith, Mary Peterson, and Alison Gray. At first we ignore the details of making each tag; instead we merely observe that three tags are needed. Let us also require that a blank line be printed between tags. Therefore our program must do these tasks:

```
Print tag for John Smith.
Print blank line.
Print tag for Mary Peterson.
Print blank line.
Print tag for Alison Gray.
```

Now if we had functions to print each tag, we could write `main` from this plan as follows:

```
main() {
    print_tag_for_John_Smith();
    printf("\n");
    print_tag_for_Mary_Peterson();
    printf("\n");
    print_tag_for_Alison_Gray();
}
```

Unfortunately we don't have any functions `print_tag_for...`; we must write them. We could write long-winded `printf` statements to print each person's tag, but functions let us do it with less effort. Only the central line of each tag is different. Each function prints the same three-line top portion, and similarly for the bottom. This suggests thinking of printing a tag as three tasks:

```
Print top section.
Print the line with the name.
Print bottom section.
```

This in turn suggests creating functions `print_top_section` and `print_bottom_section`. Thus `print_tag_for_John_Smith` might look as follows (the other two `print_tag` functions will be similar):

```
void print_tag_for_John_Smith(void) {
    print_top_section();
    printf("**            John Smith            **\n");
    print_bottom_section();
}
```

Finally, the functions printing the top and bottom have much in common — the lines of asterisks and the line with asterisks at each end. We can therefore introduce further functions for these portions. The final program is shown in Listing 2-7.

Listing 2-7

```
/* A program to print name tags.
 * Prints a tag for each of the following names:
 *      John Smith
 *      Mary Peterson
 *      Alison Gray
 */

#include <stdio.h>

/*** function declarations:  ***/
void print_top_section(void);
void print_bottom_section(void);
void print_side_border(void);
void print_stars(void);
void print_tag_for_John_Smith(void);
void print_tag_for_Mary_Peterson(void);
```

```c
void print_tag_for_Alison_Gray(void);

/* main: Prints the name tags, with a blank line between each. */

main() {
    print_tag_for_John_Smith();
    printf("\n");
    print_tag_for_Mary_Peterson();
    printf("\n");
    print_tag_for_Alison_Gray();
}

void print_tag_for_John_Smith(void) {
    print_top_section();
    printf("**              John Smith              **\n");
    print_bottom_section();
}

void print_tag_for_Mary_Peterson(void) {
    print_top_section();
    printf("**              Mary Peterson            **\n");
    print_bottom_section();
}

void print_tag_for_Alison_Gray(void) {
    print_top_section();
    printf("**              Alison Gray             **\n");
    print_bottom_section();
}

/* print_top_section: Prints the entire part of a tag above the line
                      with the name. */

void print_top_section(void) {
    print_stars();
    print_stars();
    print_side_border();
}

/* print_bottom_section: Prints the entire part of a tag below the line
                         with the name. */

void print_bottom_section(void) {
    print_side_border();
    print_stars();
    print_stars();
}

/* print_stars: Prints a row of stars to form a tag border. */

void print_stars(void) {
    printf("*********************************************\n");
}
```

```
/* print_side_border: Prints left and right parts of the vertical
                      rows of stars which form a tag border. */

void print_side_border(void) {
    printf("**                                      **\n");
}
```

The output is a tag for each person. Execution starts with the first statement in `main`, and each function call causes execution of the appropriate function. Thus the statements are performed in this order:

```
(starting in main:)
print_tag_for_John_Smith();
  (in print_tag_for_John_Smith:)
  print_top_section();
    (in print_top_section:)
    print_stars();
      (in print_stars:)
      printf("***********************************************\n");
    print_stars();
      (in print_stars:)
      printf("***********************************************\n");
    print_side_border();
      (in print_side_border:)
      printf("**                            **\n");
      (end of print_side_border - resume print_top_section)
    (end of print_top_section - resume print_tag_for_John_Smith)
  printf("**              John Smith            **\n");
  print_bottom_section();
    (in print_bottom_section:)
    print_side_border();
      (in print_side_border:)
      printf("**                            **\n");
      (end of print_side_border - resume print_bottom_section)
    print_stars();
      (in print_stars:)
      printf("***********************************************\n");
      (end of print_stars - resume print_bottom_section)
    print_stars();
      (in print_stars:)
      printf("***********************************************\n");
      (end of print_stars - resume print_bottom_section)
    (end of print_bottom_section - resume print_tag_for_John_Smith)
  (end of print_tag_for_John_Smith - resume main)
printf("\n");
print_tag_for_Mary_Peterson();
  (similar to execution of print_tag_for_John_Smith)
printf("\n");
print_tag_for_Alison_Gray();
  (similar to execution of print_tag_for_John_Smith)
(Back in main, the program terminates.)
```

By choosing self-explanatory names for functions, the need for comments is reduced — `main`, for example, almost explains itself. Programs often require certain jobs to be done in many places — such as printing the top and bottom of a tag in this case. When functions each perform a single, identifiable task, their reuse is much easier. We shall write an improved version of this program in the next chapter.

2.6 SOME FORMALITIES (SYNTAX)

Because computer languages are translated by a machine (the computer) into machine code, we must obey the rules **precisely**. In this section, we examine some rules of C concerning the features we have discussed so far. The full rules are given in Appendix F. These grammar rules are called the *syntax* of the language. When we violate them, the compiler displays a syntax error message. Another type of error is to write something with correct syntax, but which does something other than what we really want. In that case the program malfunctions when it runs, and we say it has a *logic error*.

Identifiers

Names of things such as functions are called *identifiers*. C allows any number of characters in an identifier. They may include letters, the underscore character, and, provided they do not start an identifier, digits. Some legal names would be: `total_tax`, `car62`, `pi`, and `shoes_N_sox`. Some illegal identifiers are: `total tax` (contains a space) and `5_cats` (starts with a digit). Spell an identifier exactly the same every time and be consistent in the use of upper-case and lower-case letters: `PI` and `pi` are different identifiers. Examples seen so far include `main`, `printf`, and `triangle`. Some compilers place limits on how many characters in an identifier are *significant*, that is, how many are used to distinguish one identifier from another. For example, if a compiler only allowed six significant characters, then `charles` would be the same identifier as `charley`, but not the same as `charlie`. In most cases the ANSI standard requires 31 significant characters; some older systems have limits of eight or even only six characters.

Keywords

Not all identifiers may be used freely in programs. Some, called *keywords*, have special meanings, and the compiler would misunderstand our program if we reused them. One we have already met is `void`.

The complete list of keywords is:

auto	default	float	register	struct	volatile
break	do	for	return	switch	while
case	double	goto	short	typedef	
char	else	if	signed	union	
const	enum	int	sizeof	unsigned	
continue	extern	long	static	void	

Some compilers provide extra features and so reserve extra keywords. You should check the keywords for your particular compiler in your manual. If you are using a C++ compiler or intend to learn the language C++ later on, avoid the following additional keywords from C++ (these words are not special in C).

```
asm         delete      inline      operator    public      virtual
class       friend      new         overload    this
```

You do not need to memorize all these words, but be aware of them in case you suddenly get inexplicable error messages from your compiler where everything seems okay. Then check the list.

2.7 SUMMARY

- Due to the complexity of computer systems, programs should be well-structured for ease of understanding. One useful structuring method is arrangement in *hierarchies*.
- When dealing with a hierarchical system, try where possible to deal with just one level of the hierarchy at any one time.
- In C, *functions* provide a basic tool for implementing hierarchies.
- Every C program contains a 'master function' called `main`, which:
  - is the first function to start executing in a program
  - is the function that causes all required processing to occur
  - may call other functions to perform required subtasks.
- We can pass information into a function for its use by using *arguments*.
- C provides a large *library* of standard functions; as these have already been written for us, we do not need to know how they operate in order to use them.
  - We must use `#include` to make the compiler read the appropriate header file(s).
- `printf` is one such standard function that allows us to send output to the user's screen.
  - The first argument to `printf` is a string to be printed.
- Functions can
  - be called as often as required
  - call other functions
  - contain as many statements as required
  - call themselves, directly or indirectly (recursion).
- The statements in a function are executed when (and only when) the function is *called*.
- A `void` function's purpose is to carry out the instructions in its function body (inside the braces).
- `void` function *definition*:
  ```
  void function_name (void) {
      /* statements to be executed when function is called */
  }
  ```

- void function *declaration*:
  void *function_name* (void);
- Each function should serve a single, well-defined purpose.
- Functions should have clear, explanatory names. void functions should usually be given verbs as names.
- Program layout:
  - C gives the programmer a lot of freedom in program layout, but we must not split a word or join two words.
  - We should follow layout rules to make the program easier for humans to read.
  - #include (and other # directives to be discussed later) must not be split over lines.
  - *Comments*, delimited by /* and */, let us include information for human readers, and do not alter the meaning of the program.
- *Preconditions* are statements of the conditions under which a given piece of code will work correctly; *postconditions* say what will be done by the code if the preconditions are met.
- Certain words (*keywords*) have a special meaning to the C compiler, and cannot be used for other purposes such as function names.

2.8   SELF-TEST EXERCISES

Short Answer

1 Write two calls to the printf function to output the message:

```
Computers are powerful,
but we must know the rules.
```

2 Repeat Exercise 1, but use only one printf function call.

Programming

3 The standard library contains a function called remove, whose purpose is to delete a file. Using the manual pages in Appendix D, find out how to call the remove function. Now write a program which will remove a file called "freddy" from your directory. Test the program by creating a file called "freddy" (containing junk!) and then running your program to see if the file disappears. (Whatever you do, do **not** call your program "freddy"!) (Note: on some older C systems, remove is called unlink.)

4 The function puts in the standard library copies a string to the output (i.e. the screen). By referring to Appendix D, find out how to use puts. Now write a program which does **exactly** the same thing as the program from Exercise 1 above, but using two puts calls instead of two printf calls. You will have to make a slight change to your strings, because puts does not work in exactly the same way as printf. (Hint: notice in the description of puts that it adds something to the end of the string it is asked to output.)

5 Write a function, `line_of_stars`, which prints a row of asterisks. Now write a `main` function which makes use of the function to print the following:

```
**********************************************************
Ledger line 1
**********************************************************
Ledger line 2
**********************************************************
```

2.9 TEST QUESTIONS

Short Answer

1 State whether each of the following is true or false:

    a   `main` may not call any other functions

    b   a single function can call any number of other functions

    c   no function can be called from more than one other function

    d   `main` is a function

    e   `main` is a `void` function.

2 Predict the output which results from running this program:

```c
#include <stdio.h>
main() {
    printf("/* starts a C comment\n");
    printf("and */ ends it.\n");
    /* printf("Everything in comments is ignored\n"); */
}
```

Try running it on your computer to see if you are right.

Programming

3 On your computer, use your editor to make two files with the names 'filea' and 'fileb'. Make sure they contain different text, so that you can tell them apart. Now write a C program which swaps the names. That is, `filea` should be called `fileb`, and `fileb` should be called `filea`. You will need to use the `rename` function call. After running your program, check the files using your editor to make sure that they were correctly renamed. (Hint: simply renaming `filea` to `fileb` followed by renaming `fileb` to `filea` does not work — can you see why?)

4 At a certain conference, each delegate is to wear a tag showing their name and the organization they represent. The names will be written on the tags by hand, but a page of blank tags is needed for photocopying. Write a program to print five copies of the following blank conference name tag. Use suitable functions.

```
###########################################################
###                  ANNUAL CONFERENCE                 ###
###########################################################
### NAME:                                              ###
###                                                    ###
###########################################################
### ORGANIZATION:                                      ###
###                                                    ###
###########################################################
```

5 Write a program that first prints a triangle (such as that produced by function `triangle` in the text), and then, below it, prints a square. Then write a second program that prints them side by side as follows:

```
  *       ***
 ***      ***
*****     ***
```

Were you able to re-use much of your first program in your second? Why or why not?

6 (Challenge) Write a program (without using advanced features from later chapters) that prints a diagram of the function 2^n, as follows:

```
*
**
****
********
****************
********************************
****************************************************************
```

Your program should contain only **one** '`*`' character. (Hint: 2^n asterisks is 2^{n-1} asterisks followed by another 2^{n-1} asterisks.)

7 (Challenge) Write a program, again using no features from later chapters, to print factorial 6 (i.e. 6!, or $6 \times 5 \times 4 \times 3 \times 2 \times 1$) asterisks in a (very) long row. Write a function for printing 1! asterisks (that is, just a single asterisk), then for each factorial from 2! to 6!, write a function that makes use of the previous function, given that $(n+1)!$ asterisks is $(n+1)$ lots of $n!$ asterisks. (Your computer screen must be capable of running output onto new lines when a line is full, or you won't see the entire output of your program; if you see just one screen line of asterisks, ask your instructor or check your computer manual. Failing that, try a number less than 6 — but it isn't so impressive.)

8 (Challenge) Write a program to print the words of the song, "The Twelve Days of Christmas". If you can't remember the words, make up your own. Don't forget the 'and' ("...**and** a partridge in a pear tree").

9 (Challenge) "The Towers of Hanoi" is a famous brain-teasing problem. There are three pegs, A, B, and C, with a stack of counters on peg A, the largest on the bottom,

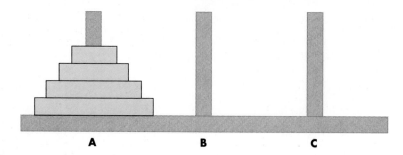

as follows.

The problem is to shift all the counters from peg A to peg C, using peg B as an intermediary. Only one counter may be moved at a time, and a larger counter may not be moved onto a smaller one. Legend has it that monks in a remote monastery are solving this problem with 64 counters, and when they finish, the world will end. We shall stick to four counters, as it is somewhat shorter and less dangerous. One way to find a solution is this: If only we could somehow get all but one counter onto B, we could pick up the final one and move it to C; then if only we could shift those on B onto C, we would have solved the problem. The two 'if only's here are themselves problems in shifting stacks, but with one fewer counters; they can be solved by a similar method, but with different pegs as the source, target and intermediary.

Write a program to print instructions for solving the problem with four counters, based on the insight above. Write a function to shift all four counters, calling two functions for shifting three counters, and one function for shifting one counter, and then write those functions in turn, inventing more functions as necessary, and so on. The functions for moving just one counter should print a simple message, such as "MOVE TOP COUNTER FROM A TO C." If you had a computer connected to a robot, and you replaced these single-move functions with instructions to the robot, you would actually have a game-playing robot.

You may want to keep your solution to this problem for reference when studying recursion later.

Compiler note (from page 19):
Some compilers issue a single warning message for each program in Chapter 2 to 7. For the time being, you can ignore this message, as it is caused by a complication that need not concern us at present. (Interested readers will find the explanation in Section 7.6.1 on page 172.)

3

Data

Objectives

Investigate how computers store data:
— representation methods
— integers, characters and floating point values
— how strings are stored in memory (string literals).

Understand why we need variables in programs:
— how variables differ from constants.

Learn how to create variables in C:
— declaring (i.e. creating) variables
— correctly positioning variable declarations
— local and global variables.

Learn how to perform calculations and change the values of variables:
— simple C expressions and assignments
— common C operators
— using function results in expressions.

See how to output values:
— using `printf` format sequences to print values:
  `%s %d %ld %c %f %e %g`.

C data types:
— `char`, `int`, `long`, `float`
— arrays of `char`s (strings).

3.1 DATA TYPES

In the previous chapter we saw how functions assist us in organizing the logic, or algorithm, of a program. The other chief consideration is the data to be processed. A common definition of *data* is that it is stored *information*. A *data type* is a particular sort of information stored in a particular way. For example, we might have twelve oranges in a bag. The fact that we have exactly twelve can be conveyed in many ways, as shown in Table 3-1.

Table 3-1   Representing twelve

Method used to represent twelve	Representation
decimal number	12
Roman numerals	XII
English	twelve, *or* one dozen
octal number	14
hexadecimal number	C
German	zwölf
binary number	1100

Each of these representations can stand for the value twelve. We could base a computer data type on any of them. To have a data type, we must know two things: the kind of information being stored, and the representation method used to store that data. Both are essential. It so happens that the binary code which makes some printers eject a sheet of paper is also 1100, or twelve. If we did not know the kind of information being stored, we would not know whether it stood for twelve oranges or the skip-page code, or any of a thousand other possible interpretations of that binary number. If we did not know the representation method, we would not know that '1100' should be decoded according to the rules of binary integers; we would not be able to decipher the value it represented.

We can summarize the relationship between data and information in either of these two ways.
- **Data is information stored using a particular representation.**
- **Information is the meaning of the data when correctly interpreted.**

Most computer languages allow a number of different types of data. C even lets us create our own data types for dealing with specialized situations which could not be anticipated by the language designers. Each data type is capable of storing a particular kind of information, and uses a suitable method to represent that information.

3.2 CONSTANTS, VARIABLES AND EXPRESSIONS

Some important data-related concepts are *constants*, *variables*, and *expressions*.

A constant is a data item with a fixed, unchangeable value. Examples are the various messages which were output by `printf` in the previous chapter (such messages are called *string literals*), and integer and fractional numbers (32, 28.4 etc.).

Variables are places in memory, referred to by a symbolic name such as `tax_rate` or `client_name`, that can have their contents altered as program execution proceeds. In C, variables are vital for real-world programming, because without them, all data values would have to be foreseen by the programmer and written as constants. The full power of computers cannot be exploited with that limitation.

In the early days of computing, when people had to program in machine language, programmers manually allocated data to memory locations. This was an onerous and error-prone task. Variables in languages such as C solve this problem because the compiler takes care of allocating the variable to a suitable location in memory. For example, the statement

```
tax_rate = 10.5;
```

stores the value 10.5 in the variable `tax_rate`. We need not (and usually do not) know the machine addresses where the variable resides. All we have to do is consistently use the right name for the right data item. In C we must *declare* variables: that is, say what names we shall be using and what types of data they will store. So, before using `tax_rate` as above, we would have to include a declaration:

```
float tax_rate;
```

to specify that `tax_rate` will hold a fractional number; `float` is a data type for storing fractional numbers using a representation method known as *floating point* (the details of which need not concern us here).

We may declare variables outside the functions (for example, just below the '`#include`' lines), or inside a function, just after the opening brace ({). Those declared outside are called *global* variables, those declared inside are called *local* variables. Global variables may be used in all functions that follow, but local variables are only available in the function that contains the declaration. It is like the difference between writing a public letter to a newspaper and writing a private one to your best friend. Thus globals are used to hold information needed in more than one function, while local variables are used to store information that has no importance to any other function. It is important to choose correctly whether to use local or global variables.

In general, **use local variables wherever possible.**

Globals violate the principle of program structure discussed in Chapter 2: only worry about one thing at a time. Since globals are accessible everywhere, it is sometimes hard to keep track of where and how they are being used.

Figure 3.1 represents a program with local and global variables. It has two functions, myfunc and yourfunc. Each has a local variable locvar. There is also a global variable, globvar. Each function has its own 'personal' copy of locvar, but there is only one globvar. Local variables declared as shown in Figure 3.1 are called *automatic* variables; the system automatically creates them on function entry and destroys them on exit.

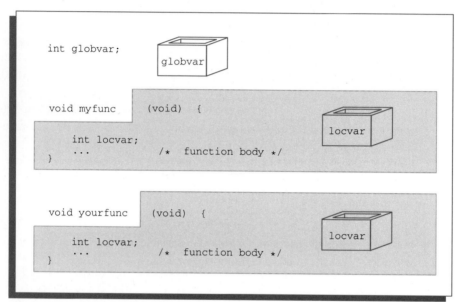

Figure 3.1 Storage allocation for local and global variables

Finally, *expressions* represent the computation of a value, and may include constants, variables, and *operators* such as plus (+), minus (−), multiply (*), and so on. We can also use functions in expressions. For example,

```
hypotenuse = sqrt(sidea*sidea + sideb*sideb);
```

uses the sqrt (square root) function to calculate the hypotenuse of a right-angled triangle, provided the variables sidea and sideb contain the lengths of the other two sides. The value computed by sqrt, which is called the function *result* (described in Section 3.6.2), is assigned to the variable hypotenuse.

3.2.1 String literals

The messages that `printf` output in the previous chapter are called *string literals*; they are sequences of characters in double quotation marks ("):

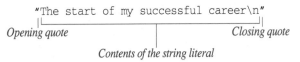

Unlike English, C does not distinguish between left and right quotation marks. We do not write

"The start of my successful career\n"

because early printers (and many modern ones), did not have two types of quotes. In C, the first quote starts a string literal, and the next closes it. The closing quote must be on the same line as the opening quote. For long strings, a special rule lets us continue over multiple lines: if we close the string, then write nothing but whitespace (i.e. no commas, etc.) and then reopen the string, it is considered to be a single string. Thus the following is identical to the string above:

```
"The start of my "
"successful career\n"
```

Each character is stored in a byte of computer memory. When we pass a string literal as an argument to a function such as `printf`, the compiler writes code to give the function the address of the first character. Thus it is able to fetch the entire string from consecutive memory locations starting at that address. Addresses are often called *pointers*.

Within string literals the backslash character (\ ) introduces an *escape sequence*, which is a group of characters with a special meaning. This overcomes the problem that not all characters represent printable (visible) text. We have already met newline, represented by \n. Another escape sequence, \ ", lets us put a quote within a string literal. Thus

```
printf("\"Hello!\" said the rabbit!\n");
```

would print

```
"Hello!" said the rabbit!
```

The \ is not actually stored in the string; it merely flags the following character as being somehow special. A related question is how to print backslash itself. You might guess this one:

```
printf("Yes, here it is: \\  <<< There it was!\n");
```

which will print

```
Yes, here it is: \  <<< There it was!
```

Don't forget that escape sequences are introduced with the backslash (\), not the forward slash (/). The full list of allowable escape sequences is given in Appendix C.

Although each escape sequence is written as more than one character, each one represents just one byte in memory, as shown by Listing 3-1.

Listing 3-1

```
#include <stdio.h>

main() {
    printf("h\"i\\low\"\n0//1/n");
}
```

This program contains the following string literal:

"h\"i\\low\"\n0//1/n"

Stored in memory, it will occupy successive bytes as follows:

| ... | h | " | i | \ | l | o | w | " | \n | 0 | / | / | 1 | / | n | • | ... |

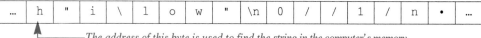
—The address of this byte is used to find the string in the computer's memory.

Comparing the picture with the string literal, we see that the compiler has placed an extra byte on the right-hand end. This byte contains a special value known as *nul*, and it is shown in the picture as a solid dot. The nul byte is used to mark the end of the string. There is an escape sequence for nul also, namely \0 (i.e. zero, not the letter O). All strings should end with a nul.

Now let us inspect the numeric values in each byte of the string. This is not quite as simple as it sounds, because not all computers use the same coding method to store characters. The most common is called ASCII (American Standard Code for Information Interchange). Although the acronym includes 'American', most countries use a similar code. About twelve of the codes are used for special national characters in other countries. Britain, for example, changes just one symbol to the pound sign (£). France changes some eleven symbols to represent special French characters like â, à, and ç. Australia, on the other hand, uses the American codes unchanged. (The full ASCII code table is given in Appendix G.) Throughout this book we shall assume that the computer being used uses ASCII codes; but don't forget that this is not always so. With ASCII coding the above string will be stored like this (although each number is actually stored in binary, of course):

| ... | 104 | 34 | 105 | 92 | 108 | 111 | 119 | 34 | 10 | 48 | 47 | 47 | 49 | 47 | 110 | 0 | ... |

There are a few surprises. For example, the code for the character 0 is **not** zero; 0 is stored as 48, and — surprise — the nul character has code zero. No, the designers of the code were not crazy. It makes good sense if every visible character has a non-zero code. Also observe how the \n character is stored in a single byte (with value 10 in ASCII).

We saw earlier that C uses the address of the first character to locate a string in memory. Suppose, for the sake of argument, that when our program runs, the string shown above is stored in memory locations numbered from 400 onwards. These would be the addresses of the bytes:

...	104	34	105	92	108	111	119	34	10	48	47	47	49	47	110	0	...
..399	400	401	402	403	404	405	406	407	408	409	410	411	412	413	414	415	416

The first byte has **address** 400, but its **content** is 104, the ASCII code for h. When the printf statement is called, it is given the address of the string, not the contents of any or all of these memory locations. Thus the value 400 would be given to printf. It is important to be quite clear about the difference between the address of a memory location and its contents.

3.2.2 Constants: integers and characters

C allows us to write integer constants using the usual decimal notation. So, if there are sixty-eight crates in a warehouse, we can write that as 68 in our program. The compiler converts such constants into a binary representation. For example, to add some integers and print the total, we might proceed as in Listing 3-2.

Listing 3-2

```
/* A program to print the sum of 65, 87, and 33. */

#include <stdio.h>

main(void) {
    printf("The sum of %d, %d, and %d is %d\n", 65, 87, 33, 65+87+33);
}
```

The output is

```
The sum of 65, 87, and 33 is 185
```

This program uses an expression containing the plus (+) operator to perform the calculation. Note how we make printf output numeric values. In the first argument, the format string, each %d sequence is replaced in the output by the value of a subsequent argument; %d is recognized by printf as a command to output a value as a decimal integer. The value used is the next available argument from the printf argument list. Apart from %d, there are many other allowable *format sequences*, including %c (which treats a value as a character code and prints the character that code represents), and %s (which prints a string).

Note the difference between escape codes starting with \, and format sequences starting with %. An escape code such as \n is recognized by the compiler itself and converted into a single character. A format sequence, for example, %d, is treated like any other character sequence by the compiler, and is stored in a string as separate characters, % and d.

We can represent a single character by surrounding the character concerned with single quotes. Thus, 'a' represents the character a, '4' the character 4, and so on. As with string literals, these are stored as numeric binary codes (again, usually ASCII), and the same backslash escape sequences may be used. The difference is that a character in single quotes stands for the ASCII code of just one character; a sequence of characters in double quotes is a nul-terminated string literal. Don't confuse them!

Since character constants are stored internally as numbers, and integer constants are also stored that way, you might ask whether there is really any difference between them. For example, if a memory location contains the binary code for 68, is there any way of knowing whether it represents the sixty-eight crates in the warehouse, or whether it stands for the letter D, whose ASCII code happens to be 68? In fact there is no difference. The two notations, 68 and 'D' both stand for the same internal binary value. As far as the compiler is concerned, we can use them interchangeably. But for human readers, obviously we should use decimal constants when we are thinking of such things as sixty-eight crates, and character constants when we are thinking of printable letters. There is no law in C against doing it the perverse way — although some other programming languages are more finicky — but it is not very sensible.

We can use the equivalence of these two notations to write a program to tell us which character has a certain ASCII code, and, conversely, which code is assigned to a particular character. Listing 3-3 uses the different behavior of the %c and %d format sequences to do this.

Listing 3-3

```
/* Prints the code for the letter 'A', and the character with code 64.
   Note: these will be ASCII only if the computer uses ASCII codes.
*/

#include <stdio.h>

main() {
    printf("Character %c has ASCII code %d.\n", 'A', 'A');
    printf("ASCII code %d belongs to character %c.\n", 64, 64);
}
```

The output, provided the computer uses ASCII codes, is

```
Character A has ASCII code 65.
ASCII code 64 belongs to character @.
```

The same value ('A' in the first `printf`, or 64 in the second) looks very different depending on whether it is treated as a character code (using `%c`) or as a decimal number (using `%d`).

3.3   `char` AND `int` VARIABLES; `char` ARRAYS

To use a variable, we must first declare it. This tells the compiler, among other things, what type of variables we want, and what names they will have. C's data types `char` and `int` both denote variables that can store integer values, but the compiler allocates more memory for an `int` than for a `char`; a `char` is stored in a single byte, whereas an `int` usually has two or four bytes. Therefore an `int` can store a larger value than a `char` can. C guarantees at least the range 0 to 127 for `char`s, and −32,767 to 32,767 for `int`s (but individual compilers may provide larger ranges). Due to the restricted range, `char` is often used for storing character codes — hence the name 'char'. To declare variables, we write the data type name followed by names of the variables we require. For example:

```
char first, second;
```

declares two `char` variables called `first` and `second`. C allows us to write mathematical expressions using various arithmetic and other operators. Among other things, we can use the *assignment operator*, =, to assign a value to a variable:

```
first = 'A';
```

This will copy the constant 'A' into the memory location reserved for `first`. Never forget that the = operator in C is used to **copy a value into a variable**.

Never pronounce '=' as 'equals' when reading a program: pronounce it as 'gets' or 'becomes'. The above assignment, read aloud, should be "first **gets** character A" or "first **becomes** character A", but **not** "first **equals** character A". This is a very important warning; forgetting it can cause lot of confusion.

Following the above assignment, we can use the stored value, for example by printing it. So

```
printf("%c", first);
```

will print the A we placed in `first`. This does not destroy the stored value; we may use the same stored value many times: the only way to lose the value in a variable is to overwrite it by storing a different value there.

Variables can each hold just one value at a time, although we can alter that value whenever we wish with an assignment. But what if we want to store, say, a string? Strings contain many characters, and so will not fit in a single `char` variable. No problem — we declare an *array*, which can store many values. Thus

```
char ch;           /* Declares a character variable, ch. */
char cha[5];       /* Declare a character array, cha. */
```

creates two variables: a simple variable, `ch`, which can hold just one value, and an array, `cha`, which can hold five values. We can think of a simple variable as a box in which a value can be stored, and an array as a whole row of boxes. We could picture the above two declarations as in Figure 3.2.

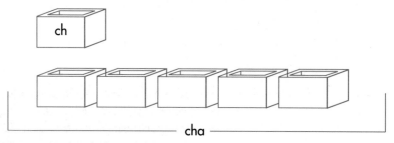

Figure 3.2   Box concept of a variable and an array

This simple picture is surprisingly accurate in so far as the behavior of a computer is concerned. Although it really works electronically, it behaves as if it contained little boxes where values may be stored.

To store a string in a `char` array, we first declare it to be sufficiently large for the string in question. Thus

```
char buffer[100], buffer2[300];
```

causes space for 100 `char`s to be allocated for `buffer` and 300 for `buffer2`. Strings are stored in arrays in exactly the same manner as in string literals. In particular, the end of the string is marked by the presence of a nul immediately after the last character forming part of the string. Thus a string in an array may be shorter than the length of the array, depending on the position of the nul. The need for the nul means that the storage needed is always one byte more than the number of meaningful characters in a string. Therefore:

Always declare `char` arrays at least one longer than the maximum length string which might be stored there.

The declared size of an array must be a constant expression: that is, one containing no variables.

The assignment operator, `=`, cannot be used to assign an entire array, therefore we cannot store a string in a `char` array using the assignment operator (`=`). Instead, we use the library function `strcpy`. It has two arguments, the name of the array to copy the string into, and a string to be copied, either a string literal or another array name. Thus

```
strcpy(buffer, "Bill Shakespeare");
```

copies `Bill Shakespeare` into `buffer`. This uses 17 bytes, not forgetting the nul. We may leave parts of an array unused if we have some way to tell where the used part ends — in this case nul serves that purpose. Now we could write

```
strcpy(buffer2, buffer);
```

and copy `Bill Shakespeare` into `buffer2` also. We can print a string (either a literal or one in an array) with the `printf` format, `%s`. So

```
printf("Our friend %s wrote Macbeth.\n", buffer2);
```

prints the string we placed in `buffer2`, as follows:

```
Our friend Bill Shakespeare wrote Macbeth.
```

Use of `strcpy` requires the inclusion of the header `<string.h>`:

```
#include <string.h>
```

Can a variable always be used wherever a constant is allowed? There are some places where only constants are allowed, but they are few, and in this text they will be well advertised. In general, use whatever types of values you wish wherever you wish.

3.4 `printf` FACILITIES FOR DATA OUTPUT

Although `printf` is very useful, we must be careful to call it correctly. The first argument **must** be a string (either a literal, or one in a `char` array). `printf` prints that string, and then terminates. Other arguments are only printed if the first string contains format specifiers that request `printf` to take a value from the argument list and output it. We have met format specifiers `%c`, `%d` and `%s`; we shall meet others shortly: `%ld` for type `long`, and `%f`, `%g` and `%e` for types `float` and `double`.

In a format specifier we can tell `printf` how to format the output values. We may specify a *width* between the `%` and the letter (`s`, `d`, etc.). This is the amount of space to allocate for the value. Thus the statements:

```
printf(";%4d;%3d;%2d;%1d;\n", 187, 187, 187, 187);
printf(";%4s;%3s;%2s;%1s;\n", "hi", "hi", "hi", "hi");
```

specify successive widths equal to 4, 3, 2, and 1 characters, and print:

```
; 187;187;187;187;
;  hi; hi;hi;hi;
```

Notice how, if we underestimate, more space is allocated automatically, and if we overestimate, `printf` fills unused columns with blanks on the left. In other words the width is the *minimum* number of characters printed.

Since blank padding is usually added to the left of the printed value with the value on the right, this is called right justification. To put the printed value on the left with the blank padding to the right (left justification), place a minus sign before the width. Thus

```
printf(";%8s;%-8s;\n", "right", "left");
```

outputs

```
;   right;left    ;
```

A second formatting value called the *precision* may be added. The precision follows a full stop. Thus, if we write `%.4s`, then the 4 is the precision, but if we write `%4s` then the 4 is the width. We may supply any combination of width and precision:

```
"%1.2s  %.3d %5s"
```

precision

width

The effect of the precision depends on the format specifier. For `%s`, it is the maximum number of characters to output; if a string is longer than the precision, the excess characters will not be printed. We may combine this with the width to specify both a minimum and a maximum:

```
printf(";%2.4s;%2.4s;%2.4s;%2.4s;%2.4s;\n",
                "a", "ab", "abc", "abcd", "abcde");
```

specifies a minimum of two characters and a maximum of four, and will print:

```
; a;ab;abc;abcd;abcd;
```

For integers, the precision is the minimum number of digits to be printed. It is used to force the printing of leading zeroes. For example if we were printing hours and minutes in 24-hour format, we might write

```
printf("%.2d:%.2d\n", hours, minutes);
```

If `hours` is 18 and `minutes` is 6, it will print

```
18:06
```

To print a percentage sign (`%`), include two of them in the format string; `%` is special only in the format string. Thus

```
printf("%%  %c  %s\n", '%', "%%");
```

prints:

```
%   %   %%
```

Only the `%%` in the format string prints as a single character.

It is **our** responsibility as programmers to ensure that the values in the argument list are consistent with the format specifiers in the format string. Thus, if the format string is "`%s %d`", the next argument should be a string (for the `%s`), and the one after should be an integer (for the `%d`). So

```
printf("%s %d", "Number of apples:", 387);
```

is correct, but

```
printf("%s %d", 387, "apples");
```

is absolutely wrong! Take special care to check `printf` statements carefully, as few C compilers can spot these errors.

To allow us to vary the width or precision dynamically (i.e. as the program runs), precisions and/or widths may be taken from an argument if an asterisk (*) is used instead of a number. Thus

```
printf("%.*s\n", n, "Goodbye");
```

requests that the precision be taken from the next argument. It will print

```
G
```

if n is one, but

```
Go
```

if n is 2, etc.

3.5 EXAMPLE: NAME TAGS WITH SEAT NUMBERS

We return to the problem of printing name tags, but first let us make it a bit harder, and demand that, as well as the name, each tag must have a three-digit seat number, for example:

```
**************************************************
**************************************************
**                                              **
**                John Smith     (seat 100)   **
**                                              **
**************************************************
**************************************************
```

We shall make the program compute the seat numbers starting with seat 100, and allocate seats in ascending order.

We could follow the same plan as in Chapter 2, with a separate function for each name, but using variables we can do better. If we have variables to store the name and seat number, we can write a function to print a tag containing whatever name and number those variables hold. Let us call this function print_tag. Then all we need do is change the contents of those variables and call the same function again; it will now print the second name and number. We repeat this process for each required tag.

To begin, we shall decide what variables are needed. The seat number, being integral, can be placed in an int: seat_num, say. The name, however, consists of more than one character, so it must be stored in an array of chars. If we allow, say, 20 characters in a name, the array must be 21 characters long. (Don't forget the trailing nul in every string.) Thus the variable declarations might be:

```
char name[21];  /* Holds the name to be put on the tag - max 20 chars */
int seat_num;   /* Holds the seat number to be put on the tag. */
```

print_tag must contain a line that prints the contents of the variables name and seat_num. We must make sure that both variables contain correct values each time print_tag is called. Looking at seat_num first, we notice two distinct problems: making sure that the first number printed is 100, and then making sure the number increases by one for each successive tag. The first problem is easily dealt with by assigning 100 to seat_num in main prior to the first call to print_tag.

We could solve the second problem similarly, by having successive assignments of the numbers 101, 102, etc., interleaved between the calls to `print_tag`, but there is another way to do this: we compute the next value from the preceding one. In `print_tag`, after printing the seat number, we alter the value in `seat_num`, making it one larger than it was before. In summary, our logic in `main` and `print_tag` must be:

main:
    Set **seat_num** to 100.
    Set **name** to "John Smith".
    Call **print_tag** (which increments **seat_num** to 101).
    Print blank line.
    Set **name** to "Mary Peterson".
    Call **print_tag** (which increments **seat_num** to 102).
    Print blank line.
    Set **name** to "Alison Gray".
    Call **print_tag** (which increments **seat_num** to 103 (not used)).

print_tag:
    Print top section.
    Print name line using current values of **name** and **seat_num**.
    Print bottom section.
    Add one to **seat_num**.

Before looking at the C code for this, a few details need consideration. Setting `seat_num` to 100 is simple:

```
seat_num = 100;
```

Adding one to `seat_num` inside `print_tag` involves computing the new value from the old. Well, `seat_num+1` is one larger than `seat_num`; we should assign it to `seat_num`, overwriting its previous value, as follows:

```
seat_num = seat_num + 1;
```

Thus the seat number will automatically be incremented after every tag. In mathematics, where = means 'equals', this statement is wrong, as nothing can be equal to itself plus one. But in C, where = means 'copy the value on the right into the variable on the left', it makes perfect sense, making the value in `seat_num` one greater than before.

As for the name, we can use `strcpy` prior to each call to `print_tag`, placing a different name in `name` each time. Thus

```
strcpy(name, "John Smith");    /* Set up first name */
print_tag();                   /* Print first tag */
```

prints a tag for John Smith. Inside `print_tag`, we can print our two variables like this:

```
printf("**      %20s   (seat %3d)  **\n", name, seat_num);
```

The `%20s` format specifier prints `name`. The width of 20 forces `printf` to use at least 20 characters. Shorter names will be padded with blank spaces on their left. This ensures that the `**` on the righthand end of the line falls in the right place to make the printed tag look correct. A similar trick on the %d format ensures that at least three digits are printed for each seat number.

Finally, since the two variables are used in both main and print_tag, they must be global, not local. It is now straightforward to develop the complete program shown in Listing 3-4.

Listing 3-4

```
/* A program to print name tags with seat numbers. Seats are allocated
 * consecutive numbers starting with 100
 * Prints a tag for each of the following names:
 *        John Smith
 *        Mary Peterson
 *        Alison Gray
 */

#include <stdio.h>
#include <string.h>

/*** Global variables: ***/
char name[21];  /* Holds the name to be put on the tag - max 20 chars */
int seat_num;   /* Holds the seat number to be put on the tag. */

/*** Function declarations: ***/
void print_tag(void);
void print_side_border(void);
void print_stars(void);

/* main: Prints the name tags, with a blank line between each. */
main() {
    seat_num = 100;                  /* First seat is no. 100 */
    strcpy(name, "John Smith");      /* Set up first name */
    print_tag();                     /* Print first tag */
    printf("\n");                    /* Blank line between tags */
    strcpy(name, "Mary Peterson");   /* Second name */
    print_tag();                     /* Second tag */
    printf("\n");                    /* Blank line */
    strcpy(name, "Alison Gray");     /* Third name */
    print_tag();                     /* Third tag */
}

/* print_tag: Prints a name tag with seat number.
   On entry: The name (max. 20 chars) must be in the global array 'name'.
             The seat number must be in the global integer 'seat_num'.
   After printing tag, increments the seat number ready for the next tag.
*/

void print_tag(void) {
    /* Top section:  */
    print_stars();
    print_stars();
    print_side_border();
```

```
    /* Line containing the name and number:  */
    printf("**          %20s    (seat %3d)  **\n", name, seat_num);

    /* Bottom section:  */
    print_side_border();
    print_stars();
    print_stars();
    seat_num = seat_num + 1;
}

/* print_stars: Prints a row of stars to form a tag border. */

void print_stars(void) {
    printf("************************************************\n");
}

/* print_side_border: Prints left and right parts of the vertical rows
                      of stars which form a tag border. */

void print_side_border(void) {
    printf("**                                          **\n");
}
```

The output is

```
************************************************
************************************************
**                                          **
**               John Smith     (seat 100)  **
**                                          **
************************************************
************************************************


************************************************
************************************************
**                                          **
**             Mary Peterson    (seat 101)  **
**                                          **
************************************************
************************************************


************************************************
************************************************
**                                          **
**              Alison Gray     (seat 102)  **
**                                          **
************************************************
************************************************
```

3.6 EXPRESSIONS

3.6.1 Operators

C provides an extensive range of operators for use in expressions, including operators for common purposes such as division, subtraction and multiplication.

Table 3-3 Some useful C operators

C operator	Purpose
+	Perform addition
−	Perform subtraction and negation
*	Perform multiplication
/	Perform division
%	Find the remainder
=	Assignment to a variable

Note that the multiplication operator may **not** be omitted. The use of the asterisk for multiplication and slash for division may seem odd. These choices were made because the multiplication symbol (×) could not be used because of the possibility of confusion with the letter x, and the usual division symbol (÷) is not available on many computer display devices. In fact, ÷ does not even have an ASCII code. We may use expressions made up with these and other operators wherever we wish to calculate a value.

The *remainder* operator (%), when used between two positive integers, gives the remainder when the first is divided by the second. For example, 22%5 is 2, because 5 divides evenly into 20, and 22–20 equals 2.

When using expressions we must follow the arithmetic operator *precedence* rules: multiplication and division are performed before addition and subtraction, unless the latter are protected by parentheses. The precedence rules play an important part in C, and we shall return to the topic in future chapters. Here are some examples of arithmetic expressions in both normal mathematical, and C formats.

Table 3-4 Equivalent C and mathematical expressions

Example number	Mathematical expression	Equivalent C expression
1	$x + y$	x + y
2	$5 + 2x$	5 + 2 * x
3	$x(x - y + 7)$	x * (x - y + 7)
4	$\dfrac{x + y}{4xy}$	(x + y) / (4 * x * y)
5	$x \div 6$	x / 6

The above are *binary* (or *dyadic*) operators, meaning that they take two *operands*. (In x+y, x and y are the operands.) There are also *unary* (or *monadic*) operators which have only one operand. For example, the minus operator (−) can be used as a unary operator to negate a value, as in

```
x = -y;
```

which, if y contained 6, say, would store −6 in x.

C provides many operators to make life easier. For example, we often need to add one to a variable. The ++ unary operator does this. Thus, instead of writing

```
total = total + 1;
```

we just write

```
total++;
```

or

```
++total;
```

There is a slight difference between writing the operator before or after the variable, but for the present we shall ignore it. As you might guess, there is a −− operator for subtracting one from a variable. Unary − and ++ and −− when written before an operand are called *prefix* operators; ++ and −− written after an operand are called *postfix* operators.

There is also a shortcut for adding a number other than one: the += operator. So, instead of writing

```
total = total + 57;
```

we can just write

```
total += 57;
```

There are shortcut operators similar to this for subtraction, multiplication, division, and remainder, as shown in the following table. Remember that these shortcuts are provided mainly for convenience; we do not have to use them if we do not want to.

Table 3-5   Shortcut equivalents for common calculations

Example calculation	Shortcut equivalent
`total = total + 9;`	`total += 9;`
`diff = diff - 2;`	`diff -= 2;`
`prod = prod * 3;`	`prod *= 3;`
`quot = quot / 16;`	`quot /= 16;`
`rem = rem % 12;`	`rem %= 12;`

3.6.2 Function results

Function results allow C functions to be used in much the same way as functions in mathematics. For example, the exponential, trigonometric, and square root functions in mathematics have their analogs in the standard C library. To see how to use functions in expressions, let us look at the square root function. If I write

```
root = sqrt(4.0);
```

the `sqrt` library function executes, computing the square root of 4.0 and *returning* it as the result of the function call, `sqrt(4.0)`. How does the program use this result? To know the answer, imagine the result written into the program in place of the function call. If we do this, we get:

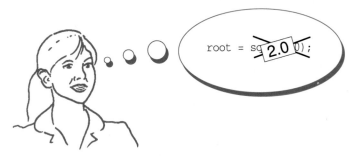

and it is obvious the statement assigns 2.0 to the variable, `root`.

Function results also parallel the everyday activity of answering questions. For example, if I ask my accountant "How much tax will I need to pay?", I expect to receive an answer: "You need to pay $*n*." The C equivalent would be to write a function, say, `tax_payable`, which computes the answer to my question and returns it as the function result. I might use the function in a statement such as:

```
my_tax = tax_payable();
```

which assigns the answer (how much tax) to the variable `my_tax`, which should be declared previously. For now we shall be content to use results of library functions, and postpone for later the question of writing our own functions that yield results.

3.7 OTHER DATA TYPES

In this section we shall briefly introduce some of the more useful data types in C.

3.7.1 Floating point data: `float` and `double`

There are many problems where we need to deal with fractional numbers, particularly in science and engineering. For example, if we are measuring voltage, we are as likely to get a value such as 3.8 as we are to get an integer value like 6. Since `int`s are restricted to integral values, C also provides the `float` and `double` data types. The difference between these two is their precision. Since storing the digits of a number consumes memory, there will be a limit to how accurately the computer can store a value. While floats on most computers are accurate to around seven decimal digits, doubles, because they occupy more memory, are usually accurate to around fifteen decimal digits. These types can hold positive or negative numbers with magnitudes from 10^{-37} to 10^{37}, and zero. Some compilers allow larger ranges than these.

floats and doubles are declared in the normal way. For example,

```
float f, g, radius;
```

creates three float variables, f, g and radius. We can assign values to such variables in the obvious way, but the values may be fractional:

```
f = 2.8;
g = -1.684;
radius = f + g;
```

As well as the familiar fractional notation above, constants can be written in floating point notation, which is a variation of the standard scientific style of writing numbers. In chemistry, Avogadro's number is approximately 6.02×10^{23}. In a C program, we would write it as 6.02E23 or 6.02e23. The E or e is short for 'times ten to the power'. The power (in this number, 23) is called the *exponent*.

We can use the *, /, +, and − operators (and their shortcut equivalents) with floats and doubles, and they give the same type of results. We cannot use %, however, as that is an integer remainder operator only. (But see Appendix D for the fmod function, which performs a floating point remainder operation.)

How do we decide whether to use int or float variables to store a data value? Although there are exceptions, a useful guide is:

- int variables are integral. Use them for values obtained by **counting**: how many apples, how many atoms, etc.
- float and double variables allow fractions. Use them for values obtained by **measuring**: your weight, the length of a girder, etc.

We may assign integers to floating variables and vice versa. No problems arise assigning integers to floating variables: the integer value is simply converted into the equivalent floating-point representation. Going the other way, though, there is a trap for the unwary. Consider

```
intvar = 6.99995;
```

C always discards the fractional part to convert floating point to integer format. Thus 6 will be assigned to intvar. This is called *truncation*. Most likely, though, we would want the nearest integer to the original value. A simple trick will do this, if we know the floating value is positive: add 0.5 before assigning to the int:

```
intvar = 6.99995 + 0.5;
```

This is called *rounding*.

Outputting `floats` and `doubles`

We can output these values (either constants, variables or expressions) using `printf`'s `%f`, `%e`, and `%g` formats, which work for both `floats` and `doubles`: `%f` always prints a normal fractional number, without exponent; `%e` always prints a number with an exponent; and `%g` tries to choose a neat appearance, depending on the value being printed.

For all three format specifiers, the width is, as usual, the total number of characters to be printed. The precision, for `%e` and `%f`, is the number of digits after the decimal point; for `%g`, it is the total number of significant digits. Listing 3-5 shows some examples of these formats.

Listing 3-5

```
#include <stdio.h>

main() {
    float f, g, radius, Avogadro;
    f = 2.8;
    g = -1.684;
    radius = f + g;
    Avogadro = 6.02e23;
    printf("%f %6.3f %8.2f\n", radius, -12.81963, Avogadro / 1e19);
    printf("%e %6.3e %8.2e\n", radius, -12.81963, Avogadro / 1e19);
    printf("%g %6.3g %8.2g\n", radius, -12.81963, Avogadro / 1e19);
}
```

The output is

```
1.116000 -12.820 60200.00
1.116000e+00 -1.282e+01 6.02e+04
1.116  -12.8      6e+04
```

The first value on each line shows the default format. The second shows how decimal digits are properly rounded to fit into the specified precision. The extra digits are not simply chopped off; what you see printed is the closest to the actual value which can be shown in the requested precision.

Mathematical functions

The header file `<math.h>` contains definitions for a host of functions needed for mathematical and scientific problems. Most of them have arguments and results of type `double`, but they will also accept `float` arguments. Among these functions are:

`cos(x)`	returns cos x (the cosine function)
`sin(x)`	returns sin x (sine)
`tan(x)`	returns tan x (tangent)

`cosh(x)`	returns cosh x (the hyperbolic cosine function)
`sinh(x)`	returns sinh x (hyperbolic sine)
`tanh(x)`	returns tanh x (hyperbolic tangent)
`acos(x)`	returns $\cos^{-1} x$ (the inverse cosine function)
`asin(x)`	returns $\sin^{-1} x$ (inverse sine)
`atan(x)`	returns $\tan^{-1} x$ (inverse tangent)
`atan2(y,x)`	returns $\tan^{-1} y/x$ (inverse tangent of the quotient of two numbers)
`log(x)`	returns ln x (natural logarithm of x)
`log10(x)`	returns $\log_{10} x$ (logarithm to base 10 of x)
`exp(x)`	returns e^x (exponential)
`pow(x,y)`	returns x^y (x to the power y)
`sqrt(x)`	returns $\sqrt{x}$ (square root of x)
`fabs(x)`	returns $|x|$ (absolute value of x)
`abs(i)`	returns $|i|$ (absolute value of i; i is `int`, `int` result)
	Note: defined in the header `<stdlib.h>`
`labs(l)`	returns $|l|$ (absolute value of l; l is `long`, `long` result)
	Note: defined in the header `<stdlib.h>`.

For a brief example, to print the cosine of the angle stored in the `double` variable `theta`, we would write

```
printf("Cos(theta) is %f\n", cos(theta));
```

Note: the trigonometric functions (sin, cos etc.) require an argument in radians, not degrees. Degrees are converted to radians by multiplying by π and dividing by 180, as there are π radians in 180°: π is approximately 3.141592654. Examples of these functions in complete programs are given in subsequent chapters.

3.7.2 The type `long`

Like `int`s, `long` variables are integers, but they are guaranteed to have a large range of permissible values. (Recall that `int`s are only guaranteed to allow values between −32,767 and 32,767.) `long` values may range from −2,147,483,647 to 2,147,483,647. Again, a particular compiler may allow a larger range. They are useful whenever large integers might be encountered. For example, programs dealing with the time of day need to allow for the fact that there are 86,400 seconds in a day. `long` constants are written as normal decimal values with an 'l' (el, not one) or 'L' immediately after the final digit, for example `381673L`. `long` values may be output with `printf` by using the `%ld` (el-dee, not one-dee) format specifier.

Some compilers do not distinguish between the sizes of `int`s and `long`s, allowing the former to be as large as the latter. Even so, if a problem needs large numbers, `long` should be used, because one day that program might be compiled with a compiler that does not permit big values in `int`s.

3.8 SUMMARY

- *Data* is *information* represented according to well-defined rules.
- C has many data types for storing *integer* values.
  - Characters are stored as integer codes (usually ASCII).
  - The `char` type is used to store an integer code for any character.
  - The `int` type can store values from −32,767 to 32,767 inclusive. Some compilers let us store larger numbers than this.
  - The `long` data type is like `int`, but allows a larger range of values.
- *String literals* consist of readable text in double quotes.
  - The same type of quotation mark both opens and closes a literal.
  - The opening and closing quote must be on the same line.
  - Each character is stored in one computer memory byte.
  - Special characters are represented with *escape sequences*, such as:
  - `\n`   newline
  - `\"`   the quote character itself
  - `\\`   the backslash itself
  - `\0`   the *nul* character.
  - A string is terminated by a *nul* character.
- *Variables* are named places in memory where a data value of the appropriate type may be stored.
  - Variables must be *declared* before they are used.
  - A variable can only store one value at a time.
  - A variable may be given a value using the *assignment operator*, =.
- Local variables:
  - are declared inside a function, and can only be used inside that function
  - should be used wherever feasible.
- Global variables:
  - are declared outside functions
  - may be accessed by any function
  - should only be used for data needed by more than one function.
- An *array* is a place in memory which can store many values.
  - A `char` array may be used to store a string.
- `printf` can output data using format sequences in the format string.
  - Some format sequences are: `%s` (for strings), `%c` (for character codes), `%d` (for integers), `%ld` (for `long` integers), or `%f`, `%e` and `%g` (for `floats` and `doubles`).
  - For each format sequence, a suitable argument to be output must be supplied following the format string.
  - Format sequences can have length specifications to control formatting of output:
  - The *width* is the minimum number of characters to print, for all format types.
  - For `%s` formats, the *precision*, written after a period, is the maximum number of characters to print.
  - For `%d`, the precision is the minimum number of digits to print.

- For %f and %e, the precision is the number of places after the decimal point; for %g it is the total number of digits.
    - %% is used in the format string **only**, to print the % character.
- Calculations may be performed by writing expressions.
    - Operators include +, −, *, / and, for integers only, %.
    - Shortcut assignment operators: ++, −−, +=, −=, *=, /=, %=.
    - Function *results* may also be used in expressions.
    - A range of mathematical functions are provided in the standard library.
- Variable names are *identifiers*, which may include letters, underscores and digits, but may not commence with a digit. Upper and lower case letters are considered to be different.

3.9 SELF-TEST EXERCISES

Short Answer

1 What happens if you assign to a variable a value which is too big for it to store? Write a program which assigns the value 10,000 to a char variable, then print the value of the variable. What happened?

2 On a certain programming project, you discover that your program needs to be able to remember which day of the week it is. Devise a rule for storing this information in a char variable.

3 You have been asked to write a program by a card player. How would you store information about playing cards? For example, how would you store the fact that a certain card is the ace of hearts? (You may use more than one variable if you wish.)

4 Based on your knowledge of local and global variables, predict the output of the following C program:

```
#include <stdio.h>

void func(void) {
    char xx;
    xx = 'Q';
}

main() {
    char xx;
    xx = 'Z';
    func();
    printf("%c\n", xx);
}
```

After you have answered this question, try running it on the computer. Good C compilers will give a warning message during compilation.

5   Rewrite the following using combined arithmetic/assignment operators such as
    +=. Assume all identifiers are legitimate declared variables.

```
a = b + a;
b = b - c;
ww = ww / 5.8;
```

6   Rewrite the following without using combined arithmetic/assignment operators
    such as +=. Assume all identifiers are legitimate declared int variables.

```
a += 23;
sbc -= (a+4);
q += 1;
r /= 2;
z /= z;
i %= i;
```

Some of these can be simplified even further after making substitutions for the
combined operators, so be alert.

Programming

7   Write a C program that outputs the message:

```
In C we can print with "printf".
```

8   Write a program that divides 100 by 7, and then multiplies the result by 7 and
    prints out the final answer. What do you notice? Why?

9   Write a program that has two int variables, dollars and cents. Assign
    12,705 to cents. Convert this into the whole dollar part (stored in dollars)
    and the cents left over (stored in cents). Then use printf to display these
    variables in money format, as $127.05.

10 Can your system store values larger than 32,767 in an int? Write a program to
    find out.

11 The text shows a simple way of rounding a fractional value to the nearest integer
    when the value is positive. Read about the ceil function in Appendix D, and
    devise an assignment statement that always rounds, whether the fractional value is
    negative or positive.

12 The circumference of a circle with radius R is $2\pi R$, where π is approximately
    3.1415926. Using a %f format in printf, find the circumference of a circle
    whose radius is 2 meters.

3.10 TEST QUESTIONS

Short Answer

1 State whether the following are true or false.

  a   Global variables may be accessed by any function in the program.

  b   Local variables may be accessed by any function in the program.

  c   Variables should be local if possible.

  d   The precondition is the statement of the things we can rely on a function doing for us.

  e   When the program starts executing, functions are executed in the order they appear in the program text.

  f   Function names should be as short as possible — one or two letters, preferably.

  g   Anything which can be written using a combined arithmetic/assignment operator can be written without it.

2 Explain the difference between the C operators == and =.

3 Explain the purpose of the ++ and -- operators. Can you do without them? If so, how?

4 Assign the value 145.86 to a `float` variable. Assuming that this value represents dollars, print it using a suitable `%f` format so that it prints as `$145.86`.

Programming

5   Write a C program that outputs the message:

```
C strings can include these special escape sequences:
    \n    newline
    \"    the quote character itself
    \\    the backslash itself
    \0    the nul character.
```

6   Write a program that prints the following message exactly as shown (be careful!).

```
When using printf:
Use "%s" for strings
and "%d" for integers
and "%c" for characters.
```

7   Write a program to compute and print the value of the following formula:

$$\frac{5 + 7}{5 - 2}$$

8   Write a program to compute five-twelfths of 68. The exact answer is just over 28. In integer arithmetic, which you are using when you use `int`s, the answer you will get is 28. Does your program give that, or some other answer — 25 maybe? If your answer is not 28, think carefully about how the division operator works in integer arithmetic.

9 Sometimes money amounts are stored in integer variables as cents (or pennies etc.) to keep the figures accurate. Write a program which stores such a value in a variable (e.g. 2453 for $24.53). Then print the value in dollar and cent format by computing the dollar and cent components (using the / and % operators) and printing them with a dollar sign before and a point in between.

10 Write a program which has an int variable called amount. In the program, assign a single-digit number (6, say) to amount. Now write a call to printf which will print the value stored in amount. Now devise another output statement which uses the putchar function (see Appendix D), and also correctly reports the single-digit value stored in amount. (Hint: the ASCII code values allocated to the digits 0 to 9 are consecutive; for example, the code allocated to '6' is 6 larger than the code allocated to '0'.)

11 If you solved the previous question, here is a tougher one. Write a program with a global int variable, amount, and assign a two-digit integer to it in main. Write a function which uses putchar twice, once to print each digit in the decimal representation of the number. For example, if you had assigned 45 to amount, then the putchar calls should print a 4 and then a 5.

12 Write a program to compute and print the date of Easter Sunday in 1992. The output should be in the form: Month n, day m, where n is the month number (3 for March, 4 for April), and m is the date in the month. The date for Easter Sunday is March (22 + A + B), where

$A = (19C + 24)$ remainder 30
$B = (2D + 4E + 6A + 5)$ remainder 7
$C = $ Year remainder 19
$D = $ Year remainder 4
$E = $ Year remainder 7

If the computed date is greater than 31, the date is in April. Those who have peeked ahead to the chapter on if statements will know a simple way to test for this, but there is another way to compute the month and date properly using the division and remainder operators. Use this other (no if statement) method in your program.

13 Write a program to print squares and square roots of all the integers from 1 to 81, which happens to be 3^4. On each line print a number, its square, and its square root. Do not use any features from future chapters, especially loops. With thought, this can be done using just four simple functions and a global variable. Hint: the list 1...81 is the list 1...27 followed by the list 28...54, then the list 55...81.

14 A company uses four-letter codes to encode the expiry date on its products. The first letter is the tens digit of the day, coded as a letter from A to J (A = 0, J = 9), the second the units digit, similarly coded. The third is the month, represented by a letter from A to L. The last is the year, where A is 1990, B 1991, etc. Given global `char` variables `day_tens`, `day_units`, `month` and `year`, write a function to convert these to the usual numeric values (i.e. day from 1 to 31, month from 1 to 12, etc.) and display the date in the normal numeric format. Call this function from a suitable `main` function that tests it thoroughly.

15 Write a function that does the inverse of the previous one. Given global `int` variables `iday`, `imonth` and `iyear`, compute the coded date representation and store in the global `char` variables `day_tens`, `day_units`, `month` and `year`. Test with a suitable `main` function.

16 As an exercise in manual reading, find out what the library `strlen` function does, either from Appendix D or from a C manual. Now modify the name tag program in Listing 3-4 to correctly place the name and seat number in the centre of the tag, however long or short the name (within the limit of the string size, of course).

4

Repetition

Objectives

Understand the concept of *looping*: making program instructions execute repeatedly.

Appreciate why loops are needed in most programs.

Understand the two types of loops: *pretest* and *posttest*.

Learn how to write loops in C: `while`, `for` and `do...while` loops.

Take a first look at logical tests:
— comparison operators
— operator priority.

Learn standard techniques for computing sums and products.

Study some techniques for creating quality programs:
— giving constants descriptive names with the `#define` preprocessor statement; the operation of the preprocessor
— program correctness proofs: verifying the correctness of a loop — loop invariants, loop postconditions.

4.1   INTRODUCTION

In programming, a task often has to be performed many times over. For example, we have already written a program which printed name tags, one for each person who needed a tag. We wrote a function to print one tag, and then called it once per person. That worked well in that case because we did not require many tags, but if we had needed, say, 10,000 tags, that scheme would have needed 10,000 function calls, which is clearly impractical. What we need is a program statement which effectively says "Do such-and-such 10,000 times." *Loops* do just this. We write out (just once) the statements to be repeated, and we give instructions specifying how often, or under what conditions, they should be repeated.

Looping capitalizes on the high speed of computers. Instructions that might take us a day to plan might be executed once by the computer in, say, a ten-thousandth of a second or less. Obviously we can only make full use of the power of a computer if we can keep it busy — making it repeat our commands thousands or millions of times. The number of repetitions depends on the details of the problem we are solving. Some examples might include: adding numbers (a loop executes once for each number), controlling a heating system (a loop executes once every second, say, to check the temperature), and processing a company's payroll (a loop executes once for each employee). Looping is also called *iteration*.

4.2   TYPES OF LOOPS

A loop has two parts, the *loop test* and the *loop body*. The loop body contains the instructions to be repeated. The loop test decides whether the loop should continue. To execute the loop, the computer performs the loop test and, if the result of the test indicates that the loop should continue, it executes the loop body once and then tests again, and so on. Thus the test and the body alternate repeatedly as long as the test indicates that the loop should continue. For example, to add a list of numbers, the loop test would be an expression meaning "Are there still numbers remaining to be added?" The loop body would be statements meaning "Add one more number into the total." When a test indicates that a loop should continue, we say the test has *succeeded*, otherwise we say it has *failed*.

There are two main types of loops. The difference is whether we start the loop with the loop test (the pretest loop), or with the loop body (the posttest loop). Schematically we can illustrate these two possibilities as in Figure 4.1.

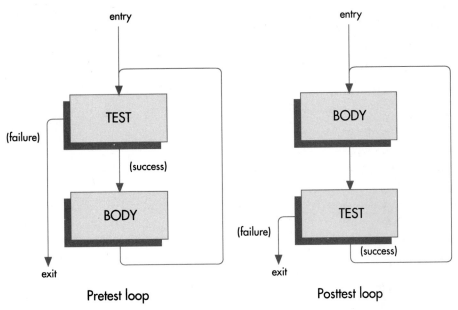

Figure 4.1   The two main types of program loop

C provides two pretest loops, namely the `while` and `for` statements. There is one posttest loop, the `do...while` statement.

4.3   WRITING LOOPS IN C

4.3.1   The `while` loop

The `while` statement is the most important looping statement in C. It is the basic pretest looping command. It must have the following form:

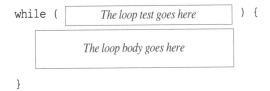

This form shows that a `while` statement consists of the word `while`, a pair of parentheses (round brackets), and a pair of braces (curly brackets). The loop test is written inside the parentheses, and the loop body is written inside the braces. (There are certain limited circumstances where the braces may be omitted, but in this text we shall never do that, as it makes the program harder to read.)

It is time to look at a programming example. So we can focus on the behavior of the loop itself, we shall avoid serious applications for the time being, and instead write a light-hearted program that pretends to be an English policeman. As everyone knows,

English policemen are fond of saying "Allo Allo Allo!" We could write a program without a loop very easily as follows:

```
#include <stdio.h>

main() {
    printf("Allo\nAllo\nAllo\n");
    printf("We always say %d 'Allo's\n", 3);
}
```

and the output would be:

```
Allo
Allo
Allo
We always say 3 'Allo's
```

This program looks satisfactory, but that is only because we want so few repetitions. It is not uncommon to require thousands, or millions, of repetitions in serious programs. So let us write a version which has just one statement to write 'Allo', and which uses a loop to execute it repeatedly. Controlling this loop is essentially a counting problem. We want to be able to count 1-2-3, printing 'Allo' once for each number as we count. The key insight is that we can use a variable to remember how many times our loop has executed. Before starting the loop, we set the variable to zero, which will stand for the fact that we have not yet executed the loop body at all. Every time the loop body executes, we must add one to the variable — this step is part of the loop body. The loop test asks whether the variable has reached the final value (three, in this case). Such a variable is called a *loop counter*. Our new program will therefore contain statements such as:

```
        .
        .
int counter;                /* Declare the loop counter */
        .
        .
counter = 0;                /* Set the loop counter to zero */
while ( counter < 3 ) {     /* Check whether counter has reached 3 */
        .                   /* (The statements to be repeated) */
        .
    counter = counter + 1;  /* Add one to counter */
}                           /* End of while loop */
```

The three steps discussed above are shown here in bold type. The first bold statement (counter = 0) sets the counter to zero; this is called *initializing* the counter. The second bold section is the loop test. It is written as a claim, or *assertion*, which might be true or false — such assertions are often called *boolean*, or *logical*, expressions. This one uses the less-than operator, <, to assert that counter is less than 3. If it is, then the test is true, so the loop body is executed and the test performed again. The final bold section adds one to counter, so that next time the test executes, counter will be one larger than before.

We now have C statements which will execute something three times. If we want "Allo" printed three times, obviously the thing to do three times is to print "Allo" once. Here is a complete program which does just that:

Listing 4-1

```
/* The English policeman program */

#include <stdio.h>

main() {
    int counter;            /* Declare the loop counter variable */
    counter = 0;            /* Set the loop counter to zero */
    while ( counter < 3 ) { /* Make sure loop executes three times */

        printf("Allo\n");       /* Print "Allo" once */
        counter = counter + 1; /* Add one to counter */

    }                       /* End of while loop */

    printf("We always say %d 'Allo's\n", 3);
}
```

The output is the same as before. Note that the final step, printing "We always say...", should only be done once; therefore the printf statement to do that is **after** the loop, not inside the loop body. To be absolutely clear how this program works, here are the program steps written out in the order the computer executes them:

`int counter;`	Allocates a memory location for the variable `counter`.
`counter = 0;`	`counter` now contains zero.
`while ( counter < 3 ) {`	This is **true**, because 0 is less than 3. Therefore the loop will execute.
`printf("Allo\n");`	Prints "Allo" the first time.
`counter = counter + 1;`	Sets `counter` to 0 + 1, that is, 1.
`( counter < 3 ) {`	This is **true**, because 1 is less than 3. Therefore the loop will execute.
`printf("Allo\n");`	Prints "Allo" the second time.
`counter = counter + 1;`	Sets `counter` to 1 + 1, that is, 2.
`( counter < 3 ) {`	This is **true**, because 2 is less than 3. Therefore the loop will execute.
`printf("Allo\n");`	Prints "Allo" the third time.
`counter = counter + 1;`	Sets `counter` to 2 + 1, that is, 3.

```
( counter < 3 ) {
```
This is **false**, because 3 is not less than 3. Therefore the loop will not execute again.

```
printf("We always say %d 'Allo's\n", 3);
```
As the loop has finished, the computer moves on to the next statement.

Following the execution of a program in this manner is called *tracing*.

In the listing, note how the body of the `main` function is indented four spaces. This helps to make it stand out visually for easy understanding. The loop body is indented a further four spaces. This makes it easy to see at a glance where the loop starts and finishes. It is considered most unprofessional to have bad, or no, indentation. Opinions differ on exactly how many spaces to indent. The really important thing is to be absolutely consistent — use the same size indentations throughout. Inconsistent indentation wrecks the clarity of a program.

Some pitfalls

The indentation rules above are an aid to humans reading the program; to the compiler they mean nothing. The compiler only understands the meaning from the sequence of C tokens (`while`, `(`, etc.) in the program — it ignores the layout completely.

Structural errors such as forgetting braces are handled poorly by many compilers. To illustrate this, I omitted the brace at the end of the `while` loop in the program given in the main text. Trying this on one compiler gave the following error message:

```
line 18: syntax error
```

If you ever get strange or obscure errors from your compiler, check carefully that your braces and parentheses match correctly. If all looks correct, make sure every comment ends properly with `*/`.

4.3.2 The `for` loop

The `for` loop is not strictly necessary to write programs. It is just a convenient way to write certain kinds of `while` loop. Pretest loops with initialization, test and increment (such as in our 'Allo' program) are very common, and it would be nice to have a shorthand way to write them. So, whereas such a `while` statement looks like this:

```
initialize;
while ( test ) {
    body;
    increment;
}
```

the equivalent `for` loop looks like this:

```
for ( initialize ; test ; increment ) {
    body;
}
```

Collecting the three steps into one line can produce a clearer and more compact program. The while and for programming styles shown above mean exactly the same thing. Here is the 'Allo' program rewritten using a for loop:

Listing 4-2

```
/* The English policeman program using a for loop */

#include <stdio.h>

main() {
    int counter;              /* Declare the loop counter variable */

    /* A for loop to execute the printf three times: */
    for (counter = 0 ; counter < 3 ; counter = counter + 1) {
        printf("Allo\n");     /* Print "Allo" once */
    }

    printf("We always say %d 'Allo's\n", 3);
}
```

The initialization, test, and increment expressions that control the execution of a for loop need not be as simple as the ones shown here; they can be any legal C expressions. Also, we may omit any or all of them: if no initialization is needed, we can omit the initialization expression, and the same with the increment. If the test is omitted, the loop repeats forever. This is usually a mistake, and is called an *infinite loop*, but occasionally we omit the test deliberately — we might know that some outside influence will stop the loop. For example we might want the program to run until the computer is turned off. Alternatively, C provides statements which we can use inside our loop to stop it independently of the test.

4.3.3 The do...while loop

The do...while statement is used to write posttest loops. The general form of the do...while statement is:

do {

> *The loop body goes here*

} while (*The loop test goes here*) ;

As an example, here is our old friend again:

Listing 4-3

```
/* The English policeman program using a do...while loop */

#include <stdio.h>

main() {
    int counter;            /* Declare the loop counter variable */
    counter = 0;            /* Set the loop counter to zero */

    do {

        printf("Allo\n");       /* Print "Allo" once */
        counter = counter + 1; /* Add one to counter */

    while ( counter < 3 ) {    /* Make sure loop executes three times */

    printf("We always say %d 'Allo's\n", 3);
}
```

Apart from the fact that the test and the body have interchanged, it would appear that this program works exactly as before. Indeed, the output is identical. Nevertheless, there is a difference. Many beginners are surprised by this, but the do...while loop is nearly always the wrong one to use. Why? Suppose we wanted only two Allos. In all three versions, we could get this by replacing 3 with 2 in the loop test. If we wanted only one Allo we could do it by replacing 3 with 1. But what if we wanted no Allos at all? In the while or for versions, we can do that by replacing 3 with 0. But if we do that in the do...while version, it still prints one Allo. The reason is that it executes the body before testing, so if we already have all the Allos we want (none) when the loop first starts, we still get another one thrown at us. In other words, the do...while loop malfunctions if we want the body executed zero times.

But why on earth would we ever want to write a loop that will never be executed? Indeed, in the Allo program it would be pointless. Its real usefulness is when the target number of iterations of the loop is not a constant, such as 3, but a variable. For example a business might automatically run a program every midnight to add the values of all sales during the day. If the business is closed for some reason (e.g. a holiday) there will be no sales figures to add; the addition loop, on this occasion, must execute zero times.

A good rule of thumb is: **avoid the do...while statement unless you specifically want a loop to always execute at least once**.

4.4 MORE C OPERATORS

4.4.1 Comparison operators

Our short Allo program, in its three variants, demonstrated the use of loop tests and illustrated one logical operator, <. A major function of computers is to be able to make decisions, and loop tests are just one place where that is done. The following table shows the operators available to us when comparing values in C.

Operator	Tests for
<	less than
<=	less than or equal
>	greater than
>=	greater than or equal
==	equal
!=	not equal

These all work in a similar manner to <, which we have already met. For example, to find out if the variable K was greater than or equal to seven, we could write: K >= 7.

> **Important warning**
> The 'equal' comparison operator is ==. **Do not confuse it with the assignment operator =**. The assignment operator copies a value into a variable. The equality test, ==, compares two values to see if they are equal. In C it is legal to put = (becomes) in a test, although it still means **copy**, not **comparison**. This means that we might not get a warning from the compiler if we confuse these two. So, when writing = and ==, be very careful to choose the right one: use **= to copy** a value, and **== to compare** values. Be fanatical about always pronouncing = as 'becomes', and == as 'equals'.

4.4.2 Operator precedence

All comparison operators have a lower precedence than the arithmetic ones introduced in Chapter 3. (So, for example, j<k+7 means j<(k+7), not (j<k)+7.) The following table shows the precedence of all operators met so far.

Precedence	Operators
highest	unary − ++ −−
	* / %
	+ −
	< > <= >=
	== !=
lowest	=

Remember, a higher precedence means that an operator is performed before those of lower precedence. Precedence is sometimes called *priority*.

4.5 EXAMPLE: COMPUTING PRODUCTS AND SUMS

For a more realistic example of looping than the Allo problem, let us write a program to calculate the sum and product of a sequence of numbers. One useful function in mathematics is the factorial, which is the product of all the integers from 1 up to the integer concerned. Thus, factorial 5 (in mathematical notation, 5!) is $1 \times 2 \times 3 \times 4 \times 5$, or 120. Let us write a program to print the numbers from 1 to 10, and their factorials, in a table with headings. After the table we shall print the sum of the numbers and the sum of the factorials. In other words, we want this:

```
Number  Factorial
======  =========
     1          1
     2          2
     3          6
     4         24
     5        120
     6        720
     7       5040
     8      40320
     9     362880
    10    3628800
================
Sum of 1..10: 55
Sum of factorials: 4037913
```

This problem illustrates many important programming techniques. The loop will produce the detail lines in the table using a counter to advance from 1 to 10, in a similar way to the loop in the Allo program. The counter will tell us, at the start of the loop body, the next number we must process; let us call it next_number. Since the first number to process is 1, we set next_number to 1 before the loop.

The headings in the table columns must be printed before the loop starts, and the totals must be printed after the loop finishes. Thus the program will have this structure:

```
1  print headings,
2  prepare variables for the loop,
3  produce detail lines in a loop,
4  print sums.
```

Step 2 is needed because of the way we shall calculate the factorials and the sums. To produce a sum we must initialize a variable to zero before we enter the loop, and then add a value to it each time through the loop (i.e. inside the loop). At the end of the loop it will contain the total of all the added values. In this case we want two sums, so we will need two summing variables, and we will have to follow this strategy with each one separately. Let us call these two variables sum_numbers and sum_factorials.

To calculate a product, a slightly different strategy is needed: initialize a 'product' variable to one (not zero) before entering the loop, and in the loop, multiply a value into the product. In this program the product will be the factorial of the number — let us call it `factorial`. Always initialize a summing variable to zero and a product variable to one. These two plans are shown schematically below. The identifiers `tot_var` and `prod_var` can be replaced by any variable names you like.

To compute a total	To compute a product
`tot_var = 0;`	`prod_var = 1;`
Then inside a loop:	*Then inside a loop:*
`  tot_var = tot_var + ...;`	`    prod_var = prod_var * ...;`
After the loop, `tot_var` *contains the sum of the added values.*	*After the loop,* `prod_var` *contains the product of the multiplied values.*

We can now produce a design for our program, as follows:

```
/* Output the column headings */
/* Set totals and factorial variables to initial values. */
next_number = 1;  /* first number to process */
while (next_number <= 10) {
    /* Update the totals and factorial. */
    /* Print a detail line for the number prepared */
    next_number = next_number = 1;
}
/*** Now print the grand totals. ***/
```

Since this is only our basic plan, many steps are represented only as comments; these can be expanded into full C as we proceed. The first step prints the headings. The second must ensure that the sums and the product are correct on first entry to the loop, as discussed above. The loop test checks that we have not yet passed the final desired value (10). If not, we enter the loop and update **all** the variables. `next_number` is added to `sum_numbers`, and multiplied onto `factorial`. This latest factorial is then added to `sum_factorials`. We then print a detail line, update `next_number`, and end the loop. Only after the program has cycled through the loop the required number of times can we print the grand totals; this step must therefore be **after** the loop.

This design can now be expanded into a full program, shown in Listing 4-4. A few simple functions have been used for some steps to keep `main` readable.

Listing 4-4

```
/* A program to print a table showing the numbers 1..10 and their
   factorials, then the sum of these numbers and the sum of the factorials.
*/

#include <stdio.h>

/*** global variables ***/
int next_number,              /* The next number to be processed */
    sum_numbers;              /* Progressive sum */
long factorial,               /* Factorial of latest number to process */
    sum_factorials;           /* Sum of the factorials */

/*** Function declarations ***/
void print_heading(void);
void update_totals_and_factorial(void);

/*** Function definitions ***/

main() {

    /* Output the column headings */
    print_heading();

    /* Set totals and factorial variables to initial values. */
    factorial = 1;                    /* Factorial(0) is 1 */
    sum_factorials = sum_numbers = 0;  /* Sum of nothing is zero. (This
                                          statement shows how you can assign
                                          a value (0, here) to two or more
                                          variables in one statement.) */

    /* In a loop, print the detail lines in the table */
    next_number = 1;                  /* first number to process */
    while (next_number <= 10) {       /* Keep going while the next_number
                                          is within the range we require. */

        /* At this point:
                factorial == (next_number-1)!    (! is factorial fn)
                sum_numbers == sum of 1..(next_number-1)
                sum_factorials == sum of 1! .. (next_number-1)!
        */

        update_totals_and_factorial();

        /* Print a detail line for the number prepared */
        printf("%4d%11ld\n", next_number, factorial);

        next_number = next_number + 1; /* Update loop counter */
    }                                 /* End of the while loop */
    /* After the loop:
            factorial == 10!
            sum_numbers == sum of 1..10
            sum_factorials == sum of 1! .. 10!
    */
```

```
    /*** Now print the grand totals. ***/
    printf (
        "=================\nSum of 1..%d: %d\n",
        10,
        sum_numbers
    );
    printf("Sum of factorials: %ld\n", sum_factorials);

} /* of main */

void print_heading(void) {
    /* Prints the headings over the columns in the table */
    printf("Number  Factorial\n======  =========\n");
}

void update_totals_and_factorial(void) {
/*      Updates factorial and sum for the next number in ascending order.
        On entry: factorial and sums are correct for 1..(next_number-1).
        On exit:  factorial and sums are correct for 1..next_number.
*/
    factorial = factorial * next_number;
    sum_numbers = sum_numbers + next_number;
    sum_factorials = sum_factorials + factorial;
}
```

The variables involving factorials are `long`, not `int`, as `int`s are only guaranteed to go up to 32,767. The statement

```
sum_factorials = sum_numbers = 0;
```

is called a *multiple assignment*, and is a convenient way to assign one value to two or more variables.

4.6 CREATING QUALITY PROGRAMS: GIVING NAMES TO CONSTANTS (#define); THE PREPROCESSOR

Most programs involve constants; our Allo program used 3 as the number of Allos required, and Listing 4-4 used the number 10 in two places. What if in Listing 4-1 we decided we wanted, not three, but five, Allos? Simple. Use the editor to alter 3 to 5, and recompile. But there are two places where 3 occurs in the program — the loop test, and the final `printf`. We might change it in the loop, but mistakenly miss the `printf`, or vice versa; in making a simple modification, we would have put an error into a previously working program.

To overcome this problem, C allows us to give symbolic names (i.e. identifiers) to constants. So instead of writing 3 in both places, we could write a descriptive word such as ALLOS_WANTED. By using the #define facility, we can stipulate that this word always means 3. #define specifies that a certain identifier should always be replaced, wherever it appears, by a certain sequence of replacement tokens. A *token* is any word or symbol allowable in C programs, such as identifiers, numbers, operators, braces, parentheses, and so on. Listing 4-5 is a modification of Listing 4-1, showing how #define can specify that ALLOS_WANTED always stands for 3.

Listing 4-5

```
/* The English policeman program, illustrating the use of #define */

#define ALLOS_WANTED 3          /* The number of repetitions of Allo */

#include <stdio.h>

main() {
    int counter;               /* Declare the loop counter variable */
    counter = 0;               /* Set the loop counter to zero */

    while (counter < ALLOS_WANTED) {
                               /* Ensure loop executes wanted no. of times */

        printf("Allo\n");      /* Print "Allo" once */
        counter = counter + 1; /* Add one to counter */

    }                          /* End of while loop */

    printf("We always say %d 'Allo's\n", ALLOS_WANTED);
}
```

The program uses ALLOS_WANTED in two places. In both places the value 3 will be used, because that is the replacement given in the #define line at the start. If we changed that one 3 to something else, both occurrences of ALLOS_WANTED will now stand for that new value. We are thus protected against overlooking a 3 somewhere in the program. This may not seem very important, but in large programs, where a constant might be used tens or hundreds of times, this facility is of great importance. We can do a similar thing with the value 10 in Listing 4-4.

The syntax of #define is

```
#define identifier <space> substitution-tokens
```

The identifier being defined must be followed by a space. After that, the rest of the line is the list of tokens to be used wherever the identifier occurs in the program. It is important to realize that #define causes substitutions without regard to the meaning of the tokens being substituted. To illustrate this, here is a common mistake:

```
#define ALLOS_WANTED 3;
```

wrong

Note the erroneous semicolon. The preprocessor will change the `if` statement to:

```
while ( counter < 3; ) {
```

The spurious semicolon occurs because the replacement token list consists of 3 and `;` instead of just 3. A syntax error will result, and we might have trouble spotting the cause. One can specify any sequence of replacement tokens in a `#define` command. This is very useful, but it can also be misused, giving rise to unintelligible programs. The smart programmer uses this facility to make programs clearer rather than to be 'clever'.

Names defined in `#define` statements are called *macros*; `#define` lines are processed by the preprocessor, which we met briefly in Chapter 2 in connection with the `#include` command. The program text is examined by the preprocessor before it is seen by the compiler proper; lines commencing with # are processed and removed by the preprocessor. The `#include` command, for example, is completely replaced by the text of the included file — the compiler proper simply sees the text of the included file at that point and compiles it normally. The `#define` commands are also completely deleted by the preprocessor, but it remembers the names thus defined and substitutes for them wherever they occur in the program from then on.

To clarify how this works, consider these two short files:

File `first.c`	**File `second.c`**

```
#define fred 148                    printf("hello %d\n", fred);
main() {                           printf("fred+1:%d",i+1);
    int i = fred;
#define di {printf("%d",fred);}
#include "second.c"
    di;
}
```

If we ask the compiler to compile `first.c`, the preprocessor will first include `second.c` where indicated, and substitute for `fred` and `di`. Thus the compiler proper will use the following modified text for compilation:

```
main() {
    int i = 148;
printf("hello %d\n", 148);
printf("fred+1:%d",i+1);
    {printf("%d",148);};
}
```

All preprocessor commands are gone, `second.c` has been inserted where requested, and except inside strings, character constants, and comments, all occurrences of `fred` and `di` have been replaced.

It is clear from this example that macros are **not** the same as variables. A variable is the name of a storage location **in the running program** where we can store a value; a macro is a name which is replaced by something else (the replacement tokens) **before the program is compiled**.

Because macros are not the same as variables, we cannot write something like this:

```
#define VALUE 10
...
VALUE = VALUE + 1;
```

because, before compilation, the assignment will be turned into

```
10 = 10 + 1;
```

which is illegal, as it attempts to alter the constant 10.

4.7 PROGRAM VERIFICATION: CORRECTNESS OF A LOOP (OPTIONAL)

In Chapter 2 we mentioned a mathematical method, called program verification, for assuring the correctness of programs. Producing mathematical proofs of correctness is beyond the scope of this book, but some of the techniques can be applied without mathematics, to decrease our chances of making errors. We shall now look at how verification theory checks program loops for correctness. We won't be formally checking our loops, but we will learn a useful way of thinking about them.

The method is based on this insight: an algorithm is a list of instructions for performing a task in a **finite** number of steps. Thus a correct algorithm must stop with the right answer (or having performed the right actions, or printed the right output, or whatever). So, in order to work correctly, a loop

- must stop, and
- **if** it stops, it must have done what we wanted.

We shall use a five-point checklist to determine whether these conditions are met. Two points concern making sure the loop stops, and three concern ensuring that if it stops, it works.

We check that a loop will stop using a *bound function* (using 'function' in its mathematical sense). This is not necessarily a function in the C sense; it might never actually occur in the program at all. It is an integer function (it must not be real) that could (but does not have to) be calculated every time round a loop. The loop should be written so that it can only execute if the bound function is positive. If the bound function falls to or below zero, we must be able to show that the loop stops repeating. For example, in Listing 4-4 our loop is:

```
    next_number = 1;
    while (next_number <= 10) {
        ...
        next_number = next_number + 1;
    }
```

A suitable bound function *b* is *b* = 11 − *next_number*. Since the loop can only execute when *next_number* ≤ 10, *b* must be positive. If *b* ever falls to zero, *next_number* must be as large as 11 and the loop will stop. The existence of such a bound function is our first check. The second check is that the bound function must decrease every time the loop iterates. If each execution of the loop decreases *b*, and if the loop stops when *b* reaches zero, then obviously the loop must eventually stop. In the above, the loop increment `next_number = next_number + 1;` guarantees the decrease in the bound function. For loops written according to the style shown above, the existence and decrease of a suitable bound function is assured; but notice that the function is not actually computed as part of the program. So, the first two points of the five-point checklist for correctly working loops are:

1　**Can we find an integer bound function which must be positive if the loop continues?**
2　**Is it guaranteed to decrease each time through the loop?**

The next part of the checklist verifies that the loop will have worked correctly when it terminates. We will use assertions similar to the preconditions and postconditions we write for each function. Our first task is to decide precisely what we want the loop to do for us. Looking at Listing 4-4, we see the following comment immediately after the end of the loop:

```
/* After the loop:
        factorial == 10!
        sum_numbers == sum of 1..10
        sum_factorials == sum of 1! .. 10!
*/
```

That is the *loop postcondition*: what the loop must achieve. We now have to find a special assertion called the *loop invariant*. The invariant is an assertion that is true immediately upon entry to the body of the loop, every time the body is executed. In Listing 4-4, the comment inside the loop that says

```
/* At this point:
        factorial == (next_number-1)!    (! is the factorial fn)
        sum_numbers == sum of 1..(next_number-1)
        sum_factorials == sum of 1! .. (next_number-1)!
*/
```

is the loop invariant. We can verify that it is true every time the loop body starts execution:

- It is true the first time, as then `next_number` is 1, so `next_number-1` is 0; `factorial` is 1 (which is the factorial of 0), and both sums are 0 (which is the sum of the zero numbers from 1 to 0).
- It is true every subsequent time: inside the loop, we adjust the factorial and the totals to include `next_number`. (This happens inside `update_totals_and_factorial`.) Immediately after doing this, the invariant is no longer true, as the totals etc. are now true for 1..next_number, not for 1..next_number-1. But at the end of the loop body we increment `next_number`, restoring the truth of the invariant ready for the next iteration of the loop.

Finally, the loop stops executing with the invariant true and `next_number` equal to 11. When `next_number` is 11, the invariant is exactly the same as the postcondition. Therefore the postcondition will be true when the loop completes.

Our final three checkpoints are revealed by the above discussion. First, we must devise a postcondition for our loop: a statement of what it is meant to achieve. Then we devise an invariant: an assertion which will be true each time round the loop immediately after the loop test. Using these, we perform the next three checks, which are the final three points of the five-point checklist for correctly working loops:

3 **Make sure the invariant is true on first entry to the loop**. We do this by including initializing statements prior to the loop, or, in a `for` loop, in the special initialization section of the loop heading.

4 **Check a single execution of the loop, making sure that if the invariant and the loop test are both true at the start of one execution, the invariant will be true at the start of the next**.

5 **Check that if the loop test stops the loop, the falsity of the loop test and the truth of the invariant are sufficient to prove that the postcondition is true**. We can be sure the invariant is true immediately the loop finishes because it is true according to (4) right after the test, and there are two places right after the test — just inside the loop (if the test succeeds) and just after the loop (if it fails).

Figure 4.2 shows diagrammatically why these five checks help us detect errors in a loop. In short, (3) says "Have you properly prepared for this loop? Are things as you expect them to be?" Check (4) says "Make sure a single iteration of the loop body returns us to the 'known' state where our invariant is true." Check (5) says "Make sure the answer is correct when the loop stops."

It is simple common sense that it is far easier to decide what to do and then do it, than to do something or other, and then try to figure out what you did. In other words, when programming a loop, decide on the postcondition and invariant first, then write the loop to achieve your postcondition by intermediate stages, as represented by the invariant.

Don't panic if this all seems hazy. Developing and using invariants and other assertions is a subject in itself. We are just trying to appreciate the 'flavor' of the subject, to make writing programs a little less haphazard. Remember: finding a postcondition is just making sure we know what we are trying to do. If we can't write a comment saying what we expect to have achieved when the loop finishes, then we don't have a clear idea of our goal. Programming is a goal-oriented activity. If nothing else, try to develop the habit of writing clear postconditions. Devising an invariant is a way of keeping track of what is going on in our loop. Each iteration of a loop should achieve some definite partial goal towards the postcondition.

Whether we apply full loop verification techniques or not, the invariant and loop postcondition are excellent just as plain comments. The postcondition tells readers what the loop should do, and the invariant tells them why the programmer expects the loop to work.

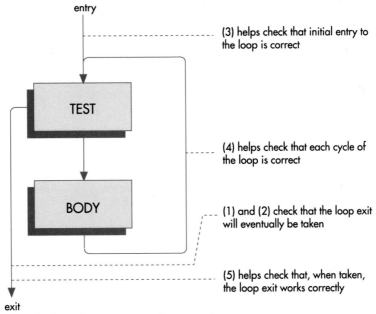

entry

(3) helps check that initial entry to the loop is correct

TEST

(4) helps check that each cycle of the loop is correct

BODY

(1) and (2) check that the loop exit will eventually be taken

(5) helps check that, when taken, the loop exit works correctly

exit

Figure 4.2   Checking the correctness of a pretest loop

Finally, David Gries writes in *The Science of Programming*: *"The wise programmer develops a program with the attitude that a correct program can and will be developed, and then tests it thoroughly with the attitude that it must have a mistake in it."* In other words, use correctness techniques to develop a sound program, but still test the program thoroughly to see that it works properly.

To students who wish to pursue correctness proofs further

While still learning the basics of programming, it is probably a good idea just to use the ideas given above as and when you feel you can, without being too concerned if you cannot do the complete job. If you wish to learn more, a very good text is The Science of Programming *by David Gries (Springer-Verlag 1981).*

In such texts the invariant is usually written at the end of the loop body, rather than at the front as above. Various complications in C convinced me that it is harder to prove C loops with invariants at the end. C was not designed with program verification in mind, so it is possible that a good-looking proof will have a fault due to some odd feature of C. The best insurance is to **keep it simple**. *Don't be seduced into writing obscure one-liners (incredibly tricky C statements that do a huge amount of work).*

Another difference between the simplified method given here and the full mathematical method is that in the full method, one does not even trace through a single iteration of the loop: the whole thing is demonstrated entirely from the static program text.

4.8 SHORT EXAMPLES

Lorentz contraction

The theory of relativity predicts that when a body is moving relative to an observer, its length in the direction of motion contracts. For a one-meter-long object travelling at a fraction u of the speed of light, its length will contract to

$$\sqrt{1 - u^2} \text{ meters}$$

The task is to print a table showing the length of this object at speeds from 0.1 to 0.9 of the speed of light, in steps of 0.1. We need the sqrt function to do this. (See Listing 4-6.)

Listing 4-6

```
/* Program to show table of object length at various speeds,
   computed according to the Lorentz contraction. */

#include <stdio.h>
#include <math.h>

main() {
    float frac_c;
    printf("A one-meter long object contracts to:\n");

    for (frac_c=0.1; frac_c<0.95; frac_c+=0.1) {
        printf (
            "%f meter at %3.1f of the speed of light\n",
            sqrt(1 - frac_c * frac_c),
            frac_c
        );
    }
}
```

The sqrt function result is passed to printf for output. The printout is

```
A one-meter long object contracts to:
0.994987 meter at 0.1 of the speed of light
0.979796 meter at 0.2 of the speed of light
0.953939 meter at 0.3 of the speed of light
0.916515 meter at 0.4 of the speed of light
0.866025 meter at 0.5 of the speed of light
0.800000 meter at 0.6 of the speed of light
0.714143 meter at 0.7 of the speed of light
0.600000 meter at 0.8 of the speed of light
0.435890 meter at 0.9 of the speed of light
```

The loop test is `frac_c<0.95`. Why not `frac_c<=0.9`? Unfortunately, floating point values are not absolutely exact. The successive additions of 0.1 to `frac_c` might mean that it becomes, say, 0.9000001 instead of 0.9 in the final iteration. The loop test would then fail one iteration early. Thus the strange test. Another way to minimize the problem is to use integer loop control variables, as in the following problem.

Radioactive decay

Radioactive elements decay according to the function Me^{-Kt}, where M is the original mass, t is the time, and K is a constant characteristic of the particular element. The half-life of a radioactive element is the time needed for the original sample to be reduced to half due to radioactive decay into other elements. If we know the half-life T_h, it is possible to calculate $K = (\log_e 2)/T_h$. The half-life of uranium is about 4.5×10^9 years (4,500,000,000 years). Given a pound of uranium, we require a program to print the remaining mass for times from 0 to 10^{10} (10,000,000,000) years in steps of 10^9 (1,000,000,000) years. It would be convenient to use an integer loop counter, but these numbers are far too big for `int`s, and on most computers, even `long`s. The solution is to use an `int` counter that advances modestly by ones, and, inside the loop, multiply it by 10^9 to compute the 'true' loop increment. This also works for small increments much less than one.

Listing 4-7

```
/* Table of uranium radioactive decay remnant quantity. */

#include <stdio.h>
#include <math.h>

#define HALF_LIFE 4.5e9
#define TIME_GAP 1.0e9

main() {
    float mass, years, K;
    int epoch;

    mass = 1.0;   /* one pound, that is */
    K = log(2.0)/HALF_LIFE;

    for (epoch=0; epoch<=10; epoch=epoch+1) {
        years = TIME_GAP * epoch;
        printf (
            "After %11.0f years, %f pound of uranium remains.\n",
            years, mass * exp(-K*years)
        );
    }
}
```

With large numbers like the ones in this example, be careful to multiply an `int` (epoch, here) by a `float` or `double` value, so that the computer performs the multiplication using floating point arithmetic. The output is:

```
After            0 years, 1.000000 pound of uranium remains.
After   1000000000 years, 0.857244 pound of uranium remains.
After   2000000000 years, 0.734867 pound of uranium remains.
After   3000000000 years, 0.629961 pound of uranium remains.
After   4000000000 years, 0.540030 pound of uranium remains.
After   5000000000 years, 0.462937 pound of uranium remains.
After   6000000000 years, 0.396850 pound of uranium remains.
After   7000000000 years, 0.340198 pound of uranium remains.
After   8000000000 years, 0.291632 pound of uranium remains.
After   8999999488 years, 0.250000 pound of uranium remains.
After 10000000000 years, 0.214311 pound of uranium remains.
```

The inaccuracy of floating arithmetic is apparent in the second-last line of the output. Your computer might give slightly different results, as it may have more or less accurate arithmetic. Use of a `double` variable for the years would improve this situation. Floating point constants (such as 1.0, 4.5e9, 0.69314718 etc.) are `double` by default, so one only needs to worry about the declaration of the variables in order to get things right.

4.9   SUMMARY

- A *loop* is a section of a program which is repeated zero or more times.
- The main loop types are *pretest* and *posttest*:
  - pretest loops perform the *loop test* before executing the *loop body*
  - posttest loops perform the *loop test* after executing the *loop body*.
- C statements for creating loops include `while`, `for`, and `do...while`.
  - `while` is a pretest loop
  - `for` is a convenient form of `while`
  - `do...while` is a posttest loop.
  - Unless the loop body must execute at least once, avoid the `do...while` loop.
- Loop tests consist of logical assertions which may be true or false.
  - In all three C looping statements, a true test result causes the loop to execute again, whereas a false result causes the loop to cease.
  - One way to write a test is with comparison operators: <, <=, >, >=, ==, !=.
- A common way to program a loop is to set a variable to an initial value, and increment it until the test indicates it has reached the final value.
- Pretending to be a computer and executing a program by hand is called *tracing* the program.
- To **add** a list of values, set a totalling variable to **0** first, and add one value to it each time round a loop.
- To **multiply** a list of values, set a totalling variable to **1** first, and multiply one value into it each time round a loop.

- The preprocessor transforms the text of a program before it is compiled by the C compiler proper. All lines starting with # are directives to the preprocessor.
- The #define directive tells the preprocessor to substitute a constant (or some other piece of text) for a *macro* name wherever it occurs, except inside string literals.
- A *multiple assignment* allows a value to be stored in two or more variables.
- Care needs to be taken when using floating point variables as loop counters, as slight inaccuracies may cause the loop to malfunction.
- Loop correctness can be checked using a *bound function*, a postcondition, and an *invariant*.
- The five-point checklist:
  1 Is there an integer bound function which must be positive if the loop continues?
  2 Is it guaranteed to decrease each time through the loop?
  3 Is the invariant true on first entry to the loop?
  4 Will any one iteration of the loop re-establish the truth of the invariant?
  5 Will the truth of the invariant, and the fact that the loop stopped, establish the truth of the postcondition?
- Try to write postconditions, bound functions, and (if you can) invariants, even if you do not perform the full loop checking.
  - Write the postcondition and invariant *before* you write the loop.
  - Incorporate them in the program as comments.

4.10 SELF-TEST EXERCISES

Short Answer

1 What test would you use in a while loop that should repeat as long as the variable k is not equal to the variable j?

2 What is probably wrong with the test in this while loop?

```
while ( z = 7 ) {
    ...
}
```

3 The variable j contains a certain value, and we want it to be one larger. Write three different ways to accomplish this.

4 What loop test would I use if I wanted the loop to keep repeating as long as the variable state_tax was greater than or equal to seven?

5 Write a for loop which does exactly the same thing as this while loop:

```
j = k + 6;
while ( j >= k ) {
    ...
    j = j - 2;
}
```

6   Points 3 to 5 of the loop verification checklist, as presented in the text, are tailored to checking pretest loops. Revise them to make them suitable for checking posttest loops.

Programming

7   Write a 'Nervous English Policeman' program that prints:

```
A
Al
All
Allo
```

You may not do this by writing out the full output; use a loop which prints one line each time through.

8   Create a program that prints the numbers from 10 to 1 in descending order. Test your program using your C compiler.

9   Write a program that prints all the even numbers from 10 to 20 inclusive, one number per line. Place a heading, "Even Numbers" above the list, and the sum of the numbers below.

10 Write a program to print all characters with codes from 'A' to 'Z' inclusive. (You can use a char variable, and increment it, in the same way as we used ints in the text examples.)

11 Write a program to print a graph of a sine wave on its side, as follows:

```
            *
              *
               *
                *
                 *
                *
              *
            *
          *
        *
      *
     *
    *
     *
       *
         *
```

4.11 TEST QUESTIONS

Short Answer

1 How many times will this loop execute? What does it print? Assume `i` is an `int`.

```
i = 10;
while ( i != 2 ) {
    printf("%*s\n", i, "*");
    i--;
}
```

2 Write a `while` loop which does exactly the same thing as this `for` loop. Assume `i` is an `int`.

```
for ( i=5; i>=0; --i ) {
    printf("%d\n", i*i);
}
```

3 Describe the difference between pretest and posttest loops. Explain one problem that can arise if posttest loops are used thoughtlessly.

4 Explain the purpose of the braces (`{` and `}`) in C looping statements.

5 The following program is supposed to print all numbers less than 100 which are divisible by three. Without running it on a computer, explain what it actually does.

```
#include <stdio.h>
main() {
    int n;
    n = 3;
    while (n<100) {
        printf("%10d\n", n);
        n == n + 3;
    }
}
```

If you are certain you know how to stop a program that is in an infinite loop, try it to see if you are right.

6 Assuming `i`, `j`, and `k` are `int` variables, show a short way to store 894 in all three.

7 Run the program below and, by examining its output carefully, describe your findings about the operation of multiple assignments.

```
#include <stdio.h>
main() {
    float r, s;
    int i;
    r = i = s = 9.4;
    printf("r: %6.4f,  i: %d,  s: %6.4f\n", r, i, s);
}
```

Programming

8   Write a program to print all powers of two from 2^0 to 2^8. (Hint: $2^0 = 1$, $2^1 = 1 \times 2$, $2^2 = 1 \times 2 \times 2$, and so on. So 2^8 can be computed by starting with 1 in a variable, and multiplying by 2 eight times. Each time you multiply by 2, print the value in the variable.)

9   Write a program to print a translation table showing the upper-case letters 'A' to 'Z', one per line, and, next to each one, the code value of the letter. Place headings over each column saying 'CHARACTER CODE'. If your computer uses ASCII character codes (as most do), the simplest program for this job will print all the capital letters consecutively. The value of 'A' is 65 in ASCII. If your printout has other characters intermixed between the letters, your computer probably uses the EBCDIC code system.

10 Modify your program for the above question to do the same thing for lower-case letters 'a' to 'z'. By comparing the code values for upper-case letters and lower-case letters, can you see a simple way to translate an upper-case letter into the corresponding lower-case letter? (There is a C library function `tolower` which does this job, but for this exercise, assume it doesn't exist.)

11 A business executive in a retail store is in charge of ten departments, which have department numbers 60 to 69. Each week every department must report their total sales and total expenditure. The executive wants a computer-generated blank form to write these figures on. The form must look like this:

```
                    WEEKLY SALES REPORT
    Department number    |    Sales    |   Expenses
==================================================
            60           |             |
==================================================
            61           |             |
==================================================
            62           |             |
        ... etc.
```

Write a program to create such a blank form for the executive.

12 A palindrome is a word or number that reads the same forwards and backwards. Examples are 'deed' and '4994'. Write a program which will print out all four-digit palindrome numbers. The first is 1001, followed by 1111, and so on up to 9889, 9999. (Hint: the first two digits are just the numbers 10 to 99.)

13 A Fibonacci sequence is a sequence of numbers formed by starting with any two integers, and making the next number in the sequence by adding the two immediately preceding values. Mathematically, we can write:

$$F(n) = F(n-1) + F(n-2)$$

The usual two starting numbers are 1 and 1. In that case the sequence starts:

1 1 2 3 5 8 13 21 ...

Write a program that prints this sequence as far as possible. As it is an infinite sequence, the program obviously cannot compute it all, so it must be made to stop sooner or later. Make the program stop as soon as it prints a value greater than 15,000. (You will be surprised how soon it does that.)

14 An engineer is designing a system that incorporates weights on each end of a cable passing over a pulley, as in the following picture.

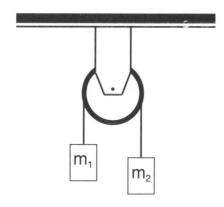

For a frictionless pulley, the tension in the cable is

$$T = \frac{2gm_1m_2}{m_1 + m_2}$$

where m_1 and m_2 are the masses of the weights in kilograms, g is gravitational acceleration, 9.80665 m s^{-2}, and T is the tension in newtons. Write a program to print a table showing the tension for all combinations of m_1 and m_2, with m_1 ranging from 1.0 kg to 10.0 kg in steps of 1.0 kg, and m_2 ranging from 0.5 kg to 5.0 kg in steps of 0.5 kg. Include a function whose purpose is to print one single line of the table.

15 In an electrical circuit, the formula relating voltage V, current I, and resistance R is $V = IR$. Print a table showing, for voltages from 1 volt to 10 volts in steps of 0.5 volt, the resistance (in ohms) necessary to maintain a current of 0.5 amp. Place suitable headings above the columns of the table.

16 The series

$$\sum_{k=0}^{\infty} \frac{1}{k!}$$

converges to e, the base of natural logarithms. Write a program that computes and prints the first ten partial sums of the series.

17 Write a program to print squares and square roots of all the integers from 1 to 81. On each line print a number, its square, and its square root. You may, of course,

use a loop. If you solved the equivalent problem in the previous chapter, compare your two programs. Which is better, and why?

18 An approximation to the factorial function can be obtained from Stirling's formula:

$$N! = \sqrt{2\pi N}\left(\frac{N}{e}\right)^{N}$$

Write a program to print a table showing values of the factorial function, $N!$, for N ranging from 1 to 10. On each line, display N, $N!$ calculated the usual way, and $N!$ calculated with Stirling's formula. Provide suitable headings to the table.

19 Write a program to print out a rectangular table showing the square roots of all integers from 0 to 99, as follows:

```
           Table of Square Roots of Numbers from 0 to 99
        0      1      2      3      4      5      6      7      8      9
     ====== ====== ====== ====== ====== ====== ====== ====== ====== ======
 0: 0.0000 1.0000 1.4142 1.7321 2.0000 2.2361 2.4495 2.6458 2.8284 3.0000
10: 3.1623 3.3166 3.4641 3.6056 3.7417 3.8730 4.0000 4.1231 4.2426 4.3589
20: 4.4721 4.5826 4.6904 4.7958 4.8990 5.0000 5.0990 5.1962 5.2915 5.3852
30: 5.4772 5.5678 5.6569 5.7446 5.8310 5.9161 6.0000 6.0828 6.1644 6.2450
40: 6.3246 6.4031 6.4807 6.5574 6.6332 6.7082 6.7823 6.8557 6.9282 7.0000
50: 7.0711 7.1414 7.2111 7.2801 7.3485 7.4162 7.4833 7.5498 7.6158 7.6811
60: 7.7460 7.8102 7.8740 7.9373 8.0000 8.0623 8.1240 8.1854 8.2462 8.3066
70: 8.3666 8.4261 8.4853 8.5440 8.6023 8.6603 8.7178 8.7750 8.8318 8.8882
80: 8.9443 9.0000 9.0554 9.1104 9.1652 9.2195 9.2736 9.3274 9.3808 9.4340
90: 9.4868 9.5394 9.5917 9.6437 9.6954 9.7468 9.7980 9.8489 9.8995 9.9499
```

Include a function whose purpose is to print just one line of the table.

20 The *polar coordinates*, (r, θ) of a point P measure the distance from the origin and the angle to the x axis, as shown below.

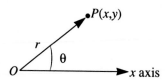

Polar coordinates can be converted to rectangular coordinates as follows:
$$x = r \cos \theta$$
$$y = r \sin \theta$$

Now use these formulae in a program that prints the rectangular coordinates of twenty points equally spaced around the circumference of a circle with a radius of one.

21 Write a program to find an approximation to the sum of the infinite series

$$1 + \frac{1}{2} + \frac{1}{4} + \frac{1}{8} + \frac{1}{16} + \ldots$$

Your program should keep adding terms into the total (which should be `float`) until the total changes by less than 0.0001 between one iteration and the next. Is the approximation computed by your program what you expect?

22 Write a program that calculates and prints the first twenty partial sums of the following continued fraction

$$1 + \cfrac{1}{1 + \cfrac{1}{1 + \cfrac{1}{1 + \ddots}}}$$

The easiest method is to find a way to compute P_{k+1} from P_k, where P_k is the kth partial sum.

23 Write a program that uses a loop to count the digits in a given positive integer. Write two versions, one using a pretest loop, and one a posttest loop. Make sure it works if the number is zero.

5

Input:
obtaining data
from outside
the program

Objectives

Investigate what happens when a program inputs data:

— data conversion.

Learn how to use some C library functions to do basic input tasks:

— the `scanf` function: integer, floating point, and character input formats
— detecting illegal input: the `scanf` function result
— the `getchar` function.

Inputting names and other strings:

— `scanf` string input: `%s`
— the function `gets`.

Master some common ways to process input:

— a fixed number of input data values
— input until a particular event happens
— input with error checking.

A short digression. How to do input and output redirection when running programs.

5.1 INTRODUCTION — HOW INPUT HAPPENS

In Chapter 1 we saw how important input is in professional software. We often use the word *read* for input. Never forget that the reading is being done from the computer's point of view. If I am writing my latest thriller with a word processor, even though I am writing, the computer is inputting data, so we say the program is *reading*. Similarly, we use *write* when a computer outputs data.

To understand input, we must remember that the computer's processor is thousands or millions of times faster than most input or output devices: if we type on our keyboard at, say, five characters per second, the processor of an ordinary personal computer would execute about a million instructions in between each keystroke! The processor will therefore quickly overtake the various input and output devices attached to it. So when a program inputs data, the processor usually has to wait until the data is ready. For example, a program might execute these steps:

```
1   Print a message asking for some data.
2   Input the data.
3   Do some calculations using the data.
4   Output the results of the calculations.
```

When the program runs, Step 1 happens immediately. But at Step 2, there might be no data to input, in which case the computer waits until we enter it. When we finish, the data is made available to the program and the computer can race on to Step 3 and then Step 4. When the program runs, we see the message from Step 1 printed, and then the computer appears to stop. If we decide it's time for coffee and donuts, the computer will sit and wait. It continues to wait until we enter the data, stop the program, or turn off the computer. But if we come back suitably full of refreshments, and type the data, we then see the results, most likely immediately (depending on how much work we ask it to do in Step 3). To summarize: we see Step 1 happen, we type the data, and we see Step 4 happen. The message printed in Step 1 is called a *prompt*. Computers can input data from all sorts of devices: keyboards, disks, mice, modems, other computers, etc. But whenever a program inputs information from a human user, it is important that the program displays a prompt explaining what to do next.

Various factors complicate this. On timesharing computers (large computers processing many people's work simultaneously) the processor never stops and waits; it just gets on with someone else's work instead. But to us, it still appears to be behaving as described above. Another complication that concerns us a little more is *buffering*. Most operating systems collect input data in regions of memory called *buffers*, and give the data to the program in bulk, rather than a character at a time. We have to be aware of this for one particular reason: when we are typing a line of data on a keyboard, it is likely that the program will not be given any data until we have finished typing the entire line. This can cause perplexing effects if we do not know what is happening.

> **A warning for former BASIC programmers**
> Unfortunately, BASIC misuses the word 'read'. BASIC's READ statement is **not** an input statement. The data for a READ in BASIC comes from DATA statements within the program, so BASIC's READ statement is really an unusual assignment statement.

5.2 INPUT IN C PROGRAMS

The standard C library provides many functions for doing input. The `scanf` function is one of the most widely used; others include `getchar` and `gets`.

5.2.1 Using the `scanf` library function to read `int`s

To read numbers we usually use the function `scanf`. A call to `scanf` looks similar to a call to `printf`. As with `printf`, the first argument is a format string which specifies the types of data we want to handle. The remaining arguments tell `scanf` the variables in which to store the input data. `scanf` is like a delivery service, delivering input data to the computer's memory. But there is a complication: every delivery service needs to know the address to which the items should be delivered. Thus the second and subsequent arguments to `scanf` must be addresses of places where the various data values should be put. All memory locations have addresses, and C provides a special operator, `&`, to use when we need an address. In C, `&` means 'the address of'. So to find the address of a variable `i`, we would write `&i`. We seldom care what the actual numeric value of the address is, but we can be confident that, whatever it is, the C compiler will use the right value. Remember that addresses are often called pointers. So, the address of `i` is often called a pointer to `i`.

Let us see how this works by solving a simple problem. Suppose the mint, where coins are produced, has machines that can each make 93 coins per minute. A program is needed that, given input specifying how many coins are needed per minute, tells how many machines must be operating to equal or exceed that figure. We shall perform the four steps mentioned in the previous section, as follows.

1   The program should ask how many coins are needed per minute.
2   It should input an integer from the terminal.
3   It should calculate how many machines must operate.
4   It should print a message: "*x* machines must operate". (Where *x* is the value computed in Step 3.)

The calculation in Step 3 is a little tricky. Suppose Step 2 stores the number of coins needed in the variable `coins`. We should be able to use the integer division operator (`/`) somehow to divide `coins` by 93, but there is a snag. If we need between 1 and 93 coins/minute, one machine will do. Production of between 94 and 186 coins needs two machines, and so on. Yet if `coins` is between 1 and 92, `coins/93` is 0. For `coins` between 93 and 185, `coins/93` is 1, etc. For the answer to be correct, we must add 92 to `coins` before doing the division. Listing 5-1 shows this program.

Listing 5-1

```
/* A program to tell how many machines the mint must run to
   obtain a required output, at 93 coins/minute per machine. */

#define MACHINE_OUTPUT 93   /* coins per minute per machine */
#include <stdio.h>

main() {
    /* Declare a variable, coins, to store the coins required
       and another, machines, for the number of machines to run. */
    int coins, machines;

    /* Print a message requesting the required output/minute. */
    printf("How many coins are needed per minute? ");

    /* Input answer into coins */
    scanf("%d", &coins);

    /* Calculate the machines required. */
    machines = (coins + (MACHINE_OUTPUT - 1))/MACHINE_OUTPUT;

    /* Print the answer */
    printf("%d machines must operate.\n", machines);
}
```

In the call to `scanf`, the first argument is the format specifying which input conversions are to be performed; `%d` means that characters representing an integer are to be read and converted into an `int`. For each `%d` in the format string, a subsequent argument must supply the address of an `int` variable (not a `char`, `long`, or anything else) in which a number is to be stored.

Where is the input data? A common mistake is to try to write the data in the program text somewhere. **This is entirely wrong**. None of the steps in a program (input, processing, or output) occurs until the program is executed, therefore the data must be entered when we run the program.

Here is a sample run, with characters typed by the user shown in **bold**. We shall always use the convention that bold text is the user input, and normal text is the program output.

```
How many coins are needed per minute? 750
9 machines must operate.                    ↑
```
(The computer stops and waits for input here.)

In this run the user typed the characters 7, 5, and 0, followed by a newline (on many keyboards, labeled 'enter', 'return', or '↵'); `scanf` input the 7, 5 and 0, and converted them into a binary integer which it stored in the variable `coins`. This variable was then used in the ensuing computations in the usual way.

5.2.2 Reading other numeric data types

scanf can input all numeric data types, provided the correct '%' format is specified. One must take even more care using scanf than printf, choosing **exactly** the correct input format for the particular data type, as listed in Table 5.1.

Table 5-1: Matching input format to data type

Data type	scanf format sequences	
int	%d	input a signed decimal integer
long	%ld	(el-dee) input a signed decimal integer
float	%e, %f, %g	input a floating point value written either in C floating point or C integer format
double	%le, %lf, %lg point or integer format	input a floating point value written in C floating

A *width* is also allowed in a format sequence to specify the maximum number of characters to be converted to obtain a value. For example, in this scanf call,

scanf("%3d", &coins);

the width is 3, so if the following input data is entered:

750148

only the 7, 5 and 0 will be read, and the value 750 assigned to coins. The remaining characters (1, 4, and 8) will still be waiting to be input.

Warning
Unfortunately, unlike printf, scanf does not allow the use of an asterisk for specifying dynamically variable widths. The asterisk has another meaning when used with scanf format sequences.

5.2.3 Reading chars, whitespace

The scanf format %c specifies that the input shall be a character. The code for the character typed is stored in the char variable whose address is supplied. The program in Listing 5-2 reads a character and reports its code value.

Listing 5-2

```
/* A program to tell the code value for a typed character */

#include <stdio.h>

main() {
    /* Declare a variable, ch, to store the typed character */
    char ch;

    /* Print a message requesting a character. */
    printf("Please enter a character: ");

    /* Input the character into ch */
    scanf("%c", &ch);

    /* Print the value as a character and as a number */
    printf("The code for '%c' is %d\n", ch, ch);
}
```

In Listing 5-2, `scanf` gets a single character code from the input, and we have given it the address of the `char` variable `ch` to place it in. The final `printf` is similar to those in Listing 3-3. Here is a sample run:

```
Please enter a character: D
The code for 'D' is 68
```

Run this program on your computer. If it does not print 68 as the code for D, then your computer does not use ASCII codes. The advantage of using input to provide values for the program is that we can run the program again without altering or recompiling it. For example:

```
Please enter a character: !
The code for '!' is 33
```

When reading `int`s, `scanf` skips whitespace as it searches for an integer value to input. However, when reading a character with `%c`, it always takes the next available character, no matter what that is. Sometimes we must be sure that `%c` will only read a printable character. For example, if we ask users to answer a yes/no question, but they happen to type a space before their 'y' or 'n', we want to skip that space and read the character they really intend as the answer. We can make `scanf` do this by placing a space in the format string before the `%c`. Then it will skip over all whitespace in the input up to the next printable character. `scanf` will do this whenever it finds a whitespace character in the format. Thus, in Listing 5-2, we might alter the `scanf` call as follows:

```
scanf(" %c", &ch);
```

Another function for reading characters is `getchar`, which returns as its result a single character input from the keyboard. It is simple and efficient. For example, the following is equivalent to the `scanf` call in Listing 5-2:

```
ch = getchar();
```

5.2.4   Some important warnings

Always give addresses to `scanf`

The second and subsequent arguments to `scanf` must be addresses, so we must not forget the & operator before a variable name. Many C compilers are notoriously bad at detecting illogical calls to functions. If we forget the &, the compiler might not warn us, and the program might even run. But something will surely go badly wrong. If we left out the & in Listing 5-2, `scanf` would be given the contents of `ch` instead of its address. It would treat whatever number is in `ch` as if it were an address, and plop the input into the memory location that happened to have that address. It might be an illegal memory location, and some computers will give a cryptic error message and stop the program. Worse, it might be a valid, but incorrect, address, in which case the program will misbehave in some odd way, and we will have no indication of the reason. Such bugs can take hours or days to find. The only way to fix them efficiently is never to make the mistake in the first place.

> *Never forget the & operator before a simple variable name in the* `scanf` *argument list.*

Having given the warning not to forget the &, it must now be added that some things in C are already addresses, and so & should not be added to them. That is the reason for the word "simple" above. "Simple" variables include things declared with such statements as `char ch;` or `int i;` etc.

Never assume the answer to a question when writing the program

As we have seen, the big advantage to using input is the ability to make a program respond correctly to whatever data a user gives it. If we assume the answer when writing the program, we throw away this advantage. For example, here is an incorrect version of Listing 5-2.

```c
#include <stdio.h>
main() {
    char ch;
    printf("Please enter a character: ");
    scanf("%c", &ch);
    printf("The code for 'D' is %d\n", ch);
}
```

In this incorrect version, the final `printf` assumes that the input will be the letter D. If it is, then all will be fine. If it is not, the program will malfunction. For example:

```
Please enter a character: E
The code for 'D' is 69
```

Here the user has typed E, and the program has blithely proceeded to lie to us about the code value of D. So, if the user does not enter D, the program fails. But if D is the only value it works for, why waste the user's time asking them to input it?

5.3 INPUTTING AND OUTPUTTING STRINGS

When we use string literals, the sequence of characters is built in to the program and cannot be changed. But many programs have to deal with strings in their input data. For example, a supermarket checkout system might input the names of products from a data file for printing on the customer's receipt. Since a supermarket sells thousands of items, and since the inventory changes from day to day and week to week, it is obviously impractical to write all the product names as string literals in the program; it must be able to deal with whatever comes along. For such problems we need character arrays.

Two library functions can help us here: `scanf` and `gets`. `scanf` has a convenient way of inputting characters that make up a single word, where a word is any sequence of printable (visible) characters (i.e. not whitespace). On the other hand, `gets` inputs a complete line, no matter how many words are on the line. These functions (and all others in the C library that handle strings) correctly handle the nul byte which ends the string.

5.3.1 Inputting words with `scanf`

`scanf` has a `%s` option which reads a single word into a character array. If we declare:

```
char item[50];
```

then `item` is the address of a block of 50 characters. It can hold a string with a maximum of 49 characters, after allowing for the nul byte. We can ask `scanf` to accept a word from the user and store it in the array:

```
scanf("%s", item);
```

There is no & (address-of) operator before `item` above! The reason needs to be studied closely. As you know, when simple variables are used as function arguments, a copy of the value stored in the variable is passed to the function. However, this is **not done** with array arguments. When an array name is used as a function argument, only the address of the start of the array is passed to the function. The function can then access the original (and only) copy of the array via its address. (As noted in Chapter 3, this rule also applies to string literals, which can be thought of as a special kind of `char` array.) The rule means that `item` in the `scanf` call above already stands for an address, without the need to include an &. We must therefore extend our previous warning about &:

> Never **forget** the & operator before a simple variable name in the scanf argument list, but never **include** the & operator before the name of an array in the scanf argument list.

Listing 5-3 shows a program to input a word and repeat it back to the typist.

Listing 5-3

```
/* Echo a single word on the terminal */
#include <stdio.h>

main() {
    char item[50];
    scanf("%s", item);
    printf("%s\n", item);
}
```

The following sample run shows what is meant when we say that the %s format inputs one word:

Morning folks
Morning

Here the user typed a few blanks before starting the message. scanf skipped the blanks, then read the longest non-whitespace sequence it could, and placed it in the item array. Although it is not obvious from Listing 5-3, scanf stopped processing the input at that point, leaving the rest of the line unread. We can verify this in Listing 5-4, where another scanf is inserted to read the following word.

Listing 5-4

```
/* Echo two words on the terminal */
#include <stdio.h>

main() {
    char item[50];
    scanf("%s", item);      /* Input the first typed word */
    printf("%s\n", item);
    scanf("%s", item);      /* Overwrite it with the second word */
    printf("%s\n", item);
}
```

After the first `printf` has displayed the first word, the second `scanf` inputs the second word into the same array. This is allowable because the first word is no longer needed. Any variable may be re-used after we have finished with its existing contents — but do not overdo this, as it can make programs hard to understand. Storing in a variable always overwrites (and hence erases) the previous value. With the same input as before, the run is as follows:

```
Morning folks
Morning
folks
```

What happens if the word is longer than the array? Unfortunately the system will probably not detect the fact, and the data will overflow the end of the array. This kind of problem causes obscure errors. We can solve it by supplying a width in the format string. This specifies the maximum number of characters to process. The width does **not** include the trailing nul. This is demonstrated in Listing 5-5.

Listing 5-5

```c
/* Echo two words on the terminal */
#include <stdio.h>

main() {
    char item[5];
    scanf("%4s", item);    /* Input the first typed word */
    printf("%s\n", item);
    scanf("%4s", item);    /* Overwrite it with the second word */
    printf("%s\n", item);
}
```

Here is the run:

```
Morning folks
Morn
ing
```

The first input reaches the specified maximum of four characters. Remembering the nul, the five-character array will be completely full. The second input finds the end of the word after only three characters, so the input stops early. In serious programs one must anticipate every way in which a program might malfunction. Trouble with input is a common cause of problems, so specifying maximum input widths is a necessity.

5.3.2 Inputting lines with `gets`

The `gets` function has one argument, the address of the array where the input is to be placed. It reads characters until it meets a newline character. Listing 5-6 demonstrates the use of `gets`.

Listing 5-6

```
/* Echo two lines on the terminal */
#include <stdio.h>

main() {
    char item[81];
    gets(item);              /* Input the first line */
    printf("%s\n", item);
    gets(item);              /* Overwrite it with the second line*/
    printf("%s\n", item);
}
```

A sample run:

Ye banks and braes o' bonnie Doon,
Ye banks and braes o' bonnie Doon,
  How can ye bloom sae fresh and fair?
  How can ye bloom sae fresh and fair?

However long the line, gets will read it. Unfortunately, if the target array is not large enough, gets will place data beyond the its final element, causing memory *corruption,* which means placing data where the system does not expect it. Soon you will know enough C to use a better function, fgets, but until then be careful not to type overlong lines to gets.

5.4 PROGRAMMING EXAMPLES AND SOME USEFUL TECHNIQUES

5.4.1 Example: Rearranging names

Our problem is changing names such as 'Joe Bloggs' into the 'Bloggs, J.' format. This kind of manipulation is frequent in commercial systems. The input will be five lines, each of which contains a first name and a last name. We shall use a for loop to execute a single input and output sequence five times over, truncating the first name by specifying a maximum output width in the printf call. See Listing 5-7.

Listing 5-7

```
/* A program to convert five names from first-name, last-name
   format into last-name comma first-initial format.
*/
#include <stdio.h>

main() {
    char first_name[41], last_name[41];
    int counter;      /* To count the five iterations of the loop */

    /* Loop five times, one name each time */
    for (counter = 0; counter < 5 ; counter ++) {
        /* Input a name */
        scanf("%40s%40s", first_name, last_name);
        /* Output it rearranged */
        printf("%s, %.1s\n", last_name, first_name);
    }
}
```

Sample run:

Joe Bloggs
Bloggs, J
Mary Smith
Smith, M
Sanjay Rao
Rao, S
Heather Green
Green, H
Carbon Monoxide
Monoxide, C

This program, like all others, has no common sense. It rearranges "Carbon Monoxide" as easily as the proper names before it. If we make even more drastic mistakes in the input, it will still follow its instructions faithfully:

Peter Smith
Smith, P
Anne Boleyn
Boleyn, A
Hey diddle diddle, the cat and the fiddle
diddle, H
the, d
and, c

The program has only read three lines of input, as the third line had enough data to satisfy the last three input requests.

5.4.2 Example: Processing until a certain event happens

Suppose the owners of a building supplies store wish to purchase stock, but only have a certain amount of money available. They need to know how much they can order with the funds they have. One way to solve this problem is to list the items they wish to purchase in decreasing order of importance, and enter the cost of each purchase along with the name of the item of that cost. Then a report can be prepared showing a progressive total cost next to each item name. The owners will know when to stop buying by looking for the item where the progressive total first exceeds the money available.

We must make a plan before proceeding. Our program will repeatedly read and write data. When should it stop? Why not make the program stop at the first item that exceeds the limit, as in the following design?

```
Ask for and input the money available, in whole dollars.
While money remains,
    Read an item name and cost in whole dollars,
    Print the name and progressive total cost.
(After the money runs out) Print a message explaining this.
```

How do we know the progressive total cost? This is a case of the general problem of forming a sum, as explained in Chapter 4. We can expand our plan to include this more explicitly:

```
Ask for and input the money available, in whole dollars.
Set the cost total to zero.
While money remains,
    Read an item name and cost in whole dollars,
    Update the cost total,
    Print the name and progressive total cost.
(After the money runs out) Print a message explaining this.
```

Now that we have a plan we can design the program. It is a fatal mistake to just launch into writing program statements as they come to mind, especially as problems get harder. Unfortunately many programmers do just that: they struggle with the problem, writing code, testing, debugging, fixing mistakes, and so on, until the program finally works. Then they think, "Hmm, better throw in a few comments", and they read through the listing trying to dream up comments that might be useful. Two things have gone wrong for these people. First, having comments actually helps get the program right in the first place. Second, comments written after the fact are seldom the ones most useful in maintaining the program when (inevitably) changes or new features are required. The most useful comments are the very ones that would have really helped in writing the program; to write the program we must understand it, and to modify an existing program we must understand it. So a comment that helps in the first case should help in the second. A comment invented to look good after the fact is likely to be nothing more than extra waffle to be plowed through by the person who must maintain the program later on.

So where do we get these great comments? The answer is that we have already written them. See our program design sketch above. All we need do is write it in comment form and include an introductory comment summarizing the purpose of the program:

```
/* A program to produce a progressive total cost listing for items
   supplied as input.
   The program first asks the amount of money available, and then
   inputs item names and purchase costs, and writes a progressive
   total cost listing. The program stops when the progressive
   total exceeds the money available.
*/

      /* Ask for and input the money available, in whole dollars. */
      /* Set the cost total to zero. */

      /* While money remains */
          /* Read an item name and cost in whole dollars */
          /* Include the item cost in the cost total */
          /* Print the name and progressive total cost */

      /* (The money has run out) Print a message explaining this. */
```

For use as program explanation, some of the original wording has been slightly tidied up; no one gets things right first time, so don't be afraid to go back and improve your original ideas. We can now write C code next to each comment. We will need some variables, and their names should be as self-explanatory as possible. Even so, comments may be needed to supply additional information. The result is shown in Listing 5-8.

Listing 5-8

```
/* A program to produce a progressive total cost listing for items
   supplied as input.
   The program first asks the amount of money available, and then
   inputs item names and purchase costs, and writes a progressive
   total cost listing. The program stops when the progressive
   total exceeds the money available.
*/

#include <stdio.h>

main() {
    char item_name[21];    /* To store the name of each item entered. */
    int progressive_cost_total;
    int money_available;

    /* Ask for and input the money available, in whole dollars. */
    printf("How many dollars are available? ");
    scanf("%d", &money_available);
```

```
/* Set the cost total to zero. */
progressive_cost_total = 0;

/* While money remains */
while (progressive_cost_total < money_available) {
    int item_cost;
    /* Read an item name and cost in whole dollars */
    scanf("%20s%d", item_name, &item_cost);

    /* Include the item cost in the cost total */
    progressive_cost_total = progressive_cost_total + item_cost;

    /* Print the name and progressive total cost */
    printf("%20s %5d\n", item_name, progressive_cost_total);
}

/* (The money has run out) Print a message explaining this. */
printf("\nThat last item exceeded the amount available.\n");
}
```

We can now test the program with a run:

```
How many dollars are available? 1000
hammers 300
                hammers    300
nails 250
                  nails    550
bolts 115
                  bolts    665
saws 302
                   saws    967
wrenches 85
               wrenches   1052

That last item exceeded the amount available.
```

The program worked, but one problem is that the user is not told what to do after entering the number of dollars available. To conduct a run, the user has to know what the program is waiting for. This is a design problem, not a programming mistake. We should fix it by returning to the original design description and correcting it to include a suitable prompt asking the user to enter the items and costs. Only then should we modify the program to bring it in line with the corrected design. That way we will always have a design document that accurately reflects the condition of the software. This is essential in writing large software projects.

Exercise
Carry out these alterations to the design and program.

5.4.3   Short example: Skipping incorrect input

We often want a program to ask a question and read an answer. However, it may be that not all possible answers are sensible. For example, in an engineering problem we might want the user to input the mass of an object. Negative masses cannot exist, so if the user types a negative number we should explain the error and ask again. The user might enter further negative numbers, so we should loop until a correct value is entered. For the sake of having a complete program, let us say that we shall ask for a non-negative mass in whole kilograms; when we have finally obtained a correct response, we shall simply print it back and stop. Of course, in a real problem we would want to do something more important than that with the value. Our design thus looks like this:

```
Ask the user for a non-negative mass in kilograms.
Input the answer.
while the answer is negative:
     Explain the error and ask for another value.
     Input another mass value.
Print the mass back at the user.
```

An input statement precedes the loop, and another is placed just before the end of it. This guarantees that the input statement happens at least once. A `while` loop will be used. Some readers will naturally ask, "But surely the `do...while` loop is designed especially for the case where a loop executes at least once; why not use it here?" The problem is the step that prints the error message. It is harder to use a `do...while` loop and also print that message at the right time. For example, if we wrote:

```
do
     Explain the error and ask for another value.
     Input another mass value.
while the answer is negative.
```

then there would be an error message before the user entered any data. Or if we wrote:

```
do
     Input another mass value.
     Explain the error and ask for another value.
while the answer is negative.
```

then there would be an error message after the correct value was entered, which is wrong. It can be done with an `if` statement (which we shall study later) in addition to a `do...while`, but at the price of added complexity. Such problems tend to diminish even further the usefulness of the `do...while` statement. So, using the original plan above, we can develop a program such as Listing 5-9.

Listing 5-9

```
/* A program to test consistency-checking of user inputs. Asks for
   a non-negative mass, and repeatedly complains until it gets one.
   Then it prints the final value back out again as a check.
*/

#include <stdio.h>

main() {
    float mass_in_kilos;
    /* Ask the user for a non-negative mass in kilograms. */
    printf("What is the mass in kilograms? ");

    /* Input the answer. */
    scanf("%f", &mass_in_kilos);

    /* while the answer is negative: */
    while (mass_in_kilos < 0.0) {
        /* Explain the error and ask for another value. */
        printf("Sorry, masses cannot be negative. Please re-enter: ");

        /* Input another mass value. */
        scanf("%f", &mass_in_kilos);
    }

    /* Print the mass back as a check. */
    printf("The mass is %f kg.\n", mass_in_kilos);
}
```

Here is a sample run:

```
What is the mass in kilograms? -2
Sorry, masses cannot be negative. Please re-enter: -0.38
Sorry, masses cannot be negative. Please re-enter: 4.52
The mass is 4.520000 kg.
```

5.4.4 *The* scanf *function return*

When inputting data, the characters typed by the user might not make sense when scanf tries to convert them using the specifications in the format string. For example, if the format is %d, scanf expects something that represents an integer. If the user types, say, a name, scanf will be unable to convert it into an int. If we are unaware that something has gone wrong, the program's future calculations will be unreliable. scanf therefore uses its return value to tell the calling function how successful it was at processing its input. More precisely, it returns a count of the number of variables it successfully assigned values to. Thus, in the following call

```
scanf("%d %d %d", &i, &j, &k)
```

113

if the user types

12 AAARG!!! 37

then scanf will assign the value 12 to i. It will be unable to assign anything to j, as the next character, A, cannot form part of an integer. It gives up at that point, returning **1** as its result (because it successfully assigned a value to **one** variable, namely i). The rest of the input line (AAARG!!! 37) remains unprocessed: the next scanf call will attempt to read it again. In serious work, we should always check the result returned by scanf. (It should be 3 in the above call, because we have listed three variables to read values into.) If it is incorrect, we must do three things:

1   Get rid of the rest of the erroneous input line, reading it a character at a time until we read the newline character at the end (the getchar function is convenient for this purpose).

2   Print a message telling the user the problem and asking them to try again.

3   Re-read the input.

These steps assume that the program is to be used *interactively*, that is, with a human user. Errors in programs intended for automatic operation pose greater difficulties and require careful planning. Listing 5-10 demonstrates the above operations.

Listing 5-10

```
/* Demonstration of input with checking */

#include <stdio.h>

main() {
    int num_input, i, j, k;
    printf("Enter three values: ");
    num_input = scanf("%d %d %d", &i, &j, &k);
    while (num_input < 3) {
        /* An error has occurred. */

        /* First throw away the rest of the input line; we use
           the simple function, getchar, for this. getchar() reads
           one character from the input and returns it as its result.
        */
        while (getchar() != '\n'  /* i.e. newline */ ) {
            /* keep looping until getchar gets the newline. */
        }

        /* Now print the message */
        printf("You only typed %d values correctly.\n", num_input);
        printf("Try again: ");

        /* Re-read */
        num_input = scanf("%d %d %d", &i, &j, &k);
    }
```

```
/* Here the values must be correct. */
    printf("Your correct input was %d, %d, and %d\n", i, j, k);
}
```

We can analyze the `scanf` call as follows:

```
num_input = scanf("%d %d %d", &i, &j, &k);
```

The `scanf` *function result is assigned to* `num_input`.

The input data is assigned to the listed variables.

This must be considered carefully to avoid confusion. The data typed at the terminal is converted and assigned to the arguments; a count of the number of arguments given values is returned as the function result. Here is a sample run:

```
Enter three values: qqqqq
You only typed 0 values correctly.
Try again: 3 ttttt
You only typed 1 values correctly.
Try again: 76 34 ,
You only typed 2 values correctly.
Try again: 65 78 -432
Your correct input was 65, 78, and -432
```

5.4.5   Example: Report of purchases and sales

A warehouse is processing records of its total purchases and sales of various commodities. Input for each one consists of records containing:

Commodity code	A unique integer assigned to a commodity
Commodity name	A single word identifying the commodity
Purchase cost	Cost of each item in fractional dollars (e.g. 5.86)
Total purchases	Number of items purchased
Selling price	Selling price of each item in fractional dollars
Number sold	Number of items sold to date

We do not know how many records are to be processed, but the final one has a commodity code of zero and should not be processed. We are to print one line of information for each input record, showing the commodity name, code, the total amount spent on the commodity, the total value of sales so far, and the remaining stock of that commodity. After processing all records, the total expenses and income to date are to be printed. Headings are to be placed over the output columns. Here is some sample input and the desired output.

Sample input
```
5162 Sprockets 1.54 1000 2.45 504
2222 Monitors 390 400 642 400
1101 Printers 156 400 256 385
7264 Wringldongers 3.89 800 5.60 640
0
```

Desired output

Commodity Name	Code Number	Commodity Cost ($)	Commodity Sales ($)	Quantity Remaining
=========	======	=========	=========	=========
Sprockets	5162	1540.00	1234.80	496
Monitors	2222	156000.00	256800.00	0
Printers	1101	62400.00	98560.00	15
Wringldongers	7264	3112.00	3584.00	160

```
Total expenses to date: $223052.00
Total income to date:   $360178.81
```

In fact I have cheated; this output comes from the completed program. You may notice that the total income to date ends with 1 cent, but all the commodity sales figures end with zeros. This is due to the inaccuracies of floating point numbers, and your computer might not do this. (Performing money calculations accurately is discussed in Chapter 16.)

There are many details in this problem, such as doing the input and handling the calculations. To keep things simple, we should at first look only at the overall program structure. We know that (a) headings must appear before detail lines, (b) because there are many detail lines, there must be a loop, and (c) we cannot know the total figures until we have seen all the data. Thus the program structure must be as follows:

```
Print the headings.
Repeatedly process records until a zero commodity code is read.
Print the total expenses and income so far.
```

Next we must decide what type of loop to use, and how to work out the totals. We might expand the design along the following lines:

```
Print the headings.
Zero accumulators for the totals.
Read the commodity code
While the code is not zero:
    Process a record (including output and totaling).
    Read the next code.
Print the total expenses and income so far.
```

Most of this is straightforward, but 'process a record' contains many finicky details. It is sensible to do that task in a separate function. Three variables occur in the design: the code, and two accumulators for totals. All of these will be needed in processing a record, so all should be global. Furthermore, they should be the **only** globals. We can now write our `main` function and global declarations completely, as in Listing 5-11a.

Listing 5-11a

```
/* Program to produce an itemized income and expenses report for
   items in stock */
#include <stdio.h>

/*********** Globals: ***********/
int   commodity_code;
float total_expenses_to_date, total_income_to_date;

/***** Function Declaration *****/
void process_a_record(void);

/********** Functions ***********/

main() {
    /* Print the headings. */
    printf("Commodity      Code    Commodity  Commodity  Quantity\n");
    printf(" Name         Number   Cost ($)   Sales ($)  Remaining\n");
    printf("=========     ======  =========  =========  =========\n");

    /* Zero accumulators for the totals. */
    total_expenses_to_date = total_income_to_date = 0.0;

    scanf("%d", &commodity_code);

    while (commodity_code != 0) {
        process_a_record();      /* (including output and totaling) */
        scanf("%d", &commodity_code);
    }

    /* Print the total expenses and income so far. */
    printf("\nTotal expenses to date: $%4.2f\n", total_expenses_to_date);
    printf("Total income to date:   $%4.2f\n", total_income_to_date);
}
```

Before writing `process_a_record`, we should be clear what it must do. Thus we write a description in precondition/postcondition form:

```
/** process_a_record:
    Processes one input record.

    On Entry: commodity_code must contain the record's code no.
              Other input values are waiting to be read.
              total_expenses_to_date & total_income_to_date must
              contain totals for all records prior to this one.
              Assumption: No commodity name exceeds 80 characters.
    On Exit:  Remaining input fields for this record have been read.
              One-line summary for this record has been printed.
              total_expenses_to_date & total_income_to_date have
              been updated to include this record.
**/
```

117

The comment preceded by "On Entry" is the precondition, and that preceded by "On Exit" is the postcondition. They help us understand each function individually, without concern for the inner workings of any other. When writing `main`, we need not read the code of `process_a_record` to see what it does. When programming `process_a_record`, we only need to check that it achieves the postconditions whenever the preconditions hold, without concern for how it will be used by `main`. In large systems this separation of concerns is essential, as we just don't have the brainpower to understand everything at once. In such systems these comments would form part of the system design documents as well as (or instead of) being comments in the program. We can now write a design for this function:

```
/* Input remaining fields for this item */
/* Calculate totals for this item */
/* Print report line */
/* Update grand totals */
```

The headings, looping, printing grand totals etc. have been done already in `main`, so this function's logic only has to deal with a single record. We can complete it as shown in Listing 5-11b. 5-11a and 5-11b together form the complete program.

Listing 5-11b

```
/** process_a_record:
    Processes one input record.

    On Entry: commodity_code must contain the record's code no.
              Other input values are waiting to be read.
              total_expenses_to_date & total_income_to_date must
              contain totals for all records prior to this one.
              Assumption: No commodity name exceeds 80 characters.
    On Exit:  Remaining input fields for this record have been read.
              One-line summary for this record has been printed.
              total_expenses_to_date & total_income_to_date have been
              updated to include this record.
**/

void process_a_record(void) {

    /* Input fields: */
    char commodity_name[81];
    float cost_per_item;      /* Amount paid for each item */
    float income_per_item;    /* Amount received for each item sold */
    int   num_sold_to_date;   /* Number of items sold so far */
    int   num_bought_to_date; /* Number bought (should be >= no. sold) */

    /* Working variables: */
    float full_cost, full_income;  /* for the items in this record */

    /* Input remaining fields for this item */
```

```
scanf (
    "%80s%f%d%f%d",
    commodity_name,
    &cost_per_item,
    &num_bought_to_date,
    &income_per_item,
    &num_sold_to_date
);

/* Calculate totals for this item. */
full_cost = cost_per_item * num_bought_to_date;
full_income = income_per_item * num_sold_to_date;

/* Print report line */
printf (
    "%13s %5d %10.2f %10.2f     %5d\n",
    commodity_name,
    commodity_code,
    full_cost,
    full_income,
    num_bought_to_date - num_sold_to_date  /* qty remaining */
);

/* Update grand totals */
total_expenses_to_date += full_cost;
total_income_to_date   += full_income;
}
```

All extra variables that `process_a_record` uses during processing are declared locally inside the function. The `printf` and `scanf` calls are so long that they are split over several lines. Since the C compiler completely ignores layout, splitting these makes no difference to the program's operation. The layout for splitting these calls follows the same indentation pattern used for writing loops.

5.5   INPUT AND OUTPUT REDIRECTION

If you run the program in Section 5.4.5 and type the input on the keyboard, you will see the input and the output intermixed, for example

```
Commodity      Code    Commodity  Commodity  Quantity
   Name       Number   Cost ($)   Sales ($)  Remaining
=========     ======  =========  =========  =========
5162 Sprockets 1.54 1000 2.45 504
     Sprockets  5162     1540.00    1234.80         496
2222 Monitors 390 400 642 400
     Monitors   2222   156000.00  256800.00           0
1101 Printers 156 400 256 385
     Printers   1101    62400.00   98560.00          15
7264 Wringldongers 3.89 800 5.60 640
Wringldongers  7264     3112.00    3584.00         160
0
Total expenses to date: $223052.00
Total income to date:   $360178.81
```

This looks poor. Such a program would usually be run with input coming from a file, so that the output looks tidy. Most operating systems have some means of making a program read data from a file instead of the keyboard; this is called *input redirection*. Under the MS-DOS and Unix operating systems this is done with the < symbol on the command line. For example, if the above program is called lst5-11, and the data is in the file lst5-11.dat, then this command will make the program process the data file:

```
lst5-11 < lst5-11.dat
```

You could create lst5-11.dat with the same editor you use to write your C programs.

A similar thing can be done with output if we want to record a program's output on a file — just use > (under DOS or Unix) instead of <. You can even do both at once. Try it.

Input and output redirection are not part of the C language; they are provided by the operating system. To write C programs that are guaranteed to get their data from files, we must use special C library functions.

5.6 SUMMARY

- The purpose of input is to allow programs to respond to outside information, especially information not available when the program is written. All realistic programs make use of input.
  - Input is often called *reading*.
  - When inputting, the program waits until the input data is available, and then converts it into internal form and assigns it to the variable(s).
- When accepting input from a human, display a *prompt* explaining what the human is supposed to do next.
- Never assume the answer the user will give to a question — write programs that work properly no matter what the user answers.
- An array name used as a function argument represents the address of the array's allocated memory.

- `scanf` provides many different input data conversion facilities. In particular:
  - it will accept characters representing numbers and convert them into the computer's internal `int` (and other) numeric formats
  - it will accept a single character and assign it to a `char` variable (`%c`)
  - a whitespace character in the format string causes it to skip **all** whitespace in the input up to a printable character
  - a non-whitespace, non-% character will accept an input character only if it matches exactly. To specify a `%`, use `%%`
  - it will accept characters making up a word and assign to a character array (`%s`)
  - maximum widths may be specified to limit the number of characters `scanf` will read from the input
  - the `scanf` function return tells how many argument variables were successfully given values from the input.
- `gets` provides a simple facility for reading an entire line of text into a `char` array.
- `getchar` is a simple function to read a single character.
- When using `scanf` to assign to simple variables, **always** put the 'address-of' operator, `&`, before the variable name.
- When using `scanf` to assign to `char` arrays, **never** put the address-of operator before the array name.
- Programming techniques discussed:
  - processing a fixed number of input values
  - processing input until a certain event happens
  - checking an input value for errors
  - program design, comments.
- Many operating systems, including MS-DOS and Unix, provide some way of performing input redirection.

5.7   SELF-TEST EXERCISES

Short Answer

1   Describe what happens when the computer executes the following statement (`intvar` is some `int` variable).

```
scanf("%d", &intvar);
```

2   Given these declarations:
```
char car[50];
char ch;
int i;
float f;
```
state which of the following are correct, and which are incorrect. For the incorrect ones, say why.

```
a   scanf(car)
b   scanf("%40s", car)
c   scanf("%40s", &car)
d   scanf("%49s", car)
e   scanf("%50s", car)
f   scanf("%d", car)
g   scanf("%d", i)
h   scanf("%c", &ch)
i   scanf("%5d", &i)
j   scanf("%d%30s", &i, car)
k   scanf("%d", &f)
l   scanf("%d %f", &i, &f)
m   scanf("%f", &f)
```

3   When inputting from a human user, what should the program first do?

4   When does a program perform its input?
   a   when it is being written
   b   when it is being typed into the computer
   c   when it is being compiled
   d   when it is being executed.

5   Name three C library functions that perform input.

6   What is a prompt?

7   Write a declaration for a `char` array only just big enough to hold words of up to eight printable characters.

8   Write a call to `scanf` to read a character into the `char` variable `bzzt`, and an integer into the `int` variable `mzlfmph`. (Those names were picked to remind you that identifiers have no inherent meaning.)

Programming

For all numeric input in the problems, include checks for invalid input.

9   A meteorologist is reading temperatures from a thermometer marked in Fahrenheit, and wishes to convert them into Celsius. The answers are needed to the nearest degree. Write a program that will ask the meteorologist to type a temperature in Fahrenheit degrees, and then print the equivalent value in Celsius. The formula for converting Fahrenheit to Celsius is

$$C = \frac{5(F-32)}{9}$$

The program should continue asking for, and converting, temperatures until the meteorologist enters the value −999. When that value is entered, the program should stop without printing a converted value for the −999.

10 Write a function that prints Fibonacci numbers. It should use the values in the global `int` variables `F1` and `F2` as the two starting numbers, and the global variable `num` should specify how many numbers in the sequence to compute beyond the first two given numbers. Write a `main` function that asks the user the values of `F1`, `F2` and `num`, and then calls the function to generate the required printout.

11 Write a program that computes interest on a bank account over a number of years. The input is the initial account balance, the number of years, and the interest rate. Also input the name of the account holder and the account number. The output should be a table showing on each line the balance at the start of the year, the interest in dollars, and the balance at the end of the year. The table should have headings that include the name and account number. Include a function that does all the processing for a single year.

5.8 TEST QUESTIONS

Short Answer

1 Briefly describe *buffering*.

2 Name a C function that can read a line of text into a `char` array.

3 Briefly explain why the address-of operator is needed in some arguments to `scanf` but not in others.

4 Which of the following statements are true, and which are false?
 a `scanf` is an output function.
 b To do input in C, one must use `scanf`.
 c "Input" refers to the process whereby computers obtain data from the outside.
 d The first argument to `scanf` is a format string.
 e Most serious programs perform some input.
 f Input in C alters the values of the variables to which data is input.
 g When `scanf` is called, it obtains data from the variables named in its argument list.
 h When accepting data from a human, it is wise to display instructions.
 i `scanf` will not function unless the program previously displays a prompt.
 j The `&` operator must be placed before the names of simple variables in the `scanf` argument list.
 k The `%s` format is used in a `scanf` call to input into `char` arrays.
 l A single call to `scanf` may not input more than one type of value.

5 `%1s` and `%c` are both used in `scanf` to request input of one character. So what are the differences? (There are at least two.) You might have to think carefully to find the answer — but you do have all the information.

Programming

6   It is fairly straightforward to make the computer print a diamond:

```
  *
***
  *
```

Write a program that asks the user how many diamonds to print, and that then prints that many in a vertical line.

7   (Harder) As in the above problem, ask the user how many diamonds to print, but then print that many in a horizontal line. Reject requests for more than eight diamonds, and re-input the number. For example, a user who asks for four diamonds should get

```
  *       *       *       *
***     ***     ***     ***
  *       *       *       *
```

8   Write a program that asks for the user's name and then prints an award for the user:

```
*********************************************
**              AN AWARD TO            **
**              Joe Bloggs             **
*********************************************
```

9   An old-fashioned baker sells bread in baker's dozens (thirteen loaves). The bread is baked on trays which hold three loaves each. Write a program that will ask how many trays are available, and then tell the baker how many complete baker's dozens can be baked on those trays. Ignore extra loaves that do not make a complete baker's dozen. For example, if 9 trays are available, 27 loaves can be baked, so your program should print 2.

10 Write a program that asks for two integers, n and m, and then prints the mth power of n.

11 An Australian investor wishes to sell some gold coins in America. A program is needed that will report the value of the gold in the coins to be sold. The newspapers print both the daily gold price in US dollars and the exchange rate between Australian and US dollars. (For example, gold might be $US367.65 per troy ounce, and one $A might be 71.05 US cents.) These values will be entered into the computer first. Then, on each line, the investor will enter a coin's gold weight and the number of those coins to be sold. For example, the investor might have five American eagles ($10) each containing .5159 oz gold, and twenty Australian or British sovereigns each containing .2354 oz gold. For each input line, the gold value in both Australian and US dollars is to be printed. At the end the investor will enter a coin weight of zero, and the program should report the grand total price in both currencies.

12 A physicist wishes to test whether a certain gaseous chemical behaves like an ideal gas. The pressure, volume, and temperature (P_1, V_1 and T_1) have been measured for a certain sample of the gas. The physicist intends to alter the volume and temperature and measure the new value for pressure. These new figures will be called P_2, V_2 and T_2. The measured pressure will be compared manually with the predicted value for an ideal gas. This will be done repeatedly for various values of temperature and volume. Your job is to write a program that provides the pressure values as predicted by the ideal gas equation. It must first ask for and read the values P_1, V_1 and T_1. Then it should repeatedly ask for and read values for V_2 and T_2, and compute and print the corresponding predicted value of P_2. The program should stop when the entered value for V_2 is zero. The formula for calculating P_2 is

$$P_2 = \frac{P_1 V_1 T_2}{T_1 V_2}$$

13 An engineer's data-sampling instrument prints a voltage level and the time a measurement was taken. Unfortunately the time is printed in seconds since midnight. Write a program that asks the user to type a time in seconds, and then prints out the time in hour-minute-second format, hh:mm:ss (using the 24-hour clock). (Hint: Use the / and % operators.) Some days have an extra leap second; don't worry about that.

14 Write a program that does the inverse of the previous one. That is, it converts hh:mm:ss format into seconds since midnight.

15 Write a program that echoes the input to the output until a line is entered that commences with an asterisk (*) in column one. The line with the asterisk should not be printed.

16 Write a program that reads ten numbers and prints the ratios between successive pairs (meaning that only nine ratios are printed).

17 A shopkeeper needs a program to calculate change. Write one that asks for the purchase value in cents and the amount tendered in cents and then prints how many coins of each denomination must be given in change such that the minimum number of coins are needed. Coin values are 1c, 5c, 10c, 25c and 50c.

18 The area of a circle is πR^2, where R is the radius. Write a function that looks in the global variable D for the diameter of a circle and then prints a line like this:

```
The diameter is ____, the radius is ____, and the area is ____.
```

with the blanks filled in appropriately. Allow for non-integer values. Now write a main function that repeatedly asks the user for a diameter, and calls the function to print the above line. It should stop when the user enters a diameter less than zero.

19 A lecturer wants a program to compute the final grades for a class. Each student is represented by a line containing a one-word surname followed by five floating point numbers, representing the results in four assignments and an exam. The first two assignments are worth 5% of the total, the next two are worth 10%, and the exam is worth the rest. Write a program that first asks how many students are in the class, and then reads that many lines of input and prints the students' names and final percentages. Finally an average percentage for the class should be printed. (This is the total of all percentages divided by the number of students.) Include a function that completely processes just one set of student marks. Be careful in deciding which variables should be global.

20 The arctangent of x, if $|x| < 1$, can be computed using the following series

$$x - \frac{x^3}{3} + \frac{x^5}{9} - \frac{x^7}{7} + \ldots$$

Write a program that inputs x with validation that it is within range, inputs the number of terms required, and then displays the arctangent computed to the requested number of terms. Also display the result computed using the library atan function for comparison.

21 A common problem for home buyers is choosing a repayment option that doesn't cost too much per month and yet repays the loan in a reasonable period. Your task is to write a program that allows a borrower to enter values for the amount borrowed and the number of months over which the loan should be repaid, and to print the monthly repayment that would be needed to pay off the loan in that time. Use the following formula. If A is the amount borrowed, n is the number of months, r is the interest rate per month, and P the repayment amount, then

$$P = \frac{Ar\left(1 + \frac{r}{100}\right)^n}{\left(1 + \frac{r}{100}\right)^n - 1}$$

You should solve this problem as follows: first, write a function that uses the values of the global variables A, n, and r to calculate the repayment amount, and stores it in the global variable P. All variables should be floating point dollars. Then write a main function that sets r to 5 (for 5% interest), and then asks the user for A and n values repeatedly, printing the matching repayment, until the user enters zero for A.

22 A geometric sequence is one where the ratio of each term to the one before is a constant, as in 1, 3, 9, 27, ... The common ratio in this case is 3. Write a program that asks for the first term, the common ratio, and the number of terms to print out. Then call a function to print the requested number of terms of the series. The numbers might not be integers.

23 A number is triangular if that many dots can be arranged in a triangle. For example, our `triangle` function shows that 6 is a triangular number. There are two smaller ones, 1 and 3. Similarly a number is square if that many dots can be arranged in a square, for example 9:

★★★
★★★
★★★

Write a program to print the first ten triangular and square numbers. The nth triangular number is $(n^2 + n)/2$, and the nth square number is of course n^2.

24 Write a program that evaluates $\sin^2 x$ according to the formula

$$\sin^2 x = x^2 - \frac{2^3 x^4}{4!} + \frac{2^5 x^6}{6!} - \cdots = \sum_{n=1}^{\infty} \frac{(-1)^{n+1} 2^{2n-1} x^{2n}}{(2n)!}$$

Note that each term equals the preceding one multiplied by

$$\frac{-(2x)^2}{2n(2n-1)}$$

The purpose of the program is to find out how many terms are needed to calculate $\sin^2 x$ accurate to 1 in 1,000,000. It should input a value for x, with validation that its magnitude is less than $\pi/2$, and then calculate and add terms until a term is smaller than .000001 of the calculated sum of terms so far. Then it should print the final sum of terms, the number of terms used (including the final one), as well as a comparison value computed using the library `sin` function.

25 Write a program that reads figures showing average salaries for each year from 1975 to 1992 and displays the figures in a histogram format where each asterisk stands for $1000 or part of $1000. For example

```
Year    Salary in $1,000s ==>
1975    ************************
1976    *************************
1977    ****************************
...etc.
```

To get a clean display of the histogram, you may wish to use input redirection from a file of salary data.

6

Making choices: the conditional statements `if` and `switch`

Objectives

Understand the nature and purpose of *conditional* statements in programming.

Be aware of the principles of structured programming and the three control constructs: *sequences, iterations,* and *selection (conditionals)*.

Be able to use `if` statements to make decisions.

Master C logical expressions:

— `&&` (and), `||` (or) and `!` (not) operators

— execution and evaluation of logical expressions

— string comparison functions: `strcmp` and `strncmp`.

Be able to manipulate logical expressions — *Boolean algebra.*

See how the `switch` statement can conveniently express certain limited kinds of decisions.

6.1 CONDITIONAL STATEMENTS

It has been proved that any algorithm whatsoever can be programmed using just three different programming control methods. We have met two of these: *sequencing* (writing one statement after another) and *iteration* (looping). The final one is the *selection*, or *conditional* statement. The programmer writes two or more alternative instructions, and supplies a test which the program uses to decide which alternative to execute. For example, if the user is selecting an option from a menu, the program must test the user's answer to see which option was chosen.

Sometimes we need more than one test: for example, a program reading characters may have to do different things depending on whether the character is alphabetic, numeric, punctuation, whitespace, and so on. Such a situation demands one test after another: "If it is alphabetic, do this, but if not, see if it is a digit, and if so, do that, but if not, ..." and so on. Figure 6.1 shows some conditional situations diagrammatically.

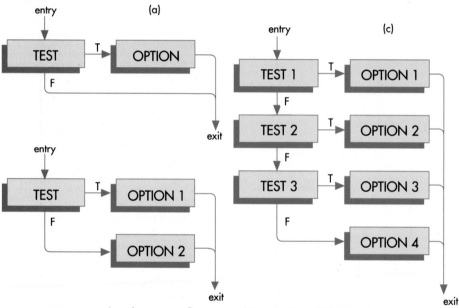

Figure 6.1   Examples of execution flow in conditional statements

Figure 6.1(a) shows a test being used to decide whether to execute some statements (shown as OPTION). The branch marked T (for true) is taken if the test is satisfied, and the code is executed. If the test fails, the F (false) branch bypasses the code. Slightly more complicated is the situation in 6.1(b). There, the test is used to choose between two different pieces of code (OPTION 1 and OPTION 2). Figure 6.1(c) shows a situation with many tests. If one succeeds (T path taken) the matching option is executed. If the first test fails the second test is made, and so on until a test succeeds. If no tests succeed, the final option is taken. C's if statement allows us to program any of these possibilities.

6.2 if: C'S MAIN SELECTION STATEMENT

6.2.1 Simple if statements

The if statement in C is similar to sentences starting with 'If' in English. We might say "If it is raining, bring the umbrella." The expectation is that the umbrella will only be brought if the statement "It is raining" is true. Similarly, in C, we supply a test, or *condition*, which might be true or false. The truth or falsity determines which statements are executed. The simplest case is analogous to (a) in Figure 6.1, and to the umbrella example. There is one test and one optional statement. The format of such an if statement is

```
if (    test goes here    ) {

           statements for conditional
              execution go here

}
```

Listing 6-1 illustrates this. It asks the user to enter a number representing temperature in kelvin. If it is negative, it prints "Temperatures can't be negative!"

Listing 6-1

```
/* Program to input a temperature and print a warning if the number
   is negative. */

#include <stdio.h>

main() {
    float temperature;

    /* Print a prompt for the user */
    printf("Please enter the temperature in kelvin: ");

    /* Input number and check. */
    scanf("%f", &temperature);
    if (temperature < 0.0) {
        printf("Temperatures can't be negative!\n");
    }

    /* (A touching farewell message) */
    printf("Temperature processed.\n");
}
```

Output (first run):
```
Please enter the temperature in kelvin: 35
Temperature processed.
```

Output (second run):
```
Please enter the temperature in kelvin: -89.9
Temperatures can't be negative!
Temperature processed.
```

The program has executed the statements inside the `if` statement only when `temperature` is negative.

The next situation is where there are two possible actions, and the program must select one, as in Figure 6.1(b). The syntax for this sort of `if` statement is

```
if (    test goes here    ) {

        Statements for conditional execution when
              the test succeeds go here.

} else {

        Statements for conditional execution when
              the test fails go here.

}
```

C uses `else` where in English we might use 'otherwise'. For example, we might say "If it is raining stay at home, otherwise go to the beach." To illustrate this type of `if` statement, it is easy to modify the previous program to print a message for both the negative and non-negative cases.

Listing 6-2

```
/* Program to input a temperature and print a warning if the number
   is negative, or confirmation otherwise. */

#include <stdio.h>

main() {
    float temperature;

    /* Print a prompt for the user */
    printf("Please enter the temperature in kelvin: ");

    /* Input number and check. */
    scanf("%f", &temperature);
    if (temperature < 0.0) {
        printf("Temperatures can't be negative!\n");
    } else {
        /* We are doing this in two statements just to prove we can. */
        printf("OK: ");
        printf("Non-negative temperatures are realistic.\n");
    }
```

```
    /* (A touching farewell message) */
    printf("Temperature processed.\n");
}
```

```
Please enter the temperature in kelvin: 21.75
OK: Non-negative temperatures are realistic.
Temperature processed.
```

Output (run 2)

```
Please enter the temperature in kelvin: -6
Temperatures can't be negative!
Temperature processed.
```

The statements included in the `if` can be any C statements whatsoever. For example, we might decide that if the test succeeds we need to call half a dozen functions, and if it fails we need to execute a `for` loop 1000 times. No problem — just place the appropriate statements in the two places. "Anything whatsoever" includes further `if` statements, or even a collection of many different types of statements. What matters is that it should be logically correct and easily understood.

6.2.2 A remark about program layout rules

Some readers will be aware that the braces in the various structured statements (`for`, `while`, `if`, etc.) are not strictly necessary if only one statement is being included in the structured statement. For example, many texts would print the `if` statement in Listing 6-2 as follows:

```
if (temperature < 0.0)
    printf("Temperatures can't be negative!\n");
else
{
    printf("OK: ");
    printf("Non-negative temperatures are realistic.\n");
}
```

The braces can be omitted from the first part of Listing 6-2 because it contains only one statement. This omission does not alter the meaning of the `if` statement. You need to know about this because you will often have to work with programs written by other people, but I strongly recommend that you **never** omit the braces.

Also note: in this code fragment, the opening brace after the `else` is on a separate line. Never do that either. The reasons for these recommendations are explained in Appendix E.

6.2.3 Multiple-test conditionals

These correspond to Figure 6.1(c). We can generalize our previous `if` syntax to include more than one test, as follows.

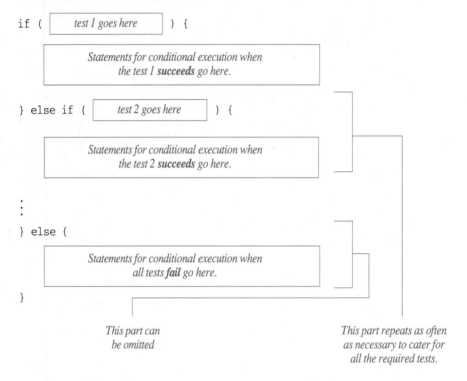

Don't worry! It looks worse than it is. Let us use it to solve a realistic problem. A well-known problem in mathematics is finding the roots of a quadratic equation. The standard quadratic is $y = ax^2 + bx + c$. For given a, b, and c, we wish to know what values of x, if any, make y zero. The answer is given by the formula

$$x = \frac{-b \pm \sqrt{b^2 - 4ac}}{2a}$$

Any of the following things can happen:
1   a can be zero, in which case the equation is not quadratic and the formula doesn't work
2   $b^2 - 4ac$ can be negative, in which case we cannot take the square root, and there are no real solutions
3   $b^2 - 4ac$ can be zero, in which case there is one solution
4   $b^2 - 4ac$ can be positive, and there will be two solutions.

Our task is to ask the user for the values a, b and c, and then decide which case applies. Let us commence by seeing how the logic fits the pattern in Figure 6.1(c). Figure 6.2 shows that pattern as it applies to this particular problem.

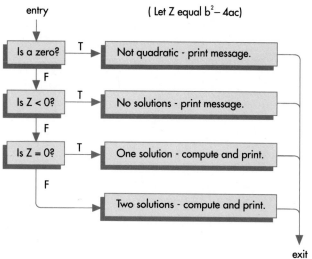

entry   (Let Z equal $b^2 - 4ac$)

Figure 6.2   The logic for finding quadratic roots

Using the `if` statement syntax given above, this can be programmed as shown in Listing 6-3.

Listing 6-3

```
/* Given three input real numbers representing the coefficients of a
   quadratic equation (y = a*x*x + b*x + c), decides what sort of
   solution the equation has, and prints the solutions if any.
*/
#include <stdio.h>
#include <math.h>

main() {
    float a, b, c, Z;
    /* Input coefficients: */
    printf("Enter the three coefficients of the quadratic,\n");
    printf("x-squared coefficient first: ");
    scanf("%f %f %f", &a, &b, &c);
    Z = b*b - 4*a*c;   /* to save recalculation */

    if (a == 0) {
        printf("The coefficients do not represent a quadratic.\n");

    } else if (Z < 0) {
        printf("The quadratic has no solutions.\n");

    } else if (Z == 0) {
        printf("There is one solution, x = %f\n", -b / (2.0 * a));

    } else {   /* b*b-4*a*c must here be greater than zero */
        printf (
```

```
            "There are two solutions, x = %f, and x = %f\n",
            (-b + sqrt(Z)) / (2.0 * a),
            (-b - sqrt(Z)) / (2.0 * a)
        );
    }
}
```

Four example runs

```
Enter the three coefficients of the quadratic,
x-squared coefficient first: 0 1 1
The coefficients do not represent a quadratic.

Enter the three coefficients of the quadratic,
x-squared coefficient first: 1 1 1
The quadratic has no solutions.

Enter the three coefficients of the quadratic,
x-squared coefficient first: 1 -2 1
There is one solution, x = 1.000000

Enter the three coefficients of the quadratic,
x-squared coefficient first: 1 0 -1
There are two solutions, x = 1.000000, and x = -1.000000
```

6.3 LOGICAL EXPRESSIONS

The various tests we have been using in loops and if statements are in fact logical expressions, just as numeric computations are arithmetic expressions. It might come as a surprise that C does not distinguish between logical and arithmetic expressions. Logical expressions yield numeric values in C, 1 for true, and 0 for false. (This is not true in many other languages such as Pascal.) For example, the logical expression $7<1$ yields 0 because it is false, but $7!=1$ yields 1 because it is true. We could even have an if statement commencing "if (1) {" and it would behave just as if we wrote, say, "if (3>2) {". If 0 is false and 1 is true, what if we wrote "if (385) {"? The answer is that whenever a logical value is needed (such as in an if statement), C regards any non-zero value as true. Some programmers use this quirk of C to write very odd-looking tests. It is certainly better, though, to write tests that look like tests. Thus, when we have a variable (say length) that holds a value that we use as a number (such as a counter, or a length, or money, etc.), to find out if it is non-zero, write

```
if (length != 0) {
```

instead of

```
if (length) {
```

even though they actually mean exactly the same thing. (Do they? Think about it.) The first says exactly what it means; the meaning of the second is only apparent after a moment's thought. Remembering the importance of keeping things simple, why make the reader hesitate (even for an instant) when a clearer formulation is just as easy? Don't be misled if you hear or read arguments about the second being more efficient than the first. Human time is more important than computer time, so wasting a second of human effort to save a millionth of a second of computer effort is not good business, especially if it causes an error that wastes hours of both sorts of effort. Also, most modern compilers are smart enough to recognize that the two statements are equivalent, and to write the same code in both cases.

The other side of this coin is when we have a variable intended to hold a logical value. For example, in a large program, we might find, deep in the processing, that an error has occurred, and we need to know this at other places in the program. If we have an `int` called, say, `an_error_occurred`, and set to zero initially, then we need only assign 1 to it when we first discover the error. At the point in the processing where we need to check back and find out if an error happened, we can write

```
if (an_error_occurred) {
    ...
```

Such situations should not use the form

```
if (an_error_occurred != 0) {
    ...
```

because conceptually, the variable does not hold a number, it holds a logical value (1 for true, 0 for false). Many people include the following statements at the head of their programs:

```
#define TRUE (1)
#define FALSE (0)
```

so that they can write such things as

```
an_error_occurred = TRUE;
```

Once again the reason is clarity.

6.3.1 More logical operators

C provides operators for combining logical values, the most important being **and** (written `&&`), **or** (`||`) and **not** (`!`). Again, these can be used in C in a manner analogous to their use in English sentences such as "If it is raining, **or** it is snowing, stay indoors." For a C example, suppose we wish to be sure that the value in the `char` `ch` does not represent a digit. (There is a library function to test this, but we shall ignore that for the time being.) Characters are **not** digits if their value is less than the ASCII code for `'0'`, **or** greater than the code for `'9'` (since either occurrence rules out its being a digit). Thus we might write

```
scanf("%c", &ch);
if (ch < '0' || ch > '9') {
    printf("Not a digit\n");
}
```

Similarly if a given character **is** a digit, its code must be both greater than or equal to '0', **and** less than or equal to '9':

```
scanf("%c", &ch);
if (ch >= '0' && ch <= '9') {
    printf("A digit\n");
}
```

It is obvious from the above examples that the priorities of the && and || operators are less than those of the comparison operators. In fact, && has a higher priority than ||, and this should be borne in mind when mixing ands and ors in the same expression. ! (not), on the other hand, has a high priority (the same as the other unary operators). So, to find out if ch is not less than '0', we could either write ch >= '0' or (using !) we could write !(ch < '0'). The parentheses are essential in the latter version, due to the high priority of !. The results of these operators for all combinations of operand values are shown in the following tables.

A && B	A==0	A!=0
B==0	0	0
B!=0	0	1

A || B	A==0	A!=0
B==0	0	1
B!=0	1	1

! A	
A==0	1
A!=0	0

Warning: We cannot write ch ! < '0', even though we can say it that way in English. There is nothing illogical about the way C requires it; it is exactly analogous to the way the arithmetic negation operator, unary −, is used. But what about ! = ? Well, != is a single operator, the test for inequality; it is not an application of the ! operator

One more thing needs to be said about && and ||: they are what is known as *short-circuit* operators. That is, they only do as much computation as necessary to decide the result. For example, in the && table above, we can see that if A is zero, the result must be zero irrespective of the value of B. In that case B would not be evaluated. This is a subtlety, but there are places where it is important. For example, if evaluating B changes something important, then it might be critical that we know whether B has been computed. Again, this causes most trouble for people who write unnecessarily convoluted, complicated programs.

6.3.2 Reasoning about logical expressions

It is useful to know a few simple manipulation rules for logical operators. Here are a few of the most important. In mathematics, these apply to the Boolean (logical) values, true and false; in C, they apply to the values 1 and 0 (or any C expression evaluating to 1 or 0).

Rules involving not (!)

```
! (a < b)     ==    (a >= b)
! (a <= b)    ==    (a > b)
! (a > b)     ==    (a <= b)
! (a >= b)    ==    (a < b)
! ! a         ==    a           (provided a is 0 or 1)
```

These rules are a source of confusion for many beginners. Many people naturally assume, for example, that if *a* is not greater than *b*, *a* must be less than *b*. But it might be equal to *b*, as the above table shows. Never forget about the 'equal' case.

De Morgan's laws

We frequently need to know the conditions under which some event does **not** occur. For example, let us say we must leave the building if there is a fire **or** if there is an earthquake. When can we stay? Obviously, if there is **no** fire **and** if there is **no** earthquake. You now know De Morgan's laws! Here they are symbolically:

```
! (A && B)    ==    (!A || !B)
! (A || B)    ==    (!A && !B)
```

In other words, when we logically negate an expression connected by `&&` or `||`, we must negate each component, and change `&&` to `||` and vice versa.

Example

A year is a leap year if it is divisible by 4, except when it is divisible by 100 but not by 400. For example 1980, 1992, 2000, and 1600 are leap years, but 1981, 1990, and 1900 are not. Our task is to write an expression that yields true (i.e. 1) if the variable `year` contains a leap year, and false (i.e. 0) otherwise. The condition just given sounds complicated, so let's simplify it. Let DIV4 stand for '`year` is divisible by 4', and similarly for DIV100 and DIV400. Using this notation, the test is

```
DIV4 except when (DIV100 but not DIV400)
```

What are we to make of 'except when' and 'but not'? In fact they both mean the same as 'and not'. They seem to mean something different, but when we really look hard at them the difference is entirely emotional, not logical. So our test can be rephrased:

```
DIV4 and not (DIV100 and not DIV400)
```

Or using C notation,

```
DIV4 && ! (DIV100 && ! DIV400)
```

Using De Morgan's law,

```
DIV4 && (! DIV100 || ! ! DIV400)
```

Since two **not**s cancel,

```
DIV4 && (! DIV100 || DIV400)
```

We can now write out the DIV4 etc. in full; `year` is divisible by 4 if the remainder when divided by 4 is zero, that is, `year % 4 == 0`.

```
year % 4 == 0 && ( ! (year % 100 == 0) || year % 400 == 0)
```

and removing the `!`, the required expression becomes

```
year % 4 == 0 && (year % 100 != 0 || year % 400 == 0)
```

Further manipulations could be performed, but they would destroy the clarity of the expression, and would therefore be unwise.

6.4 THE `switch` STATEMENT

Sometimes we need a convenient way to handle the common situation where a multi-way choice depends on the value of a single expression. For example, we might present users with a menu with eight options, and ask them to enter a value in the range 1 to 8 to indicate their choice. We could then read their response into an `int` variable (`choice`, say) and execute a different piece of code for each possible value of `choice`. The `if` statement could handle this situation, but the `switch` statement does it more neatly. It has the following structure:

```
switch (choice) {
case 1:
```
┌───┐
│   *Code for choice == 1 case goes here.*   │
└───┘
```
      break;
case 2:
```
┌───┐
│   *Code for choice == 2 case goes here.*   │
└───┘
```
      break;
   .
   .
   .
case 8:
```
┌───┐
│   *Code for choice == 8 case goes here.*   │
└───┘
```
      break;
default:
```
┌───┐
│   *Code for any other value of choice goes here.*   │
└───┘
```
}
```

The word `switch` introduces the statement. Then in parentheses, we may write any integer expression. It is evaluated, and the value determines which option, each marked by the word `case`, will be selected. After the word `case`, we must write a **constant** expression (i.e. one that contains no variables or function calls). Finally, the `default` option is executed if the value of `choice` is not one of the values mentioned in a `case`. After executing the desired option, execution proceeds to the next option in the statement, rather than to the end of the `switch`. Thus if `choice` were 1, case 1 would be selected, and the execution would flow on through case 2, then 3, and so on. This is almost certainly **not** what we want. The `break` statement rectifies this; it is a special C statement for getting out of loops and switches. We shall avoid it in loops in this book, but we have to use it to break out of switches. After executing a `break` statement, execution continues with the statement after the end of the `switch`. It is very easy to forget a `break`, and the `switch` will then malfunction, so we have to be particularly careful.

We can of course leave out `break` if we really want execution to flow from one case to the next. There is only one situation where this is wise, namely where two or more cases have exactly the same code. So if, in the above, cases 5 and 6 both required execution of the same code, we might write:

```
case 5:
case 6:
```

```
        Code for when choice == 5 or
        choice == 6 goes here.
```

```
break;
```

The advantage of `switch` is its convenience; its disadvantages are the need to remember `break`, and the need for the various case options to be constant. The `if` statement, on the other hand, is safer, and allows fully general tests of any kind.

One final remark to save you hours of frustration: **Never misspell** `default`! The compiler will almost certainly not warn you — for various reasons better not gone into — but the logic will go haywire.

6.4.1 Example: Telephone charges

Consider the problem of producing a telephone account. Suppose there are four call types: local, long distance A, long distance B, and international, represented by the letters L, A, B, and I respectively. Local calls are $0.40 per call, long distance A are $0.40 per minute, long distance B are $0.60 per minute, and international are $0.50 + $0.80 per minute. Input consists of a line containing the client's name, then lines of information on calls made. Each line will have a letter (L, A, B, or I) as above, and a fractional number representing the length of the call in minutes. A final line will start with the letter Z to mark the end of the data. We are required to print an itemized account showing all calls, totals for each call type, and a grand total. Our first approach to a solution might be:

```
Zero variables for storing totals.
Read client name, and print heading, including name.
Get the letter starting the next line.
While the letter is not Z,
    Process one line of the account
    Get the letter starting the next line.
Print all totals.
```

This is sufficient to develop a `main` function, as in Listing 6-4a.

Listing 6-4a

```
/* A program for producing a telephone account.
   Input must consist of
   a)  A line containing a client name,
   b)  Multiple lines, each describing a phone call:
       a character (L, A, B or I) indicating call type
       a fractional number representing call duration in minutes.
   c)  A line commencing with a Z

   Output is a phone account with a heading including the client name, then
   an itemized list of calls showing individual cost, and finally
   totals for all four call types, and a grand total cost.
*/

#include <stdio.h>

/**** Function declarations ****/
void process_heading(void);
void Process_one_call_record(void);
void print_all_totals(void);

/**Globals**/
float total_L, total_A, total_B, total_I;
    /* Totals for Local, long dist A, l.d. B, International. */
char call_type_code;    /* letter specifying type of call */

main() {
    /* Zero variables for storing totals. */
    total_L = total_A = total_B = total_I = 0.0;

    /* Read client name, and print heading, including name. */
    process_heading();

    /* Get the letter starting the next line. */
    scanf(" %c", &call_type_code);

    while (call_type_code != 'Z') {
        /* Process one line of account (including updating totals) */
        Process_one_call_record();

        /* Get the letter starting the next line. */
        scanf(" %c", &call_type_code);
        /*      ^       That space is vital! */
    }
    print_all_totals();
}
```

Will it work? That depends on whether the three functions do their jobs properly. We should describe exactly what they do, in precondition/postcondition form:

```
/***** process_heading:
 On entry: The next line of input contains the name of the client.
 On exit:  A heading for the bill is printed which includes the
           client's name.  Headings for the columns in the itemized
           part are printed.
*****/
```

```
/***** Process_one_call_record:
 On entry: call_type_code contains the identifying letter for the
           call type of the present call.
           Input contains the duration in fractional minutes.
           Totals contain summed costs for all previous calls.
 On exit:  An item line is printed showing call type code, duration,
           and cost of call.
           Totals contain summed costs for all previous, AND THIS, call.
*****/
```

```
/***** print_all_totals:
 On entry: Totals contain summed costs for all calls.
 Operation:Totals are printed.  The grand total is computed and printed.
*****/
```

Now we can check the logic of the main program. The headings come out first, and the description of `process_heading` guarantees to take care of the first line of data (the name). The data will be correctly read, since our loop reads the class code letter, and `Process_one_call_record` reads the rest of a record. The totals are zeroed in `main`, so logically they are the totals of the first **zero** records. The description of `Process_one_call_record` guarantees that if the totals are up-to-date for all previous records, it will make them up-to-date for all records including the current one. So, as we process records one by one starting with the first, the totals will stay up-to-date, and they will be correct at the finish. That is all `print_all_totals` needs to be able to print them. Thus we can be reasonably sure the program will function properly when the missing functions are programmed. The final part of the program is shown in Listing 6-4b.

Listing 6-4b

```
/***** process_heading:
 On entry: The next line of input contains the name of the client.
 On exit:  A heading for the bill is printed which includes the
           client's name.  Headings for the columns in the itemized
           part are printed.
*****/

void process_heading(void) {
    char client_name[81];    /* Assume no client name > 80 chars */
    gets(client_name);
```

```
    printf("\t\tSupa Phone Incorporated.\n");
    printf("Phone bill for\n%s\n\n", client_name);
    printf("Call Code   Duration   Cost($)\n");
    printf("=========   ========   =======\n");
}


/***** Process_one_call_record:
 On entry: call_type_code contains the identifying letter for the
           call type of the present call.
           Input contains the duration in fractional minutes.
           Totals contain summed costs for all previous calls.
 On exit:  An item line is printed showing call type code, duration,
           and cost of call.
           Totals contain summed costs for all previous, AND THIS, call.
*****/

void Process_one_call_record(void) {
    float call_duration, call_cost;
    scanf("%f", &call_duration);

    /* Evaluate call cost based on category & adjust total */
    switch (call_type_code) {
    case 'L':
        call_cost = 0.40;                          /* 40 cents */
        total_L += call_cost;
        break;
    case 'A':
        call_cost = 0.40 * call_duration;       /* 40c / minute */
        total_A += call_cost;
        break;
    case 'B':
        call_cost = 0.60 * call_duration;       /* 60c / minute */
        total_B += call_cost;
        break;
    case 'I':
        call_cost = 0.50 + 0.80 * call_duration; /* 50c + 80c/min */
        total_I += call_cost;
        break;
    default:
        printf("Warning: illegal call type code:\n");
        call_cost = 0;
    }

    /* Print bill detail line */
    printf (
        "%5c    %10.2f  %8.2f\n",
        call_type_code, call_duration, call_cost
    );
}
```

```
/***** print_all_totals:
 On entry: Totals contain summed costs for all calls.
 Operation:Totals are printed.  The grand total is computed and printed.
 *****/

void print_all_totals(void) {
    /* Note the use of if statements to ensure that only those
       lines with nonzero totals are reported. */

    printf("================================\n");
    if (total_L != 0.0) {
        printf("Total cost of local calls:     $%6.2f\n", total_L);
    }
    if (total_A != 0.0) {
        printf("Total cost of long distance A: $%6.2f\n", total_A);
    }
    if (total_B != 0.0) {
        printf("Total cost of long distance B: $%6.2f\n", total_B);
    }
    if (total_I != 0.0) {
        printf("Total cost of international  : $%6.2f\n", total_I);
    }
    printf (
        "==================\nTotal amount due: $%4.2f\n\n",
        total_L + total_A + total_B + total_I
    );
}
```

Input for test run
```
Freda Blogginwithers
L 12
L 10
L 1
L 56
L 72
Q 94
L 14
I 2
L 12
L .5
L 21
B 5.7
B 1.5
Z
```

Program output

```
     Supa Phone Incorporated.
Phone bill for
Freda Blogginwithers

Call Code    Duration    Cost($)
=========    ========    =======
    L          12.00       0.40
    L          10.00       0.40
    L           1.00       0.40
    L          56.00       0.40
    L          72.00       0.40
Warning: illegal call type code:
    Q          94.00       0.00
    L          14.00       0.40
    I           2.00       2.10
    L          12.00       0.40
    L           0.50       0.40
    L          21.00       0.40
    B           5.70       3.42
    B           1.50       0.90
=================================
Total cost of local calls:     $  3.60
Total cost of long distance B: $  4.32
Total cost of international  : $  2.10
==================
Total amount due: $10.02
```

When I wrote the functions, I was able to do it without glancing even once at the `main` function which called them. This is because I already had in existence a clear statement in precondition/postcondition format of the required behaviour. All I had to do was look at that description and make sure I wrote suitable code. As that was the same description I used to check out the `main` function, I could be confident that `main` and the functions would interact properly. However, I **might** have made a mistake, because English descriptions, no matter how good, are still ambiguous. If I find the program has a bug, I should recheck these things before resorting to such methods as program tracing.

6.5 THE STRING COMPARISON FUNCTIONS

We often need to know if one string is alphabetically before, the same as, or after another. The function `strcmp` compares two string arguments, returning a negative value if the first is alphabetically before the second, 0 if the strings are identical, and a positive value if the first is after the second. This is often used for alphabetic comparison, but in reality `strcmp` uses the character codes of the characters in the strings in making its decision. This is usually good enough, but there are some problems. If strings have mixed upper and lower case characters, or contain some of the special European letters (e.g. á, ä, ç etc.), then some surprises are in store. A thorough job can only be done by writing your own function (and it is quite tricky to do it just right). Listing 6-5 shows a simple program that uses strcmp to input two words and output them in alphabetic order, looping until the first input word is END.

Listing 6-5

```
/* Program that places input words in alphabetical order.  */

#include <stdio.h>
#include <string.h>   /* necessary for using any str... function */

main() {
    char word1[31], word2[31];   /* max length 30 each */
    printf("Enter two words: ");
    scanf("%30s %30s", word1, word2);
    while (strcmp(word1, "END") != 0) {
        printf("    In order they are: ");
        if (strcmp(word1, word2) <= 0) {
            /* word1 belongs before, or is the same as, word2 */
            printf("%s %s\n", word1, word2);
        } else {
            /* word2 belongs before word1 */
            printf("%s %s (swapped)\n", word2, word1);
        }
        printf("Enter two words: ");        /* prompt and... */
        scanf("%30s %30s", word1, word2);   /* get next two words */
    }
    printf("Detected END word\n");
}
```

The output is

```
Enter two words: word processing
        In order they are: processing word (swapped)
Enter two words: never never
        In order they are: never never
Enter two words: wild west
        In order they are: west wild (swapped)
Enter two words: ENDWORD found?
        In order they are: ENDWORD found?
Enter two words: end found?
        In order they are: end found?
Enter two words: END found!
Detected END word
```

A variant of strcmp is strncmp, which, instead of comparing the entire two strings, only looks at a specified number of characters at the start. See Appendix C.13 or your C manual for more information about strncmp. Both functions require the <string.h> header file to be included.

6.6   STRUCTURED PROGRAMMING

As mentioned at the start of the chapter, just three control constructs (sequences, loops, and conditionals) allow any algorithm to be programmed. When we restrict ourselves to them, as we do in this text, we can keep our programs simple and easy to understand with a minimum of effort. This is what is meant by *structured programming*. It is quite easy in C to create poorly structured programs, most notably by using the `goto` statement, which is banished to the appendix for this reason.

There is one place where we trod dangerously — the `switch` statement: leaving out (or forgetting!) the `break` at the end of a `case` option allows control to 'fall through' from one option to the next. This is a violation of the structured programming principle, and should be avoided. The temptation to do this is almost always a sign that one's thinking is a bit scrambled. Most algorithms can not only be programmed in a structured way, they can actually be programmed better (that is, clearer and simpler) that way than any other. In particular, it is hard to write preconditions and postconditions for sections of code if the various pieces intertwine like a bowl of spaghetti (thus the common slang term, 'spaghetti code'). There are exceptions, but they are rare.

6.7   SUMMARY

- `if` statement syntax

```
if ( condition ) {
    statements executed when condition true
} else if ( next condition ) {          — Zero or more
    next group of statements            ⌐ repetitions.
...
} else {                                 — else-part
    statements for when all conditions fail   ⌐ is optional
}
```

- `switch` statement syntax

```
switch ( integral expression ) {
case integral constant :
    statements when expression          One or more
    equals the constant                 repetitions
    break;
...
default:
    statements when the expression      optional
    equals none of the constants
}
```

- C regards all non-zero values as being logically true, and zero as false.
- C logical operators for combining simpler conditions: `&&` (and), `||` (or), and `!` (not).
  - `&&` and `||` are *short-circuit* operators.

- Logical manipulations:

```
! (a < b)    ==    (a >= b)
! (a <= b)   ==    (a > b)
! (a > b)    ==    (a <= b)
! (a >= b)   ==    (a < b)
! ! a        ==    a    (if a is 0 or 1)
```

- De Morgan's laws:

```
! (A && B)   ==    (!A || !B)
! (A || B)   ==    (!A && !B)
```

- All algorithms can be programmed using only *sequences*, *loops*, and *conditionals*. This is called *structured programming*.
  - Structured programs are usually simpler to write, easier to understand, and contain fewer bugs.
- All C statements — conditionals, loops, etc. — can be combined in any sensible way desired by the programmer.
- Consistent use of program layout rules is important for program clarity.
- Strings are compared with the functions strcmp and strncmp. These are defined in the <string.h> header.

6.8   SELF-TEST EXERCISES

Short Answer

1   Write the following as a C if statement.
    If the variable *i* is 5, set *k* to 8, otherwise if *j* is 7 and *k* is less than 13, print "hello", otherwise do nothing.

2   Write the following as a C switch statement.
    If *k* is 2 or 4, print "hello"; if it is 7, set *j* to 67, otherwise set *m* to 72.

3   Can you do everything with an if that you can do with a switch? Explain.

4   Describe the operation of the && and || operators.

5   What is the value of !7?

6   What is the value of !0?

7   Write a simple assignment statement that sets *k* to 1 if and only if it is non-zero, leaving it zero otherwise. This can be done without any if or switch statements.

8   The variable alert must be set to true (1) if the pressure is greater than 120, unless yellow_alert is non-zero, in which case alert is set if pressure is greater than 100 or temperature is greater than 350. In all other cases alert should be false (0). Write a single assignment statement (no ifs or switches) to do this.

Programming

9 Write a program that calculates the salary owing to each of a company's employees. It should input the number of hours each employee worked, and compute and print their salaries on the basis of $25.00 per hour for not more than 40 hours, and $35.00 per hour for all hours over 40. (Thus an employee who worked 41 hours would be paid for 40 hours at $25.00, and one hour at $35.00.) The program should repeatedly process data until −1 is entered for the hours worked.

10 Write a program to help a scientist who wishes to make a number of measurements of light intensity during a light-generating chemical reaction. The measurements are to be entered into the computer as the reaction proceeds, and an average is to be printed at the end. (The last measurement entered will be followed by a zero value.) There is just one hitch: the scientist wants some safeguard against typing mistakes, so if an entered value differs by more than 0.1 from the previous one, the program must print a prominent message, and allow the user to (a) accept the entered values, (b) alter the last one, or (c) alter the second-last one.

6.9 TEST QUESTIONS

Short Answer

1 What will these statements print?
   a `printf("%d\n", 7 <= 4);`
   b `printf("%d\n", ! (7 <=4));`
   c `printf("%d\n", 1 + 2 + 3 == 6);`
   d `printf("%d\n", 1 && 2);`
   e `printf("%d\n", 0 || 0 && 8);`

2 Write the shortest possible C statement that will store 1 in n if k is greater than 3, and zero otherwise. (Hint: an `if` statement is not needed.)

3 In computing, `||` (or) is *inclusive*, that is, it is true if one or both operands are true. Sometimes in normal English, 'or' is used *exclusively*: that is, it is true if exactly one operand is true. (As in "You can have this or that" — but by implication, not both.) Design a C `if` test to see if k>7 **exclusive-or** j==5. (Hint: it is probably simpler than you think.)

4 Write a simple assignment statement that stores 1 in k if m equals 8, and zero otherwise. Do not use an `if` or `switch` statement.

5 Write an assignment statement that leaves k as it is if it is non-zero, and that sets it to 1 otherwise.

Programming

6   Write a program that asks the user for two numbers, and then, no matter what order the numbers were typed in, prints them out with the larger number first.

7   An editor wants to check manuscripts for excessive punctuation. Write a program that will read data until it sees a # character at the start of a line, and then print the number of characters read, and the number which were punctuation (for this problem, any of the characters . , ; : ! ?). If the punctuation exceeds 5% of the total, print a warning for the editor.

8   Often tables are printed with duplicate entries blanked out for simplicity. Write a program that will generate and print a multiplication table as shown below. (There is more than one way to do this — some ways with if statements, some without.)

```
    1  2  3  4  5  6  7  8  9
1   1  2  3  4  5  6  7  8  9
2      4  6  8 10 12 14 16 18
3         9 12 15 18 21 24 27
4           16 20 24 28 32 36
5              25 30 35 40 45
6                 36 42 48 54
7                    49 56 63
8                       64 72
9                          81
```

9   A professor wants a program to compute the final grades for a class. Each student is represented by a line containing a one word surname followed by five floating point numbers representing the results in four assignments and an exam. The first two assignments are worth 5% of the total, the next two are worth 10%, and the exam is worth the rest. Write a program that first asks how many students are in the class, and then reads that many lines of input and prints the students' names and final percentages and grades. The grades to be awarded are: F (below 50%), C (50% up to but excluding 65%), B (65% up to but excluding 80%), and A (80% and above).

10 A formula for finding the date of Easter was given in the test questions for Chapter 3. Write a program to ask the user for a starting and finishing year, and then print the date of Easter for each year between the start and finish, inclusive. The date should be printed as the name of the month (March or April), day number, comma, and year.

11 Write a program to print a graph of a sine wave on its side (x axis vertical), including the axes, as follows:

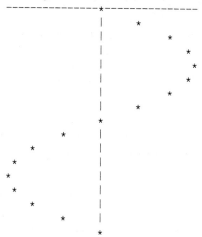

12 Write a program that inputs a positive integer not greater than 100, and prints it in Roman numerals.

13 Given two numbers, the greatest common denominator (GCD) can be found by subtracting the smaller from the larger repeatedly until the two numbers are equal, at which point that value is the GCD. Write a program to input two numbers and print the GCD, computed as described. Don't forget that after a subtraction, the number that was previously greater might now be smaller.

14 A bank offers 10% per annum compound interest on accounts, unless the balance is below $500, in which case the interest rate is only 5%. Interest is calculated on balances at the end of each day. Write a program that reads transaction details for an account and prints the balance (a) after each transaction and (b) at the end of a 100-day period. Input lines consist of a day number within the 100-day period and a positive or negative amount (for a deposit or a withdrawal). The program adds the amount to the balance on the day specified, and prints the latest balance and the interest since the previous transaction. A message should be printed if a withdrawal would result in a negative balance, and the transaction should be discarded. Transactions must be in ascending order, and the program should insist that the first one is on day 1. End of data is indicated by a day number greater than 100.

15 The area of a triangle with sides of lengths a, b, and c can be computed using this formula:

$$\text{area} = \sqrt{s(s-a)\,(s-b)\,(s-c)}\,, \qquad \text{where } s = \frac{a+b+c}{2}$$

If the portion under the square root is negative, it means the three lengths cannot form a triangle. Write a program to accept measurements of the sides of a triangle and either print an error message or print the area of the triangle.

16 Write a program to input a positive integer, and report whether it is a perfect square, that is, its square root is integral. One can use the sqrt function in the library, but must beware floating point inaccuracies; for example, sqrt(4.0) might return 1.99999, not 2.0. To get around this, take the nearest integer to the square root returned by sqrt, square it, and see if it equals the original number.

17 Having solved the previous problem, write a program to find all integer solutions i, j, k, to the equation $i^2 + j^2 = k^2$, subject to the restriction that i and j are less than 15.

18 A prime number is an integer greater than 1 which has no factors except itself and 1. Write a program to print all prime numbers less than 1000. Include a function that tests a single value for being prime.

19 Write a program to input a paragraph of ordinary text, and output it reformatted so that it fits within 40 columns; that is, as many words as possible should be placed on each line, going to a new line when a word is too large to fit. A # sign marks the end of the input. You may assume no word is longer than 32 characters, but your program should not crash (although it is allowed to give wrong output) if a longer word is entered.

20 Newton's method is a way to find the location of the zero of a mathematical function, $f(x)$. If one imagines a graph of the function concerned, the method works by guessing the x location of the zero, computing the function's value at that point, and, if it is not zero, drawing a tangent to the curve and 'sliding down' it to the x axis; this gives a better estimate of the zero. This process is repeated until it ceases to make significant changes to the estimate of x. This is illustrated below; x_0 is the original guess, x_1 the first refinement, x_2 the second, and so on.

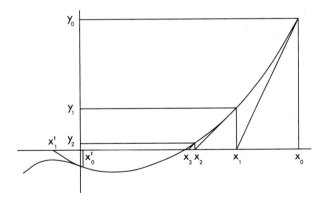

Each estimate is computed from the previous one as follows:

$$x_{n+1} = x_n - \frac{f(x_n)}{f'(x_n)}$$

where $f'(x)$ is the derivative of the function. Write a program that will accept the coefficients of any fifth-order polynomial, the coefficients of its derivative, and an initial guess x_0, and then find the zero of the polynomial using this method; the iterations should be repeated until one iteration differs from the previous one by less than 10^{-7}. The most serious problem with the method is the possibility that sliding down the tangent moves further away from the solution (as in the figure above if x'_0 is the initial guess). This can cause the method to fail to converge. Include a test that successive x values are getting closer together, and print a suitable message and stop if this test fails.

21 Write a simple program to edit a list of words. The program should ask for a search word and a replacement word. Then it should read and echo input words, with all occurrences of the search word changed to the replacement word. Stop when an input line commences with the 'word' #.

7

Writing functions with arguments and results

Objectives

Examine how arguments make functions much more flexible and convenient to use.

Learn how to write C functions that have arguments:
— simple arguments — `int`, `char`, etc.
— array arguments — `char` arrays.

Understand how the computer implements passing arguments to functions.
— why simple arguments and array arguments behave differently.

Learn to write functions that return results.
— returning a result from `main`, and program termination status.

Throwing away function results.

Be aware of the 'old' C method of declaring functions.
— why the old method should be avoided where possible.

Writing quality programs: creating personal function libraries.

7.1 INTRODUCTION

While calling library functions in previous chapters, we have used two very important C features. First, we have used arguments to pass information to a function. For example, in the statement

```
printf("%d\n", i);
```

the arguments are "`%d\n`" and i. Arguments are also called *parameters* — the two terms mean the same thing. Second, we have used function results. For example, in

```
y = sin(theta);
```

the value computed by the `sin` function and assigned to `y` is the result, or *return value*, of the function `sin`.

Our task now is to learn to write our own functions with both these features. A key use of arguments and results is to avoid global variables. Whenever we use a global variable to pass information to or from a function, we must remember which global to use, make sure we know which functions access which globals, and avoid name clashes (i.e. inadvertent re-use of a variable for an incompatible purpose). All these are easy in small programs, but onerous in big ones where it really matters.

Finally, although both arguments and results help us in the goal of avoiding complexity in our programs, we must **never confuse the two**; they are entirely separate features of C, and we are free to use neither, either, or both, as we please.

7.2 WRITING FUNCTIONS WITH SIMPLE ARGUMENTS

The benefits of function arguments can be seen in the following situation. Dates often need to be displayed in commercial programs, but if a company plans to sell a program internationally, it must accommodate varying ways of writing dates around the world. Three common methods are

(0)   month/day/year   (e.g. 4/26/93 — USA)
(1)   day/month/year   (e.g. 26/4/93 — Britain, Australia)
(2)   year/month/day   (e.g. 93/4/26)

A function can help, as the logic, though straightforward, should not concern us every time a date is to be printed. Here is a function, **without** parameters, for printing dates. The format is determined by the global integer `date_format`, which should be 0, 1, or 2. The date is transmitted to the function by setting the globals `day`, `month`, and `year`.

```
void display_date(void) {
    /* Select correct display method */
    switch (date_format) {
    case 0: /* US format */
        printf("%d/%d/%d", month, day, year);
        break;
    case 1: /* European format */
        printf("%d/%d/%d", day, month, year);
        break;
    case 2: /* Year-first format */
        printf("%d/%d/%d", year, month, day);
    }
}
```

A program using this function must find out what the date format should be, and set date_format once only when the program starts up. Then every time a date is wanted the three variables day, month, and year will be set, and the function called. Listing 7-1 shows a program that alternates printouts of today's date with dates input from the user. This is intended to simulate the fact that in serious programs a function can be used for various purposes in the one application; a doctor's billing program, for instance, might have to print today's date and the dates of consultations.

Listing 7-1

```
/* Test the parameterless display-date function on input dates */
#include <stdio.h>

#define MDY_FORMAT 0       /* Explanatory names    (US)     */
#define DMY_FORMAT 1       /* for the              (British) */
#define YMD_FORMAT 2       /* date format codes    (other)   */

int date_format, day, month, year;
void display_date (void);

main() {
    int today_day, today_month, today_year;
    int then_day, then_month, then_year;

    /* First set the country code */
    printf("Enter the date code (0=US, 1=Europe, 2=year-first): ");
    scanf("%d", &date_format);

    printf("Date today (day month year)? ");
    scanf("%d %d %d", &today_day, &today_month, &today_year);

    printf("Date to be printed (day month year)? ");
    scanf("%d %d %d", &then_day, &then_month, &then_year);

    while (then_day != 0) {
        printf("Today is ");
        day = today_day;
```

```
        month = today_month;
        year = today_year;
        display_date();

        printf("     The other date is ");
        day = then_day;
        month = then_month;
        year = then_year;
        display_date();

        printf("\nDate to be printed (day month year)? ");
        scanf("%d %d %d", &then_day, &then_month, &then_year);
    }
}

void display_date(void) {
    /* Select correct display method */
    switch (date_format) {
    case MDY_FORMAT:                           /* US format */
        printf("%d/%d/%d", month, day, year);
        break;
    case DMY_FORMAT:                           /* European format */
        printf("%d/%d/%d", day, month, year);
        break;
    case YMD_FORMAT:                           /* Year-first format */
        printf("%d/%d/%d", year, month, day);
    }
}
```

Sample run
```
Enter the date code (0=US, 1=Europe, 2=year-first): 0
Date today (day month year)? 27 5 92
Date to be printed (day month year)? 25 12 89
Today is 5/27/92     The other date is 12/25/89
Date to be printed (day month year)? 4 7 93
Today is 5/27/92     The other date is 7/4/93
Date to be printed (day month year)? 26 1 91
Today is 5/27/92     The other date is 1/26/91
Date to be printed (day month year)? 0 0 0
```

Listing 7-1 is easy to criticize. Setting up the date variables and calling the function is clumsy and long-winded, and we have to remember to declare the global variables and hope that no other function uses them for a conflicting purpose. Things would be much tidier if we could pass the date values as arguments. To do this, instead of writing (void) after the function name in the function definition, we write a list of variable declarations. Then the function can be called with arguments just like the library functions. Listing 7-2 does this.

Listing 7-2

```
/* display-date function with arguments, tested on input dates */
#include <stdio.h>

#define MDY_FORMAT 0          /* Explanatory names    (US)      */
#define DMY_FORMAT 1          /* for the              (British) */
#define YMD_FORMAT 2          /* date format codes    (other)   */

int date_format;     /* Note: only one global now */
void display_date(int day, int month, int year);
                     /* Note: formal parameters listed in parentheses */

main() {
    int today_day, today_month, today_year;
    int then_day, then_month, then_year;

    /* First set the country code */
    printf("Enter the date code (0=US, 1=Europe, 2=year-first): ");
    scanf("%d", &date_format);

    printf("Date today (day month year)? ");
    scanf("%d %d %d", &today_day, &today_month, &today_year);

    printf("Date to be printed (day month year)? ");
    scanf("%d %d %d", &then_day, &then_month, &then_year);

    while (then_day != 0) {
        printf("Today is ");
        display_date(today_day, today_month, today_year);

        printf("    The other date is ");
        display_date(then_day, then_month, then_year);

        printf("\nDate to be printed (day month year)? ");
        scanf("%d %d %d", &then_day, &then_month, &then_year);
    }
}

void display_date(int day, int month, int year) {
    /* Select correct display method */
    switch (date_format) {
    case MDY_FORMAT:                          /* US format */
        printf("%d/%d/%d", month, day, year);
        break;
    case DMY_FORMAT:                          /* European format */
        printf("%d/%d/%d", day, month, year);
        break;
    case YMD_FORMAT:                          /* Year-first format */
        printf("%d/%d/%d", year, month, day);
    }
}
```

The output from Listing 7-2 is the same as for Listing 7-1, but the program is shorter and it is obvious in `main` how much easier it is to make the revised function print a date. The argument variables in the function definition (in this case `day`, `month` and `year`) are called *dummy arguments*, or *formal parameters*, and they look similar to ordinary local variable declarations. In fact, arguments do behave just like ordinary local variables, with one important difference: when we first enter the function, normal locals start out containing rubbish (which is why we must initialize them inside the function); arguments, however, are automatically given an initial value when we enter the function. This initial value comes from the place in the program where we call the function. Whatever values we write inside parentheses at the function call are copied into the corresponding argument variables when the function starts executing. The first value supplied in the call is copied into the first argument variable, the second into the second, and so on. Whenever the function is called, the values supplied must match, in number and type, the arguments in the function definition; Figure 7.1 shows a typical function call.

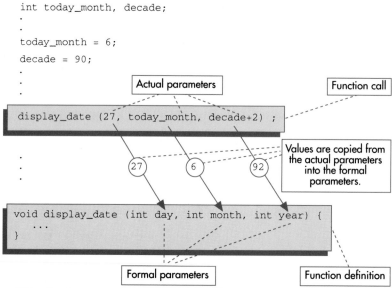

Figure 7.1   Passing arguments in a function call

The first argument in the call in Figure 7.1 is a constant, the second a variable, and the third a general expression — any type of argument is acceptable, as long as it can be converted (as in an assignment) to the correct type (in this example, `int`). These values supplied in the call are called the actual parameters or, if there is not likely to be any confusion, simply the arguments. The actual parameters are evaluated and copied into the formal parameters, which thereafter act like any other local variables.

One weakness in C is the possibility of undetected errors in the types of arguments in function calls. To avoid this, **the call must be preceded by a declaration or definition for the function being called**. This declaration or definition should be in the modern ANSI style as taught throughout this text, not the old style discussed in Section 7.7. (For library functions, this is achieved by including the appropriate .h header file.) If this advice is heeded, a C compiler will detect and report all parameter incompatibility errors. C++ compilers make this advice compulsory, thus providing full protection against errors. This is a good reason for using a C++ compiler, even for compiling ordinary C programs.

In `display_date`, `date_format` was left as a global; this shows that a single function can access both arguments and global variables. `date_format` could have been a parameter also, although we would then need to think about it every time we called the function, instead of just once at the beginning. This is because the date format is part of the overall environment in which the program works, whereas the day, month, and year are specific to each call to the function. It takes experience to choose well between globals and arguments. Most beginners use globals much too often — probably to avoid the trouble of figuring out how to write an argument. To avoid this it is a good idea to completely avoid global variables until you are thoroughly proficient at using function arguments.

Summary

Rule 1 In the call you must supply the same number of actual parameters as the function has formal parameters. (Obviously, if they are being copied one-for-one, this is the only way each formal parameter will get a value, with no actual parameters left over.)

Rule 2 Each actual parameter must be a value that can legitimately be assigned to the corresponding formal parameter. It doesn't matter whether the actual parameter is a constant, variable, or expression, so long as it is of a suitable type.

Rule 3 The formal parameters can only be used inside the function they belong to. (After all, they act like local variables, and local variables can only be used in the function in which they are defined.)

Fact If, inside a function, you change the value of a formal parameter (perhaps by assigning a different value or reading a value into it), the actual parameter is not altered — arguments pass information into a function, not out of it. This should be obvious from the above description of how arguments work.

Good advice Avoid global variables.

> ### Note about other computer languages
> The above fact is not true in all computer languages. Some use different argument-passing methods, so readers familiar with another language should be careful not to get confused here. Pascal programmers should note that C's simple arguments (as described above) work the same as Pascal's when the Pascal reserved word VAR is **not** used in the Pascal formal parameter.

7.3 WRITING FUNCTIONS WITH ARRAY ARGUMENTS

In Section 3.2.1 we saw how `printf` accesses its format string argument. Since strings are `char` arrays, C functions must in general be able to handle array arguments. Listing 3-4 showed a program to print name tags for conference delegates. In that program the function `print_tag` printed the name in the global `char` array called name. Just as with simple variables, a global used only to carry a value into a function is ideal for replacement by a parameter. Listing 7-3 shows how to rewrite Listing 3-4 to do just that.

Listing 7-3

```
/* A program to print name tags with seat numbers. */

#include <stdio.h>
#include <string.h>

void print_tag(char name[]); /* << Note how to write an array argument */
void print_stars(void);
void print_side_border(void);

int seat_num;    /* Holds the seat number to be put on the tag. */

/* main: Prints the name tags, with a blank line between each. */

main() {
    seat_num = 100;                /* First seat is no. 100 */
    print_tag("John Smith");       /* Print first tag */
    printf("\n");                  /* blank line between tags */
    print_tag("Mary Peterson");    /* second tag */
    printf("\n");                  /* blank line */
    print_tag("Alison Gray");      /* third tag */
}

/* print_tag: Prints a name tag with seat number.
   On entry: Its parameter is a string with the name to be printed.
             The seat number must be in the global integer 'seat_num'.
   After printing tag, increments the seat number ready for the next tag.
*/

void print_tag(char name[]) {
    /* Top section:  */
    print_stars();
    print_stars();
    print_side_border();

    /* Line containing the name and number:  */
    printf("**        %20s    (seat %3d)  **\n", name, seat_num);

    /* Bottom section:  */
    print_side_border();
```

```
    print_stars();
    print_stars();
    seat_num = seat_num + 1;
}

void print_stars(void) {
    printf("**********************************************\n");
}

void print_side_border(void) {
    printf("**                                        **\n");
}
```

Whereas previously we had ponderous statements such as:

```
    strcpy(name, "John Smith");     /* Set up first name */
    print_tag();                    /* Print first tag */
```

we now have the much snappier:

```
    print_tag("John Smith");        /* Print first tag */
```

Let us see how `print_tag` handles the array parameter:

```
    void print_tag(char name[]) {
```

Indicates array parameter

This looks like a formal parameter for a simple variable, except for the square brackets after the variable name. This is clearly intended to resemble an array variable declaration, so it raises an obvious question: why isn't there a number inside the brackets? The answer comes from understanding what happens when arrays are passed as parameters. In Chapter 3 we saw that C uses the address of the start of an array to tell where the array is located in memory. Therefore when an array is passed as a parameter, all that needs to be copied into the function is the **address** of the array. Since an address is a single number, the compiler doesn't care how big the array is that the address refers to. Provided we put in the brackets, it knows all it needs to know: that the parameter is the address of an array, not a simple variable.

This raises yet another question. What happens if, inside the function, we try to alter the contents of the array (for example, by using `strcpy` to copy a different name into it)? The function will use the address to locate the original array and place the new data there. Thus a function is able to pass information back to the caller by modifying an array parameter. Recall from the previous section that it cannot do this with simple variables. Listing 7-4 illustrates this.

Listing 7-4

```
/* Demonstration of parameter modification. */

#include <stdio.h>
#include <string.h>

void modparms(int i, char buf[]);
/* modparms will attempt to alter the value of both its arguments. */

main() {
    int k;
    char strng [100];

    k = 27;
    strcpy(strng, "First name");
    printf("Before modparms, k==%d, strng==%s.\n", k, strng);

    modparms(k, strng);

    printf("After modparms, k==%d, strng==%s.\n", k, strng);
}

void modparms(int i, char buf[]) {
    printf("    Start of modparms, i==%d, buf==%s.\n", i, buf);

    i = 999;
    strcpy(buf, "different");

    printf("    End of modparms, i==%d, buf==%s.\n", i, buf);
}
```

The output from Listing 7-4 is:

```
Before modparms, k==27, strng==First name.
    Start of modparms, i==27, buf==First name.
    End of modparms, i==999, buf==different.
After modparms, k==27, strng==different.
```

The variables k and strng are both given values prior to entering modparms, and these are printed before and after the call; modparms tries to alter them both by changing the values in both its formal parameters. However, at the end we find that modparms has succeeded in altering strng, but not k. As i and k are two different int variables, changing i cannot affect k. But buf, being an array parameter, is actually the address of the array strng. This is shown in Figure 7.2.

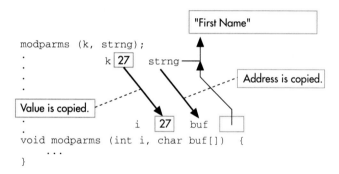

Figure 7.2   The difference between simple and array parameters

The heavy arrows represent the copying that occurs when the function call is made. **Every parameter results in something being copied**: if a parameter is a simple variable, its value is copied, but if the parameter is an array, its address is copied.

The address `strng` is shown in Figure 7.2 as a thin arrow pointing to the memory where the array is stored, and it is clear that, after copying that address into `buf`, both arrows (being the same address) point to the same place. So when we modify the array `buf` refers to, we really modify the array `strng`.

Returning to the question of the missing number in the array parameter declaration: since the function doesn't know how big the array really is, it may allow us to access storage beyond the array's end. This is a source of errors, and they can be difficult to find. The cure is never to make the mistake in the first place. Make sure that you never try to put more in an array than its declaration permits it to hold.

> ### Note for Pascal programmers
> *Readers familiar with Pascal will object that Pascal very definitely does want to be told the size of an array parameter. The reason is that Pascal protects the programmer against accidentally using more space than is allocated in the array, whereas C compilers usually do not. This is considered by many to be a serious failing in C. In fact it is a trade-off. C is a very powerful language, but like electricity, it must be handled carefully. C's array arguments work the same as Pascal's when the Pascal reserved word VAR is used in the Pascal formal parameter. This is the opposite of the case with simple variables.*

7.4   EXAMPLE

None of the name-tag programs so far has been truly realistic. A more useful version would allow us to input as many names as we pleased, printing a name tag for each one. Listing 7-5 shows a revised `main` function to replace that in Listing 7-3.

Listing 7-5

```
main() {
    int no_of_tags;              /* How many tags to print */
    int i;
    char name[21];               /* Holds the name for the tag */
    seat_num = 100;              /* First seat is no. 100 */

    printf("How many tags are needed? ");
    scanf("%d%*c", &no_of_tags);

    for (i=0; i<no_of_tags; i++) {
        printf("Enter name for tag (max. 20 chars): ");
        gets(name);
        printf("\n");            /* blank line between tags */
        print_tag(name);         /* Print first tag */
        printf("\n");            /* blank line between tags */
    }
}
```

Sample run

```
How many tags are needed? 2
Enter name for tag (max. 20 chars): Bill Buthwittle

************************************************
************************************************
**                                          **
**          Bill Buthwittle   (seat 100)    **
**                                          **
************************************************
************************************************

Enter name for tag (max. 20 chars): Mary Peterson

************************************************
************************************************
**                                          **
**          Mary Peterson    (seat 101)     **
**                                          **
************************************************
************************************************
```

No trouble will arise from the local variable in `main` called `name`, even though `name` is also the name of the formal parameter to `print_tag`. This is because parameters act like local variables: their names are not available outside the function they are declared in, and we are free to re-use the identifier in another function if we wish. It is vital to understand that these two uses of the one identifier are absolutely unrelated: in `main`, `name` is a local array; in `print_tag`, `name` is a formal parameter. Although this might seem confusing, it is in fact a powerful aid to clarity: when reading one function, we never need worry about local declarations in other functions, as there can be no interference whatever from them.

Listing 7-5 uses one new C feature: an asterisk in a `scanf` format. After asking how many tags are needed, the program reads the answer with this `scanf` call:

```
scanf("%d%*c", &no_of_tags);
```

The `%d` reads an integer and assigns it to `no_of_tags`, as usual. But in order to type the number that answers that question, we must also type a newline character to end the line, otherwise the computer will just sit there waiting. However, that newline is not processed by the `%d` format, which stops reading after the final digit in the number. Unless that newline is input somehow, it will still be waiting to be read when the program encounters the next input function, which happens to be `gets`. `gets` processes input until it reads a newline — and that is exactly what it would immediately encounter. The outcome is that the name for the first tag will be an empty string, and so a blank name tag will be printed. (To see this, change the `scanf` format to `%d`, and compile and run the program.)

This problem is cured by the `%*c` in the `scanf` call: `%c` means "read one character and assign it to a variable"; `%*c` means "read one character, and **throw it away**". In the above `scanf` call, it inputs and discards the newline after the number. The asterisk can be placed in any `scanf` format specifier; so, for example, to read a `float` and throw it away, we would write `%*f`.

7.5 WRITING FUNCTIONS THAT RETURN RESULTS

In Chapter 2 we saw how functions allow us to package a list of instructions, and how a function call makes the computer execute the instructions in the package. That allowed us to write the equivalent in C of the familiar notions of recipes, instruction books, and so on. But some functions we have used from the C library do not fit this pattern: `sin` and `sqrt`, for example, correspond to the familiar notion of answering a question. The expression `sqrt(x)`, for example, effectively answers the question "What is the square root of x?" To answer a question, it is necessary to know how to find the answer, so these functions still consist of a list of instructions as before, but in addition, they must specify what the answer, or result, will be.

In C, functions that return results can still do all the things other functions do. For example, they can have *side-effects*. A side-effect is a change external to the function that is not apparent from the function call. Such changes might include modifying global variables, or outputting or inputting data.

Now we shall write a function that returns a result. To keep things simple, let us write a function called `five` that merely returns the number 5 every time it is called. (But note that in serious work there is little call for functions that return a fixed value.) The first thing to decide is what sort of value is being returned. Since 5 is an integer, the function should return an `int`. The function heading will be:

```
int five(void) {
```

Here the word `int` is used where previously we wrote `void`. The meaning of that first `void` was "This function returns no result." (This is why such functions are often called *void functions*.) By replacing `void` with `int`, the above function heading says "This function returns an `int` result."

Having specified the type of result, we must now provide it. We do that with the `return` statement. After the word `return`, we write the value to be used as the result. Our complete function is:

```
int five(void) {
    return 5;
}
```

Listing 7-6 uses this function in an assortment of ways, to show how versatile function calling can be.

Listing 7-6

```
/* Test of the five() function */
#include <stdio.h>
#include <math.h>    /* because we call sqrt() later */

int five(void) {
    return 5;
}

main() {
    int i;

    /* Assign a function result to a variable */
    i = five();

    /* check */
    printf("i should be five: %d\n", i);

    /* Include a function result in an expression */
    printf("25 is %d\n", 4 * five() + 10 - five() );

    /* compare a function result */
    if (five() == 5) {
        printf("five() is returning 5 correctly.\n");
    }

    /* function in a function call in a function call... */
    printf("Square root of 5 is %f\n", sqrt(five()));

    /* Throw away a function result */
    five();
    printf("Where did it go??\n");
}
```

The output is

```
i should be five: 5
25 is 25
five() is returning 5 correctly.
Square root of 5 is 2.236068
Where did it go??
```

Most of this program should be self-explanatory, except perhaps the final section. In C, we are allowed to throw away a function result. We do this as shown, by writing a call to the function as if it were of type `void`. We have often done this with `scanf`.

There are at least three situations where a function call is not allowed. The first is as the target of the assignment operator, as in

```
five() = 27;     /* WRONG!! */
```

This is because a function result is a value, not a variable, so it does not represent a memory location where a value can be stored.

The second situation is where the function returns the wrong type of value. For example, the first argument to `printf` should be a string (the format), so since `five` returns an `int`, we should not put `five` as the very first `printf` argument.

Finally, there are some situations where only constants are allowed. Since a function result is computed at run time, it is not considered constant (not even our trivial `five` function). For example, we are not allowed to use a function to specify the size of an array, as C only allows arrays to have constant sizes.

7.5.1   A larger example of a function returning a result

Suppose you are writing a program where you have to ask the user to input a `float` in response to a question. You might just use `scanf` directly. But it might be that you want to check the user's input to ensure that it falls within a certain range, asking the user to try again if the input is out of range. If this job is done more than once, it may be worth programming it as a function.

The function could be called `checked_float`. The result type is obviously `float`. Thus `checked_float` will commence

```
float checked_float (
```

Now it is necessary to decide what arguments are needed. They must include sufficient information to allow the function to work flexibly, irrespective of any details of the program it is used in. `checked_float` will ask the user a question, the text of which could be passed as an argument in a `char` array. The input must fall within certain limits; these also can be parameters, and they will be the same type as the number being read; that is, `float`. Our completed function heading can therefore be

```
float checked_float (
    char question[],      /* the question to ask the user */
    float minval,         /* minimum legal response */
    float maxval          /* maximum legal response */
) {
```

This function has both arguments and a result. It is important not to confuse the two ideas. The **arguments** are the items in the parentheses **after** the function name. The **result** has the type written **before** the function name. There is no necessary correlation between the types of the arguments and the type of the result. You may choose both freely, in any way that makes sense in solving the problem at hand.

The logic of the function is straightforward: ask the question, input a value, and loop until the value is within range. We should also print an error message if the value is invalid, otherwise the user will not realize the computer is waiting for another number. Listing 7-7 shows the completed function, along with a simple `main` function for testing.

Listing 7-7

```c
#include <stdio.h>
#include <stdlib.h>     /* for abort() */

/* checked_float - Prints a prompt, and inputs a value.  Unless the
value is within a specified range, continues to object and ask for
the value to be re-input.  Returns the final legal value as the
function result. */

float checked_float (
    char question[],      /* the question to ask the user */
    float minval,         /* minimum legal response */
    float maxval          /* maximum legal response */
) {
    float in_value;

    /* First a quick check that the arguments make sense - stop
       the program if not. */
    if (maxval < minval) {
        printf("ERROR: Bad arguments to checked_float.\n");
        abort();
    }

    /* Display question, with valid range.  Read answer. */
    printf("%s (range %g to %g): ", question, minval, maxval);
    scanf("%f", &in_value);

    /* Repeatedly object until the answer is legitimate. */
    while (in_value<minval || in_value>maxval) {
        /* error message */
        printf (
            "Your answer must be between %g and %g. Try again: ",
            minval, maxval
        );
        /* input another value */
        scanf("%f", &in_value);
    }
```

```
/* Here we have a legal input value; return it */
return in_value;
}

/************** Simple test main function *************/

main() {
    float f;
    f = checked_float("Wazza numba?", 2.5, 10.7);
    printf("\nThe input number is %g\n", f);
}
```

In the test `main` function, the result of a call to `checked_float` is assigned to a `float` variable, f. The following sample run shows how the function adapts its printout to the arguments supplied in the call, and finally returns as the result the last number the user entered.

```
Wazza numba? (range 2.5 to 10.7): 0
Your answer must be between 2.5 and 10.7. Try again: 10.9
Your answer must be between 2.5 and 10.7. Try again: -34.7
Your answer must be between 2.5 and 10.7. Try again: 10.7

The input number is 10.7
```

For extra 'stamina' the function checks if the maximum is less than the minimum, and calls the library function `abort` if so, as such parameters mean that there is no legitimate answer the user can give. This is so clearly nonsensical that it is wise to take drastic action if that ever happens. `abort` stops the program immediately and prints an error message. We have not used `abort` previously, but it is in the standard library. Due to the size of the library, few programmers can memorize everything in it, so browsing through to find useful functions like `abort` is a key skill in C programming.

7.6 USING `return`

The simplest way to use the `return` statement is to put it at the end of a function, as in the previous example. However, we are allowed to place it anywhere we wish in the function; we can even have more than one. `return` does two jobs at once: it specifies the value to be returned and it ends the execution of the function. That is, if the program encounters a `return`, it immediately stops work on the present function and returns to the one that called it.

It is common to write functions that check for errors before carrying out their task. A skeleton for such a function might be as follows.

```
if (...something is wrong...) {
    return ...a value meaning 'error'... ;
}
...do the main task...
return ...a value meaning 'everything is OK'... ;
```

Even `void` functions can use `return`. Since they have no result, the only effect will be to terminate the function and return to the calling function. In a `void` function, therefore, the `return` statement is written simply as

```
return;
```

7.6.1   Using `return` *inside* `main`*: program exit status*

If `return` is used in the `main` function, the entire program terminates. As `main` is an `int` function, we may supply an integer return value in that `return` statement. That value is called the program's *exit status* or *termination status*. In many operating systems and other programming environments, the exit status is used to tell whether the program succeeded or failed at doing its task. To indicate success, the value 0 should be returned; this will be the normal case, and from now on, all programs in this text will end with `return 0;` as the final statement in `main`.

The `return` statement cannot be used to terminate the program from a function other than `main`. In that case, the library function `exit` must be used; it takes an `int` parameter which also indicates the exit status.

In either case (`return` from `main`, or `exit` from any function), failure of the program may be signaled by using the macro `EXIT_FAILURE` as the exit status. For example

```
exit(EXIT_FAILURE);
```

will terminate the program and signal failure. Use of `exit` or `EXIT_FAILURE` requires inclusion of the header `<stdlib.h>`.

7.7   OLD-STYLE FUNCTION DEFINITIONS AND DECLARATIONS

Before the ANSI/ISO C standard was devised, a different way was used to specify arguments in function headings. The easiest way to appreciate the old style is to see the two together.

New style
```
void putout(int number, char whichchar) {
```

Old style
```
void putout(number, whichchar)
    int number; char whichchar;
{
```

In the old style, only the list of argument names is placed in the parentheses; the declarations showing their types are given between the) and the {. Even when there are no arguments, there is still an old style and a new style:

New style
```
void do_something(void) {
```

Old style

```
void do_something() {
```

Modern C compilers can handle both methods, but many older compilers can only accept the old style. This change was not made just because someone thought it looked better the new way. The problem was that it was harder for compilers to properly check the logic of function calls under the old style. Programmers therefore had to be meticulously careful to make no errors in calling functions, as the compiler was unable to report problems, and programs would malfunction at runtime. Since we want the compiler to do the best job it can on checking our logic, we should always use new-style function headings. We should only use the old style if we have an old compiler that doesn't recognize the improved method. Of course, in reading old C programs we will often encounter it as well. Changing the style in such old programs can often show up errors which have gone unnoticed for years.

> ### *Note to readers using a C++ compiler*
> *C++ prohibits the old-style function heading. In this respect it is a very much safer language than C, as you cannot forget to properly specify a function. There are some subtle differences between C new-style and C++ function headings, but they are unlikely to cause problems in straightforward programming.*

7.8 FUNCTION LIBRARIES

There is nothing magic about the standard C library. Thoughtful C programmers can set up libraries of their own functions for re-use in program after program. Any time you find yourself writing a function similar to one you have written previously, perhaps you have a candidate for your personal function library.

Arguments and results are important aids in writing re-usable functions. Functions that make us place values in global variables are much harder to reuse. When planning a function to put in a library, try to think beyond the particular problem that prodded you into writing the function. Suppose we wanted to make our name tag function part of a re-usable library. We might ask whether we will always want name tags the same size, for example. If not, then some parameters will be needed specifying how big the tag should be. It takes practice to become really good at deciding how general to make the function and what the function parameters and result will be. Even with experts designing them, many functions in the standard library have been criticized for design faults, so don't feel too concerned if you find you have to go back and re-design a function.

To set up a re-usable library, you need to write a .h file along the lines of files such as <stdio.h>. Your file should contain function declarations (but not the function bodies) for the functions in your library. For example, if we placed the function `print_tag` from Listing 7-3 in a library, our `.h` file would contain the following line:

```
void print_tag(char name[]) ;
```

The `.c` files containing the actual functions must be compiled separately; this step is done differently depending on the particular C compiler being used, so it cannot be described here. Having set up a `.h` file, it should be included in any program that needs a function in the library. If we wrote a library called `mylib`, for example, we should put the following at the head of our program:

```
#include "mylib.h"
```

Note the use of quotes instead of angle brackets. Angle brackets are used to `#include` standard system files, while quotes are used for our own personal libraries.

7.9 A BRIEF STOCK-TAKE

So far we have seen how to write functions that can be fed any amount of information via parameters. They can return information to the calling function in two ways: `char` arrays can be modified within the function, and a result can be provided of any simple type (`int`, `float`, etc.). So apart from `char` arrays, we can only make a function return a **single** piece of information to the calling function, as there can only be one function result. For the time being, if we want a function to return two or more `int`s, `float`s etc. we will still be forced to use global variables. Later we shall use pointers to eliminate this remaining restriction.

7.10 SUMMARY

- Arguments are declared inside parentheses in the function heading; each declaration looks similar to a normal variable declaration.
- The argument variable declared in the function heading is called a *formal parameter*, or *dummy argument*.
- The values passed to the formal parameters when we call a function are called *actual parameters*.
- When we call a function, every argument requires that something be copied from the actual parameters to the formal parameters.
  - If the formal parameter is a simple variable, a value of that type is copied into the formal parameter from the actual parameter.
  - If the formal parameter is an array, the address of the actual parameter (which must also be an array) is copied.
- If we change a simple variable argument within the function, the actual parameter is **not** altered.

- If we change an array argument within the function, the actual parameter **is** altered.
- Formal and actual parameters must be compatible, in the sense that the actual parameter must be something that can be legitimately copied into the formal parameter.
- C has both a new style and an old style for declaring functions. Unless we are forced to use the old style (by having to use an old compiler, for example), we should always use the new-style arguments.
- A function *result* is a special value calculated by a function and returned to the calling function by the `return` statement.
- Function heading syntax:

  type_of_result function_name (*...arguments...*) {

- The `return` statement does two jobs:
  - it specifies the value to be returned, that is, the function result (omitted in a `void` function)
  - it terminates execution of the function, and causes execution to return to the calling function.
- `return` statements may be used wherever desired in a function, and may occur many times in the one function. The first one to be encountered ends execution of the function.
- A function may be used wherever a value of its result type makes sense.
- A *side-effect* is an effect external to the function other than its result.
- A function result may be thrown away by calling a function as if it were of type `void`.
- A result returned from `main` acts as the program's *termination status*.
  - The termination status may also be set by calling the function `exit`, which terminates the program.
- Functions can be written with any mixture of arguments and result: arguments but no result, result but no arguments, neither, or both. If both, the arguments may be the same type as the result, but they need not be. The arguments and the result are two independent features and should not be confused.
- Arguments and results are useful in designing functions to put in our own personal function libraries.
- To set up a function library, create a `.h` file containing the function headings for the functions in the library. Then include it at the head of any program that uses functions in that library.

7.11 SELF-TEST EXERCISES

Short Answer

1 State whether the following are true or false.
  a When we call a library function, the values we write inside the parentheses are called actual parameters.
  b Parameters replace all possible uses of global variables.
  c Parameters and arguments are two different things.
  d Dummy arguments are the same as formal parameters.
  e When calling a function, each actual parameter results in a value being copied into the corresponding formal parameter.
  f If a dummy argument is a simple variable, it behaves just like a local variable, except that it is initialized when the function is called to the value of the actual parameter.
  g With simple variable parameters, changing the formal parameter within the function permits one to alter the actual parameter.
  h With array parameters, changing the formal parameter within the function permits one to alter the actual parameter.
  i Library functions cannot have parameters.
  j The number of actual parameters supplied in a function call must be the same as the number of formal parameters in the function definition.

2 True or false?
  a A function result returns a single value to the calling function.
  b Function parameters return a single value to the calling function.
  c If a function has a result (i.e. is not `void`), it must not have any parameters.
  d If a function has a result (i.e. is not `void`), it must have at least one parameter.
  e Only library functions may give a result.
  f It is legal to throw away a function result by using the function as if it were a `void` function.
  g No function may take more than one parameter.
  h No function may give more than one result.

3 Predict the output of the following program.
```
#include <stdio.h>
int twice(int x) {
    x *= 2;
    return x;
}
main() {
    int x;
    x = 6;
    twice(x);
    printf("%d\n", x);
}
```

4   Predict the output of the following program.

```
#include <stdio.h>
int twice(int x) {
    x *= 2;
    return x;
}
main() {
    int x;
    x = 6;
    printf("%d\n", twice(x)+1 );
    printf("%d\n", twice(x+1) );
}
```

Programming

5   Write a function for printing name tags that would be a suitable candidate for inclusion in a function library. It cannot access a global variable, as the one given in the text does, nor can it assume that we want to print seat numbers in ascending order. It should be able to print tags of various sizes. Test the function in a suitable main function.

6   Write a function, imax2, that returns the larger of its two int arguments. Write a program to test it extensively.

7   A company wants to send promotional literature to customers that is suitable for the customer's age. If a customer is younger than 7, they do not want to mail at all. If the age is between 7 and 15, they want to mail their toy catalog; above 15 and below 25, the youth catalog; between 26 and 50 the adult catalog; and above that, the mature-age catalog. Write a program that asks the user to input first name, surname, and age, and that prints " ... ... should be sent the ... catalog.", or else " ... ... should be deleted from the mailing list." Blanks are to be filled in appropriately, of course. Include a function with a suitable parameter, that prints the message.

8   We say *A implies B* if, whenever A is true, B is also true. Write a function, impl(A,B), where A and B are integers, which returns true unless A is true and B is false. Test your function with critical cases; for example:

impl(x>7,x>5) should return true for any value of x, but
impl(x>5,x>7) should return false if x is 6 or 7.

7.12 TEST QUESTIONS

Short Answer

1 State whether the following are true or false.
   a No library functions have parameters, but they do have arguments.
   b If a formal parameter is an `int`, the actual parameter must be an `int` constant.
   c If a formal parameter is an `int`, the actual parameter may be an `int` constant.
   d If a formal parameter is an `int`, the actual parameter may be an `int` expression.
   e If a formal parameter is an `int`, the actual parameter may be an `int` variable.
   f Provided the formal parameter is a `char` array, the actual parameter may be a string literal.
   g A function with parameters may not be called more than once.
   h Formal parameters can only be used in the function they belong to.
   i In a function call, you must supply more actual parameters than formal parameters.

2 True or false?
   a `void` functions cannot return a result.
   b A `void` function may only return a result if a `return` statement is included.
   c If a function is of type `float`, at least one of its arguments must be a `float`.
   d Only one function in a program is allowed to return a result.
   e All functions must perform some input or output.

Programming

3 In addition to the following problems, many of the programming problems given in previous chapters could be improved by using parameters and/or results in functions. Look back at your earlier work and see if you can find any good candidates for improvement. If so, rewrite those programs.

4 If your computer uses ASCII codes, write a `char` function `letter(i)` which, if `i` is between 1 and 26, returns which letter of the alphabet is in position `i`. If `i` is outside that range, it should return a '!' character.

5 The C trigonometric functions work in radians, yet most people prefer degrees. Write two functions, `degtorad` and `radtodeg`, to reduce your programming woes.

6 Write a function, `imax3`, that returns the largest of its three `int` arguments. Test it extensively.

7 Write a function, `geomean`, that returns the geometric mean of its two floating point arguments. The geometric mean is the square root of the product of the numbers.

8   Write a function, `fac`, to evaluate and return the factorial of its integer argument. Use it in a program that calculates and prints the sum of the factorials of the numbers from 1 to 7. Use `double`s to obtain a larger range; the result for very large values will, of course, be only approximate, due to the fifteen or so digit accuracy of doubles.

9   The number of possible combinations of r items chosen from a population n without duplication is given by

$$\frac{n!}{r!(n-r)!}$$

Write a `double` function, `C(n,r)`, to evaluate and return an approximation to this number. `C` should use `fac` from the previous question. A competition requires entrants to predict which six numbers from 1 to 36 will be drawn from a barrel. Use `C` to find out your chances of winning.

10   Write a function with an argument representing temperature in degrees Celsius, that returns the same temperature in degrees Fahrenheit. The conversion formula is $F = 1.8C + 32$.

11   Write a function to return the number of bacteria present in a culture. Arguments should be the time t at which the number is required, the initial number present, N, and the reproduction rate, k. The expression that yields the desired number is Ne^{kt}. (e here represents the exponential function.) The C library's `exp` function can be used to evaluate an exponential.

12   Write a function called `round` that rounds a `float` to a specified number of decimal places. For example, `round(18.8725,1)` should return `18.9`, and `round(21.2723,2)` should return `21.27`. The library functions `ceil` and/or `floor` may be helpful. Test your function extensively.

13   Write a function, `is_prime`, that checks its integer parameter, `number`, to see if its value is prime. A prime is a number greater than one which is divisible only by itself and 1. The function should return 1 if the argument is prime, 0 otherwise. Include the function in a program that asks the user how many primes they want, inputs a positive integer, and keeps re-asking them until the answer they type is positive. It should then print the number of primes the user requested, starting with the first one (2). Since `is_prime` returns a logical value, it should be called in a manner suitable to logical values.

14   In chess the king is in check if it is on a square that an enemy piece can move to. The queen in chess is able to move to any unobstructed extent from its present position along a diagonal, row, or column. Write a program that will input the positions of the black queen and white king, each as two numbers, a row and column position. (The chess board is 8 rows by 8 columns.) The program should print whether the white king is in check from the black queen. Assume that all

rows, columns and diagonals are clear of any other pieces. Include a suitable function with at least one argument.

15 Write a program that reads a list of Roman numerals, one per line, and prints each one in decimal notation. Roman numbers consist of the letters M (1000), D (500), C (100), L (50), X (10), V (5) and I (1). If a numeral is followed by one of higher value, it is subtracted instead of added. Thus MLX is 1060 (1000 + 50 + 10), but MXL is 1040 (1000 − 10 + 50). Include a suitable function.

16 Write a program that asks for a person's birth date in the form day number, month number, year number, and then for today's date in the same format. Then the program should print the person's age in whole years, disregarding extra months and days. Include a suitable function with at least one argument.

17 An algorithm for finding the greatest common denominator (GCD) of two numbers is described in the test questions for Chapter 6. Write a general-purpose function called gcd, suitable for inclusion in a library, which returns the GCD of any two integers. Write a header file that includes a declaration for this function. Find out how to create a library on your system, build one containing this function, and test the function and the library by writing a program to input two numbers and print their GCD.

18 In electrical circuits, when two resistors follow each other in series, as follows,

the overall resistance is the sum of the individual resistances, i.e. $R_1 + R_2$. However, if the resistors are in parallel, as follows,

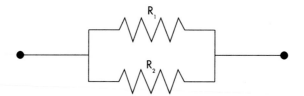

then the formula for the total resistance is

$$R_{tot} = \frac{1}{1/R_1 + 1/R_2}$$

Write a function paplus, which, given two resistances R1 and R2, returns the overall resistance for the two resistances in parallel. Using this function and the ordinary '+' operator only, write a main function that evaluates and prints the overall resistance of the following electrical component:

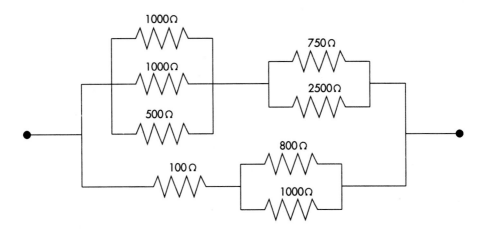

Note: this can be computed in a single expression.

19 In dealing with real numbers, due to inaccuracies in measurements, we often want to ignore small discrepancies when doing comparisons. For example, we might want two reals that differ by only a small amount to be considered equal. We might call this 'fuzzy' comparison. Write fuzzy functions `feq` (fuzzy equal) and `fne` (fuzzy not equal). Both should take three arguments: two numbers to compare, and an accuracy parameter, `eps`. `feq` should return true if the two numbers are within `eps` of each other; `fne` returns true if they are not within `eps` of each other.

20 Write a function that finds and returns the cube root of its argument. Given an initial guess $r = 1$, repeatedly replace r with

$$\frac{2r + x/r^2}{3}$$

until $r^3 - x$ is within 0.00001 of zero; use the function `feq` from the previous question to perform this check.

8

Top-down programming: choosing the program structure

Objectives

Understand what top-down programming is, and appreciate that we have been doing it all along.

See some non-trivial programs developed using top-down methods.

Learn and practice some techniques for finding a sound solution for a given problem.

Briefly look at object-oriented programming and how it fits in with top-down programming techniques.

See some ways in which testing and debugging can be performed on larger programs.

8.1 TOP-DOWN PROGRAMMING

We have emphasized throughout that we should only ever try solving one problem at a time, and that using hierarchies — where a function uses more specific functions to perform subtasks — is a good way to separate the various problems so that we can examine each one separately. In the hierarchy, there will be one overall task at the top (in C, coded in the `main` function) and many very specific functions for performing specialized tasks at the bottom. In between will be various layers consisting of tasks of intermediate generality. An obvious question is, should we start by writing all the tiny functions at the bottom and then write the functions that call them, and so on all the way up to the top (writing the `main` function last), or should we write `main` first, then the functions it calls, and so on down to the lowest level functions? Starting with the lowest layer first is called *bottom-up programming*. Starting with the highest function (`main`) is called *top-down programming*.

There is nothing inherently wrong with either method, and most professional programmers tend to use both, often swapping from one to the other while writing a single program. Bottom-up programming is most useful when you know you will need a collection of general utility functions. For example, you might want a program to respond to a mouse connected to the computer. You will need functions for checking the position of the mouse, whether and which buttons are pressed, when they are released, and so on. You may not know in advance exactly how these will be used, but you know that they will be needed somewhere. It makes sense to write them first, and test and debug them in simple throw-away test programs. When you are sure they work, you can use them in the important programs with confidence, just as with the C library functions.

When you write the bulk of the program, though, you will probably want to do it top-down. The reason is that the top (overall) level is closest to the statement of the problem. For example, suppose you have to read some data and produce an itemized report. It doesn't much matter what the data is or what the report should look like, the solution will be roughly like this:

```
print required headings.
initialize any required totaling variables, etc.
while (not all the input has been processed) {
    process some more.
}
print the totals, summary, etc.
```

Even with such a vague specification, the structure of the `main` function can be decided. Thus starting at the top is much easier than starting at the bottom; even if we had the problem specified in great detail, we might not have a clear idea of the lowest-level functions needed, nor could we be sure that if we wrote them a certain way, they would fit together properly to make a complete working program. It is very much like a jigsaw puzzle, where we have all the pieces and we need to fit them together (a bottom-up process). But they only fit because someone started with the whole picture and cut it up (a top-down process).

8.2 DESIGNING A GOOD PROGRAM STRUCTURE

You may have felt while reading preceding chapters that, although the programming examples made sense, you did not have the confidence to do it yourself. Programming, like many practical activities, is a combination of knowledge and practice. This chapter presents some tips and observations that can help guide us when we try to map out the overall plan of our programs. There is nothing mystic about designing programs; the skills just need to be learned and practiced.

That said, let us start with a useful rule-of-thumb:

> *Make the structure of the program similar to the structure of the problem being solved.*

To see what this means, let us look at a small example. A pack of playing cards has 52 cards (13 of each suit: clubs, hearts, diamonds, spades). A certain parlour trick involves quickly looking through a deck of **51** cards, and immediately saying which card is missing. This looks like a brilliant piece of memory work, but in fact there are simple arithmetic tricks for solving this problem. One such trick is to remember two numbers while looking at the cards; the first is between 1 and 10, and tells the suit. Add 1 for a spade, 2 for a club, 3 for a diamond, and 4 for a heart; if the total exceeds 10, drop the 'tens' digit. At the finish, 10 minus the remembered number shows the suit of the missing card. To find the missing card's number, form a second total counting Ace as 1, the numbers at face value, and Jack as 11, Queen as 12, and King as 13. Each time this goes above 12, subtract 13. At the end, 13 minus this total is the required number.

If we had to do this problem on a computer, how should we do it? Should we program that simple mathematical trick, or should we do it the hard way, which is to laboriously make a list of all 52 cards, check off each one we see, and then look for the one not checked off?

Many people would opt for programming the simple trick method. But the laborious method is closer to the structure of the problem. The problem concerns 52 cards, so our program should contain some representation of all 52 cards, rather than a sneaky computation. What does it matter? Suppose we are now asked to find two missing cards in a deck of 50. The sneaky trick now fails completely, and a program that used it would need to be completely rewritten. But the plodding method can be easily adjusted to find two missing cards rather than one. If we stick close to the way real life is, and do things in the most obvious way, we will usually not go far wrong. It is very common indeed to write a program, only to find soon after that a small change is necessary to solve a slightly different problem. Such changes are easier if one does the original job in a straightforward way.

8.3 EXAMPLE: A SIMPLE CALCULATOR

Our problem is to program a simple calculator to perform arithmetic calculations and print the answers. The rules will be simplified to reduce the size of the job: we shall disallow parentheses and allow only addition, subtraction, and multiplication operators. The end of a line will mark the end of an expression and cause the program to print its value. We will ignore the usual operator priorities, and do each operation in order as it comes. Let us also say that when the user types # at the start of a line, the program stops. Sample input might be

```
5+1*4-3
91-7*6
1+2+3
4-5*7
#
```

The first line, for example, should give the answer 21. If the user types something unexpected the program should print an error message and stop.

Finding the right structure is our first task. At each stage we shall keep the program structure the same as the problem structure. But what is the problem structure?

> **In many situations, the problem structure can be deduced from the structure of the input or the output.**

Since the data consists of one computation per line, the input (using the above example) can be structured as follows:

```
5+1*4-3
```
```
91-7*6
```
```
1+2+3
```
```
4-5*7
```
```
#
```

Each line, including the final #, can be thought of as a single unit. We do not yet look within the boxes, as that would violate our rule of solving one problem at a time. Thus a possible solution is:

```
Print instructions.
while the next line of input doesn't start with '#'
    Process one calculation (i.e. one line of input)
```

We can be more specific about this. How will we know whether a line starts with #? Obviously we have to read the first character. So we can rewrite the above:

```
    Print instructions.
    Read a character into next_char.
    while next_char is not '#' (i.e. this line isn't the last)
        Process one calculation (i.e. one line of input).
        Read a character into next_char.
```

We have not addressed the most worrying problem: how to interpret the input lines and perform the calculations; we are not ready for that yet. Instead we want to start with the 'big picture' and write a main function styled on the above plan. This is shown in Listing 8-1a.

Listing 8-1a

```c
/* A simple 'desk calculator' program.
   Input: Lines of text, each representing an arithmetic expression.
          Allowed operators are '+', '-', and '*'.  No whitespace allowed.
          All operators have the same priority, no parentheses allowed.
          A final line commencing with '#' signals the end of the data.
   Output:At the end of each line, the value of the expression is printed.
          If input is incorrect, program halts with an error message.
*/

#include <stdio.h>

int eval_expr(char next_char, char terminator);

main() {
    char next_char;      /* Holds the first character in a line
                            immediately on entry to eval_expr */

    /* Give user instructions... */
    printf("Enter expressions, one per line, no blanks.  # to finish.\n");

    /* Read the first character of the first expression. */
    scanf("%c", &next_char);

    while (next_char != '#') {    /* Another expression to process... */
        /* Process one calculation (i.e. one line of input). */
        printf("Result: %d\n", eval_expr(next_char, '\n'));

        /* Read first character of following line. */
        scanf("%c", &next_char);
    }

    return 0;           /* success */
}
```

In `main`, postponing the problem of doing calculations is achieved by inventing a function, `eval_expr`, to return the value of an expression; the returned value is displayed. As it will need to know the first character on the line, this is passed as a parameter. The character expected to end the expression is also passed so `eval_expr` can print an error message if an unexpected character is encountered. What exactly should `eval_expr` do? Listing 8-1b shows a heading comment.

Listing 8-1b

```
/********** eval_expr: *********************************
   On entry: Parameter next_char contains first char of the expression.
             Terminator contains the char expected to end the expression.
   On exit:  If the line is a valid expression, the entire line
             including its terminator, will have been input and the
             value of the expression will be returned.
             If the expression is invalid or the terminator incorrect, an
             error will have been printed and the program stopped.
*/
```

This comment says nothing about how `eval_expr` will work. Being the interface between `eval_expr` and the calling function (i.e. `main`), it says only what is necessary to check for a correct call in `main`.

Correctness check (optional)

The postcondition of the loop in `main` is

> *All lines correctly processed.*

Using the five-point checklist for correctness from Chapter 4 (revise it now) our bound function is

> *The number of input lines remaining.*

As `eval_expr` promises to process an input line (or, if the input is invalid, stop) we know the bound function keeps decreasing (provided `eval_expr` works) — points 1 and 2 are verified. Our invariant is

> *First character of the current line is in `next_char`, and all previous lines have been correctly processed.*

At initial entry, nothing has been processed and there are no previous lines, and we loaded `next_char` before entering the loop — point 3 is verified. Then during a single loop iteration, `eval_expr` processes one line, and we again load `next_char` — point 4 is verified. At last, we stop because we detect the final line, so "all previous lines" in the invariant means at the end "all lines" — point 5 is verified.

End of correctness check.

Now we can write `eval_expr`. We have the first character already, and it should be a digit. Keeping that in mind, we can now look within an input line to see its structure:

We can regard the structure as alternating operands and operators as shown, with a terminator (`\n`) at the end. A loop is necessary and we need a variable to store the progressive computed result; we shall call that `value_so_far`. Also we need to store each operator somewhere; we can call that variable `Operator`[1]. So our logic to handle this can be

```
How to eval_expr:
    Evaluate the first operand; store in value_so_far.
    Get a character in Operator.
    While Operator is not the terminator,
        Deal with the operator and its following operand, updating
            value_so_far.
        Get a character in Operator for next loop iteration.
    (After while loop:)
    Return value_so_far to caller.
```

Each loop iteration commences with the next operator already read, but the following operand not yet read. There are two tasks mentioned above that we might like to postpone by inventing more functions: "Evaluate the first operand", and "Deal with the operator and its following operand". This makes `eval_expr` simple, as shown in Listing 8-1c.

Listing 8-1c

```c
int eval_expr(char next_char, char terminator) {
    int process_op_operand(int value_so_far, char Operator); /* Note: We
        can include a function declaration (heading) inside a function. */
    int operand_value(char next_char);
    int value_so_far;    /* Holds the progressive calculation result. */
    char Operator;       /* Holds a character read where an operator
                            is expected. */

    /* Evaluate first operand, store in value_so_far.*/
    value_so_far = operand_value(next_char);
```

[1] We avoid `operator` (with a lower-case o) because readers with a C++ compiler will encounter trouble — it is a C++ keyword.

```
/* Next char should be an operator. */
scanf("%c", &Operator);

/* Process operator-operand pairs until terminator seen. */
while (Operator != terminator) {  /* The expression continues... */
    /* Deal with the operator and its following operand.
       I.e. compute its effect on value_so_far. */
    value_so_far = process_op_operand(value_so_far, Operator);

    /* Prepare to process next operator */
    scanf("%c", &Operator);
}
/* Expression has been processed and answer is in value_so_far. */
return value_so_far;
}
```

The function `operand_value` needs `next_char` as an argument, as `next_char` is part of the operand to be evaluated. The program will be stopped inside `operand_value` if `next_char` is erroneous, so if `operand_value` returns to `eval_expr`, things must be OK. A heading comment should now be written describing the operation of `operand_value`. However, this will not appear in the program until `operand_value` is written (see Listing 8-1e).

In the loop, `value_so_far` is modified by the line

```
value_so_far = process_op_operand(value_so_far, Operator);
```

which passes the current value of the expression and the latest operator as arguments; the latest operand will be input inside `process_op_operand`. The modified expression value is returned as the function result, so this function will be of type `int`, not `void`. Its heading comment is shown in Listing 8-1d.

Exercise (optional): Verify the correctness of the loop in Listing 8-1c.

Notice how we have repeated the plan we used to write `main`: any time we run into something difficult, postpone the problem by inventing a suitable function. We can handle the remaining functions without inventing any others. `process_op_operand` must input the operand and decide which arithmetic operation to perform:

```
How to process_op_operand:
    Switch depending on Operator:
        Operator is '+': Get next operand and add to value_so_far,
            store in new_value.
        Operator is '-': Get next operand and subtract from
            value_so_far, store in new_value.
        Operator is '*': Get next operand and multiply by
            value_so_far, store in new_value.
        otherwise print error (illegal character) and stop.
    Return new_value as the function result.
```

We can program the above algorithm, as in Listing 8-1d.

Listing 8-1d

```
/*********** process_op_operand: **************************************
     On entry: Parameter Operator contains a character from the input,
               which is supposed to be one of (+, -, or *) telling which
               operation to perform.  The following operand has not
               been read yet.  Parameter value_so_far must contain the
               progressive total for previous calculations.
     On exit:  If operator is not valid, an error message will have been
               printed and execution stopped.
               Otherwise, the next operand has been read, and if it is
               valid, the function returns the updated value so far to
               reflect this latest calculation.  If not valid, an error
               message is printed and the program stopped.
*/
#include <stdlib.h>     /* for exit() */

int process_op_operand(int value_so_far, char Operator) {
    int operand_value(char next_char);
    char next_char;
    int new_value;   /* The updated value of the calculation after
                         processing this operator. */

    /* At this point value_so_far holds one operand, Operator holds the
       operator. */
    switch (Operator) {
    case '+':
        scanf("%c", &next_char);             /* Get next operand char */
        new_value = value_so_far + operand_value(next_char);
        break;
    case '-':
        scanf("%c", &next_char);             /* Get next operand char */
        new_value = value_so_far - operand_value(next_char);
        break;
    case '*':
        scanf("%c", &next_char);             /* Get next operand char */
        new_value = value_so_far * operand_value(next_char);
        break;
    default:
        printf("Error: Illegal character: \"%c\".\n", Operator);
        exit(EXIT_FAILURE);
    }
    return new_value; /* Send updated result back to calling function. */
}
```

Now for the final function, `operand_value`. The first character of the operand is in `next_char`, and it must be a digit as it is the first character of a number. To evaluate that we shall use the function `ungetc` from the standard library. `ungetc` pushes a character back into the input so that the next input function re-inputs the character. The logic is:

```
How to calculate the operand_value:
    if next_char is not a digit
        print an error message.
        stop.
    Push the digit back into the input stream.
    Call scanf to input the no. and return it as the fn. result.
```

This function is shown in Listing 8-1e.

Listing 8-1e

```
/********** operand_value: ********************************
   On entry: next_char is the character commencing the operand.
   On exit:  returns the value of the operand.
*/
int operand_value(char next_char) {
    int value;
    if (next_char < '0' || next_char > '9') {
        printf("Error: \"%c\" should be a digit.\n", next_char);
        exit(EXIT_FAILURE);
    }
    /* Now push that char back into the input, so that the entire integer
       is waiting to be read, and use scanf to input the entire number. */
    ungetc(next_char, stdin); scanf("%d", &value);
    return value;
}
```

The full program is the concatenation of Listings 8-1a to 8-1e, in order. In using `ungetc` I have cheated, because its parameter, `stdin`, will not be studied until Chapter 10. This raises the problem of what we could have done if no such function existed. We could have built up the number manually, as follows:

```
value = 0;
while (next_char>='0' && next_char<='9') {
    value = 10*value + (next_char-'0');
    scanf("%c", &next_char);
}
```

(The phrase `next_char-'0'` converts a character code for a digit to the equivalent integer.) However, after the above fragment executes, we have the character following the number in `next_char`; since that is not expected by the other functions, we would have to use `ungetc` anyway. Without `ungetc`, the program structure would fail, requiring adjustment higher up, perhaps in `eval_calc`. Because such an occurrence would, in a large program, cause great inconvenience, the tasks assigned to lower-level functions must be realistic. This problem is considered further in the next example.

Sample Run 1
```
Enter expressions, one per line, no blanks.  # to finish.
21-48+4
Result: -23
19+1*2
Result: 40
41
Result: 41
#
```

Sample Run 2
```
Enter expressions, one per line, no blanks.  # to finish.
1+2+3
Result: 6
5+B
Error: "B" should be a digit.
```

Sample Run 3
```
Enter expressions, one per line, no blanks.  # to finish.
8+8-15
Result: 1
1+2/4
Error: Illegal character: "/".
```

8.4 EXAMPLE: PRINTING A MONTH IN A CALENDAR

This example is chosen because it poses some challenging problems in designing the program structure. We want to input the number of days in a month and the day of the week on which the first day falls, and get a printout of a nicely formated picture of the month such as we see on printed calendars. So if we input 31 and Tuesday, we should obtain:

```
* * * * * * * * * * * * * * * * * * * * * * * * * * * * * * * * * * * * * * * * *
*   1     *   2     *   3     *   4     *   5     *
*         *         *         *         *         *
*         *         *         *         *         *
* * * * * * * * * * * * * * * * * * * * * * * * * * * * * * * * * * * * * * * * * *
*  6    *  7    *  8    *  9    * 10    * 11    * 12    *
*      *      *      *      *      *      *      *
*      *      *      *      *      *      *      *
* * * * * * * * * * * * * * * * * * * * * * * * * * * * * * * * * * * * * * * * * *
* 13   * 14   * 15   * 16   * 17   * 18   * 19   *
*      *      *      *      *      *      *      *
*      *      *      *      *      *      *      *
* * * * * * * * * * * * * * * * * * * * * * * * * * * * * * * * * * * * * * * * * *
* 20   * 21   * 22   * 23   * 24   * 25   * 26   *
*      *      *      *      *      *      *      *
*      *      *      *      *      *      *      *
* * * * * * * * * * * * * * * * * * * * * * * * * * * * * * * * * * * * * * * * * *
* 27   * 28   * 29   * 30   * 31   *
*      *      *      *      *      *
*      *      *      *      *      *
* * * * * * * * * * * * * * * * * * * * * * * * * * * * * * * * * * *
```

We shall not restrict the days in a month to the range 28 to 31, as some calendar systems do not follow the usual Western pattern, but we shall restrict the number of days to eight or more, guaranteeing at least two weeks or part-weeks in a month.

We can use the structure of the input to devise the logic for the main function, as follows:

```
Input the number of days and the starting day of the week.
Make sure the input is sensible, ask user to re-enter until it is.
Print the picture of the month.
```

We can store the number of days in an int called last_day. The day of the week can be represented as a number from 0 to 6 (0=Sunday, 6=Saturday) and stored in an int called start_weekday. Each step in this plan can be implemented by a function. Listing 8-2a shows main and the functions for the first two steps, as these are all straightforward.

Listing 8-2a

```
/* Program to print a picture of a calendar month.

   Input must be the number of days in a month, and the day in the
   week of the first day of the month.  There must be at least 8
   days in a month, and the day in the week must be from 0 to 6
   (0=Sunday, 6=Saturday).

   Output is a 'calendar' style picture of the month.
*/

#include <stdio.h>
```

```
/***** Global variables to specify calendar required *****/

int last_day;          /* Number of days in the month */
int start_weekday;     /* Week day of the first of the month */

/********************* Functions *********************/

void obtain_user_input(void);
void check_input_legality(void);
void print_calendar_month(void);

main() {
    /* Input the number of days and the starting day of the week. */
    obtain_user_input();

    /* Make sure input is legal, ask user to re-enter until it is. */
    check_input_legality();

    /* Print the picture of the month. */
    print_calendar_month();

    return 0;
}

/***************** obtain_user_input *****************
    Gets user's values for last_day and start_weekday.
*/

void obtain_user_input(void) {
    printf("How many days are in the month? ");
    scanf("%d", &last_day);
    printf("Which week day is the first of the month?\n");
    printf("(0=sun, 1=mon, 2=tue, 3=wed, 4=thu, 5=fri, 6=sat)\n");
    scanf("%d", &start_weekday);
}

/*************** check_input_legality ***************
    Makes sure user has entered last_day >= 8 and start_weekday
    between 0 and 6.
    Note: last_day is not restricted to 28..31 because some
    calendars used in the world have months of other lengths.
*/

void check_input_legality(void) {
    void obtain_user_input(void);
    while (
        last_day < 8        ||
        start_weekday < 0   ||
        start_weekday > 6
    ) {
```

```
        if (last_day < 8) {
            printf("The month must have eight or more days.\n");
        }
        if (start_weekday < 0  ||  start_weekday > 6) {
            printf("The starting week day must be between 0 & 6\n");
        }
        printf("Please re-enter both values.\n");
        obtain_user_input();
    }
}
```

The missing function, `print_calendar_month`, can be specified as follows:

```
/*********** print_calendar_month ****************************
    Prints the calendar picture.

    On entry:
        last_day is the number of days in the month, and must be
        greater than seven.
        start_weekday is the day-of-the-week of the first of the
        month, and must indicate a valid week day (0 to 6).
*/
```

How do we program this? We have no more input, so we must turn elsewhere to get clues about the problem structure. When input fails, try output. The output consists of a square for each day, so maybe the function should look like this:

```
while we haven't printed all the squares
    print another square representing a day
```

This certainly reflects the fact that the calendar is made of squares. Unfortunately each physical line of output contains only part of a square. Even worse, each line contains parts of up to seven squares. If we were using a plotter or graphics screen this wouldn't matter, but on a normal text screen or printer we must print each text line completely before moving on to the next. The above plan is incompatible with that aspect of the problem. This emphasizes how important it is to choose a sound program structure. If we used the above plan and went ahead and wrote a program based on it, it just couldn't work. It is fundamentally unsound, and no amount of tinkering will fix it.

Perhaps we should start with the output lines as the key part of the problem structure. Each picture consists of many lines of printing, so we could try

```
while we haven't printed the whole calendar
    print another line
```

Well, it is workable, but some problems are apparent. The various lines are not all equivalent. Some lines represent borders between rows, some have day numbers, some don't. In short, this structure tries to solve many problems at once in the printing step, and will be hard to develop into a full solution.

We clearly have to pay attention to both the division of the calendar into squares **and** the need to print it a line at a time. Each row of squares represents a single week, which is a fundamental part of the structure of the problem. Furthermore it is a unit we have some hope of programming correctly, because each row of boxes is printed in its entirety as a unit (that is, not intermixed with bits and pieces from other rows). So perhaps we could try

```
while we have not printed the squares for the final week
    print the squares for another week.
```

This looks promising, although there are still some important questions. Consider the lines of asterisks between two rows of squares. Do they belong to the squares above or those below? Further, there is one more line of asterisks than rows of squares, as we have a line of asterisks above the top week as well as below the bottom one. Also, the length of the very first row of asterisks depends on the used days in the row of squares below, but the length of the bottom row of asterisks depends on the used days in the row of squares above; others are full-length. We have the start of a workable plan, but we are not out of the woods yet.

We need a way to look at this problem that makes the most of its repetitive aspect (one week after another) but we still have to watch those special conditions at the start and finish. Let us define a 'calendar row' to be all the lines making up a row of squares, except the asterisks above and below. We can expand our plan as follows.

```
print the top line of asterisks.

while we have not printed the second-last calendar row
    print another calendar row
    print a full line of asterisks.

print the last calendar row
print the bottom line of asterisks.
```

How will we know how long to make the first and last line of asterisks? Also, how do we know where we are up to, for detecting the second-last calendar row and for knowing which row we are supposed to print? Suppose that, whenever we were ready to print a calendar row, a variable (sun_date, say) contained the date of the Sunday in the week we were printing. It would be easy to program the while loop test by comparing sun_date with the number of days in the month, and it would provide all the information needed to print a calendar row. This suggests the following refinement of the plan:

```
Set up sun_date correct for week 1.
print the top line of asterisks.

while sun_date not within final week
    print another calendar row
    Add 7 to sun_date.
    print a full line of asterisks.

print the last calendar row
print the bottom line of asterisks.
```

Sunday in week 1 is on or before the first of the month. If the month does not commence on Sunday, the Sunday for week 1 will not be within the month. This is circumvented by inventing fictitious dates prior to the first. So if, for example, the first of the month is Wednesday (start_weekday is 3) then sun_date will be −2, as in this diagram:

Day of the week:	Sun	Mon	Tue	Wed	Thu	Fri	Sat
Number of week day:	0	1	2	**3**	4	5	6
Date in month of day:	**(−2)**	**(−1)**	**(0)**	1	2	3	4

Clearly then, to set up sun_date for week 1, we must write

```
sun_date = 1 - start_weekday;
```

If sun_date is less than 1, Sunday is not in the month, so some blank days will be printed in the first week. Now we must decide the test for the while loop. We have reached the last week if sun_date is within the final seven days of the month. Therefore we have **not** reached the last week if

```
(sun_date < last_day - 6)
```

We can now program print_calendar_month, inventing functions for the parts we still can't do, and remembering to pass as parameters the values they will need to do their jobs. The functions needed and their parameters are:

print_top_asterisks: Prints the top line of asterisks. It must know where the first week starts, so its parameter is start_weekday.

print_calendar_row: Prints a calendar row. It must know what dates to include, and (for the last week) where the dates stop, so parameters are sun_date and last_day.

print_full_line_asterisks: Always prints a complete line of asterisks, so it needs no parameters.

print_bottom_asterisks: Prints the final line of asterisks, so it must compute how long this should be, requiring parameters sun_date and last_day.

print_calendar_month is shown in Listing 8-2b.

Listing 8-2b

```
/*********** print_calendar_month ****************************
    Prints the calendar picture.

    On entry:
        last_day is the number of days in the month, and must be
        greater than seven.
        start_weekday is the day-of-the-week of the first of the
        month, and must indicate a valid week day (0 to 6).
*/

void print_calendar_month(void) {
    void print_top_asterisks(int start_weekday);
    void print_calendar_row(int sun_date, int last_day);
    void print_full_line_asterisks(void);
    void print_bottom_asterisks(int sun_date, int last_day);

    int sun_date;       /* date of Sunday in the week to be printed */

    /* prepare to print the first week.
       (The date of Sunday of week 1 is on or before the first of the
       month.  Since start_weekday is the 1st of the month, Sunday (0)
       must be the (1-start_weekday)st.  If this is less than 1, Sunday
       is not in the month, so some blank days will be printed.) */
    sun_date = 1 - start_weekday;

    /* print the top line of asterisks. */
    print_top_asterisks(start_weekday);

    /* while we have not printed the second-last row, print another.
       (We have reached the last week if sun_date is within the final
       seven days of the month.) */
    while (sun_date < last_day - 6) {
        /* Here sun_date is Sunday's date in the week to be printed. */

        print_calendar_row(sun_date, last_day);

        sun_date += 7;         /* prepare for the next week */

        print_full_line_asterisks();
    }

    /* print the last calendar row */
    /* Here sun_date is Sunday's date in the final week. */
    print_calendar_row(sun_date, last_day);

    print_bottom_asterisks(sun_date, last_day);
}
```

The function `print_calendar_row` is a little complicated. We shall invent some `#define` constants, `SQUARE_WIDTH` for the full width of each square (the space within plus one asterisk), and `SQUARE_HEIGHT` for the number of lines to be printed by `print_calendar_row`. Each square in the first line contains a date if it represents a day within the month (from 1 to `last_date`). The output structure is a number of lines, each of which prints a segment for each day in the week. The nature of the segment depends on whether the day is within the month and whether this is the top line. This suggests a `for` loop executing once for each line in the calendar row, and within that a loop executing once for each day. Finally, within that loop would be an `if` statement deciding exactly what should be printed. With these decisions made, we can now finish the program, as shown in Listing 8-2c; another small function, `putout`, is invented to repeatedly output characters.

Listing 8-2c

```
/**************************************************************/
/*       Functions for outputting the calendar         */

/* The following #defines allow us to change our minds about the
   appearance of the calendar with minimal effort. */

/* Full width of a square (cannot be less than 4):   */
#define SQUARE_WIDTH 9

/* Height of area BETWEEN rows of asterisks (must be at least 1): */
#define SQUARE_HEIGHT 3

void putout(int number, char whichchar);

/*********************** print_calendar_row: **********************
   On entry: sun_date is the date of Sunday in the week to be printed.
            If this is the first week, sun_date can be less than one.
            If so, sun_date should be 1 - start_weekday so that the
            first falls on start_weekday.  last_date must be correct.

   Prints a calendar row (i.e. minus top & bottom asterisks) for the
   indicated week.  If a day has a date less than 1 or greater than
   last_day, its square in the calendar is blanked (as the day is not
   within the month).
*/

void print_calendar_row(int sun_date, int last_day) {
    int line, day;

    for (line=1; line<=SQUARE_HEIGHT; line++) {
        /*Print one text line */

        for (day=sun_date; day<sun_date+7; day++) {
            /* Print the segment belonging to a single day */
            if (day<1) {
```

```
                    /* day is before start of month - print blanks */
                    putout(SQUARE_WIDTH, ' ');
                } else if (day>last_day) {
                    /* day is beyond end of month - print nothing */
                    /* NOTHING TO DO */
                } else {
                    /* day is within month - print square pieces */
                    putchar('*');                    /* print left asterisk */

                    if (line==1) {
                        /* First line needs a number */
                        printf("%3d", day);
                        putout(SQUARE_WIDTH - 4, ' '); /* rest of square */
                    } else {
                        /* other lines are an empty box */
                        putout(SQUARE_WIDTH - 1, ' ');
                    }
                }
            }
        }
        printf("*\n");    /* Terminate final box and add a newline */
    }
}


/******************** putout ************************
A short utility function to output repeated characters.
   On entry: number is how many characters to print, whichchar is
             the character to be printed.
   Prints whichchar, number times.
*/

void putout(int number, char whichchar) {
    int i;
    for (i=0; i<number;i++) {
        putchar(whichchar);
    }
}
```

Now we have the simpler output functions to write. These are shown in Listing 8-2d.

Listing 8-2d

```
/***************** print_top_asterisks: ************************

  On entry: start_weekday is the weekday of the first of the month.

  Prints a row of asterisks to cover the top of the 'used' squares
  in the first week.
*/
```

```
void print_top_asterisks(int start_weekday) {
    /* There are start_weekday blank squares at the start,
       then (7 - start_weekday) used squares. */
    /* SQUARE_WIDTH blank characters per blank square: */
    putout(start_weekday * SQUARE_WIDTH, ' ');

    /* Now ditto for asterisks, plus one to cover the right hand
       vertical column of asterisks */
    putout((7 - start_weekday) * SQUARE_WIDTH + 1, '*');

    putchar('\n');      /* Complete the line */
}


/******************* print_full_line_asterisks: *******************
  Prints a full line of asterisks to separate calendar rows.
*/

void print_full_line_asterisks(void) {
    putout(7 * SQUARE_WIDTH + 1, '*');
    putchar('\n');      /* Complete the line */
}


/******************** print_bottom_asterisks: ********************
  On entry: sun_date is the date of Sunday in the final week of the
            month, and last_day is the last day in the month.

  Prints asterisks to underline days sun_date to last_day.
*/

void print_bottom_asterisks(int sun_date, int last_day) {
    putout((last_day - sun_date + 1) * SQUARE_WIDTH + 1, '*');
    putchar('\n');      /* Complete the line */
}
```

A useful guide when developing solutions to complex problems is:

Always start with the big picture — postpone looking at details as long as possible.

Thus we commenced with the overall division of the calendar into rows, instead of with the details of how to print a row. Provided we have a sound plan, we can safely postpone any uncomfortable details by assigning them to a subsidiary function. Unfortunately most beginners tend to focus first on the tricky details, because they are the bits that seem the most worrying. Getting sidetracked by details will result in (a) failure, or (b) a very convoluted, error-prone and obscure program.

8.5 OBJECT-ORIENTED PROGRAMMING

Object-oriented programming techniques are a further development of the theme of solving separate problems separately. They are in the main beyond the scope of this book, but as they are becoming increasingly well known and used, it is important to be clear how they fit in with the top-down programming techniques presented here.

In the early years of programming, even small routines were major programming challenges, but the development of high-level languages and top-down programming techniques made previously difficult projects feasible. Writing many types of small-to-medium systems is now routine — the problem of writing small or medium programs is essentially solved. Very large systems, however, still frequently over-run budgets and deadlines, or even fail to materialize. One goal of object-oriented programming is to improve this situation.

Object-oriented programming starts by asking, not what the program must do, but rather what *objects* it does things to. For example in a commercial system objects might include clients, suppliers, payments, accounts, and so on. These objects have behaviors (a supplier can supply things, send bills, etc.). The behaviors of the objects are programmed in a self-contained manner, quite apart from any use we might have for these behaviors. Then, to write a program to actually get things done, we ask the various objects to activate their in-built behaviors, or *methods*. So if we asked our programmed 'supplier' object to supply something, the program code in the supplier object might write out an order to a real-life supplier for the items we require, and it might also tell an 'account' object to debit itself the cost of the items.

This way of doing things holds out great hope for being able to re-use software components in new projects long after the project they were originally written for has seen its last days. Top-down programming techniques fit in with the object-oriented philosophy in the programming of the object methods. Each method must achieve some task for the object, and still presents the same programming challenges as the self-contained programs we have been studying. Methods tend to be simpler than complete non-object-oriented programs. This means that people will no longer try to use top-down techniques on gigantic, monolithic software projects. The object-oriented method splits that single big project into, say, a hundred separate manageable ones.

These comments are greatly simplified, especially as object-oriented techniques work best in languages specially designed for them, and cannot easily be illustrated in C. C++ is an object-oriented language based on C, with the addition of object-oriented support. Other popular object-oriented languages include Eiffel and Smalltalk. Objective C is another C-based object-oriented language.

Bertrand Meyer's text (mentioned in the bibliography) may be useful if you are interested in learning more about object-oriented methods.

8.6 PROGRAM DEBUGGING

As soon as we start to write large programs, errors will happen. There are two basic ways to find and eliminate them: testing, and correctness verification. Here we look at the former method. By trying our program, we discover situations where it fails, then we investigate to find out why. Just as there are two ways to write a program (top-down and bottom-up) so there are the same two ways to test and debug it.

In bottom-up debugging, one takes low-level functions and calls them from specially written dummy `main` functions that exercise them with various inputs to see that they do the right thing in all circumstances. When the low-level functions work, one places them in a higher function, and tests that to see if that works. If we know that the lower functions work, any bugs which turn up must be caused by the higher function. One fixes it and puts it in place in an even higher function, and so on. For example in the previous section we might start by testing the functions to print lines of asterisks and `print_calendar_row` then, when we are sure they work, put them in place in `print_calendar_month` and test it. The problem with bottom-up testing is that, if we write our program top-down as we normally should, we have to wait until it is complete before starting the testing. If we have a serious error in a high-level module, it might cause us to write a lot of misguided low-level code that would take a lot of work to fix.

Top-down debugging works by trying to ensure the correctness of the top-level functions first. Thus one can be sure the overall plan is workable even though most of the program is as yet unwritten. This is a very good way to proceed, but we have to be careful. If the lower-level functions are as yet unwritten, how can we test the operation of the higher functions? Many writers urge the use of *stub functions*. These are simple dummy versions of the lower functions which do not actually work, but can be called to see if the higher function is calling the right functions at the right time. For example, in the previous program, we might have made `print_calendar_row` a stub function, printing a simple message like

```
***** calendar row here *****
```

If it is being called in the right manner we would expect to see this 'calendar':

```
How many days are in the month? 29
Which week day is the first of the month?
(0=sun, 1=mon, 2=tue, 3=wed, 4=thu, 5=fri, 6=sat)
3
                              ********************************
***** calendar row here *****
***************************************************************
***** calendar row here *****
***************************************************************
***** calendar row here *****
***************************************************************
***** calendar row here *****
***************************************************************
***** calendar row here *****
***************************************************************
***** calendar row here *****
********************************
```

We can see that the calendar has the right form, even though the rows are not being fully printed, so this would be a suitable place to use a stub function. But what if, in our first example (the simple calculator), we had tried replacing the function `process_op_operand` by a stub function? Try it. You will find it is very hard to write a simple stub to verify that the function above (`eval_expr`) is correct. Why does the method work in one case and not the other? Well, `print_calendar_row` is purely an output function; whether it works does not affect the further processing of the rest of the program. But `process_op_operand` returns a crucial value used further on. If that is not returned properly, we have no reason to believe the other functions will work even if they are written correctly.

Where stub testing fails, it is often better to test the entire thing as a single unit. When an error is found, we may see the problem anyway. If we can't pinpoint it, we can still find out which function is misbehaving, and then take that function out if necessary and test it separately. We can decide which function is going wrong by inserting test printouts in strategic places. Even better, special debugging programs are available on many systems which allow you to watch the execution of your program and look at the values of variables as they are changed. This is especially true on personal computers, where it is becoming almost compulsory for the compiler vendor to offer a good debugger.

Another way to use stub testing is to write the program top-down, but write only part of the program completely. For example, if your program offers the choice of five options on a menu, write the code for just one option fully, from top to bottom. If even that is too much (in a really large program, for example) then the option probably has sub-options. Write just one of those. The other menu options should all be stubs, but in this case the stubs should never be called, as they are not part of the section we are testing. In other words, write a full top-to-bottom development of just a piece of the entire system. Then debug it fully before moving on. Most big programs can be subdivided usefully in some way.

When doing the testing, we have to decide what data to try on our program. There are two ways to do this. One way is to look at how the program works and design tests that try out every aspect of the program's logic. For example, in the calendar program there is a test for whether `sun_date` is within seven of the end of the month. This suggests picking a month in which the last Sunday is the exact last day (and then the previous one will differ by exactly seven), and one where the last day is Saturday (and the previous Sunday differs by six). These tests will show up a 'one-off' error — for example, if I have written a < test where I should have written <=.

The other way is to just throw random tests at the program. For example, can I print a month of 173 days starting on Tuesday? This is called *black-box* testing, because we ignore how it works internally. Both methods find errors, but neither method seems to find them all.

8.7 SUMMARY

- *Top-down programming* techniques start by designing the highest level modules first (e.g. main).
  - In general, it is the preferred technique.
  - Start with the 'big picture' before moving on to details.
- *Bottom-up programming* starts with the lowest level modules.
  - This is useful where we have a clearly defined purpose for the low level modules, and/or where they are re-useable in many programs.
- Design the program structure to match the structure of the problem:
  - match the format of the input and/or
  - match the format of the output and/or
  - (in some problems) match the way calculations must be performed.
- Write the preconditions and postconditions of lower-level functions as you decide you need them. Check that these comments alone are enough to convince you the function you are now writing is correct. They should be sufficiently precise that you can later program the functions from these comments alone.
- Testing and debugging can also be done top-down or bottom-up, and not necessarily the same direction as the program was written.
- Stub functions can help you test just part of a program, but they are not always suitable.
- Testing an entire program which does part of the job is sometimes easier than testing a part of a program which does the full job.
- Test and debug thoroughly, because we are all fallible!

8.8 SELF-TEST EXERCISES

Short Answer

1 When developing a program, should we:
   a pay careful attention to every detail of the problem at all times, or
   b only worry about one aspect of the problem at a time?

2 When developing a function, should we:
   a pay careful attention to every situation in which the function is called, or
   b write the function by referring to its precondition and postcondition?

3 State whether each of the following is true or false.
   a A function should not be written unless the function that calls it has already been exhaustively tested.
   b No function should be called from more than one place.
   c Function definitions enable us to put our functions in a more readable order.
   d No function should be written unless its precondition and postcondition have already been written.

Programming

4 Write a program that prints the numbers from 0 to 99 as a square matrix of 10 by 10 numbers, with the numbers running down each column as follows:

```
0 10 20 30 40 50 60 70 80 90
1 11 21 31 41 51 61 71 81 91
2 12 22 32 42 52 62 72 82 92
3 13 23 33 43 53 63 73 83 93
4 14 24 34 44 54 64 74 84 94
5 15 25 35 45 55 65 75 85 95
6 16 26 36 46 56 66 76 86 96
7 17 27 37 47 57 67 77 87 97
8 18 28 38 48 58 68 78 88 98
9 19 29 39 49 59 69 79 89 99
```

5 Enhance the calendar program in Section 8.4 by placing headings (Sun, Mon, Tue, etc.) over the columns. Be sure to do it in such a way that if the constant SQUARE_WIDTH is altered, the headings will still be placed correctly over the columns.

8.9 TEST QUESTIONS

Short Answer

1 State whether each of the following is true or false.
   a The precondition specifies the circumstances that a function requires in order to work properly.
   b When writing code that calls a certain function, we should ignore that function's preconditions and postconditions.
   c Bottom-up programming should always be avoided.
   d Bottom-up testing should always be avoided.
   e It is necessary to test a program in the same direction (top-down or bottom-up) as it was written.
   f A program should be written completely, no matter how large it is, before any testing is done.

Programming

2 When the computer reads a line of text, it gives you the opportunity to backspace, thus erasing previously entered characters. Write a program that partly simulates this function of the operating system by reading characters from the keyboard and delaying their output by one character. Use the $ character as a backspace command. Allow only a single backspace at a time. Thus if the input is ABCDEFG the output should be ACDFG.

3 Numerical integration (finding the area under a curve) can be performed by the trapezoidal method, which involves adding the areas of small trapezoid approximations to the area of parts of the curve, as shown in the following figure.

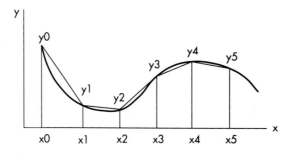

If the distance between successive x points is Δx, then the sum of the areas from x_0 to x_n is

$$\sum_{i=1}^{n} (y_{i-1} + y_i)\frac{\Delta x}{2}$$

Write a program that inputs n, Δx, and $n+1$ y values, and computes the area under the curve.

4 A business employs many part-time employees who, over the course of a month, work various hours at various times. Write a program that will print total hours worked for each employee. Input is lines consisting of a four-digit employee number followed by a number of hours. There can be any number of lines for a single employee, and times on all of them must be added to produce that employee's total. However, all lines for a single employee are consecutive in the input. The final line has employee number 0.

5 A company wishes to process sales figures from their regional representatives. Input consists of an integer telling how many representatives there are, and then blocks of data, one block for each representative. A block of data for a representative starts with a line containing the representative's name, then a line with a number telling how many sales that representative made last month. Following that there is, for each sale, a floating point number standing for the value of the sale in dollars. Write a program to process this input, printing each representative's name and total sales. Then finally print the total sales for all representatives. Here is an example of correct input.

```
2
Mary Schmidt
3
31100.50
10608.00
8008.68
Joe McCallum
2
18342.64
2000.00
```

6 The base of natural logarithms, e, calculated to twelve decimal places is 2.718281828459. Using `float` variables, calculate e by adding terms of the series:

$$e = 1 + 1 + 1/2! + 1/3! + 1/4! + ...$$

Each term is smaller than the preceding one. Write a program that evaluates e using this series. Keep adding terms until your value for e differs from its previous value by less than 0.00001. Compute the factorials using floating point numbers also.

7 In professionally printed calendars, the last few days of the month are often placed on the top left of the first row. This only works if the first week and last week have no days in common, of course. For example, March 1991 had the 1st on Friday and the 31st on Sunday; thus the 31st could be tucked away on the top line. However, July 1991 started on a Monday and ended on a Wednesday. Thus Monday, Tuesday and Wednesday overlapped, so the final week had to be printed on a separate row at the bottom. Modify the calendar program in Section 8.4 to check whether the last and first weeks can be printed together, and do so if possible.

8 Write a calendar program that prints the weeks vertically, rather than horizontally. That is, row one shows all the Sundays, row two all the Mondays, and so on. You may have to limit the maximum number of days in a month so the display fits your screen or printer. Place day name abbreviations (Sun, Mon, etc.) to the left of the rows.

9 Write a program that prints a sine wave, with x and y axes. The x axis should be horizontal.

10 Most word processors, unfortunately, use their own individual file formats — one word processor will not be able to process a different one's files unless they are converted specially. This is caused by the presence of various codes that only make sense to the program that created them. To help work around this problem, a generic file format exists that many word processors can read. It keeps paragraphs and tab codes, but discards most others. The generic format is prepared as follows: newlines within a paragraph are replaced by a single blank space, and the end of a paragraph is marked by a single newline. Write a program that accepts normal text

input, and outputs it in generic format. In the input, a completely empty line (i.e. two newline characters in a row) marks the end of a paragraph, and should be replaced by a single newline in the output. All other newlines are within a paragraph and should be replaced by a space in the output. Stop processing input when you see three newlines in a row. By using output redirection you can store the output in a file and test it in a word processor (if you have access to one that can read generic format).

11 In handling *peripheral* devices (devices attached to a computer) a common problem concerns *escape sequences*; these are special sequences of characters that have special meanings for the devices. For example, terminals have escape sequences to clear the screen, turn attributes such as bold on or off, and many more. Unfortunately, different brands use different sequences, which makes writing programs trickier. Your task now is to write a program that simulates the logic of a computer terminal. Your program is to input normal characters from the keyboard, and output to the screen. The typed input, we shall pretend, is the output received by the terminal from a remote timesharing computer. The purpose of the program is to scan the computer 'output' (i.e. your program's input) looking for certain escape sequences that affect the display on the screen. We are looking for the following sequences of characters:

offt Makes the terminal go to 'quiet' mode; that is, all further data is suppressed (not displayed) until an `ont` sequence is detected.

ont Cancels the effect of `offt`. When your program starts, '`ont`' should be the default state.

onb Makes the terminal print following text in bold. If you can find out the true escape sequence to do this on your screen, output it, and all following output will be bold. If not, just simulate the effect by displaying the characters <BOLD>.

offb Cancels the effect of `onb`. Again, use the correct escape sequence if you know it, or display <NORMAL> if not.

Note: none of these escape sequences should be echoed on the screen.

A problem with the design of our terminal is that these character sequences can never be printed normally; this will upset words like onto, for example. In real terminals, the first character of escape sequences is a special non-printing one (usually 'escape', which has ASCII code 27).

One way to do this problem is to have a variable to record the current state. For example, state 0 might mean "printing normal text". State 1 might mean "we have seen an o when in state 0". State 2 might mean "We have seen an f when in state 1" and so on. For each state there will be a series of special characters to look for, and actions to be taken if they are found, and a new value for the state. This can be done with conditional statements. This way to solve tricky logical problems is quite common, although the information is usually stored in an array called a lookup-table, rather than being programmed using conditionals.

9

Arrays

Objectives

Look at some of the sorts of problems that can be solved using arrays.

Understand how the C compiler handles arrays and array names.

Learn how to access the individual components of an array.
— linear arrays
— multi-dimensional arrays
— dangers of exceeding array bounds.

Gain skill in using some common programming techniques involving arrays.
— collecting values in an array
— searching for values in an array
— arrays of totals
— rearranging and sorting array elements.

How to decide whether an array is needed to solve a problem, and if so, how it should be used.

A C feature: initializing a variable at its declaration.

9.1 INTRODUCTION

We have previously seen in connection with strings that an array is a place in memory where we can store many values of a given type. They are needed in problems involving multiple data items that must be stored *concurrently* (i.e. at the same time). For example, we might need to *sort* data (i.e. rearrange it in some order). Names might be sorted in alphabetical order, and numbers might be sorted in ascending or descending numeric order. Sorting methods involve comparing each data item with various others, and are most easily done when all the data is loaded in memory at once.

We have already used arrays to store character data. Thus, in the array declared

```
char buf[50];
```

we can store up to 50 values of type `char`, remembering that to use this array as a string, the last `char` will be the terminating nul. You can create arrays of one or more elements containing any sort of data (subject to limitations such as the available memory in the computer). For example, to create an array that can store at least eight `floats`, we write

```
float fltarr[8];
```

We can store or retrieve values in any of the eight individual `floats` that make up this array. We call these individual `floats` the *elements* of the array. For example, `fltarr[5]` is element number 5 within the array declared above. To store a value there, we might write

```
fltarr[5] = 72.8;
```

and to retrieve it (for example, for printing) we could then write

```
printf("%f\n", fltarr[5]);
```

When we follow an array name by square brackets containing a number, as in these examples, we say we are *subscripting* the array. The number in brackets is called the *subscript*, or *index*. The subscripts start at zero (not one, as in many other languages), and the final subscript is one less than the number of elements. So, the subscripts of `fltarr` declared above will range from 0 to 7 (not 8). `fltarr[5]`, therefore, is actually the sixth element in the array.

We can think of an array as a collection of boxes, or pigeonholes, where we can store values, one per box. When handling array elements, do not confuse the **subscript** with the **contents**. We can think of the subscripts as numbers stuck to the outside of the boxes, as shown in Figure 9.1; they help us to locate a particular element in the array. In this respect they are exactly like the room numbers that a hotel fixes to the pigeonholes where they keep the room keys. The content of an array element is a value stored there; think of storing a value in an array element as equivalent to placing something in one of the boxes in Figure 9.1.

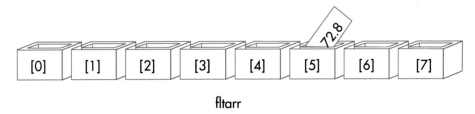

fltarr

Figure 9.1 An array is like a collection of boxes, each of which can store a single item

We are nearly ready to solve some problems using arrays, but there is one further fact of the greatest significance: **array subscripts do not have to be constants.** Thus, if the variable i, say, contains the number of the element we want to access, we may write fltarr[i] and the computer will look in i to decide which array element to use — if i contained 3, for example, this would be equivalent to writing fltarr[3]. This point is responsible for 99% of the usefulness of arrays.

9.2 STORING NUMERIC DATA

Consider the following problem. The program is to compute and display the mean (average) of a list of numbers entered by the user. Then it will display all numbers less than the mean. If the numbers represented student scores in a test, such a program might be useful in identifying those requiring extra tuition.

The difficulty with this problem is that we don't know the mean until we have examined every number. But any number might be less than the mean, even the very first one, so we need to look at each number twice: once to compute the mean and then again to compare it with the computed mean to see if we need to display that number for the user. Without arrays we would have to ask the user to type all the numbers twice. With an array we can remember all the input numbers. After computing the mean we can look through the array for the numbers that need to be displayed. Since an array has a maximum size, we must agree beforehand how many numbers the user will be allowed to type. Let us set a limit of 500 numbers.

As usual we start with main. The mean is the sum of the numbers divided by the number of numbers. Thus the program logic must be:

```
/* Ask the user how many numbers will be entered */
/* Read numbers into an array, summing and counting as we go. */
/* Divide the sum by the count to get the mean, and display. */
/* Look for, and display, numbers less than the mean. */
```

Listing 9-1a shows the program so far.

Listing 9-1a

```
/* A program to print numbers less than average.
   Input:  A number, N, at most MAXIMUM, then a list of N floats.
   Output: A message giving the mean of the numbers, then a list of
           those values less than the mean.
*/

#include <stdio.h>
#define MAXNUM 500        /* maximum number of numbers */

float enter_and_sum(float nums[],int amount_used); /* Returns the sum of
                                                      the entered values */

void display_low_values(float numbers[], float mean, int amount_used);

main() {
    float numbers[MAXNUM];  /* The numbers entered by the user */
    float mean, sum;
    int amount_used;

    /* Ask the user how many numbers will be entered */
    printf("How many numbers do you wish to enter? ");
    scanf("%d", &amount_used);

    /* Check that the user's request is OK */
    while (amount_used > MAXNUM) {
        printf("Sorry, that's too many.  Try again: ");
        scanf("%d", &amount_used);
    }

    /* Read numbers into array, summing and counting as we go. */
    sum = enter_and_sum(numbers, amount_used);

    /* Divide the sum by the count to get the mean, and display. */
    mean = sum/amount_used;
    printf("The mean is %f\n\nNumbers below mean:\n", mean);

    /* Look for, and display, numbers less than the mean. */
    display_low_values(numbers, mean, amount_used);
    return 0;
}
```

We have used a macro, MAXNUM, for the number of elements in the array. This is good practice as it makes the program easy to alter if some other value is required. We force the user to enter a number no bigger than MAXNUM, as it is a serious error to allow data to overflow an array. enter_and_sum stores the input values in numbers, and returns the sum of these values as its function result. Listing 9-1b shows enter_and_sum.

Listing 9-1b

```
/* enter_and_sum:
    Reads 'amount_to_read' input values, summing and counting the values.
    Does not check for erroneous input.
    Stores the values in its argument array, nums, and returns the sum
        as the function result.
*/
float enter_and_sum(float nums[], int amount_to_read) {
    int count;
    float sum;

    sum = 0.0;
    printf("Enter %d input numbers:\n", amount_to_read);
    for (count=0; count<amount_to_read; count++) {
        scanf("%f", &nums[count]);
        sum += nums[count];
    }

    return sum;
}
```

enter_and_sum follows the usual methods: the summing variable is zeroed before the loop, and progressively added to within it. Its parameter, nums, is really the array numbers, as that is the actual parameter given in the call in main. Then scanf reads one value into nums[count]; since count is incremented each time through the loop, the successive elements of nums, starting at element zero, are loaded with data. We do not necessarily fill up the entire array; if amount_to_read is less than MAXNUM, some array elements will be left unused. This is perfectly all right as long as we never try to use the elements in which we have placed no data. (They will contain garbage.)

display_low_values, which completes the program, is shown in Listing 9-1c.

Listing 9-1c

```
/* display_low_values:
    Looks at the first 'amount_used' numbers in the array 'numbers',
    displaying any that are less than the mean.
*/
void display_low_values(float numbers[], float mean, int amount_used) {
    int i;
    for (i=0; i<amount_used; i++) {
        if (numbers[i] < mean) {
            printf("%g\n", numbers[i]);
```

```
            }
        }
    }
```

Here is a sample run.

```
How many numbers do you wish to enter? 7
Enter 7 input numbers:
1.2
7.6 9.88
-.2
4.555
2.44
15.77
The mean is 5.892143

Numbers below mean:
1.2
-0.2
4.555
2.44
```

All problems like this which involve filling an array with data will have the same basic structure:

```
Set a counter to 0.
while (...not yet finished...) {
    ...Store a value in array[counter]...
    ...Add 1 to counter...
}
```

In the above problem this is done using a `for` loop instead of a `while` loop, but that is only a cosmetic difference. Increments to a counter alternate with assignments to array elements. Make sure the first step executed is an assignment, or element 0 of the array will contain garbage.

When should we use an array?

If we can solve a problem by accessing data values one at a time in the order they appear in the input, an array is not necessary; we can use a single variable, storing a value in it, processing it, and then simply overwriting it with the next value when we have finished. Arrays should only be used if no straightforward non-array solution is possible.

Deciding the length of an array

An array only needs to be large enough to store the exact number of items that will be placed in it. Do not be misled by the fact that `char` arrays used for holding strings are one larger than the maximum length string — this is because the terminating nul requires that extra character. For most other purposes using a special terminating value is not a good idea. A much better plan is to have a separate variable (such as `amount_used` in Listing 9-1a) for recording the number of items stored in the array.

9.3 USING ARRAY ELEMENTS TO REPRESENT CATEGORIES

Arrays are also used where the input data must be divided into various categories and some salient feature of each category is computed. For example, a professor might allocate student marks as integers in the range 0 to 10, and might wish to know how many students obtained each mark. In this case, each mark is a category. We allocate an array element to each of the eleven possible marks (0 to 10). Thus element 0 stores a fact about mark 0 (namely, how many students scored 0), element 1 about mark 1, and so on. As we input the marks, we use each one to tell us which array element must be altered. This is quite different from the plan in the previous section, where we stored the data itself in the array; there the data was used as array **contents**, but here it will be used as array **subscripts**. To make the problem slightly harder, let us print the professor's totals as a histogram, rather than as bare numbers.

It is clear that if each array element is a total (the number of students who scored a certain mark) they should all be zeroed before commencing. Our plan will therefore be

```
/* Zero all array elements. */
/* For each input number: */
    /* Add one to the appropriate array element. */
/* Display the histogram. */
```

Let us make a rule that a mark less than 0 signals the end of the data. This allows us to create the main function from the above plan, as shown in Listing 9-2a.

Listing 9-2a

```
/* Histogram of student marks.
   Input:  Integers representing student marks between 0 and 10.
   Output: A warning for any mark not between 0 and 10, and
           a histogram of number of students scoring each mark.
*/

#include <stdio.h>
#define MAXMARK 10       /* marks lie between 0 and MAXMARK */

void histogram(int mark_totals[]);   /* Display histogram of marks */
```

```
main() {
    int mark_totals[MAXMARK + 1];      /* note the "+1"! */
    int i, mark;

    /* Zero all array elements (ready for use as totals) */
    for (i=0; i<=MAXMARK; i++) {
        mark_totals[i] = 0;
    }

    /* Request input */
    printf("Enter the student marks, a negative value to end.\n");

    /* For each input number (no error check): */
    scanf("%d", &mark);
    while (mark >= 0) {
        /* Add one to the appropriate array element. */
        if (mark<=MAXMARK) {        /* Always guard against overflowing
                                       the array!! */
            mark_totals[mark]++;
        } else {
            printf("Warning: mark %d out of range.\n", mark);
        }
        /* Get next number */
        scanf("%d", &mark);
    }

    /* Display the histogram. */
    histogram(mark_totals);
    return 0;
}
```

Notice how the input value is used in the subscript position:

```
scanf("%d", &mark);
...
        mark_totals[mark]++;
```

This is because the input tells us which array element to modify. In histogram the situation is different, as the totals are the data we want plotted. For example, if marks[0] is 5, we want five asterisks on the 'zero' line of the histogram. Thus the array element becomes the upper limit of a for loop. Listing 9-2b completes the program.

Listing 9-2b

```
/* histogram: prints a histogram of mark totals */
void histogram(int mark_totals[]) {
    int mark, student;
    printf("\nHistogram of Students scoring each mark.\n\n");
    printf("Mark   Number of Students -->>\n");

    /* Print a line for each mark. */
    for (mark=0; mark<=MAXMARK; mark++) {
        /* Print a line:
            print the mark, and an asterisk for each student. */
        printf("%4d   ", mark);
        for (student=0; student<mark_totals[mark]; student++) {
            putchar('*');
        }
        /* end the line */
        putchar('\n');
    }
}
```

Sample run
```
Enter the student marks, a negative value to end.
2 4 6 7 1 5 2 4 5 6 7 8 2 5 4 6 4 5 5 7 10
0 11 6 5 9 2 2 5 8 7 7 7 6 4 5 8
Warning: mark 11 out of range.
2 6 7 5 9 8 5 6 3 -1

Histogram of Students scoring each mark.

Mark   Number of Students -->>
   0   *
   1   *
   2   ******
   3   *
   4   *****
   5   **********
   6   *******
   7   *******
   8   ****
   9   **
  10   *
```

As the structure of this program is so different from the one in the previous section, you may be tempted to try to learn various program types by rote. It can't be done. The only way to devise a correct program structure is to understand what is going on and why the right structure works. This program, for example, is the computerized equivalent of a well-known method of counting by hand. For road usage investigations, the government might send out spotters with a list of the various vehicle types, and every time the spotters see, say, a bus, they would put a tick in the 'bus' column on their counting sheet. The columns of the sheet are like the elements of the array above. Adding a tick in a column on paper is equivalent to adding one to the appropriate array element in the program. Just as seeing a bus tells the spotter which column to adjust, so reading a mark tells our program which array element to increment. If the spotters think they must write down 'bus' for every bus, 'car' for every car, etc., they are doing it wrongly, and their work is wasted. Similarly, if we had mistaken the nature of this problem as being the same as the one in the previous section, we would use the array wrongly, and no matter how long we toiled at it we would never get the program to work.

9.4 SEARCHING AND SORTING

Searching and sorting are two tasks commonly performed in circumstances where bulk data is involved, such as in arrays. *Searching* is looking for one or more items in the data. We have already seen an example of this in Listing 9-1, where we displayed items less than the average. We can think of that as the problem of finding those less-than-average items. The method we used — looking at every item for the ones we wanted — is called *sequential* searching, and is the simplest, but least efficient, method.

Sorting is rearranging the data in order. There are many kinds of 'order'. Character data is often sorted in alphabetic order, while numeric data is usually placed in either ascending or descending order. Searching and sorting are related topics because it is possible to search ordered data much faster than unordered data. Before writing a simple sorting program, let us start by solving a simpler problem: finding the largest value in an array.

Our problem will be as follows. Write a function `maxindex` that, given a `float` array, a low index, and a number of elements, searches for the largest value in the specified number of elements of the array starting at the low index; the function result will be the index of that value. For example, assuming `arr` is a `float` array, `maxindex(arr,2,3)` will return the index of the largest value in elements 2, 3, and 4 of the array. This is illustrated by the picture below.

*maxindex(arr,2,3) searches these elements,
and returns 3, the index of the element
in the range with the largest value.*

One way to do this is to remember the first value and its subscript, then compare the remaining values with it. Each time a larger value is found, replace the remembered value with the larger value, and the remembered subscript with the subscript where that larger value was found. When we get to the end, our remembered subscript is the place where the largest value is located. Listing 9-3 shows this function.

Listing 9-3   (Not a complete program)

```
/* maxindex: Tell which array element in a range has the largest value.
   Parameters: values:   the array to search,
               lowindex:  the index of the first element to examine,
               numvalues: the number of elements to examine.
   N.B. lowindex+numvalues must not exceed the declared
        array size, nor may numvalues be below 1, or lowindex
        below 0.
   Function result: the index of the largest element with a subscript
                    in the range lowindex ... lowindex+numvalues-1
                    inclusive.
*/
int maxindex(float values[], int lowindex, int numvalues) {
    int i, index, latest_max_index;
    float current_max;

    current_max = values[lowindex];     /* remember 1st value */
    latest_max_index = lowindex;        /* remember 1st index */

    /* Now loop, looking at numvalues-1 elements, starting just AFTER
       the element remembered above.  Note the use of two initializers
       and two increment assignments in the for loop heading.  This
       trick is accomplished using the 'comma' operator (','), which
       lets us write two expressions where normally only one would
       be allowed.  See appendix C. */

    for (i=1, index=lowindex+1; i<numvalues; i++, index++) {
        if (values[index] > current_max) {  /* found a bigger one... */
            current_max = values[index];     /* update max */
            latest_max_index = index;        /* update index */
        }
    }
    return latest_max_index;
}
```

It is easy to write a short test program to verify that this function works; this is left as an exercise. We shall now use it to write a function that sorts an array into descending order. In a list of numbers in descending order, what do we know about the first element? Right, it is the biggest. How about the second element? It is the second biggest — and so on. This suggests a way to proceed: first search the whole array for the largest value; the above function can do this. When we know where it is, swap it with the value in the first element. That will put the largest first. Then do the same again, but with one fewer values commencing at the second element. That will place the second largest value second. If we keep repeating this process until we have put the second smallest value in second last place, the array will be sorted. (We need not look at the smallest value, as it must be in the right place: a list of one item is always sorted.)

The following diagram shows this process being used to sort a list of five values. The sorted elements are shown in **bold**.

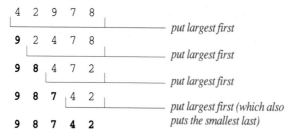

In this example it turns out that the list is sorted after the third scan. This is a variation known as the *selection* sort. Listing 9-4 shows a function, sort, that performs this sort, along with a test main function. The function maxindex from Listing 9-3 is also needed, but is not repeated in 9-4 for brevity. This is the easiest sorting method to understand, but unfortunately it is not very efficient on large arrays. For more than say, 50 items a better method would usually be preferable. Another simple but inefficient sort is *bubble sort* (see Exercise 2 in 9.7); faster sorting methods include *shell sort* and *quick sort*.

Listing 9-4

```
/* The function sort(), with a test main().
   Input:   A list of at most MAXNUM (see below) floats typed by the
            user.  The end is detected by looking for an illegal number,
            for example, the letter 'X'.
   Output: (Generated by a 'temporary' printf inside sort) the array
            after each pass of the sorting algorithm, ending with
            the fully sorted array.
*/

#include <stdio.h>
#include <stdlib.h>
#define MAXNUM 500      /* maximum number of numbers */

int enter_and_count(float nums[]);
int maxindex(float values[], int lowindex, int numvalues);
void sort(float data[], int count);

main() {
    float numbers[MAXNUM];   /* The numbers entered by the user */
    int count;

    /* Read numbers into array, summing and counting as we go. */
    count = enter_and_count(numbers);

    sort(numbers, count);
    printf("Array sorted\n");
    return 0;
}
```

```
/* enter_and_count:
   Reads input, counting the values, stopping when scanf fails to read
   a number.  Stores the values in its argument array, nums, and
   returns a count of the number of items input.
*/
int enter_and_count(float nums[]) {
    int scan_status, count;
    float x;
    printf("Enter all input numbers:\n");
    count = 0;
    scan_status = scanf("%f", &x);
    while (scan_status == 1 /* scanf input OK */) {
        if (count >= MAXNUM) {            /* Too many numbers? */
            printf("ERROR: Too many input numbers\n");
            exit(EXIT_FAILURE);
        }
        nums[count] = x;                  /* Store number in array */
        count++;                          /* Count that number */
        scan_status = scanf("%f", &x);    /* get next number */
    }
    return count;
}


/* sort: sorts its argument array in descending order.
   Arguments:
       data: the array to sort.  count: number of values in data.
*/
void sort(float data[], int count) {
    void display(float data[], int count); /* Function to output array */
    int num_of_passes,      /* Num. of passes needed to sort the array */
        completed_passes,   /* how many passes are complete */
                            /* NB: also the index of the first item */
                            /* to scan in a pass */
        items_to_scan,      /* no. of items to examine this pass */
        max_item;           /* index of max. item in relevant region */
    float temp;             /* a temporary. */

    /* temporary output, just to demonstrate how it works: */
    printf("Initial order: ");
    display(data, count);

    /* Set up for pass one. */
    num_of_passes = count - 1;
    completed_passes = 0;   /* none done yet */
    items_to_scan = count; /* on first pass, scan all elements */

    while (completed_passes < num_of_passes) {
        /* Invariant: data[0] to data[completed_passes-1] are sorted,
           and larger than any item in data[completed_passes] to
           data[count-1].
        */

        /* Locate the biggest item */
        max_item = maxindex(data, completed_passes, items_to_scan);
```

```
        /* Now swap the biggest item with the first. */
        temp = data[completed_passes];  /* store first item */
        data[completed_passes] = data[max_item];
                                        /* put largest first */
        data[max_item] = temp;          /* put old first item where
                                           max item used to be. */

        /* prepare for next pass */
        completed_passes++;
        items_to_scan--;

        /* temporary output, just to demonstrate how it works: */
        printf("After pass %2d: ", completed_passes);
        display(data, count);
    }
}

void display(float data[], int count) {
    int i;
    for (i=0; i<count; i++) {
        printf(" %5.2f", data[i]);
    }
    putchar('\n');
}
```

Sample run

```
Enter all input numbers:
1.1 9.8 4.5 7.66 5.0 5.55
X
Initial order:    1.10   9.80   4.50   7.66   5.00   5.55
After pass  1:    9.80   1.10   4.50   7.66   5.00   5.55
After pass  2:    9.80   7.66   4.50   1.10   5.00   5.55
After pass  3:    9.80   7.66   5.55   1.10   5.00   4.50
After pass  4:    9.80   7.66   5.55   5.00   1.10   4.50
After pass  5:    9.80   7.66   5.55   5.00   4.50   1.10
Array sorted
```

9.5 MULTI-DIMENSIONAL ARRAYS; INITIALIZATION

In C we can have an array of any type of data. We are even allowed to have arrays whose individual elements are themselves arrays. If we do this, we have what is called a *multi-dimensional* array. There are generous limits (which you are not likely to exceed) to the depth to which you can nest arrays within arrays. Thus there are two-dimensional arrays (an array of arrays, sometimes called a *matrix* or *table*), three-dimensional arrays (an array of arrays of arrays), and so on. One use of two-dimensional arrays is storing mathematical matrices. For example, this matrix

```
1    3    2
4   -8    7
```

is a 2-by-3 matrix (two rows of three columns). A C array capable of storing it would be declared as follows:

```
float mat[2][3];
```

Such an array can be imagined as a rectangular array of boxes, as Figure 9-2 illustrates.

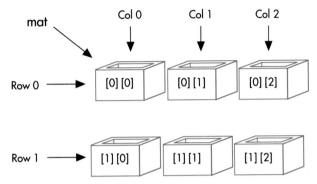

Figure 9.2 Layout of elements in a two-dimensional array

We can initialize `mat` to the matrix above with assignment statements

```
mat[0][0] = 1;
mat[0][1] = 3;
mat[0][2] = 2;
mat[1][0] = 4;
mat[1][1] = -8;
mat[1][2] = 7;
```

or input the values in a nested loop (assuming `i` and `j` are `int` variables):

```
for (i=0; i<2; i++) {
    for (j=0; j<3; j++) {
        scanf("%f", &mat[i][j]);
    }
}
```

The user would type the values in the order: 1 3 2 4 –8 7.

Important difference between C and other languages

In C, to refer to an element of a two-dimensional array we must write

```
arrayname[subscript][subscript]
```

as in the examples above. We cannot write

```
arrayname[subscript,subscript]
```

as this is not a two-dimensional array reference in C, even though it is in many other languages. Instead, in C it is a usage of the 'comma' operator, an example of which occurred in Listing 9-3.

9.5.1 *Initialization during declaration*

There is yet another way to set up the previous array to contain the above matrix. It is possible to initialize any variable at the time we declare it. This is sometimes useful with simple variables, but it is a great boon when arrays are involved. Let us first see how to do it with a simple variable. Instead of writing

```
int number;    /* the declaration of number */
number = 5;    /* the initialization */
```
we are allowed to write

```
int number = 5;  /* combined declaration and initialization */
```

The initialization expression must be constant, except for simple local variables, for which non-constant expressions are allowed. Arrays are initialized by a list of values in braces, as follows:

```
int values[5] = { 3, 5, 18, -6, 2 };
```

We need not provide a value for every element, but we should never rely on the contents of uninitialized elements. (C automatically initializes some variables to zero, namely those that exist for the duration of the program execution (called *static* duration). Normally this means that global variables, but not local variables, are automatically initialized. We shall never use this feature in this text, as it is much clearer to explicitly initialize all variables whose values we rely on.) When initializing in a declaration, we may omit the array size, in which case the compiler assumes it is the same as the number of elements provided for initialization. So the above could be simplified as:

```
int values[] = { 3, 5, 18, -6, 2 };
```

We can do a similar thing with two-dimensional arrays, this time with two levels of braces. Therefore the simplest way to declare the above array mat and initialize it to the matrix shown is:

```
float mat[2][3] = {
    { 1,  3, 2 },
    { 4, -8, 7 }
};
```
Don't forget this semicolon.

When initializing multi-dimensional arrays, only the first subscript may have its size omitted, as otherwise the compiler is not sure of the array's shape and so cannot generate correct machine code. Thus instead of mat[2][3] in the previous example, we may write mat[][3], but we may not write mat[][] or mat[2][].

Another use of two-dimensional arrays involves strings. Since a string needs an array of char, obviously an array of strings must be a two-dimensional array of char. For example

```
char names[3][21];
```

provides space to store three names, each of up to 20 usable characters. Here is how we might declare and initialize it:

```
char names[3][21] = {
    { 'F', 'r', 'e', 'd', '\0' },
    { 'M', 'a', 'r', 'y', '\0' },
    { 'S', 'u', 'e', '\0' }
};
```

We have loaded individual characters just as we loaded individual floats earlier. Luckily there is a shortcut when initializing an array of char:

```
char names[3][21] = {
    "Fred",
    "Mary",
    "Sue"
};
```

Each string is used to initialize a single row of the array.

When using an array, we may write expressions with fewer subscripts than the array possesses. For example, although the array mat used earlier has two subscripts, we might write

```
some_function(mat[i]);
```

This has the same effect as the name of an array of **one fewer dimensions**. So, as mat is a two-dimensional table, mat[i] is the name of a one-dimensional row. Thus the imaginary function some_function, called above, would have to be declared

```
void some_function(float some_name[]);
```

Extending this principle to three dimensions, suppose we have an array declared:

```
int Any[4][2][3];
```

Any is an array of ints with four layers, each with two rows of three columns. So Any[2], for example, refers to layer 2 (i.e. the third layer) which is a two-dimensional array of two rows of three columns. Any[2][0] is row 0 of layer 2 of Any, that is, a single-dimension array of three elements. Any[2][0][1] is not an array at all; it is an int variable at position 1 in row 0 of layer 2 of Any. This is illustrated in Figure 9-3.

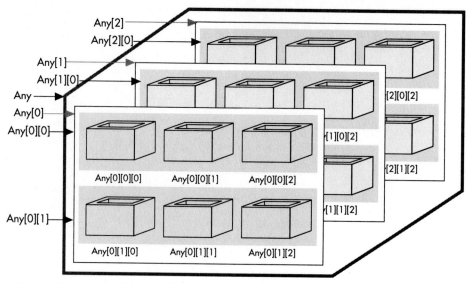

Figure 9.3 Layout of a three-dimensional array

We might use a three-dimensional array to store a collection of matrices (where each individual matrix is two-dimensional); in general, whenever we need a collection of something else, where that something is an array, our collection will need one more dimension than the things being collected.

9.5.2 Example: Matrix multiplication

We shall now write a program to multiply two matrices and output the product. If you haven't seen matrix multiplication before, just trust it and look at how the calculations are written in C. We shall limit the matrix sizes to a maximum of 5×5. When forming the product C of two matrices A and B, the elements of the product matrix are

c_{ik} = the sum over all j of $(a_{ij} \times b_{jk})$

This means that A must have the same number of columns as B has rows. We must check that also. We shall use an array of character strings to print our user prompts. The program plan will be:

```
Ask size of matrix A, check size.
Ask size of matrix B, check size.
Check sizes of A and B are compatible.
Input matrix A.
Input matrix B.
Multiply A and B giving matrix C.
Display matrix C.
```

Listing 9-5a shows a partly developed program following this specification.

Listing 9-5a

```
/* Program to input, multiply, and print two matrices. */

#define MAX 5    /* maximum row & column sizes */
#include <stdio.h>
#include <stdlib.h>    /* for exit() */

int rowsizes[2], colsizes[2]; /* row and column sizes of the
                                 input matrices. */
char matrix_name[2][8] = {    /* names for the input matrices */
    "first",
    "second"
};

float A[MAX][MAX], B[MAX][MAX], C[MAX][MAX];  /* the matrices */

/* function definitions: */
void get_size_and_check(int which_matrix) ;
void input_matrix(int which_matrix, float mat[MAX][MAX]);
void form_product(void);
void display_result(void);

main() {
    int i;
    /* Ask and check sizes of matrices. */
    for (i=0; i<2; i++) {
        get_size_and_check(i /* which matrix */);
    }

    if (colsizes[0] != rowsizes[1]) {  /* Sizes compatible? */
        printf("Matrix sizes are not compatible.\n");
        exit(EXIT_FAILURE);
    }

    /* Input matrices. */
    input_matrix(0 /* which matrix */, A);
    input_matrix(1 /* which matrix */, B);

    form_product();       /* Multiply giving matrix C. */

    display_result();     /* Display matrix C. */
    return 0;
}

void get_size_and_check(int which_matrix) {
    printf (
        "Enter row and column sizes for the %s matrix: ",
        matrix_name[which_matrix]
    );
    scanf("%d%d", &rowsizes[which_matrix], &colsizes[which_matrix]);
    if (rowsizes[which_matrix] > MAX || colsizes[which_matrix] > MAX) {
```

```
        printf("Error: maximum %d rows and columns.\n", MAX);
        exit(EXIT_FAILURE);
    }
}
```

Notice how in get_size_and_check, printf is given the expression matrix_name[which_matrix] to fill a %s format. Since matrix_name is a two-row matrix, matrix_name[which_matrix] refers to just one of those rows — in other words, a single string (either 'first' or 'second', depending on whether which_matrix is 0 or 1). Initialized arrays of strings are very useful if a program has many messages to generate and the appropriate message can be selected according to the value of some integer. Listing 9-5b shows the remaining three functions.

Listing 9-5b

```
void input_matrix(int which_matrix, float mat[MAX][MAX]) {
    int row, col;
    printf("Enter %s matrix:\n", matrix_name[which_matrix]);
    for (row=0; row<rowsizes[which_matrix]; row++) {
        for (col=0; col<colsizes[which_matrix]; col++) {
            scanf("%f", &mat[row][col]);
        }
    }
}

void form_product(void) {
    int i, j, k;
    for (i=0; i<rowsizes[0]; i++) { /*for each row in the matrix C*/
        for (k=0; k<colsizes[1]; k++){ /*for each column in the matrix C*/
            /* sum the partial products */
            float sum = 0.0;
            for (j=0; j<colsizes[0]; j++) {
                sum += A[i][j] * B[j][k];
            }
            C[i][k] = sum;
        }
    }
}

void display_result(void) {
    int r, c;
    printf("Product:\n");
    for (r=0; r<rowsizes[0]; r++) {        /* for each row, */
        for (c=0; c<colsizes[1]; c++) {  /* print all columns, */
            printf("%6.2f ", C[r][c]);
        }
        putchar('\n');                    /* and go to a fresh line */
    }
}
```

Sample run
```
Enter row and column sizes for the first matrix: 2 2
Enter row and column sizes for the second matrix: 2 2
Enter first matrix:
1   2
3   4
Enter second matrix:
1   0
-1  1
Product:
 -1.00   2.00
 -1.00   4.00
```

9.6 SUMMARY

- An array is a region of memory capable of storing many data values of some given type.
  - The array declaration specifies how many values the array must be able to hold.
  - The individual *elements* of the array may be referred to by their *subscript*, for example `a[i]`.
  - Subscripts range in value from zero to one less than the size of the array.
  - It is wrong to try to access an array element with a subscript outside the above range. Program errors will result.
- Arrays may be used when a problem requires the storage of bulk data. This is likely if
  - the data will be referred to out of order or more than once, or
  - many similar pieces of information must be calculated, for example, totals of values falling within various categories.
- An array with one subscript is called a *linear* array.
  - Example of declaration: `char buf[50];`
  - Example of access: `printf("%s %c", buf, buf[25]);`
- An array with two subscripts is called a *rectangular* array.
  - Example of declaration: `char buf[5][50];`
  - Example of access: `printf("%s %c", buf[4], buf[3][15]);`
  - Useful for storing matrices, tables of data, and lists of strings.
- Array subscripts may be variables or expressions. Therefore we can compute on-the-fly which element we wish to access. Most programs using arrays rely heavily on this feature.
- *Searching* is looking for some particular value, or group of values, in an array.
- *Sorting* is rearranging an array in some order, for example, ascending or descending numeric order, or (for strings) alphabetically.
  - To search for something in an unsorted array, we must look at every array element.
  - There are ways of searching sorted arrays that are much faster.

- A variable or array may be initialized at the same time as it is declared. For example, `int group[5] = {2, 4, 3, 76, -4};`
  - We do not have to initialize the entire array.
  - We may omit the first array subscript size, in which case the compiler assumes the array has the same number of elements as we supply values, e.g. `int group[] = {2, 4, 3, 76, -4};`

9.7 SELF-TEST EXERCISES

Short Answer

1 State whether the following code fragments are legal or illegal. For the illegal ones, say why.

```
a   char fred [][5] = {"Hi", "there"};
b   char fred [][6] = {"Hi", "there"};
c   char fred [][] = {"Hi", "there"};
d   char fred [2][6] = {"Hi", "there"};
e   char fred [2][] = {"Hi", "there"};
f   int x[7]; x[6] = 2;
g   int x[6]; x[6] = 2;
h   int x[6] = {3, 54, 19};
i   int x[2] = {3, 54, 19};
j   char buf[20]; scanf("%19s", buf);
```

Programming

2 Write a program to input a list of at most 20 `floats` and sort and output them in ascending order. It should include a sorting function that uses the *bubblesort* method. Bubblesort works as follows: scan through the array, comparing each element with the one following (be careful not to look beyond the end of the array). If any comparison shows that the earlier element is larger than the later one, exchange the two elements. If this process is performed $n-1$ times, where n is the array size, then the array will be sorted. If you think about the process carefully, you will see that the range to be sorted can be reduced by one on each pass.

3 In the espionage business, one of the things you simply must do is send all your messages in code, and your opponents have to try to break your code. One thing you need to break a code is a table showing the relative frequencies of the various letters as they occur in normal English text. Write a program to input normal text until it encounters a blank line. The program should, for each letter (a–z), record how many times it occurs, and how many times it occurs at the start of a word (i.e. not preceded by another letter). After reading the text, print out a table with headings, showing each letter and these two frequencies expressed as a percentage of the total number of letters seen overall. Do not distinguish between upper-case and lower-case letters; count them both together.

9.8 TEST QUESTIONS

Short Answer

1   An array is to be used to hold three tables of fractional numbers, where each table has 40 rows of 10 columns each. How many dimensions must the table have? Write a suitable C declaration.

2   State whether the following are true or false.

a   An array may have no more than three dimensions.

b   When assigning a value to an array element, as in

```
x[3][10] = 2.8;
```

we are allowed to omit the first subscript to the array.

c   An array declared int x[100]; provides room for exactly 99 ints.

d   A char array may be used to store a string.

e   No char array may be longer than 80 characters.

f   If we don't know when writing the program how big an array will be, we may use a variable for the size in the declaration, for example

```
int xx[j];
```

g   The last element of an array must always contain the largest value.

h   The first element in a one-dimension array has subscript zero.

i   It is allowable to use only a part of an array.

j   The following code sets all elements of the array bb to one:

```
int bb[10], i;
for (i=9;i>=0;i--) {
    bb[i] = 1;
}
```

k   The following code sets all elements of the array bb to one:

```
int bb[10], i;
bb[0] = 1;
for (i=1;i<=9;i++) {
    bb[i] = bb[i-1];
}
```

l   The following code sets all elements of the array bb to one:
```
int bb[10], i;
bb[0] = 1;
for (i=0;i<=8;i++) {
    bb[i] = bb[i+1];
}
```

3   Draw a picture similar to Figure 9.3 showing the structure of the two-dimensional array matrix_name declared in Listing 9-5a.

Programming

4 Write a program that allows you to input up to 20 names of maximum length 40, and sorts these names into alphabetic order and outputs them.

5 Write a program that inputs up to 100 positive `ints` (a negative value ends the input) and outputs them in reverse order.

6 Write a program to help an investor predict the movement in the value of a company's stock. Your program should input daily stock prices for up to sixty days, and display them in a histogram chart, printed in the normal horizontal direction (the hard way!). For example, if the input values ranged from $10.10 to $10.50, the output might be:

```
$10.50 |                    **
$10.40 |               ****  **              **
$10.30 |    *    ****     ****** ***    *   ***   ****
$10.20 |*** ********  ************    **  ***** *******
$10.10 |***********************************************
       +---------------------------------------------
```

The minimum and maximum values to plot, and the labels, should be determined by the program from the input values.

7 Pascal's triangle is a triangle of numbers computed according to the following rule: The first line has a single number, 1, and each successive line has another 1 added to the end. Each number on a line except the end numbers is the sum of the two numbers above. Here are the first few lines of the triangle:

```
        1
      1   1
    1   2   1
  1   3   3   1
1   4   6   4   1
```

Mathematics students will recognize these values as being very important indeed. Write a program to input the number of lines of the triangle required, up to a maximum of ten, and to generate and print that many lines.

8 Write a program that reads input until it sees a line commencing with a '~'. It should print whatever it reads in two 'newspaper' columns thirty characters wide and twenty lines deep, with eight spaces between columns. That is, each successive line of input goes below the previous line in the same column, and when the first column is full, the next line starts at the top of the second column. If any input line is longer than thirty characters, fold it (i.e. the line is split after thirty characters, and the rest is placed in the next row). This might need repeating multiple times for very long lines. When a page is full, leave a four-line gap. You might want to use input redirection to test this program, as typing lots of text to do a single test will be quite painful. Don't forget, the final page might not be completely full.

9   *Insertion sort* works by starting with an empty array, and placing values in it one by one. Each value is placed in its correct position among the elements placed previously. So, if at some point the array has, say, six items (i.e. elements 0 ... 5 contain data) and a value occurs that belongs, say, at position 3, then the existing contents of elements 3 ... 5 are shifted to positions 4 ... 6 to make room, and the new value is inserted at position 3. Write a program that uses insertion sort to sort a list of input integers. Warning: be careful how you do the shifting of existing elements.

10 Write a simple program to do matrix computations. It should commence by inputting two 2×2 matrices, then asking which operation to perform. The user should be able to respond with +, −, or *, and then the program should print the appropriate computed matrix.

11 (More challenging.) Write a more realistic matrix manipulation program. It should contain room for storing ten matrices up to size 5×5, and should recognize and respond to the following commands:

I0 ... I9	Input a matrix. It should ask the user the size of the matrix, then input the appropriate matrix. That is, the command I0 inputs matrix zero, I1 inputs matrix 1, and so on.
P0 ... P9	Output a matrix. Prints the specified matrix (0 to 9).
*ijk	(where i, j, and k are one-digit integers) Multiplies matrices i and j, storing the result in matrix k.
+ijk	Ditto for addition.
−ijk	Subtracts matrix j from matrix i, storing the result in matrix k.
Q	Quit.

12 Similar to the above question, but instead of matrices, write a complex number calculator. You can have an additional command in this one, /ijk, which divides i by j giving k.

13 For some problems the range of values that can be stored in an `int`, or even a `long`, is insufficient. Write a program that allows you to input two numbers of up to 200 decimal digits each, and that adds them and prints the total. Each number can be stored in an array of `char` or `int`, one digit per element, and the addition can be performed by adding corresponding digits from the two numbers, starting with the least significant (righthand side) digit, and carrying 1 to the next place along whenever necessary — in other words, an automated version of the addition method we learn in school as children.

14 Write a function with two `float` array parameters that will input the coefficients of a polynomial into an array, and then compute and place into a second array the coefficients of the derivative of the polynomial. In each array, element zero should store the constant term, element one the linear term, element two the square term, and so on. Use the fact that the derivative of ax^n is anx^{n-1}. The function will also need an `int` parameter telling how many terms are in the polynomial. After

testing this function, place it in your personal function library, with an entry in your personal .h header file.

15 Using the function described in the previous question, write a more general version of Newton's method for finding the zero of a polynomial (described in Test Question 20 in Chapter 6). Your program should allow the user to enter a polynomial of up to ten terms, along with an initial guess of the location of the zero. Then it should find the location of the zero accurate to 0.000001 or report failure if the solution does not converge.

16 In processing customer orders a business wishes to ensure that all items ordered are valid. Write a program that first inputs the code numbers, prices, descriptions, and quantity on hand, of up to 100 products. Code zero indicates the end of the list. Then it should input customer name, and code numbers and quantities for items ordered by the customer. An invoice should be printed with detail lines showing the name and code for each item ordered, quantity supplied, and the total cost. Place headings over the columns, and include a title that contains the customer's name. Finally a grand total cost should be displayed. Include error messages if the code for an item ordered does not match any item in stock, or if more items are ordered than are in stock (supply as many as possible).

17 An ancient way for finding prime numbers is called the *sieve of Eratosthenes* after the Greek mathematician who discovered it. He wrote down a long list of numbers starting with 2. (The more written down, the more primes one can find.) The number 2 is the first prime number. Since no multiple of 2 can be prime, Eratosthenes crossed out every multiple of 2 on his long list. Looking at the list, he saw that 3 was not crossed out; 3 is therefore also prime, but none of its multiples can be, so all multiples of 3 must be crossed out. Looking ahead, 5 is the next number still uncrossed, so it must be prime, and so on. Write a program to print prime numbers that uses this method. It is easy to automate. Allocate an array element to each number from 2 to n (where n can be any value, limited only by computer storage and time available; for example, 1000 should work fine). Initialize them all to the same value, say 1. That will stand for an uncrossed-out value. Then, to cross out a value, change the corresponding array element from 1 to 0.

18 An ancient way to encrypt messages is to translate each letter of the alphabet into some other letter. Nowadays this is considered a 'toy' encryption method; it is quite easy to break, even by hand, but still it will probably fool half the people half the time. Write a program that uses a translation table to encode a message read from its input. A translation table is an array that has an entry for each letter of the alphabet, containing some other letter. The message is translated by looking up each letter in the table and finding out which other letter to substitute. For simplicity, characters that are not letters should be output unmodified. The program can be run with input and output redirection to read and write on files. The decoder is the same program, but with an inverse translation table — one that undoes the effect of the first.

19 For a more useful version of the previous program, do not include a fixed translation table. Instead, use the library `rand` (random number) function to initialize the table randomly. Ask the user for a code number, and use it in conjunction with `srand` to set a random starting point for `rand`. (See `rand` and `srand` in Appendix D.) This will take some thought to do properly. The decoder will have to first set up the same table as the encoder and deduce the inverse table from it. Of course, unless the same code number is entered by the user, the inverse table will not correctly decode the message. Finally, there is a simple way to make the inverse table the same as the forward table, which means that one does not need a separate decoder program. Can you see how?

20 A guessing game that used to be popular was Moo. The computer 'thinks' of a four-digit number, and the player must guess it. For each digit that the player guesses correctly and in the correct position, the computer records a "bull"; for each correct digit in the wrong position, it records a "cow". Then it shows the number of bulls and cows. Here is a sample game.

```
Your guess? 1234
BC
Your guess? 1256
miss!
Your guess? 3784
BBCC
Your guess? 3874
CORRECT! 4 guesses is pretty darn good!
```

Get the digits for the number using `rand`. `srand` can be initialized by asking the user for the seed value. Encourage the player with the following messages: "Pretty darn good!" for fewer than five guesses, "Quite good!" for five or six guesses, "Reasonable." for seven to nine guesses, and "Not the best I've seen." for ten or more guesses.

21 Test Question 11 in Chapter 8 simulated the behavior of a processor controlling a terminal or other device. Rewrite your solution to that problem to use a lookup table for state changes instead of a series of conditional statements. A two-dimensional array is needed; for example, there could be one row for each possible character (256 entries), each row having one entry for each possible state. The table contains the new state to be adopted when the given character is seen in the given state. For example, if our table is called `new_state`, and we see character `ch` when in state `state`, we can update `state` with a statement such as

```
state = new_state[ch][state];
```

This will replace the conditionals needed previously. This array will be fairly large, and most entries will be zero, so to set up the table it might be easiest to initialize it all to zero, and then assign just the non-zero entries. A table used this way is called a *transition matrix*. It is usually more efficient, but for complex problems it may need a very large table. Methods exist for compressing such tables to reduce the wastage of so many zero entries.

22 Conway's *Life* is a special kind of game called *cellular automata*. It isn't a game against an opponent, rather just a spectator sport. It is played out on an infinite chess board, where each square is either alive or dead. A live square stays alive if it has two or three live neighbors, and dies otherwise; a dead square comes alive if it has exactly three live neighbors. All births and deaths take place simultaneously. Write a program to allow you to input locations of live squares on a 20 by 20 board (no, we can't really have an infinite one — assume that squares beyond the boundaries are dead) and then print out subsequent 'generations' of the pattern. Show live squares by an asterisk, dead ones by a blank. You will need two arrays to do this properly; load the initial pattern into one array and compute the next generation in the other. Print the new pattern, and then have the arrays change places for the next cycle. If your program is working properly, the following pattern will show a glider hitting a brick:

```
**
**


   ***
   *
    *
```

23 It is said that if a deck of cards is given perfect shuffles enough times it will return to its original order. A perfect shuffle is done by splitting the deck exactly in half and interleaving the cards from the two halves; that is, the first card is from the first half, the second from the second half, the third from the first half, and so on. Write a program to find out if this is true, for up to 20 perfect shuffles. The program should display the original deck order and the order after each shuffle. For example

```
AH  2H  3H  4H  5H  6H  7H  8H  9H  10H  JH  QH  KH
AC  2C  3C  4C  5C  6C  7C  8C  9C  10C  JC  QC  KC
AD  2D  3D  4D  5D  6D  7D  8D  9D  10D  JD  QD  KD
AS  2S  3S  4S  5S  6S  7S  8S  9S  10S  JS  QS  KS

AH  AD  2H  2D  3H  3D  4H  4D  5H  5D  6H  6D  7H
7D  8H  8D  9H  9D  10H  10D  JH  JD  QH  QD  KH  KD
AC  AS  2C  2S  3C  3S  4C  4S  5C  5S  6C  6S  7C
7S  8C  8S  9C  9S  10C  10S  JC  JS  QC  QS  KC  KS
```

…etc. If the original order is restored, print out how many shuffles were needed.

Text files

Objectives

Appreciate the importance of storing data in files.

Know what text files are, and how to access them in C.
— FILE pointers
— opening and closing files – `fopen`, `fclose`.

Be able to input text data from files.
— the **end of file** concept – detecting end of file
— file input functions: `getc`, `fscanf`, `fgets`
— the standard input, `stdin`.

Be able to create text files and write data to them.
— file output functions: `putc`, `fprintf`, `fputs`
— the standard output, `stdout`
— he standard error output, `stderr`.

Study some important techniques used in processing files.

(Optional) Study formatted in-memory conversion functions, `sprintf` and `sscanf`.

10.1 STORING DATA IN FILES; TEXT AND BINARY FILE TYPES

This chapter deals with one of the two main types of computer files — text files. *Text files* store readable character data; this includes any file that can be created with a normal text editor, such as the C source programs you will have written while studying earlier chapters. They also include files containing Shakespearian sonnets, numbers represented in readable form, letters to clients, and so on. The other main type, *binary files*, are the subject of another chapter, but briefly, they contain data represented in the computer's internal formats — mainly binary numbers. Binary files are not intelligible by humans unless the data is converted into character form. The distinction between text and binary files does not depend on the sort of information in a file — a file of numbers can still be a text file, provided the numbers are represented as readable ASCII characters. This distinction is examined further in Chapter 16.

In studying text files, you will be pleased to hear that you already know almost the entire story. Merely by entering a C source program with an editor you have created a text file. In using input or output redirection you have caused your programs to read and write such files. All that remains is to learn how to write programs that can control the reading and writing of files without resorting to the trick of redirection. This makes some powerful data processing techniques available to us.

10.2 OVERVIEW OF FILE PROCESSING IN C

C, unlike many programming languages, does not contain any built-in facilities for input-output (including file processing). Everything is done using functions in the standard library. The library facilities use a data type called the `FILE`. (The word must be written in capital letters.) A variable of this type contains all the information needed by the library functions to read or write data in a file. We never need to know anything about what is stored in a `FILE` variable — in fact, we never actually create these variables ourselves, as the library functions take care of the entire job. Our job is to simply follow a fixed pattern of operations whenever we want to use a file; if we follow the standard 'plan', the C library will ensure that everything works. The plan has four steps:

1 Declare a `FILE` *pointer variable*. (We have not studied pointer variables yet, so we shall take a 'sneak preview' of them in this section.)
2 *Open* the file using the library function, `fopen`. This connects our `FILE` pointer to an actual file. We can tell `fopen` the name of the file, whether we wish to read or write it, and other details. In this step we also check that the file is opened successfully. A connection to a file via a `FILE` pointer is called a *stream*.
3 Process the data in the file using suitable library functions. Probably this step will involve a loop to read or write many items in the file.
4 When we have completely finished with the file we close it with the function `fclose`. This step disconnects our program from the file and makes sure that the file is left in a proper state. This is especially important when writing a file; if we

forget to close a file we may find it is left in a corrupt state; for example, data may be missing.

Steps 2 to 4 all use the `FILE` pointer declared in step 1. The `FILE` pointer is the means of telling the various library functions which file to operate on. We can operate on more than one file at a time; we simply declare a `FILE` pointer for each one and follow steps 2 to 4 for each file. A common processing pattern is to have two files, one for input and one for output; open them both and, in a loop, read data from one file, process it, and write results to the other file. Then both files are closed.

Preview of pointer variables

From Chapter 3 you will be aware that a pointer is an address of a location in memory. We can declare variables to store such addresses by placing the pointer symbol, `*`, before a variable name in a declaration. Thus

```
int i, *ip;
```

declares two variables, a normal `int` called `i` and an `int` **pointer** called `ip`. `ip` is not itself an `int`; rather, it stores the address of an `int`. Moving on to `FILE`s, then, if we plan to input from one file and output to another, we will need two `FILE` pointer variables, so we might write

```
FILE *in_file, *out_file;
```

which declares two `FILE` pointers, `in_file` and `out_file`. **The pointer symbol must be repeated for each variable**. This is all we need to know about pointers for now, as the library functions do all the required manipulations of these pointers behind the scenes.

10.3 FILE OUTPUT

Both input and output operations on files closely parallel the normal input-output operations we have been using until now. In many cases the only difference is that we call a differently named function and supply an extra argument, the `FILE` pointer. For example, instead of calling `printf`, which outputs to the screen, we call `fprintf` (f for file). Listing 10-1 shows a program that writes an ASCII character code table to a file called "ascii".

Listing 10-1

```
/* Program to generate a file called "ascii" containing a
   table of ASCII codes. This requires a computer using ASCII
   codes in order to work correctly.
*/

/* We use the fact that the first printable ASCII character is
```

```
    the space, and the last is '~'.  For other character code
    conventions (such as EBCDIC), this must be changed.
*/
#define FIRSTCHAR (' ')
#define LASTCHAR ('~')

#include <stdio.h>
#include <stdlib.h>
void create_table(FILE *f);

main() {

    /* Step 1: declare the FILE pointer. */
    FILE *outfile;

    /* Step 2a: attempt to open the file for writing. */
    outfile = fopen("ascii", "w");
        /* Note: first parameter is file name, second is access
                 mode ("w" means "write").  */

    /* Step 2b: check whether we succeeded in opening the file. */
    if (outfile == NULL) {
        printf("ERROR: Could not open file \"ascii\"\n");
        exit(EXIT_FAILURE);
    }

    /* (Here we are sure the file is open for writing.)
        Step 3: Write all required information to the file. */
    create_table(outfile);

    /* Step 4: close the file. */
    fclose(outfile);

    /* At this point, the completed file should exist on the disk. */
    return 0;
}

/******* create_table ********
 Creates a table showing ASCII codes for all printable characters
 in five columns, with headings.
 On Entry: 'outfile' must refer to a file correctly opened for output.
           The file must not end with a partially-complete output line.
 On Exit:  The table will be appended to the file, which is still open.
*/

void create_table(FILE * outfile) {
    int ch, i;

    /* Heading */
    fprintf (
        outfile,
        "char code  char code  char code  char code  char code\n"
        "==== ====  ==== ====  ==== ====  ==== ====  ==== ====\n"
    );
```

```
/* Detail lines.  'ch' is the character code, i is the number
   printed so far (used to break lines every five characters).
*/
i = 0;
for (ch=FIRSTCHAR; ch<=LASTCHAR; ch++) {
    fprintf(outfile, " '%c' %3d", ch, ch);    /* write char and code */
    i++;                                        /* That's one more! */
    if (i % 5 == 0) {                           /* Even multiple of 5 */
        putc('\n', outfile);                    /* Puts a single char */
    } else {
        fputs("   ", outfile);                  /* Puts a string */
    }
}
putc('\n', outfile);              /* Ensure final line complete */
}
```

Let us review the four steps of the plan, as performed in this program.

Step 1: Creating the file pointer variable

This is done in the line:

```
FILE *outfile;
```

There is no connection between the name of the FILE pointer and the name of the actual file. In this program, for example, the FILE pointer is called outfile, but the file being written is called "ascii". The identifier outfile is a variable name within the program, just like the integer i. In both cases, these names have no significance outside the program. The name of the file is specified, not by the variable name, but by the fopen call in step 2.

Step 2: Opening a file for output

In Listing 10-1, this is done with the line:

```
outfile = fopen("ascii", "w");
```

The first parameter to fopen must be the name of the file to open. It can be a string literal, as above, or it can be a string stored in a char array. The latter possibility allows us to decide the file name at runtime, for example by asking the user for the name of the file. The sketch of the logic for doing this is:

```
char name_buf[80];
...
printf("What is the name of the output file? ");
scanf("%79s", name_buf);
outfile = fopen(name_buf, "w");
```

At the scanf step, the user can type a filename of up to 79 characters, and that name will be stored in name_buf. Then in the fopen step, the contents of name_buf will be used as the name of the file required.

The second `fopen` parameter, called the access mode, tells how the file will be used; `"w"` means "The file will be written to"; `fopen` will create a new, empty file to take the data written by the program. If a file of the same name exists beforehand, its contents are lost. A variation is the parameter `"a"`, which means "Append". `"a"` differs from `"w"` in that, if the file exists beforehand, the data written by the program is added to the end of the existing contents. This allows us to create a data file in stages. For example, a scientific experiment might be conducted over a period of many weeks, with data arriving at infrequent intervals. To avoid leaving a file open for weeks on end, a program might open it only when a data value is available, and close it immediately after writing the value. So that the `fopen` does not destroy the previous measurements stored in the file, the program would open it with `"a"`, not `"w"`.

If `fopen` succeeds in opening the file, it creates the `FILE` variable somewhere, and returns its address. Therefore, the `fopen` function result must be assigned to the `FILE` pointer. All calls to `fopen` must, therefore, have this form:

```
FILE_pointer_variable = fopen(file_name, access_mode);
```

We must also check that the `fopen` step succeeded, as in these lines from Listing 10-1:

```
if (outfile == NULL) {
    printf("ERROR: Could not open file \"ascii\"\n");
    exit(EXIT_FAILURE);
}
```

`NULL` is a macro name defined in `<stdio.h>` and some other header files. It is a special value that can be stored in a pointer, meaning "This pointer points nowhere". If `fopen` fails, it returns `NULL` instead of the address of a `FILE`. The kinds of events that can cause `fopen` to fail would include trying to write to read-only devices or files, no spare room on the disk, missing disk (in the case of floppy disks), etc.

Step 3: Writing the data to the file

In Listing 10-1 a number of functions were illustrated which wrote to the file. The mainstay of file output is `fprintf`:

```
fprintf(outfile, " '%c' %3d", ch, ch);
```

A similar call to `printf` would be

```
printf(" '%c' %3d", ch, ch);
```

If you can use `printf`, you can use `fprintf`. The only difference is the insertion of the `FILE` pointer as the first parameter. The format string becomes the second parameter, and so on.

A simple way to write one character to a file is to use `putc`, for example:

```
putc('\n', outfile);
```

The first parameter is the character to write, the second is the `FILE` pointer. This is analogous to `putchar`, which writes to the screen.

Finally, Listing 10-1 shows a call to `fputs`, which writes a string to a file:

```
fputs("    ", outfile);
```

The first parameter is the string to be written, the second is the `FILE` pointer.

10.4 FILE INPUT

File input follows a similar four-step plan to that used for file output. To illustrate, we shall write a program that reads a file of names and salaries, and displays any whose salary is above a limit input from the terminal. Let us throw a twist into the problem: we shall require headings over the terminal output, provided at least one entry in the file requires printing. Otherwise, we want a message saying that there were no such entries. We cannot just print the headings before launching into the loop that processes the data (why?); we must wait until we find the first entry to be displayed. Luckily, we should be able to postpone worrying about this until we write the code to process the data in the file. The `main` function skeleton will be:

```
Declare the FILE pointer.  (Plan step 1)
(Ask the user the name of the file with the data.)
Open the file.  (Plan step 2)
(Ask the user the salary threshold limit.)
Read all the data, displaying those above the threshold.(Plan step 3)
Close the file.  (Plan step 4)
```

In this skeleton, the four steps we must always do when reading file data are numbered. The other two steps are specific to this particular program, and are shown in parentheses.

It is a good idea to put the logic for opening a file into its own function, rather than cluttering up `main`. It makes `main` easier to follow, and if done properly, it helps simplify things when we write programs that open many files. The first part of the program is shown in Listing 10-2a.

Listing 10-2a

```
/* Program to locate employees paid more than a user-supplied threshold.
   Input: the name of the file with the employee data, and the threshold
          amount.  The file must contain names in the first 30 columns,
          then the salary as a float.  A final line containing only a '#'
          marks the end of the file.
*/

#include <stdio.h>
#include <stdlib.h>
#define TRUE (1)
#define FALSE (0)

/* Declaration for functions called in main:  */
FILE * file_open(char name[], char access_mode[]);
```

```
void process_file(FILE * fin, float threshold);

main() {
    FILE * fin;                    /* Declare the FILE pointer (1). */
    char filename[81];
    float threshold;

    /* Ask the user the name of the file with the data. */
    printf("Name of file to read? ");
    scanf("%80s", filename);

    /* Open the file (using our own function - see below) (2). */
    fin = file_open(filename, "r");

    /* Ask the user the salary threshold limit. */
    printf("Salary threshold amount? ");
    scanf("%f", &threshold);

    /* Read all the file data, displaying those above the threshold (3). */
    process_file(fin, threshold);

    /* Close the file (4). */
    fclose(fin);
    return 0;
}
```

The file is opened in our own function, `file_open`, rather than directly using `fopen`. This is because, in many programs, we will want to do precisely the same thing if the file open step fails: print a message and stop the program. By packaging the logic for this in a little function of our own, we can add it to our own personal function library, and never worry about it again.

Listing 10-2b

```
/******* file_open *******
    Works like fopen, but checks for errors, and if so, stops with an
    error message.
*/

FILE * file_open(char name[], char access_mode[]) {
    FILE * f;
    f = fopen(name, access_mode);
    if (f == NULL) { /* error? */
        /* Library function perror prints an informative message. */
        perror("Cannot open file");
        exit(EXIT_FAILURE); /* Terminate after printing error message. */
    }
    return f;                  /* Only happens if fopen succeeded. */
}
```

The function `perror` used here is a library function that prints an informative error message. On many systems, but unfortunately not all, this can include specific information about errors detected by `fopen`. We haven't yet finished writing the program, but let's see how `perror` might work by previewing the program output.

Sample run

```
Name of file to read? FrednBarney
Cannot open file: File Not Found
```

`perror` combined the string supplied in the call (`Cannot open file`) with a specific explanation of the error — in this case, `File Not Found`. This is not entirely satisfactory, as the message does not include the name of the file that the message applies to. We shall fix this problem at the end of this chapter with a better version of `file_open`.

The other function called in Listing 10-2a is `process_file`, which does the main work of processing the information in the file, printing headings, etc. Its heading comment is shown in Listing 10-2c.

Listing 10-2c

```
/******* process_file *******
On entry: fin refers to a file opened for input.  It must contain
          names and salaries.  The name must occupy the first 30
          chars of the line.  The last line starts with '#'.
On exit:  Will have listed all lines with salary greater than the
          threshold.  Prints a heading before the first such line,
          or an informative message if none are found.  No error
          checking is done.
*/
```

From the precondition (on entry), we see the function assumes that the file will contain names and salaries. If it does not, the program will malfunction, as nowhere else do we do any checking of the type of data in the file. Provided the file is correct, the postcondition (on exit) guarantees correct operation. To program the function, we clearly must have a loop, stopping when the final line is detected:

```
while ...line doesn't start with '#'...
    ...process a line...
```

How do we know what character starts the line? We must read it. If we input the name before each cycle of the loop, we can check its first character. The plan becomes:

```
Input the name.
while ...name doesn't start with '#'...
    input the salary
    ...process name and salary...
    input the next name
```

To process a name and salary we test whether it needs displaying; we can expand our plan to:

Input the name.
while ...name doesn't start with '#'...
    input the salary
    if salary is over the threshold
        display name and salary
    input the next name

But this ignores the heading. If we find a detail line that needs displaying, we must know whether to print the heading. Therefore we have to know, on any cycle round the loop, whether the heading has been printed yet. This must be done with a variable — let us call it no_previous_listings. We set this to true at the start, and change it to false if we find a line we must display. A heading is only printed if no_previous_listings is true. The same goes for the failure message at the end if we find no suitable entries. The final plan therefore is:

Set no_previous_listings to true
Input the name.
while ...name doesn't start with '#'...
    input the salary
    if salary is over the threshold
        if no_previous_listings
            Print the headings
            Set no_previous_listings to false
        display name and salary
    input the next name
if no_previous_listings
    Print the failure message.

It is now a mechanical job to translate this plan into C, as shown in Listing 10-2d, which completes the program.

Listing 10-2d

```
#define NAME_SIZE (30)

void process_file(FILE * fin, float threshold) {
    int no_previous_listings = TRUE;  /* Used to decide when to
                                    print the heading etc. */
    char employee_name[NAME_SIZE + 1];
    float salary;

    /* Load the first name */
    fgets(employee_name, NAME_SIZE+1, fin);

    while (employee_name[0] != '#') {  /* does not start with "#" */
        /* Load salary and following character (to skip the '\n') */
        fscanf(fin, "%f%*c", &salary);
```

```
      /* Decide whether to print. */
      if (salary>threshold) {
          if (no_previous_listings) {  /* Do we need headings? */
              printf("Staff with salary over $%4.2f:\n", threshold);
              printf(                    "Name%*sSalary\n====%*s======\n",
                  NAME_SIZE-4, " ",
                  NAME_SIZE-4, " "
              );
              no_previous_listings = FALSE;
          }
          printf("%*s$%4.2f\n", NAME_SIZE, employee_name, salary);
      }

      /* Load the next name */
      fgets(employee_name, NAME_SIZE+1, fin);
  }
  /* Check whether anything was printed. */
  if (no_previous_listings) {
      printf("No staff have salaries over $%4.2f\n", threshold);
  }
}
```

In the headings, note the use of `%*s`, with corresponding arguments `NAME_SIZE-4` and `" "`. This displays a space within a field of `NAME_SIZE-4` spaces. `NAME_SIZE-4` is of course 26, but by using `*` as the format width (see Section 3.5) we avoid actually writing 26 in the program text; if we ever needed to alter the width, we could edit the program simply by changing the `#define` line for `NAME_SIZE`.

The name is input with `fgets`, which inputs a string:

```
fgets(employee_name, NAME_SIZE+1, fin);
```

The first parameter is the name of the array to receive the input. The second is the maximum size of the array, including room for a string-terminating nul. `fgets` stops reading characters after a newline, or when the input string fills the array (whichever comes first). The third parameter of `fgets` is the `FILE` pointer. `fgets` is the safer version of `gets` (see Chapter 5) because it lets us specify the size of our array, and it will never read more data than the array can store. Unlike `gets`, if `fgets` encounters a newline, it **is** stored as the last character in the string — see the sample run for Listing 10-3 in the next section. Thus, in the above call, `fgets` will read up to 30 characters, which is the length of the employee name field. Afterwards, the file will be positioned after the name, ready to input the salary. This is done with the statement:

```
fscanf(fin, "%f%*c", &salary);
```

Just as `fprintf` parallels `printf`, so `fscanf` parallels the operation of `scanf`, with the extra `FILE` pointer parameter at the start. Therefore, everything you know about `scanf` you can now apply to `fscanf`. For example, you can test `fscanf`'s result to check for correct processing of file input.

For testing, a data file called `lst10-2.dat` is required. This can be made with your normal program editor.

Sample run
```
Name of file to read? 1st10-2.dat
Salary threshold amount? 60000
Staff with salary over $60000.00:
Name                       Salary
====                       ======
Blumpph, Lord John.        $100000.00
Featherstonehaugh, Bill    $61000.00
Philpott, Juliet           $75050.00
```

Sample run
```
Name of file to read? 1st10-2.dat
Salary threshold amount? 100000
No staff have salaries over $100000.00
```

Contents of data file `lst10-2.dat`
```
Blumpph, Lord John.        100000
Bloggs, Frederick, the 2nd 35000
Featherstonehaugh, Bill    61000
Philpott, Juliet           75050
#
```

Another handy function is `getc`, which inputs a single character. It works similarly to `getchar`. For example, to read a single character into an `int` called `ch` from a file opened with `FILE` pointer `fin`, we would write

```
ch = getc(fin);
```

See the next subsection for an example.

10.4.1 End of file (EOF)

There is a problem with Listing 10-2. It requires a data file to have a final line starting with #. We have done this kind of thing before when reading from the terminal, but it is a much less satisfactory requirement for file input because users would have to remember to add the # to the end of every file. A better solution is to simply stop when we run out of data. This is called *end of file*, or *EOF* for short. All C input functions let us test for EOF. For example, `fscanf` informs us via its function result. Normally, `fscanf`'s result tells how many data values were successfully assigned, but if EOF is encountered (that is, the file runs out of data), a special negative value is returned. The macro EOF (defined in `<stdio.h>`) can be used to test for this value. Listing 10-3 inputs a list of integers from the file `1st10-3.dat`, and displays its function return after each input. It checks both for errors and for EOF.

Listing 10-3   (requires `file_open` from Listing 10-2b)

```
/* Demonstration of error and EOF checking.  Attempts to read integers
   from lst10-3.dat.  Displays any line in error, and stops at EOF */

#include <stdio.h>  /* This contains the definition for the EOF macro */
#include <stdlib.h>
FILE * file_open(char name[], char access_mode[]);

main() {
    FILE * intfile;
    int intval, result;
    char buf[81];

    /* Open file with file_open from lst10-2 (not repeated for brevity) */
    intfile = file_open("lst10-3.dat", "r");

    /* Read first value, remembering the fscanf result. */
    result = fscanf(intfile, "%d", &intval);

    /* Loop as long as fscanf result is not EOF */
    while (result != EOF) {
        /* But perhaps fscanf hit an error (a non-integer in the file.
           Input the troublemaker as a string, and display.
        */
        if (result != 1) {    /* Since correct input assigns value 1 */
            /* Read the line as a string. */
            fgets(buf, 81, intfile);
            /* Display error message. */
            printf("fscanf result %d! Input was: \"%s\"\n", result, buf);
        } else {  /* Fscanf must have worked - just print the integer. */
            printf("fscanf result %d. Integer is %d\n", result, intval);
        }
        /* Input next value. */
        result = fscanf(intfile, "%d", &intval);
    }

    /* After the loop, let's find out what value fscanf returned. */
    printf("After last input, fscanf result was %d.\n", result);
    return 0;
}
```

Contents of data file `lst10-3.dat`

```
23
  147
 -36
How now brown cow!
2965  99
0
-1
44
```

Sample run

```
fscanf result 1. Integer is 23
fscanf result 1. Integer is 147
fscanf result 1. Integer is -36
fscanf result 0! Input was: "How now brown cow!
"
fscanf result 1. Integer is 2965
fscanf result 1. Integer is 99
fscanf result 1. Integer is 0
fscanf result 1. Integer is -1
fscanf result 1. Integer is 44
After last input, fscanf result was -1.
```

Notice how for successful inputs fscanf returned 1 (the number of variables assigned by the fscanf), and for unsuccessful inputs it returned a smaller value (zero). The final fscanf call which hit end of file returned the special EOF value, which our printout shows as –1. The EOF value is always negative, but one should not rely on its being precisely –1.

Since fscanf closely parallels the operation of scanf, you might wonder whether EOF tests can be done on the results of scanf calls. Indeed they can. Although the terminal is not a genuine file on a disk it is treated like a file by the standard library functions. Most operating systems provide a way to type an end of file signal when entering input. For example, MS-DOS uses control-Z (^Z), and Unix normally uses control-D (^D); if you type the appropriate character at the start of a line, terminal input comes to an end, and scanf will return the EOF value.

getc also returns EOF if it fails to read due to end of file. Listing 10-4 illustrates this; it uses getc to make an exact copy of any ASCII file.

Listing 10-4   (requires file_open from Listing 10-2b)

```c
/* Program to make a copy of any ASCII file.  Asks user for filenames. */

#include <stdio.h>
#include <stdlib.h>
FILE *open_user_file(char message[], char file_access_mode[]);

main() {
    FILE *f_in, *f_out;
    int ch;

    /* Call our own function to query user for filename & open file. */
    f_in = open_user_file("Copy which file?", "r");

    /* Ditto for output */
    f_out = open_user_file("Copy data to which file?", "w");

    /* Now copy characters one at a time until end of file on input. */
    ch = getc(f_in);
    while (ch != EOF) {
```

```
        putc(ch, f_out);
        ch = getc(f_in);
    }

    /* Now copied; close files. */
    fclose(f_in);
    fclose(f_out);
    printf("File has been copied\n");
    return 0;
}

/******* open_user_file *******
    Prints the specified message, and reads a filename from the user.
    Then opens that file in the specified file access mode.  If the
    open fails, the function stops the program with an error message.
*/

FILE *file_open(char name[], char access_mode[]);

FILE *open_user_file(char message[], char file_access_mode[]) {
    char filename[81];
    FILE *f;

    printf("%s ", message);
    scanf("%80s%*c", filename);

    f = file_open(filename, file_access_mode);

    return f;
}
```

The function `open_user_file` in Listing 10-4 carries out a common task, so it is another candidate for inclusion in a personal function library.

Sample run
```
Copy which file? lst10-3.dat
Copy data to which file? fred
File has been copied
```

After the above run, `fred` will be an exact copy of `lst10-3.dat`.

To detect end of file when using `fgets` is a little different. Instead of returning EOF, it returns a special pointer value called NULL. To illustrate, Listing 10-5 is a rewritten version of Listing 10-2d, which eliminates the need to put a special flag value (in Listing 10-2d, #) on the end of the data file.

Listing 10-5   (not a complete program)

```
#define NAME_SIZE (30)

void process_file(FILE * fin, float threshold) {
    int no_previous_listings = TRUE;   /* Used to decide when to
                                          print the heading etc. */
    char employee_name[NAME_SIZE + 1];
    float salary;
    char *result;

    /* Load the first name */
    result = fgets(employee_name, NAME_SIZE+1, fin);

    while (result != NULL) {
        /* Load salary and following character (to skip the '\n') */
        fscanf(fin, "%f%*c", &salary);

        /* Decide whether to print. */
        if (salary>threshold) {
            if (no_previous_listings) {   /* Do we need headings? */
                printf("Staff with salary over $%4.2f:\n", threshold);
                printf(
                    "Name%*sSalary\n====%*s======\n",
                    NAME_SIZE-4, " ",
                    NAME_SIZE-4, " "
                );
                no_previous_listings = FALSE;
            }
            printf("%*s$%4.2f\n", NAME_SIZE, employee_name, salary);
        }

        /* Load the next name */
        result = fgets(employee_name, NAME_SIZE+1, fin);
    }

    /* Check whether anything was printed. */
    if (no_previous_listings) {
        printf("No staff have salaries over $%4.2f\n", threshold);
    }
}
```

The data for Listing 10-5 will be the same as for Listing 10-2, minus the final line consisting only of #. The output will be the same. The skeleton of the logic for using fgets is

```
char *result;               /* Declare a char pointer. */

result = fgets(employee_name, NAME_SIZE+1, fin);
                            /* Store fgets result in the char pointer */

while (result != NULL) {  /* Loop only if result is not NULL */
    ..../* Do whatever processing is required. */
    result = fgets(employee_name, NAME_SIZE+1, fin);
                            /* Load the next value */
}
```

Some simplifications

Some readers may be concerned about the duplication of the input function call, once before the loop and once at the end of it, as in the preceding program skeleton. If the function result is used only in the loop test, the function call can be placed within the loop test itself. For example, the above skeleton can be simplified to

```
while (fgets(employee_name, NAME_SIZE+1, fin) != NULL) {
    ..../* Do whatever processing is required. */
}
```

With fscanf there is an extra problem, as the function result is needed for both end of file testing and error testing. For example, the structure of the loop in Listing 10-3 is

```
result = fscanf(intfile, "%d", &intval);
while (result != EOF) {
    if (result != 1) {
        .../* Display error message. */
    } else {
        .../* Normal processing */
    }
    result = fscanf(intfile, "%d", &intval);
}
```

Therefore we must assign the function result to a variable. Nevertheless, there are still ways to simplify the coding. First, we can use the comma operator, which was introduced in Listing 9-3. This allows us to write two expressions in a row inside the while loop test. The structure of the loop becomes:

```
while (
    result = fscanf(intfile, "%d", &intval) , /* <<the comma */
    result != EOF
) {
    if (result != 1) {
        .../* Display error message. */
                                   (the comma operator)
    } else {
        .../* Normal processing */
    }
}
```

The other way to write the loop uses what is known as 'assignment within an expression'. All C operators yield a result. For example, 5+7 yields the result 12. Similarly, even the assignment operator, =, yields a result, namely the value assigned to the variable. So, i=8 yields the result 8. This means we can use assignment operators inside a larger expression. Thus

```
j = 6 + (k = 2 + 3);
```

assigns 5 to k, and 11 to j. Because = has lower priority than any other operator except comma, we must parenthesize the assignment to k. Some people over-use this feature and create very convoluted programs. But if used in moderation it can help shorten our code without becoming difficult to follow. Thus the above loop skeleton can be written as follows: (the assignment within an expression is shown in bold)

```
while ( ( result = fscanf(intfile, "%d", &intval) ) != EOF ) {
    if (result != 1) {
        .../* Display error message. */
    } else {
        .../* Normal processing */
    }
}
```

Don't forget the parentheses around the assignment.

A useful scanf format

A useful format specifier in scanf and fscanf is %[. This is a string format, like %s, but whereas %s reads just one word of non-whitespace characters, %[lets you specify the characters you wish to read. Just supply a list of characters ending with a bracket (]). For example

```
fscanf(fin, "%[A^*]", stringbuf);
```

will read only the characters A, ^, and * into the char array stringbuf (as many of them as it finds before encountering some other character). Naturally we can supply a width. Thus

```
fscanf(fin, "%15[A^*]", stringbuf);
```

will read at most 15 chars (so stringbuf should have at least 16 chars).

We can reverse the logic of %[, making it read any characters **except** those specified, by making ^ the first character after [:

```
fscanf(fin, "%15[^\n]", stringbuf);
```

will read any characters **except** a newline, to a maximum of 15. You can even include a], provided it is the first character. Thus

```
fscanf(fin, "%15[^]A]", stringbuf);
```

will read anything except] or A, to a maximum of 15 characters.

This format is useful for skipping over bits of input. For example, to read and throw away the rest of the current input line, we can write:

```
fscanf(fin, "%*[^\n]");getc(fin);
```

`%*[^\n]` means "read everything up to (but excluding) a newline, and throw away"; `getc(fin)` reads one character (that is, the newline) and throws it away. The `%[` format is used in Listing 11-1.

10.5 PREDEFINED `FILE` POINTER NAMES

C automatically provides every program with three opened files, and the good news is that you already know about two of them! There are standard `FILE` pointer names for the normal terminal output and input as used in such functions as `printf`, `scanf`, `putchar` etc. The normal terminal output channel is called `stdout`, and we can use functions such as `fprintf` to write to the terminal by using `stdout` as the `FILE` pointer name. So

```
fprintf(stdout, "Hello world");
```

has the same effect as

```
printf("Hello world");
```

Similarly the name `stdin` refers to the normal terminal input channel. So

```
fscanf(stdin, "%d", &some_int);
```

means the same thing as

```
scanf("%d", &some_int);
```

We might ask what use these names are — after all, can't we simply use `printf` and `scanf`? One situation where they are handy is when we write a complex function for doing output or input, and we want to use it to access a file and also the terminal. Suppose `pretty_print` is a function doing output. We could give it a `FILE` pointer parameter and make it write to the stream attached to that `FILE` pointer as follows:

```
void pretty_print(FILE *f, ...other arguments...) {
    ...
    fprintf(f, ...);
    ...
}
```

Now suppose, in `main`, we have a `FILE` pointer called `outchan` open for output. We can make `pretty_print` output to both `outchan` and the terminal by calling it twice as follows:

```
pretty_print(outchan, ...);
pretty_print(stdout, ...);
```

Another important need for `stdin` in particular is to enable us to call `fgets` rather than `gets` for terminal input. As explained in Section 10-4, `fgets` is safer than `gets` because it allows us to specify the size of the `char` array, thus preventing memory overflow. We can call `fgets` for terminal input as follows:

```
fgets(char_array_name, array_size, stdin);
```

The third standard `FILE` pointer is `stderr`. It is mainly used to print error messages, and we shall use it for all error messages from now on. Unlike `stdout`, output to `stderr` is usually not affected by output redirection.

These three file pointers (`stdin`, `stdout` and `stderr`) are opened and closed automatically; do not call `fopen` or `fclose` for them.

10.6 EXAMPLE: FILE MERGE

Merging files is one of the classic problems in computing: two files containing ordered sequences have to be read and merged into a single ordered output file. One use for file merging is sorting large quantities of data. For example, a computer may not have enough memory to sort a large data file. But the file can be split into sections which are sorted separately, and the sorted pieces can then be merged, giving a single sorted file.

Let us suppose a business has two files containing product codes and names. The product codes will be alphanumeric sequences of up to six characters, and the names will be strings of up to thirty characters. The product codes in each file will be in alphabetic order with no duplicates. We wish to read both files and merge them, giving a single ordered output. If any given product code occurs in both files, we want to check that the names are the same. If not, we warn the user and ask which of the two names to write to the output file.

Obviously we have to read both input files while writing the new one; we therefore need three `FILE` pointers. If we have one record in memory from each of the input files, we can compare them and write the one with the earlier code to the output, then fetch another input record from the appropriate input file to replace the one written out. This suggests the following plan:

```
Open files.
Load record from file A.
Load record from file B.
while not all records written:
    if record A should be output next:
        write record A to file C
        load another record from file A.
    else if record B should be output next:
        write record B to file C
        load another record from file B.
    else (record codes equal)
        if record names are the same:
            Write code and name to file C.
        else (names are different)
            Ask user which name to write
            write code and the name the user selected to file C.
        Load new records from both files A and B.
Close files.
```

Let us do a quick informal check on the correctness of this loop. The loop stops when all records are written, and every branch of the `if` statements does write at least one record and read a replacement; we can therefore be sure the loop terminates. Our loop invariant is that whatever has been written so far to the output file is ordered. We see that (1) it is ordered at the beginning, since it is empty; (2) each iteration keeps it ordered, as the lower record in memory is written each time (this relies on the input files being ordered); and (3) when the loop stops, all records have been written, so the output is the complete merge of all the input data.

Unfortunately the programming for this plan is somewhat trickier than it seems at first sight. The problem is that the files will eventually run out of data, and we don't know which will do so first. One solution is to execute the loop as long as either file still has data. Therefore, immediately upon entering the loop, we might have records available from one file or the other or both; the situation should be immediately examined to decide which of the three alternatives of the `if` statement should be executed.

The `main` function can now be written using this plan. Additional functions can be introduced; for example, the logic for loading a record should be a separate function (`load_record`, say). It must return three values to `main`: the name, the code, and a value specifying whether a record was successfully read. The first two values can be passed back to `main` in array arguments, and the last can be the function result. `main` is shown in Listing 10-6a.

Listing 10-6a

```
/* Program to perform file merge of product codes and names.
   Input: Two files, "lst10-6a.dat" and "lst10-6b.dat", containing
          codes and names.  Codes are in range 0 - 999,999, names are from
          1 to thirty characters.  Input files must be in ascending order.
          No duplicates.  Incorrect entries are echoed to the screen and
          to the file "lst10-6.err".
   Output: A file, "lst10-6c.dat" containing merged data in ascending
           order.  If both input files contain the same codes and different
           names, the name selected by the user is written.
*/

#include <stdio.h>
#include <string.h>      /* For string comparisons */
#include <stdlib.h>
#define NAMELENG (30)
#define CODELENG (7)

FILE * file_open(char name[], char access_mode[]); /* See listing 10-2b */

int load_record(FILE *in_file, char code[], char name_buffer[]);
    /* reads name & code from file; returns 1 (success), or 0 (failure). */

void write_user_choice (
    /* Asks user which code & name to write; writes choice to file. */
```

```
    char code[],      /* The code for which two different names occur */
    char nameA[],     /* 1st name choice for user */
    char nameB[],     /* 2nd name choice for user */
    FILE *outfile     /* file to write to */
);

main() {
    FILE *inA, *inB, *outC;
    char codeA[CODELENG], codeB[CODELENG];
    char nameA[NAMELENG+1], nameB[NAMELENG+1];
    int A_nonempty, B_nonempty; /* == 1 iff data loaded from file */
    int ordering;               /* <0 if record from file A should be
                                   output next, ==0 if codes equal, >0 if
                                   record from file B should be output next.*/


    /* Open files. */
    inA = file_open("lst10-6a.dat", "r");
    inB = file_open("lst10-6b.dat", "r");
    outC = file_open("lst10-6c.dat", "w");

    /* Load record from file A. */
    A_nonempty = load_record(inA, codeA, nameA);

    /* Load record from file B. */
    B_nonempty = load_record(inB, codeB, nameB);

    while (A_nonempty || B_nonempty) {       /* have more data? */
        /* First set the ordering: A goes first if B was empty or if A
           comes before B; vice versa for B.
        */
        ordering = B_nonempty - A_nonempty;  /* -1 (B empty), 1 (A empty)
                                                0 (neither empty). */
        if (ordering == 0) {                 /* both files nonempty? */
            ordering = strcmp(codeA, codeB); /* choose correct ordering */
        }

        if (ordering < 0) {                  /* A goes first */
            fprintf(outC, "%6s %s\n", codeA, nameA);    /*write record A*/
            A_nonempty = load_record(inA, codeA, nameA); /*reload from A*/

        } else if (ordering > 0) {           /* B goes first */
            fprintf(outC, "%6s %s\n", codeB, nameB);    /*write record B*/
            B_nonempty = load_record(inB, codeB, nameB); /*reload from B*/

        } else {                             /* (record codes equal) */
            if (strcmp(nameA, nameB) == 0) { /* record names are equal */
                /* write either record */
                fprintf(outC, "%6s %s\n", codeB, nameB);
            } else {                         /* (names are different) */
                /* Ask user which name to write, and write the code
                   and the name the user selected to file C.
                */
                write_user_choice(codeA, nameA, nameB, outC);
            }
            /* Load new records from both files A and B. */
```

```
                A_nonempty = load_record(inA, codeA, nameA); /*reload from A*/
                B_nonempty = load_record(inB, codeB, nameB); /*reload from B*/
        }
    }  /* end of while */

    /* Close files. */
    fclose(outC);
    fclose(inA);
    fclose(inB);

    return 0;
}
```

Two functions are used by `main`; here are their specifications as required to make sure `main` works correctly.

```
/******** load_record ***********
On Entry: Parameter in_file refers to a correct open input file.
On Exit:  A code and name will have been read from the input file.
          The name is stored in the parameter name_buffer, and the
          code in parameter code.  If a name is too long, it
          will be truncated and a warning printed to the screen and
          to "lst10-6.err".  Returns 1 for success, 0 for failure.
*/

/*********** write_user_choice ************
On Entry: outfile is the open output file.
On Exit:  The user will have been warned that two different names have
          the same code, and the code, with the name of the user's
          choice, will be written to outfile.
*/
```

The plan for `load_record` will have to check for end of file and correct input of the name, as in the following:

```
Try reading the code.
If end of file,
    Return 0 (failure).
(Otherwise code was input correctly.)
Read a string into name_buffer.
If last character in name_buffer is newline (entire line read okay):
    Delete it from the end of the name_buffer.
    Return 1 (success).
If the next character in the input is newline (again all okay):
    Return 1 (success).
(The name is too long)
Print warning to screen and error file.
Copy the rest of the input line to the screen and error file.
Return 1 (success).
```

Now the C code can be written; a few more short functions may be needed, but they will be straightforward. The rest of the program is shown in Listing 10-6b. In particular, notice how to decide whether the name is too long — look for the newline: it should be in the name string or immediately after it; otherwise we have an error. Also, to write records to the error file, we open it specially in append mode, and close it again straight after; this ensures it is always up-to-date, and since it is not opened in write mode, it collects messages correctly if the program is run two or more times.

Listing 10-6b

```
#include <ctype.h>        /* for tolower() */

/******** load_record ***********
On Entry: Parameter in_file refers to a correct open input file.
On Exit:  A code and name will have been read from the input file.
          The name is stored in the parameter name_buffer, and the
          code in parameter code.  If a name is too long, it
          will be truncated and a warning printed to the screen and
          to "lst10-6.err".  Returns 1 for success, 0 for failure.
*/

void warning(FILE *, int inchar, char code[], char name[]);
void echo_line(FILE *infile, FILE *outfile);

int load_record(FILE *in_file, char code[], char name_buffer[]) {
    int status, length, inchar;
    FILE * err_file;

    status = fscanf(in_file, "%6s ", code); /* Try reading the code. */
    if (status == EOF) {
        return 0;                           /* (function terminates). */
    }

    /* (Here code was input correctly.) */
    /* Read a string into name_buffer.  No need to check EOF (will be
       caught next time when reading the code). */
    fgets(name_buffer, NAMELENG+1, in_file);

    length = strlen(name_buffer) - 1;       /* Get position of last char */

    /* If last character in name_buffer is newline (entire line read OK): */
    if (name_buffer[length] == '\n') {
        name_buffer[length] = '\0';         /* Delete it from name_buffer. */
        return 1;
    }

    /* If the next character in the input is newline (again all OK): */
    inchar = getc(in_file);
    if (inchar == '\n') {
        return 1;
    }
```

```
    /* (name is too long) - Print warning to screen and error file. */
    err_file = file_open("lst10-6.err", "a");
    warning(stderr, inchar, code, name_buffer);   /* warning to screen */
    warning(err_file, inchar, code, name_buffer); /* warning to err_file */

    /* Copy the rest of the input line to the screen and error file. */
    echo_line(in_file, err_file);
    fclose(err_file);

    return 1;
}


/*********** warning **************
On Entry: f is an open output file.  inchar is the first data char to write
          after the warning, code is the code, name is the part name.
On Exit:  Warning for name too long is written to f.
*/
void warning(FILE *f, int inchar, char code[], char name[]) {
    fprintf (
        f, "WARNING: Code %s, Name too long:\n       %s%c",
        code, name, inchar
    );
}


/*********** echo_line **************
On Entry: infile open for input, outfile open for output.
On Exit:  Rest of current line copied from infile to outfile & to screen */

void echo_line(FILE *infile, FILE *outfile) {
    int ch;
    /* Must copy at least 1 char (the return) therefore do...while. */
    do {
        ch = getc(infile);
        if (ch==EOF) {     /* Shouldn't happen, but check anyway. */
            return;
        }
        putc(ch, outfile);
        putc(ch, stderr);
    } while (ch != '\n');
}


/********** write_user_choice ************
On Entry: outfile is the open output file.
On Exit:  The user will have been warned that two different names have
          the same code, and the code, with the name of the user's
          choice, will be written to outfile.
*/

void write_user_choice (
    /* Asks user which code & name to write; writes choice to file. */
    char code[],        /* The code for which two different names occur */
    char nameA[],       /* 1st name choice for user */
    char nameB[],       /* 2nd name choice for user */
    FILE *outfile       /* file to write to */
) {
```

```
char choice;
fprintf(stderr, "ERROR: Code %s has two different names,\n", code);
fprintf(stderr, "A: \"%s\" and B: \"%s\"\n", nameA, nameB);
do {
    fprintf(stderr, "Please select A or B: ");
    scanf(" %c", &choice);
    choice = tolower(choice);   /* (See tolower in Appendix D.) */
    getchar();   /* Throw away the return after the user's choice */
    switch (choice) {
    case 'a':
        fprintf(outfile, "%6s %s\n", code, nameA);
        break;
    case 'b':
        fprintf(outfile, "%6s %s\n", code, nameB);
        break;
    default:
        fprintf(stderr, "You must answer A or B.\n");
    }
} while (choice!='a' && choice !='b');
}
```

Here are the data files and screen dialog from a run of the program.

Sample data file `1st10-6a.dat` (created with text editor)
```
AC1894 Widgets
B28566 Small but beautiful sprockets with shiny gold bearings
B29965 6 inch model unicorns.
B29966 7 inch model unicorns.
K66773 99-year calendar
K66775 101-year calendar
```

Sample data file `1st10-6b.dat` (created with text editor)
```
AC1100 flea detectors
AD0012 size 2 thimbles
B28741 paper clips
B29965 6 inch model unicorns.
B29966 7 inch mdel unicorns.
K10022 magnifying glass
```

Program run — screen dialog
```
WARNING: Code B28566, Name too long:
     Small but beautiful sprockets with shiny gold bearings
ERROR: Code B29966 has two different names,
A: "7 inch model unicorns." and B: "7 inch mdel unicorns."
Please select A or B: a
```

Output file `lst10-6c.dat` **(created by program)**
```
AC1100 flea detectors
AC1894 Widgets
AD0012 size 2 thimbles
B28566 Small but beautiful sprockets
B28741 paper clips
B29965 6 inch model unicorns.
B29966 7 inch model unicorns.
K10022 magnifying glass
K66773 99-year calendar
K66775 101-year calendar
```

Error log file `lst10-6.err` **(created by program)**
```
WARNING: Code B28566, Name too long:
        Small but beautiful sprockets with shiny gold bearings
```

10.7 DATA CONVERSION FUNCTIONS (OPTIONAL)

In text input-output, two things happen: data is converted from or to a readable format, and it is read or written on a device. C provides two functions that allow us to do just the first of these two steps — that is, we can convert data to or from text form without actually inputting or outputting it to a file or the terminal. These functions are `sscanf` and `sprintf` (s for string). They use a string variable as the source or target of the text data, just as `fscanf` and `fprintf` use a file for the text data. For example, if a `char` array called `buf` contains the string "`12 243 -89.6`", then (assuming that `i` and `j` are `int`s and `f` is a `float`) the statement

```
sscanf(buf, "%d%d%f", &i, &j, &f);
```

converts the `12` into a binary integer with the value twelve, and stores it in `i`, and similarly converts and stores the `234` in `j`, and the `-89.6` (this time as a `float`) in `f`. In other words, the function is 'reading' from a string variable. `sscanf` is often used in problems where there are a number of possible formats for lines of input data; one can read the entire line with, say, `fgets`, then examine it and decide which of a number of alternative `sscanf` formats to use to convert the data into internal form. We can even process the data two or more times with different formats.

The `sprintf` function works similarly, but in the opposite direction; binary data is written to a string in text form. We shall illustrate this function with a useful application. Remember from the sample run after Listing 10-2b, how the error message generated by `perror` did not contain the filename? We can fix that using `sprintf`. Listing 10-7 shows a revised version of function `file_open` that will give a better error message; the modified parts are shown in **bold**.

Listing 10-7

```
FILE *file_open(char name[], char access_mode[]) {
    FILE *f;
    char message_buf[80];
    f = fopen(name, access_mode);
    if (f == NULL) {          /* error? */
        int e = errno;        /* Save any error number set by fopen. */
        /* Library function perror prints an informative message. */
        sprintf(message_buf, "Cannot open file \"%.60s\"", name);
        errno = e;            /* Restore error number */
        perror(message_buf);
        exit(EXIT_FAILURE); /* Terminate after printing error message. */
    }
    return f;                 /* Only happens if fopen succeeded. */
}
```

Do not be concerned by the assignments involving the variable errno; it is a global variable provided in the standard library. It contains a number indicating which error was last recorded by a library function. perror uses its value to decide which error message to print, and we want to be sure that the message applies to the fopen call, and not to any error number set by the sprintf call. Therefore, errno is saved before the sprintf step, and restored after. Now if we try opening a non-existent file, we get

```
Name of file to read? qwqwqw
Cannot open file "qwqwqw": File Not Found
```

10.8 A WARNING

Since C has had a long association with the Unix operating system, many C systems provide input-output functions that directly access Unix input-output services. Even C compilers running under other operating systems often provide functions that mimic these Unix services. It is not a good idea in general to use these functions, as they are not part of the ANSI C standard and they needlessly tie the program to a specific operating system. None of these Unix-related functions are documented in this text, but as you might need to use a manual that does include them, it is important to know how to tell the ANSI functions from the Unix ones. All the ANSI input-output functions use the FILE pointer, so if the function description mentions that, it is probably ANSI. On the other hand the Unix functions use a thing called a file descriptor, which is an int; any functions using file descriptors are not ANSI functions and should be avoided if possible. C compilers under MS-DOS also provide various DOS-only functions, which should also be avoided where possible.

If you must use a non-standard function (perhaps because no standard function does the job) call it only once within a special function of your own. Then wherever you need that non-standard function, call your own function. That way you can, if you need to shift to a different operating system, just rewrite the one function rather than having to search the entire program for things that need fixing. Such functions would be ideal for placing in a personal function library; that way, by rewriting the library and recompiling it and the programs that use it, all your programs are adjusted with only modest effort.

10.9 SUMMARY

- Computer files are of two main types, *text* and *binary* files.
- *Text* files contain readable character data, e.g. any file created with a text editor.
- C programs access files using library functions.
- The FILE pointer data type is used when accessing a file.
  - A *stream* is a connection to a file using a FILE pointer.
- Four-step plan for accessing a file:
  1. Declare a FILE pointer variable, e.g.

     ```
     FILE *file_ptr_var;
     ```

  2. *Open* the file — that is, specify an actual filename to be accessed via the FILE pointer, and prepare it for input or output.
  3. Perform all required input or output on the file; the FILE pointer is used to specify which file is being manipulated.
  4. *Close* the file — that is, disconnect the actual file from the program.
- Open a file with fopen, e.g.

  ```
  file_ptr_var = fopen (filename, accessmode);
  ```

  - *filename* is a string or string variable containing the filename.
  - accessmode is a string or string variable containing
    "r" to read a file,
    "w" to write a new file, or
    "a" to append to the end of an existing file, or create a new one if the file does not exist.
- File output functions (after fopen(...,"w") or fopen(...,"a")):

  ```
  fprintf(file_ptr_var, format, other arguments );
  putc(character, file_ptr_var );
  fputs(string, file_ptr_var );
  ```

  These three are similar to the terminal output functions printf, putchar, and puts.

- File input functions (after fopen(...,"r")):

  result = fscanf(file_ptr_var, format, other arguments...);
  character = getc(file_ptr_var);
  result = fgets(string_var, string_size, file_ptr_var);

  These three are similar to the terminal input functions scanf, getchar, and gets. But fgets is safer than gets, and should be used even for terminal input — e.g. fgets(stringvar, size, stdin).
  - End of file detection: fscanf, scanf, getc and getchar function results are EOF if the function fails due to hitting end of file. fgets and gets function results are NULL at end of file.
- Closing a file: fclose(file_ptr_var);
- Predefined FILE pointer names: stdin (standard input — usually terminal), stdout (standard output — usually terminal), stderr (standard error message output — almost certainly terminal).
- Assignment within an expression — an assignment to a variable is made as part of a larger expression. This is a general C feature, but is useful when doing input in a loop.
- Another scanf format: %[...] reads a string consisting of a specified list of characters. %[^...] reads all **except** a specified list.
- The data conversion functions sscanf and sprintf allow reading and writing on a string instead of a disk file.

10.10 SELF-TEST EXERCISES

Short Answer

1   Assuming the following declarations:

    char buffer[20];   FILE *f, *g; int i, j; float r;

    write statements to:
    a   Open f for input from a file called fred.
    b   Read a string of the maximum possible length from f into buffer, using fgets.
    c   Read a single word of the maximum possible length from f into buffer, using fscanf.
    d   Read a string of the maximum possible length from the terminal into buffer, using fgets.
    e   Read a single word of the maximum possible length from the terminal into buffer, using fscanf.
    f   Read a float from f into r.
    g   Read an integer from f into i, storing the scanf return value in j.
    h   Open g for output to a file called "sue".
    i   Write up to ten characters from buffer to g.

j   Write the entire contents of `buffer` to the terminal using `fprintf`.

2   Explain the purpose of the `.60` in the `sprintf` format in Listing 10-7.

Programming

3   Modify the file merge program in the text so that it detects whether the input files are in order, and stops with an error message if not.

4   Write a program that reads a list of `float` numbers from a file. At end-of-file the program should print the total of the user's numbers. Rely only on `fscanf`'s result to decide when the input is complete; do not ask any extra questions or rely on any special 'end' value. Also check if the user has made an error, and print a warning if so.

5   Write a program that lists any text file to the screen, stopping at end-of-file. Each line listed should be preceded by a line number. It should use the library functions `getc` and `putc`.

10.11 TEST QUESTIONS

Short Answer

1   After reading about the library functions `strcat` and `strncat` in Appendix D, write another version of `file_open` (shown in Listing 10-7) that does not use `sprintf`, yet has the same effect.

2   Write code fragments to do the following tasks.
a   Declare `FILE` pointers `fin` and `fout`.
b   Open `fin` to input from the file `sales.dat`; if that fails, try `purchase.dat`; if that fails, print an error message and stop.
c   Open `fout` to output in append mode to the file `transact`; if that fails, print an error message and stop.
d   Lines in `sales.dat` and `purchase.dat` consist of: a date in yyyymmdd format, a five-digit product code, a four-digit price in whole dollars, and a three-digit quantity. For example

    19920812123450132023

represents a sale on 12 August 1992, for product number 12345 at $132 each, for 23 items. Write statements to read such a record from `fin`, and write to `fout` the date, product code, quantity, unit price and total price, in a human-friendly format.
e   Read three `int`s, `i`, `j`, and `k`, from `fin` in a single `fscanf` call. If end of file is detected, stop. If an error is detected, flush (i.e. read and ignore) the rest of the current input line. If there are no errors, add the three `int`s and display the total.

3 The following code fragment will **not** list the file `freddy` on the screen. Without trying it, say why not. (There are four faults.)

```
char ch; FILE *f;
f = fopen("freddy", "w");
while (ch=getc(f) != EOF) {
    putchar(ch);
}
fclose("freddy");
```

Programming

4 Questions in previous chapters handled all input and output using the standard input-output channels. Many of these, especially those where redirection is useful, are ideal candidates for reading or writing files using the functions discussed in this chapter. Identify those programs that you feel would most benefit from file input-output, and rewrite them suitably.

5 Write another version of the program shown in Listing 10-1, which creates a file containing an ASCII code table. Your program should read the name of the file to create from the user, and it should write the codes down the columns instead of across the rows (i.e. B is beneath A, etc.).

6 Palindromes are words or numbers that read the same forwards or backwards, for example, "16461" and "Able was I ere I saw Elba". Write a program to ask for a filename, and echo its contents to the terminal, until either end of file, or a non-palindromic line is detected. Ignore case differences in deciding whether a line is a palindrome. Assume no line is longer than 80 characters.

7 Write another version of the `file_open` function which, if the file cannot be opened, gives the user the opportunity to specify a different file or to quit. This should happen as often as desired; if the second file cannot be opened, it should ask again, etc. Write a suitable `main` function to test `file_open`.

8 A variation of the file merge problem is the master file update problem. A master file contains records of some kind (stock, clients, etc.) and a secondary merge file contains commands for updating the records in the master file (e.g. insert, modify, delete). The problem is to read both files and produce a new master file modified according to the commands in the secondary merge file. Write a master file update program to operate on a customer name data file. The master records (both the old and new) have a customer number in columns 1 to 5 (in ascending order), then a customer name in columns 6 to 45. The secondary merge file records have a customer number in columns 1 to 5, then either a D (delete) or an A (add) in column six. For 'D' records, the corresponding record in the old master file is to be suppressed in the new master. 'A' records also have a customer name, and are to be added to the new master. For example, if the old master contained

```
11213Jones, William
11435Bailles, Marilyn
```

and the secondary merge file contained

```
11213D
23132ASmithers, Buckley
```

then the new master created by the program should contain

```
11435Bailles, Marilyn
23132Smithers, Buckley
```

Report errors (such as adding a customer number that is already present) but keep on processing.

9 Add an option to the program written for the previous question that allows someone to change their name.

10 Write a program that asks for the names of two files, and compares their contents. It should either print "Files are identical", or report the line and column at which the first difference occurs.

11 Write a *pretty printer* — a program to tidy up the appearance of a C program. Your pretty printer should read a C program and indent lines following a { by four spaces, and vice versa for lines commencing with }. This can be a little tricky if you are ambitious enough to ignore braces within comments and string literals.

12 Write a program to input a file of normal English text, and write a new file in which lines are fully left and right justified (i.e. straight margins, as in a book). Output lines should be exactly 65 characters long. If words will not fit on a line, they should be carried over to the line below, and if a line is too short, it should take words from the line below. Since lines will seldom exactly fit the 65-character width, the number of spaces between words will have to be padded with extra blanks. A line immediately before a completely blank line is the end of a paragraph, and should not be right-justified.

13 One facility of many word processors is the ability to generate personalized letters from a file containing the letter text and a file of names and addresses. Write a program that reads two such files and generates multiple personalized letters. The name file should start with a number saying how many lines of data apply to each person, then have exactly that many lines per person. The letter file should contain special sequences (@@1, @@2, etc.) for the various entries in the name file. Each such sequence is replaced with the corresponding line of one person's details from the name file. You will need to read the letter file once for each person. Either `fclose` and re-`fopen` it, or check out the `rewind` function in Appendix D.

14 Sometimes programs must record details about their users. Write a demonstration program that asks the user's name, then tells them how many times they have previously run the program.

11

Structuring data

Objectives

Appreciate the need to properly organize data.
— data types
— structures.

Study C facilities for building structures and data types.
— building structures with `struct`
— naming data types with `typedef`
— declaring structured variables
— arrays of structures.

11.1 INTRODUCTION

In daily life we are quite accustomed to the idea of packaging lots of small pieces of data under a larger name. 'Exam results', for example, might really mean a grade for computing, a grade for chemistry, a grade for history, and so on. To the police 'the file on Squeaky Louie' might really mean a vast amount of information on Louie's nefarious activities. Think how difficult it would be if a detective, instead of simply asking for Louie's file, had to ask individually for Louie's address, his convictions, his mother's maiden name, and so on. This same problem arises in programming: we can have so many pieces of data to worry about that the program becomes long and hard to understand.

Consider a business storing data about its employees. Employees have names, addresses, ages, salaries, and lots of other attributes of interest to an employer. Any programs that manipulate employee data (such as the payroll program) will have to handle all these details. Any time the program passes information about a staff member to a function, or copies the information, dozens of variables will probably need to be handled. It appears that so far, our C programs have not caught up with our everyday speech, which allows us to easily ask for Louie's police file, and be given all the relevant information in one hit.

Two concepts are needed to allow this easy talk about Squeaky Louie's police file. First, we should be able to create our own data types. 'A police file' is a certain kind of data object; we expect to find certain things in it. We can talk about it in English because the English language lets us invent new data types: a credit rating, a bank account, a resumé, etc. Similarly in C, we should not be stuck forever with `int`s, `float`s, `char`s etc.: we must be able to invent new data types of our own. The `typedef` declaration is provided for this purpose. Second, we must be able to collect different kinds of information into a single data object. Louie's file contains many different types of data: numbers (his age etc.), names, addresses, plain text information, and so on. In C, the `struct` declaration handles this by allowing us to collect many different data items into one large object. (Arrays cannot be used to solve this problem because all elements in an array have the same type.)

11.2 CREATING NEW DATA TYPES (`typedef`)

As explained in the previous section, we are allowed to create our own data types in C. These then take their place alongside the built-in types (`int`, `float`, etc.) and may be used in the same way to declare variables. Consider the following common problem. When declaring pointers, people often forget a pointer symbol (`*`). To declare two `FILE` pointers, instead of

```
FILE *infile, *outfile;
```

we might accidentally write

```
FILE *infile, outfile;
```
wrong

which is wrong because it declares `outfile` as a `FILE` instead of as a `FILE` pointer. To forestall this mistake, we can use `typedef` to create a new type which means 'FILE pointer':

```
typedef FILE * FILEptr;
```

Apart from the word `typedef` at the start, this looks like a variable declaration. But variables and types are very different; a variable is a particular example of a type.

Do not confuse types with variables. In the previous police file example, 'a police file' is the type; "the file on Squeaky Louie" is an actual example of a police file — a police file 'variable', if you like, as it can be used to store information, in this case about Louie; `FILEptr` declared above is a type, just like `int`, `float`, etc.

We can use `FILEptr` to make variables:

```
FILEptr infile, outfile;
```

Now `infile` and `outfile` are **both** `FILEptr` variables (i.e. `FILE` pointers).
To reiterate the difference between types and variables, in the declaration

```
int count;
```

`int` is a type and `count` is a variable. `int` is the name of a sort of thing, not the name of a particular thing. `count` is a particular `int` that can be used to store data. Similarly in the case of `FILEptr`, `FILEptr` is the type and `infile` and `outfile` are variables. It is a good idea to declare a type name using `typedef` for any pointer types you use (such as `FILE` pointer).

Exercise

Why do I need `typedef` at all? Why not just write

```
#define FILEptr FILE *
FILEptr infile, outfile;
```

You will find the explanation in Section 4.6. Do not read the answer below until you think you understand the reason.

Answer

Section 4.6 stated: "It is important to realize that `#define` causes substitutions without regard to the meaning of the tokens being substituted." So by using `#define`, `FILEptr` becomes just another way to write the tokens `FILE *`. So the second line above becomes

```
FILE * infile, outfile;
```

which we know is wrong; `typedef` is **not** equivalent to `#define`.

Here is another example. Many people like to document their programs by using more explanatory declarations. For example, sometimes an `int` is used to remember true/false information. Since Boolean algebra concerns the rules governing logical data, we could write:

```
typedef int bool;
```

Now `bool` is a type which happens to mean exactly the same thing as `int`. But because we have another type name available, we can write our declarations more expressively:

```
int number_of_items;
bool eof_detected;
```

Both `number_of_items` and `eof_detected` are really `int`s, as `bool` is the same type as `int`. But the above lines give the reader the clear signal that the former will be used for numeric data, the latter for logical data. Some programmers put the following lines in the `.h` file for their personal function library:

```
typedef int bool;
#define TRUE (1)
#define FALSE (0)
```

These are simple yet useful examples of user-created types. The real power comes when we also create our own structures, as described in the next section.

11.3 CREATING STRUCTURES (`struct`)

We have already seen the need for data objects that combine many different types of data into a single entity. Such a collection is usually called a *record*. In C usage it is sometimes called a *structure* because the C keyword for creating records is `struct`. The syntax of a `struct` declaration is

struct | structure_name | {

| ...declarations for the components making up the structure... |

```
};
```
    └─── (**Must** end with a semicolon!)

For example, suppose we wish to package an `int`, a `float`, and a `char` array in a single entity. We might write

```
struct fruit_case {
    int number;
    float average_weight;
    char name[21];
};
```

The variables that make up the structure are called *fields*. (So, the fields of structure `fruit_case` are `number`, `average_weight`, and `name`.) The structure `fruit_case` thus created is similar to a type, in that we can declare variables using it:

```
struct fruit_case orange_case, apple_case;
```

This is a little clumsy, however, as we must repeat the word `struct` every time we declare a variable. We can eliminate this by using `typedef`. If we say

```
typedef struct fruit_case fruitcase;
```

then the new type `fruitcase` describes a structure. Thus our variables could instead be declared

```
fruitcase orange_case, apple_case;
```

Either way, we get two variables, `orange_case` and `apple_case`; each one contains the three components `number`, `average_weight`, and `name`. They can be represented pictorially as follows:

orange_case:

number:	
average_weight:	
name:	

apple_case:

number:	
average_weight:	
name:	

We can store data in the components that make up these two variables. Because the names of the fields are not unique, we cannot assign to them just by using their field names. If we wrote:

```
average_weight = 4.8;
```

wrong

the compiler would not know whether we meant to store 4.8 inside `orange_case` or `apple_case`. We therefore have to say which variable we mean, using an operator called *dot*, or *field selection*. To put values in `orange_case`, then, we might write:

```
orange_case.average_weight = 4.8;
orange_case.number = 64;
strcpy(orange_case.name, "Oranges");
```

We can do to a field in a structure anything we could do to a simple variable of the same type. For example, as `orange_case.name` is a `char` array, we can copy a name into it with `strcpy`, just as we would with any other `char` array. The result of these assignments is:

orange_case:

number:	64
average_weight:	4.8
name:	"Oranges"

apple_case:

number:	
average_weight:	
name:	

Because a structure is a single variable (even though it contains many smaller variables, or fields), we can treat it as a single variable in assignment statements, function parameters, and so on. So we can copy the entire contents of `orange_case` to `apple_case` by writing

```
apple_case = orange_case;
```

The contents of the variables will now be

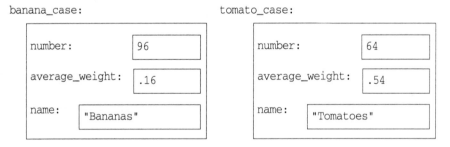

orange_case: apple_case:

number:	64
average_weight:	4.8
name:	"Oranges"

number:	64
average_weight:	4.8
name:	"Oranges"

The importance of this cannot be underestimated. It means we only need worry about the fields in a structure where we actually do something that concerns a specific field. For example, we only ever need mention `name` if the name itself concerns us for some reason. (For instance, the `name` field of `apple_case` is incorrect. Can you fix it?)

We can initialize structure variables as they are declared, in a manner analogous to that used to initialize arrays. For example

```
fruitcase banana_case = {96, .16, "Bananas"},
          tomato_case  = {64, .54, "Tomatoes"};
```

would declare and initialize the following variables:

banana_case: tomato_case:

number:	96
average_weight:	.16
name:	"Bananas"

number:	64
average_weight:	.54
name:	"Tomatoes"

There is complete freedom in mixing and matching various C data types. For example, we can declare an array of structures

```
fruitcase cases[5];
```

Now we have five `fruitcases`. All the usual things can be done with these; here is a selection.

```
cases[2] = banana_case;          /* Assign to an array element */
cases[3].number = 56;            /* Assign to a field in an element */
scanf("%d", &cases[1].number);   /* Input a field in an element */
printf("%d", cases[1].number);   /* Output a field in an element */
cases[0] = cases[3];             /* copy an element */
strcpy(cases[4].name, cases[0].name);  /* copy a string field */
```

To clarify how arrays and structures interact, let us analyze the argument to the `printf` statement above.

> `cases`   is the name of an array of `fruitcases`

therefore

> `cases[1]`   is a single `fruitcase`

therefore

> `cases[1].number` is the `number` field inside this `fruitcase`.

We know that both arrays and structures can be initialized on declaration, so we should be able to initialize an array of structures. Indeed we can, and it all works the obvious way. Here is a declaration for four initialized `fruitcases`.

```
fruitcase caselist[4] = {
    {24, .08, "Strawberry"},
    {96, .16, "Bananas"},
    {64, .54, "Tomatoes"},
    {64, 4.8, "Oranges"}
};
```

Finally, it is possible to combine the definitions of structures and types into a single declaration, with the following syntax.

`typedef struct` | *structure_name* | `{`

| *...declarations for the components making up the structure...* |

`}` | *type_name* | `;`

*(**Must** end with a semicolon!)*

If you do not plan to use the structure name, you can leave it out. Using this syntax, we could have declared type `fruitcase` as follows:

```
typedef struct {
    int number;
    float average_weight;
    char name[21];
} fruitcase;
```

Finally, there are a few rules that C imposes when using structures.
- We may not have two fields of the same name in the one structure.
- We may have two fields of the same name in different structures.
- A structure must have at least one field.

- Fields in structures may have the same names as other objects (variables, functions, etc.).
- Structures and types may have the same name. That is, we may write such things as

```
typedef struct person person;
```

- A variable can have the same name as a structure.
- A structure may contain fields which are themselves structures, but it may not contain another copy of itself.
- A structure can contain arrays, and arrays can have structures as elements.

11.4 EXAMPLE: SORTING EMPLOYEE RECORDS

Our task is to sort a file containing a company's employee data. Each record contains information about a single employee (such as name, address, salary, etc.). All data about a single employee can be collected in a structure and given a type name, as follows.

```
typedef struct {
    char    surname[SURNAME_SIZE];
    char    given_names[GIVEN_NAME_SIZE];
    char    address1[ADDRESS_SIZE];
    char    address2[ADDRESS_SIZE];
    char    title[TITLE_SIZE];
    long    payroll_no;
    int     age
    int     department;
    double  salary;
    char    sex;
} staff_data;
```

Here the type name is `staff_data`. An array of these structures is needed, as we must store information about many employees:

```
staff_data staff[MAX_STAFF];
```

Given this array of structures, each function in the program that deals with the employees can be given one argument, `staff`, and thereby gain access to all the employee information.

The natural structure for the `main` function is

```
load the data.
sort the data.
output the data.
```

These three steps can be written as functions. Each one needs access to the `staff` array, which must therefore be an argument to all three. The function to load the data must count the employee records and return this value as its function result; the other two functions must be given this count as an argument. Therefore the function declarations must be

```
int load_data(staff_data staff[]);
void sort_data(staff_data staff[], int numb_staff);
void write_data(staff_data staff[], int numb_staff);
```

In function `sort_data` the swapping of all data relating to two employees can be accomplished as simply as if the `staff` array contained some simple data type such as `int`:

```
temp_employee = staff[j-1];        /* Swap elements */
staff[j-1] = staff[j];
staff[j] = temp_employee;
```

The variable `temp_employee` used here must be declared to have type `staff_data`, as that is the type of the individual elements of the array `staff`.

The individual fields of the `staff` array elements must be considered in functions `load_data` and `write_data`, because `scanf` and `printf` can only operate on built-in data types. For example, the `fprintf` call in `write_data` will be

```
fprintf (
    outf, "%-*s%-s\n%-s\n%-s\n%-*s%ld %d%c %4.2f %d\n",
    SURNAME_SIZE-1, staff[i].surname, staff[i].given_names,
    staff[i].address1, staff[i].address2, TITLE_SIZE-1,
    staff[i].title, staff[i].payroll_no, staff[i].age,
    staff[i].sex, staff[i].salary, staff[i].department
);
```

Listing 11-1 shows the program in full.

Listing 11-1

```
/* Program to sort a file, "lst11-1.old", into a new file, "lst11-1.new".
   Files contain employee data records (max 100).  Records have four lines:
   (1) Surname (20 chars), Given names (50 chars)
   (2) Address line 1 (60 chars)
   (3) Address line 2 (60 chars)
   (4) Position title (40 chars), Payroll no. (long), age (int),
       Sex (char, M or F), salary (double), Department no. (int).
   File to be sorted on: surnames, then given names, then payroll no.
   (Uses a structure to encapsulate all data belonging to one employee.)
*/
#include <stdio.h>
#include <string.h>
#include <stdlib.h>
#define MAX_STAFF (50)

#define ADDRESS_SIZE (61)
#define SURNAME_SIZE (21)
#define GIVEN_NAME_SIZE (51)
#define TITLE_SIZE (41)

/* The following are format strings used in function "load_data".
   If the above #define sizes are altered, these must also be changed.
*/
```

```
#define address_format "%60[^\n]%*c"    /* meaning: read up to 60 chars, */
                                        /* stopping at a newline, then */
                                        /* read and discard the newline. */
#define name_format "%20[^\n]%50[^\n]%*c"
#define title_format "%40[^\n]%ld%d %c%lf%d%*c"

/**** staff_data: The main structure used to store employee data. ****/

typedef struct {
    char    surname[SURNAME_SIZE];
    char    given_names[GIVEN_NAME_SIZE];
    char    address1[ADDRESS_SIZE];
    char    address2[ADDRESS_SIZE];
    char    title[TITLE_SIZE];
    long    payroll_no;
    int     age;
    int     department;
    double  salary;
    char    sex;
} staff_data;

/* Function Declarations: */

FILE *file_open(char name[], char access_mode[]);    /* See Listing 10-7 */
int load_data(staff_data staff[]);
void sort_data(staff_data staff[], int numb_staff);
void write_data(staff_data staff[], int numb_staff);

/******* The functions themselves: *******/

main() {
    staff_data staff[MAX_STAFF];   /* Data for all employees */
    int numb_staff;                /* How many employee records are read */
    numb_staff = load_data(staff);
    sort_data(staff, numb_staff);
    write_data(staff, numb_staff);
    return 0;
}

/* load_data: Fills the array with data from lst11-1.old, until MAX_SIZE
              items read or EOF.
              Returns a count of the number of employee records input.
              If an input error (except for EOF) occurs, a message is
              printed and the program terminates.
*/
int load_data(staff_data staff[]) {
    int number=0;            /* How many employee records are read */
    int status;              /* result of fscanf call */
    FILE *inf;
    inf = file_open("lst11-1.old", "r");          /* See Listing 10-7 */
    do {                     /* Load one record at a time until failure */
        status = fscanf (
            inf, name_format, staff[number].surname,
            staff[number].given_names
```

```
        );
        if (status >= 0) {        /* EOF not detected on first fscanf */
            if (
                status < 2
            ||
                fscanf(inf, address_format, staff[number].address1) < 1
            ||
                fscanf(inf, address_format, staff[number].address2) < 1
            ||
                fscanf (
                    inf, title_format, staff[number].title,
                    &staff[number].payroll_no, &staff[number].age,
                    &staff[number].sex, &staff[number].salary,
                    &staff[number].department
                ) < 6
            ) {
                /* This branch is selected on error in any of the fscanf
                   calls, and on EOF in any call except the first one.
                */
                fprintf(stderr, "Error in input file, record %d\n", number);
                exit(EXIT_FAILURE);
            }
        }
        number++;
    } while (number<MAX_STAFF && status>=0);
    fclose(inf);
    return number - 1;            /* The loop counted one too many. */
}

int in_wrong_order(staff_data staff[], int which);
    /* Compares items at indices which & which+1, tells if disordered. */

void sort_data(staff_data staff[], int numb_staff) {
    staff_data temp_employee;
    int i, j;

    for (i=numb_staff-1; i>0; i--) { /* scan numb_staff-1 times */
        for (j=1; j<=i; j++) {    /* Scan the elements still unsorted. */
            if (in_wrong_order(staff,j-1)) {
                temp_employee = staff[j-1];        /* Swap elements */
                staff[j-1] = staff[j];
                staff[j] = temp_employee;
            }
        }
    }
}

int in_wrong_order(staff_data staff[], int which) {
    /* Compares items at indices which & which+1, tells if disordered.
       Do three tests, stop at the first where the items differ.
    */
    int order;  /* will be <0 for less, 0 for ==, >0 for greater */
    order = strcmp(staff[which].surname, staff[which+1].surname);
    if (order==0) {       /* surnames ==, must compare given names. */
```

```
        order = strcmp(
            staff[which].given_names, staff[which+1].given_names
        );
        if (order==0) {        /* given names ==, must compare payroll. */
            return (staff[which].payroll_no>staff[which+1].payroll_no);
        }
    }
    return (order>0); /* Since (order>0) means they are wrongly ordered. */
}

void write_data(staff_data staff[], int numb_staff) {
    FILE *outf;
    int i;

    outf = file_open("lst11-1.new", "w");                /* See Listing 10-7 */
    for (i=0; i<numb_staff; i++) {
        fprintf (
            outf, "%-*s%-s\n%-s\n%-s\n%-*s%ld %d%c %4.2f %d\n",
            SURNAME_SIZE-1, staff[i].surname, staff[i].given_names,
            staff[i].address1, staff[i].address2, TITLE_SIZE-1,
            staff[i].title, staff[i].payroll_no, staff[i].age,
            staff[i].sex, staff[i].salary, staff[i].department
        );
    }
    fclose(outf);
}
```

In passing, it is worth noting the organization of function `load_data`. It requires four `fscanf` calls to read an entire record. EOF is only accepted as legitimate in the first of these, as EOF on any other indicates an incomplete record, which should be flagged as an error. Illegal input is erroneous on any of the four `fscanf`s. Now for a sample run.

Sample input file, `lst11-1.old`

```
Jones                Jimmy
Orange Blossom Lane
Happy Valley
Gopher                              123456 27M 35000 14
Jones                Alison
Orange Blossom Lane
Happy Valley
Order Clerk                         123568 28F 37000 14
Jones                Alison
Tofu Crescent
Happy Valley
Sales Representative                100241 37F 57000 19
Farquharson          Benjamin P. Rudolph
Floppy Disk Drive
Horseless Gulch
Military Advisor                    740021 57M 42000 13
```

Corresponding output file, lst11-1.new

```
Farquharson          Benjamin P. Rudolph
Floppy Disk Drive
Horseless Gulch
Military Advisor                            740021 57M 42000.00 13
Jones                Alison
Tofu Crescent
Happy Valley
Sales Representative                        100241 37F 57000.00 19
Jones                Alison
Orange Blossom Lane
Happy Valley
Order Clerk                                 123568 28F 37000.00 14
Jones                Jimmy
Orange Blossom Lane
Happy Valley
Gopher                                      123456 27M 35000.00 14
```

11.5 EXAMPLE: VECTORS

Vectors provide a realistic illustration of the use of structures to solve scientific and engineering problems. If you are are unfamiliar with them, you can safely skip this section. Alternatively, if you take the mathematics on faith, you may wish to follow the example anyway, as the programming methods are relevant to many kinds of problems.

The task is to develop a library of functions that perform common operations on two-dimensional vectors. This will involve a .h header file and a C source file for the functions in the library. Tasks in a program that deals with vectors may include:

- inputting and outputting vectors
- adding, subtracting, and negating vectors
- multiplying by a scalar
- finding the length of a vector
- finding the angle made to the x axis.

Since it is hard to predict how a particular program will need to input and output vectors, those tasks are perhaps best omitted from a general-purpose library. Other tasks can be added to the list as necessary. The first problem is how to represent a vector as a structure. Each vector has x and y components, so one possibility is

```
typedef struct {
    float x, y;
} vector;
```

On the other hand, it might be wise to anticipate the possibility that we might later need to deal with vectors having three or more dimensions, and therefore adopt a structure that can be more easily expanded to higher dimensions, such as

```
#define VECDIM (2)
```

```
typedef struct {
    float v[VECDIM];
} vector;
```

Here the two components of the vector are represented as a two-element array. Because the array is enclosed in a structure, it can be handled as a single variable. Whichever method is used, we want to be able to use functions for the various vector operations. For example

```
vector a, b, c;
...
c = vAdd(a, b);
```

where vAdd is a vector addition function. If we define vector using the first of the above methods, this function would be written

```
vector vAdd(vector a, vector b) {
    vector c;
    c.x = a.x + b.x;
    c.y = a.y + b.y;
    return c;
}
```

If we defined vector using the second of the above methods, we would write the function as

```
vector vAdd(vector a, vector b) {
    vector c; int i;
    for (i=0; i<VECDIM; i++) {
        c.v[i] = a.v[i] + b.v[i];
    }
    return c;
}
```

By using a loop, we have the opportunity to alter the value in the definition of VECDIM from 2 to 3, or 4, or whatever and thus obtain a package of functions for some other vector dimension. Although this is an attractive possibility, we shall pursue this example using the first method of defining vector; that is, we shall write a package for two-dimensional vectors only.

Listing 11-2 shows the contents of vector2.h, a header file for two-dimensional vector arithmetic.

Listing 11-2   File vector2.h

```
/* Header file for programs using two-dimensional vectors. */

typedef struct {
    float x, y;
} vector2;
```

```
vector2 v2Add(vector2 a, vector2 b);    /* Sum of 2 vectors */
vector2 v2Sub(vector2 a, vector2 b);    /* Difference */
vector2 v2Neg(vector2 a);               /* Negative of vector */
vector2 sv2Mul(float f, vector2 v);     /* Multiply by a scalar */
vector2 v2Polar(float len, float angle);
                        /* Compute vector from its length and direction */
float v2Len(vector2 v);                 /* Length of vector */
float v2Arg(vector2 v);                 /* Angle of vector with x axis */
```

The vector type is called `vector2`, standing for two-dimensional vectors. The first five functions defined in Listing 11-2 perform operations that yield a vector answer, so their function type is `vector2`; the other two give real answers, so their function type is `float`.

Listing 11-3 shows the file `vector2.c`, containing the C code for the functions. Readers unfamiliar with vectors need not worry if they can't follow the mathematical reasons why the statements work; in fact, we soon shall see how to use the package perfectly well without understanding how it operates.

Listing 11-3   File `vector2.c`

```
/* vector2.c: Package for manipulating 2-dimensional vectors */

#include "vector2.h" /* For the vector structure declaration */
#include <math.h>    /* For sqrt, sin, cos & atan2 functions */

vector2 v2Add(vector2 a, vector2 b) {    /* Sum of 2 vectors */
    vector2 c;
    c.x = a.x + b.x;    /* Adds the x components */
    c.y = a.y + b.y;    /* Adds the y components */
    return c;
}

vector2 v2Sub(vector2 a, vector2 b) {    /* Difference */
    vector2 c;
    c.x = a.x - b.x;    /* Subtracts the x components */
    c.y = a.y - b.y;    /* Subtracts the y components */
    return c;
}

vector2 v2Neg(vector2 a) {               /* Negative of vector */
    a.x = -a.x;  /* Negate x; this does not alter the actual parameter a */
    a.y = -a.y;  /* Negate y; this does not alter the actual parameter a */
    return a;
}

vector2 sv2Mul(float f, vector2 v) {     /* Multiply by a scalar */
    v.x *= f;    /* Multiply x by scalar; does not alter actual parameter */
    v.y *= f;    /* Multiply y by scalar; does not alter actual parameter */
```

```
        return v;
}

float v2Len(vector2 v) {                    /* Length of vector */
    return sqrt(v.x * v.x + v.y * v.y);  /* Pythagoras' rule */
}
/* (A better version of the function v2Len is given in chapter 16.) */

float v2Arg(vector2 v) {                     /* Angle of vector with x axis */
    return atan2(v.y, v.x);   /* Note: meaningless if v.y & v.x both zero */
}

vector2 v2Polar(float len, float angle) {
    /* Compute vector from its length and direction */
    vector2 v;
    v.x = len * cos(angle);
    v.y = len * sin(angle);
    return v;
}
```

Let us try out the vector package on a suitable problem. A motorcycle stunt rider is planning a trick involving riding up a ramp, becoming airborne, and landing on a ledge, as shown in Figure 11.1. He wishes to enter values for the height of the ledge, ramp angle, distance of ledge from the ramp, and motorcycle speed. The program should print out horizontal and vertical position and speed every tenth of a second until the cycle either lands on the ledge or crashes; then it should say which of these outcomes happened and, if it clears the ledge, at what angle it landed.

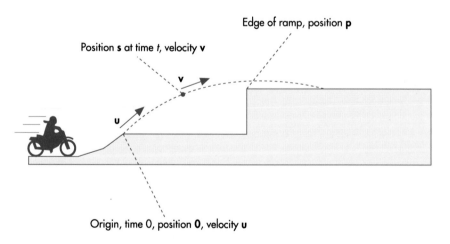

Origin, time 0, position **0**, velocity **u**

Figure 11.1 *Motorcycle stunt (vectors in bold)*

The main function will be easy; it just calls functions to ask the user the initial velocity and ledge position, then another to print the results. The function to input the initial velocity, get_init_vel, say, must ask the motorcycle speed and the angle of the ramp, and compute the initial velocity **u**. Function v2Polar will do that job, but it would be nice if the user could enter the speed in miles/hour. Internally, however, the program must use consistent units, so everything must be converted to units involving feet and seconds. Also, like all the trigonometric functions, v2Polar wants its angle in radians, but the user will wish to enter it in degrees, so this too will need converting.

Computing the edge of the ledge, **p**, is easy: since the origin is at the end of the take-off ramp as shown in Figure 11.1, the distance of the ledge from the ramp is p.x and the ledge height is p.y. The function to obtain **p**, get_ledge_edge, say, can simply input these quantities in feet. The first half of the program is shown in Listing 11-4a.

Listing 11-4a

```
/* Program to compute trajectory of object projected from a ramp towards
   a ledge, and to tell if it lands correctly.
*/

#include <stdio.h>
#include <math.h>
#include "vector2.h"
#define FALSE (0)
#define TRUE (1)

float RAD_FACTOR;                        /* Degree to radian conversion factor */
#define FPS_FACTOR (5280.0/3600.0) /* mph to ft/sec conversion factor */
vector2 get_init_velocity(void);
vector2 get_ledge_edge(void);
void produce_results(vector2 p, vector2 u);

main() {
    vector2 p,                       /* Position of ledge edge from ramp */
            u;                       /* Initial velocity */
    RAD_FACTOR = atan(1.0)/45.0;     /* Initialize using the ratio of 45 */
                                     /* degrees to its radian value. */

    u = get_init_velocity();
    p = get_ledge_edge();
    produce_results(p, u);           /* Computes and prints solution */
    return 0;
}

/**** Functions to get initial settings: Compute from user input ****/

vector2 get_init_velocity(void) {
    vector2 u;
    float speed, angle;
    printf("Enter vehicle speed (mph): ");
    scanf("%f", &speed);
    printf("Enter angle of ramp to horizontal (degrees): ");
```

```
    scanf("%f", &angle);
    u = v2Polar(speed*FPS_FACTOR, angle*RAD_FACTOR);
    return u;
}

vector2 get_ledge_edge(void) {
    vector2 p;
    printf("Enter distance of ledge from ramp (feet): ");
    scanf("%f", &p.x);
    printf("Enter height of ledge above ramp (feet): ");
    scanf("%f", &p.y);
    return p;
}
```

Now for the function `produce_results`. For our present purposes (seeing how to use the vector package) we shall use simplified formulae to avoid obscuring the important issues, so the program's predictions will probably differ from what would actually happen — real stunt riders please note, this program is **not** for you! Assuming constant acceleration **a**, the equations for displacement **s** and velocity **v** of a body after a time t are

$$\mathbf{s} = \mathbf{u}t + {}^1\!/_2\,\mathbf{a}\,t^2 \qquad (1)$$

and

$$\mathbf{v} = \mathbf{u} + \mathbf{a}t \qquad (2)$$

Normally, we might work out horizontal and vertical components of **s** and **v** separately, but with the vector library we can do both together. Thus the bold symbols in the equations can be vectors whose x and y components stand for the horizontal and vertical components of the quantity.

The vertical acceleration due to gravity is 32 ft/sec^2. Thus the vector **g**, representing acceleration due to gravity, is the constant $(0,-32)$; in C, `a.x` equals 0 and `a.y` equals -32. We could declare this and initialize it as follows:

```
vector2 g = {0, -32.0};
```

Although **g** is constant, we have to store it in a variable, as C does not allow `struct` constants. (There is a special keyword, `const`, for these situations, but we can ignore it for now.)

We shall assume that over each 0.1 second, air resistance slows the speed by 0.2 percent. This represents an **a** value (change in velocity during 1 second) of 0.02**u**. However, this is a variable acceleration, whereas the acceleration **a** in equations (1) and (2) above must be constant. Therefore, over long times the results will be inaccurate. Nevertheless, we can get an approximate answer by treating **a** as constant for a short time (say 0.1 second) and recomputing it after that time. For example, to find the position **s** after 6 seconds, we do not use equation (1) over a single time interval of $t=6$ seconds; instead we use it over sixty time intervals, each with $t=0.1$ second, recomputing **a** in between each application of the equation. The total displacement after 6 seconds will be the sum of the **s** values for all of these short intervals. This is a simple example of a numerical method for solving differential equations. For better results a more advanced method should be used. Solving equations numerically is a complex subject in its own right, and for good results the method used must be suitable for the problem being solved.

In the program we shall assume for simplicity that the user does not enter absurd values — for example, a negative or zero horizontal speed. We can therefore program the function as a loop that repeats until the cycle either hits the ledge or lands on it.

```
Set time t to 0.
Set distance to 0.
Set initial position to (0,0).
Print headings.
while the cycle is in the air:
    Print details,
    Increment t by 0.1,
    Calculate a for this interval,
    Recompute cycle position s and velocity v,
    Add s to distance (to compute total distance traveled),
    Update u for next iteration.
Compute and print final outcome information.
```

It would be nice if, as soon as the cycle is above the ledge, we were told of this in the printout. We need only know the first time that the cycle position is over the ledge. It is easy to check for this, but so that the program prints a message only once, we need a flag to tell us if we have printed a message previously. An expanded plan might be:

```
Set time t to 0.
Set distance to 0.
Set over_ledge to FALSE.
Set initial position to (0,0).
Print headings.
while the cycle is in the air:
    Print details,
    If over_ledge is FALSE and we are now over the ledge:
        Print message,
        Set over_ledge to TRUE.
    Increment t by 0.1,
    Calculate a for this interval,
    Recompute cycle position s and velocity v,
    Add s to distance (to compute total distance traveled),
    Update u for next iteration.
Compute and print final outcome information.
```

Listing 11-4b shows this function, which completes the program. The vector calculations automatically evaluate both the x and y components. In a large scientific program doing many computations it is very convenient to be able to directly program mathematical concepts such as vectors. To compile this program it must be linked with the `vector2` routines shown in Listing 11-3; details on how to do this vary from compiler to compiler, so you must check with your instructor or your compiler manual.

Listing 11-4b

```
/**** produce_results: Compute and display behaviour of cycle. ****/

void produce_results(vector2 p, vector2 u) {
    vector2 g = {0, -32.0};          /* gravity (constant) */
    #define DELTA_T (0.1)            /* the length of each time interval */
    float t = 0;                     /* time since cycle took off. */
    vector2 v;                       /* velocity at end of time interval */
    vector2 s;                       /* distance traveled in time interval */
    vector2 a;                       /* Assumed constant acceleration during
                                        a short time interval */
    vector2 total_s = {0.,0.};       /* distance from origin at time t. */
    int over_ledge = FALSE;          /* Not yet over ledge at the start */

    /* Print headings */
    printf(
        "\n Time   Horizontal    Vertical    Horizontal    Vertical\n"
        " (sec) Position(ft) Position(ft)  Speed(mph)  Speed(mph)\n"
    );

    /* while the cycle is in the air, either it has not reached the ledge,
       or it has reached it, but is above it.
    */
    while (total_s.x < p.x  ||  total_s.y > p.y) {
        /* Print details */
        printf(
            "%5.1f   %8.2f    %8.2f    %8.2f    %7.2f",
            t, total_s.x, total_s.y, u.x/FPS_FACTOR, u.y/FPS_FACTOR
        );
        if ( (! over_ledge) && total_s.x >= p.x) {
            printf("  Now over the ledge!");
            over_ledge = TRUE;
        }
        printf("\n");

        /* Recalculate a for the next short time interval */
        a = v2Sub(g, sv2Mul(0.02, u));    /* a = g - 0.02u */

        t += DELTA_T;                     /* Advance the total time */

        /* Compute distance traveled in time interval */
        s = v2Add(sv2Mul(DELTA_T, u), sv2Mul(0.5*DELTA_T*DELTA_T, a));
                                          /* s = ut + .5att */

        total_s = v2Add(total_s, s);      /* add s to total */

        /* Compute velocity at end of time interval */
        v = v2Add(u, sv2Mul(DELTA_T, a));/* v = u + at */
        u = v;                            /* This v is next iteration's u */
    }

    /* Compute and print final outcome information. */
    if (! over_ledge) {
        printf(
```

```
              "\nCycle FAILED to reach ledge! Missed by %3.1f ft.\n",
              p.y - total_s.y
          );
      } else {
          printf(
              "\nCycle made the ledge! Landed at angle %2.0f deg.\n",
              /* Convert landing angle to degrees, then make positive. */
              - v2Arg(v)/RAD_FACTOR
          );
      }
  }
```

Sample run 1

Enter vehicle speed (mph): **30**
Enter angle of ramp to horizontal (degrees): **30**
Enter distance of ledge from ramp (feet): **35**
Enter height of ledge above ramp (feet): **12**

Time (sec)	Horizontal Position(ft)	Vertical Position(ft)	Horizontal Speed(mph)	Vertical Speed(mph)
0.0	0.00	0.00	25.98	15.00
0.1	3.81	2.04	25.93	12.79
0.2	7.61	3.75	25.88	10.58
0.3	11.40	5.14	25.83	8.38
0.4	15.18	6.21	25.77	6.18
0.5	18.96	6.95	25.72	3.99
0.6	22.73	7.38	25.67	1.80
0.7	26.49	7.48	25.62	-0.39
0.8	30.24	7.26	25.57	-2.57
0.9	33.99	6.73	25.52	-4.75

Cycle FAILED to reach ledge! Missed by 6.1 ft.

Sample run 2

Enter vehicle speed (mph): **35**
Enter angle of ramp to horizontal (degrees): **30**
Enter distance of ledge from ramp (feet): **30**
Enter height of ledge above ramp (feet): **10**

Time (sec)	Horizontal Position(ft)	Vertical Position(ft)	Horizontal Speed(mph)	Vertical Speed(mph)	
0.0	0.00	0.00	30.31	17.50	
0.1	4.44	2.40	30.25	15.28	
0.2	8.87	4.48	30.19	13.07	
0.3	13.30	6.24	30.13	10.86	
0.4	17.71	7.67	30.07	8.66	
0.5	22.12	8.78	30.01	6.46	
0.6	26.51	9.57	29.95	4.27	
0.7	30.90	10.03	29.89	2.08	Over ledge!
0.8	35.28	10.17	29.83	-0.11	

Cycle made the ledge! Landed at angle 4 deg.

11.6 SUMMARY

- New data types can be created with `typedef`.
  - Put the word `typedef` before something that would otherwise be a variable declaration, and it creates a type instead of a variable.
  - The type thus created can be used to declare variables, function argument types, and function result types.
- A *structure*, also called a *record*, lets us package a collection of data items in a single variable.
  - Structure types are declared with `struct`:

    ```
    struct structure_name {
         ...declarations for fields within the structure...
    };
    ```

- `typedef` and `struct` can be combined to create a structured data type:

    ```
    typedef struct structure_name {
         ...declarations for fields within the structure...
    } structure_type_name ;
    ```

  - The fields in a structure can be simple variables, arrays, or even other structures.
- A structure type name can be used to declare variables, and function argument and result types.
- A structured variable can be used in most places where a simple variable can be used:
  - assignments (copies the entire contents of the structure)
  - function arguments
  - function return statements.
- A structured variable can be initialized as it is declared. The initializer consists of a list of constant values (one for each field of the structure) inside braces e.g.

    ```
    fruitcase froot = {50, .1, "Lemons"};
    ```

- A field in a structured variable can be accessed using the *dot*, or *field selection*, operator: `structured_variable_name.field_name`
- We may **not** have two fields with the same name in a single structure.
- We **may** have two fields with the same name in different structures.
- A structure must have at least one field.
- Fields in structures may have the same names as other objects.
- Structures and types may have the same name.
- A variable can have the same name as a structure.
- A structure may contain fields that are themselves structures, but it may not contain another copy of itself.
- A structure can contain arrays, and arrays can have structures as elements.

11.7 SELF-TEST EXERCISES

Short Answer

1   Write a declaration to create a type containing two fields: (a) an `int` called `size`, and (b) a `char` array of maximum size 50 called `name`. Show how to use this type to declare a variable. Then write a function that returns a value of this type. The function should input a string from the keyboard, store it in the structure, and set the size to the actual length of the string. Finally, show how to call the function to assign the function result to the variable declared earlier.

2   Show how to declare an array of 50 structures, each containing an `int` and a `float` field. Now show how to declare a structured variable containing an `int` and an array of 50 `floats`.

3   Because we cannot write a structured constant outside a combined declaration and initialization, it would be convenient in the `vector2` package to have a function to build a `vector2` from two floats, as in

```
somevector = vec2(12.4, 19.8+radius);
```

Write such a function; explain how to add it to the `vector2` library.

4   State whether the following are true or false.
    a   Structures cannot have two fields with the same name.
    b   Structures cannot have two fields of the same type.
    c   Structures must have at least two fields.
    d   A field in a structure cannot itself be a structure.
    e   Every variable of a given structured type has its own copy of the data fields defined in the structure.

Programming

5   Design a structure capable of storing positive integers of up to 500 digits. Write functions to add and multiply two such numbers. Then write a program that allows the user to input numbers and add or multiply them.

11.8 TEST QUESTIONS

Short Answer

1   State whether the following are true or false.
    a   The names of fields of a structure may be accessed using the dot (.) operator.
    b   A `typedef` name and a `struct` name may be the same.
    c   An array that is a field in a structure cannot have elements that are themselves structures.
    d   The name of a structure refers to the entire structure, so assigning one

structured variable to another of the same type will copy the entire contents of the structure.

e   `typedef` may only be used in conjunction with `struct`.

2   A chessboard is eight squares by eight, and chess pieces consist of white or black kings, queens, bishops, knights, rooks, and pawns. A programmer writing a chess-playing program wishes to store in a single structure a 'snapshot' of a chess game at a certain point in play. In addition to recording which pieces are on which squares, this also involves remembering how many moves have elapsed since the start of the game, how many since the last capture or pawn move, and whose move is next (white's or black's). Design a C structured type that will allow the programmer to declare variables capable of holding complete chess game snapshots.

3   Design a structured type capable of storing the time. Write a function that accepts two such values, computes the elapsed time between the two, and returns this value as its function result.

Programming

Use appropriate structures in all problems.

4   In Section 11.5 another method of developing a vector library was sketched out. Using that or a different method, develop a library for handling three-dimensional vectors. Include functions capable of computing the dot and cross products of two vectors (be careful to choose the correct result types for these functions). Write a program that thoroughly tests the correct operation of your package.

5   Write a program that maintains a telephone number database. The database should be a normal text file, as created with your usual editor. Each line should contain surname, first name, area or zip code, and phone number, with spaces between. The file will have a maximum of 500 entries. Write a program that reads this file and answers queries from the user, who should be able to ask for the number matching a given surname or given name, or the name matching a given number.

6   Write a program that answers questions about the planets of the solar system. For each planet, maintain information about its name, diameter, average distance from the sun, radius, mass, and number of moons. Also record the names and diameters of up to four moons per planet. Allow the user to enter a planet's name or number (closest to the sun is number 1) when asking for information.

7   Write a program to help the police with the likes of our friend Squeaky Louie. The program should read from a text file such information as height, weight, hair color, eye color, age, and sex. The police should be able to enter any item and see all matching names; then, if requested, the full file on any name should be displayed. Allow up to 200 entries.

8   Write a library package that allows C programs to do complex arithmetic. Include a suitable complex type, and functions for all the usual arithmetic operations. Write a program to test it exhaustively.

9   Write a program that can input information about two poker hands, and report which one wins.

10 An information service in a city wishes to answer phone queries about restaurants, such as type of food (Chinese, Indian, fast, etc.), neighbourhood, price range (low, medium, high), rating, address, phone number, etc. Callers will usually ask for either a certain type of food, a certain neighborhood, a certain price range, or a combination of these, and they will need to be told the names of suitable restaurants. Sometimes they will ask about a restaurant by name and should be told all the available information about it. Write a program to handle this problem using data stored in a text file. Remember that some restaurants have more than one type of food; allow up to five food types per restaurant, and up to 1000 restaurants.

11 A coin collector wishes to keep a catalog of coin values. Items of interest are denomination (e.g. $1, 50c), year, mintmark (up to ten characters), condition (VG (very good), F (fine), VF (very fine), EF (extremely fine), UNC (Uncirculated), or PRF (Proof)). The data will initially be entered as a text file with an editor, each line containing denomination, year, mintmark, and six values for the six possible conditions. The program should allow the collector to track changes in the coin market by rescaling (a) all values by any specified percentage, (b) all values for a particular denomination, or (c) all values for a particular condition. After each run the program should rewrite the modified file.

12 A maze can be represented in a computer by recording for each room which of the four walls contains a door to another room. Write a program that can read a maze description from a data file, and then describe how to get from the entrance to the exit. It should output a picture of the maze with the successful path. A method for finding the solution is to always turn the same way (say, left) at every opportunity; at dead ends, go out the way you came in. Provided the maze has exactly one entry connected somehow to one exit, this will eventually work. Allow for mazes of up to 15 by 15 rooms.

12

Memory addresses: pointers

Objectives

Review uses of pointers already encountered.

Examine further uses for pointers.

Learn how to manipulate pointers in C.
— pointer variables
— 'address-of' operator, &
— indirection ('follow-the-pointer') operator, *
— pointer arithmetic and operator priorities
— calling functions that return pointers
— pointers and arrays
— pointers and structures
— writing functions that modify their parameters.

12.1 INTRODUCTION TO POINTERS

You may be surprised to learn that every program you have written so far has used pointers, whether you knew it or not. A pointer may be thought of as a memory address. We have seen how `scanf` must be given pointers to the various variables it loads with input data. Every assignment statement is converted by the compiler into code involving the address of the target variable. We have also seen that an array name can stand for the address of the start of the array. In addition to these uses for pointers, C allows us to explicitly declare variables to store them, and to manipulate the data referenced by pointers.

Suppose we have a `float` variable called `radius`. The expression that tells us the address of that variable is

```
&radius
```

which uses the address-of operator, `&`. (We have already met this operator in connection with the `scanf` function.) The type of the above expression is pointer-to-`float`, because an address is a pointer, and it is the address of a `float`. We can declare variables to hold such values using the *indirection* symbol, `*`, as in

```
float *radius_addr;
```

We have met this previously when declaring `FILE` pointers. Using an assignment, we can copy the expression into the variable.

This works because an assignment can copy any type of data into a suitable variable; as the types on both sides of the `=` operator are the same, the assignment works. Suppose that the variable `radius` is located at address 4000 and contains 12.86, and that the variable `radius_addr` is at address 2000. Here is the effect of the above assignment:

```
radius_addr (at location 2000):          radius (at location 4000):
        ┌──────────────┐                         ┌──────────────┐
        │     4000     │                         │    12.86     │
        └──────────────┘                         └──────────────┘
```

The address of `radius` (4000) was stored in `radius_addr`. The **contents** of `radius` (i.e. 12.86) were not copied. To avoid inventing example addresses when illustrating pointer variables, it is usual to show a pointer as an arrow starting in the pointer variable and ending at the thing pointed to. Thus, we can redraw the previous picture as follows:

```
radius_addr :                                     radius:
        ┌────────┐                                ┌──────────────┐
        │   ●────┼───────────────────────────────▶│    12.86     │
        └────────┘                                └──────────────┘
```

Under this pictorial convention, **an arrow from A to B means that variable A contains the address of variable B**. The solid dot is located in the variable that holds the address. Suppose we had another float pointer, `another_addr`. Our picture would be

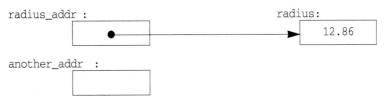

If we execute the statement

```
another_addr = radius_addr;
```

the contents of `radius_addr` are stored in `another_addr`. They both now contain the same address, so the picture becomes

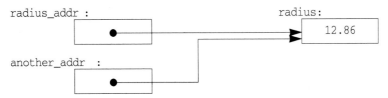

It is possible to make a pointer point nowhere; this is done with the macro `NULL`:

```
radius_addr = NULL;
```

This changes the picture to

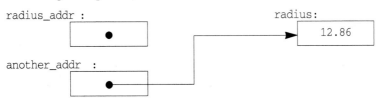

The macro `NULL` is defined in `<stdio.h>`, `<stddef.h>`, `<locale.h>`, `<stdlib.h>`, `<string.h>`, and `<time.h>`. A `NULL` pointer is shown pictorially as a dot with no arrow.

To access the variable pointed to by a pointer, C provides the *indirection*, or 'follow-the-pointer' operator, `*`. For example, suppose we want to print the value in the variable whose address is stored in `another_addr`. (In the above picture, the variable pointed to is `radius`, but pretend we don't know that.) We use `*` to find which variable `another_addr` points to:

```
printf("%f\n", *another_addr);
```

12.86 will be printed. For another example, consider the following

```
float *fptr1, *fptr2, float1, float2 = 10.5;
fptr1 = &float1;
fptr2 = &float2;
```

This creates the following situation:

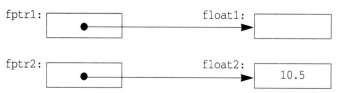

The following assignment, which includes the * operator,

```
*fptr1 = *fptr2;
```
alters the picture to

fptr1:   float1:   10.5

fptr2:   float2:   10.5

Thus the * operator causes the change to happen to the things pointed at, not to the pointer variables themselves. Conversely, omitting it causes the normal effect: the variables themselves are accessed. Thus

```
fptr1 = fptr2;
```

copies the address stored in fptr2, resulting in:

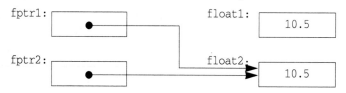

It is not correct to do either of the following.

```
fptr1 = *fptr2;  /* Incorrect: tries to store a float in a pointer */
*fptr1 = fptr2;  /* Incorrect: tries to store a pointer in a float */
```

12.2 IMPORTANT EXAMPLE: MODIFYING FUNCTION ARGUMENTS

Suppose we need to write a function to swap two floats. Here is something which will **not** work.

Listing 12-1

```c
#include <stdio.h>
void swapfloats(float a, float b) {
    float temp;
    temp = a;
    a = b;
    b = temp;
}

main() {
    float first=2, second=1;
    swapfloats(first,second);
    printf("%f %f\n", first, second);
    return 0;
}
```

The problem is that each formal parameter is assigned a **copy** of the corresponding actual parameter; after that there is no further connection between the two. When swapfloats is called from main, we have the situation in Figure 12.1. The argument copies inside swapfloats are exchanged, leaving the variables in main unaltered.

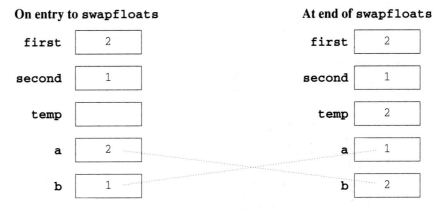

Figure 12.1 The effect of executing swapfloats in Listing 12-1

The cure is to pass to the function, not the float values, but the addresses of the float variables. The function will then be able to get at the original variables using the * operator, as shown in Listing 12-2.

Listing 12-2

```
#include <stdio.h>

typedef float * floatptr;

void swapfloats(floatptr a, floatptr b) {
    float temp; /* This is still float, because we are swapping floats */
    temp = *a;   /* Note the '*'s - get the float pointed to by a. */
    *a = *b;     /* Copy the float b points at into the variable a points at*/
    *b = temp;   /* Copy the float in temp into the variable b points at. */
}

main() {
    float first=2, second=1;
    swapfloats(&first,&second);     /* Note the 'address-of' operators */
    printf("%f %f\n", first, second);
    return 0;
}
```

Listing 12-2 works properly, swapping `first` and `second`. Pictorially, the operations are as shown in Figure 12.2.

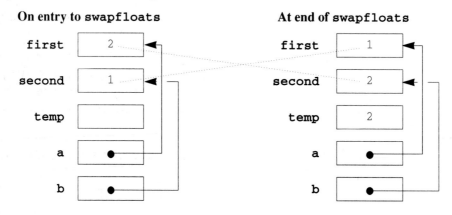

Figure 12.2 The effect of executing `swapfloats` in Listing 12-2

This technique for altering parameters to functions is of the greatest importance in C because, apart from function results and global variables, it is the only way to get a function to modify an external simple variable.

12.3 POINTERS, ARRAYS, AND POINTER ARITHMETIC

The connection between pointers and arrays is very important in C, and needs special attention. Therefore you should study this section with extra care.

Section 7.3 examined array arguments to functions. We saw that in that situation, the system passes the array's address to the function; it does not copy the entire array. This is an effect of a general rule that applies whenever we use an array name as a value in an expression; the function argument is just one particular case of this general rule. Another situation where the rule applies is when an array name is on the right hand side of an assignment. To understand this rule, consider these declarations:

```
char buffer[4];
char *chptr;
```

The rule states that the word `buffer`, when used as a value in an expression, stands for the address of `buffer[0]`, the first element in the array. Since an array is located at a fixed place in memory, this address is fixed. Therefore we can think of the name of an array as acting like a constant pointer pointing at the first element in the array; `chptr`, on the other hand, is a simple pointer variable. We can represent this as follows.

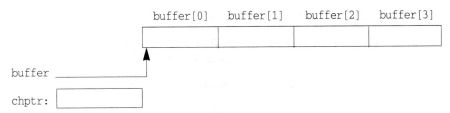

This diagram shows that we can use the word `buffer` as a pointer to `buffer[0]`, but it **is not a variable**: unlike `chptr`, we cannot assign a value to `buffer`. However, since the name `buffer` acts like a pointer to `char`, we should be able to assign it to a pointer-to-`char` variable. Therefore, the following statement

```
chptr = buffer;
```

will copy the address represented by `buffer` into `chptr`, giving

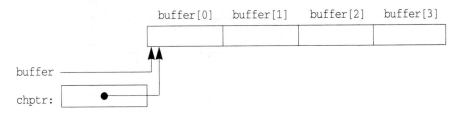

Now since `buffer` and `chptr` are the same kinds of values (pointer to `char`), anything we can do with one we should be able to do with the other (except assign to `buffer`). One thing we can do with `buffer` is give it a subscript. Sure enough, we can also add a subscript to `chptr`:

```
chptr[1] = 'A';
```

Conversely, since we can 'follow-the-pointer' from `chptr` by writing `*chptr`, we should be able to do that with `buffer`.

```
*buffer = 'B';
```

Indeed, both the above statements work correctly, and leave us with this situation:

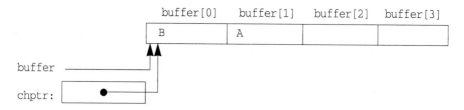

These examples lead us to conclude that in expressions, we may use array names and pointer variables in similar ways, except that array names act like constants, so we may not assign to them. For a complete explanation of this topic, see Appendix C.5.

12.3.1 Pointer arithmetic

C allows us to do arithmetic with pointer values. In particular, we can add integers to pointers. The effect is to advance the pointer through memory by an appropriate amount. For example, in the previous section `chptr` was a pointer to `char`, so adding, say, 2 to `chptr` will advance it through memory by two `chars`. Subtracting an integer from a pointer works similarly, but in the opposite direction. Continuing the example in the previous section, the statement

```
chptr += 2;
```

results in

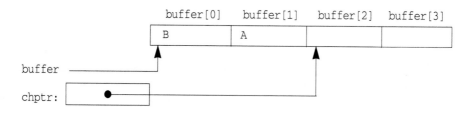

so the statements

```
chptr[0] = 'Y';
chptr[1] = '\0';
```

result in

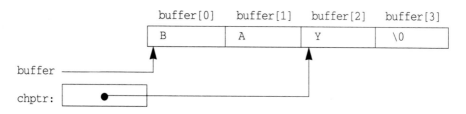

Using pointer arithmetic, we are allowed to advance a pointer until it is **only just** beyond the end of the array in which it was originally placed. (That is, it can point to the very first memory location that is not part of the array.) Thus if we added another 2 to `chptr`, we would have

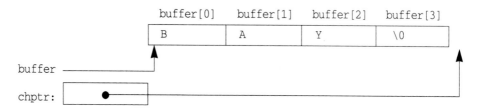

When a pointer is beyond the end of the array, we are not allowed to use the indirection operator `*`, or array subscripts, to access the memory there: it is not allocated to the array, and such access could cause unpredictable alterations to unrelated data. Why, then, are we allowed to make the pointer go just beyond the end of the array at all, if we cannot use the memory there? The reason is that sometimes it helps us to write simpler code. For example, in the previous picture we could find out how many `char`s were between the start of the array and `chptr` by using another feature of pointer arithmetic, subtraction of two pointers. Thus

```
printf("chptr skipped %d characters\n", chptr - buffer);
```

will print

```
chptr skipped 4 characters
```

Pointer subtraction finds the number of items between two pointers. In all pointer arithmetic, the compiler correctly accounts for the type of data item concerned. For example, if we subtract two `float` pointers, we get the number of `float`s between them; if we subtract two `int` pointers, we get the number of `int`s between them. This is in spite of the fact that `int`s, `float`s, `char`s, etc. all use different amounts of storage; the C compiler worries about that, not us.

To store the difference between two pointers in a variable, include the header `<stddef.h>`, and declare your variable to have the type `ptrdiff_t`. This is an integral type, either `int` or `long`, but we don't know which, as it can be different on different computers. On some computers, an `int` might be large enough to hold any possible difference between pointers, but on others, a `long` might be needed. So that you don't have to guess which is the right one, the macro `ptrdiff_t` is defined in the header as either `int` or `long`, whichever is appropriate on your computer.

A related macro is `size_t`; it should be used to declare any variable that will store the size of a memory region (for example, the size of an array). It is provided for the same reason as `ptrdiff_t`, and is defined in `<stddef.h>`, `<stdio.h>`, `<stdlib.h>`, and `<string.h>`. (You only need to `#include` one of these headers.) Use of `ptrdiff_t` and `size_t` is illustrated in the example in Section 12.3.2.

Array subscripts and pointer arithmetic

The array and pointer notations provide two ways to write accesses to array elements. For example, to print the A in the second element of `buffer`, we might write

```
printf("%c", buffer[1]);
```

or we might write

```
printf("%c", *(buffer+1));
```

In fact, these two notations are defined to mean exactly the same thing. That is, the array subscript notation is provided purely for convenience and appearance; it provides no extra capabilities beyond that obtainable using pointer addition and pointer indirection.

12.3.2 Library string and memory functions

The standard library provides string-manipulation and other functions that either return pointer results or rely heavily on pointer arithmetic. Some such functions are listed in Table 12.1.

Table 12.1 Library string and memory manipulation functions

Function prototype	Purpose
`strchr(s, c)`	Returns the address of the first occurrence of the `char` c in the string s.
`strpbrk(s1, s2)`	Returns the address of the first character in the string s1 which is also in s2.
`strrchr(s, c)`	Returns the address of the last occurrence of the `char` c in the string s.
`strstr(s1, s2)`	Searches s1 looking for s2. Returns the address of the first occurrence of the string s2 in s1.
`memmove(s1, s2, n)`	Copies n characters from the object pointed to by s2 into the object pointed to by s1. s1 and s2 may point to overlapping memory regions. s1 and s2 are not treated as strings: that is, a nul in s2 does not stop the copying, and no terminating nul is appended to s1.
`memcpy(s1, s2, n)`	As memmove, except that the two memory regions may not overlap.

The first four of these return a pointer: if the item being searched for is not found, NULL is returned. The following example illustrates the use of `strstr` and `memcpy`; the others can be used in analogous ways.

Example: Editing a string

The task is to write a function to search a string for every occurrence of a given substring, and replace them all with some other string. This is a common task in text editing. The function heading will be

```
int str_repl(
    char dest[], char src[], char pattern[],
    char repl[], size_t size
);
```

The function will copy `src` to `dest`, but with every occurrence of `pattern` replaced by `repl`. `size` indicates the size of the `dest` array: if exceeded, the result is truncated and the function returns 1; if everything fits without truncation, the function returns 0.

The function `strstr` can be used to locate the `pattern` substrings within `src`. We can regard the `src` string as consisting of sections of 'plain' text (i.e., not containing the pattern — to be copied verbatim) alternating with copies of the `pattern`. (If two copies of `pattern` occur side-by-side, we can think of the plain text in between as having zero length.) This suggests the following algorithm:

```
while another copy of the pattern can be found in src
    copy the plain text preceding it,
    copy the replacement text,
    skip the pattern.
Finally copy any plain text after the final pattern.
```

For the moment we shall ignore the need to check for overflow of the `dest` array. The basic loop requires a `char` pointer to indicate the location within `src` of the latest piece of plain text: `plain_start`, say. Another pointer, `pattern_start`, say, will mark the start of the pattern following that plain text; when the loop fails to locate any more copies of the pattern, `pattern_start` will be NULL, meaning that plain text extends to the end of the string. A third pointer, `target`, say, will indicate the place within `dest` where the next piece of text should be copied. Thus the algorithm could be coded in C as follows.

```
char *plain_start;    /* Start of a section of plain text */
char *pattern_start;  /* Start of a pattern (at end of plain) */
char *target;         /* Where to put the text in dest */
size_t pattern_leng;  /* Length of the pattern string */
size_t repl_leng;     /* Length of the replacement string */

pattern_leng = strlen(pattern); /* Compute once only before loop */
repl_leng = strlen(repl);       /* ditto */
plain_start = src;              /* First plain section at start of src */
target = dest;                  /* First copy is to the beginning of dest */
```

```
    while ( (pattern_start = strstr(plain_start, pattern)) != NULL ) {
        memcpy(target, plain_start, pattern_start - plain_start);
                                           /* Copy the plain text */
        target += pattern_start - plain_start; /* Update target */
        memcpy(target, repl, repl_leng);       /* Copy the replacement */
        target += repl_leng;                   /* Again update target */
        plain_start = pattern_start + pattern_leng; /* next plain section*/
    }
    strcpy(target, plain_start); /* The final plain section - also adds
                                    the string-terminating nul. */
```

Remembering the need to check for overflowing `dest`, we note that checks must be made before the `memcpy` and `strcpy` steps. If we have a `size_t` variable remembering how much free space remains in `dest` (`free_space`, say) then at each copy we can subtract the amount to be copied and make sure `free_space` is still non-negative. The algorithm can therefore be expanded to

```
set free_space to size-1 (to allow for the trailing '\0').
while another copy of the pattern can be found in src
    check & adjust free_space, & copy across the plain text preceding it,
    check & adjust free_space, & copy the replacement text,
    skip the pattern.
Check & adjust free_space, & copy any plain text after the final pattern.
```

The 'check & adjust & copy' steps will return early if the destination fills. This is programmed in Listing 12-3. A short `main` function is also provided for testing.

Listing 12-3

```
/* str_repl: Function to replace all copies of a given pattern within
    a string.
On entry:   dest is the destination array; size is its length.
            src is the source array containing a string.
            pattern and repl contain strings.
On exit:    dest contains a nul-terminated string which is a copy of src,
            with all occurrences of pattern replaced by repl.
            Returns 0 if everything fitted in dest, 1 if result was truncated
            to fit.
*/

#include <string.h>
#include <stddef.h>

int str_repl(
    char dest[], char src[], char pattern[], char repl[], size_t size
) {
    char *plain_start;        /* Start of a section of plain text */
    char *pattern_start;      /* Start of a pattern (at end of plain) */
    char *target;             /* Where to put the text in dest */
    size_t pattern_leng;      /* Length of the pattern string */
    size_t repl_leng;         /* Length of the replacement string */
    ptrdiff_t chunksize;      /* size of a piece */
```

```
/* Note: size will be initially set to the maximum string length that
   the destination can hold (not counting the nul), and will be
   reduced as the array is filled. Thus at any given time it indicates
   the free space left in dest; when it is zero, there will still be
   room for the string-terminating nul.
*/
if (size == 0) {
    return 1;                       /* Success is impossible: no room for nul */
}
size--;                             /* Reserve room for the nul */

pattern_leng = strlen(pattern);  /* Compute once only before loop */
repl_leng = strlen(repl);         /* ditto */
plain_start = src;                /* First plain section at start of src */
target = dest;                    /* First copy is to the beginning of dest */

while ( (pattern_start = strstr(plain_start, pattern)) != NULL ) {

    /* Pattern was found - Copy preceding plain section */
    chunksize = pattern_start - plain_start;  /* This will be >= 0 */
    if (chunksize >= size) {                  /* dest overflow? */
        memcpy(target, plain_start, size);    /* Yes - truncate */
        target[size] = '\0';                  /* nul at end of string */
        return 1;                             /* report failure */
    }
    memcpy(target, plain_start, chunksize);   /* OK: Copy plain text */
    target += chunksize;                      /* Update target */
    size -= chunksize;                        /* adjust free count */

    /* Copy replacement pattern */
    if (repl_leng >= size) {                  /* dest overflow? */
        memcpy(target, repl, size);           /* Yes - truncate */
        target[size] = '\0';                  /* nul */
        return 1;                             /* report failure */
    }
    memcpy(target, repl, repl_leng);          /* OK: Copy replacement */
    target += repl_leng;                      /* Again update target */
    size -= repl_leng;                        /* adjust free count */

    plain_start = pattern_start + pattern_leng; /* next plain section*/
}

/* Copy the final plain text section. */
chunksize = strlen(plain_start);              /* length of final section */
if (chunksize >= size) {                      /* dest overflow? */
    memcpy(target, plain_start, size);        /* Yes - truncate */
    target[size] = '\0';                      /* nul at end of string */
    return 1;                                 /* report failure */
}
strcpy(target, plain_start); /* OK: Copy entire plain section - also
                                add the string-terminating nul. */

return 0;                       /* Success */
}
```

```
/*********** main function for testing purposes ************/

#include <stdio.h>

main() {
    char src[51], dest[51], pattern[21], repl[41];
    int result;
    printf("Enter src:         ");
    scanf("%50[^\n]%*[^\n]", src);getchar(); /* Load line, flush to '\n' */
    /* Load entire line, flush '\n' */
    printf("Enter pattern:     ");
    scanf("%20[^\n]%*[^\n]", pattern);getchar();
    printf("Enter replacement: ");
    scanf("%40[^\n]%*[^\n]", repl);getchar();
    result = str_repl(dest, src, pattern, repl, 51);
    printf("String: \"%s\"\nResult: %d\n", dest, result);
    return 0;
}
```

Sample run 1 (no overflow)

```
Enter src:         Spelling erers: The worst sort of erer.
Enter pattern:     erer
Enter replacement: error
String:  "Spelling errors: The worst sort of error."
Result: 0
```

Sample run 2 (overflow)

```
Enter src:         The poor program was very poor to follow clearly.
Enter pattern:     poor
Enter replacement: difficult
String:  "The difficult program was very difficult to follow"
Result: 1
```

12.4 POINTERS AND STRUCTURES

We are permitted in C to declare pointers to any sort of data item, including structures. In Listing 11-1, we created a structure called staff_data:

```
typedef struct {
    char    surname[SURNAME_SIZE];
    char    given_names[GIVEN_NAME_SIZE];
    char    address1[ADDRESS_SIZE];
    char    address2[ADDRESS_SIZE];
    char    title[TITLE_SIZE];
    long    payroll_no;
    int     age;
    int     department;
    double  salary;
    char    sex;
} staff_data;
```

A pointer to such a structure (`staff_ptr`, say) is declared, as with all pointers, as

```
staff_data *staff_ptr;
```

We can combine in the one program all the features of both pointers and structures, provided we take care. For example, suppose we have a `staff_data` variable to which `staff_ptr` is pointing, and further, suppose we wish to print the `age` field of that variable. We might try this:

```
printf("%d", *staff_ptr.age);
```
wrong

Unfortunately, if we check the operator priorities in Appendix D, we find that the . operator has a higher priority than the * operator, so the above really means

```
printf("%d", *(staff_ptr.age));
```
wrong

and the problem is that `staff_ptr`, being a pointer and not a structure, does not have any field called `age`. The cure is to parenthesize the indirection operation.

```
printf("%d", (*staff_ptr).age);   /* Correct */
```

This now means: Follow the pointer to the structure being pointed at, **then** select the `age` field from that structure. It turns out that this is a very common combination of operations, so common that C provides a special operator, `->` that combines the * and . operations. Here is that same `printf` statement, using `->`:

```
printf("%d", staff_ptr->age);   /* Correct */
```

To illustrate these features, we can improve the program in Listing 11-1 using pointers. The `staff_data` structure is a large object due to the various arrays within it. When these structures are sorted they are copied and recopied many times, wasting a lot of processing time. For example, the program would rearrange three structures as follows

Before sorting

Very large structure 1
Very large structure 2
Very large structure 0

After sorting:

Very large structure 0
Very large structure 1
Very large structure 2

The cure for this inefficiency is to create an array of pointers to the structures, and sort the array of pointers instead. Pictorially, this looks as follows

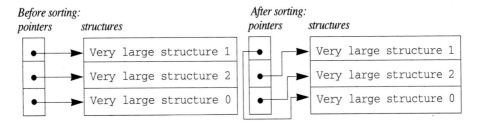

A pointer is a single value. Therefore it is more efficient to rearrange pointers than to rearrange large structures, yet it has the same effect: by following the pointers in order, the structures can be accessed in the correct order also. Doing this to the program in Listing 11-1 requires an array of pointers to `staff_data` objects, correctly initialized to point to the corresponding elements in the array of structures. Also, the calls to the `sort_data` and `write_data` functions must be modified to pass the pointer array rather than the structure array. Listing 12-4a shows the modified `main` function, with alterations in bold. Nothing prior to the section listed is altered in any way.

Listing 12-4a

```
void sort_data(staff_data *staff[], int numb_staff);
void write_data(staff_data *staff[], int numb_staff);

main() {
    staff_data staff[MAX_STAFF];
    staff_data *pstaff[MAX_STAFF]; /* array of pointers to staff_datas */
    int numb_staff;               /* How many employee records are read */

    /* Set up pointers: */
    for (numb_staff=0; numb_staff<MAX_STAFF; numb_staff++) {
        pstaff[numb_staff] = &staff[numb_staff];
    }

    numb_staff = load_data(staff);
    sort_data(pstaff, numb_staff);
    write_data(pstaff, numb_staff);
    return 0;
}
```

Finally, the functions `sort_data` and `write_data` must be modified to access the data via the pointer array. Instead of 'dot' field selection on the structure, as in

```
staff[i].age
```

they must use the `->` operator to follow the pointer and then select the field, as in

```
pstaff[i]->age
```

To swap elements, `sort_data` must swap the pointers, not the structures. `load_data` need not be modified, because the initial order of the pointers is the same as that of the structures. The altered functions are shown in Listing 12-4b, again, with the modified sections in bold.

Listing 12-4b

```
int in_wrong_order(staff_data *pstaff[], int which);
    /* Compares items at indices which & which+1, tells if disordered. */

void sort_data(staff_data *pstaff[], int numb_staff) {
    staff_data *temp_ptr;
    int i, j;

    for (i=numb_staff-1; i>0; i--) { /* scan numb_staff-1 times */
        for (j=1; j<=i; j++) {  /* Scan the elements still unsorted. */
            if (in_wrong_order(pstaff,j-1)) {
                temp_ptr = pstaff[j-1];           /* Swap elements */
                pstaff[j-1] = pstaff[j];
                pstaff[j] = temp_ptr;
            }
        }
    }
}

int in_wrong_order(staff_data *pstaff[], int which) {
    /* Compares items at indices which & which+1, tells if disordered.
       Do three tests, stop at the first where the items differ.
    */
    int order;  /* will be <0 for less, 0 for ==, >0 for greater */
    order = strcmp(pstaff[which]->surname, pstaff[which+1]->surname);
    if (order==0) {      /* surnames ==, must compare given names. */
        order = strcmp(
            pstaff[which]->given_names, pstaff[which+1]->given_names
        );
        if (order==0) {     /* given names ==, must compare payroll. */
            return (pstaff[which]->payroll_no>pstaff[which+1]->payroll_no);
        }
    }
    return (order>0); /* Since (order>0) means they are wrongly ordered. */
}

void write_data(staff_data *pstaff[], int numb_staff) {
    FILE *outf;
    int i;

    outf = file_open("lst11-1.new", "w");           /* See listing 10-7 */

    for   (i=0; i<numb_staff; i++) {
        fprintf (
            outf, "%-*s%-s\n%-s\n%-s\n%-*s%ld %d%c %4.2f %d\n",
            SURNAME_SIZE-1, pstaff[i]->surname, pstaff[i]->given_names,
            pstaff[i]->address1, pstaff[i]->address2, TITLE_SIZE-1,
            pstaff[i]->title, pstaff[i]->payroll_no, pstaff[i]->age,
            pstaff[i]->sex, pstaff[i]->salary, pstaff[i]->department
        );
    }
    fclose(outf);
}
```

The output of the modified program is the same as for Listing 11-1.

Matrix manipulation is another application where this style of processing can be convenient, as it is possible to write general-purpose functions with more flexibility in the sizes of the arrays they handle. For example, a function to invert a matrix would normally need at least one of the two dimensions of its square array parameter specified:

```
void invert(size_t size, float dest[][4], float src[][4]);
```

This means that we are restricted to using (in this case) 4 × 4 arrays, and perhaps allowing size to specify a subset of the array for actual manipulation. This sad circumstance is avoidable if a row of pointers is used for the array representation:

```
void invert(size_t size, float *dest[], float *src[]);
```

The actual array elements can be laid out in a one-dimensional array of floats. The float pointer array elements will be used to point to the start of successive rows of the matrix in the float array. Pictorially, if src is the array of float pointers and srcbuf is the array of floats, we would have this situation:

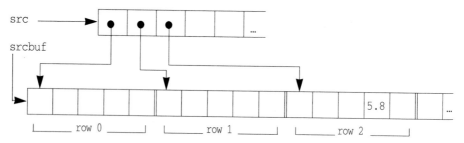

The pointers can be set up subject to overall array size constraints, but independent of any restriction on the individual subscripts, as follows:

```
float srcbuf[100], *src[20]; /* Max overall size, 100 elts, max rows 20 */
for (i=0; i<3; i++) {           /* Set up a 3-row matrix */
    src[i] = &srcbuf[5*i];      /* with 5 columns/row: total 15 elements. */
}
src[2][3] = 5.8;                /* Use the matrix 'src' in the normal way. */
```

Another benefit of this technique is that rows of a matrix can be swapped by exchanging the pointers, which is faster than exchanging the contents of the rows themselves. For example, to swap rows 1 and 2 of src above, we could write

```
float *temp;
...
temp = src[1]; src[1] = src[2]; src[2] = temp;
```

Organizing matrices in this way is pursued in the Self-test Exercises.

12.5 SUMMARY

- A *pointer* is an address of a variable or other item.
- The address of a variable is found with the operator &, as in:

    `&radius`

- A variable to hold a pointer to a given data type is declared

    `given_data_type *pointer_variable_name;`

    e.g.

    `float *radius_addr;`

- To access the variable pointed to by a pointer, use the *indirection* operator, *, as in

    `printf("%f", *radius_addr);`

- To allow a function to modify an argument, (a) declare the argument as a pointer to the appropriate data type, (b) use the indirection operator within the function, and (c) pass the address of the actual data when calling the function; e.g.

    ```
    void zero(int *v) {
    ```
    └──────── *Declare argument as a pointer*

    ```
        *v = 0;
    ```
    └──────────────── *Use indirection within the function*

    ```
    }
    …
    zero(&i);
    ```
    └──────── *Pass an address (in this case, of an **int**) in the call*

- Addition or subtraction of an integer to or from a pointer makes the pointer point to a variable higher or lower in memory; e.g. adding 3 to an `int` pointer makes it point three `int`s further on in memory.
    - In portable C programs, never access memory beyond the end of an array.
- Subtraction of two pointers tells how many data items apart they are. For example in an array `arr`, `&arr[5]-&arr[3]` equals 2.
- An array name used as a value in an expression acts like a pointer constant, pointing always at element zero of the array.
    - You may therefore use indirection, pointer arithmetic, and array subscripting on both array names and on pointers.
    - Array subscripting is the same as a combination of pointer arithmetic and indirection; e.g. `arr[5]` is the same as `*(arr+5)`.
- The library functions `strchr`, `strpbrk`, `strrchr`, and `strstr` all return pointers to characters within a string.
- `memmove` and `memcpy` copy a specified number of characters, but do not treat the data as a nul-terminated string.

- You may declare pointers to structures in the usual way.
  - Given a pointer `pstr` pointing to a structure containing a field `fld`, you may access `fld` either by combining `*` and `.` as in

    ```
    (*pstr).fld
    ```

    or by using the 'follow-and-select' operator, `->`:

    ```
    pstr->fld
    ```

12.6 SELF-TEST EXERCISES

Short Answer

1 Explain the operation of this line from Listing 12-3:

    ```
    scanf("%40[^\n]%*[^\n]", repl); getchar();
    ```

2 What is printed by the following statements?

    ```
    char buf[]="The quick brown fox jumped over the lazy dog";
    char *chp1, *chp2, ch1, ch2;
    chp1 = strrchr(buf, 'd');
    chp2 = strchr(buf, ' ');
    printf("%.*s\n", chp1-chp2, chp2+1);
    ch1 = *buf;
    ch2 = buf[0];
    printf("%d\n", ch2 - ch1);
    ```

3 What is printed by the following statements?

    ```
    char buf[]="The quick brown fox jumped over the lazy dog";
    char *chp;
    chp = buf; putchar('(');
    while (*chp != '\0') {
        if (*chp != ' ') {
            putchar(*chp); chp++;
        } else {
            printf(")("); chp++;
        }
    }
    printf(")\n");
    ```

Programming

4 At the end of the main text of this chapter, a method was sketched out for storing matrices using an array of pointers to the individual matrix rows. Write a function that provides the caller with the address of such an array of pointers, set up to the dimensions specified by the caller. This address, being the address of a `float *` array, will be of type `float **`, a pointer to a pointer. (Remember, we can have pointers to any type of data.) Your function should use a global array of 1000 `floats` and a global array of 100 `float` pointers, and should be callable more than once, each time cutting out another matrix from these global arrays. If there

is insufficient room in either array to fill a request, the function should return NULL to indicate failure. For testing purposes, make it fill the allocated floats with a different value for each array. On printing the contents of the matrices and the global float array, you should be able to verify correct operation of the function.

12.7 TEST QUESTIONS

Short Answer

1   Given the declarations

```
long **lpp, *lp, l;
```

show how to assign the address of l to lp, and the address of lp to lpp. Then show, in a statement that mentions only the variable lpp, how to assign the value 5 to l.

2   Write a function with two arguments that inspects two int variables and ensures that the larger value is in the second argument variable.

3   Write statements that, for a given filename, will devise a 'backup' filename. On some systems this is done by replacing everything after the last dot in the name with "BAK", or, if the name has no dot, adding ".BAK".

4   Given the following,

```
typedef struct struc {int pi; float pf;} struc;
struc ss, *p; int pi; float f, fa[5];
p = &ss;
```

which of these statements are incorrect, and why?

```
a    *p = 57;
b    pi = 2;
c    p->pi = 2;
d    f = 5.1;
e    ss.pf = 5.1;
f    (*p).pf = 5.1;
g    p->pf = 5.1;
h    p.pf = 5.1;
i    ss->pf = 5.1;
j    fa = &f;
k    *fa = 5.1;
l    p = &f;
m    pi = p->pi;
n    printf("%f",*(fa+2));
```

Programming

5 Write a function `suppress(str,pat,n)` that removes the nth occurrence of the string `pat` from the string `str`.

6 Write a function `ctran(str,old,new)` using the library function `strpbrk`, which performs character translation on the contents of the string `str`. Each occurrence in `str` of a character in the string `old` should be replaced with the corresponding character from `new`. If `old` is shorter than `new` and the character position for replacement is beyond the end of `new`, delete the old character from `str`. (Note: this method will be inefficient for long strings.)

7 Write a program that inputs a list of up to 1000 `float`s from a file and then prints the longest non-decreasing sequence within that input. Use pointers as appropriate.

8 Write a function, `mystrchr`, that works the same as `strstr`, but calls no library functions. Use pointer notation only.

9 Write a function, `mystrcmp`, that works the same as `strcmp`, but calls no library functions. Use pointer notation only.

10 Write a function, `mystrncpy`, that works the same as `strncpy`, but calls no library functions. Use pointer notation only.

11 Write a function, `samestr`, that accepts two `char` pointer parameters and reports whether the second parameter points to a place within the string pointed to by the first parameter.

12 Write a function that, from a string, computes a 'sound-alike' string. This is done by removing all vowels. Such strings are often computed by spelling checkers when presenting a list of possible words in response to a wrongly-spelled word. (The actual algorithm used is slightly more complicated, but the principle is the same.)

13 Write a function, `wordloc`, that locates a word in a string. Unlike `strstr`, it should not locate words that are part of a larger word.

14 Write a program that allows the user to find their way through a 10×10 maze of rooms. The rooms in the maze are numbered as follows:

```
0  1  2  3  4  5  6  7  8  9
10 11 12 13 14 15 16 17 18 19
20 21 22 23 24 25 26 27 28 29
...
```

The maze should be input from a file, each line representing the connections available to one room in the maze. The first line describes room 0, the second room 1, and so on. On each line, the numbers of the rooms connected to the room being described are listed; so if the first line contained the numbers 1 and 10, it would mean that room 0 was connected to rooms 1 and 10. The program should start the user in room 0, and award a win upon entering room 100. At each stage, the user should be told the number of the current room and the numbers of the available rooms, from which a choice should be entered. The maze is much more interesting if 'wormhole' connections are allowed, for example, if room 2 is connected to room 47.

Write this program in two different ways, one where the connections are stored as array indices for the connecting rooms, and one where pointers are used. When both versions are working, which do you prefer?

15 Modify the previous program to devise its own maze, a different one each time it runs. Be sure that a solution is possible; this can be done by first getting the program to lay down a trail from room 1 to room 100, and then placing a large number of misleading connections.

16 The Life Game was described in Test Question 22 in Chapter 9. Write a version of the Life Game where, instead of the squares being automatically connected to the adjacent four squares, a `square` data structure contains four pointers to the adjacent `squares`. Wire these pointers up so that, within the interior of the grid, squares are connected as normal to the adjacent squares, but at the edges the squares along the top are connected to the squares at the bottom, and squares on the left are connected to the ones on the right, and vice versa. This means there are no edges: a glider exiting on the left should appear on the right, and so on. This can be thought of as playing the game on an infinite grid where the starting pattern repeats indefinitely in all directions. It can also be thought of as playing on an elastic board stretched over the surface of a donut with a hole in the middle. Strange but true!

13

Advanced programming with pointers

Objectives

Learn to use C facilities for dynamic allocation of memory:
— the *heap*, the `malloc` and `free` functions
— `sizeof` function
— `void` pointers.

Employ pointers in complex situations without risk of getting confused:
— use `typedef` to simplify declarations
— casts.

Make a brief preview of *Data Structures*.

See how to process command-line arguments.
— `argc` and `argv`.

Examine pointers to functions.

Learn how to understand arbitrarily complicated C declarations.

13.1 DYNAMIC MEMORY ALLOCATION

So far we have seen how, by using the address-of operator &, a pointer variable can be made to point at some other suitable variable declared in the program. There is one problem with that arrangement — storage for every piece of data must be declared in the program text. In other words, we must, when writing the program, anticipate how much data the program will be called on to handle. In general this is difficult or impossible to do. Consider the problem posed in the previous chapter about declaring matrices; sometimes we need a small matrix, sometimes a big one. One solution would be to declare the matrix to have a huge size and then use only a part of it. Unfortunately, if our program needs many different arrays and we declare them all to be enormous, we can easily run out of memory, especially on microcomputers.

A glimpse of a solution to this difficulty can be seen in Exercise 5 in Section 12.6. The problem was the creation of many two-dimensional arrays of various unanticipated sizes. The answer was to declare a single large array for the data elements, and allocate pieces of it to the individual matrices being created. That way we only have trouble when the total storage requirement exceeds the available space, not when an individual storage requirement exceeds a limit. For example, we might estimate that a program needs 100 matrices, each at most 10×10. That is a total of 10,000 elements. If we declare 100 separate 10×10 arrays, then, if it turns out we need, say, only ten arrays, each 11×11, our program fails, yet we have used only 1,210 of the 10,000 elements in the declared arrays. But by putting the 10,000 elements in a single store, we could easily allocate the ten 11×11 arrays.

This kind of consideration was apparent to the designers of C. Accordingly, the C library includes functions that provide us with memory allocated from a large memory pool called a *heap*. At any time during execution, the program can call the library function `malloc` to request a memory allocation of any required size. If a large enough piece of memory is available, the function returns its address. If not, it returns NULL to warn the program of the problem. Another function, `free`, lets the program tell the system that a certain allocated chunk of memory is no longer needed; `free` then marks that chunk as being available for satisfying further requests to `malloc`. This combination of `malloc` and `free` provides remarkably flexible management of program data storage.

To use `malloc` and `free`, first include the header file `<stdlib.h>`. (In some non-standard C systems you may have to include `<malloc.h>`, so if you find one name doesn't work, try the other.) A call to `malloc` usually takes the form

```
pointer_variable = (type_of_pointer_variable) malloc(space_required);
if (pointer_variable == NULL) {
    ...Handle situation where allocation fails.
}
```

For example, to dynamically allocate space for a 50-character string, we might proceed as in Listing 13-1.

Listing 13-1

```
#include <stdio.h>
#include <stdlib.h>
#include <string.h>
main() {
    char * str;
    str = (char*)malloc(51 * sizeof(char)); /* (not forgetting the nul) */
    if (str == NULL) {
        fprintf(stderr, "ERROR: no space left.\n");
        exit(EXIT_FAILURE);
    }
    printf("Allocation succeeded!\n");
    strcpy(str, "Up to 50 characters"); /* Use str like any char array */
    return 0;
}
```

The call to `malloc` can be analyzed as follows.

```
str = (char*)malloc(51 * sizeof(char));
```
                                      amount of space required
              type cast to type of pointer variable
        pointer variable

Here, `sizeof` is a special operator that calculates the amount of storage needed to store one element of a given data type. As `str` is a `char` pointer, `sizeof` is used to evaluate the amount of storage required by **one** character. Multiplying this by 51 gives the space needed for the required 51 characters, and this value is passed as the argument to `malloc`. The writers of `malloc` did not know what kind of data we would want to store in the memory it allocates for us, so the return type of `malloc` is a special kind of pointer called a `void` pointer. A `void` pointer is a memory address like all other pointers, but the C compiler assumes nothing about the kind of data a `void` pointer points at. To use the space pointed to by a `void` pointer, it must be converted into a normal pointer of some kind. In the above, as the space is to be used as `chars`, it is appropriate to convert the `void` pointer into a `char` pointer. This is done by the type cast, `(char*)`. (Although C compilers do not strictly require a type cast here, many readers will be using C++ compilers, and these have more rigid requirements.) Finally, the address is assigned to the `char` pointer, `str`.

To see how this works in a practical example, we turn again to the problem of creating matrices of arbitrary size. Again, we shall use an array of pointers to the individual rows, but we shall not declare this array with a fixed size; rather we shall allocate both it and the array for the individual elements using `malloc`. All that need be declared as a normal named variable is a single pointer: `mat`, say. Using `malloc`, we shall connect `mat` to a two-level structure as shown below for a 3-row, 4-column matrix.

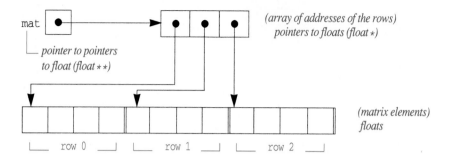

Organized arrangements of data such as this are called *data structures*; these are investigated further in Chapter 15. As shown in the diagram, the elements themselves are floats. Therefore the elements of the array of row addresses must be pointers to floats. The mat pointer will contain the address of one of those addresses, so it is a pointer to a pointer to a float, declared as follows:

```
float **mat;
```

Writing more than one * like that can get confusing, so it is a good idea to introduce a typedef and do things a little differently:

```
typedef float **matrix;
matrix mat;
```

This declaration for mat creates only the variable mat, not the entire system shown in the above diagram. Setting up this structure is a task for a function in our personal library: mat_create, say. mat_create will return a matrix suitable for assignment to a matrix variable. To do this it needs to know the row and column sizes, which should be arguments (row and column, say). There are row*column elements in the matrix, so the array of matrix elements should be created with a malloc call such as

```
(float*)malloc(row*column*sizeof(float))
```

The smaller matrix, the array of row pointers, contains row elements of type float*, so it should be allocated with the call:

```
(float**)malloc(row*sizeof(float*))
```

These must both be checked for success, and the array of row addresses must be set up with the appropriate pointers, as shown in Listing 13-2.

Listing 13-2 `mat_create` **function (not a complete program)**

```
#include <stddef.h>
#include <stdlib.h>

typedef float **matrix;

matrix mat_create(int row, int column) {
    float *elements, **rows; int i;

    /* First allocate the elements: */
    elements = (float*)malloc(row*column*sizeof(float));
    if (elements == NULL) {
        return NULL;      /* failure to allocate the element array */
    }

    /* Now allocate the rows: */
    rows = (float**)malloc(row*sizeof(float*));
    if (rows == NULL) {
        free(elements);     /* First return the allocated elements
                               to the available space. */
        return NULL;
    }

    /* Now load the rows with addresses of the appropriate elements.
       Successive rows are 'column' floats apart. */
    for (i=0; i<row; i++) {
        rows[i] = &elements[column*i];
    }

    return rows;     /* The address of the initialized row array */
}
```

The second test for failure in Listing 13-2 illustrates the use of the other main dynamic memory function, `free`. At that point the first allocation has succeeded, giving us an `elements` array; but if the second allocation fails, the `elements` array is useless because there is no `rows` array. We should return the space occupied by `elements` to free storage using `free`, as that space may be needed for some other purpose in the program. A call to `free` has the following format:

```
free(address_of_allocated_space);
```

Once a storage region has been freed, it is illegal to make any further use of it. If space is required later, another `malloc` call should be issued.

> **Note:** A pointer passed to `free` must have been previously allocated using `malloc` or the similar function, `calloc`, described in Appendix D. If any other pointer is given to `free`, failure of the program can be expected.

We shall now employ `mat_create` in a brief example: a program to input two matrices and print their matrix sum. The program will read the file `lst13-3.dat` that contains the row and column sizes and the matrices, and will print the sum on the terminal. The `matrix` data structure may be used like a normal 2-dimensional array, which greatly simplifies the coding. Listing 13-3 shows this program; it uses the function and data type declared in Listing 13-2. To compile it, either Listing 13-3 should be added to the end of Listing 13-2, or the declarations from Listing 13-2 added via a `.h` file.

Listing 13-3

```
/*** Program to input two matrices and print their sum ***/
#include <stdio.h>

void read_matrix(matrix m, FILE *f, int rows, int columns);
void sum_matrices(matrix sum, matrix a, matrix b, int rows, int columns);

main() {
    matrix a, b, c;
    int rows, columns, i, j;
    FILE * inf;
    inf = fopen("lst13-3.dat", "r");
    if (inf==NULL) {
        fprintf(stderr, "File open failure\n"); exit(EXIT_FAILURE);
    }
    fscanf(inf, "%d %d", &rows, &columns);
    a = mat_create(rows, columns);
    b = mat_create(rows, columns);
    c = mat_create(rows, columns);
    if (a==NULL || b==NULL || c==NULL) {
        fprintf(stderr, "Could not create matrices\n"); exit(EXIT_FAILURE);
    }
    read_matrix(b, inf, rows, columns);
    read_matrix(c, inf, rows, columns);
    fclose(inf);
    sum_matrices(a, b, c, rows, columns);
    /* Now print the sum matrix */
    for (i=0; i<rows; i++) {
        for (j=0; j<columns; j++) {
            printf("%8.4f ", a[i][j]);
        }
        printf("\n");
    }
    return 0;
}
void read_matrix(matrix m, FILE *f, int rows, int columns) {
    int i, j;
    for (i=0; i<rows; i++) {
        for (j=0; j<columns; j++) {
            fscanf(f, "%f ", &m[i][j]);
        }
```

```
        }
    }
}
void sum_matrices(matrix sum, matrix a, matrix b, int rows, int columns) {
    int i, j;
    for (i=0; i<rows; i++) {
        for (j=0; j<columns; j++) {
            sum[i][j] = a[i][j] + b[i][j];
        }
    }
}
```

Sample data file `lst13-3.dat`
```
3 4
1 2 3 4
0 2 3 3
1 1 1 1

0 0 1 1
2 2 2 2
3 3 4 5
```

Program output
```
1.0000   2.0000   4.0000   5.0000
2.0000   4.0000   5.0000   5.0000
4.0000   4.0000   5.0000   6.0000
```

> **Exercise**
> *Although it is not necessary in Listing 13-3, in some programs it may be necessary to free the storage allocated to a* `matrix`*. Explain exactly why the following statements do this to a* `matrix m`*:*
> `free(*m);`
> `free(m);`
> *Can the statements be interchanged? Why or why not?*

Note that in Listing 13-3 the values `rows` and `columns` are passed to every function. In a large program this might be a source of confusion or error. One way out would be to make these variables global. If a program used the same size matrices throughout, this might be a good approach. If, however, a program uses matrices of varying sizes, it may be better to package the size of a matrix along with the matrix itself; this can be done by using a structure like this:

```
typedef struct {
    matrix m;
    int rows, cols;
} scaled_mat;
```

Listing 13-4 shows the previous program rewritten to use such a structure to package the array itself with its size. As with Listing 13-3, it uses the matrix datatype defined in Listing 13-2. Output is the same as from Listing 13-3.

Listing 13-4

```
/*** Program to input two matrices and print their sum ***/
#include <stdio.h>

typedef struct {
    matrix m;
    int rows, cols;
} s_mat;

s_mat s_mat_create(int row, int column);
void read_matrix(s_mat m, FILE *f);
void sum_matrices(s_mat sum, s_mat a, s_mat b);

main() {
    s_mat a, b, c;
    int rows, columns, i, j;
    FILE * inf;
    inf = fopen("lst13-3.dat", "r");
    if (inf==NULL) {
        fprintf(stderr, "File open failure\n"); exit(EXIT_FAILURE);
    }
    fscanf(inf, "%d %d", &rows, &columns);
    a = s_mat_create(rows, columns);
    b = s_mat_create(rows, columns);
    c = s_mat_create(rows, columns);
    if (a.m==NULL || b.m==NULL || c.m==NULL) {
        fprintf(stderr, "Could not create matrices\n"); exit(EXIT_FAILURE);
    }
    read_matrix(b, inf);
    read_matrix(c, inf);
    fclose(inf);
    sum_matrices(a, b, c);
    /* Now print the sum matrix */
    for (i=0; i<a.rows; i++) {
        for (j=0; j<a.cols; j++) {
            printf("%8.4f ", a.m[i][j]); /* Note use of field m */
        }
        printf("\n");
    }
    return 0;
}

void read_matrix(s_mat m, FILE *f) {
    int i, j;
    for (i=0; i<m.rows; i++) {
        for (j=0; j<m.cols; j++) {
            fscanf(f, "%f ", &m.m[i][j]);
```

```
                }
        }
}

void sum_matrices(s_mat sum, s_mat a, s_mat b) {
        /* N.B.: Assumes all three are the same size!! */
        int i, j;
        for (i=0; i<sum.rows; i++) {
                for (j=0; j<sum.cols; j++) {
                        sum.m[i][j] = a.m[i][j] + b.m[i][j];
                }
        }
}
s_mat s_mat_create(int row, int column){
/* Failure is detected by checking the '.m' field for NULL */
        s_mat s;
        s.rows = row;
        s.cols = column;
        s.m = mat_create(row, column);
        return s;
}
```

13.2 CREATING LINKED DATA STRUCTURES

With pointers it is possible to build large interlinked data structures. For example, a *linked list* is a data structure consisting of a sequence of items, where each item in the sequence contains a pointer to the next one (and, in a *doubly linked list*, to the previous one also). The individual items are called *nodes*. Each node in the list is a C struct data item. There is an unfortunate re-use of the word 'structure' here: on the one hand, in C, a single struct data item is called a structure, and on the other hand, an entire collection of interlinked structs is called a 'data structure'.

Take great care to distinguish between a C (struct) structure, and a data structure.

Consider a program that displays and manipulates graphic shapes. A polygon, for example, is a list of points defining the vertices. If the user deletes a point a node must be removed from the list, and vice versa if a point is added. Such manipulations are well suited to linked lists. We start by defining a structure suitable for storing a single point. On a typical computer screen, this will require x and y co-ordinates for the location of the point; since a screen is a grid of points, these will be integers, usually measured from the top left corner:

```
typedef struct {
        int x, y;     /* x,y co-ordinates, top left == 0,0 */
} point;
```

The linked list of points that constitutes a polygon will have nodes containing a `point` and a pointer to the next node. The next node is, of course, another item of the same kind, and defining the data type needs a slight trick:

```
typedef struct vertex {
    point p;
    struct vertex * next;
} vertex;
```

The trick is that we have to give the `struct` itself a name for use in declaring the pointer `next`. We have thus created a type suitable for a node in a list:

The `next` field in a node points to the node that should follow. In the final node, `next` will be `NULL`. A variation of this scheme is to make the final `next` field point back to the first node; lists in which this is done are called *circular lists*.

It is perfectly legitimate for a node to contain a pointer to another node of the same kind. However the following, although it looks similar, is very wrong indeed.

```
typedef struct vertex {
    point p;
    struct vertex next;
} vertex;
```

*Here an attempt is being made to include within a `vertex` another `vertex` which would itself contain a `vertex`, and so on. It is like those trick pictures of someone holding a photo of themselves holding a photo of themselves holding... In short, it is perfectly okay for a `vertex` to **point** to another `vertex`, but it is wrong for a vertex to **contain** another vertex.*

To manage the entire linked list of `vertexes`, all we need is a pointer to the very first one, and for convenience, a pointer to the last one; these should be declared as ordinary variables — `phead` and `ptail`, say:

```
vertex *phead, *ptail;
```

The final `vertex` will have its `next` pointer set to `NULL` to indicate that no more `vertexes` follow. Thus an entire linked list will be represented as follows (this example containing two points):

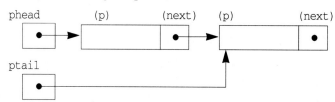

An empty list is represented by setting `phead` and `ptail` to NULL. The obvious question is how we actually build a list as illustrated above. Suppose we wish to add a fourth vertex at the end of the list. This would involve calling `malloc` to obtain space for a `vertex`, and then altering the links of the above list to produce this situation:

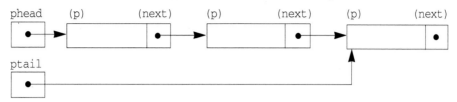

To do this the `next` field of the node at the end of the existing list must point to the new node, as must the `ptail` pointer, and the `next` field of the new node must be NULL:

```
ptail->next = (vertex*)malloc(sizeof(vertex)); /*Create new node */
...Check for failure...
ptail = ptail->next; /* ptail now points to the new node */
ptail->next = NULL;   /* The end of the list is marked correctly */
```

The `point p` in the new `vertex` should also be assigned *x,y* values. Adding to an empty list needs different processing, as shown below:

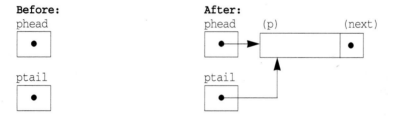

The steps needed are:

```
phead = (vertex*)malloc(sizeof(vertex));
...Check for failure...
ptail = phead;
ptail->next = NULL;
```

All these steps should of course be encapsulated in a suitable function. Since a list is represented by its `phead` and `ptail` values, it makes sense to package these in a structure also. Then we can have more than one list in a program if we wish:

```
typedef struct {
    vertex *phead, *ptail;
} point_list;
point_list poly1, poly2; /* creates 2 variables for lists. */
```

Now the variables `poly1` and `poly2` are both capable of storing a list of points because they both have `phead` and `ptail` fields. At least two facilities will be needed to manipulate these lists: a way to specify an empty list to initialize the `point_list` variables prior to use, and a function to add a node at a specified place in the list. The easiest way to initialize the lists is to do it as the list variables are declared, using a macro, so the above declaration should be altered to

```
#define EMPTY_LIST {NULL, NULL}
point_list poly1 = EMPTY_LIST, poly2 = EMPTY_LIST;
```

A node might need adding anywhere in a list — front, middle, or end — so a function to add a node needs to know which list to add to, where to add, and what to add. Although there are many ways to achieve this, the following fills the bill.

```
int add_node(point_list *plist, vertex *where, point pt);
```

Here `plist` is the list in which an addition is to be made, `where` points to the node preceding the spot where the new node is to be added, and `pt` is a `point` value for the new node. If `where` is NULL, the node should be added at the front. The function will return 0 on success, or 1 on failure.

We must now decide on the algorithm for this function. As failure can only occur if `malloc` fails to obtain space, it makes sense to test for that first and only proceed if space is obtained. Turning to the problem of actually adding the node to the list, recall that we found the need for two different sets of logic depending on whether the list was empty or not. The real reason for that was that in one case, the `next` field of a preceding node needed altering, and in the other, the `phead` pointer needed altering. Therefore what really matters is whether the node is being added at the front. This suggests the following algorithm:

```
Try to obtain space for the new node.
Return 1 if this fails.
Copy the point into the new node's p field.
if where is NULL
     add the new node at the start
else
     add the new node after where
Update the ptail pointer if the node was added at the end
Return 0.
```

To add a node at the start, `phead` must point to the new node, and the `next` field of the new node must point where `phead` pointed previously. Similarly, when adding after `where`, `where->next` must point to the new node and the `next` field of the new node must point where `where->next` pointed previously. In either case, everything still works if insertion is at the end of the list. Listing 13-5a shows the start of the graphics program, including function `add_node` and the other declarations decided on so far.

Satisfy yourself that it works correctly by tracing its operation when adding nodes at the front, middle and end of a list, and to an empty list.

Listing 13-5a

```c
#include <stdio.h>
#include <stdlib.h>

typedef struct {
    int x, y;          /* x,y co-ordinates, top left == 0,0 */
} point;

typedef struct vertex {
    point p;
    struct vertex * next;
} vertex;

typedef struct {
    vertex *phead, *ptail;
} point_list;

#define EMPTY_LIST {NULL, NULL}

/****** add_node ******  Adds a node to a point_list.
On entry: plist points to a point_list.
          where points to a node in that list, or is NULL.
          pt is a point to be stored in the new node.
          NB: None of these requirements are checked!
On exit:  EITHER: A new node, containing a copy of pt, is added to plist's
          list after node where. (If where is NULL, the new node
          is at the front.) The function returns 0. (normal return)
          OR: plist's list is unaltered, add_node returns 1. (error return)
*/
int add_node(point_list *plist, vertex *where, point pt) {
    vertex *newnode;
    /* Try to obtain space for the new node. */
    newnode = (vertex*)malloc(sizeof(vertex));
    if (newnode == NULL) {              /* Allocation failed - Return 1. */
        return 1;
    }
    newnode->p = pt;                    /* Fill the new node with data */
    if (where == NULL) {                /* Adding at head of list? */
        /* Add the new node at the start */
        newnode->next = plist->phead;   /* Previous 1st entry is now 2nd */
        plist->phead = newnode;         /* new entry is first */
    } else {                            /* Add the new node after where */
        newnode->next = where->next;    /* new node points to node that was
                                           previously straight after where */
        where->next = newnode;          /* where->next points to new node */
    }
    if (newnode->next == NULL) {        /* Was the node added at the end? */
        plist->ptail = newnode;         /* If so, it becomes the tail node */
    }
    return 0;
}
```

A professional graphics program would undoubtedly allow us to manipulate images using a mouse, but for this demonstration of linked lists we have to keep the length reasonable. Accordingly, let us specify that the program inputs a single polygon from a file, displays it, and then presents a menu allowing the user to add, delete, or move a point specified by number (1st, 2nd, etc.), or quit. After the user performs one of these, the program redisplays the polygon and queries the user again.

Before doing a top-down design for the program, it will be useful to have some list-manipulating functions that can be called wherever necessary. A function to locate the *n*th point and a function to delete a point will be required:

```
vertex *find_pt(point_list *plist, int which);
void del_pt(point_list *plist, vertex *which);
```

find_pt locates a point by advancing through the list the required number of times. If which is 0 or greater than the number of vertices in the list, the function returns NULL. If a pointer (pnode, say) points to a node in a list, the statement

```
pnode = pnode->next;
```

will make pnode point to the following node; this statement must be placed in a loop to advance the required number of times. Listing 13-5b shows function find_pt.

Listing 13-5b

```
/****** find_pt ******
 Locates the which'th vertex in a list.
 On entry: plist points to a point_list, which is the index of the node to
           locate (0=before first, 1=first, etc.).
 On exit:  Returns pointer to vertex, or NULL if which<=0 or > no. vertices
*/
vertex *find_pt(point_list *plist, int which) {
    vertex * pnode;                  /* To be used to advance through list */
    if (which <= 0) {
        return NULL;
    }
    pnode = plist->phead;       /* Pointer to first node */
    which--;                    /* which now == no. of nodes to skip. */
    /* Loop, decrementing which, until which==0 or we fall off the end */
    while (pnode != NULL && which > 0) {
        pnode = pnode->next;    /* Skip one node */
        which--;                /* One fewer left to skip */
    }
    return pnode;
}
```

del_pt must be written to delete the node **after** the one pointed to by its parameter which. There is an important reason why. (See the Self-test Exercises in Section 13-7.) If which is NULL it deletes the first node. Node deletion involves altering which->next to skip over the following node, and then using free to reclaim the space occupied by that following node. Also, if the final node is deleted, the ptail pointer should be updated. del_pt is shown in Listing 13-5c.

Listing 13-5c

```
/****** del_pt ******
Disconnects a node from the list, and destroys it.
On entry: plist points to a list, which points to a node in the list, or
          is NULL to indicate the list head.
On exit:  The node AFTER the node indicated by which is deleted.
          If there is no such following node, nothing happens.
*/
void del_pt(point_list *plist, vertex *which) {
    vertex * next_node;
    if (which == NULL) {              /* Disconnect the very first node */
        next_node = plist->phead;
        if (next_node != NULL) {      /* There is a node there to delete */
            plist->phead = next_node->next;    /* Yes, disconnect it */
            if (next_node == plist->ptail) {   /* Deleting the final node? */
                plist->ptail = NULL;           /* yes, list empty-alter ptail*/
            }
            free(next_node);                    /* Reclaim space */
        }
    } else {                          /* Disconnect a subsequent node */
        next_node = which->next;
        if (next_node != NULL) { /* There is a node there to delete */
            which->next = next_node->next;      /* Yes, disconnect it */
            if (next_node == plist->ptail) { /* Deleting the final node? */
                plist->ptail = which;        /* yes - set ptail to new tail*/
            }
            free(next_node);                 /* Reclaim space */
        }
    }
}
```

We can now turn to the top-down design of the graphics program. The operations given earlier in English can be formalized as

```
Input the polygon.
do
    Display polygon.
    Display menu of choices (add, delete, move or quit).
    Get valid choice from user.
    if choice is not quit
        process choice.
while choice is not quit.
Output the modified polygon.
```

A main function developed from this skeleton is shown in Listing 13-5d.

Listing 13-5d

```
point_list input_points(void);
void display_shape(point_list);
void display_menu(void);
char user_choice(void);
void add_point(point_list *ppoly);
void delete_point(point_list *ppoly);
void move_point(point_list polygon);
void output(point_list polygon);

main() {
    point_list polygon;           /* The list of points in the polygon */
    char choice;
    polygon = input_points();
    do {
        display_shape(polygon);
        display_menu();           /* choices (add, delete, move or quit) */
        choice = user_choice();
            if (choice != 'q') {
                switch (choice) {
                    case 'a': add_point(&polygon); break;
                    case 'd': delete_point(&polygon); break;
                    case 'm': move_point(polygon); break;
                }
            }
        } while (choice != 'q');
    output(polygon);
    return 0;
}
```

In this `main` function, the variable `polygon` is passed as an argument to most of the other functions. Those that will need to alter it, such as `add_point` (which, if a point is inserted first or last, will alter the `phead` or `ptail` fields), are given the address of `polygon`; those that merely need the value, such as `move_point`, can be passed a copy. It is often wise to always pass the address in any case, because often structures are quite large, and it is inefficient to make a copy. Listing 13-5e shows all remaining functions except `display_shape`. Displaying the polygon requires functions for manipulating graphics, but these are not provided in the standard C library. Although many C compilers provide graphics functions, they are often incompatible. The file on the student disk for this book contains `display_shape` functions for a variety of C compilers, but they are not listed here in the text.

Listing 13-5e

```
void display_menu(void) {
    printf(
        "\n\n\tOptions:\n\n"
        "A Add a point to the polygon\n"
        "D Delete a point from the polygon\n"
        "M Move a point in the polygon (alter its position on screen)\n"
        "Q Quit.\n\nEnter choice (A, D, M or Q):"
    );
}

#include <ctype.h>      /* For function tolower() */
#include <string.h>
char user_choice(void) {
    /* Inputs user's menu choice. Insists on a correct answer. */
    char choice;
    /* Input the choice, and discard the rest of the input line: */
    scanf("%c%*[^\n]", &choice);getchar();
    choice = tolower(choice);       /* Convert to lower case letter */

    while (strchr("admq", choice) == NULL) { /* while choice not in the
                                                allowed options */
        printf("You must answer one of A, D, M or Q:");
        /* Input the choice, and discard the rest of the input line: */
        scanf("%c%*[^\n]", &choice);getchar();
        choice = tolower(choice);   /* Convert to lower case letter */
    }
    return choice;
}

void add_point(point_list *ppoly) {
    /* Adds a point to the polygon at location entered by user */
    int where; point pt; vertex *v;
    printf("After which point in the polygon should the point be added?\n");
    printf("(0=before 1st point, 1=after 1st, 2=after 2nd, etc.)? ");
    scanf("%d", &where);
    printf("Enter x,y co-ordinates of point (0,0 = top left): ");
    scanf("%d %d%*[^\n]", &pt.x, &pt.y); getchar();
    v = find_pt(ppoly, where);
    if (add_node(ppoly, v, pt)) {        /* failure */
        fprintf(stderr, "ERROR: space for list exhausted - hit Enter\n");
        getchar();
    }
}

void delete_point(point_list *ppoly) {
    /* Deletes the point nominated by the user */
    int where; vertex *v;
    printf("Which point in the polygon should be deleted?\n");
    printf("(1=1st, 2=2nd, etc.)? ");
    scanf("%d%*[^\n]", &where);getchar();
```

```
    if (where < 1) {
        return;
    }
    v = find_pt(ppoly, where-1);  /* The point BEFORE the one to delete */
    if (where != 1 && v == NULL) {
        return;             /* Off the end of the list - nothing to delete */
    }
    del_pt(ppoly, v);
}

void move_point(point_list polygon) {
    /* Relocates the co-ordinates of a point nominated by user */
    int where; point pt; vertex *v;
    printf("Which point in the polygon should be relocated?\n");
    printf("(1=1st, 2=2nd, etc.)? ");
    scanf("%d", &where);
    v = find_pt(&polygon, where);
    if (v == NULL ) {
        return;           /* No such point */
    }
    printf(
        "Point is currently at %d,%d\n Enter new co-ordinates: ",
        v->p.x, v->p.y
    );
    scanf("%d %d%*[^\n]", &pt.x, &pt.y); getchar();
    v->p = pt;
}

point_list input_points(void) {
    /* Inputs a list of x,y pairs representing a polygon from a file */
    char fname[81]; FILE * f; int status;
    point_list poly = EMPTY_LIST; point pt;
    do {
        printf("Input file: ");
        scanf("%s%*[^\n]", fname);getchar();
        f = fopen(fname, "r");
    } while (f==NULL);
    while (fscanf(f,"%d %d", &pt.x, &pt.y) == 2) {   /* 2 items read */
        /* Add the new item after the existing last node in the list */
        status = add_node(&poly, poly.ptail, pt);
        if (status) {    /* error allocating list node */
            fprintf(stderr, "ERROR: space for list exhausted\n");
            exit(EXIT_FAILURE);
        }
    }
    fclose(f);
    return poly;
}
void output(point_list poly) {
    /* Outputs a list of x,y pairs representing a polygon to a file */
    char fname[81]; FILE * f;
    vertex *vp;
    do {
        printf("Output file: ");
```

```
        scanf("%s%*[^\n]", fname);getchar();
        f = fopen(fname, "w");
    } while (f==NULL);

    /* Now traverse the list from head to tail, printing each node's
       point in turn.
    */
    vp = poly.phead;
    while (vp != NULL) {
        /* Print the point at the current node in the list */
        if (fprintf(f, "%d %d\n", vp->p.x, vp->p.y) < 0) { /* error */
            fprintf(stderr, "ERROR writing file\n");
            fclose(f);
            exit(EXIT_FAILURE);
        }
        vp = vp->next;
    }
    fclose(f);
}
```

13.3 PROCESSING COMMAND-LINE ARGUMENTS

Suppose we wish to delete a file called fred. With some operating systems, we would type the command

```
rm fred
```

and on others

```
del fred
```

or something similar. The command (rm or del) is given a *command-line argument*, fred. To write the rm command in C, we have to know how to find out what command-line arguments the user typed. This provides an example of using an array of pointers. Also, it allows us to write our own utility programs to respond to one-line commands. For example, suppose we need a program, calc, that either adds or multiplies a list of numbers. To add, we might give the command

```
calc + 2 6.7 25.8 -4
```

and similarly for multiplication, but with * as the operator. In other words, the first argument is the operator (+ or *), and the remainder are the values to add or multiply; all arguments are separated by spaces. We shall write the calc program in the next section.

In C, access to command-line arguments is obtained by giving main two parameters, usually (but not necessarily) called argc and argv. argc must be an int, and is a count of the number of command-line arguments, including the command name itself; thus, the rm or del commands mentioned earlier each have a count of 2, and the above calc command has a count of 6. argv is an array of char pointers, each one pointing to a string containing the appropriate argument. This array is terminated by a NULL pointer. Thus the appropriate declaration for `main` when command-line arguments are to be accessed is

```
main(int argc, char *argv[]) {
    ... etc.
```

For the above `calc` command, these variables would be set up by the system shown below.

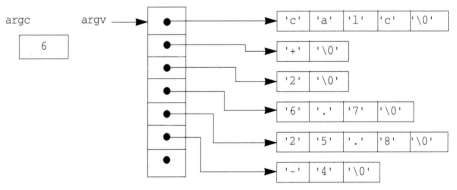

`argv[0]` points to the name of the command, and `argv[1..argc-1]` point to the successive command argument strings. Let us verify the above by writing a short program, `yousaid`, that lists the arguments. `yousaid` is shown in Listing 13-6.

Listing 13-6 yousaid.c

```
/* yousaid: program to print out its command line arguments. */

#include <stdio.h>

main(int argc, char *argv[]) {
    int i;
    printf("argc is %d\n", argc);
    for (i=0; i<argc; i++) {
        printf("argv[%d]:  \"%s\"\n", i, argv[i]);
    }
    return 0;
}
```

Sample session (running under the DOS operating system)
```
C:> yousaid a mouthful!
argc is 3
argv[0]:  "C:\CBOOK\PRG\YOUSAID.EXE"
argv[1]:  "a"
argv[2]:  "mouthful!"
```

In this sample session, note that `argv[0]` has been altered by the system to show the full pathname of the executable file (under DOS, executable files end in ".COM" or ".EXE"). Not all operating systems make such changes. In fact, some are unable to supply a value for `argv[0]` at all. Further, some environments alter the other arguments before passing them to the program. For example, under the Unix operating system, wildcard filenames are usually expanded into a full list of all matching files; thus, if the disk had files called f1.c and f2.c, and the command-line argument `*.c` was entered, the program would be given two separate arguments, `"f1.c"` and `"f2.c"`. This is useful when writing programs that operate on a list of files, such as `rm`. Under DOS, the program must expand wildcards itself; there are no standard ANSI C library functions for doing this, but interested readers should check their C compiler library for functions with names like `_dos_findfirst` and `_dos_findnext`, or something similar.

Note that `main` must have either zero or two arguments; no other combination is legal in ANSI C. Some compilers allow us to access a third argument, but this will not concern us here.

13.4 POINTERS TO FUNCTIONS

Just as a variable has an address, so too does a function. Thus we can have pointers to functions in the same way as we can have pointers to data. We declare such pointers using the normal '`*`' indirection operator. For example, a pointer to a function `func` with two `int` parameters yielding a `float` result is written

```
float (*func)(int, int);
```

This cryptic-looking declaration can be understood as follows: if we first follow the pointer (indicated by `(*func)`), and execute the function at that location giving it two `int` arguments (indicated by `(int, int)`), then the result will be a `float`. Designing complicated C declarations such as this is explained further in the next section.

Having created a pointer, `func`, to a function, we make it point to an actual function by assigning to it a function's name. Just as an array name stands for a pointer to the array, so a function's name stands for a pointer to the function:

```
func = somefunction;
```

where `somefunction` is the name of a function of two `int`s with a `float` result. **Note the absence of the function-call parentheses.** Finally, the function can be called via the pointer in the usual way:

```
somefloat = func(someint, someotherint);
```

The `calc` program described in the previous section provides an application of function pointers. There are two possible operations, + and *, to perform, but (apart from the operation to be done) the logic of calculating the result is identical. Thus we can write a function to calculate the result (`process`, say) but instead of directly coding into it a + or * operation, we make it execute a function for the required operation via a function pointer. The function pointer is previously assigned the address of a function to do the required operation. First we must create functions for the required calculations, such as the following for addition:

```
double add(double a, double b) {
    return a + b;
}
```

Then, if addition is the required operation, assign this function's address to a suitable function pointer:

```
double (*func)(double, double);
...
if (strcmp(argv[1], "+") == 0) {          /* + */
    func = add;
}
```

func can then be used to perform whichever operation is selected (in this case, addition). The numbers come from the command-line arguments, which must be converted from string format into numeric format; the library function sscanf can be used to do this. The program calc is shown in Listing 13-7.

Listing 13-7 calc.c

```
/* Program to perform a specified operation on all its command line args.
   First arg is the operation, '+' or '*', and the rest are the values.
   The program prints the result of operating on the listed values.
*/

#include <stdio.h>
#include <string.h>
#include <stdlib.h>

double add(double, double);
double mul(double, double);
void process(double (*func)(double, double), int argc, char *argv[]);

main(int argc, char *argv[]) {
    double (*func)(double, double);

    if (argc < 3) {
        fprintf(stderr, "To use, list the operation and at least ");
        fprintf(stderr, "one value:\n calc +or* values...\n");
        exit(EXIT_FAILURE);
    }

    /* See whether + or * */
    if (strcmp(argv[1], "+") == 0) {                /* + */
        func = add;
    } else if (strcmp(argv[1], "*") == 0) {         /* * */
```

```
            func = mul;
    } else {
        fprintf(stderr, "First argument must be '+' or '*'\n");
        exit(EXIT_FAILURE);
    }

    /* Now process the other arguments */
    process(func, argc, argv);
    return 0;
}

double add(double a, double b) {
    return a + b;
}

double mul(double a, double b) {
    return a * b;
}

void process(double (*func)(double, double), int argc, char *argv[]) {
    /* Performs the specified func on all arguments from argv[2] onward,
        and prints the result.
    */
    double result1, result2;
    int i=2, count; char dummy;

    count = sscanf(argv[2], "%lf%c", &result1, &dummy);
    /* argv[2] should contain a number & nothing else, so things are
        correct if the above call FAILS to assign to dummy or assigns '\0'.
    */
    for (i=3; i<argc && (count==1 || count == 2 && dummy == '\0'); i++){
        count = sscanf(argv[i], "%lf%c", &result2, &dummy);
        result1 = func(result1, result2);   /* either add or mul */
    }
    if (count < 1 || count == 2 && dummy != '\0') {
        fprintf(stderr, "Error in argument %d\n", i - 1);
        exit(EXIT_FAILURE);
    }
    printf("%f\n", result1);
}
```

Sample session under DOS

```
C:> calc 1 4 6
First argument must be '+' or '*'

C:> calc
To use, list the operation and at least one value:
    calc +or* values...

C:> calc * 1 4 6
24.000000

C:> calc + 1 4 6
11.000000

C:> calc + -5.8 99.8 20 -6
108.000000
```

13.5 'COMPLICATED' C DECLARATIONS

All C declarations can be understood by considering them as examples of how the identifier being declared will be used. Consider for example

```
float *fp;
```

This means that if you write `*fp` in an expression, the result will be a `float`. Therefore `fp` must be a pointer to a `float`. In other words, the collection of operators, function arguments, array subscripts, etc. surrounding the variable name in the declaration are an example, or pattern, of how to use the variable in an expression in order to get a value of the type that starts the declaration. That's quite a mouthful, but it should become clearer by looking at the examples in the following table.

Table 13-1 Examples of C declarations

C declaration	Meaning and reason
`int i;`	i is an `int` variable, because writing i in an expression will yield an `int`.
`int *ip;`	ip is a pointer to an `int`, because writing `*ip` in an expression will yield an `int`.
`int ia[5];`	ia is an array of `int`s, because writing `ia[some_value]` in an expression will yield an `int`. (This example is slightly idiosyncratic; we cannot actually write `ia[5]` in an expression, because the subscripts range from 0 to 4. Nevertheless, `ia` followed by an array subscript will be an `int` value.)

`int ifn(float);`	`ifn` is a function of a `float` argument giving an `int` result, because calling `ifn` with a `float` parameter gives an `int`.
`int (*ifnp)(float);`	`ifnp` is the address of (i.e. pointer to) a function of a `float` argument giving an `int` result, because first following the pointer from `ifnp`, then executing a function with a `float` argument, gives an `int` result.
`int *(ipfn(float));`	`ipfn` is a function of a `float` argument, giving a result of type pointer-to-`int`, because calling `ipfn` with a `float` argument, then following the pointer, gives an `int`.
`int *ipfn2(float);`	this is the same as `ipfn`, because function parentheses have a higher priority than the pointer `*`, making this mean the same as the previous declaration.
`void (*af[5])(int);`	`af` is an array of five pointers to functions, each with an `int` argument and a `void` result, because first writing a subscript (subscripts have higher priority than `*`), then following a pointer, then executing a function with an `int` parameter, yields `void`.
`float *aff[5](int);`	ILLEGAL! This attempts to create an array of functions, each yielding a `float *` result, because it says that if we write a subscript, then call a function (because function call has higher priority than `*`), then follow a pointer, we get `float`. This is illegal because it is impossible to have an array of functions.

You should have no immediate use for some of the more esoteric examples in the above table. However, the point is that whatever you want to declare, application of the principle of declaration by example will let you do it. Note, though, that the brain strain can often be reduced by suitable use of `typedef`. For example, rather than worrying about whether

```
float *ax[10];
```

really is or is not an array of pointers to `float`s, rewrite it using `typedef` to remove all doubt:

```
typedef float *floatptr;
floatptr ax[10];
```

13.6 SUMMARY

- Dynamic memory allocation from a pool of memory called the *heap* is performed by the function `malloc`. Memory is returned to the heap using `free`.

```
pointer_variable = (*type_of_pointer )malloc(size_of_array *
                                    sizeof(type_of_pointer ));
...Use the space thus allocated...
free(pointer_variable );
```

  - After `malloc`, `pointer_variable` is NULL if storage is unavailable.
  - Include <stdlib.h> when using `malloc` and `free`.
  - Values passed to `free` **must** have been allocated using `malloc`.
- A `void` pointer is a pointer to memory where the type of data being stored is not known to the compiler.
- An organized arrangement of data is called a *data structure*.
- A *linked list* is a list of nodes such that each node contains a pointer to the next one.
  - If each node also points to the previous one, the list is a *doubly-linked list*.
  - If the final node points back to the first one, the list is a *circular list*.
- *Command-line arguments* are the arguments typed on the command line when invoking a program from the operating system prompt.
- These arguments are accessed by including two parameters to `main`:

```
main(int argc, char *argv[]) {
    ...etc.
```

  - `argc` is a count of the number of arguments, including the command name itself
  - `argv` is an array of `argc+1` pointers
    `argv[0]` points to the command name.
    `argv[1]`... `argv[argc-1]` point to the arguments proper.
    `argv[argc]` is NULL.
- Pointer variables can point to functions, and are declared:

```
function_result_type (*pointer_variable_name)
    (function_argument_types);
```

  Such pointers may be assigned the address of a function:

```
pointer_variable_name = function_name ;
```

  and then the function can be called via the pointer variable:

```
pointer_variable_name(arguments );
```

- C declarations use a principle of declaration-by-example: the operators surrounding the identifier being declared show how the identifier could be used to obtain the data type at the start of the declaration. For example:

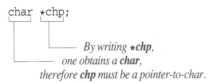

```
char *chp;
```

By writing *chp,
one obtains a char,
therefore chp must be a pointer-to-char.

13.7 SELF-TEST EXERCISES

Short Answer

1 State which `free` calls in the following code are not correct, and why.

```
#include <stdlib.h>
...
char buf[50], *chp1, *chp2, *chp3, ch;
chp1 = buf; chp2 = (char*)malloc(sizeof(char)*50); chp3 = &ch;
if (chp2!=NULL) {
    /* A: */        free(chp1);
    /* B: */        free(chp2);
    /* C: */        free(chp3);
    /* D: */        free(chp2);
}
```

2 Show how to create an array of `doubles` whose size is input from the user at runtime.

3 A programmer wishes to create a five-row triangular `float` array, where the first row has one element, the second two, and so on. Show how to do this. Draw a picture of the data structure.

4 Classify each labelled statement in the following code into the categories (1) correct, (2) nonsensical but harmless, and (3) incorrect and/or dangerous. Do not worry about the overall purpose of the code. Assume all `malloc`s succeed.

```
#include <stdlib.h>                         /* A */
...
int *ip, *ip2;
float *fp1;
fp1 = (float*)malloc(10*sizeof(char));      /* B */
...
free(fp1);                                  /* C */
ip = (int*)malloc(sizeof(int));             /* D */
*ip = 5;                                    /* E */
...
free(ip);
ip2 = ip;                                   /* F */
*ip2 = 8;                                   /* G */
```

5 Write C declarations for the following objects
   a A pointer to a function of two arguments, one a `float`, the other an `int` array; the function returns `void`.
   b A function of two arguments, one a `float`, the other an `int` array; the function returns a pointer to `void`.
   c A function of two arguments, one a pointer to a `float`, the other an `int` array; the function returns a pointer to a `char`.
   d An array of ten pointers to `void` functions with no arguments.
   e A structure type containing an `int` and a pointer to a `float`; then, an array of twenty such structures.

6 Function `del_pt` in Listing 13-5c was written to delete the node **after** the one pointed to by its parameter `which`. Why not the one pointed to by `which`?

Programming

7 Bearing in mind that the `argv` array of pointers ends in a `NULL`, rewrite the program `yousaid` (Listing 13-6) so that it does not rely on the value of `argc`.

8 At a certain rail junction, trains are assembled by adding or removing boxcars from either end. Write a program that records the numbers of the boxcars in a train being assembled. Input consists of the commands `AH` for 'add at the head of the train', `AT` for 'add at the tail', `RH` for 'remove from the head', and `RT` for 'remove from the tail'. The `AH` and `AT` commands will be followed by the serial number of the boxcar being added (an `int`). Finally, the `D` (departure) command causes the program to print the serial numbers of all vehicles in the train from head to tail, and then quit. Use a doubly linked list to keep track of the boxcars in the train.

13.8 TEST QUESTIONS

Short Answer

1 A certain C compiler uses one byte for a `char` and two for an `int`. Using that compiler, the following statement will allocate the correct space for a 100-element `int` array. Nevertheless, what criticism should be offered about the statement?

```
intptr = (int*)malloc(200*sizeof(char));
```

2 Reading a program, you notice the following two lines concerning an `int` pointer `ip`. What is your criticism?

```
free(ip);
printf("%d", *ip);
```

3 A trucking company wants to represent their routes in a program as a linked data structure. Any given city will be represented by a node containing the city name as well as pointers to nodes for up to ten other cities to which the company runs services. There must also be a way to tell how many such nodes are connected.

Further, there will be an array of pointers to every city node, alphabetically ordered by city name. Show declarations for all types and variables needed to implement this system.

4   Devise C declarations for the following:
  a   A type representing a pointer to the address of an `int`.
  b   A 4 by 4 array of `floats`.
  c   A 4 by 4 array of pointers to `floats`.
  d   A function of an `int` and a `float`, returning a pointer to a `double`.
  e   A pointer to a function of an `int` and a `float`, returning a `double`.
  f   A pointer to a function of an `int` and a `float`, returning a pointer to a `double`.

Programming

5   For a computer with a floppy disk drive, write a program to copy a text file from a floppy disk to a different disk in the same disk drive. Store the data in dynamic memory so the user can change disks between the reading and the writing steps. Include error checking.

6   An office wishes to schedule its activities according to their urgency, so as each job is received it is assigned a description (a string of less than 80 characters) and a priority (a number from 1 to 9, 1 being the highest priority). Write a program that assigns tasks according to priority. If an A (add task) is entered, the program should ask for the priority and the description, and add the task to a list sorted according to priority order. If a D (do task) is entered, it should print out and remove the first task in the list (which will, of course, have the highest priority). An S (save) command will cause the program to prompt for a filename and save remaining tasks to the file specified. Conversely, an L (load) command will read tasks from a file and add them to the existing task list. P should print the current task list to the screen, and Q should quit.

7   Write a program to reverse the order of the links in a singly linked list. Input a list of integers and print it in reverse to test your logic.

8   Twelve people decide to play a game. They stand in a circle, and starting with the first person, count round n positions; the person in that position then leaves the circle. This is repeated until only one person remains, who is declared the winner. Write a program to play this game. The value n should be chosen using `rand`, and the numbers of the people expelled should be printed as the game progresses. Use a circular linked list.

9   Write a program that stores polynomials in linked lists. Each node in a list is one term of the polynomial, and should contain the coefficient and the power; terms should be in descending order. Allow the user to input polynomials and assign them to variables labelled A to Z. The user must also be able to request that any two polynomial variables be added or multiplied with the result being stored in another variable. Finally, the user must be able to display any variable.

10 Add differentiation to the previous program.

11 Write a program, `entab`, which takes a filename on its command line and writes its contents to `stdout`, transforming spaces to tabs. That is, any sequence of two or more spaces ending on a tab stop (columns 9, 17, etc.) are turned into a tab (`\t`).

12 Write a program, `detab.c`, which works in reverse to `entab`; that is, it transforms tabs to a suitable number of spaces.

13 Write a program, `chmatch`, that takes a name of a C program on its command line and checks that program to see that the number of left braces (`{`) matches the number of right braces (`}`).

14 Write a 'safe delete' command, `safdel`, which deletes each file listed on its command line, but only after listing the filename and asking the user whether it should be deleted. This is particularly useful under Unix, where filename expansion is performed.

15 (Hard) Write a program to compare two text files and print the differences. Lines can be compared with `strcmp`, and all goes well as long as the files match. When a difference is encountered, lines read from then on should be kept in two linked lists, one for each file. Lines are read alternately from the two files, and each one read is compared with all the lines stored from the other file. If a match is found, the difference can be printed, the files resynchronized, all lines in the lists up to the synchronization point deleted, and the comparison continued. There may be lines in one or the other list still unused, so after a match, be careful where the data comes from. If a large difference is encountered the program may run out of memory, in which case it should stop with an informative message.

16 (Even harder) Serious file comparison programs worry about the problem of false matches: that is, short lines or sequences that cause a faulty decision to resynchronize. Blank lines commonly do this, as do common lines such as '`}`' in C programs. To counter this, when a match is discovered the program should look ahead two or more lines to see if the match continues. Modify the program from the previous question to resynchronize after seeing three matching lines. Do not print the matched lines as part of the difference.

17 (Challenge) A permuted index is intended for such things as manual entries. It is alphabetically arranged according to key words, and provides a short context phrase so that the reader will know whether the index entry is useful for their purposes. For example, here is a short part of a permuted index:

```
            using the   library catalog                    57
     introduction to   library functions                   41
           providing   library support to programs        297
   changing the time   limit of a process                  36
language restrictions and   limitations                   184
```

Each entry in the index may appear many times; for example the second line above would also appear under 'introduction' and 'functions'.

Write a program that can build a permuted index from an input file of key phrases. In the file, each line will contain a page number, a single space, and then a phrase of up to 50 characters. Allow up to 500 entries in the index, and declare an array of reference structures, each containing two pointers, one pointing to a structure containing a phrase/line number pair, and the other pointing to the start of the particular word within the phrase that is being indexed. As each entry is input, allocate space for it dynamically and generate multiple references to it, one for each key word. Finally, the program should sort this array and generate an index. Use a simple bubble sort or, if you wish, study and use the `qsort` library function. For an extra challenge, eliminate words such as 'the', 'it', and 'a' by having a short list of common words which should not be indexed.

14

Recursion

Objectives

Understand the principle of recursion.

Learn to design correct recursive algorithms.

Be able to program recursive algorithms in C.

14.1 INTRODUCTION

Recursion is the use of functions that call themselves. The subject is not difficult if you follow the various principles stressed throughout this book — in particular, properly structuring programs, ensuring that functions perform a single, self-contained task, and writing clear comments for functions in precondition or postcondition form. Readers who have taken the effort to master these principles will almost certainly find recursion quite straightforward; some people even invent it for themselves without realizing it is anything special, and then wonder what all the fuss is about.

A natural response to the idea of recursion is to worry about getting confused. If a function calls itself, of all things, surely the program will tangle itself in knots when it runs; how can we possibly keep track of it all? The answer is simple: yes, the program will tangle itself in knots in a sense, but because we should always worry about only one thing at a time (namely the function we happen to be writing right now) we just don't worry about the contortions the program undergoes when it runs. That may seem a cavalier attitude, but it is nothing other than the way we should have been thinking all along: **we** write the functions that make up a program, ensuring that each one is correct, and then the **computer** executes the program and makes everything happen properly. To help us in our part of the job, there are some simple design principles (explained in the following sections) that make writing a correct recursive function as easy as writing any other function.

One (but not the only) effect of recursion is to cause program statements to be executed more than once. This is because, when a function calls itself, the function's code is activated a second time. Therefore, recursion can be used to replace iteration (looping) and vice versa. We can choose whichever method gives the best and simplest solution for the particular problem at hand.

14.2 EXAMPLE: PARSING ARITHMETIC EXPRESSIONS

In Chapter 8 we wrote a program (see Listings 8-1a to 8-1e) to evaluate arithmetic expressions entered by the user. The simplified case considered there consisted of numbers separated by operators, with no way to indicate operator priority. By extending the program to allow parentheses, it can be made more useful and at the same time provide a good example of recursion. Whereas previously we only permitted expressions such as

```
1+2*4-3
```

we shall now also allow parentheses:

```
1+(2*4)-3
```

Since all operators have equal priority, the two expressions above are not the same. In Chapter 8 we treated expressions as consisting of alternating operators and operands. If we look only at the outer operators (those not within parentheses) we can still do that; since a parenthesized expression is reduced to a single value we can think of it as a single operand:

This way of looking at expressions allows us to use the majority of the previous program unaltered. However, the function `operand_value`, which previously only had to evaluate numbers, must now evaluate parenthesized expressions. Without recursion, we might be tempted to write a new function to handle that; with recursion, we simply note that the parenthesized expression has the same form as the overall expression, and we recall that we have a function, `eval_expr` (see Listing 8-1c), that evaluates such expressions. All we need do is call it if we see a left parenthesis. `eval_expr` has a parameter, `terminator`, specifying the character that should end the expression; this should clearly be the right parenthesis. Therefore the revised algorithm for `operand_value` should be

```
if next char is a '('
     Input following char (the first char in the parenthesized
        expression)
     Call eval_expr to evaluate expression, with ')' as terminator, and
        return the value returned from eval_expr.
else (it should be a normal digit)
     check that next char is a digit, error if not.
     convert number to int format.
```

This algorithm is shown in Listing 14-1. Sure enough, this is sufficient to implement parenthesized expressions, and is the only change needed in the program in Listing 8-1.

Listing 14-1   Modified version of Listing 8-1e (changes in bold)

```
/********* operand_value: ********************************
On entry: next_char is the first character of the operand.
On exit:  returns the value of the operand; all characters of
          the operand have been input.
*/
int operand_value(char next_char) {
    int value;
    if (next_char == '(') {        /* A parenthesized subexpression */
        scanf("%c", &next_char); /* Get first char of expression */
        return eval_expr(next_char, ')');
                                   /* Process expression ending on a ')' */
    } else {                       /* We should have a single number */
        if (next_char < '0' || next_char > '9') {
            printf("Error: \"%c\" should be a digit.\n", next_char);
            exit(EXIT_FAILURE);
        }
        /* Now push that char back into the input, and use scanf. */
        ungetc(next_char, stdin); scanf("%d", &value);
        return value;
    }
}
```

Sample run

```
Enter expressions, one per line, no blanks.  # to finish.
99
Result: 99
12*12-(11*11)
Result: 23
100-(90-(80-(70-(60-(50-(40-(30-(20-10)))))))))+1000
Result: 1050
100-(90-(80-(70-(60-(50-(40-(30-(20-10))))))))))+1000
Error: Illegal character: ")".
```

It may seem surprising that the small addition shown in Listing 14-1 is sufficient to permit deeply nested parentheses. However, once we call `eval_expr` to handle a parenthesized expression, all the same possibilities are available inside the parentheses as were available outside — including a further level of parentheses. This logic repeats indefinitely.

The recursion in the above example is called *indirect recursion* because no function calls itself directly; the recursion comes from the cycle: `eval_expr` calls `operand_value` which calls `eval_expr` etc. If we had written a call to `eval_expr` in `eval_expr` itself, it would be *direct recursion*. Both forms are equally valid.

It is worth asking what enabled us to discover the recursive solution given above. Certainly we did not trace through an example such as the complex nested parentheses in the sample run for Listing 14-1. Indeed, that would almost certainly have confused rather than helped us develop a solution. In fact the answer came from trusting the insight that, since the inside of a set of parentheses has the same form as the overall expression, the same function (`eval_expr`) must be capable of handling both. This is a common experience with recursion: we observe some property and trust that wherever that property holds, a function written to handle it will work — even if called from within itself.

When a function is called recursively, it is active twice (or more) at the same time. The computer deals with this problem by effectively duplicating the function, including all local variables, parameters, and so on. Thus each execution of the function has its own variables which do not interfere with the variables used by another execution of the function. It is as if we wrote two functions with different names but identical code inside. For example, consider the following partially evaluated expression:

```
10+9-(3*4...
```

Immediately after processing the 4, there are two copies of `eval_expr` in execution. The first is processing the outer calculations, and its copy of the variable `value_so_far` contains 19. That execution of `eval_expr` is temporarily suspended while a second execution of the function evaluates the inner expression; that second execution also has a variable, `value_so_far`, which at the point shown above would contain 12. Since each execution has its own variables, these do not interfere. Now suppose the expression concludes as follows:

```
10+9-(3*4)
```

At the), the inner execution of `eval_expr` concludes and returns the 12 as its result. That will return via `operand_value` to `process_op_operand`, which subtracts it from the 19 and returns it to the outer execution of `eval_expr`, which in turn updates its copy of `value_so_far` to 7.

Although it can be reassuring to examine nested recursive calls in this way, it is not a good policy to do it as a normal step in designing a program, because each execution of a function is solving its own problem, and each single problem should be considered separately. Often the best way to deal with recursion is to stop being overly concerned about it: under suitable circumstances, feel free to call any function that does a useful job — even the function you are writing right now.

14.3 DESIGNING RECURSIVE ALGORITHMS: WHAT WORKS AND WHAT DOESN'T

Recursion, properly understood and applied, can be a very simple and useful technique, as the example in Section 14.2 demonstrated. However, serious mistakes are possible if it is used carelessly. Suppose we wish to write a function, specified as follows, for summing the elements of an array:

```
/***** sumarray: Sums specified elements of a float array *****
On entry: A is the array whose elements are to be summed,
          L specifies the first element of the array to include in the sum,
          H specifies the last element to include.
On exit:  Returns the sum of array elements A[L] to A[H].
*/
float sumarray(float A[], int L, int H);
```

This specification should be sufficient to enable us to call `sumarray` any time we wish to sum array elements; in particular, we should not need to see the coding of the function in order to use it. (After all, we do not usually have available the source code for the standard library functions, yet we use them successfully.) Therefore, if we are writing a function (`fred`, say) that needs to sum some array elements, we can call `sumarray` to do the job:

```
float fred(float A[], int L, int H) {
    float t;
    int lo, hi;
    ...
    t = sumarray(A, lo, hi);
    ...
}
```

Considering the call in detail, execution proceeds through `fred` until it encounters the call; then `fred` suspends execution, `sumarray` is executed, and when it returns, `fred` continues as shown in Figure 14.1. (The flow of control is shown by the solid line.)

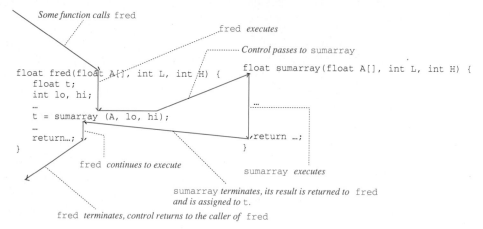

Figure 14.1 Tracing the execution of fred as it calls sumarray

We don't have to worry about the called function (sumarray) while writing fred; all we need do is get the logic of fred correct on the assumption that any functions fred calls will work correctly. This applies no matter which function we are writing. Any time we want some array elements added, we can call sumarray. But what if we are actually writing sumarray itself? Is it possible to have the situation shown in Figure 14.2?

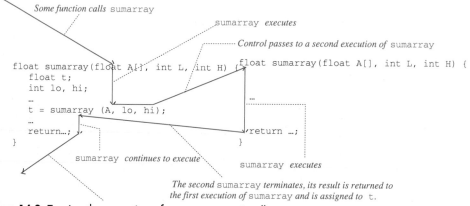

Figure 14.2 Tracing the execution of sumarray as it calls sumarray

It may seem mind-boggling to have sumarray calling sumarray, but the situation in Figure 14.2 is exactly the same as that in Figure 14.1; we must make sure that it makes sense to call sumarray where we do, but there is no reason why a function should not call itself under appropriate circumstances. That said, here is a circumstance where a recursive call is not appropriate:

```
float sumarray(float A[], int L, int H) {
    return sumarray(A, L, H);
}
```

wrong

This function exhibits the problem most beginners fear about recursion: the solution is never obtained because `sumarray` calls `sumarray` which calls `sumarray`, etc. etc. forever. The cause of the trouble is that the recursive call is trying to solve exactly the same problem as the original call. Remembering the connection between recursion and iteration, this is analogous to a `for` loop in which the programmer forgot to increment the counter: the program never makes any progress and so loops forever.

Our goal is to find an algorithm for `sumarray` that includes a sensible recursive call to itself. In order for the recursive call to make progress, it must, in some sense, be asked to solve a simpler problem than the original one. If that is done, then eventually the recursive call becomes so simple that no further recursive calls are needed to get the answer. The usual summing algorithm (adding each element in turn to a total) is iterative because it requires a loop that sums one array element per iteration. That solution is obtained by considering what we have to **do** to get the total. A recursive solution is more likely to come from considering some **property** possessed by the total. For example, the sum of the entire array is the sum of the first half plus the sum of the second half. We can write this using the mathematical sigma (Σ) notation as follows:

$$\sum_{i=L}^{H} A_i = \sum_{i=L}^{(H+L)/2} A_i + \sum_{i=((H+L)/2)+1}^{H} A_i \tag{1}$$

For readers unfamiliar with it, the sigma notation is just a convenient shorthand for writing 'the sum of'; for example, the first Σ in equation (1) means the sum of all elements `A[i]` of A where `i` assumes all values from L to H — in other words, the sum of all elements of A from `A[L]` to `A[H]`.

If we are careful, the property described by equation (1) can be used as the basis for a C function to add array elements. In this equation the sum is expressed in terms of two smaller sums. The function `sumarray` would appear to do in C exactly what the Σ operation does in equation (1). Furthermore, summing half the array is simpler than summing the entire array. Can we then really just write the code of `sumarray` as a direct translation in C of equation (1), as follows?

```
float sumarray(float A[], int L, int H) {
    int M;
    M = (L+H)/2;
    return sumarray(A, L, M) + sumarray(A, M + 1, H);
}
```
wrong

Unfortunately, this is still not correct. To see why, let us analyze the definition according to equation (1) of a simple sum, namely the first two elements of an array:

$$\sum_{i=0}^{1} A_i = \sum_{i=0}^{0} A_i + \sum_{i=1}^{1} A_i \tag{2}$$

So far, so good: summing the elements from 0 to 1 involves adding the sum of elements from 0 to 0 to the sum of elements from 1 to 1. That is certainly true, but what happens next? Let us now apply the same rule again to each of the two smaller sums:

$$\sum_{i=0}^{1} A_i = \left(\sum_{i=0}^{0} A_i + \sum_{i=1}^{0} A_i \right) + \left(\sum_{i=1}^{1} A_i + \sum_{i=2}^{1} A_i \right) \tag{3}$$

It is apparent that, in applying the rule to the sum of just one element, something goes wrong. In the first of the two sums, for example, the sum of elements 0 to 0 is expressed as the sum from 0 to 0 plus the sum from 1 to 0. The sum from 1 to 0 is zero, because the lower bound is greater than the upper and so the range is empty. Mathematically, equation (3) is correct, but computationally it is a disaster, because the C function above will try to calculate the sum from 1 to 0, and when it does it will split it into further sums, as follows:

$$\sum_{i=1}^{0} A_i = \sum_{i=1}^{0} A_i + \sum_{i=1}^{0} A_i \tag{4}$$

In other words, the computer will try to calculate the sum by calling `sumarray` twice more, giving it exactly the same problem to solve as before. This will go on forever, and is clearly no better than our first, obviously wrong, version.

The above faulty recursive function is the equivalent of an infinite loop; there is no way out. Just as a loop must have a loop test to decide whether to continue, so a recursive function must have a test to decide whether the recursion is necessary. The cure is to change our mathematical definition of summation:

$$\sum_{i=L}^{H} A_i = \sum_{i=L}^{(H+L)/2} A_i + \sum_{i=((H+L)/2)+1}^{H} A_i \qquad (if\ H > L) \tag{4}$$
$$= A_L \qquad\qquad (if\ H = L)$$
$$= 0 \qquad\qquad (if\ H < L)$$

This definition contains tests for the two cases where recursion serves no purpose: the sum of one element (where the sum is just the value of that single element) and the sum of no elements (where the sum is zero). Using this modified definition, recursion is only used when adding two or more elements. Sure enough, a C function using the definition in equation (5), as shown in Listing 14-2, will work correctly.

Listing 14-2   A correct recursive function to sum array elements

```
float sumarray(float A[], int L, int H) {
    if (H < L) {                       /* nothing to sum */
        return 0;                          /* answer 0 */
    } else if (H == L) {               /* one element in range */
        return A[L];                       /* answer is that element */
    } else {                           /* Multiple elements */
        int M;                             /* answer is the sum of */
        M = (L+H)/2;                       /* the two halves */
        return sumarray(A, L, M) + sumarray(A, M + 1, H);
    }
}
```

To understand how this recursive function operates, let us insert some diagnostic printouts (this involves some minor rewriting of the algorithm) and call it from a simple `main` function, as shown in Listing 14-3. The basic algorithm is shown in bold.

Listing 14-3

```
/* A Recursive function to add elements of an array, with diagnostic
   printouts and a short main function for testing.
*/

#include <stdio.h>
int level = 0;      /* This will tell us the nesting level of the
                       recursive function calls. */

float sumarray(float A[], int L, int H) {
    printf("%*.*sEntering sumarray level %d, L==%d, H==%d\n",
          level*4, level*4, " ", level, L, H);
    if (H < L) {                            /* nothing to sum */
        printf("%*.*sExiting sumarray level %d, result==0\n",
           level*4, level*4, " ", level);
        return 0;
    } else if (H == L) {                    /* one element in range */
        printf("%*.*sExiting sumarray level %d, result==%.1f\n",
           level*4, level*4, " ", level, A[L]);
        return A[L];
    } else {                                /* Multiple elements */
        int M; float answer1, answer2, answer;
        M = (L+H)/2;
        level++;    /* Bump up the level for the recursive call */
        answer1 = sumarray(A, L, M);
        answer2 = sumarray(A, M + 1, H);
        answer = answer1 + answer2;
        level--;    /* Restore previous level */
        printf("%*.*sExiting sumarray level %d,result==%.1f+%.1f==%.1f\n",
           level*4, level*4, " ", level, answer1, answer2, answer);
        return answer;
    }
}

float arr[] = {1., 2., 3., 4., 5., 6.};

main() {
    float total;
    total = sumarray(arr, 0, 5);
    printf("\nThe total is %f\n", total);
    return 0;
}
```

Note that the variable `level`, intended to tell how deeply nested the recursion gets, is

global; therefore there is only one copy of this variable, and it is used by all the various executions of `sumarray`. However, variables such as M are **local**, so each execution of `sumarray` has its own individual copy which does not interfere with any other. The test run set out in Figure 14.3 shows the program output with explanatory comments added.

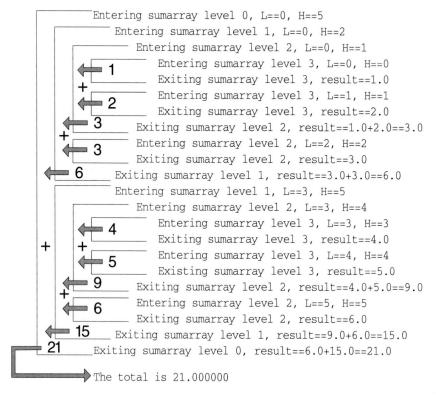

```
Entering sumarray level 0, L==0, H==5
    Entering sumarray level 1, L==0, H==2
        Entering sumarray level 2, L==0, H==1
            Entering sumarray level 3, L==0, H==0
    1       Exiting sumarray level 3, result==1.0
    +       Entering sumarray level 3, L==1, H==1
    2       Exiting sumarray level 3, result==2.0
    3   Exiting sumarray level 2, result==1.0+2.0==3.0
    +       Entering sumarray level 2, L==2, H==2
    3       Exiting sumarray level 2, result==3.0
    6   Exiting sumarray level 1, result==3.0+3.0==6.0
        Entering sumarray level 1, L==3, H==5
            Entering sumarray level 2, L==3, H==4
                Entering sumarray level 3, L==3, H==3
    4           Exiting sumarray level 3, result==4.0
    +           Entering sumarray level 3, L==4, H==4
    5           Existing sumarray level 3, result==5.0
    9       Exiting sumarray level 2, result==4.0+5.0==9.0
    +           Entering sumarray level 2, L==5, H==5
    6           Exiting sumarray level 2, result==6.0
    15      Exiting sumarray level 1, result==9.0+6.0==15.0
    21  Exiting sumarray level 0, result==6.0+15.0==21.0
The total is 21.000000
```

Figure 14.3 Test run showing sequencing of recursive calls

14.3.1 Some general principles for writing correct recursive functions

The preceding discussion has shown that there is no intrinsic problem with the idea of recursion as such. Unfortunately, not all recursive functions work correctly. We cannot easily trace the execution of recursive programs, so if we are to write them with confidence, we must have a way to know at the outset whether a given recursive algorithm is workable. Three checks will ensure this.

Checking whether a recursive algorithm is workable

Check 1

Ensure the called function's precondition is satisfied before the call, and the postcondition is suitable for the situation after the call.

> This is just the normal check we should always perform for any function call. The next two checks ensure that the recursive call eventually returns with an answer.

Check 2

Ensure there is a possible path through the recursive function that does **not** involve a further recursive call.

> If the recursion is to eventually stop (which it has to do in a correct program) it must be possible to execute the recursive function without a further recursive call. In Listing 14-1, this path is provided by the `else` option on the `if` statement, which detects the case where a normal number occurs; these are processed non-recursively. In Listing 14-2, the first two branches of the `if` (dealing with zero and one elements to be added) involve no recursion.

Check 3

Ensure that every recursive call involves a situation that is closer to the case or cases handled non-recursively.

> 'Closer' means that the recursive call poses a simpler problem than the original call. For example, in Listing 14-2, the recursive calls (in the final branch of the `if`) ask for the sum of only half as many array elements as before. If each recursive call halves the number of elements to be added, we must eventually arrive at the case where only zero or one elements are to be summed; then the simple non-recursive options take over. In Listing 14-1, the call to `eval_expr` deals with the contents of a set of parentheses; unless the user keeps on typing nested parentheses forever (which is not likely), we must sooner or later find the innermost nested expression, which will contain no more parentheses. Each operand at that point will be a simple number, handled non-recursively.

Let us design an algorithm by conscious application of these three principles. We shall try a simple, if not very realistic, problem so we can see how the checks assure us of a solution. Our problem is to read a list of numbers from the keyboard and print it in reverse order. Our insight is this: **if we can read the first number, reverse the rest of the list, and then print the first number after the rest, we have reversed the entire list** (see Figure 14.4).

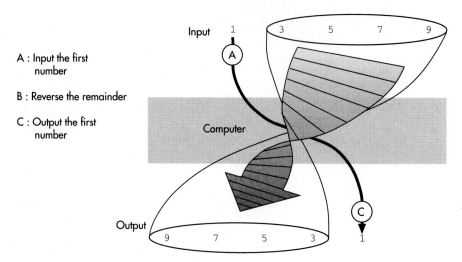

Figure 14.4 How to reverse a list recursively

Let us start by designing the preconditions and postconditions of a function to reverse a list of input numbers.

```
/******** reverse: ****************
On entry: The standard input stream contains a list of integers, until
          end of file.
On exit:  The input will have been read to end of file, and the output
          will be the input integers in reverse order.
*/
```

This describes the preconditions and postconditions of the overall program, so a call to `reverse` from `main` satisfies check 1. In the function, check 2 requires that a possible path involves no recursion. When the input is exhausted there is nothing to be printed, as the reverse of nothing is nothing. This case can be non-recursive, so the function can commence:

```
void reverse(void) {
    int num;
    if (scanf("%d", &num) < 1) {  /* Error or no data left */
        return;                   /* Do nothing */
    }
    /* Now ready for the general case. */
    ....
```

The general case (at least one input number) will obey the algorithm shown in Figure 14.4. Having read the first number, we are faced with a list of input numbers that is now one number shorter. If we call `reverse` recursively to reverse this shorter list, eventually successive recursive calls will use up all the input, and the simple 'do nothing' option will be taken. This satisfies checks 1 and 3. The `main` function does little more than call the recursive function (see Listing 14-4).

Listing 14-4

```
/*********reverse: ***************
On entry: The standard input stream contains a list of integers, until
          end of file.
On exit:  The input will have been read to end of file, and the output
          will be the input integers in reverse order.
*/

#include <stdio.h>

void reverse(void) {
    int num;
    if (scanf("%d", &num) < 1) {  /* Try to input number.  Failure? */
        return;                   /* Error or no data left : Do nothing */
    }
    /* We have the first number.  Now ready for the general case. */
    reverse();                    /* Reverse the rest of the list */
    printf(" %d", num);           /* Tack the first number on the end */
}

/* main function to reverse the overall input */
main() {
    printf("Please enter a list of integers for reversal:\n");
    reverse();
    putchar('\n');   /* End the output line */
    return 0;
}
```

Test run
```
Please enter a list of integers for reversal:
1 4 2 6
^Z
 6 2 4 1
```

For the final time we shall consider the order of execution of the steps in a recursive algorithm. The following traces the nested executions of reverse as it processes the above test run.

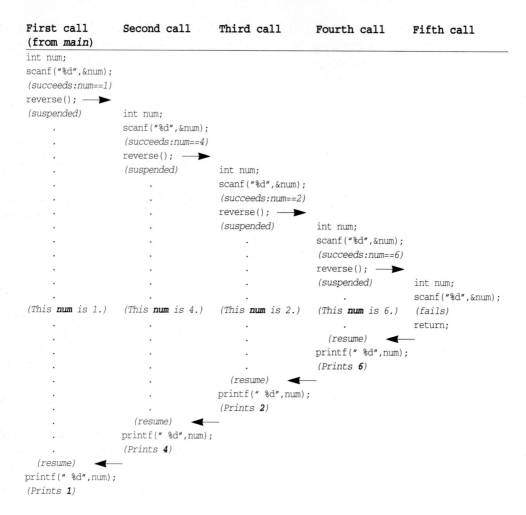

First call (from *main*)	Second call	Third call	Fourth call	Fifth call

```
int num;
scanf("%d",&num);
(succeeds:num==1)
reverse();  ───▶
(suspended)
                 int num;
                 scanf("%d",&num);
                 (succeeds:num==4)
                 reverse();  ───▶
                 (suspended)
                                  int num;
                                  scanf("%d",&num);
                                  (succeeds:num==2)
                                  reverse();  ───▶
                                  (suspended)
                                                   int num;
                                                   scanf("%d",&num);
                                                   (succeeds:num==6)
                                                   reverse();  ───▶
                                                   (suspended)
                                                                    int num;
                                                                    scanf("%d",&num);
(This num is 1.)  (This num is 4.)  (This num is 2.)  (This num is 6.)  (fails)
                                                                    return;
                                                   (resume)  ◀───
                                                   printf(" %d",num);
                                                   (Prints 6)
                                  (resume)  ◀───
                                  printf(" %d",num);
                                  (Prints 2)
                 (resume)  ◀───
                 printf(" %d",num);
                 (Prints 4)
  (resume)  ◀───
printf(" %d",num);
(Prints 1)
```

14.3.2 Some pitfalls

Although the considerations mentioned in the previous section allow us to write correct recursive functions, we might nevertheless still write an impractical function.

Theoretical computer science research has shown that any problem solvable by recursion is also solvable by iteration, and vice versa, but the two ways will not necessarily be equally obvious, easy, or efficient. Recursion is often easier to program but less efficient (although this is not always so). For example, sumarray in Listing 14-2 involves a division at each step, and division is a slow operation. We would therefore expect sumarray to be significantly slower than a normal iterative function.

Many people also baulk at the mere fact that recursion involves function calls. The argument is that function calls are expensive, meaning that they take a lot of time. Sometimes yes, sometimes no: this varies widely among different types of computers. Some are very efficient indeed at calling functions, so the cost is negligible. My opinion is that any time there is a clear advantage to writing a recursive function, it is mostly counterproductive to worry overmuch about the supposed slowness of recursion. Of course, if an iterative solution is just as simple, you might as well use it.

There are, however, certain considerations that should be taken into account as they concern fundamental principles. We turn to them now.

Function calls require memory

Every function call uses computer memory. At a minimum, function parameters, local variables, and the *return address* (the address of the place from which the function was called) must be stored. Since each recursive invocation has its own copy of these, it isn't a good idea to have a million nested recursive calls! Remember, though, that the space used when a function is called is also reclaimed when it exits, so it is only the number of nested calls (calls within calls) that matters. For example, consider the recursive call to `eval_expr` in Listing 14-1. A user might type the following expression:

```
1+(2-3)+(4*5)-(6*3)
```

The function `eval_expr` will be called once for the overall expression and once for each set of parentheses, making four calls in all. But the nesting level is only two because each of the three calls for the parentheses exits before the next one is entered. Therefore space for only two executions of `eval_expr` is required to evaluate this expression. Listing 14-1 is an example of a 'good' recursion: a lot of functionality is obtained with little effort and little cost in time or space.

Careless recursion can be grossly inefficient

Consider the Fibonacci sequence: *fib*(0) and *fib*(1) are both 1, and each subsequent value is the sum of the two preceding values, i.e. $fib(n) = fib(n-1) + fib(n-2)$. This sequence can be obtained iteratively very efficiently by remembering two values and computing the next one in a loop, as shown in Listing 14-5.

Listing 14-5

```
/* Iterative program to print Fibonacci sequence.  doubles are used,
   as the values get big fast.
*/

#include <stdio.h>

main() {
    double prev1=1, prev2=1, next;
    printf("%2.0f\n%2.0f\n", prev1, prev2);  /* Display first two terms */
    do {
        next = prev1 + prev2;                /* Compute next term */
        printf("%2.0f\n", next);             /* display */
        prev1 = prev2; prev2 = next;         /* advance the saved terms */
    } while (next < 1000.0);
    return 0;
}
```

Printout

```
1
1
2
3
5
8
13
21
34
55
89
144
233
377
610
987
1597
```

An alternative program can be developed recursively directly from the definition of *fib*, as shown in Listing 14-6.

Listing 14-6

```
/* Recursive program to print Fibonacci sequence. */

#include <stdio.h>

double fib(int n) {
    if (n == 0 || n == 1) {     /* First two terms */
        return 1.0;             /* fib is 1 */
    } else {                    /* Otherwise sum the 2 previous terms */
        return fib(n-1) + fib(n-2);
    }
}

main() {
    double value; int n=0;
    do {
        value = fib(n);
        printf("%2.0f\n", value);      /* display */
        n++;                           /* move on */
    } while (value < 1000.0);
    return 0;
}
```

The recursive version produces the same output as before, but runs at a snail's pace. This is caused by the two recursive calls in `fib`, which force recomputation of the same values many times over. Whereas the iterative version calculates each value from the immediately preceding ones, the recursive version does a mushrooming amount of work. For example, calculating *fib*(6) involves evaluating *fib*(5) and *fib*(4), but calculating *fib*(5) involves calculating *fib*(4) and *fib*(3). Therefore *fib*(4) is evaluated twice. Lower values are evaluated even more often, as shown in Figure 14.5. Thus going just one step further nearly doubles the amount of work. This is called an *exponential* increase, and causes grinding inefficiency.

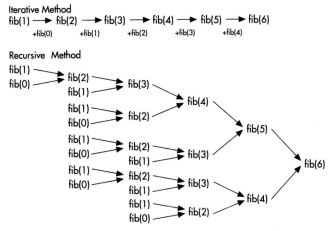

Figure 14.5 Iterative and recursive evaluation of the Fibonacci sequence

Watch out for global variables

Sloppy programmers often make all variables global, probably because it saves a short amount of time learning how to use local variables properly. In ordinary programs this is bad, because programs are hard to understand and prone to inadvertent misuse of a variable. In recursive programs, it is fatal. Recursive functions rely on the rule that local variables are duplicated for each recursive call. There is only one copy of a global variable; all activations of a recursive function will access the same variable.

You can demonstrate this for yourself by making num *a global in Listing 14-4 and running the program. You should be able to predict what you will see.*

14.4 EXAMPLE: MATCHSTICK PUZZLE

Recursion is particularly effective for problems where there is no obvious iterative solution. This matchstick puzzle is one such problem. Two opposed rows of three (or whatever) matches have a space between just large enough to take a single match. The objective is to exchange the two rows of matches. We can push a match one place forward (towards its head) or jump a single match but we cannot move a match backwards. The starting and ending positions are shown in Figure 14.6.

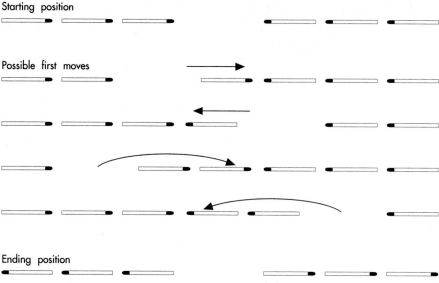

Starting position

Possible first moves

Ending position

Figure 14.6 The matchstick game

We can start our analysis with the observation that at any given time in the game, there are up to four possible moves, as the two pieces either side of the vacant space might be shifted into it. If the space is near the end or if a match is pointing the wrong way, the number of moves will be fewer than four. If there are no possible moves the game is blocked, as reversing direction is impossible; when this happens, either the matches are in the end state (we win) or they are not (we lose). The brute force approach is to try every possible combination of moves until a winning sequence is found. Thus at any stage in the game we can try a move, see if it leads on to victory, and if not, try another one. With this observation, a recursive function (seek_win, say) might operate as follows:

```
How to seek_win from a given game position:
    For each possible move from the present position:
        seek_win from the new position.
        If a win was found by seek_win,
            (This game position is on the route to victory:)
            Display the match positions.
            Return, indicating a win to the caller.
    (After trying each possible move, game must be blocked:)
    Check if matches are in the final position, if so,
        Display the match positions,
        Return, indicating a win to the caller.
    else
        Return, indicating failure to the caller.
```

This looks good, but it has a problem: it is impossible to know whether a given move will succeed until after it is tried, so the display of the game position is after the return from the recursive call to seek_win. In this regard, the function has the same structure as the function reverse in Listing 14-4, and will have the same effect: the moves will be displayed in reverse order. This hiccup is easily overcome by displaying the matchsticks pointing the wrong way. This is not elegant, but it works, because the game is the same whether played forwards or backwards, apart from the direction of movement of the matches.

It will probably be convenient to package all information about the match positions in a structure of type gamestate, say. This can contain a signed char array with a place for every possible match position, +1 standing for a match pointing right, −1 for one pointing left, and 0 for the unoccupied space. If we make the number of matches variable up to some limit (8, say) the main function need do no more than ask the size of the problem, initialize the gamestate, and call seek_win to find and display the solution.

It would be natural to pass the gamestate as a parameter to seek_win, but each move causes an extra level of recursion, which would involve a separate copy of the gamestate structure. This would restrict the size of problem the program can handle. We can get around this by using a global variable (current, say) but at the cost of being very careful indeed (see the previous subsection); seek_win must **completely** undo any changes it makes to current so that the nested executions of this function do not spring nasty surprises on each other. This involves some alteration of the algorithm; in particular, the state of the game as stored in current will be altered before the recursive call and reset immediately afterwards. Resetting the state can be done without recording a lot of information if we keep track of the location of the vacant space; a field for this must be added to the gamestate structure. The remaining functions, such as one to display the game, are straightforward. The program, with the description of the revised algorithm, is shown in Listing 14-7.

Listing 14-7

```
/* Program to solve the matchstick game for up to 7 matches.  */

#define MAXSIZE (7)      /* Max. matches on each side of the space */

#include <stdio.h>
#include <stdlib.h>      /* for exit() */

typedef struct {
    signed char piece[MAXSIZE*2+1];      /* MAXSIZE each way + space */
    /* Note: a 'piece' is either a matchstick or the vacant space. */
    char spaceloc;                       /* where is the space? */
} gamestate;

gamestate current, win_state;   /* The game during play & target position */
int gamesize;                   /* matches each way */
int positions;                  /* Size of playing area (gamesize*2+1) */

void initialize(void);          /* Sets up current & win_state */
int seek_win(void);             /* Returns 1 for win, 0 for failure */
```

```
main() {
    printf("   The Matchstick Game\nHow many matches (max %d)? ", MAXSIZE);
    do {
        scanf("%d", &gamesize);
        if (gamesize>MAXSIZE) {
            printf("Too big (maximum %d), please re-enter: ", MAXSIZE);
        }
    } while (gamesize>MAXSIZE);
    positions = gamesize*2 + 1;
    initialize();      /* Set up current and win_state to represent
                          the first and final state of the matches. */
    seek_win();        /* Do it all! */
    return 0;
}


/****** initialize: ************************
On entry: gamesize is the number of matches each way, positions is
          gamesize*2+1.
On exit:  Variables current & win_state are set up to represent the
          initial & final states respectively for a game of size gamesize.
*/
void initialize(void) {
    /* current should be as shown below. (e.g. for gamesize == 3):
       +----+----+----+----+----+----+----+
       | 1 | 1 | 1 | 0 | -1 | -1 | -1 |
       +----+----+----+----+----+----+----+
       The win_state has the match directions reversed.
    */
    int i, rhs;
    rhs = gamesize + 1;
    for (i=0; i<gamesize; i++) {
        current.piece[i] = win_state.piece[rhs+i] = 1;
        win_state.piece[i] = current.piece[rhs+i] = -1;
    }
    current.piece[gamesize] = win_state.piece[gamesize] = 0;
    current.spaceloc = win_state.spaceloc = gamesize;
}


/****** seek_win: ************************
On entry: The global current tells the existing game state, win_state
          tells the state needed for a win, gamesize is the number of
          matches each way, positions is gamesize*2+1.
On exit:  If a win is found, all game positions from the win backward to
          the current will be displayed backwards, resulting in a printout
          that appears to be moving forwards from the start; returns 1.
          If a win is not found, nothing is displayed; returns 0.
          All globals will be exactly as they were on entry.
*/
int move_is_legal(char spaceloc, char current_spaceloc);
void alter_position(char spaceloc, char current_spaceloc);
void undo_changes(char spaceloc, char current_spaceloc);
int found_a_win(void);
void display_position(void);
```

```
int seek_win(void) {
    /* How to seek_win:
        For each possible move from the present position:
            Alter the position.
            seek_win from the new position.
            Undo the change to the position.
            If a win was found by seek_win,
                (This game position is on the route to victory:)
                Display the matches.
                Return, indicating a win to the caller.
        (After trying each possible move, game must be blocked:)
        Check if matches are in the final position, if so,
            Display the matches,
            Return, indicating a win to the caller.
        else
            Return, indicating failure to the caller.
    */
    /* We can undo a move easily if we remember the old location of the
       space: whatever is there after moving must have come from where the
       space is now; undo by putting it back where it came from.
    */
    char spaceloc, current_spaceloc;    /* Space location after & before */
    current_spaceloc = current.spaceloc;/* Remember 'before' location */

    /* Try all possible new locations of the space: up to 2 either side. */
    for (
        spaceloc = current_spaceloc - 2;
        spaceloc <= current_spaceloc + 2;
        spaceloc++
    ) {
        if ( move_is_legal(spaceloc, current_spaceloc) ) {
            int we_won;
            alter_position(spaceloc, current_spaceloc);
            we_won = seek_win();
            undo_changes(spaceloc, current_spaceloc);
            if (we_won) {
                display_position();
                return 1;                        /* Indicate win */
            }
        }
    } /* end of for loop */

    /* Here, nothing has worked, so check if we are at the final position */
    if (found_a_win()) {
        display_position();
        return 1;                                /* win */
    } else {
        return 0;                                /* failure */
    }
}

/****** move_is_legal: *********************
On entry: spaceloc is location of match to be moved into the space now
          at current_spaceloc.
```

```
On exit:   Returns 1 if the following tests are passed, 0 otherwise:
              spaceloc is within the limits of the game
              spaceloc is not the same as current_spaceloc (because a
                 piece MUST be moved)
              the shift will move a match forwards.
*/
int move_is_legal(char spaceloc, char current_spaceloc) {
    return (
         spaceloc >= 0 &&                 /* Space not fallen off LHS */
         spaceloc < positions &&          /* Space not fallen off RHS */
         spaceloc != current_spaceloc &&  /* Space HAS been moved */
         current.piece[spaceloc] * (current_spaceloc-spaceloc) > 0
                       /* Matchstick is moving forward. (Think about it.) */
    );
}

/****** alter_position: *****************
On entry: spaceloc is location of match to be moved to current_spaceloc.
On exit:  current structure updated to reflect the move.
*/
void alter_position(char spaceloc, char current_spaceloc) {
    current.piece[current_spaceloc] = current.piece[spaceloc];
                                         /* Shift piece into space */
    current.piece[spaceloc] = 0;         /* Set its old spot empty */
    current.spaceloc = spaceloc;         /* Record new position of space */
}

/****** undo_changes: *****************
On entry: spaceloc is the old location of the match that was moved into
          the space at current_spaceloc.
On exit:  current structure updated to undo the move.
*/
void undo_changes(char spaceloc, char current_spaceloc) {
    current.spaceloc = current_spaceloc; /* Reset space position */
    current.piece[spaceloc] = current.piece[current_spaceloc];
                                         /* Reverse piece */
    current.piece[current_spaceloc] = 0; /* Put space where it was before */
}

/****** found_a_win: *****************
On entry: current is the current state of the game, win_state is the
          target state (the position when a win is found).
On exit:  Returns 1 if current is the winning position, 0 otherwise.
*/
int found_a_win(void) {
    int pos;
    if (current.spaceloc != win_state.spaceloc) {
        return 0; /* If the spaces are at different places, states differ */
    }
    for (pos=0; pos<positions; pos++) { /* Check all match positions */
        if (current.piece[pos] != win_state.piece[pos]) {
            return 0;                    /* Found a difference */
        }
    }
    return 1;                            /* Passed all tests, have win. */
}
```

```
/**** display_position ****
On entry: current tells the state to be displayed.
On exit:  A 'picture' of the current state is shown on the screen,
          but with directions of the matches reversed.
*/
void display_position(void) {
    /* Draw forward matches as "<---" and reverse matches as "--->" */
    int i;
    for (i=0; i<positions; i++) {
        switch (current.piece[i]) {
        case -1:
            printf("---> ");
            break;
        case 0:
            printf("     ");
            break;
        case 1:
            printf("<--- ");
        }
    }
    putchar('\n');          /* End the line */
}
```

Program run

```
    The Matchstick Game
How many matches (max 7)? 8
Too big (maximum 7), please re-enter: 3
---> ---> --->           <--- <--- <---
---> ---> ---> <---            <--- <---
---> --->           <--- ---> <--- <---
--->           ---> <--- ---> <--- <---
---> <--- --->           ---> <--- <---
---> <--- ---> <--- --->           <---
---> <--- ---> <--- ---> <---
---> <--- ---> <---            <--- --->
---> <---           <--- ---> <--- --->
          <--- ---> <--- ---> <--- --->
<---           ---> <--- ---> <--- --->
<--- <--- --->           ---> <--- --->
<--- <--- ---> <--- --->           --->
<--- <--- ---> <---           ---> --->
<--- <---           <--- ---> ---> --->
<--- <--- <---           ---> ---> --->
```

Although the program works, it would be a clever person who could follow all the detailed steps it takes in finding the solution. The only way to have confidence that the program is correct is to understand the insight behind function seek_win as described above. The program will investigate every possible game that can be played until it stumbles onto the winning one. Chess-playing programs could be written the same way, but in chess there are so many possible games that an exhaustive search is impossible; therefore other techniques are used to try to identify promising moves and only investigate those. The skill of a human grand master in chess includes the uncanny ability to sense, instinctively, the best moves for detailed study. So although modern computers can investigate many thousands of times more moves than a human can, they still find it hard to beat a human expert.

14.5 SUMMARY

- A *recursive* function is one that calls itself.
  - *Direct recursion* means the function contains a direct call to itself.
  - *Indirect recursion* means the function calls itself via other functions; for example it calls another function that calls the first one.
- Recursive calls work in the same way as other function calls.
- Certain precautions ensure that recursive calls eventually return successfully:
  - there must be a possible path through the function that avoids the recursion
  - the recursive call(s) must pose a simpler problem than the original (that is, they must be closer to the nonrecursive case)
  - the normal function preconditions and postconditions must be suitable.
- Recursion works because all parameters, local variables, etc. are replicated for each nested recursive call. Global variables are **not** replicated; all recursive functions access the same copy of a global variable.
- As each nested function call requires memory, very deep recursion can cause memory problems, depending on the particular computer.
- It is easy to inadvertently write very inefficient recursive functions, especially if they contain more than one recursive call, which causes an exponential tree of function calls. Sometimes, of course, the problem is inherently complicated, and more than one recursive call is needed to find a solution.
- Some ways to devise recursive algorithms are:
  - Split a problem into two problems of half the size and recursively solve each one. This does not cause inefficiency because repeatedly dividing a problem in two causes an exponential reduction in complexity which balances the exponential increase due to recursing twice (e.g. Listing 14-2 sums an array by adding the sums of the two halves).
  - First think out how to do one step of a problem, and then call recursively to perform all remaining steps (e.g. Listing 14-1 evaluates all nested expressions within a pair of parentheses).
  - Call recursively to do all but one step, and then do the remaining step (e.g. see the factorial function in the Self-test Exercises).
  - Do part of one step, do all remaining steps, and do the rest of the first step. This usually causes some sort of reversal of order (e.g. Listing 14-7 makes one move and then tries to make all remaining moves, and after finding success, displays the move made).

14.6 SELF-TEST EXERCISES

Short Answer

1   Explain why the following `sumarray` function is inferior to the one in Listing 14-2:

```
float sumarray(float A[], int L, int H) {
    if (H < L) {                            /* nothing to sum */
        return 0;
    } else if (H == L) {                    /* one element in range */
        return A[L];
    } else {                                /* Multiple elements */
        return A[L] + sumarray(A, L + 1, H);
    }
}
```

Programming

2   The factorial function, $n!$, or `fac(n)` in C notation, is defined to be 1 if n equals 0 or 1, and $n \times (n-1)!$ if n is greater than 1. Write recursive and iterative versions of `fac`, and test them both.

3   Recursively reprogram question 6 of the Test Questions in Chapter 2 (the diagram of the function 2^n), developing your algorithm from the hint given in that question.

4   The Towers of Hanoi problem described in question 9 of the Test Questions in Chapter 2 is a classic problem used to illustrate recursive techniques. The recursive solution comes from this insight: We can shift a stack of n counters on peg A to peg C, by first moving $n-1$ counters from A to B, then shifting the one remaining counter from A to C, and lastly shifting that stack of $n-1$ counters from B to C. Program Towers of Hanoi using that recursive algorithm.

14.7 TEST QUESTIONS

Short Answer

1   Explain why we must be wary of very deeply nested recursion.

2   What is wrong with the following function to sum the numbers from 1 to n? Explain in terms of an important general principle.

```
int sum_1_to(int n) {
    return n + sum_1_to(n-1);
}
```

Programming

3   Listing 14-6 shows an inefficient recursive Fibonacci function. By using a global array to remember values previously calculated, design an efficient recursive function.

4   The matchstick program in Listing 14-7 displays the positions in the reverse order to that in which it finds them. This works because the game is the same in reverse as forwards. This is not true of more complex games such as Chess or Go. Pretend it is not true of the matchstick game, and rewrite the program so that it stores the forward moves in an array and prints them forwards in `main` after completion of `seek_win`. (Extra challenge: you are now close to having a non-recursive version of the matchstick game. Can you see how to obtain it?)

5   Write a program that asks the user values for two integers n and r, and then displays all combinations of the first n integers taken r at a time.

6   The greatest common denominator (gcd) of two positive integers M and N is N if N divides exactly into M, otherwise it is $gcd(N, R)$, where R is the remainder when M is divided by N. From this definition, write a recursive `gcd` function.

7   Consider an n-dimensional grid of points, with unit spacing between points in all directions. Further, suppose that an n-dimensional hypersphere of radius r lies with its centre at the origin (r need not be integral). Write a program to ask the user n and r, and then calculate and print the number of grid points lying on or within the hypersphere. That is, the program must count all points p (each point having n co-ordinates $(p_1, p_2, ... p_n)$) which satisfy $p_1^2 + p_2^2 + ... + p_n^2 \leq r^2$. (Hint: think of all integral values of p_n^2 that are less than or equal to r^2, and for each one, ask how many grid points lie within an $n-1$ dimensional hypersphere of radius $r^2 - p_n^2$.)

8   Ackermann's function is a very convoluted mathematical function of two integers, defined as follows:

$$\text{ack}(M, N) \quad = \quad \begin{cases} N + 1, & \text{if } M=0 \\ \text{ack}(M-1, 1), & \text{if } M \neq 0 \text{ and } N=0 \\ \text{ack}(M-1, \text{ack}(M, N-1)), & \text{if } M \neq 0 \text{ and } N \neq 0. \end{cases}$$

It is extraordinarily complicated and can only be evaluated for very small values of M and N. Write a recursive function to evaluate Ackermann's function, and include a printout on entry to tell you what the parameters are. You will be very surprised indeed. Start out with simple examples like `ack(1,1)`. You will see that the same function values are evaluated repeatedly. Next, try to speed up `ack` by having a global two-dimensional array to store values already calculated; `ack` should, upon entry, check the array first to see if these parameter values have been evaluated before. If so, use the stored number; if not, use the recursive definition to evaluate the function and store the result in the array for future reference.

9   You sit down at your computer one day and discover that the multiplication operator has stopped working. Luckily, you know that if m is zero, $m \times n = 0$, and if m is greater than 0, $m \times n = n + (m-1) \times n$. If m is less than 0, $m \times n = -((-m) \times n)$. Write a program to input two integers and display their product, using these facts.

10 (Interesting challenge) Noughts and Crosses is a two-player game just simple enough to be solved by exhaustive analysis of all possibilities. Write a program to play the game. On the computer's move, try each possible move, and for each one try all possible games following that move. If a win is reported, make the move. If a draw is reported, remember the move, and make it if no win is found in investigating other moves.

In the process of investigating all possible games, each alternating level of the recursion belongs to the human opponent, and for those moves a win (for the human) is actually a loss for the computer, so if any win is found for the human's move, a loss must be reported to the level above. This game can be made infuriating by, on the first occasion the computer finds a win, predicting the win and saying how many moves away it is.

11 Transport companies often have to work out the shortest distance between two cities. For up to 20 cities, represent roads from city i to city j by the value j and the distance. There can, of course, be up to 19 such entries per city, so a square array will be needed; also a corresponding entry should be made for city j (unless it is a one-way road). Such a matrix, plus city names, can be read in from a data file. Write a program to answer queries for the shortest route between any two input cities. The method is to set the length of the shortest route found so far to a very big value, then for each road from the start, move to the next city, add the distance traveled to a route total, and see if it exceeds the shortest route so far. If so, scrap it and try another route. Either we get to the destination or we recurse. Because of the possibility of loops, we must never revisit a city already on the current route.

12 A partition of an integer n is a sequence of integers adding to n; for example, the partitions of 4 are (4), (3,1), (2,2), (2,1,1), and (1,1,1,1). Write a program that inputs an integer n and prints all its partitions. You might notice that if the first digit of a partition of n is m, then the rest of that partition is a partition of $(n-m)$. To prevent repetitions, ignore such sub-partitions whose first element is greater than m.

15

Data structures and abstract data types

Objectives

Introduce the concept of an abstract data type.

Examine further examples of data structures, as implementations of abstract data types.

Investigate key issues concerning abstract data types:

— data hiding

— functional specification

— relation to object-oriented programming.

15.1 INTRODUCTION

In Chapter 13 we briefly previewed data structures. In a sense, we are still merely previewing these and the related concept of an abstract data type. Complete books are devoted to these subjects, so this chapter can obviously be no more than an introduction.

A data structure is any coherent collection of data. For example, an array organized for a particular purpose is a data structure. The `matrixes` and `point_lists` of Chapter 13 are also data structures, as they comprise collections of data organized according to some defined scheme. In these cases, pointers connect the separate parts, so they can be called *linked* data structures.

When programmers first started designing complex data structures, programs were often hard to understand and modify. The reason was that having gone to the trouble of designing all the arrays, `struct`s, and pointer connections that comprised a data structure, the programmers naturally felt entitled to use them. Thus their programs relied heavily on the way the data structures were designed, which in turn meant that, if a change was needed in the data structure, all sections of the program that relied on the previous arrangement had to be located and modified. That was no fun.

Abstract data types were a response to this problem. To see how, consider the type `FILE`, defined in `<stdio.h>`. We declare `FILE` pointers, and through them, perform all manner of operations on files. Yet we never need to know what is actually in the `FILE` structure nor the details of the algorithms used in the various operations such as `fopen`, `fclose`, etc. All we need to know are the advertised specifications of the various input/output functions, and we can then confidently write a program that will work as intended.

This is so because `FILE`s have both public and private properties. Public properties include the behavior of the various functions. Private properties include the arrangement of the fields in the `FILE` structure and the algorithms used to implement the functions.

Portable, maintainable programming with a data type makes **free** use of the public properties, but **no** use of the private properties.

If we obey this rule, we are using a type as an abstract data type. In other words, an abstract data type, or *ADT*, is a data type which we only use via a specified set of advertised, public properties. Each property is usually implemented by either an operator (in the case of built-in types) or a function. To design an abstract data type of our own, we must first design the *public interface*: the set of functions programmers will use to access the ADT. For example, a *stack* is an ADT with the property that the last item entered must be the first item removed; this is the same as the behavior of a stack of plates in a restaurant.

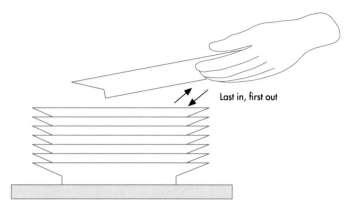

Last in, first out

Figure 15.1 The behavior of a stack

The public behavior of a stack might include functions to create one, tell whether it is empty, put an item in (push), and remove an item (pop). To implement the stack in a computer, it might be stored in either an array or a linked list, but if we use only the ADT public interface, we need never know which. Therefore, if the implementation of a stack needs changing, it need not upset any program we have written using it. This key idea is further developed in object-oriented programming (see Section 8.5).

15.2 EXAMPLE: THE STACK AS AN ABSTRACT DATA TYPE

Our goal is to define an abstract data type, `stack`, and implement it in two different ways: an array-based data structure, then a linked list. Both implementations will represent the same ADT, and an application should work correctly using either.

The first task is to define a datatype to store a stack and a set of functions that perform the required operations. These definitions will be collected in a `.h` file for inclusion in any program that needs a stack. The datatype that will actually hold the stack information will be a `struct` type (`struct stacktype`, say). However, so that we do not reveal the internal details of the required datatype, the `.h` file should only contain a declaration for a pointer type (`stack`, say) that points to this `struct` type. The `struct` type itself will not be defined in the `.h` file, and so programs will be prevented from making unauthorized use of the internal details of the `struct`. Because the `struct` type is not fully defined, it is called an *incomplete type*. We can declare a pointer to point to an incomplete type and we can declare (but not define) functions that return an incomplete type. However, we cannot actually create or use variables of the incomplete type itself. Later we shall write a `.c` file that actually implements the stack functions; in that file, the incomplete type must be completed by providing a full `struct` declaration for it.

Listing 15-1 shows a `stack.h` file showing suitable functions.

Listing 15-1 `stack.h`

```
/******** stack.h: Definition of the Abstract Data Type, stack. ********/

typedef struct stacktype *stack;    /* The incomplete type - we haven't
                                        said what a 'struct stacktype' is */

/**** stack_init: ******
 On entry: size is the maximum number of elements to be stored in stack.
 On exit:  Returns a correctly initialized empty stack, or NULL if the
           initialization fails.
*/
stack stack_init(int /*size*/);

/**** stack_free: ******
 On entry: stk is an empty stack.
 On exit:  Any space used by stk has been freed.  stk may no longer be used.
*/
void stack_free(stack /*stk*/);

/**** stack_push: ******
 On entry: stk is an initialized stack, item points to an item to be added
           to the stack.
 On exit:  If item has been added to the top of the stack, returns 1.
           If addition failed, returns 0.
*/
int stack_push(stack /*stk*/, void * /*item*/);

/**** stack_empty: ******
 On entry: stk is an initialized stack.
 On exit:  Returns 1 if stk is empty, 0 otherwise.
*/
int stack_empty(stack /*stk*/);

/**** stack_pop: ******
 On entry: stk is an initialized stack.
 On exit:  If stack not empty, returns top item and removes it from stk,
           otherwise returns NULL.
*/
void *stack_pop(stack /*stk*/);

/**** stack_top: ******
 On entry: stk is an initialized stack.
 On exit:  If stack not empty, returns top item (not removed from stk),
           otherwise returns NULL.
*/
void *stack_top(stack /*stk*/);

/**** stack_count: ******
 On entry: stk is an initialized stack.
 On exit:  Returns count of number of items in the stack.
*/
int stack_count(stack /*stk*/);
```

In the `stack.h` file, the names of all function parameters have been commented out. This prevents clashes if a programmer includes the file in a program that has used one of these names as a macro.

The plan for using a `stack` is similar to that for using `FILE` pointers; just as a `FILE *` variable must be assigned a value with `fopen`, so a `stack` must be assigned a value with `stack_init`. We should be able to use `stacks` without knowing anything about how they are implemented; the preconditions and postconditions of the stack functions tell us everything we are entitled to know about them.

Now consider the postcondition for `stack_init`: there is something odd about it. The precondition mentions that `size` is the size of stack, yet the postcondition makes no promise that the stack will hold the amount of data requested. If this requirement were included, it would almost force us to implement the stack in an array, as successfully `malloc`ing a suitable array will guarantee the stack capacity very conveniently. By omitting this requirement we have the option of using dynamic linked storage for the stack. This has the advantage that the stack will be allowed to expand as much or as little as necessary, as long as free memory remains.

To use a stack, the program must `malloc` storage for each item and pass its address to `stack_push`, which remembers the address but does not copy the data itself into the stack. When we ask for a value with `stack_pop` or `stack_top`, the address of the top item is returned; in the case of `stack_pop`, we should `free` the memory once we are finished with the data. This is illustrated in Figure 15.2.

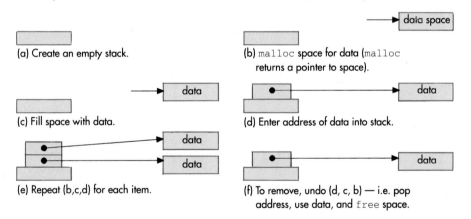

(a) Create an empty stack.

(b) `malloc` space for data (`malloc` returns a pointer to space).

(c) Fill space with data.

(d) Enter address of data into stack.

(e) Repeat (b,c,d) for each item.

(f) To remove, undo (d, c, b) — i.e. pop address, use data, and `free` space.

Figure 15.2 Steps for storing data in a stack

Our application problem will be a simple one to avoid obscuring the main issues. We shall write a program to input names, one per line, and output them in reverse order. By stacking each name as it arrives until end of file, and then unstacking and displaying the entire contents of the stack, we achieve this effect. The program is shown in Listing 15-2.

Listing 15-2

```
/*Program to reverse a list of names using the stack package */

#include <stdio.h>
#include <stdlib.h>
#include <string.h>
#include "stack.h"

void fatal(char message[]);
int can_load_name(stack stk);
void unload_name(stack stk);

main() {
    stack s;                         /* Declare stack variable */
    s = stack_init(100);             /* Initialize */
    if (s == NULL) {
        fatal("Cannot initialize stack");
    }
    printf("Enter names:\n");
    while (can_load_name(s)) {        /* Try to load another name */
        /* Try again */
    }
    printf("Names are:\n");

    /* Here all names are loaded into stack; now unload and output. */
    while (! stack_empty(s)) {        /* Still more in stack? */
        unload_name(s);              /* yes - pop and print */
    }
    stack_free(s);    /* Not necessary in this program, but good practice
                         to free any memory not required further. */
    return 0;
}

/* fatal: print error and stop */
void fatal(char message[]) {
    fprintf(stderr, "ERROR:%s!\n", message);
    exit(EXIT_FAILURE);
}

/* can_load_name: Read a name & push; return 1 (success), or 0 (fail) */
int can_load_name(stack s) {
    char buf[80], *nam;    /* Temporary buffer, and pointer for the name */

    if (scanf("%79[^\n]%*[^\n]", buf) < 1) {  /* Try to read name. Fail? */
        return 0;                             /* Report failure */
    }
    getchar();                    /* Input '\n', ready for next name input */

    nam = (char*)malloc((strlen(buf)+1) * sizeof(char)); /* get space */
    if (nam == NULL) {                                   /* fail? */
        fatal("No space for name");
    }
```

```
    strcpy(nam, buf);              /* copy string into nam */
    if (! stack_push(s, nam)) {    /* Try pushing buffer's address - fail? */
        fatal("No room on stack");
    }
    return 1;                      /* Report success */
}

/* unload_name: Assumes there is a name in the stack; removes & prints it */
void unload_name(stack stk) {
    char *buf;
    buf = (char*)stack_pop(stk);
    printf("%s\n", buf);
    free(buf);                     /* Reclaim space malloc'ed above. */
}
```

15.2.1 Array-based stack implementation

We can't run this program yet because we do not have an implementation of the stack ADT, and in particular the type `struct stacktype`. The first implementation will employ an array. An `int` field in the structure will record how many items are used, and another the stack's capacity. We require two objects: an array of `void` pointers for the stacked addresses, and a structure with the two `int`s and a pointer to the array. The latter will be type `struct stacktype` itself; the array will be linked onto the structure, and it in turn will contain the pointers to the user's data, as shown in Figure 15.3.

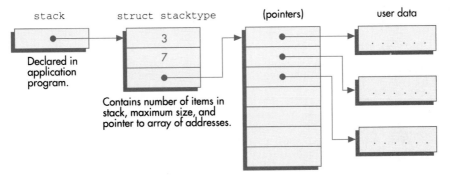

Figure 15.3 Stack of maximum size seven, holding three items.

Given these decisions, the `struct stacktype` structure can be defined and the various functions declared in `stack.h` can be programmed; these will be in their own source file, as shown in Listing 15-3.

Listing 15-3 `stackarr.c,` **an array-based stack implementation**

```c
/* Array-based implementation of the ADT stack. */
#include "stack.h"
#include <stdlib.h>                 /* for malloc, etc. & NULL */

typedef struct stacktype {
    int size, sp;                   /* Maximum size and current size */
    void **items;                   /* Pointer to an array of void pointers */
} stacktype;

stack stack_init(int size) {
    stack stk;

    stk = (stack)malloc(sizeof(stacktype)); /* space for the stack. */
    if (stk == NULL) {                       /* no space? */
        return NULL;
    }

    /* Now try for the array of void pointers */
    stk->items = (void**)malloc(size*sizeof(void*));
    if (stk->items == NULL) {                /* no space for array? */
        free(stk);                           /* Undo first allocation */
        return NULL;                         /* report failure */
    }

    /* Set up housekeeping fields of stack structure. */
    stk->size = size;                        /* Maximum size */
    stk->sp = 0;                             /* Stack starts out empty */
    return stk;                              /* initialized stack */
}

void stack_free(stack stk) {
    free(stk->items);                        /* Free array of pointers */
    free(stk);                               /* Free stack */
}

int stack_push(stack stk, void *item) {
    /* Detect overflow by checking the size limit. */
    if (stk->sp >= stk->size) {
        return 0;                            /* fail */
    }
    stk->items[stk->sp] = item;              /* Record address in array */
    stk->sp++;                               /* Count it */
    return 1;                                /* succeed */
}

int stack_empty(stack stk) {
    return (stk->sp == 0);                   /* If true, stack is empty */
}
```

```
void *stack_pop(stack stk) {
    void *item;
    if (stack_empty(stk)) {                 /* Check for item on stack */
        return NULL;
    }
    item = stack_top(stk);                  /* Get top item. */
    stk->sp--;                              /* Pop it from stack */
    return item;
}

void *stack_top(stack stk) {
    if (stack_empty(stk)) {                 /* Check for item on stack */
        return NULL;
    }
    return stk->items[stk->sp-1];           /* Return recorded address */
}

int stack_count(stack stk) {
    return stk->sp;
}
```

By compiling Listings 15-2 and 15-3 and linking them together we obtain a complete program which we can now test.

Test run
```
Enter names:
Montreal
New York
London
Mexico City
Brisbane
^Z
Names are:
Brisbane
Mexico City
London
New York
Montreal
```

15.2.2 Stack implementation using a linked list

This implementation will use a linked list similar to the one written as part of Listings 13-5a to 13-5c, but it will be much simpler due to the limited range of operations that must be performed: addition and deletion at the head of the list are all we need. The structure `stacktype` will need a pointer to the linked list and an `int` field to hold the count of the number of nodes held in the stack. In addition, the linked list will need its own `listnode` type. Listing 15-4 shows this implementation of the stack ADT.

Listing 15-4 `stacklnk.c`

```c
/* List-based implementation of the ADT stack. */
#include "stack.h"
#include <stdlib.h>                          /* for NULL */

typedef struct listnode {                    /* type for items in list */
    struct listnode *next;
    void *item;
} listnode;

typedef struct stacktype {                   /* basic stack type */
    listnode *list;
    int itemcount;
} stacktype;

stack stack_init(int size) {
    stack result;
    result = (stack)malloc(sizeof(stacktype));/* space for stack struct */
    if (result == NULL) {
        return NULL;                         /* no space available */
    }
    result->list = NULL;                     /* No nodes */
    result->itemcount = 0;                   /* so count is 0 */
    return result;
}

void stack_free(stack stk) {
    listnode *p, *q;
    p = stk->list;                           /* set p to first node */
    while (p != NULL) {                       /* while nodes remain */
        q = p->next;                         /* remember next node */
        free(p);                             /* free this one */
        p = q;                               /* set p to next node */
    }
    free(stk);                               /* free stack structure */
}

int stack_push(stack stk, void *item) {
    listnode *p;
    p = (listnode*)malloc(sizeof(listnode)); /* space for list node */
    if (p == NULL) {
        return 0;                            /* no space for node */
    }
    stk->itemcount++;                        /* count extra node */
    p->item = item;                          /* record user data ptr */
    p->next = stk->list;                     /* p precedes current list */
    stk->list = p;                           /* and becomes new head */
    return 1;                                /* success */
}
```

```
int stack_empty(stack stk) {
    return (stk->itemcount == 0);
}

void *stack_pop(stack stk) {
    listnode *p;
    void *result;
    if (stk->list==NULL) {
        return NULL;                       /* No node, so no data! */
    }
    stk->itemcount--;                      /* one fewer items */
    p = stk->list;                         /* address of head node */
    result = p->item;                      /* recover user's data ptr */
    stk->list = p->next;                   /* disconnect head node */
    free(p);                               /* free discarded node */
    return result;                         /* return user's data ptr */
}

void *stack_top(stack stk) {
    if (stk->list==NULL) {
        return NULL;                       /* No node, so no data! */
    }
    return stk->list->item;                /* return user's data ptr */
}

int stack_count(stack stk) {
    return stk->itemcount;
}
```

To compile Listing 15-2 using this implementation, compile and link `lst15-2.c` and `stacklnk.c`. The output is exactly the same as before.

15.3 KEY ISSUES CONCERNING ABSTRACT DATA TYPES

The previous examples have shown that it is possible to separately program an ADT and an application program that uses it, without at either stage peeking at the coding of the other part to make sure everything will work properly when combined. Certain principles make this possible. The most obvious is the use of *functional specification*: the **behavior** of the ADT is defined, but the details of how it will work or how it will be stored are not. The best way to define the behavior is by using preconditions and postconditions: the 'On entry' and 'On exit' clauses in the heading comments for the functions. (These specifications need not actually be in the code; they might be in a separate manual, for example.) By following this format, we force ourselves to describe only the requirements to be met when calling a function and the promises to be fulfilled by the function. If the details of the algorithm used to implement a function are not clear, explain them with further comments elsewhere, but do not mix such explanations in with the promises.

For example, here is a bad specification for function `stack_free`:

```
/**** stack_free: ******
    Deletes all the nodes in a stack by setting a pointer to the first
    and advancing it through the list, deleting one node at a time.
    Always make sure no node is freed until its next pointer is saved
    in a temporary variable.
*/
```

This specification confuses the two jobs of specifying the function and internally documenting it. Therefore it is suitable for neither purpose. Another kind of 'specification' in wide usage is the one-liner — a brief remark that gives us a vague idea of the job done by a function, but which is not specific enough to rely on. This forces us to read the code to find out what is going on. Here is such a one-liner:

```
/** stack_free: deletes a stack **/
```

I suspect that many programmers write one-liners because they never properly think out what their functions are meant to do. This is especially true when, in a hurry to get things working, programmers decide to forge ahead with the coding and "leave the comments till later". It is hard to persuade people not to do this, even though it can double or treble the time needed to complete a project, or even kill it off altogether. (Yes, this really happens.)

The next principle used in the previous ADTs is *data hiding*. Like functional specifications, this erects a 'fire wall' between the application and the abstract data type's internal logic. The field `next` in type `listnode` is an example — it is not mentioned in the functional specification and its use is forbidden to application programs. Unfortunately, C has quite weak facilities for enforcing this discipline: it is easy to gain unauthorized access to this field if one really wants to. But when, in a major system, a change is made to the implementation and programs unexpectedly fail, it is a considerable headache putting things right. Some languages such as C++ allow one to specify certain fields as public or private, and the compiler itself then helps to prevent unauthorized access.

The above principles are important in object-oriented programming (see Section 8.5). For example, with a linked list like that developed in the preceding section, certain operations are efficient and others are not. We might like a different implementation (say, using an array) for some purposes. With an object-oriented language like C++, we could define `stack` as a *base class* (which we shall not explain further here) and develop other specialized classes from it. Then the stack implemented as a linked list might be just one of many different types of stack for various special purposes. All stacks, however, will obey the specifications of the type `stack` no matter how they are implemented. This is called *inheritance* (again, not explained further here) and is a central object-oriented feature which makes object-oriented programming so much more productive for large systems than non-object-oriented programming. But be warned: the further along the road we go towards these powerful techniques, the more important it becomes to avoid sloppy programming methods.

15.4 SUMMARY

- A data structure is any coherent collection of data.
- Two main ways to construct data structures are
    - to store successive elements in contiguous storage (arrays)
    - to connect related parts using pointers (linked storage).
- A definition of an *abstract data type* is a set of definitions of operations we may perform on the data.
- The ADT definition is the *public* component of an implementation of the ADT. Internal operations, data fields, etc. should be *private*.
- The *stack* ADT is a data structure where the last item inserted is always the first item removed.
- An ADT should be defined in terms of the preconditions and postconditions of the functions that access the data.
- If an ADT is defined well, it should be possible to implement it in different ways without affecting application programs that use the ADT.
- When defining functions, avoid mixing the *specification* of the function with the explanation about how it works.
- Avoid 'one-liner' comments — vague remarks that cannot be fully understood without reference to the program source.
- ADTs rely on *data hiding* — restricting access to internal fields and functions that do not form part of the ADT definition (the interface).

15.5 SELF-TEST EXERCISES

Short Answer
1 Write a definition for an ADT that provides the facilities of an array. (Think out the tasks you can do with an array, and define functions to provide them. Array subscripting will be provided via function calls, not the usual [ ] notation.)

Programming
2 Using the ADT definition from question 1, write an implementation. You should be able to do one easily by using normal C arrays within your implementation. If this seems pointless, try the next question!

3 Using the ADT definition from question 1, write an implementation that provides infinitely expandable arrays (that is, arrays that automatically grow as data is inserted, subject only to overall memory limitations).

15.6 TEST QUESTIONS

Short Answer

1 Write an ADT definition for a string datatype that automatically sizes itself to fit the string assigned to it. (Hint: You may need to define a function to do the assignment operation.)

2 Write an ADT definition for a type that holds arbitrarily large non-negative integers. Provide at least the assignment, addition, subtraction, and multiplication operations; division too if you like.

Programming

3 Implement the string ADT from question 1 above.

4 Using the ADT definition from question 1 in the Self-test Exercises, write an implementation that provides `float` *sparse arrays* (arrays for which only the non-zero entries are recorded). (These are useful in certain matrix and other algorithms where a large proportion of zero values occur.)

5 Program the ADT you defined in question 2 above.

6 Define and implement an ADT for an array that includes file storage and retrieval operations for an entire array. You may wish to restrict your ADT to a particular type of element, e.g. `float`.

7 Define and implement an ADT for arrays where the user can specify both lower and upper bounds; that is, the lowest subscript need not be zero.

8 Repeat question 7 for two-dimensional arrays.

9 Write a program that reads normal text from a file and makes and prints a concordance of each word occurring in the text, along with every line the word occurs on. Use the `list` ADT from the text to hold lists of the words and, for each word, have a `list` of all the line numbers. The program will therefore contain many lists.

10 Define and implement a matrix ADT, with functions for the common matrix operations as well as input and output. Use your ADT in a program that implements a matrix calculator.

16

Further issues concerning numeric computation

Objectives

Study the full set of C numeric data types.

— `short`, `signed`, and `unsigned` types

— type promotion and demotion rules

— extra ways to write constants

— further `printf` and `scanf` formats.

Be aware of some pitfalls in performing numeric computations.

— overflow, underflow, accuracy

— differences between compilers

— calculations involving money.

16.1 INTRODUCTION

When writing real-life programs — programs that will be relied upon in commerce, science or industry — the programmer must consider the choice of appropriate data types and the possibility of errors arising during calculations. All data types have size limits, for example, and if they are exceeded the program results can be meaningless. In such circumstances professional programs must either prevent the problem or at least detect it and take suitable action, such as warning the user. Therefore we must examine the full range of numeric data types available in C, consider the circumstances under which each one is appropriate, and investigate their pitfalls.

16.2 INTEGRAL DATA TYPES

We have looked at the basic integral data types `char`, `int`, and `long`. However, there is also another type, `short`. The differences among `char`, `short`, `int`, and `long` concern the number of bits allocated for a variable; `char` has the fewest and `long` has the most. Therefore, a `long` variable, for example, will be able to hold a number selected from a much larger range than a `char` variable. Variables of each type may also be declared to be `signed` or `unsigned`, in the following way:

```
signed int i;
unsigned char j, k;
signed short p;
unsigned long q;
```

The main difference between `signed` and `unsigned` concerns the treatment of negative numbers. The `signed` variables allocate one bit to stand for + or −; `unsigned` variables use that bit as just another binary digit in the value. This means that the `unsigned` variants cannot store negative values but they can store twice the range of non-negative values. The ANSI/ISO C standard requires all C compilers to provide at least a certain minimal range for each type. Table 16-1 shows these minimal ranges.

Table 16-1 Guaranteed minimum and maximum values for integral data types

Type name	Minimum possible value	Maximum possible value
signed char	at most −127	at least 127
unsigned char	exactly 0	at least 255
signed short	at most −32,767	at least 32,767
unsigned short	exactly 0	at least 65,535
signed int	at most −32,767	at least 32,767
unsigned int	exactly 0	at least 65,535
signed long	at most −2,147,483,647	at least 2,147,483,647
unsigned long	exactly 0	at least 4,294,967,295

Compilers may give you more than is indicated in Table 16-1 but they cannot give you less; a compiler can let you use `signed shorts`, for example, for values up to 80 quadrillion (although this isn't likely) but it cannot cut you off even one short of the guaranteed 32,767. Your programs can find out the ranges allowed by your particular compiler by including the header `<limits.h>` which defines names that equal the actual limits allowed on your system. The names of these values are shown in Table 16-2.

Table 16-2 Names defined in `<limits.h>` specifying the limits on the ranges of integral types

Type name	Name of minimum allowed value	Name of maximum allowed value
signed char	SCHAR_MIN	SCHAR_MAX
unsigned char	(always 0)	UCHAR_MAX
char	CHAR_MIN	CHAR_MAX
signed short	SHRT_MIN	SHRT_MAX
unsigned short	(always 0)	USHRT_MAX
signed int	INT_MIN	INT_MAX
unsigned int	(always 0)	UINT_MAX
signed long	LONG_MIN	LONG_MAX
unsigned long	(always 0)	ULONG_MAX

One situation that gives rise to an expanded range arises because many computers use the twos complement number system for doing integral arithmetic. This system allows one more negative number than positive ones. Another common extension concerns the `int` type: some compilers define it to be as large as `long`. So if both these situations apply to you, you might find that in `<limits.h>` on your computer, INT_MAX is 2,147,483,647 and INT_MIN is –2,147,483,648.

What if we leave out the word `signed` or `unsigned` in a declaration? Except for `char`, this is the same as writing `signed`. (Thus, for example, `int` means the same thing as `signed int`.) For `chars`, however, this depends on the particular compiler, so if you want negative `chars` be sure to declare a `signed char`, and if you want `chars` with values beyond 127, declare an `unsigned char`. This is summarized in the following table.

Table 16-3 Equivalents of plain data types

Plain type	Equivalent
char	either `signed char` or `unsigned char` (Your compiler manual will say which.)
short	signed short
int	signed int
long	signed long

Finally, in declarations involving the words `signed`, `unsigned`, `short` or `long`, the word `int` can be included or omitted according to personal preference. For example:

```
short int i;      is the same as    short i;
unsigned u;       is the same as    unsigned int u;
long int l;       is the same as    long l;
```

16.2.1 Choosing the right integral type

The obvious rule for deciding on a type for a variable is to simply pick one that is big enough. So if the variable's value can never go outside the range 0–159, for example, `unsigned char` is good enough. The issue becomes puzzling when we notice that the ranges for the `short` types (listed above) are the same as for the `int` types. Why have two types with the same ranges? The answer concerns the fact that a `short` can be stored in 16 binary digits, and a `long` in 32. Many popular computers (e.g. older industry-standard PCs) use 16-bit internal logic, and so 16-bit variables are handled efficiently. Other computers, including most minicomputers such as the VAX, use 32-bit internal logic, and so 32-bit variables are handled efficiently. The idea behind these datatypes is that compiler writers should make `short` a bare 16-bit variable, they should make `long` at least a 32-bit variable, and they should make `int` the most efficient datatype for the computer concerned. Thus, most PC C compilers make `int` the same as `short`, but most minicomputer compilers make it the same as `long`.

People draw different conclusions from the above facts. Some recommend that you never use `int`, always choosing from `short` or `long`, as required; their argument is that the common variation in the size of `int` means you might be unnecessarily using a variable that is much too big for the value to be stored. I believe that this advice is wrong, and that you should normally select from `int` or `long`. My reason is this: if you need numbers beyond the guaranteed `int` range, you must use `long` — no argument. But if either a `short` or an `int` will do, `int` is better because it gives you the compiler writer's estimate of the best all-round datatype for normal applications. For example, `int` is the type used in the standard library for small numeric values. `short` should be reserved for use where some specific reason exists for minimizing storage, such as in a very large array.

Finally, when choosing datatypes, you will get the maximum portability by relying on the datatype ranges given in Table 16-1, not on any expanded ranges that a particular compiler might allow you to use. For example, you might want to store values up to 200,000 and you know you are running on a 32-bit computer where `int` means `long`. Still, you should declare variables `long`, not `int`, because otherwise, if you need to transfer the program to a computer where `int` means `short`, all `int` variables will malfunction.

16.2.2 Integral constants

In Chapter 3 we looked at the character (e.g. `'A'`), and the decimal (e.g. `5132`) ways of writing integral constants. Like variables, constants have a type. The type of a decimal constant depends on its value, and in general it is the 'smallest' type that will correctly hold the value. If the value will fit in an `int`, it has type `int`. If not, but it will fit in a `long`, then it has type `long`; or if its value exceeds even that, it has type `unsigned long`. This usually means that a constant has the right type automatically, but sometimes it is necessary to specify a constant's type. This is done with suffixes, as follows.

Specifying a constant's type using suffixes

Unsigned constants

We can force a constant to have an unsigned type by appending `u` or `U`. For example, `5132u` is of type `unsigned int`.

Long constants

We can force a constant to be `long` by appending an `l` or `L`. Thus `5132L` has type `long`. We can do both at once: `5132LU` and `5132UL` both stand for the same `unsigned long` value.

The main reason we need to force constants into a particular form is so that when they are combined with variables in arithmetic expressions, the expression result has the desired type. We shall return to this point after looking at floating-point types in the next section.

It is also possible to write constants to bases other than 10. You may not need to do this, so this point can be skipped on first reading. Octal (i.e. base 8) constants are written with a leading zero followed by octal digits (0 – 7). For example, `0521` is $(5 \times 8 \times 8) + (2 \times 8) + 1$, which is decimal 337. Hexadecimal (base 16) constants use the sixteen symbols (0 – 9, A – F) for the values 0 to 15 (A is ten, B is eleven, etc.). They are written as `0x` or `0X` followed by a hexadecimal number. Thus `0xa1f` is $(10 \times 16 \times 16) + (1 \times 16) + 15$, which is 2591 in decimal. These forms are often used when writing programs for performing manipulations of individual bits within computer words, and are often unsigned. They may also be given the `unsigned` or `long` suffixes explained above, but the rules regarding the resulting types are slightly different. All this is summarized in Table 16-4 which shows the various ways to write integral constants and the possible types that constants written in those ways can possess. (Each set of examples in the table uses the same three values: 2,396, 42,396, and 3,000,000,000. In some cases they appear in octal or hexadecimal.)

Table 16-4 Possible forms of decimal constants

Suffix	Possible typeset†	Examples	
		Value	Type
None on decimal constant	1) `int` 2) `long int` 3) `unsigned long int`	2396	`int`
		42396	`long int`
		3000000000	`unsigned long int`
None on octal or hexidecimal constant	1) `int` 2) `unsigned int` 3) `long int` 4) `unsigned long int`	04534	`int`
		0xa59c	`unsigned int`
		0xb2d05e00	`unsigned long int`
u or U on any constant	1) `unsigned int` 2) `unsigned long int`	2396u	`unsigned int`
		42396u	`unsigned int`
		3000000000U	`unsigned long int`
l or L on any constant	1) `long int` 2) `unsigned long int`	2396L	`long int`
		42396L	`long int`
		3000000000L	`unsigned long int`
Both u or U and l or L on any constant	1) `unsigned long int`	2396ul	`unsigned long int`
		42396Lu	`unsigned long int`
		3000000000uL	`unsigned long int`

† Each constant has the first type in the list that is capable of holding its value.

C also permits character-format constants containing more than one character, but this form is used so infrequently that we shall omit it here.

16.3 FLOATING-POINT DATA TYPES

C provides three floating-point data types: `float`, `double`, and `long double`. Like integral types, they have guaranteed ranges, but the situation is complicated by various intricacies concerning the internal representation of the floating-point values, such as the precision to which results are stored and the internal *radix* in which the exponent is represented. (In a floating-point number, such as 1.6×10^{12}, 10 is called the radix, and 12 the exponent.) A full description of the specification of floating-point numbers is too complex to include here, so this section is somewhat simplified.

Briefly, in storing a floating-point number such as `1.23456E27`, the computer stores the significant digits (`1.23456`, called the *significand*) and the exponent (`27`) as separate values within the `float` (or `double` or `long double`) variable. Firstly, we are guaranteed a certain number of significant digits in the significand. For floats, this is 6; it means that any float of six or fewer significant digits can be input (using scanf, say) and stored in the internal floating-point format accurately enough that it can be reconverted into decimal (by printf, say), and will print as exactly the same decimal number. This does not mean that any floating-point value of 6 or fewer digits can be represented exactly. In fact, even the number .1 cannot be stored exactly in a binary format. It can, however, be stored accurately enough that, to six digits, it prints as .100000, and not, say, .100001 or .0999999. There is also a guaranteed minimum range for the exponent, which for floats is from –37 to +37. Therefore 1E-37 is the smallest float guaranteed to be representable and 1E37 is the largest.

There is an international standard for floating-point arithmetic known as ANSI/IEEE 754–1985, and many C implementations conform to it. (We shall call this arithmetic standard IEEE for short.) It allows a wider range of values than the minimal requirements of the ANSI C standard. Also, just as with integral arithmetic, a C program can find out the characteristics of the floating-point numbers provided by any particular C compiler. In this case, the relevant information is in the header <float.h>. Table 16-5 summarizes the ANSI C and IEEE requirements for the floating types and also lists the names defined in <float.h> that tell a program the values of these limits for the particular compiler being used. For convenience, it also includes the minimum and maximum values storable in standard floating-point variables.

Table 16-5 Guaranteed ranges of values for the floating-point data types

Property	Attribute	float	double **and** long double
Significant digits	<float.h> name	FLT_DIG	DBL_DIG, LDBL_DIG
	ANSI C value	6	10
	IEEE value	6	15
Minimum exponent	<float.h> name	FLT_MIN_10_EXP	DBL_MIN_10_EXP, LDBL_MIN_10_EXP
	ANSI C value	–37	–37
	IEEE value	–37	–307
Maximum exponent	<float.h> name	FLT_MAX_10_EXP	DBL_MAX_10_EXP, LDBL_MAX_10_EXP
	ANSI C value	+37	+37
	IEEE value	+38	+308
Minimum value	<float.h> name	FLT_MIN	DBL_MIN, LDBL_MIN
	ANSI C value	1E-37	1E-37
	IEEE value	1.17549435E-38	2.2250738585072014E-308
Maximum value	<float.h> name	FLT_MAX	DBL_MAX, LDBL_MAX
	ANSI C value	1E+37	1E+37
	IEEE value	3.40282347E+38	1.7976931348623157E+308
Epsilon†	<float.h> name	FLT_EPSILON	DBL_EPSILON, LDBL_EPSILON
	ANSI C value	1E-5	1E-9
	IEEE value	1.19209290E-7	2.2204460492503131E-16

†Epsilon is the positive difference between 1 and the smallest number greater than 1 that can be represented in the given data type. It is another measure of the accuracy of the numbers.

Although the ranges shown for the IEEE `doubles` look impressive, many numeric applications require their full 15-digit precision. Some numeric applications require even more, and that is why `long double` exists; although `long double` is not required by the C standard to do more for you than `double`, some compilers intended for heavy numeric work make `long double` even more accurate.

16.3.1 Floating-point constants

The basic format of floating-point constants was explained in Chapter 3. A constant written according to the rules given there is in fact of type `double`, not `float`. Internally, C does much floating-point work in `double` format. For example, the parameters and results of all the transcendental functions (`sin`, `cos`, etc.) are `double`. To obtain a `float` constant, append an `f` or `F` to the end (e.g. `1.5f`). Similarly, append `l` or `L` to obtain a `long double` constant (e.g. `1.8122238612E300L`).

16.4 ADDITIONAL `printf` AND `scanf` FORMATTING FEATURES

We can input and output all of the various data types discussed in previous sections, in any format (e.g. octal, hexadecimal, etc.). The following tables summarize the format specifiers necessary.

16.4.1 `printf, fprintf,` and `sprintf`

Table 16-6 `printf, fprintf,` and `sprintf` formats

Format specifier	Data types printed	Explanation
`%d` `%i`	`signed char,` `int, short`	Printed as a signed decimal number.
`%u`	`unsigned int`	Prints an unsigned decimal value.
`%o`	`unsigned int`	Prints an unsigned octal value.
`%x` `%X`	`unsigned int`	Prints an unsigned hexadecimal value; any letters A–F in the number are printed in the same case as the `x` in the specifier.

`%f`
`%e`
`%g`
	`float,`
	`double`
		See Chapter 3; these are actually `double` formats, but `floats` are converted to `double` automatically when used as `printf` arguments.

The letter l (ell, not one) may be inserted to signify a long int or an unsigned long int, as follows: %ld, %lu, %lo, %lx, and %lX. Similarly, h signifies a short int in the formats %hd, %hu, %ho, %hx, and %hX. (The h modifier is usually unnecessary. For the reason, see the remark about it in Section 16.5.) Finally, L signifies a long double, with the formats %Le, %LE, %Lf, %Lg, and %LG.

Fine control over the output is obtained with flag characters, as listed in Table 16-7, which may be mixed and matched.

Table 16-7 printf, fprintf, and sprintf format flags

Flag	Meaning
–	The value is output left-justified. For example, "%3lu" prints 6UL as *<space><space>*6, but "%-3lu" prints it as 6*<space><space>*. (*<space>* here means that a space is printed.)
+	Always print a sign, even for positive numbers. Thus, "%-+3ld" prints 6L as *+6<space>*.
<space>	Always print positive numbers with a leading space. Thus, "% d" prints −6 as *–6*, but it prints 6 as *<space>6*.
#	Use an alternative format: for %o, the output will always have a leading zero, for %x (or %X) a leading 0x (or 0X). For floating formats, a decimal point will always be printed, even if no digits follow. Also, for %g and %G, trailing zeros will not be suppressed.
0 (zero)	The field is zero-padded instead of space-padded. Thus, "%03d" prints 6 as *006*.

There are other formats available with printf, but the rest are very uncommon or specialized; check your C compiler manual for the complete list.

16.4.2 scanf, fscanf, *and* sscanf *formats*

Although the scanf formats roughly parallel the printf ones, they are unfortunately just sufficiently different to mean that we have to study them separately.

Table 16-8 scanf, fscanf, and sscanf formats

Format specifier	Data types	Explanation
%d	int	Inputs a signed decimal number
%i	int	Recognizes and inputs any C-format constant (decimal, octal, or hexadecimal)
%u	unsigned int	Inputs an unsigned decimal value
%o	unsigned int	Inputs an unsigned octal value
%x %X	unsigned int	Inputs an unsigned hexadecimal value
%f %e %g	float	See Chapter 3

Certain modifiers may be used with these formats. The letter l may be inserted to signify a long int, an unsigned long int, or a double, as follows: %ld, %lu, %lo, %lx, %lX, %lf, %le, and %lg. Unlike printf, the bare floating-point specifiers ("%f", "%e", and "%g") stand for type float, not type double. The letter h may be inserted to specify a short int in the formats: %hd, %hu, %ho, %hx, and %hX. Finally, L signifies a long double, with the formats: %Le, %Lf, and %Lg. All floating format letters will accept any floating format; in other words, %e, %E, %f, %F, %g, and %G all behave in exactly the same way.

16.5 MIXING TYPES IN EXPRESSIONS

C allows great flexibility in mixing and matching types in arithmetic expressions. To do this, the compiler will on occasions automatically adjust the type of a value. For example, in the following code fragment

```
float a; int i;
...
printf("%f", a+i);
```

the compiler, seeing the attempt to add an int to a float, *widens* the value of the int i into a float before doing the addition. The addition is therefore a floating-point addition, not an integer addition, and so a float result is obtained. Thus it is necessary to use "%f", not "%d", in the printf call. Such conversions are called *type promotion*. The type of any expression involving mixed types can be predicted if a few rules are remembered. The following is a slight simplification of the actual rules in the C standard, but has the same effect in virtually all cases.

Rules governing the mixing of types in an expression

1 No expression yields a result of type `char` or `short`; these types (and also `int` bit-fields, which are not covered here) are all converted to `int`s. (This rule explains why `printf`'s h format modifier is usually unnecessary: `printf` will never receive an unconverted `short` value.)

2 If the two operands have the same type, the result is that type.

3 In general, if the operand types differ, the narrower type is converted to the wider type. For this purpose, the types may be considered to have an order. If, on your computer, `int`s have a smaller range than `long`s, the order (from narrowest to widest) is:

```
int → unsigned int → long → unsigned long → float → double →
long double
```

For example, if an `int` is multiplied by a `double`, the `int` is converted to `double` first, because `double` is further along the list than `int`.

If `int`s are the same as `long`s, the order is:

```
int → long or unsigned int → unsigned long → float → double →
long double
```

In this case, if one value is `long` and the other is `unsigned int`, they both become `unsigned long`.

Promoting values through these sequences preserves the value, unless:

- a negative value of a signed type is promoted to an unsigned type, or
- an integral value is converted to a floating-point type, and it has more digits than the floating type can handle accurately.

Examples

The examples in Table 16-9 assume these declarations:

```
char ch1, ch2; int i; unsigned u; long l;
unsigned long ul; float f; double d; long double ld;
```

Table 16-9 shows the expression, the result, and (to show how the result is obtained) an equivalent expression with all conversions written as explicit casts.

Table 16-9 Examples of the effect of the type promotion rules on arithmetic expressions

Expression	Result type	Equivalent expression
`ch1 + ch2`	int	`(int)ch1 + (int)ch2`
`(u + d) / f`	double	`((double)u + d) / (double)f`
`(u + f) / d`	double	`(double)((float)u + f) / d`
`i + u - ul +ld`	long double	`(long double)( (unsigned long)( (unsigned)i + u) - ul) + ld`
`i / l * f`	float	`(float)((long)i / l) * f`

Operand conversions are only performed if necessary for the immediate operation to be applied to that operand. Thus, in the final example in Table 16-9, the division is integer division because its operands are integral types; thus any fractional part is discarded before the conversion to type `float`.

Another type of conversion occurs in assignments. The type of the evaluated expression on the right side is converted (if necessary) to the type of the variable on the left side before assignment. This might involve type promotion, but if the expression is of a wider type than the variable it is to be stored in, the inverse process, *type demotion*, occurs. The main effect of type demotion is that when converting to a narrower type, if the value cannot be represented in the narrower type it will be altered to a value that can be represented.

Type demotion occurs in accordance with the following guidelines.

- If the value is too large to represent in the narrower type, the demoted value will be incorrect. In fact, attempting to convert a value to a signed integral or floating-point type is illegal if the value is too large to fit. Not all C implementations will detect this error.

- For floating types, even if the value is within the range of the narrower type, its precision will still be reduced; it will be approximated to the next higher or next lower value that can be represented.

- When converting floating types to an integral type, the fractional part will be discarded.

- For integral types, if the value is within the range of the narrower type, it will be exactly correct after demotion.

16.6 OVERFLOW, UNDERFLOW, AND ACCURACY

Since it is impossible for computers to store infinitely large or small numbers, numeric calculations can fail by performing a calculation whose result is too large (*overflow*) or too small (*underflow*) to fit in a variable. The full details of how to handle these problems is beyond the scope of this book. Unfortunately the C standard gives a lot of latitude in how programs should behave if these errors happen during execution of expressions. Many of the standard `<math.h>` functions set a global variable called `errno` to a non-zero value upon detecting an error. If you set `errno` to zero, then after some computations, you can inspect it to find out if a function detected an error. If so, the `perror` function could be used to print an error message.

One of the simplest ways to guard against errors is to think about the behavior of a sequence of calculations under extreme conditions, and check that the parameters are within such limits that errors cannot happen. For example, if multiplying a number by itself produces an overflow, the number must be greater than the square root of the maximum representable number. So to guard against overflow in a multiplication we could check that the two numbers being multiplied are both less than the square root of that maximum value. Sometimes we know that things will always be okay simply because we never deal with gigantic values. Truly professional programs, however, may need extensive checking to ensure safe behavior under all conditions.

Underflow occurs when calculation produces a number very close to zero. For example, 2×10^{-20} times 3×10^{-20} gives 6×10^{-40}, which, in a `float` with the guaranteed minimum `float` exponent of -37, is too close to zero to be stored to full accuracy.

Both underflow and overflow can often be precluded by rescaling the numbers or choosing measurement units to keep them 'around' 1. For example, if we wish to solve astronomical problems such as the amount of dark matter in the galaxy, we first observe that the galaxy is about 100,000 light years wide. That is about 5.86×10^{17} miles. If we use light years in computing the volume of the galaxy, we get a value around 100,000 cubed, or 10^{15} cubic light years. If we do it in miles we get about 5.86×10^{17} cubed, or around 2×10^{53} cubic miles, so using miles is more likely to cause overflow problems. Similar considerations in reverse apply to very small numbers, such as atomic diameters. This sort of investigation can usually be performed before starting the programming.

Accuracy concerns the fact that floating values can only be stored to a certain number of digits, and, as most computers store them in a binary format, this means that many short decimal numbers are not stored exactly. This can cause some surprises; for example, on my computer, the following program prints the word "No".

```
#include <stdio.h>
main() {
    double a = 0.1;
    if (a*9 == .9) {
        printf("Yes\n");
    } else {
        printf("No\n");
    }
    return 0;
}
```

In repeated calculations this small imprecision can slowly build as the errors in successive steps compound each other. Other traps lie in wait for the unwary, as in this program:

```
#include <stdio.h>
main() {
    float a = 0.1, b = 0.00000234567, c = .100002, d, e;
    d = (c - a); e = (b + c);
    printf("%.12f\n%.12f\n", b + d, e - a);
    return 0;
}
```

The output on my computer is:

```
0.000004342426
0.000004343688
```

Both numbers represent c − a + b, yet they differ after three significant places on a computer which boasts seven-digit accuracy. According to normal arithmetic rules, it should not matter what order the calculation is performed in, so the two output numbers above should be the same. The trouble is that with the limited accuracy of computer variables, if we add or subtract a very tiny number from a much larger one, most of the digits of the small number fall off the end of the resulting answer. In general it is better to subtract large numbers from each other, or add small ones together, before combining the large and small numbers. This is a reason why we often use doubles or long doubles even though we might only need an answer to, say, six figures. Here is the output if we change the declaration float to double in the above program:

```
0.000004345670
0.000004345670
```

Example: Length of a vector

Listing 11-3 included a simple float function (v2Len) to calculate the length of a vector. It used the fact that the hypotenuse h of a right-angled triangle with sides a and b is $h = \sqrt{a^2 + b^2}$). Assuming for simplicity that a is no smaller than b (switch them around if not), h will always be between a and $a\sqrt{2}$. This is not much larger than a, so we would be unlucky if the calculation overflowed. Unfortunately, a simpleminded application of that formula can easily cause numeric overflow even when a is much smaller than the largest allowable float (i.e. FLT_MAX). The trouble is the calculation of a^2, which can overflow even if a is many orders of magnitude smaller than FLT_MAX. Similarly, if a is much smaller than 1, underflow can occur.

All these troubles can be avoided by paying attention to the likely problems and suitably rearranging the formula. To avoid overflow and underflow when computing a^2, calculate h using the formula $h = a\sqrt{1 + (b/a)^2}$. Also, b/a should not be evaluated if a equals 0. Listing 16-1 shows a better version of v2Len that observes these precautions.

Listing 16-1

```c
#include <float.h>
float v2Len(vector2 v) {                    /* Length of vector */
    float a = fabs(v.x), b = fabs(v.y), c;  /* absolute values */
    if (b > a) {                            /* wrong one larger ? */
        c = b; b = a; a = c;                /* exchange */
    }                                       /* Now a is larger */
    if (a == 0.0) {
        return a;                           /* Both components are zero */
    }
    b /= a;                                 /* compute b/a */
    if (b < FLT_EPSILON) {
        return a;                           /* Answer very close to a */
    }
    return a * sqrt(1.0 + b*b);             /* full Pythagoras' rule */
}
```

16.7 REPRESENTING MONEY

Until now, we have been content to solve money problems by using `floats` for whole dollars, with two decimal digits of the fraction for the cents. (We call the major money unit a dollar, and the minor one a cent — but of course it can just as easily be pounds and pence, marks & pfennigs, or francs and centimes.) That is fine for short and simple programs, but for serious work with money there is an obvious flaw: `floats` might only hold numbers to six digits, and some decimal fractions are not stored exactly in floating-point datatypes. Using `doubles` helps: if the computer has IEEE arithmetic (as many do), then `doubles` will have 15-digit accuracy, which is ample in the absence of really shocking inflation. But the fractional part will still be slightly incorrect because no binary fraction can represent a typical decimal fraction exactly.

The cure for both problems is to rely only on the integral part of a `double` number: that is, use `double` variables to store the number of cents, not the number of dollars. If dollar amounts are input or output, they should be multiplied by 100 after input to convert them to cents, the various computations should be performed, and then the values should be divided by 100 before output to reconvert them to dollars.

There is still a problem in that operations such as calculating interest, etc. will result in fractional cents, so we must be careful to keep totals accurate to the cent. Before dividing by 100 to convert to dollars, the value should be rounded to the nearest cent. This is done, not because `printf` will print the wrong value (it won't), but because in commercial applications, totals of many figures usually must be kept exactly correct.

Suppose, for example, that from $100.00 (stored in cents as 10,000 cents) we have to pay two amounts of 2500.3 cents and 3000.25 cents, and then record how much money is left. If we subtract these two payments from the original sum, the balance will be 4499.45 cents. If all three figures are rounded to the nearest cent and converted to dollars they will be $25.00, $30.00, and $44.99 respectively, which do not add up to $100.00. However, by rounding the payments to whole cents first and subtracting the rounded values from the $100.00 we are left with 4500 cents — or $45.00 — which is correct.

The C library contains a function, `floor`, which returns the smallest integral value not greater than its argument; both its argument and result are `doubles`. A double value can therefore be rounded to the nearest integer by writing

```
value = floor(value + 0.5);
```

The above comments are a general guide to doing money calculations, but before writing a critically important real-life program, check carefully the exact characteristics of `floats` and `doubles` on the computer you will be using, and also make sure your program follows the financial rules of the organization. And always test your program.

16.8 SUMMARY

Topics covered in this chapter were:

- `signed` and `unsigned char`, `int`, and `long` data types (see Tables 16-1 to 16-3)
- integral constants (see Table 16-4)
- `float`, `double`, and `long double` data types (see Table 16-5)
- `printf` and `scanf` formats (see Tables 16-6 to 16-8)
- mixing data types
- overflow, underflow and accuracy
- calculating with money.

16.9 SELF-TEST EXERCISES

Short Answer

1   There are alternative ways to declare some C datatypes. Arrange the following list of declarations into categories so that all declarations in the same category declare identically-typed variables.

```
int, long double, long, float, signed short, char, signed int,
unsigned, unsigned int, unsigned char, double, long int,
unsigned short, unsigned long int, signed long int, signed char,
signed long, unsigned long, short.
```

2   Write the value 8 as
    a   a `long` constant
    b   an `unsigned` constant
    c   an `unsigned long` constant
    d   a `signed long` constant
    e   an `int` constant.

3   Assuming the following declarations:

```
char ch1, ch2; short s1, s2; int i1, i2; unsigned u1, u2;
long l1, l2; unsigned long ul1, ul2; float f1, f2;
double d1, d2; long double ld1, ld2;
```

what is the result type of each of the following expressions on a computer where `long` is longer than `int`?

    a   `i1 - i2 + 3L`
    b   `l1 + (l2 = d1 - 4.8)`
    c   `s1 + s2`
    d   `s1 + s2 + 30245`
    e   `s1 + d2`
    f   `ld1 - ld2 + 345UL`
    g   `u2 * l1`

4   Write `printf` formats to print a value of each of the following types:

   a   `char` as a character
   b   `char` as a decimal character code
   c   `int`
   d   `unsigned`
   e   `long`
   f   `unsigned long`
   g   `float`
   h   `double`
   i   `long double`.

16.10 TEST QUESTIONS

Short Answer

1   Write the value –457.98 as

   a   a `float` constant
   b   a `double` constant
   c   a `long double` constant.

2   Assuming the following declarations,

```
char ch1, ch2; short s1, s2; int i1, i2; unsigned u1, u2;
long l1, l2; unsigned long ul1, ul2; float f1, f2;
double d1, d2; long double ld1, ld2;
```

what is the result type of each of the following expressions on a computer where `long` is longer than `int`?

   a   `ch1 / s1`
   b   `ul1 * l2 - (i2 = d2) + 4`
   c   `i2 % i1`
   d   `u1 * l2`
   e   `s1 + d2`
   f   `ld1 - ld2 + 345UL`
   g   `l2 - d2`

3   Write scanf formats to input a value into variables of each of the following
    types.
    a   char as a character
    b   int
    c   unsigned
    d   long
    e   unsigned long
    f   float
    g   double
    h   long double.

Programming

4   Write a program to find the 1000th power of 1.00001 by repeated multiplication.
    Compute the answer three ways: using floats, using doubles, and using the
    library pow function. Compare the results.

17

Random-access and binary input-output

Objectives

Understand the concepts of random-access and binary input-output.
— what happens when binary data is stored in a file
— advantages of binary files
— random access to data.

Be able to write C programs to manipulate random-access and binary files.
— reading and writing binary data
— randomly accessing data
— additional features of the `fopen` function
— library functions `fread`, `fwrite`, `fgetpos`, `fsetpos`, `fflush`, `ftell`, and `fseek`
— file buffers: the `setvbuf` function
— the `ferror` function.

17.1 INTRODUCTION

So far we have investigated C's facilities for *sequential, text-mode* access to files. Sequential access means that the program reads or writes the file in sequence from start to finish. Text-mode access means that the program treats the file as a stream of readable characters — we expect to be able to examine a text file in our favorite editor, for example. But C also provides for *random* and *binary* file access. Random access means that the program can read and/or write to any place in a file in any order. Binary access means that the program treats the file as binary data; we shall examine what this means in more detail shortly. We can mix and match these features: binary data can be accessed either sequentially or randomly, and similarly for text data.

17.2 BINARY INPUT-OUTPUT AND BINARY FILES

We have seen that internally, the computer stores `ints`, `floats`, etc. in a binary format unreadable to humans. Functions `printf` and `scanf` convert that binary format to and from readable text. It is only because of that conversion operation that we are able to understand values printed by the computer (`printf` conversion from binary to text) and the computer is able to correctly use values input by us (`scanf` conversion from text to binary). An obvious question occurs: what do we get if we skip the conversion operation and output binary-format data (`ints`, `floats` etc.) as-is? What we get, if a human tries to read the data, is rubbish. But if the data is used on a later occasion by the computer itself, it will make perfect sense, as it is already in the computer's own internal format. Such input-output is called binary file access, and we often refer to files read and written in this way as binary files, and conversely for text files (although with many computers there is no way to distinguish text files from binary files other than by looking at what is stored in them).

Binary input-output is intended, among other things, for efficient storage of large quantities of data. Text-mode conversion to-and-from character format is fairly slow, especially for floating-point data. Also, unless care is taken, values can be slightly altered in the process, as Listing 17-1 and the accompanying test run show.

Listing 17-1

```
/* Program to show modification of floating data by careless text i-o */
#include <stdio.h>
#include <math.h>
main() {
    float d, e;
    d = sqrt(2.0);
    printf("Please type this number exactly: %f\n", d);
    scanf("%f", &e);
    printf("%f is ", d);
    if (d != e) {
        printf("NOT ");
```

```
    }
    printf("equal to %f\n", e);
    return 0;
}
```

Test run

```
Please type this number exactly: 1.414214
1.414214
1.414214 is NOT equal to 1.414214
```

In this test run, because `sqrt(2.0)` has no exact representation in seven decimal digits, the number typed back in converts into a slightly different binary value. So when storing data for the computer's own later use, we can either take the trouble to triple-check every `printf` format for correctness, or write, and later read, the data in binary.

To perform binary input-output we must (a) specify the fact when opening the file with `fopen`, and (b) use the special format-less input-output functions `fwrite` (for output) and `fread` (for input). For transferring single bytes, `getc` and `putc` may also be used for binary input-output. These are both illustrated in Listing 17-2, which writes and reads `sqrt(2.0)` on a file. (Error-checking is omitted for the time being for simplicity.)

Listing 17-2

```
/* Program to show correct storage of floating data by binary i-o */
#include <stdio.h>
#include <math.h>
#include <stdlib.h>
main() {
    float d, e;  FILE *f;
    d = sqrt(2.0);

    f = fopen("tempfile.dat", "wb");     /* NB: "wb" means "write binary" */
    fwrite(&d, sizeof(float), 1, f);     /* Write from d, 1 item the size of
                                            a float to file f */
    fclose(f);

    f = fopen("tempfile.dat", "rb");     /* NB: "rb" means "read binary" */
    fread(&e, sizeof(float), 1, f);      /* Read into e, 1 item the size of
                                            a float from file f */
    fclose(f);

    printf("%f is ", d);
    if (d != e) {
        printf("NOT ");
    }
    printf("equal to %f\n", e);
    return 0;
}
```

Test run
```
1.414214 is equal to 1.414214
```

As Listing 17-2 shows, the call to `fopen` includes a b (binary) in the second (mode) parameter, in addition to the w, r or a (which were explained in Chapter 10). On some systems such as Unix, the b has no effect: all files are effectively binary, even if they contain readable text. Other systems **do** distinguish the two file types, and forgetting the b can cause very peculiar errors; DOS is such a system.

Having opened a file in binary mode, we use `fwrite` to output data and/or `fread` to input data. These functions have similar arguments, as shown here:

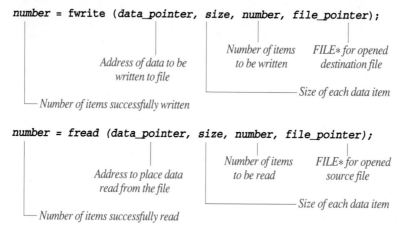

These functions do no data conversion, but simply transfer binary bits unaltered. Therefore they do not need to know the type of information being transferred. They do, however, need to know **where** the data is, **how big** it is, and **which file** to access. Thus the first parameter is the address of the variable or array in memory, the second is the size of each data item, the third is the number of data items, and the fourth is the `FILE*` for the file to be used. From the second and third arguments, the function can determine how much data to transfer.

The function return is the number of items **successfully** transferred. Errors are detected by comparing the number asked for (the third parameter) with the number actually transferred. Listing 17-3 is the same program as Listing 17-2, but with error detection inserted. The statements concerned with the success of the `fwrite` and `fread` calls are shown in bold.

Listing 17-3

```
/* Program to show correct storage of floating data by binary i-o */
#include <stdio.h>
#include <math.h>
#include <stdlib.h>
main() {
    float d, e;  FILE *f;
    size_t num_written, num_read;
    d = sqrt(2.0);
    f = fopen("tempfile.dat", "wb");     /* NB: "wb" means "write binary" */
    if (f == NULL) {
        fprintf(stderr, "Failed to open output file\n");
        exit(EXIT_FAILURE);
    }
    num_written = fwrite(&d, sizeof(float), 1, f);
    if (num_written < 1) {
        fprintf(stderr, "Data not written\n");
        fclose(f);
        exit(EXIT_FAILURE);
    }
    fclose(f);
    f = fopen("tempfile.dat", "rb");     /* NB: "rb" means "read binary" */
    if (f == NULL) {
        fprintf(stderr, "Failed to open input file\n");
        exit(EXIT_FAILURE);
    }
    num_read = fread(&e, sizeof(float), 1, f);
    if (num_read< 1) {
        fprintf(stderr, "Data not read\n");
        exit(EXIT_FAILURE);
    }
    fclose(f);
    printf("%f is ", d);
    if (d != e) {
        printf("NOT ");
    }
    printf("equal to %f\n", e);
    return 0;
}
```

Provided no errors occur, the output is the same as before. Note that the variables
num_written and num_read in Listing 17-3 are of type size_t, explained in
Section 12.3.1. These variables store the values returned by the functions fwrite
and fread. The second and third arguments to these functions are also of type
size_t.

Binary files provide a convenient way to write programs that can perform part of a
lengthy calculation, store intermediate results, and resume again later. This situation
might arise in scientific work, where a lengthy program might take many days to run

and so might only be allowed to operate at night to avoid slowing the machine during the day. The plan is to declare a structure containing all the information that needs saving from one run to the next, as in the following program skeleton (error-checking not shown).

```
typedef struct {
    ...All arrays, variables, etc. required from run-to-run are declared here.
    float whatever;     /* (for example) */
} all_data;
all_data a;
...
/* Do calculations: */
a.whatever = ... /* Prefix variable names with the structure name, a. */
...
/* Now ready to interrupt the program: write the entire structure to
    a file using fwrite:
*/
somefileptr = fopen("somename", "wb");
fwrite(&a, sizeof(all_data), 1, somefileptr);
fclose(somefileptr);
/* Close program down */

...

/* To prepare for the next run, retrieve the data from the file: */
somefileptr = fopen("somename", "rb");
fread(&a, sizeof(all_data), 1, somefileptr);
fclose(somefileptr);
...
/* Proceed with calculations as if no interruption had happened */
... = a.whatever;
```

Using this skeleton, vast amounts of data can be safely stored and retrieved between program runs; the amount transferred by the `fwrite` and `fread` calls is limited only by the `sizeof` the `struct` containing the data. The error checks discussed elsewhere should also be included.

> **Important warning**
> It is not usually possible to store pointers in files because there is no guarantee that items retrieved from a file will be placed in the same memory locations from which they were originally written. However, it is possible to store array indexes.

Binary input-output is also useful where we do not care what sort of data we are handling, as in general file-copying programs such as the Unix `cp` and the DOS `COPY` programs. Listing 17-4 shows such a program, which takes the names of two files as command-line arguments and copies the first file to the second. A buffer of 4096 bytes is used for holding blocks of data. The program requires the `file_open` function from Listing 10-2b.

Listing 17-4   `mycopy.c`

```c
/* mycopy: copies its first command-line argument file to the second. */
#include <stdio.h>
#include <stdlib.h>

FILE * file_open(char name[], char access_mode[]);
int fcopy(FILE *inf, FILE *outf);

main(int argc, char *argv[]) {
    FILE *inf, *outf;
    if (argc!=3) {                          /* Check command line */
        printf("You must supply source and destination filenames.\n");
        exit(EXIT_FAILURE);
    }
    inf = file_open(argv[1], "rb");     /* Try to open files */
    outf = file_open(argv[2], "wb");
    if (fcopy(inf, outf) != 0) {        /* Copy file */
        perror("Error writing file");   /* Error message on failure */
        fclose(inf); fclose(outf);
        exit(EXIT_FAILURE);
    }
    fclose(inf);  fclose(outf);
    return 0;
}

/***** fcopy: copies a file ******
 On entry: inf is open for binary input, outf for binary output.
 On exit:  Remaining data in inf is copied to outf; both files still open.
           Returns 0 for success, 1 for error transferring data.
*/
#define BUFMAX (4096)
int fcopy(FILE *inf, FILE *outf) {
    char buffer[BUFMAX];
    size_t num_read, num_written;
    while (
        num_read = fread(buffer, 1, BUFMAX, inf),
                        /*    ^ Note: chars always have size 1 */
        num_read > 0        /* The final block may be shorter than BUFMAX */
    ) {
        num_written = fwrite(buffer, 1, num_read, outf);
        if (num_written != num_read) {
        return 1;                           /* failure */
        }
    }
    if (ferror(inf)) {
        return 1;
    }
    return 0;                                /* success */
}
```

This program will copy the data in any file with a command line of the form

```
mycopy first second
```

In function `fcopy`, the test for continuing the loop is that the `fread` call reads **something**, not necessarily that it reads an entire buffer-full. This is because the file size most likely is not a multiple of the buffer size, and so the final buffer-load will not be full. The error check on the `fwrite`, however, is that **everything** we try to write is indeed written; if this is not so, something must be amiss. Finally, `fcopy` does not open or close the files itself. This facilitates re-use of the function in other circumstances. For example, if we later need to write a program to concatenate a number of files, we can call `fcopy` many times for the same output file (without closing it between calls) and it will construct a large combined file. Similarly, we can use it to copy only the trailing part of an input file by reading part of the file first before calling `fcopy`.

Finally, note the check in Listing 17-4 for errors while reading the input data. Normally, errors are unlikely while reading a binary file that was successfully opened. It **can** happen, though. For example, a file on a removable diskette might become unreadable if the diskette is removed from the drive prematurely. In reliable professional programs, these errors should be detected. The `ferror` function exists for this purpose: it returns non-zero if its argument `FILE*` refers to a file on which an error has occurred. It is called in `fcopy` just after the `while` loop, which is logically just after the final `fread`, that is, the one that failed to read any data. If that failure was due to normal end-of-file, `ferror` returns 0; otherwise it returns non-zero.

17.3 RANDOM-ACCESS TO FILES

When programs must access large data files, it is impractical to process the files sequentially every time an item is to be read or written. For example, a university might have academic records for thousands of students stored in a *database* (in simple terms, a database is a special data file or group of files with powerful access functions for manipulating the data). The data for a single student might be buried deep within a large file. If the database software had to read or write the entire file to alter one student's results, the system would probably be hopelessly slow from overwork. To overcome this, *random access* library functions allow any part of a file to be accessed directly. Random access is sometimes called *direct access*.

C provides two principal functions for random access: `fgetpos` and `fsetpos`. The `fgetpos` function tells us where an input-output stream (i.e. a `FILE*`) is located within a file (in other words, where the next input or output operation will occur) and `fsetpos` alters that location. We can find the location of a data item by calling `fgetpos`, and later we can access it again by passing to `fsetpos` the location information given to us earlier by `fgetpos`. The calls to these functions have the following format:

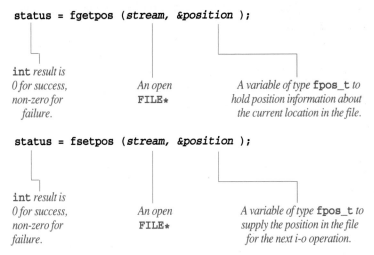

```
status = fgetpos (stream, &position );
```

int *result is*
0 for success,
non-zero for
failure.

An open
FILE*

A variable of type **fpos_t** *to*
hold position information about
the current location in the file.

```
status = fsetpos (stream, &position );
```

int *result is*
0 for success,
non-zero for
failure.

An open
FILE*

A variable of type **fpos_t** *to*
supply the position in the file
for the next i-o operation.

The datatype fpos_t is defined in <stdio.h>; we don't care what it is (although it is probably a struct of some kind); all that matters is that it can hold the information needed to locate any position in a file. We shall investigate these functions by programming a simple version of an important system: a help facility.

In a help system, information is presented that relates to whatever task the program is doing. Our help system will contain a help database in which each topic will have a one-word name, a short description, and a full explanation. A preprocessor (called helpmake, say) will analyze the help database and extract the name and short description for each help entry, placing these in a shorter index file. At the same time it will use fgetpos to find the location of the start of the full explanation and record this location in the index file. Although the index file will contain text information, it will be stored in binary to simplify storing the location information for the help entries. Each entry in the main help file will have the format of the following example:

```
::rndm C random access functions
C has two primary random access functions,
    fgetpos
and
    fsetpos
which may be used to find and alter the read/write position in a file.
```

The one-word name in this example is rndm, written on a line commencing with two colons. We shall insist this name be no longer than ten characters. The rest of the line is the short description; we shall limit its length to 50 characters. All text on succeeding lines, up to the next line starting with ::, is the full help entry. The preprocessor helpmake must read the file looking for lines commencing with ::, read the rest of that line, and while the input is poised at the start of the following line (i.e. C has... in the example) call fgetpos to obtain location information for the text description commencing there. The first line in the help file should be a : : line.

The index file will list all the short descriptions, with an fpos_t value for each. It will also be useful to measure and record the size of each full help entry. Each index entry will consist of a nul-terminated string containing the one-word name, a similar string with the short description, an `fpos_t` value, and a size (an `int`). For error-checking, we shall also include a header containing the name of the database file: a string containing ! ! followed by the filename. The outer loop of `helpmake` will process all help entries, so the algorithm will be

```
Open files.  (The names will be taken from the command line.)
If the first two input characters are not "::", print error and stop.
Write index file header entry.
do
    process a help entry
while there is another help entry (i.e. we find another "::" line).
Close files.
```

This section of the program is shown in Listing 17-5a.

Listing 17-5a `helpmake.c`, part 1

```c
/******* helpmake.c: Create the index file for a help database. *******
 Command-line parameters: the help database name (input file), and the
 help index file name (output file).  File formats described elsewhere.
*/
#include <stdio.h>
#include <stdlib.h>
#include <string.h>

#define MAXNAME 10          /* Maximum length of a help item name */
#define MAXDESCRIPTION 50   /* Maximum length of the short description */

void putstring(char *str, FILE *f);  /* Fn to write nul-terminated string */
int process_help_entry(FILE *helpdata, FILE *index);
    /* process_help_entry returns true if another entry follows this one. */
FILE * file_open(char name[], char access_mode[]);

main(int argc, char *argv[]) {
    FILE *helpdata, *index;
    int there_is_another_entry;
    /* Open files. */
    if (argc != 3) {
        fprintf(
            stderr,
            "You must supply a help database name and a name\n"
            "for the index file to be created.\n"
        );
        exit(EXIT_FAILURE);
    }
    helpdata = file_open(argv[1], "r");
    index = file_open(argv[2], "wb");

    /* Check format of help database */
    if (getc(helpdata) != ':' || getc(helpdata) != ':') {
        /* First two input characters are not "::", print error and stop.*/
```

```
            fprintf(stderr, "Incorrect format to help database.\n");
            exit(EXIT_FAILURE);
        }

    /* Write index file header entry. */
    fputs("!!", index);        /* Note: OK to write chars to binary stream */
    putstring(argv[1], index);

    do {
        there_is_another_entry = process_help_entry(helpdata, index);
    } while (there_is_another_entry);

    fclose(helpdata); fclose(index);
    return 0;
}

/**** putstring: write a nul-terminated string ****
 On entry: str is a string, f is an open output file.
 On exit:  Characters in string, including terminating nul, are written
           to file, or an error message printed and program stopped.
*/
void putstring(char str[], FILE *f) { /* Fn to write nul-terminated string */
    int leng = strlen(str) + 1;        /* +1 for the nul */
    if (fwrite(str, 1, leng, f) != leng) {
        perror("Error writing index file"); exit(EXIT_FAILURE);
    }
}
```

Now `process_help_entry` must do the main task: find the location of the entry and write it to the index file, as follows.

process_help_entry:
Read item name & description; write to index file.
Advance past end-of-line in input file.
Find file location; write to index file.
Skip & measure the size of the rest of the entry (until EOF or "::" is
    seen).
Write the size to the index file.
If EOF encountered, return 0.
Otherwise, return 1.

This section collects the disk file location information, and is shown in Listing 17-5b. The program also requires function `file_open` from Listing 10-2b (not repeated here).

Listing 17-5b `helpmake.c`, part 2

```
/**** process_help_entry: reads a help entry, and writes info to index ****
 On entry: helpdata is the help database file, open for input, positioned
           just after the "::" starting an entry.
           index is the index file, open for output in binary.
 On exit:  Writes entry to the index file.  If another entry follows this
           in the database, positions helpdata input just past its "::",
           and returns 1, else returns 0.  Terminates program on error.
*/
int process_help_entry(FILE *helpdata, FILE *index) {
    char name[MAXNAME+1], description[MAXDESCRIPTION+1], flag[3];
    int status, entry_size, ch;
    fpos_t location;

    /* Read item name & description; write to index file. */
    if (fscanf(helpdata, "%10s %50[^\n]%*[^\n]", name, description) < 2) {
        perror("Missing items in help data"); exit(EXIT_FAILURE);
    }
    putstring(name, index);
    putstring(description, index);

    getc(helpdata);                 /* Advance past end-of-line in input file */

    /* Find file location; write to index file. */
    if (fgetpos(helpdata, &location) != 0) {        /* error */
        perror("Can't find help file position"); exit(EXIT_FAILURE);
    }
    fwrite(&location, sizeof(fpos_t), 1, index);   /* error check shortly */

    /* Skip the rest of the help entry (until EOF or "\n::" is seen).
       Measure the size of the text as it is skipped.
       We are at the start of a line, skip a line at a time.
    */

    entry_size = 0;                             /* Seen nothing yet */
    status = fscanf(helpdata, "%2[^\n]", flag);/* first two chars in line */

    while (status >= 0 && strcmp(flag,"::") != 0) { /*Skip a line per loop*/
        entry_size += strlen(flag);             /* Up to 2 chars already */
        while (ch = getc(helpdata), ch != EOF && ch != '\n') {
            entry_size++;                       /* Skip & count a char */
        }                                       /* until end of line */
        if (ch == '\n') entry_size++;           /* Count end of lines */
        status = fscanf(helpdata, "%2[^\n]",flag);/* 2 chars in next line */
    }

    /* Now write entry size to index file */
    if (fwrite(&entry_size, sizeof(int), 1, index) != 1) {
        perror("Error writing index file"); exit(EXIT_FAILURE);
    }
    if (status == EOF) {                    /* If EOF encountered, return 0. */
        return 0;                           /* No more entries */
```

```
    }
    return 1;                          /* The "::" of another entry seen */
}
```

The following is a sample help database file, `helpbase.dat`; although it is short, we should pretend it is a huge file with thousands of entries (which, indeed, it would be if we were providing help for a serious system).

```
::fread Binary data input function
fread is one of the most important C functions for binary input.
getc can also be used, but it only reads one byte at a time.
fread will read a data block of any size the computer can handle.
Always make sure you put 'b' in the mode parameter of fopen when
planning to use binary file input-output.
::fwrite Binary data output function
fwrite is one of the most important C functions for binary output.
putc can also be used, but it only writes one byte at a time.
fwrite will write a data block of any size the computer can handle.
Always make sure you put 'b' in the mode parameter of fopen when
planning to use binary file input-output.
::rndm C random access functions
C has two primary random access functions,
    fgetpos
and
    fsetpos
which may be used to find and alter the read/write position in a file.
Call fgetpos to find out where you are in a file, and later use fsetpos
to return to that same position.
```

Test run

The following command line invokes `helpmake` to process the above database file:

```
helpmake helpbase.dat helpindx.dat
```

In a typical help dataset there is often a full screen or more of information for each help entry. Therefore the index file (here `helpindx.dat`) will, typically, be much shorter than the full database. Although it may be impractical to read the entire database to look for a given entry, it might not be unreasonable for the index file. It is in binary, so it cannot be listed directly here. The following is a display made by a binary file editor of this file as it was created on my computer. The left side shows bytes in hexadecimal, and the right the equivalent ASCII characters; nul (i.e. zero) bytes show as spaces on the right hand side. The `fpos_t` values are underlined, and entry lengths are double underlined.

Hexadecimal codes	ASCII characters
21 21 68 65 6C 70 62 61 73 65 2E 64 61 74 00 66	!!helpbase.dat f
72 65 61 64 00 42 69 6E 61 72 79 20 64 61 74 61	read Binary data
20 69 6E 70 75 74 20 66 75 6E 63 74 69 6F 6E 00	input function
<u>24 00 00 00</u> <u>2B 01</u> 66 77 72 69 74 65 00 42 69 6E	$ +⬤fwrite Bin
61 72 79 20 64 61 74 61 20 6F 75 74 70 75 74 20	ary data output
66 75 6E 63 74 69 6F 6E 00 <u>7A 01 00 00</u> <u>30 01</u> 72	function z⬤ 0⬤r
6E 64 6D 00 43 20 72 61 6E 64 6F 6D 20 61 63 63	ndm C random acc
65 73 73 20 66 75 6E 63 74 69 6F 6E 73 00 <u>D1 02</u>	ess functions =⬤
<u>00 00</u> <u>F7 00</u>	⬤

Note the 00 (nul) bytes ending each string (e.g. the second-last byte on the first line ending helpbase.dat). After each description my computer has inserted six bytes: four for an fpos_t value (probably an unsigned long representing the offset from the start of the full help file) and two for the int size of the full help entry. But on the right these bytes do not display as numbers, but as 'rubbish' characters, which are my printer's interpretation of those binary values as character codes.

This file would look different on a computer which stores fpos_t and int values in other formats. (Also, computers using EBCDIC or some other non-ASCII coding system will show different values on the left side for all the normal text characters.) Thus we should not worry about the exact byte-by-byte structure of binary files. Instead, we should make sure we read them in a way that is compatible with the way we wrote them. So if we write a float we should read a float, nothing else; the same is true for other data types.

Now we are ready to use the help index and database together to provide help. We can treat a help database as an abstract data type (discussed in Chapter 15) by defining a set of functions through which all access to the help information will be channeled. Here are some tasks we might want to perform in a help system:

a   open the help files
b   close the help files
c   find the first item
d   find the next item (immediately after step (c), this would of course find item 2)
e   find an item whose one-word name is known.

The 'find an item' operations might locate just an index entry, or a full help entry. As callers may want index entries without full help (e.g. to present menus of topics) it is more useful to return just an index entry, but with the information needed to later obtain the full help. We therefore need another operation:

f   given location information obtained from an index entry, retrieve the full help entry.

Based on these considerations, we might define our help access functions as in Listing 17-6. The datatype HELPSYS, like FILE in <stdio.h>, is meant to be used only within the help functions themselves; application programs declare a pointer to a HELPSYS; this pointer is given a value by help_open. To prevent applications accessing the fields of the HELPSYS datatype, it is declared as an incomplete type (see Section 15.2).

Listing 17-6 `helpadt.h`

```
/* HELPADT: Help database Abstract Data Type definition. */

#include <stdio.h>              /* for type fpos_t */
#define NAMESIZE (11)           /* Buffer size for help item name */
#define DESCRIPTSIZE (51)       /* Buffer size for a short description */

/*############### DATATYPES ###############*/

/*** help_id: Information needed to locate a full help entry. ***/
typedef struct {
    fpos_t where;
    int size;
} help_id;

/*** helpndx: Contains a help index entry ***/
typedef struct {
    char name[NAMESIZE];        /* the one-word name */
    char descript[DESCRIPTSIZE]; /* the short description */
    help_id loc;                /* location info. for full help entry */
} helpndx;

typedef struct HELPSYS HELPSYS;    /* Note: an incomplete type */

/*############### FUNCTIONS ###############*/

/****** help_open(index, helpbase, retain) - opens a help database *******
 On entry: index is the name of a help index file, helpbase is the name of
           the corresponding full help database.  retain is the number of
           index entries the help system should secretly store in memory
           to speed access to the data. ‾
 On exit:  If successful, returns a pointer to a HELPSYS structure
           identifying the opened help database.  On failure, returns NULL.
*/
HELPSYS *help_open(
    char /*index*/ [],
    char /*helpbase*/ [],
    int /*retain*/
);

/****** help_close(helpsys) - closes a help database ******
 On entry: helpsys is a HELPSYS pointer to an open help database.
 On exit:  The database is closed and all storage released.
*/
void help_close(HELPSYS * /*helpsys*/);

/****** help_next(helpsys) - supply the next index entry ******
 On entry: helpsys points to an open help database.
 On exit:  On success, returns a pointer to a structure of type helpndx,
           containing an index entry for the 'next' help item; this pointer
           is only valid until the next 'help_next' or 'help_name' function
           call. Successive calls advance item-by-item through the database.
           A call to help_next after help_open will access the first item
```

```
                    in the help database.  Returns NULL if no more items are found.
*/
helpndx *help_next(HELPSYS * /*helpsys*/);

/****** help_reset(helpsys) - reset the database ******
 On entry: helpsys refers to an open help database.
 On exit:  A following call to help_next will access the first help item.
*/
void help_reset(HELPSYS * /*helpsys*/);

/****** help_name(helpsys, itemname) - supply matching index entry ******
 On entry: helpsys points to an open help database.
 On exit:  On success, returns a pointer to a structure of type helpndx,
           containing an index entry for the help item with name itemname;
           this pointer is only valid until the next 'help_next' or
           'help_name' function call.  Returns NULL if item is not found.
*/
helpndx *help_name(HELPSYS * /*helpsys*/, char * /*itemname*/);

/****** help_message(helpsys, location) - Retrieve a full help entry ******
 On entry: helpsys points to an open help database. location is the loc
           field from a helpndx obtained from help_next or help_name.
 On exit:  Returns a pointer to a string containing the full help message.
           N.B.: This pointer should be free'd when no longer required.
           If no entry is found, returns NULL.
*/
char *help_message(HELPSYS * /*helpsys*/, help_id /*location*/);
```

In implementing these functions, we shall ignore the `retain` parameter to `help_open`; it exists only for efficiency and does not affect the behavior of the package. With this decision, we can define the type HELPSYS. FILE pointers for the two open files are needed, as well as fields of type `fpos_t` to store locations within the index file of the 'first' and 'next' entries (as defined in `help_next`). Also, a single `helpndx` variable is required for storing an index entry requested by `help_next` or `help_name`; its address will be returned by those functions. Thus, the definition of HELPSYS can be

```
typedef struct HELPSYS {
    FILE *indexf, *fullf;    /* For opened FILE pointers */
    helpndx ndxitem;         /* For one index file entry */
    fpos_t firstindex;       /* Index file position of first entry */
    fpos_t nextindex;        /* Index file position of next entry */
} HELPSYS;
```

The functions can now be programmed; only `help_message` accesses the full help file, using positioning information supplied by `help_next` or `help_name`. Its parameter, `location`, contains the position and size of the help text; `help_message` must `malloc` a sufficiently large buffer for this data and read the appropriate section of the help file. It is wise to include a consistency check: after the read, the following character should be a colon or end-of-file. Anything else probably means the user has altered the help database and forgotten to use `helpmake` to rebuild the index file. All the functions are shown in Listing 17-7. An additional feature from `<stdio.h>` is employed: the constant `FILENAME_MAX` is the size of a `char` array needed to hold the longest recommended length of a filename; it is used to declare a suitably-sized buffer in `help_open`. `fsetpos` calls occur in `help_at` and `help_message`, each relocating the next input operation, the former in the index file and the latter in the full database.

Listing 17-7 `helpadt.c`

```
/* HELPADT: Help database Abstract Data Type implementation. */

#include <helpadt.h>
#include <stdlib.h>
#include <string.h>

static int getstr(FILE *f, char buf[], int max);    /*
^^^^^^ See chapter 18 for meaning of static - ignore for now. */
static helpndx * help_at(HELPSYS *h, fpos_t *place);

HELPSYS *help_open(char index[], char helpbase[], int retain) {
    HELPSYS *hlp; char hdr[FILENAME_MAX];

    /* First try for space for the HELPSYS structure */
    if ((hlp = (HELPSYS*)malloc(sizeof(HELPSYS))) == NULL) {
        return NULL;             /* malloc failed. */
    }

    /* Open index file; if fail, free HELPSYS memory & return */
    if ((hlp->indexf = fopen(index, "rb")) == NULL) {
        free(hlp);               /* opening index file failed */
        return NULL;
    }

    /* Now error-check index file header & try to open full file;
       if any step fails, free space & close index file, & return.
    */
    if (
          getc(hlp->indexf) != '!'   /* First char isn't '!'? */
       || getc(hlp->indexf) != '!'   /* second char isn't '!'? */
       || getstr(hlp->indexf, hdr, FILENAME_MAX)   /* string missing? */
       || strcmp(helpbase, hdr) != 0 /* Is string in file the same name as
                                        the help database? */
       || (hlp->fullf = fopen(helpbase, "r")) == NULL
                                   /* Can we open the help database? */
    ) {
        fclose(hlp->indexf);      /* opening full help file failed */
        free(hlp);
        return NULL;
    }
```

```
    /* We have now read past the header of the index file; Record this
       file position for help_next and help_reset.
    */
    if (fgetpos(hlp->indexf, &hlp->nextindex) != 0) {
        fclose(hlp->fullf);      /* failed */
        fclose(hlp->indexf);
        free(hlp);
        return NULL;
    }
    hlp->firstindex = hlp->nextindex;

    return hlp;                  /* Success at last, return address of hlp */
}

/****** help_close(helpsys) - closes a help database ******
 On entry: helpsys is a HELPSYS pointer to an open help database.
 On exit: The database is closed and all storage released.
*/
void help_close(HELPSYS *helpsys) {
    fclose(helpsys->indexf);
    fclose(helpsys->fullf);
    free(helpsys);
}

helpndx *help_next(HELPSYS *h) {
    /* Uses help_at to do all the hard work */
    return help_at(h, &h->nextindex);
}

/**** help_at(h, place) - loads an index entry from the specified place ****
 On entry: h is a HELPSYS*, *place is an fpos_t in the index file.
 On exit:  *place updated to next entry in index file.
           Function return as for help_next.
*/
static helpndx * help_at(HELPSYS *h, fpos_t *place) {
    /* Set position, input name, short description, location and size, then
       test position & record. By writing as conditions in an if statement,
       if any step fails, the rest are abandoned, and the error code is
       executed.
    */
    if (
        fsetpos(h->indexf, place) ||
        getstr(h->indexf, h->ndxitem.name, NAMESIZE) ||
        getstr(h->indexf, h->ndxitem.descript, DESCRIPTSIZE) ||
        fread(&h->ndxitem.loc.where, sizeof(fpos_t), 1, h->indexf) < 1 ||
        fread(&h->ndxitem.loc.size, sizeof(int), 1, h->indexf) < 1 ||
        fgetpos(h->indexf, place)
    ) {
        return NULL;
    } else {
        return &h->ndxitem;
    }
}
```

```
void help_reset(HELPSYS *helpsys) {
    helpsys->nextindex = helpsys->firstindex;
}

helpndx *help_name(HELPSYS *helpsys, char *itemname) {
    fpos_t indexplace; helpndx *indexentry;
    /* Load each entry in the index file, until EOF or correct one found. */
    indexplace = helpsys->firstindex;
    do {
        indexentry = help_at(helpsys, &indexplace);
    } while (indexentry != NULL && strcmp(indexentry->name, itemname) != 0);
    return indexentry;
}

char *help_message(HELPSYS *hlp, help_id location) {
    char *message; int ch, i;
    message = (char*)malloc((location.size + 1));
    if (message == NULL) {
        return NULL;                               /* Cannot malloc buffer */
    }
    /* Now set position, read data; if successful, append nul. */
    if (fsetpos(hlp->fullf, &location.where)) { /* Can't locate */
        return NULL;
    }
    for (i=0; i<location.size; i++) {             /* Input characters */
        message[i] = ch = getc(hlp->fullf);
    }
    message[location.size] = '\0';
    /* Now check on file consistency. (Exercise: why does it work?) */
    if (ch == EOF || (ch=getc(hlp->fullf)) != ':' && ch != EOF) {
        fprintf(stderr, "Error: help system inconsistent; use helpmake\n");
        return NULL;
    }
    return message;
}

/****** getstr: input a nul-terminated string ******
 On entry: f is an open input file, buf is a buffer at least max bytes long.
 On exit:  A nul-terminated string is input from f; as much as will fit is
           stored in buf, always including a trailing nul. Returns 0 for
           success, 1 for failure.
*/
static int getstr(FILE *f, char buf[], int max) {
    int i=0, ch, limit = max - 1;
    /* The following loop reads the entire string, but stops advancing
       through buf after the final place - if overfull, succeeding chars
       overwrite each other in the final element of buf.
    */
    while ((ch = getc(f)) > '\0') {        /* loop until nul or EOF */
        buf[i] = ch;
        if (i < limit) {                   /* still room left? */
            i++;                           /* yes - next char in next place */
        }
    }
    if (i <= limit) {                      /* Input within string limits? */
```

```
        buf[i] = '\0';                /* nul after last data byte */
    } else {                          /* String completely full */
        buf[limit] = '\0';            /* nul in final char */
    }
    return (ch == EOF);               /* Return 1 if ch== EOF, 0 otherwise */
}
```

We can now employ these functions in an application which will give the user the choice of entering a help item name or a question mark. In the former case the program will display the entire help entry for the name given, and in the latter case the program will respond with a list of available topics. There is nothing new involved in this program, so we can inspect it without further ado in Listing 17-8. This listing and Listing 17-7 should be compiled and linked together to create the demonstration help program.

Listing 17-8

```
/* Program to issue help.  Requests the names of the two help files, and
   then allows the user to enter help topic names, or '?' for a full topic
   listing.  A blank line or EOF terminates the program.
*/
#include "helpadt.h"                        /* This includes <stdio.h> */
#include <stdlib.h>
#include <string.h>

void getname(char message[], char answerbuf[], int bufsize);
void givehelp(HELPSYS *help, char topic[]);

main() {
    char indexname[FILENAME_MAX], fullname[FILENAME_MAX], item[NAMESIZE];
    HELPSYS *help;
    getname("Enter help index filename: ", indexname, FILENAME_MAX);
    getname("Enter help database filename: ", fullname, FILENAME_MAX);
    help = help_open(indexname, fullname, 10); /* Open help files */
    if (help == NULL) {                         /* Failed? */
        fprintf(stderr, "Can't open help database.\n"); exit(EXIT_FAILURE);
    }
    while (
        getname(
            "Enter topic name, or '?' for full list, or ENTER to finish.\n",
            item, NAMESIZE
        ),
        strcmp(item, "") != 0                   /* blank line entered? */
    ) {
        givehelp(help, item);
    }
    help_close(help);
    return 0;
}
```

```
/****** getname: Prompt user and accept answer ******
 On entry: message is the question, bufsize is the size of answerbuf.
 On exit:  The user's answer to the question is in answerbuf; if EOF
           is encountered, answerbuf is the empty string.
*/
void getname(char message[], char answerbuf[], int bufsize) {
    int i, j, ch;
    fputs(message, stderr);
    j = -1; i = 0; ch = getchar();
    while (ch != EOF && ch != '\n') {      /* input line */
        if (i < bufsize-1) {               /* i.e. up to 2nd-last character */
            answerbuf[i] = ch; j = i;      /* j is position of latest char */
        }
        ch = getchar(); i++;
    }
    answerbuf[j+1] = '\0';                  /* terminating string nul */
}

void givehelp(HELPSYS *help, char topic[]) {
    helpndx *item; char *message;
    if (strcmp(topic, "?") == 0) {         /* Give list of topics? */
        help_reset(help);
        printf("\n    LIST OF TOPICS:\nNAME        DESCRIPTION\n");
        while ((item = help_next(help)) != NULL) { /* Got another topic? */
            printf("%-10s %s\n", item->name, item->descript);
        }
        putchar('\n');                     /* An extra blank line */
    } else {                               /* Help on a particular topic. */
        if ((item = help_name(help, topic)) == NULL) {  /* Cannot find? */
            printf("Sorry, that topic was not found.\n");
        } else {
            printf("\n%s: %s\n", item->name, item->descript);
            if ((message = help_message(help, item->loc)) == NULL) {
                printf("Error locating full help information.\n");
            } else {
                fputs(message, stdout); putchar('\n');
                free(message);   /* (See help_message postcondition) */
            }
        }
    }
}
```

Test run

```
Enter help index filename: helpindx.dat
Enter help database filename: helpbase.dat
Enter topic name, or '?' for full list, or ENTER to finish.
?

    LIST OF TOPICS:
NAME          DESCRIPTION
fread         Binary data input function
fwrite        Binary data output function
rndm          C random access functions

Enter topic name, or '?' for full list, or ENTER to finish.
```
fwrite

```
fwrite: Binary data output function
fwrite is one of the most important C functions for binary output.
putc can also be used, but it only writes one byte at a time.
fwrite will write a data block of any size the computer can handle.
Always make sure you put 'b' in the mode parameter of fopen when
planning to use binary file input-output.

Enter topic name, or '?' for full list, or ENTER to finish.
```
(ENTER key typed here)

Finally, it is possible to perform both reading and writing on a single file by opening it in 'update' mode. This is done by adding a + to the `fopen` mode parameter, for example, `"r+b"` or `"rb+"`. In update mode, both `fread` and `fwrite` calls may be made to the same file, but reading should not be immediately followed by writing or vice versa without an intervening call to one of the functions `fsetpos`, `fflush` (see next section), `fseek` (see next section), or `rewind` (see Appendix D.6).

17.4 ADDITIONAL FILE MANIPULATION FUNCTIONS

17.4.1 `ftell` *and* `fseek`

The `ftell` and `fseek` functions work in a similar way to `fgetpos` and `fsetpos`; `ftell` can tell the program where a stream (i.e. a `FILE*`) is located in a file, and `fseek` can alter that position. Their function calls take the following forms.

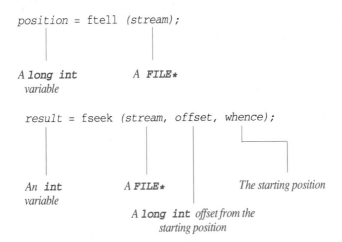

```
position = ftell (stream);
```

A *long int*
variable

A *FILE**

```
result = fseek (stream, offset, whence);
```

An *int*
variable

A *FILE**

The starting position

A *long int* *offset from the*
starting position

In the `ftell` call, the result is the current position within the open `FILE*` stream, or −1L if the call fails. For binary files, the position is the number of bytes from the beginning of the file. In the `fseek` call, `offset` is a distance from the starting position, `whence`. `whence` should be one of these three special macro values:

SEEK_SET	the beginning of the file
SEEK_CUR	the current position
SEEK_END	the end of the file.

If `whence` is SEEK_SET, then `offset` can be a `position` returned by an earlier call to `ftell`; this closely parallels the usage of `fgetpos` and `fsetpos`. The ability of `fseek` to offset from the current position or from the end of file is useful, but where possible `fgetpos` and `fsetpos` should be used instead; `ftell` and `fseek` were introduced many years ago, and because they use a `long int` for the position and offset, they may not be able to access every possible place within a file if the system allows really huge files (larger than the largest `long int` — at least 2 billion). However, `fseek` can be very flexible for shorter files. For example, if a file contains many items of the same type we can locate a particular item by calculating its position. See Self-test Exercises, question 3 for an example.

17.4.2 `fflush`

Under many operating systems, data being input or output is *buffered*. (A buffer is a block of memory in which data can be accumulated.) For example, in outputting to a file, bytes are not written to the disk individually as they are generated; instead they are collected until the buffer is full, and then the entire buffer is written in a single step. This is much more efficient, as it means fewer movements of the disk's read/write heads. Mechanical operations can be millions of times slower than processing operations, so this is a critical issue in computer performance.

There are times, however, when we must be sure that data written by the program really has been output, for example where the output is not actually a file but, say, a modem or a terminal. The `fflush` function sends any data currently in an output buffer to the operating system for transfer to the device concerned. In good C implementations, whenever the C library knows that a `FILE*` accesses an interactive device such as a terminal, it inserts `fflush` calls automatically at appropriate times. It is also called by `fclose`. The call syntax of `fflush` is

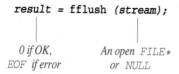

```
result = fflush (stream);
```

0 if OK,   An open FILE*
EOF if error   or NULL

If the `stream` is an open `FILE*`, that file is flushed; if it is `NULL`, all output files are flushed. Some C implementations also make `fflush` do various things to input files, but this is not standard C and cannot be relied on.

17.4.3 `setvbuf`

After a file is opened, the system allocates a buffer to it, as described in Section 17.4.2. Normally the size of the allocated buffer is well-chosen, but because buffering has such a major impact on computer performance, C allows us to specify the size of the buffer the system will use. Consider, for example, `mycopy.c` shown in Listing 17-4. Compile it and test it by copying a large file (100K or so). Now copy the same file with the copy program that comes with your computer's operating system (`COPY` in DOS or `cp` in Unix). You may find that `mycopy` is much slower than the system's copy command. If so, part of the the reason is probably the size of the buffer being used. Try inserting the following statement immediately after the `file_open` calls in `main` in Listing 17-4; this call allocates a 30,000-byte buffer to the input file.

```
if (setvbuf(inf, NULL, _IOFBF, 30000)) {
    printf("setvbuf failed\n");
}
```

If this is run on a computer with a slow disk the `setvbuf` call may substantially speed up the program. By providing a larger buffer, movement of the disk heads will be reduced and the disk will have a better chance of keeping up with the program. On a computer with a faster disk, the default buffer may be large enough for speed, in which case the `setvbuf` call will make little difference. This function is obviously fairly specialized, but it is included here because it sheds light on the buffering activities occurring in every program. The parameters for `setvbuf` are given in Appendix D.6.

17.5 SUMMARY

- *Sequential* input-output processes a file in order from start to finish.
- *Random*, or *direct*, input-output allows any part of a file to be read or written directly:
  - `fgetpos` finds out the current location in a file
  - `fsetpos` alters the current location in a file
  - after using `fsetpos`, the next input-output operation occurs at the specified location in the file
  - `ftell` and `fseek` are similar to the above, but may not work on very large files.
- *Text* input-output processes files as lines of characters, each line ending in a newline (`\n`).
- *Binary* input-output processes files as sequences of bytes which represent values (usually binary) in their unmodified internal format:
  - to perform binary access, `fopen` the file with b in the mode, e.g `"rb"` or `"wb"`
  - `fread` copies a block of data from a file into memory
  - `fwrite` copies a block of data from memory into a file
  - `fread` and `fwrite` may be used on text files if the data consists solely of characters; this needs special care
  - `getc` and `putc` may also be used to read or write single bytes from or to binary files.
- `fflush` requests the operating system to write all data currently in output buffers.
- `setvbuf` specifies the size of buffer to be allocated to a file; it must be called immediately after a successful `fopen`, before any data is transferred.
- `ferror` allows us to test whether an input-output error has occurred.

17.6 SELF-TEST EXERCISES

Short Answer

1 State whether the following are true or false.
   a If a program contains an `fsetpos` call, it must also contain an `fgetpos` call.
   b If a program contains an `fgetpos` call, it must also contain an `fsetpos` call.
   c `fgetpos` may only be used on binary files.
   d `fgetpos` may only be used on text files.
   e Binary files may contain ASCII characters, but only the characters `'1'` and `'0'`.
   f Only numeric data types may be stored in binary files.

g   Data written to a binary file with `fwrite` and read back using `fread` into the same types of variables in the same order will always be identical to the original data.

h   Data written to a text file with `fprintf` and read back using `fscanf` into the same types of variables in the same order will always be identical to the original data.

Programming

2   A restaurant wishes to store its menu on computer in a binary file. Menu items will be numbered consecutively from 1 upwards, and for each item the name (a maximum of 30 characters), short description (a maximum of 50 characters), and price (`int` cents) must be stored in a suitable `struct`. Write a program that reads a text file containing these details (created with an editor) and writes the information into a binary file as described above.

3   Write a program that allows the restaurant in exercise 2 to take phone orders and, by entering menu item numbers, obtain a printed check showing item number, item name and price for each ordered item, then a total price. Access structures in the file by using `fseek`. The nth item will be found at location $(n-1)$ times the size of the `struct`.

17.7 TEST QUESTIONS

Short Answer

1   Explain why it is hard to ensure that floating-point values are stored exactly in a text file.

2   Describe the operation of the function `ferror`.

3   In Listing 17-5b the first two characters on a line are input by `fscanf` into a string using the format `"%2[^\n]"`. Why not `"%2s"`?

4   In Listing 17-7 there is an embedded exercise. (See the comment "Why does it work?") Why **does** it work?

5   (Challenge) Devise a way, without relying on any knowledge of the particular compiler or computer, to store an `fpos_t` value as readable text in a text file. Your method should be portable in the sense that it should work on any single computer with an ANSI C compiler; it will not, of course, be able to transfer `fpos_t` values between different types of computers — but then, neither can the binary storage method.

Programming

6 Given the restaurant's binary menu file described in Self-test Exercise, question 2, write a program that produces a full menu listing. An auxiliary text file will also be required, as menus are usually grouped in categories (appetizer, first course, main course, etc.). These category names, and the menu item number they should immediately precede, should be read from a text file and inserted in the printed listing in the appropriate place.

7 Again using the restaurant's binary menu file, write a program that helps the staff answer phone queries about the menu. Either item number or name may be entered, and all information about the item should be displayed.

8 Rewrite your Life Game program (see the Test Questions for Chapter 9) so that you can stop the game and store a board position in a file. At a later time, the program should be able to retrieve the position and continue calculating from where it left off. Do not attempt to store pointers in a file.

9 (Harder) A university wishes to store student information in a binary file. Each record should contain student number, name, three address lines, and a course name. The student number should be a `long int`, and the rest should be fixed-length strings of suitable sizes, all packed into a `struct`. Write a program that allows the administration to find, add, or delete records specified by student number. To delete a record, overwrite it with a record containing student number −1. Add records to the end of the file. Write a second program that can be run occasionally to remove deleted records; it should read the file and write a new one containing no deleted records.

18

Scoping and linkage rules, storage duration, source file management, `const` **parameters**

Objectives

Understand the concepts of scope and linkage and be able to apply all relevant C facilities.

— `static, extern`

— avoiding scoping pitfalls when using pointers

— local blocks.

Be able to use additional preprocessor features:

— parameterized macros

— conditional compilation

— guarding header files against multiple inclusion.

Understand the purpose of the `const` type qualifier and be able to use it.

18.1 INTRODUCTION

This chapter considers the important concepts of scope and linkage, and looks at some useful preprocessor features; almost no significant C programming project could be completed well without a good understanding of them. We have largely been able to ignore them so far only because these features have less effect on shorter programs.

18.2 SCOPE

Throughout the text we have emphasized the importance of being able to ignore details and only consider one problem at a time. When calling `scanf`, for example, we do not need to worry about any local variables the writer of `scanf` may have used in programming that function. We have used local variables in functions through most of this book for exactly this reason; we can ignore internal details when using functions because C has *scoping rules* that restrict the visibility of identifiers.

In C, each identifier (variable or function name, etc.) has a scope — that is, its meaning is understood within a certain part of the program, but not elsewhere. Four types of scope exist in C (we have already met the first two listed):

a *block scope* (e.g. local variables); a variable declared in a function cannot be used outside it (block scope allows finer scoping than this, as we shall shortly see)

b *file scope* (e.g. global variables); a global variable may be used anywhere after its declaration up to the end of the source file, including inside any following functions

c *function scope*, used only by labels (described in Appendix C)

d *function prototype scope*, which applies to any variables in a function prototype. For an example of the latter, in

```
int fred(float a, char b);
```

a and b have function prototype scope. These are, in effect, dummy names which have no effect anywhere else in the program; they are present merely to allow the argument types to be declared, and for documentation purposes. They can be omitted without altering the program's meaning.

Block scope is used when declaring local variables in functions, but it can also be used inside any *block* (a region of code enclosed in braces, {, and }). The scope extends from immediately after the declaration of the identifier until the brace closing the block. For example, in this function skeleton

```
int fred(float a, char b) {
    long cc;
    ...
    if (cc == 25) {
        double d;
        ...
    } else {
        char buf[10];
        ...
    }
    ...
}
```

only the indentifier `fred` has file scope. (Functions must be defined at file scope level: it is illegal to try to define a function inside another function.) The scope of function parameters is the function block immediately following. Thus, a, b, and cc have block scope ending at the final brace that terminates the function. But d is declared in the block commencing after the `if` test, so its scope ends at the end of the first part of the `if` statement. Similarly, `buf` has block scope ending at the end of the `if` statement. These scopes are shown enclosed in boxes in the following diagram.

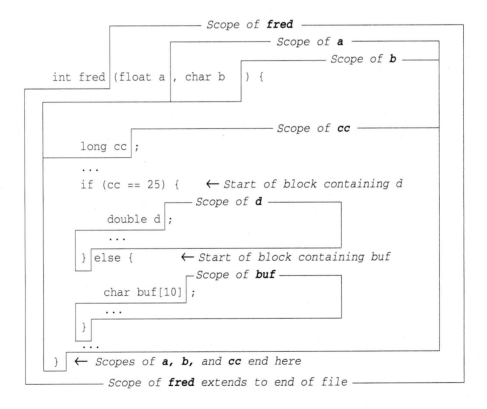

Block scopes such as those for d and buf above can be useful if you cannot avoid writing a fairly long function; variables of no concern outside a small region can be declared in a small block around that region, so that they have no effect on any other part of the function. For this purpose we can introduce a block without an accompanying if or other structured statement, as shown in the following function skeleton.

```
function bigfunc(void) {
    int int_used_everywhere;    — Scope of int_used_everywhere
    ...
    {
        char local_char;        — Scope of local_char
        ...
    }
    ...
}
```

Some compilers will create such localized variables only if the block is actually executed. This can be useful if a large array is needed only under certain conditions. By declaring the array as shown with buf in the earlier figure, it will be created only if it is actually needed.

Identifiers may be used for more than one purpose if the declarations occur in different scopes. When the identifier is used, the declaration in the smallest enclosing scope is the one that applies. Thus in the following program skeleton the int i cannot be accessed within main because the scope of the float i takes precedence.

```
int i;          ——— Scope of int i
...
void Alison(void) {
    ...
    i = 2;    /* A */
}
...
main() {
    float i; ——— Scope of float i
    ...
    i = 4;    /* B */
    Alison();
    return 0;
}
...
```

C follows static scope rules, which means we can determine the meaning of an identifier merely by looking at the program text, without trying to imagine how the program will execute. To do this for any particular identifier, look upwards in the program text from the point of use to find the closest applicable declaration. For example, in the preceding skeleton the assignment of 2 to i in Alison at point **A** assigns 2 to the global int i, not to the float i in main. We know this because the only i in scope at that point is the declaration at file level of int i.

18.3 LINKAGE

Linkage concerns how the compiler (or linker) combines the various compiled files that make up a program. There are three types of linkage: *external*, *internal*, and *none*. Global variables and functions usually have external linkage; this means that we can declare and use the identifier in more than one source file, and at runtime all declarations will refer to the same object. We have used external linkage on many occasions throughout the text when calling library functions from an application program. Although the functions are not in the program text, we can call them because their names have external linkage.

Internal linkage means that an object created in one source file is not accessible from another. For internal linkage, the object must be declared with the keyword static. A static object is only usable from code in the file in which it is declared.

External and internal linkage for both functions and data are illustrated in Listings 18-1 and 18-2. These are two source files, intended to be compiled separately and then linked together to form the executable program.

Listing 18-1   File lst18-1.c

```
#include <stdio.h>

int glob;          /* glob is accessible from any source file that is part
                      of the program. */
static int loc;    /* loc, being declared static, is only accessible from
                      this source file. */

void globfunc(void); /* globfunc is external, as the word 'static' is not
                        given in the declaration. As globfunc will be
                        defined in lst18-2.c, it is also correct to write
                        this declaration as: extern void globfunc(void);
                      */
static void locfunc(void);
                        /* locfunc MUST be declared later in THIS file, as
                          'static' makes locfunc specific to this file. */

main() {
    printf("Calling locfunc from main in lst18-1.c...\n");
    locfunc();
    printf("Calling globfunc from main...\n");
    globfunc();
    printf("Back in main; loc = %d, glob = %d\n", loc, glob);
    return 0;
}

static void locfunc(void) {
    printf("    Inside locfunc in lst18-1.c\n    storing 88 in loc\n");
    loc = 88;
}
```

Listing 18-2   File `1st18-2.c`

```
#include <stdio.h>

extern int glob;        /* This is the same glob declared in 1st18-1.c.  The
                           word 'extern' tells the compiler that there is an
                           int called glob declared in another file.
                        */
static int loc;         /* loc, being declared static, is only accessible from
                           this source file.  This is a DIFFERENT loc from
                           that in 1st18-1.c.  It would be an error to try
                           to access the loc in 1st18-1.c by using 'extern'.
                        */

static void locfunc(void) {
                        /* We can also have a function locfunc in this source
                           file, because the word 'static' prevents any other
                           file knowing about or accessing this function.
                        */
    printf("         Inside the locfunc in 1st18-2.c\n");
    printf("         Storing 77 in loc and 99 in glob\n");
    loc = 77;
    glob = 99;
}

void globfunc(void) {    /* This is the globfunc called in 1st18-1.c */
    printf("    Inside the globfunc in 1st18-2.c\n");
    printf("    Calling locfunc...\n");
    locfunc();
    printf("    Leaving globfunc; loc = %d, glob = %d...\n", loc, glob);
}
```

Test run

```
Calling locfunc from main in 1st18-1.c...
    Inside locfunc in 1st18-1.c
    storing 88 in loc
Calling globfunc from main...
    Inside the globfunc in 1st18-2.c
    Calling locfunc...
        Inside the locfunc in 1st18-2.c
        Storing 77 in loc and 99 in glob
    Leaving globfunc; loc = 77, glob = 99...
Back in main; loc = 88, glob = 99
```

This test run shows that any identifier declared `static` has effect only within the file in which it is declared; two functions called `locfunc` exist, one in each source file — and similarly for the variables `loc`. That they can be used independently without interference is apparent from the printout above. For example, the `loc` printed in the final line is the one given a value (88) in the same source file. The other `loc`, given the value 77 in the other source file, has not interfered with the first `loc`.

This feature is particularly useful when writing function libraries or abstract data types. Variables or functions intended for 'public' use should be declared without the word `static`; then, like `globfunc` and `glob` in the preceding example, they may be accessed from any source file in the program. On the other hand, variables and functions doing 'private' work within the library should be declared `static`; then there is no danger of an application programmer accidentally reusing the name and thus damaging the integrity of the library.

18.4 STORAGE DURATION

The *storage duration* of a data object such as a variable refers to the period of the program's execution for which that data object exists. There are two types of storage duration: *static storage duration* and *automatic storage duration*.

All global variables and all variables declared `static` have static storage duration. This means that the variable is created and initialized at program startup, and thereafter exists for the entire duration of the program run. Normal local variables within a function have automatic storage duration: a fresh copy is created on entry to the function or block in which the variable is declared. This means that a normal local variable within a function will not retain its value from one call of the function to the next, as the variable that exists during the second activation of the function is not necessarily in the same memory location as the variable that existed during the previous activation. The `static` keyword can be used when declaring a variable within a function, in which case the variable has static storage duration and can be used to pass a value from one activation of the function to the next. Such a variable is not accessible outside the function (even though it still exists) because of the normal scoping rules discussed in Section 18.2.

Storage duration is discussed further in Appendix C.2.1.

Problems with pointers

It is possible to circumvent the scope of an identifier by using a pointer. Sometimes this works and sometimes it doesn't: it depends on the storage class of the variable to which the pointer points. Consider this program:

```
int * ip;
void fred2(void) {
    *ip = 57; /* Assigns 57 to fred's i; OK if fred2 is called from
                  fred. */
}
void fred(void) {
    int i;
    ip = &i;   /* Stores i's address in the pointer ip. */
    fred2();
}
main() {
    fred();
    *ip = 49; /* WRONG!! fred has terminated, so i no longer exists. */
    return 0;
}
```

Inside fred, ip is made to point to the local variable i, which has automatic storage duration. From within fred, the call to fred2 is made and (via ip), 57 is stored in i. This is correct because fred is still in execution, so its local variables exist even though they are not in scope inside fred2. But when, after fred terminates, main attempts to store 49 in i, an error occurs because fred's local variable ceased to exist when fred exited. ip therefore points to a nonexistent variable. This is called a *dangling pointer*. Many compilers will not diagnose an error, but the program will malfunction just the same, and probably in a very weird manner. Finding such errors is difficult, and the best solution is not to make the mistake in the first place.

18.5 ADDITIONAL PREPROCESSOR FEATURES

Preprocessor features we have used so far include macros (#define) and file inclusion (#include). In fact the preprocessor is one of the most powerful features of C, and it has many more features which are useful when programming larger projects. We shall discuss two here: *conditional compilation* and *parameterized macros*.

18.5.1 Conditional compilation

One problem faced by software developers is maintaining two or more versions of a program. For example, we might want a program that runs on both a mainframe and a personal computer, yet these two types of computer may need different source code to handle their specialized features. Perhaps they have different rules for filenames, or perhaps different statements are needed for some advanced screen display features.

Another case requiring two program versions concerns debugging. While developing a program we might want all sorts of extra printouts, extra consistency checks on our variables, etc., yet these might be too slow or clumsy to include in the final production version. Conditional compilation allows us to write a single source program for both cases, and to conditionally compile or not compile various pieces depending on the value of a macro. The preprocessor directives allowing this are #if, #ifdef, and #ifndef.

In its simplest form, each of the above three directives appears at the start of a section of source code that ends with a #endif directive, for example:

```
#ifdef identifier
    ...source code (compiled if the identifier is defined)...
#endif
```

This #ifdef (**if def**ined) directive passes the source code to the compiler only if the identifier is a defined macro name. We may also include an alternative piece of source code for the other possibility:

```
#ifdef identifier
    ...source code (compiled if the identifier is defined)...
#else
    ...alternative source code (compiled if it is undefined)...
#endif
```

Listing 18-3 illustrates the #ifdef statement.

Listing 18-3

```
#define GLOBULE 1

#include <stdio.h>
main() {
    float GLOBULAR;
#ifdef GLOBULE
    printf("GLOBULE is defined\n");
#else
    printf("GLOBULE is NOT defined\n");
#endif

#ifdef GLOBULAR
    printf("GLOBULAR is defined\n");
#else
    printf("GLOBULAR is NOT defined\n");
#endif
    return 0;
}
```

Test run
```
GLOBULE is defined
GLOBULAR is NOT defined
```

The test run shows that GLOBULE, being a declared macro name, causes the #ifdef directive to include the printf statement that outputs the "GLOBULE is defined" message. On the other hand, GLOBULAR, not being a defined macro name, causes its #ifdef to include the printf in the #else option. Now observe that GLOBULAR is in fact a declared float variable. That makes no difference: according to the preprocessor it is undefined. All preprocessor directives (#something) operate before the program is compiled by the compiler proper, so only preprocessor macro names (#define names) are recognized in preprocessor directives.

The #if directive tests the value of an integer constant expression (one involving only constants and macro names, but not program variables) and includes the following source code if the expression is non-zero.

```
#if constant expression
    ...source code (compiled if the expression is nonzero)...
#else
    ...alternative source code (compiled if it is zero)...
#endif
```

This looks a little like the normal if statement (see Chapter 6), so it is important to understand the difference. With the normal if statement, the test is compiled into machine code and the test is made **every time** the if statement is executed **at runtime**. With #if and its variants, the test is made only **once**, **before** the program is compiled. If an if statement and a #if directive are enclosed in a loop (while, for, etc.), the if statement, being executed at runtime, is tested every time the code in the loop is executed. So the if statement might do different things on different executions of the loop. But the #if directive, because it is tested and removed before the compiler ever sees the program, is not present in the executable code. Therefore it always takes the same branch every time. This is illustrated in Listing 18-4.

Listing 18-4

```
#define MAC variable

#include <stdio.h>
main() {
    int i, MAC;
    MAC = 1;
    for (i=1; i<=6; i++) {
        if (MAC <= 3) {
            printf("(if)    MAC <= 3, MAC is %d\n", MAC);
        }
        #if MAC <= 3
            printf("    (#if) MAC <= 3, MAC is %d\n", MAC);
        #endif
        MAC++;
    }
    return 0;
}
```

Test run
```
(if)      MAC <= 3, MAC is 1
    (#if) MAC <= 3, MAC is 1
(if)      MAC <= 3, MAC is 2
    (#if) MAC <= 3, MAC is 2
(if)      MAC <= 3, MAC is 3
    (#if) MAC <= 3, MAC is 3
    (#if) MAC <= 3, MAC is 4
    (#if) MAC <= 3, MAC is 5
    (#if) MAC <= 3, MAC is 6
```

This output looks inexplicable unless the facts given above are taken into account. MAC is #defined to be variable, so the preprocessor replaces all occurrences of MAC by variable. Thus the compiler, in the declaration for MAC, is really declaring a variable called variable. Similarly the statements MAC=1, MAC++, and both printf calls really operate on variable. But the #if test does not concern the program variable called variable, as that does not yet exist when the #if preprocessor directive is acted on before the compilation proper. Instead, it is treating the identifier variable as a macro name. But variable has not been #defined as a macro. Whenever such an undefined identifier is used in a #if test, it is treated as if it were 0. As 0 is less than or equal to 3, the test evaluates as true and the preprocessor inserts the printf statement into the program; it is then compiled unconditionally, and at runtime it will execute every time through the loop, even after variable becomes greater than 3. Listing 18-5 shows the program from Listing 18-4 after processing by the preprocessor; therefore Listing 18-5 is what the compiler proper actually compiles. You should check that you understand (a) why Listing 18-5 creates the above output, and (b) why the preprocessor turns Listing 18-4 into Listing 18-5.

Listing 18-5   Program from Listing 18-4 after preprocessing

```
/* The entire contents of <stdio.h> were included here, but have
   been deleted from this listing for brevity.
*/
main() {
    int i, variable;
    variable = 1;
    for (i=1; i<=6; i++) {
        if (variable <= 3) {
            printf("(if)      MAC<= 3, MAC is %d\n", variable);
        }
            printf("    (#if) MAC <= 3, MAC is %d\n", variable);
        variable++;
    }
    return 0;
}
```

There is also a #elif (**else if**) for building multi-part conditional directives. For example, if we need three code sections corresponding to whether the macro MAC is 1, 2, or 3, and a fourth section if it is none of these, we could write:

```
#if MAC == 1
    ...source code for inclusion if MAC is 1...
#elif MAC == 2
    ...source code for inclusion if MAC is 2...
#elif MAC == 3
    ...source code for inclusion if MAC is 3...
#else
    ...source code for inclusion if MAC is not 1, 2, or 3...
#endif
```

All that remains before we can compile a specific version of the program is to include a #define directive for the appropriate value at the head of the program. Even better, most C compilers allow us to define a macro without altering the file at all; your C compiler manual will describe how to do this with your particular compiler.

18.5.2 Writing reliable header (.h) files

The preceding conditional compilation features may be used to make robust C header files, however, there is a danger of accidentally including a header more than once. In Listing 17-6, for example, the header file helpadt.h includes <stdio.h> because it needs to use standard input-output features such as the types fpos_t and FILE. But a programmer including helpadt.h in an application program might not know this, and may therefore also include <stdio.h> directly from their program. Thus the preprocessor would include <stdio.h> twice. Duplicating a declaration is sometimes harmless, but not always, so this might produce syntax errors. The cure is for each header file to protect itself against being included more than once. Suppose we want a header file to declare Boolean variables. The main text of the header should be surrounded by a protective #ifdef, as shown in Listing 18-6.

Listing 18-6   boolean.h header protected against multiple inclusion

```
/* A simple header file for boolean data. */

#ifndef _BOOLEAN_H_INCLUDED_
    #define _BOOLEAN_H_INCLUDED_

    typedef int bool;   /* Type bool is the same as int. */
    #define TRUE (1)
    #define FALSE (0)

#endif
```

The macro _BOOLEAN_H_INCLUDED_ is not otherwise used in the program. (The leading and trailing underscores make it unlikely that an application program will accidentally use this macro name and cause a conflict.) Suppose a program accidentally includes this header file twice. The first time it is entered, _BOOLEAN_H_INCLUDED_ is undefined, so the #ifndef (**if n**ot **def**ined) directive includes the source code that follows. The first line defines _BOOLEAN_H_INCLUDED_, so if this file is included again the #ifndef will not include the source code a second time. The next three lines are the definitions that the application program is really interested in — defining the type bool and the constants TRUE and FALSE. These lines will be compiled only once, no matter how often this header file is included in a program file. Finally, the #endif terminates the #ifndef statement. Every header file should be protected against multiple inclusion by a #ifndef. Needless to say, each should have a unique macro name, so a name based on the name of the header file itself is best.

18.5.3 (Optional) Parameterized macros

Macros are useful for giving short names to pieces of source code that we might need often but which are hard to remember. For example, a program might often need to input up to 50 characters into the char array buf, discarding the remainder of the input line. This can be done with the statements

```
scanf("%50[^\n]%*[^\n]", buf);getchar();
```

With a macro, we can give these statements a simple name:

```
#define get50tobuf scanf("%50[^\n]%*[^\n]", buf);getchar()
```

But what if we need to do exactly the same job on a different char array? With a parameterized macro, we can make the array name alterable:

```
#define get50(buf) scanf("%50[^\n]%*[^\n]", buf);getchar()
```

Now buf is a macro parameter. We can use any array we please when calling the macro:

```
main() {
    char first[51], second[51];
    get50(first);
    get50(second);
    ...
```

Remember that macros are replaced before the compiler compiles the program. Therefore these parameterized macros are not the same as function calls. This is clear if we look at the previous code fragment after preprocessing, but before compilation proper:

```
main() {
    char first[51], second[51];
    scanf("%50[^\n]%*[^\n]", first);getchar();
    scanf("%50[^\n]%*[^\n]", second);getchar();
    ...
```

The preprocessor has simply substituted the macro text into the program everywhere the macro name appears, but buf is replaced by the word in the macro call on each occasion. A parameterized macro may have more than one parameter (separated by commas). To write a parameterized macro definition, list the parameters in parentheses after the macro name. There must be **no spaces** between the macro name and the left parenthesis.

```
#define macro_name(arg1, arg2, ...) substitution text
```

No whitespace between the name and the ' ('!

Whitespace between the macro name and the parenthesis causes the parenthesized arguments to be taken as part of the substitution. For example, this:

```
#define get50 (buf) scanf("%50[^\n]%*[^\n]", buf);getchar()
main() {                                                    Wrong
    char first[51], second[51];
    get50(first);
    get50(second);
    return 0;
}
```

is transformed by the preprocessor into this:

```
main() {
    char first[51], second[51];
    (buf) scanf("%50[^\n]%*[^\n]", buf);getchar()(first);
    (buf) scanf("%50[^\n]%*[^\n]", buf);getchar()(second);
    return 0;
}
```

which will produce syntax errors in compilation.

When designing macros, remember that the token substitution may cause some unexpected results. For example,

```
#define double(any) 2 * any
    ...
    k = i/double(j);
```

The intention is to divide i by twice j. But the preprocessor output is

```
    ...
    k = i/2 * j;
```

which divides i by 2 and multiplies by j. To prevent this, when macros are intended to be used as expressions, enclose the definition in parentheses (( )). There is one more pitfall. Consider

```
#define double(any) (2 * any)
    ...
    k = double(j+k);
```

The intention is to double the sum of j and k. The substitution is enclosed in parentheses as advised above, but the preprocessor output is still wrong:

```
    . . .
    k = (2 * j+k);
```

This doubles j, but not k, because * has a higher priority than +. The cure is even more parentheses:

```
#define double(any) (2 * (any))
    . . .                └─┴──── (Note parentheses)
    k = double(j+k);
```

Now the expansion is correct.

```
    . . .
    k = (2 * (j+k));
           └─┴──────────── (Note parentheses)
```

Thus, to write a robust macro definition, we should bracket the entire replacement text if possible, as well as parenthesizing all argument names. Luckily, all these precautions concern the #define statement itself; once that is right it can be used confidently as often as we please.

To make macros really sturdy, there are still more pitfalls to watch out for, although these extra problems are entirely caused by failure to follow the layout rules used in this text. Can you spot the problem with the following code fragment?

```
#define get50(buf) scanf("%50[^\n]%*[^\n]", buf);getchar()
main() {
    char first[51]; int i;
    scanf("%d", &i);
    if (i < 7) get50(first);
    . . .
```

The writer of this code knew that the braces in the if statement can be omitted if there is only a single statement within the if. (We have never done this in this text, for good reason.) Unfortunately, the get50 macro represents two statements, as the macro expansion shows:

```
main() {
    char first[51]; int i;
    scanf("%d", &i);
    if (i < 7) scanf("%50[^\n]%*[^\n]", first);getchar();
    └─────────────────────────────────────────┘ └────────┘

    . . .

        The *if* statement ────────┘

    This is **not** part of the *if* statement! ────────┘
```

The layout style used in this text, because it never omits braces, cannot give rise to this problem. Nevertheless, for extra insurance against trouble, bracket macro definitions with braces ({ }) if possible. Thus, the following:

```
#define get50(buf) {scanf("%50[^\n]%*[^\n]", buf);getchar();}
main() {
    char first[51]; int i;
    scanf("%d", &i);
    if (i < 7) get50(first);
    ...
```

expands correctly into

```
main() {
    char first[51]; int i;
    scanf("%d", &i);
    if (i < 7) {scanf("%50[^\n]%*[^\n]", first);getchar();};
    ...
```

— *Note the braces*

There is one further problem caused by omitting braces. Consider

```
#define get50(buf) {scanf("%50[^\n]%*[^\n]", buf);getchar();}
main() {
    char first[51]; int i;
    scanf("%d", &i);
    if (i < 7) get50(first);
    else i = 2;
    ...
```

The `else` option causes a further error: the `if` statement expands into

```
    if (i < 7) {scanf("%50[^\n]%*[^\n]", first);getchar();};
    else i = 2;
```

which is illegal because the sequence `};  else` violates a C syntax rule. The cure is really ugly: bracket macro replacements with the sequences `do{` and `}while(0)`, as in the following:

```
#define get50(buf) do{scanf("%50[^\n]%*[^\n]", buf);getchar();}while(0)
main() {
    char first[51]; int i;
    scanf("%d", &i);
    if (i < 7) get50(first);
    else i = 2;
    ...
```

Now the `if` statement will expand into

```
    if (i < 7) do{scanf("%50[^\n]%*[^\n]", first);getchar();}while(0);
    else i = 2;
```

Now the macro definition is bullet-proof. It is ugly to have a loop that never repeats, but it does work. This is not necessary for macros contained in programs that obey the layout rules used in this text. But for macros in header files, it is important to ensure that any legal usage will work properly.

Example: Flexible macro parameters

Here is the character-input macro, parameterized for FILE* and buffer name (note the use of \ to run a long macro definition over multiple lines):

```
#define getline50(file,buf) {fscanf((file), "%50[^\n]%*[^\n]", (buf)); \
                             getc(file);}
```

Finally, it would be useful to have a version where that 50 was a parameter. Unfortunately, it is buried inside a string. Therefore, this will not work:

```
#define getline(file, buf, size) {fscanf((file), "%(size)[^\n]%*[^\n]", \
                             (buf)); getc(file);}
main() {
    char first[51], second[71];
    getline(stdin, first, 50);
    getline(stdin, second, 70);
    return 0;
}
```
                                                        ———— *Wrong*

The preprocessor output from this is

```
main() {
    char first[51], second[71];
    {fscanf((stdin), "%(size)[^\n]%*[^\n]", (first)); getc(stdin);};
    {fscanf((stdin), "%(size)[^\n]%*[^\n]", (second)); getc(stdin);};
    return 0;
}
```

Note that the size in the string has not been replaced: characters inside strings are not examined for macro replacement. One final preprocessor feature will help to fix this problem: # followed by a macro argument is replaced by a string with the argument substituted. Thus the following will work:

```
#define getline(file, buf, size) {fscanf((file), "%" #size "[^\n]%*[^\n]" \
                             ,(buf)); getc(file);}
main() {
    char first[51], second[71];
    getline(stdin, first, 50);
    getline(stdin, second, 70);
    return 0;
}
```

The result of preprocessing is

```
main() {
    char first[51], second[71];
    {fscanf((stdin), "%" "50" "[^\n]%*[^\n]", (first)); getc(stdin);};
    {fscanf((stdin), "%" "70" "[^\n]%*[^\n]", (second)); getc(stdin);};
    return 0;
}
```

This is fine because the compiler always concatenates adjacent string literals into a single longer string (see Section 3.3). For example, the compiler will treat the first input line as if it read

```
    {fscanf((stdin), "%50[^\n]%*[^\n]", (first)); getc(stdin);};
```

We might be quite pleased with the results of using parameterized macros by now, but there is still a problem. What about this?

```
#define getline(file, buf, size) {fscanf((file), "%" #size \
                                 "[^\n]%*[^\n]" ,(buf)); getc(file);}
main() {
    char first[51]; int i;
    scanf("%d", &i);
    getline(stdin, first, i);
    return 0;
}
```

Unfortunately, that parameter `size`, looking for all the world like a perfectly good general-purpose argument, only works if the substitution argument is a constant. The preprocessor output from the above is

```
main() {
    char first[51]; int i;
    scanf("%d", &i);
    {fscanf((stdin), "%" "i" "[^\n]%*[^\n]" ,(first)); getc(stdin);};
    return 0;                    └─── Invalid '%' size!
}
```

There is no way to fix this using macros. We have reached the point where the task is sufficiently complex to require a function.

18.6 THE const ATTRIBUTE

In large systems it is especially important to know which variables and function parameters may be modified and which may not. The `const` (constant) qualifier exists for this purpose. For example, in `<string.h>` we find the following declarations:

```
int     strcmp(const char *_s1, const char *_s2);
char *  strcpy(char *_dest, const char *_source);
```

In the declaration for `strcpy`, _source is stated to be a pointer to `const char`, meaning that the `char`s that _source points at may not be modified inside `strcpy`. This gives us a guarantee that we can safely give `strcpy`, as its second argument, a pointer to any of our data, without worrying that `strcpy` might alter that data behind our backs. On the other hand, the _dest parameter is stated to be a pointer to (non-const) `char`. This means (because the word `const` is absent) that `strcpy` may modify the `char`s that _dest points to. Indeed, `strcpy` copies characters into the buffer pointed to by _dest. Similarly, the declaration of `strcmp` states that **both** parameters are pointers to constant `char`, and thus `strcmp` is not permitted to modify either of the character strings pointed to by its arguments.

If the writers of the C library had omitted all `const` keywords but nevertheless written the algorithms correctly, the functions would still have operated properly. However, an important check by the compiler would not be made on the consistency of arguments. In large programming projects, the more checks the compiler can do automatically, the fewer checks we have to do manually. Although we have ignored const throughout this text, advanced C programmers will take the trouble to master its use.

Normal variables may be declared const also, but they should be initialized when they are declared. For example,

```
const int ic = 8;
```

is a constant int; its initial value of 8 cannot be modified by assignment later on. Although const may be used in declarations involving pointers, we must be clear about just what is constant: the pointer variable, or the thing it points at. There are four possibilities:

Using const with pointers

int * ip	ip is a (variable) pointer to a (variable) int. This is the usual case; ip and *ip may both be modified in the usual ways.
const int * cip	cip is a (variable) pointer to a constant int. cip may be modified to point to various ints, but these ints themselves cannot be modified.
int * const ipc	ipc is a constant pointer to a (variable) int. ipc must always point at the same int, but that int (i.e. *ipc) may be altered.
const int * const cipc	cipc is a constant pointer to a constant int. Neither cipc nor *cipc may be altered.

Another qualifier, volatile, is described in Appendix C.2.5.

18.7 SUMMARY

- The *scope* of an identifier is the region of the program in which it is known to the compiler.
  - *File scope*: the identifier is known from its declaration to the end of the file. Applies to identifiers declared outside any function.
  - *Block scope*: the identifier is known from its declaration to the end of the block. Applies to identifiers declared inside a function or block, and to function parameters, which are deemed to belong to the function's block.

- *Linkage* refers to the combining of various separately compiled source files into a single program.
  - *External linkage*: occurrences of an identifier in two or more files all refer to the same object. Applies to objects declared outside functions **without** the keyword static.
  - *Internal linkage*: occurrences of an identifier in two or more files refer to a different object in each file. Applies to objects declared outside functions **with** the keyword static.
- The *storage duration* of a variable determines the period of time for which that variable exists.
  - A variable with *static storage duration* exists for the entire program execution.
  - A variable with *automatic storage duration* is created on entry to the function or block in which it is declared and exists until that function or block is exited.
- *Conditional compilation* refers to the ability of the preprocessor to select or reject portions of the C source program for compilation.
  - #if directives allow conditional compilation depending on the value of an integer constant expression.
  - #ifdef and #ifndef directives allow conditional compilation depending on whether a macro name is defined or undefined.
  - Each conditional block is terminated by a #endif directive.
  - #else and #elif directives allow creation of multi-part conditional compilation blocks.
- *Parameterized macros* are #define statements with substitutable arguments.
- The const qualifier allows the programmer to declare that a parameter or variable refers to an object that should not be modified.

18.8 SELF-TEST EXERCISES

Short Answer

1 Three functions in a file all need to refer to an int called fred which should contain 278, must never be altered, and must not be accessible from any other source file. Declare fred.

2 Two functions in a file both need to refer to a double called dub, which should contain –826.776, must never be altered, and must be accessible from other source files. Declare dub.

3 Declare an alterable pointer pdub that can point to the constant dub mentioned in question 2.

18.9 TEST QUESTIONS

Short Answer

1 Look through the various functions in the demonstration listings in other chapters of this text, and identify any pointer arguments that should be given the `const` qualifier. Rewrite each affected function heading appropriately.

2 As well as helping document a program and allowing improved error checking, the `const` qualifier helps a compiler optimize a program for improved performance. Explain why this is so.

19

Efficiency, searching and sorting

Objectives

Examine some frequently-used searching and sorting techniques.

Be acquainted with the concept of algorithm efficiency, and the *O()* notation.

Be able to use the standard library `bsearch` and `qsort` functions.

19.1 INTRODUCTION

It is traditional in programming texts to examine many searching and sorting algorithms in depth. In C programming these tasks are less important than in other languages because C has standard library functions for each task which, under normal conditions, are sufficient. However, sometimes we must be certain of the exact characteristics of the algorithms we use. Unless we are lucky enough to have the source code for our C library, the only way to be certain is to write the search or sort function ourselves.

There are two other reasons for examining these topics — they are good examples of algorithm design, and they are well suited to illustrate the concept of *algorithm efficiency*, which is an indispensable tool when writing quality programs.

19.2 ALGORITHM EFFICIENCY

Suppose we are searching for the value 297 in an unordered array of `int`s. There is only one way to find this value: start looking at element zero, and proceed until either we find 297, or we reach the end of the array (in which case we know the number is absent). Suppose the value is absent. To discover this we would have to examine every element in the array, no matter how many there are.

This method of finding a value is called a *linear search*; the item being sought is called the *key*. It is clear from the above that the amount of work done during a linear search is proportional to the number of items to be searched. Call that number n: it might be 100, 1000, or whatever; it doesn't matter. The important thing is that a linear search requires a time proportional to n. (Thus a search of, say, 200 items needs twice the time taken by a search of 100 items.) This simple observation is summarized by saying that linear search takes time *of order n*, or that it is an *order-n* algorithm. We write this for brevity as $O(n)$ (where the O stands for 'of order').

It is important to understand that this is a statement about the efficiency of linear searches generally, not the efficiency of a particular linear search program or the sorting of a specific array. (These will vary according to the programming methods used and the size of the array.)

19.3 SEARCHING

It may seem surprising, but there are ways to either find an item in a collection or learn that it is not present, without looking at every item. *Binary search* seeks an item in a sorted array. We look first at the middle item. Either we find the item we are looking for, or because the array is sorted, we learn that it lies in the top or bottom half of the array. For example, if we are seeking 297 and the middle item is 50, we know that 297 must be in the top half (if the array is sorted in ascending order). This means that every time we inspect an item in the array we divide the size of the problem in half. When we eventually reduce the problem to just one item, we either find, or do not find, the item we seek, and the search is over. The maximum number of tests needed to find an item in arrays of various sizes are set out in Table 19-1.

Table 19-1 Number of tests needed to find an item in an array

Array size (n)	Maximum no. of tests needed (m)
1	1
3	2
7	3
15	4
⋮	⋮
4095	12
⋮	⋮

We can reduce this table to a statement about the efficiency of binary search. The numbers in the left hand column are each one less than a power of two. Thus for an array of size $n = 2^m - 1$, we may need m tests. Therefore $m = \log_2(n+1)$. Since m (the number of tests) is proportional to the efficiency, and n is the table size, we can write the efficiency as $O(\log_2(n+1))$. The +1 is insignificant, so we can simplify it as $O(\log_2 n)$. Since logarithms to one base are a scaled multiple of the equivalent logarithms in another base, the base (2) is also unimportant, so we generalize the efficiency of binary search as $O(\log n)$. The log function increases very slowly indeed, as the table shows, so $O(\log n)$ algorithms are very desirable. However, we can do better.

For many situations, a technique called *hashing* is even more efficient than a binary search. The idea is to reserve a large array (a *hash table*) for storing items, and for each item, to calculate a value called the *hash* which tells where to place the item in the array. For example, for storing text strings in a table of size T, a simple (but not very good) hash function might compute the sum S of the ASCII values of the characters in the string, and use S%T as the hash. To find whether an item is present, we calculate the hash for the item being searched for, and look in just the one place indicated by the hash. Either the item is there, or it isn't anywhere. Hashing, in the simplest case, is therefore an $O(1)$ method, because a single test is sufficient to locate an item.

Hashing is complicated by various factors such as the possibility of two items having the same hash value; this is called a *hash collision*, and needs extra steps to resolve the clash. This decreases the efficiency of the hashing method, but in a surprising manner: the efficiency of hashing still doesn't depend directly on how many items are in the table; rather, it depends on how full the hash table is (since the fuller the table is, the more likely it is that collisions will occur). For tables less than, say, 80% full, with a good hashing function, hashing can be safely considered an $O(1)$ searching method. We shall not consider hashing further here, but it is described in detail in many data structure textbooks.

19.3.1 Example: Binary search

We shall write a function, `binsearch`, to search a sorted `int` array between given lower and upper bounds looking for a given item.

```
/*********** binsearch: search an array for an item ***********
On entry: A is an array, with elements A[low]...A[high], inclusive, sorted
          in ascending order.  low is less than or equal to high+1 (this
          allows low and high to specify a search of no elements of A, by
          setting low = high+1).
On exit:  Returns the index of the first element in A[low...high] which
          is not less than the key, or high+1 if all array elements are less
          than key.
*/
int binsearch(int A[], int low, int high, int key);
```

From the above postcondition we see that if the `key` being searched for is absent, `binsearch` returns the place where it should be; this is useful if the application intends to insert the missing value. Before commencing, we should anticipate a problem: it will be almost impossible to test our function enough to convince us that it is error-free. In this regard, Jon Bentley mentions in his article 'Programming Pearls' (*Communications of the ACM*, vol 26, no 12, Dec 1983, pp 1040–1045) that the first binary search algorithm was published in 1946, but that the first **correct** version was not published until 1962. Therefore, even if we do it nowhere else, critical algorithms such as searching and sorting should be verified for correctness. The following development of `binsearch` is based on an idea from Bentley's article.

`binsearch` will obviously contain a loop, each iteration of which roughly halves the region to be searched. With two `int`s, L and U, we can mark the section of A still in doubt at any given stage during the algorithm. Initially we must search the entire region from `A[low]` to `A[high]`, so at the start, L should be set to `low` and U to `high`. Each iteration of the loop will either decrease U or increase L. The following figure shows the situation part way through a search for the value 29.

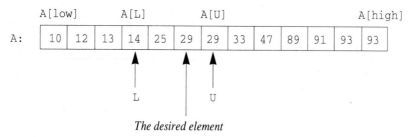

The desired element

From this picture, the region `A[L] . . . A[U]` must have the following properties: (a) no elements before `A[L]` are greater than or equal to `key`, and (b) no elements after `A[U]` are less than `key`. This will be our loop invariant, as the following diagram shows.

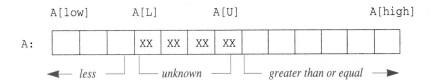

By testing array values and suitably modifying L and U, the unknown region in the diagram eventually shrinks to nothing (when L equals U+1), at which point A[L] is the first element not less than the key. Therefore, our algorithm can be written as:

```
Set L to low, and U to high.
while L <= U
    Test one array element in the range A[L]...A[U], and
    Shrink the range appropriately by modifying either L or U.
(After the loop, L is the desired array index.)
```

To perform the 'test-and-shrink' steps inside the loop, we must first select an array subscript near the centre of the Range $L...U$, such as $M=(L+U)/2$. If that element is less than the key, L can be updated to $M+1$, otherwise U can be altered to $M-1$. This must reduce the range because one of L or U is moved closer to (or just beyond) the other; therefore the loop must eventually halt. The function is shown in Listing 19-1 along with a short main function for testing purposes.

Listing 19-1

```c
int binsearch(int A[], int low, int high, int key) {
    int L = low, U = high, M;
    while (L <= U) {
        /* Invariant: A[low]...A[L-1] all < key, A[U+1]...A[high] all >= key;
                      also L <= U + 1
        */
        M = (L + U) / 2; /* M must be in range L...U (property of mean) */
        if (A[M] < key) {
            /* Here, A[low]...A[M] all < key (because array is ordered) */
            L = M + 1;    /* Re-establish invariant, L cannot exceed U+1 */
        } else {
            /* Here, A[M]...A[high] all >= key */
            U = M - 1;    /* Re-establish invariant, U cannot be below L-1 */
        }
    }
    /* Here L <= U + 1 (from invariant), and L > U (loop termination),
       therefore L == U + 1, so:
       A[low]...A[L-1] all < key, and A[L]...A[high] all >= key,
       therefore L is the subscript of the first non-lesser element.
    */
    return L;
}
```

```
/* Short main function for testing... */
#include <stdio.h>
int test[] = {1,1,3,5,5,6,8,9,9};
#define high 8      /* NB: This is the subscript of the last array element */

main() {
    int j, i;
    for (i=0; i<=high; i++) {
        printf("A[%d]=%d ", i, test[i]);
    }
    putchar('\n');
    for (i=0; i<=10; i++) {
        j = binsearch(test, 0, high, i);
        if (j > 0 && test[j-1] >= i  ||  j <= high && test[j] < i) {
            printf("ERROR! ");
        }
        if (j <= high && test[j] == i) {  /* Note test for item i found. */
            printf("Seeking %2d, found at j=%2d:\n", i, j);
        } else {
            printf("Seeking %2d, NOT found at j=%2d:\n", i, j);
        }
        if (binsearch(test, i, i-1, 5) != i) {
            printf("NULL SEARCH ERROR: %d\n", i);
        }
    }
    return 0;
}
```

Test run:
```
A[0]=1 A[1]=1 A[2]=3 A[3]=5 A[4]=5 A[5]=6 A[6]=8 A[7]=9 A[8]=9
Seeking  0, NOT found at j= 0:
Seeking  1, found at j= 0:
Seeking  2, NOT found at j= 2:
Seeking  3, found at j= 2:
Seeking  4, NOT found at j= 3:
Seeking  5, found at j= 3:
Seeking  6, found at j= 5:
Seeking  7, NOT found at j= 6:
Seeking  8, found at j= 6:
Seeking  9, found at j= 7:
Seeking 10, NOT found at j= 9:
```

19.3.2 Using the `bsearch` standard library function

`bsearch` is a C library function intended to do a binary search of an ordered array; it is declared in `<stdlib.h>`. The binary search function written in the previous section was specific to `int` data; `bsearch`, on the other hand, will locate an item in any kind of sorted array, and the way it does this is most instructive from the point of view of designing our own flexible, general-purpose functions.

Because bsearch does not know what type of data is to be sorted, it must not do anything that depends on the characteristics of particular data types. For example, it cannot contain a statement such as

```
if (A[M] < key) {
```

as used in Listing 19-1, because the compiler, when compiling bsearch, will not know what type of data is being compared by the < test (int? float? something else?) and therefore cannot write correct machine code. The solution adopted is to make the caller of bsearch supply the comparison function for the particular type of data being searched. bsearch is called as follows.

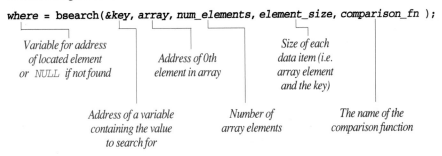

The comparison function compares two data items and returns a negative, zero, or positive value, depending on whether the first item is earlier, the same, or later in the sorting sequence, than the second. To use bsearch, we must write this comparison function, and it must have the following function definition:

```
int function_name(const void *first, const void *second );
```

The function accepts pointers to two data items, not the two items themselves — after all, bsearch knows nothing about our data items, not even the number of memory bytes they occupy. To pass the actual values, bsearch would have to know this crucial fact. However, all pointer values can be correctly converted to and from the void pointer type, no matter what they point at, so passing void pointers is feasible. It means, though, that we have to take the care to write the comparison function correctly. For example, the following is a comparison function for floats.

```
int floatcmp(const void *first, const void *second) {
    if (*(float*)first < *(float*)second) {
        return -1;
    } else {
        return (*(float*)first) > (*(float*)second);
    }
}
```

For each void* argument (first or second), the function first uses a cast ((float*)) to convert the void* to a float*, and then dereferences this with the 'follow-the-pointer' operator, * to obtain the actual float to be compared. With a similar function for int comparisons, Listing 19-2 uses bsearch to search the same array for the same values as in Listing 19-1

Listing 19-2

```
#include <stdio.h>
#include <stdlib.h>      /* for bsearch */

int intcmp(const void *first, const void *second) {
    if (*(int*)first < *(int*)second) {
        return -1;
    } else {
        return (*(int*)first) > (*(int*)second);
    }
}

int test[] = {1,1,3,5,5,6,8,9,9};
#define numb 9

main() {
    int i, *where;
    for (i=0; i<numb; i++) {
        printf("A[%d]=%d ", i, test[i]);
    }
    putchar('\n');
    for (i=0; i<=10; i++) {
        where = (int*)bsearch(&i, test, numb, sizeof(int), intcmp);
        if (where != NULL) {  /* Test for item i found. */
            printf("Seeking %2d, found at j=%2d:\n", i, where - test);
        } else {
            printf("Seeking %2d, NOT found\n", i);
        }
    }
    return 0;
}
```

The bsearch call in Listing 19-2 may be analyzed as follows:

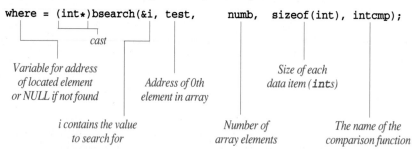

Also, note how the printf call converts the returned pointer (where) into an array index — it subtracts from where the pointer to the start of the array (i.e. the array name, test).

Test run

```
A[0]=1 A[1]=1 A[2]=3 A[3]=5 A[4]=5 A[5]=6 A[6]=8 A[7]=9 A[8]=9
Seeking  0, NOT found
Seeking  1, found at j= 1:
Seeking  2, NOT found
Seeking  3, found at j= 2:
Seeking  4, NOT found
Seeking  5, found at j= 4:
Seeking  6, found at j= 5:
Seeking  7, NOT found
Seeking  8, found at j= 6:
Seeking  9, found at j= 7:
Seeking 10, NOT found
```

Note that we cannot report where missing items belong, as we did with Listing 19-1, because bsearch returns NULL for items not found. Also, when items are found, we are not guaranteed that bsearch will find the first occurrence, as the test run shows.

Lastly, since bsearch searches an array starting at element zero, in order to search a piece of an array where the lower subscript is not zero, we must give bsearch the address of the first element we are interested in. For example, in Listing 19-2, if we had wished to search test only from test[3] to test[7], we could have written the bsearch call as

```
where = (int*)bsearch(&i, test + 3, 5, sizeof(int), intcmp);
```

19.3.3 Writing your own version of bsearch (optional)

For readers interested in knowing how bsearch is programmed to avoid all assumptions about the data being sorted, this section presents a function, oursearch, to the same specifications. If you are studying C as a first programming language, you may find it difficult to write a function of this nature yourself; however, don't be deterred from trying to follow this example. The function heading will be

```
void *oursearch(
    const void *key,       /* address of key to be found */
    const void *array,     /* address of start of array */
    size_t numb,           /* no. of elements of array to search */
    size_t elt_size,       /* size of each element */
    int (*compar)(const void *first, const void *second)
                           /* comparison fn */
);
```

The datatype size_t is explained in Section 12.3.1, and const in Section 18.6. The declaration for compar can be understood from the principles explained in Section 13.5 (Complicated C Declarations) — remember that the name of a function is the function's address (a pointer).

oursearch will be an adaptation of binsearch from Listing 19-1; the indices L, U, and M can be used as before. The main problem is the if test:

```
if (A[M] < key) {
```

In Listing 19-1, A was an array of the correct type, so the subscripting was done correctly by the C compiler. But now `array` is a `void` pointer, so the compiler does not know how big each array element is and we will have to figure out the subscripting arithmetic ourselves. If each element is `elt_size` bytes long, then the Mth element must start at address

```
((char*)array) + M * elt_size
```

The cast to `(char*)` is needed because `M * elt_size` is the number of characters, or bytes, from the start of the array. Using this as the address of element M, and remembering to call `compar` for the < test, we obtain

```
if (compar(key, ((char*)array) + M * elt_size) > 0) {
```

Finally, the specification of `bsearch` states that `NULL` shall be returned if the element is not found. Thus we should also test whether we have really found the required `key` rather than merely testing for greater than or equal. The function is shown in Listing 19-3. For the test run, we can use the same `main` function as in Listing 19-2, but with `bsearch` changed to `oursearch`; the output is identical to that from Listing 19-2.

Listing 19-3

```c
#include <stddef.h>

void *oursearch(
    const void *key,        /* address of key to be found */
    const void *array,      /* address of start of array */
    size_t numb,            /* no. of elements of array to search */
    size_t elt_size,        /* size of each element */
    int (*compar)(const void *first, const void *second) /* comparison fn */
) {
    int L = 0, U = numb - 1, M, status;
    while (L <= U) {
        M = (L + U) / 2; /* M must be in range L...U (property of mean) */
        status = compar(key, ((char*)array) + M * elt_size);
        if (status > 0) {
            L = M + 1;
        } else if (status == 0) {
            return ((char*)array) + M * elt_size;   /* address of element */
        } else {
            U = M - 1;
        }
    }
    return NULL;                            /* Key not found */
}
```

As the test run produces correct output, we might hope it is correct. But we have not verified this, and a change might have invalidated the previous verification for Listing 19-1. (See the Self-test Exercises.)

19.4 SORTING

Sorting is a common processing task. For example, an array must be sorted in order to perform binary searches on it. Most simple sorting methods, such as insertion sort and bubble sort (see Chapters 9 and 11) are very inefficient. They are in fact $O(n^2)$ algorithms, which is bad because the work needed increases according to the square of the number of items to be sorted. Suppose 1000 items can be sorted in 0.001 seconds: then 10,000 items will need 0.1 second, 100,000 items 10 seconds, 1,000,000 items 1000 seconds, etc. For large jobs this is obviously unacceptable.

The reason that simple sorts are inefficient is because they effectively compare every item with every, or nearly every, other. To measure the efficiency precisely, the detailed algorithm of a particular sort should be analyzed. For example, in bubble sort (see function `sort_data` in Listing 11-2), the largest item is bubbled to the top ($n-1$ comparisons), then the second largest is bubbled to the second-top ($n-2$ comparisons), etc., until the second-smallest item is in the second position. This is $(n-1) + (n-2) + ... + 2 + 1$ comparisons, which sums to $n^2/2$ comparisons (although stopping early if the list is found to be sorted can save some of these); ignoring the division by 2, bubble sort has $O(n^2)$ efficiency. This is true of all other simple sorting methods.

To find better sorting algorithms, it is interesting to compare bubble sort with linear search. Linear search plods along looking at one element at a time; after each inspection, the section still to be inspected is just one item shorter. Similarly, with bubble sort, one item at a time is relocated and the remaining unsorted section is just one item shorter. Binary search is better than linear search because, after each inspection, the amount left to search is only half its previous length. So whereas linear search is $O(n)$, binary search is $O(\log n)$. Can we do something like this with a sorting algorithm? In other words, can we find a way to divide the list in half with each step? Each step will still involve looking at every item, because every item must be placed in its proper place, so we will expect our improved sort to give $O(n.\log n)$ efficiency (for each of the n items, $\log n$ comparisons are needed to locate it correctly).

This would be a huge improvement. Taking that figure of 0.001 seconds for sorting 1000 items again, and assuming $O(n.\log n)$ efficiency, we would expect 10,000 items to require 0.0133... seconds, 100,000 to require 0.1666... seconds, and 1,000,000 items to require 2 seconds, which is much better than before. All advanced sorting methods are based on this divide-and-conquer strategy. There are many ways to actually do the subdivision, and each gives rise to a distinct sorting method. Here are two:

Merge sort: Split the list in two, sort the two halves separately, and then merge them together to form a sorted whole. The 'sort the two halves' steps are performed by recursive execution of the algorithm on each half.

Quick sort: Choose one particular element at random and put it in its final, correct position. Then place all other elements on their correct side of this particular element. The list will then have three parts: (1) all elements that belong before the chosen element, (2) the chosen element, and (3) all elements that belong after the chosen element. If the randomly chosen element falls somewhere near the middle, parts (1) and (3) of the original list constitute two unsorted lists of roughly half the original size. By recursively sorting these two lists the entire list is sorted.

19.4.1 Example: Quick sort

We shall write a quick sort for sorting floats. The algorithm has two steps: dividing the array in two as described in the previous section, and then quick sorting the two subdivisions, as in Listing 19-4a.

Listing 19-4a

```
int partition(float A[], int first, int last);

void quicksort(float A[], int first, int last) {
    int pivindx; /* index of the element separating the two sub-arrays */
    if (last > first) {  /* More than one element to be sorted? */
        pivindx = partition(A, first, last);
        quicksort(A, first, pivindx - 1);
        quicksort(A, pivindx + 1, last);
    }
}
```

The hard part is the partition function. This must (a) choose a random element called the pivot, (b) put it in its correct place, and (c) get all the smaller elements before the pivot and all the larger elements after. Steps (b) and (c) can be done simultaneously; indeed, the only way we know where the pivot should go is by sorting out the lesser and greater elements. This will be hard, so we must devise a loop invariant. We shall look at each element in turn: if it is less than the pivot, it will be placed before the pivot in the first section of the array; if it is not less, it will be placed in another section at the end of the array. Our invariant, presented as a diagram, will therefore be:

During the algorithm:

476

At the beginning, all elements except the pivot are unknown. We can therefore obtain the above diagrammatic invariant by placing the pivot in the first element, setting `pivindx` to `first`, and `top` to `last`:

At commencement:

At each step we should examine the element at position `top`. If `A[top]` is greater than or equal to the pivot, then it is already above the pivot where it belongs; simply decrement `top`. If it is less than the pivot, the pivot should be moved up one element to make room and `A[top]` should be placed before the pivot. The displaced element (from where the pivot has been put) should be put in the space now at `A[top]`. Eventually the unknown region shrinks to nothing, giving the following:

At the finish:

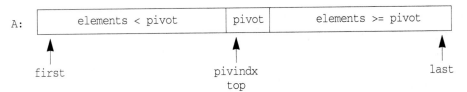

From this last diagram, we see that the loop finishes when `top` equals `pivindx`. Now we can program function `partition`, as in Listing 19-4b, which also includes a short `main` function for testing.

Listing 19-4b

```
#include <stdlib.h>      /* for rand() */

int partition(float A[], int first, int last) {
    int pivindx, top, i; float pivot;

    /* Choose a pivot: select a random index between first and last. */
    i = rand() % (last - first + 1) + first;

    /* Put the pivot first, remember pivot, initialize ready for loop. */
    pivot = A[i];                     /* remember the pivot */
    A[i] = A[first];
    A[first] = pivot;                 /* pivot now first */
    pivindx = first;
    top = last;                       /* invariant established */

    while (top > pivindx) {           /* Still unknown elements */
```

```
        /* top indicates the highest unknown element; examine */
        if (A[top] >= pivot) {
            top--;                          /* where it belongs, count as >= */
        } else {
            A[pivindx] = A[top];        /* shift down */
            A[top] = A[pivindx + 1];    /* shift displaced element up */
            A[pivindx + 1] = pivot;     /* Put pivot back */
            pivindx++;                  /* Alter record of pivot location */
        }
    }

    return pivindx;
}

#include <stdio.h>
float test[] = {9.9, 8.8, 8.5, 9.7, 8.8, 4.1, 9.9, 3.2, 4.6, 5.5};
#define size (10)

void info(void) {
    int i;
    for (i=0; i<size; i++) {
        printf("%3.1f ", test[i]);
    }
    putchar('\n');
}

main() {
    printf("Before: "); info();
    quicksort(test, 0, size - 1);
    printf("After:  "); info();
    return 0;
}
```

Test run
```
Before: 9.9 8.8 8.5 9.7 8.8 4.1 9.9 3.2 4.6 5.5
After:  3.2 4.1 4.6 5.5 8.5 8.8 8.8 9.7 9.9 9.9
```

19.4.2 Using the library qsort function

Like bsearch, the function qsort is designed to work with any type of data, and a similar type of usage is required: we must write a comparison function, and give qsort its name. A call to qsort has the following form:

```
qsort(
    array_name, number_of_elements,
    size_of_each_element, comparison_fn
);
```

To illustrate a slightly different sorting problem we shall sort a list of names, which requires a string comparison. We shall have an array of pointers to the individual strings, which can be of any length. qsort will be required to sort that array of pointers to strings. Unfortunately strcmp will not be suitable as the sorting function because of the extra level of addressing (address of address of char instead of address of char). Therefore we must write a short comparison function with the appropriate argument types: internally, it simply calls strcmp after using the * operator before each argument to get rid of that extra level of addressing. This program is shown in Listing 19-5.

Listing 19-5

```
#include <stdio.h>
#include <stdlib.h>          /* for qsort */
#include <string.h>

char *names[] = {   /* An array of pointers to string literals */
    "Mary",
    "Billy",
    "Zoe",
    "Peter",
    "Nigel",
    "Sandeep",
    "Alison"
};

int textcmp(const void *a, const void *b) {
    return strcmp(*(const char **)a, *(const char **)b);
}

main() {
    int i;
    const int count = sizeof names / sizeof names[0]; /* no. of elements */
    qsort(names, count, sizeof names[0], textcmp);
    for (i=0; i<7; i++) {
        printf("%s\n", names[i]);
    }
    return 0;
}
```

There is one new feature here: the sizeof operator is used to find the size of an array and the size of one of its elements. When using sizeof to measure the size of a variable (as opposed to the size of a type) leave out the parentheses. That is, write sizeof(*type*) but write sizeof *variable*.

Test run
```
Alison
Billy
Mary
Nigel
Peter
Sandeep
Zoe
```

19.5 CONCLUSION

Although this chapter has introduced few new features of C, you will probably agree that by combining some of the more difficult features of C, some of the examples are harder to follow than those in earlier chapters. This illustrates a major challenge to C programmers: C is such a powerful language that it is easy to write highly condensed but impenetrable programs. The goal should be to use the power but keep the program as simple as possible. In every aspect of computing — data structures, object-oriented programming, systems analysis and design, database, and so on — complexity threatens to overwhelm us. The winning strategy remains the same: be smart, keep it simple.

19.6 SUMMARY

- Algorithm efficiency, expressed in the $O(...)$ notation, indicates how the time taken by an algorithm increases with increased problem size. The variable n is the number of items the algorithm is applied to.
- Searching is the process of locating a particular value, the *key*, in a collection of values:
    - *linear* search is an $O(n)$ method
    - *binary* search is an $O(\log n)$ method
    - *hashing* can be an $O(1)$ method
    - the standard library function, `bsearch`, performs a binary search.
- Sorting is the process of arranging values in order according to some ordering function, such as 'less-than' for numbers, or alphabetic order for strings.
    - insertion and bubble sorts are $O(n^2)$ methods
    - quick sort is an $O(n.\log n)$ method
    - the standard library function, `qsort`, performs a quick sort.
- The `sizeof` operator can take a variable or expression as its operand, as in:

    `sizeof some_variable`

19.7 SELF-TEST EXERCISES

Short Answer

1 Devise an invariant for the loop in Listing 19-3, and show whether the function is correct.

2 After writing `oursearch` (Section 19.3.3), I looked at my C compiler's library source for `bsearch`, and found to my horror that, although it basically paralleled the logic in `oursearch`, it used a `do...while` loop instead of the correct `while` loop (see Chapter 4, for reasons why `do...while` is nearly always wrong). Explain the conditions under which my C compiler's `bsearch` function will produce an incorrect result.

Programming

3 *Shell sort* is a version of a bubble sort, modified for improved efficiency. The idea is that, while the array is still far from being sorted, exchange elements that are far apart instead of exchanging adjacent elements. If, as is probable, items are far from their correct place, this will probably move them closer more rapidly than if they were shifted one cell at a time. In more detail, the algorithm is:

```
Set gap to half the number of items.
while gap >= 1:
    do
        Set not_sorted to false.
        Make a pass through the array, testing item i with item i+gap;
        if wrongly ordered, exchange and set not_sorted to true.
    while still not_sorted.
    Divide gap by 2.
```

Write a program that uses Shell sort to sort an array. Test it thoroughly.

19.8 TEST QUESTIONS

Short Answer

1 Listing 19-4b shows a `partition` function for `quicksort` which keeps the `pivot` in an element of the array while it orders the other items. Since the pivot also has a variable of its own, this is inefficient. Modify the algorithm so that its efficiency is increased and the pivot is stored in only one place during the loop.

2 Believe it or not, there have actually been contests to design the most **in**efficient algorithms for performing various tasks. A problem in one of these contests was to find a bad algorithm for the `bsearch` function. One algorithm submitted in the contest was to perform a linear search on the first item; if the key is not found, perform a linear search on the first two items; if still not found, do a linear search

on the first three, and so on, until the item is found, or the final linear search of all items reveals that the item is absent. In $O()$ notation, estimate the efficiency of this search.

3   Another problem in the contest mentioned in question 2 was to rewrite the qsort algorithm. One entrant suggested finding all permutations of the values being sorted, using an algorithm that is linear per permutation; each permutation should be checked to see if it is in ascending order; if not, continue until a sorted order is found. In $O()$ notation, estimate the efficiency of this algorithm.

4   In the main text, the invariant and postcondition for the loop in Listing 19-4b are given as pictures. Write them in English or mathematical notation, and then verify the loop using the five-point checklist given in Chapter 4.

5   The following is another version of the intcmp function in Listing 19-2. Describe how it works and explain the conditions under which it will fail to work correctly.

```
int intcmp(const void *first, const void *second) {
    return (*(int*)first) - (*(int*)second);
}
```

Programming

6   One problem with the faster sorting methods is that, for very small arrays, their complexity can be a bigger time-waster than just doing things the slow and simple way. Rewrite quicksort to use a bubble sort if the array size is less than 20, and the full quick sort method otherwise.

7   By inserting statements that count comparisons and interchanges, compare the efficiency of shell sort (see Self-test Exercises) at various array sizes with bubble sort and quick sort.

APPENDIX A
Answers to self-test exercises

This appendix contains answers to the Short Answer questions in the Self-test Exercises; solutions to programming questions are supplied on the disk which is available to accompany this book.

Chapter 1

1 (c), 2 (c), 3 (b), 4 (d), 5 (d), 6 (a), 7 (d).

Chapter 2

1
```
printf("Computers are powerful\n");
printf("but we must know the rules\n");
```

2
```
printf("Computers are powerful\nbut we must know the rules\n");
```

Chapter 3

1   The value is not stored correctly. The program will print garbage or otherwise malfunction.

2   The `char` could be 0 for Sunday, 1 for Monday, etc.

3   One might encode the suit as a number from 0 to 3, and the card value as another `int`, with Jack equal to 11, etc.

4   Prints a Z alone on a line. Better compilers warn that the `char xx` in `func` is assigned a value that is never used.

5   `a += b;    b -= c;    ww /= 5.8;`

6   `a = a + 23;    sbc = sbc - (a+4);    q = q + 1;`
`r = r / 2;    z = 1;    i = 0;`

Chapter 4

1   `while (k != j) {`

2   The 'test' assigns 7 to z; 7 is the 'result' of this operation, so the loop always regards the test as true and thus repeats indefinitely.

3   `j = j + 1;    j += 1;    j++;`

4   `while (state_tax >= 7) {`

```
5   for (j = k + 6; j >= k; j = j - 2) {
        . . .
    }
```

6   The checks need no alteration.

Chapter 5

1   The computer waits for the user to enter data. It then skips any whitespace, processes as much data as can be interpreted as an `int` value, and assigns that value to the variable `intvar`.

2   a   Probably incorrect, unless the program has previously stored a legitimate format in `car`; even then, that format would have to contain no specifications which store data in variables, such as `%d`, because there are no other variables in the call.

   b   Correct.

   c   Should be incorrect, as `car` is already an address, but a quirk in the definition of C allows this to mean exactly the same as (b).

   d   Correct.

   e   Incorrect; `car` may overflow by one character (the nul).

   f   Incorrect; the `%d` format will try to store a binary integer in the first few elements of `car`.

   g   Incorrect; no `&`.

   h   Correct.

   i   Correct.

   j   Correct.

   k   Incorrect; tries to store an `int` in a `float`.

   l   Correct.

   m   Correct.

3   Issue a prompt.

4   (d)

5   `scanf, gets, getchar`

6   A prompt is a message telling the user what data the computer wishes to input.

7   `char eight[9];`

8   `scanf("%c%d", &bzzt, &mzlfmph);`

Chapter 6

```
1   if (i == 5) {
        k = 8;
    } else if (j == 7 && k < 13) {
        printf("hello");
    }
```

```
2  switch (k) {
   case 2:
   case 4:
       printf("hello");
       break;
   case 7:
       j = 67;
       break;
   default:
       m = 72;
   }
```

3 Logically, the switch statement can always be replaced by an if, but often it may not be convenient.

4 && evaluates to 0 if either operand is 0, and to 1 if both operands are non-zero; if the first operand is zero, the second is not evaluated.

|| evaluates to 1 if either operand is non-zero, and to 0 if both operands are zero; if the first operand is non-zero, the second is not evaluated.

5 0

6 1

7 k = (k != 0);

8 alert = pressure > 120 && ! yellow_alert ||
           yellow_alert && (pressure > 100 || temperature > 350);

Chapter 7

1 (a) true, (b) false, (c) false, (d) true, (e) true, (f) true, (g) false, (h) true, (i) false, (j) true normally, but see Appendix C.2.6 regarding writing functions with variable numbers of parameters.

2 (a) true, (b) false, (c) false, (d) false, (e) false, (f) true, (g) false, (h) true.

3 Prints 6.

4 Prints 13, and then 14.

Chapter 8

1 (b)

2 (b)

3 (a) false, (b) false, (c) true, (d) true if you want an easy life!

Chapter 9

1   a   Legal, but there will be no room for the nul after 'there', so the second row will not contain a valid string.

     b   Legal.

     c   Illegal; we may only omit the first array subscript.

     d   Legal.

     e   Illegal; see (c).

     f   Legal.

     g   Illegal; last array element is `x[5]`.

     h   Legal.

     i   Illegal; cannot fit three values in a two-element array.

     j   Legal.

Chapter 10

```
1  a   f = fopen("fred", "r");
   b   fgets(buffer, 20, f);
   c   fscanf(f, "%19s", buffer);
   d   fgets(buffer, 20, stdin);
   e   fscanf(stdin, "%19s", buffer);
   f   fscanf(f, "%f", &r);
   g   j = fscanf(f, "%d", &i);
   h   g = fopen("sue", "w");
   i   fprintf(g, "%10s", buffer);
   j   fprintf(stdout, "%s", buffer);
```

2   Limits to a maximum of 60 the number of characters of name that are printed.

Chapter 11

```
1  typedef struct {
       int size; char name[50];
   } structype;

   structype strucvar;

   structype func(void) {
       structype st;
       fgets(st.name, 49, stdin);
       st.size = strlen(st.name);
       return st;
   }

   strucvar = func();
```

```
2  struct {
       int i; float f;
   } first[50];

   struct {
       int i; float f[50];
   } second;
3  vector2 vec2(float a, float b) {
       vector2 v2;
       v2.x = a; v2.y = b;
       return v2;
   }
```

To include in the library, add the above function to the file `vector2.c`, and add the following declaration to the file `vector2.h`:

```
vector2 vec2(float a, float b);
```

4 (a) true, (b) false, (c) false, (d) false, (e) true.

Chapter 12

1 Reads up to 40 non-newline `chars` into `rep1` (i.e. stops at the end of line), then reads any number of non-newline characters and throws them away. The next character must be a newline, so the `getchar` reads and discards it. In brief, the first (maximum) 80 characters of a line are read into `rep1`, and the rest of the line is read and discarded.

2 quick brown fox jumped over the lazy d

   0

3 (The)(quick)(brown)(fox)(jumped)(over)(the)(lazy)(dog)

Chapter 13

1 Incorrect `free`s are A (chp1 does not point to `malloc`ed memory), C (ditto for chp3), and D (attempt to `free` memory twice).

2
```
double *dubarr; int size;
scanf("%d", &size);
dubarr = (double*)malloc(sizeof(double) * size);
```

3
```
float *arr[5]; int i;
arr[0] = (float*)malloc(sizeof(float) * 15);
if (arr[0] != NULL) {
    for (i=1; i<5; i++) {
        arr[i] = arr[i-1] + i;
    }
}
```

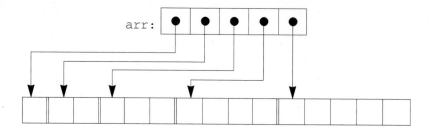

4   A 1, B 3 (should be `10 * sizeof(float)`), C 1, D 1, E 1, F 2 (the pointer in `ip` no longer points at allocated memory, and so is useless, but it is legal to copy it), G 3 (it is not correct to store data in deallocated memory).

5   a   `void (*func)(float f, int ia[]);`
    b   `void *func(float f, int ia[]);`
    c   `char *func(float *f, int ia[]);`
    d   `void (*arr[10])(void);`
    e   `typedef struct {int i; float *fp;} tstr;`
       `tstr tstrar[20];`

6   `del_pt` can free the node indicated by its parameter `which`, but then it has no way of knowing which node preceded that one (because there is no way to know which node points to a given node), and so it cannot then make that previous node point to the subsequent one.

Chapter 14

1   The version of `sumarray` in the question makes a recursive call for only one fewer elements than the original call, but in Listing 14-2, each recursive call is for only around half the number of elements. By halving the number on each call, Listing 14-2 has many fewer nested recursive calls, and so is less likely to run out of memory for large arrays.

Chapter 15

1   We must be able to create and destroy arrays, and to access individual elements. At a bare minimum, then, we need four functions in an array ADT; these use the type ARRAY, which should be defined in the implementation:

```
/**** array_create ****
On entry: size is the number of elements needed in the array.
On exit:  returns a pointer to an array, or NULL.
*/
ARRAY * array_create(int size);

/**** array_free ****
On entry: arr is a pointer to an array.
On exit:  The array has been freed.
*/
void array_free(ARRAY * arr);

/**** array ****
On entry: arr is an ARRAY, n is the index of the required element.
On exit:  Returns the value of the selected element.
*/
float array(ARRAY * arr, int n);

/**** array_set ****
On entry: arr is an ARRAY, n is the index of an element.
On exit:  Element n of arr has been assigned the value f.
*/
void array_set(ARRAY * arr, int n, float f);
```

Chapter 16

1 a int, signed int
   b long double
   c long, long int, signed long int, signed long
   d float
   e signed short, short
   f char
   g unsigned, unsigned int
   h unsigned char
   i double
   j unsigned short
   k unsigned long int, unsigned long
   l signed char

2 a 8L
   b 8u
   c 8LU
   d 8L
   e 8

3 (a) `long`, (b) `long`, (c) `int`, (d) `int`, (e) `double`, (f) `long double`,
   (g) `long`.

4 (a) "`%c`", (b) "`%d`", (c) "`%d`", (d) "`%u`", (e) "`%ld`", (f) "`%lu`", (g) "`%f`",
   (h) "`%f`", (i) "`%Lf`".

Chapter 17

1 (a) false, (b) false, (c) false, (d) false, (e) false, (f) false, (g) true, (h) false.

Chapter 18

1 `static const int fred = 278;`

2 `const double dub = -826.776;`

3 `const double *pdub;`
(pdub may be made to point to dub with an assignment: `pdub = &dub;`)

Chapter 19

1 This loop is tricky because it has two exits (the `return` within the loop, and the normal loop termination). At normal termination, the search has failed, so the postcondition is

key not present.

If present, *key* is between L and U, so the invariant is

array[0]...array[L–1] all < key, array[U+1]...array[numb–1] all > key.

The loop terminates for the same reason as in Listing 19-1. The invariant is established at the start because both ranges are empty. If the comparison yields > or <, an iteration of the loop re-establishes the invariant for the same reason as before, so on loop termination, *L>U* and therefore all elements are either less than, or greater than, the key, and so the item is not present. Thus normal termination establishes the postcondition. If the comparison is ==, the item is obviously found, so returning its address must be correct. Thus the loop is correct for both exit points.

2 By using `do...while`, the writers of my compiler's `bsearch` function forgot that the caller might ask for a search of zero elements. Their algorithm always searches one element of the array for the key, and, if the item at position zero matches the key, it will be 'found' when it shouldn't.

APPENDIX B
Sample sessions

This appendix presents some sample sessions compiling programs under Unix and DOS.

B.1 COMPILING C PROGRAMS UNDER UNIX

These sample sessions use the gcc C compiler, which is available for most computers running Unix.

Session 1: A self-contained program

The following session compiles and runs Listing 4-6, which is a self-contained program (i.e. consists of a single source file) that uses the maths library functions.

```
1% gcc lst4-6.c -lm
2% a.out
A one-metre long object contracts to:
0.994987 metre at 0.1 of the speed of light
0.979796 metre at 0.2 of the speed of light
0.953939 metre at 0.3 of the speed of light
0.916515 metre at 0.4 of the speed of light
0.866025 metre at 0.5 of the speed of light
0.800000 metre at 0.6 of the speed of light
0.714143 metre at 0.7 of the speed of light
0.600000 metre at 0.8 of the speed of light
0.435890 metre at 0.9 of the speed of light
3%
```

In the above, the number followed by % is the prompt; for example, 1% is the prompt to the programmer for the first command in the session. The typed command after 1% invokes the gcc compiler to compile lst4-6.c, and link to form an executable program. The -lm tells gcc to link in the maths library; this is only necessary for programs that need to include <math.h>. By default gcc creates an executable program called a.out, so command 2% invokes the program created by command 1%.

Session 2: A program requiring two source files

Listings 18-1 and 18-2 together form a single program; the following session compiles and runs this combined program:

```
3% gcc lst18-1.c lst18-2.c
4% a.out
Calling locfunc from main in lst18-1.c...
    Inside locfunc in lst18-1.c
    storing 88 in loc
Calling globfunc from main...
    Inside the globfunc in lst18-2.c
    Calling locfunc...
        Inside the locfunc in lst18-2.c
        Storing 77 in loc and 99 in glob
    Leaving globfunc; loc = 77, glob = 99...
Back in main; loc = 88, glob = 99
5% mv a.out lst18-1
6% lst18-1
Calling locfunc from main in lst18-1.c...
    Inside locfunc in lst18-1.c
    storing 88 in loc
Calling globfunc from main...
    Inside the globfunc in lst18-2.c
    Calling locfunc...
        Inside the locfunc in lst18-2.c
        Storing 77 in loc and 99 in glob
    Leaving globfunc; loc = 77, glob = 99...
Back in main; loc = 88, glob = 99
7%
```

Command 3% compiles both source files and links; -lm is not included as the program uses no <math.h> functions. Command 4% runs the resultant program. Command 5% uses the Unix mv command to rename the executable program to a more explanatory name, and command 6% proves that the renaming operation occurred correctly.

When developing programs with multiple source files, it often happens that a bug is discovered in one source file, while the others are correct. Suppose this happened with lst18-1. After editing lst18-1, we would need to recompile; lst18-2, however, was correct, and has already been compiled. The following command will recompile just lst18-1, using the compiled object file for lst18-2 from the previous compilation.

```
3% gcc lst18-1.c lst18-2.o
```

This uses the .o (object) file for lst18-2 created in command 3%. The reason we try to avoid recompiling is that, for large programs, we can save a lot of time. A special program, make, is available to automate this process; make decides which object files are out of date, and recompiles only as much as necessary.

Finally, we sometimes want to compile a C source file to make an object file, but do not wish to link this into an executable program. This might happen if we had a library (such as `helpadt.c` from Listing 17-7), that we wish to link into many different programs. This can be done with the $-c$ option of `gcc`:

```
8% gcc helpadt.c -c
```

This command creates a file, **helpadt.o**, for linking with other object files. Now **lst17-8.c** uses the help functions, so to compile and link that program we would type

```
9% gcc lst17-8.c helpadt.o
```

There are specialized commands in Unix for creating and using function libraries, but the method shown here is easy to follow and should be quite adequate for small to medium programs.

B.2 COMPILING C PROGRAMS UNDER DOS

Giving sample sessions for DOS presents a dilemma because many different C compilers are available, and no two seem to work the same way. These sample sessions use the Power C compiler, which is available at a modest cost.

Session 1: A self-contained program

The following session compiles and runs Listing 4-6, which is a self-contained program (i.e. consists of a single source file) that uses the maths library functions. The DOS prompt is `C:\CBOOK>`.

```
C:\CBOOK>pc/e lst4-6
Power C - Version 2.0.0
(C) Copyright 1989 by Mix Software
Compiling ...
   208 lines compiled
Optimizing ...
     1 function optimized in 1 file
Linking ...
lst4-6.EXE created

C:\CBOOK>lst4-6
A one-metre long object contracts to:
0.994987 metre at 0.1 of the speed of light
0.979796 metre at 0.2 of the speed of light
0.953939 metre at 0.3 of the speed of light
0.916515 metre at 0.4 of the speed of light
0.866025 metre at 0.5 of the speed of light
0.800000 metre at 0.6 of the speed of light
0.714143 metre at 0.7 of the speed of light
0.600000 metre at 0.8 of the speed of light
0.435890 metre at 0.9 of the speed of light

C:\CBOOK>
```

Session 2: A program requiring two source files

Listings 18-1 and 18-2 together form a single program; the following session compiles and runs this combined program:

```
C:\CBOOK>pc/e lst18-1 lst18-2
Power C - Version 2.0.0
(C) Copyright 1989 by Mix Software
Compiling ...
  286 lines compiled
Optimizing ...
    4 functions optimized in 2 files
Linking ...
lst18-1.EXE created

C:\CBOOK>lst18-1
Calling locfunc from main in lst18-1.c...
    Inside locfunc in lst18-1.c
    storing 88 in loc
Calling globfunc from main...
    Inside the globfunc in lst18-2.c
    Calling locfunc...
        Inside the locfunc in lst18-2.c
        Storing 77 in loc and 99 in glob
    Leaving globfunc; loc = 77, glob = 99...
Back in main; loc = 88, glob = 99

C:\CBOOK>
```

When developing programs with multiple source files, it often happens that a bug is discovered in one source file, while the others are correct. Suppose this happened with lst18-1. After editing lst18-1, we would need to recompile; lst18-2, however, was correct, and has already been compiled. Power C automatically detects which files are out of date, so the following line will recompile only as much as necessary to build an up-to-date executable file:

```
C:\CBOOK>pc/e lst18-1 lst18-2
```

Finally, we sometimes want to compile a C source file to make an object file, but do not wish to link this into an executable program. This might happen if we had a library (such as helpadt.c from Listing 17-7), that we wish to link into many different programs. This can be done as follows:

```
C:\CBOOK>pc helpadt
```

This command creates a file, helpadt.mix, for linking with other object files. (The Power C compiler's object files end with the .MIX extension; most DOS compilers produce files with a .OBJ extension.) lst17-8.c uses the stack functions, so to compile and link that program we would type:

```
C:\CBOOK>pc/e lst17-8 helpadt
```

Most other DOS compilers have an 'integrated environment', that is, they operate using windows and menus, and usually have a built-in help system. It is impractical to illustrate such systems here (but their manuals and built-in help are usually very good), but all compilers use the same basic compile-and-link sequence, so the same tasks must be performed somehow. Provided you understand the compilation process, it is usually straightforward to work out how to make it happen in one of the 'integrated' compilers. Just one hint: some compilers use a 'project file' for the more complex compilations (i.e. more than one source file). The project file specifies the various components of the final executable program, and is usually set up within the integrated environment.

APPENDIX C
Additional C language features

C.1 ADDITIONAL STATEMENT TYPES

C.1.1 goto *statements and labels*

The goto statement causes the program execution flow to be transferred to another place within the current function. That place is marked by a label (an identifier followed by a colon), as in the following example:

```
#include <stdio.h>
main () {
    printf("Here\n");
    goto thar;
    printf("There\n");           (Execution skips this printf statement.)
thar:
    printf("Everywhere\n");
}
```

which, when executed, produces the printout:

```
Here
Everywhere
```

The goto statement was omitted from the main text because, even though it might get us out of a difficult situation once in a while, it usually makes programs convoluted and difficult to verify for correctness.

C.1.2 break *statements in loops*

In Chapter 6, the break statement was used to terminate options in the switch statement. It can also terminate the execution of a loop (while, for, or do...while). Like the goto statement, this can lead to convoluted programs, but in moderation it can be handy, especially where a loop logically should perform a single task per iteration, but the termination condition is discovered part-way through the task. For example, to repeatedly read a number, double it, and print it, until the entered number is zero, we could use a break as follows:

```
#include <stdio.h>
main () {
    float num;
    for (;;) {  ◄─────────────────── (Infinite loop: no termination test.)
        printf("Enter number ");
        scanf("%f", &num);
        if (num == 0) {
            break;  ─────────────────────────────┐  (Jumps to the
        }                                         │   statement after
        printf("Double that is %6.4f\n", 2. * num);  │   the end of the
    }                                             │   loop.)
    printf("Finished\n");  ◄──────────────────────┘
}
```

This program will execute as follows:

```
Enter number 8.9
Double that is 17.8000
Enter number -1.1
Double that is -2.2000
Enter number 0
Finished
```

C.1.3 `continue` *statements*

The `continue` statement, which must only be used inside loops, jumps to the end of, but still inside, the loop. That is, the loop body terminates, but the loop still repeats (provided the loop test is passed). It is equivalent to using `goto` to jump to a label at the end of, but still inside, the loop.

C.1.4 *Empty statements*

The empty statement does nothing; it is written as nothing followed by a semicolon. It is commonly seen when programmers omit braces. For example, to flush a line of input, a thoughtless programmer might write

```
while (getchar() != '\n') ;
                          ▲
                          └──────── (The empty statement.)
```

The trouble is that if the semicolon is accidentally omitted, the next statement in the function is included inside the loop. Since you should always make your intentions obvious, this is better written as:

```
while (getchar() != '\n') {
    /* empty */  ◄──────── (Comment makes the empty loop body obvious.)
}
```

makes `today` an integral variable c
`today` is probably `int`, but the comp
values are to be stored. We can contr(
for example,

```
enum fluff { first, second, thir
```

makes `first` equal 0, `second` equ
`fifth` equal 27.

Some programmers make heavy us
greatly improve readability, but ma
preprocessor directives instead.

C.2.5 The `volatile` type qualifier

When the compiler optimizes a progra
change if some statement in the proj
compiler to rearrange statements f(
program's meaning. For example, a
loop, instead of being written back ir
variables, however, can be altered s
actually be a register in a real-time clo(
If the compiler optimized such a vari
the time would fail. The keyword v
described in Section 18-6) prevents
variables; each program reference to
which the variable is stored.

There are some uses for this feature
low-level feature.

C.2.6 Functions with a variable numb

Functions such as `printf` and `sca`
write such a function, its heading mus

```
void printints(int n, ...);
```

[Note: in all other places in this book,
has been omitted; in this subsection, i
in the program.]

The above means that `printint`
variable number of arguments. There
the variable arguments. These var
`va_start`, `va_arg`, and `va_end`,
declared in the header file `<stdarg.`
function must itself detect how many
compiler and the operating system usu

Another use for the empty statement is to place a label just before a `}`:

```
    ...
    goto fin;
    ...
    fin: ;
}
```

C.2 ADDITIONAL FEATURES IN DECLARATIONS

C.2.1 The `auto` and `register` storage class specifiers

`auto` storage is the default method of storing variables declared within functions; that is, the variable is created upon block entry, and destroyed on block exit. Any initialization is performed at every creation. This is known as automatic storage duration (see Chapter 18), and contrasts with the `static` storage class, as shown by the following:

```
#include <stdio.h>
static void fred(void) {
    auto int i = 5; static int j = 5;
    printf("auto: %d, static: %d\n", i, j);
    i += 5; j += 5;
}
main () {
    fred();    fred();    fred();    fred();
}
```

The execution is:

```
auto: 5, static: 5
auto: 5, static: 10
auto: 5, static: 15
auto: 5, static: 20
```

The word `auto` can be omitted without changing the effect of the program; we have used `auto` declarations throughout the text without ever using the `auto` keyword.

`register` variables are `auto` variables that include the added hint to the compiler that they should work as fast as possible. It is not legal to take the address of a `register` variable. Most modern compilers perform a full analysis of program efficiency and decide how to optimize without requiring this hint. This reduces the usefulness of the `register` keyword.

C.2.2 Unions

A union is declared in a similar way to a st
the word `struct`. Like a structure, a uni
overlapping memory locations. Therefore,
the value in all the others (since they are i
for certain low-level programming tasks;
level programming covered in this text. T
structures; values supplied in an initializ
union only.

C.2.3 Bit-fields

Like unions, bit-fields are a low-level C fe
be allocated as a `signed` or `unsigned`

```
struct {
    unsigned b1 : 5;
    signed b2   : 3;
} pack;
```

creates a structure, `pack`, containing two b
five binary digits) and b2 (a `signed in`
could be packed within a single eight-bit
scope of this text.

C.2.4 Enumeration (enum) specifiers

Enumeration specifiers provide a conveni
For example, we might want to use the nu
readability, we wish to use the normal na
declare these as:

```
enum weekday { Sun, Mon, Tue, Wed, 
```

The first value in the list is 0, the second, 2

```
printf("%d", Tue);
```

prints 2. We can store these values in a vari
if it has sufficient range to hold the valu
variable automatically if we declare it usin

```
enum weekday today;
```

For example, `printints` in the following program requires the first argument to say how many `ints` are supplied as variable arguments, and it prints each one in stars.

```
#include <stdio.h>
#include <stdarg.h>

void printints(int n, ...) {
    int i;
    va_list args;         /* A special variable used to access the
                             variable arguments. */
    va_start(args, n);    /* Call to va_start MUST be first, before
                             trying to access the arguments. Its
                             parameters are the va_list variable, and
                             the parameter immediately before the three
                             dots. */
    for (i=0; i<n; i++) {
        printf("**%d**\n", va_arg(args, int));
                          /* Each call to va_arg returns another
                             argument; Parameters are the va_list
                             variable and the type of argument
                             expected. */
    }
    va_end(args);         /* 'Cleans up' the system; this call must
                             follow the final call to va_arg. */
}

main () {
    int j = 8;
    printints(5, 23, 86, -267, j + 2, 99);
}
```

The printout is:

```
**23**
**86**
**-267**
**10**
**99**
```

The calls to `va_start` and `va_end` must be located in the function with the varying number of arguments; the calls to `va_arg` may be in a nested function to which the `va_list` variable has been passed as a parameter.

C.3 ADDITIONAL OPERATORS

C.3.1. Bitwise operators (~, >>, <<, &, |, and ^)

These operators manipulate integral values bit-by-bit. While basically a low-level feature, there are some uses for these in high-level programs.

~ is a unary complement operator: it changes all one-bits to zero-bits, and vice versa. For example, ~A is the complement of A.

<< and >> are left-shift and right-shift operators. For example, A<<5 is the value formed by shifting the bits of A left five places and moving zero bits into the vacated positions.

&, | and ^ are bitwise **and**, **or**, and **exclusive-or** operators, respectively. The operation is performed individually on each pair of corresponding bits from the two operands, as in the following tables.

A & B	A 0	A 1
B 0	0	0
B 1	0	1

A | B	A 0	A 1
B 0	0	1
B 1	1	1

A ^ B	A 0	A 1
B 0	0	1
B 1	1	0

C.3.2 The conditional (? :) operator

This operator allows conditional evaluation of one of two alternative operands. It has the form:

test ? *expression1* : *expression2*

If the `test` expression is non-zero, `expression1` is evaluated, otherwise `expression2` is evaluated. It is used to write in briefer form statements that could have been written using normal `if` statements. Here are two ways to program the same test.

```
int found_it;
...
/* "if" method */
printf("We found ");
if (found_it) {
    printf("some ");
} else {
    printf("no ");
}
printf("items.\n");

/* ?: method: */
printf("We found %s items.\n", found_it ? "some" : "no");
```

C.3.3 Priority of all operators, and sequence points

The following table shows the priority of all C operators. Operators in the same category have the same priority.

Precedence	Type	Associativity	Operators
highest	Postfix		subscripts[] function calls() field.selection indirect->selection ++ −−
	unary prefix		++ −− sizeof ~ ! − + & ∗
	cast		(cast)
	multiplicative	left	∗ / %
	additive	left	+ −
	shift	left	<< >>
	inequality	left	< > <= >=
	equality	left	== !=
	bitwise and	left	&
	bitwise xor	left	^
	bitwise or	left	|
	logical and	left	&&
	logical or	left	||
	conditional	right	?:
	assignment	right	= += −= ∗= /= %= <<= >>= &= ^= |=
lowest	comma	left	,

The #pragma directive

This directive provides a way to pass information to specific compilers. Its format and meaning are not defined in the C standard.

The # and ## preprocessor operators

These operators are used in advanced parameterized #define directives (see subsection 18.5.3). # turns a parameter into a string, and ## glues two words into one. For example, the following program:

```
#define FORMAT(n)  "%" #n "s %d\n"
#define join(a,b)  a ## b
main () {
    int bigint = 8;
    printf(FORMAT(2), "hello", join(big, int));
}
```

is transformed by the preprocessor into:

```
main () {
    int bigint = 8;
    printf("%" "2" "s %d\n", "hello", bigint);
}
```

Predefined macro names

The following macro names must be defined in all ANSI C implementations:

__LINE__	The current source file line number, as a decimal constant.
__FILE__	The name of the current source file, as a string literal.
__DATE__	The date of compilation, as a string literal.
__TIME__	The time of compilation, as a string literal.
__STDC__	The constant 1, indicating that the compiler conforms to the standard. (This macro allows a program to find out if it was compiled by a modern standard C compiler, or not.)

These names should not be altered with #define or #undef.

C.5 RVALUES, LVALUES, ARRAYS AND POINTERS

The connection between arrays and pointers in the C language has been presented in a simplified way in the main text, but after you have gained proficiency with C, you may wish to understand this subject more fully.

C recognizes two kinds of things: objects and values. A value is a temporary thing that exists for the duration of an expression and then vanishes unless it is saved in an object. For example, an int variable is an object, and 5 is a value. Thus, i=5; stores the value 5 in the object i (assuming i was declared as an int). In this statement, i is an *lvalue* (where 'l' stands for the left hand side of an assignment) and the 5 is an *rvalue* (where 'r' stands for the right hand side of the assignment). Now in the assignment i=j; the j stands in an rvalue position. Therefore, the value in the object j is retrieved as the rvalue to be assigned to i. Any context in which a value is required is an rvalue context; these include the right side of assignments, loop and if tests, arguments to functions, etc.

We now come to a quirk in the design of C: almost every type of lvalue has a corresponding rvalue, except arrays. Thus, from a simple variable object we can retrieve a simple value; from a structure or union object we can retrieve a structure value or union value respectively. But from an array object, we cannot retrieve an array value: there are no array rvalues. Therefore, even if ia and ba are both arrays of the same type and with the same number of elements, we cannot write ia=ba; to copy one array to the other. C has an important rule: **whenever an array name occurs where an rvalue (but not an lvalue) is required, it is automatically changed into a pointer to the first element of the array** (i.e. element 0).

This means that we cannot pass an array to a function, because arguments are rvalues, and so any array parameter will be converted into a pointer to the first element. Therefore, all array formal parameters in function definitions actually stand for pointers. This is unfortunate because it leads many people to believe that arrays **are** pointers, which is **wrong**. Consider:

```
char buf[50];
void func(char chuf[50]){
    char duff[50];
    ...
```

The global buf and the local duff are both arrays; they are **not** pointers. But when we call func, perhaps with:

```
func(buf);
```

the array name buf is converted into a pointer to the first element of the array buf; that is, it is the same as if we called func as follows:

```
func(&buf[0]);
```

This means that the formal parameter chuf receives a pointer as the corresponding actual parameter. Because of this, the compiler treats all array formal parameters as pointers. Thus, func could have been declared:

```
void func(char *chuf){
```

Function formal parameters are the only place where an array declaration creates a pointer. All other declarations of arrays have nothing to do with pointers. This is proved by using an array name as an lvalue: no conversion to a pointer occurs. For example, if we wrote sizeof duff, we would find that it is 50 (the size of 50 characters), not the size of a char pointer. This is because the sizeof operator never evaluates its arguments: it uses them as lvalues only, and array lvalues are perfectly legitimate.

This is a difficult subject, so don't be too worried if you find it hard to follow. Many experts consider that the lack of array rvalues is a significant fault in the design of C.

Descriptions of frequently-used standard library functions and macros

This appendix contains short descriptions of most functions and some macros in the C standard libraries. Due to space restrictions, the descriptions here are sometimes not the entire story; a full C library manual should be consulted where accuracy is critical. The following standard functions are not described, as they are unlikely to be needed except in advanced or specialized applications:

```
setlocale localeconv signal raise freopen setbuf vfprintf vprintf
vsprintf realloc mblen mbtowc wctomb mbstowcs wcstombs strcoll
strxfrm strtok
```

Some functions are described in more detail elsewhere in the text, and so have abbreviated entries in this appendix.

D.1 COMMON DEFINITIONS (*include* `<stddef.h>`)

This header defines some standard macro names, which include:

ptrdiff_t	The integral type resulting from subtracting two pointers.
size_t	The integral type of the result of the `sizeof` operator.
NULL	The null pointer constant.
offsetof(*type, field*)	A `size_t` value giving the offset of the field `field` within a structure of type `type`.

D.2 CHARACTER HANDLING (*include* `<ctype.h>`)

`int isalnum(int c);`
   Returns true if `c` is alphabetic or a digit (alphanumeric).

`int isalpha(int c);`
   Returns true if `c` is alphabetic.

`int iscntrl(int c);`
   Returns true if `c` is a control character.

`int isdigit(int c);`
> Returns true if c is a digit.

`int isgraph(int c);`
> Returns true if c is any printable character except space.

`int islower(int c);`
> Normally returns true if c is alphabetic lower case.

`int isprint(int c);`
> Returns true if c is any printable character including space.

`int ispunct(int c);`
> Returns true if c is any printable character except space or an alphanumeric.

`int isspace(int c);`
> Returns true if c is a whitespace character.

`int isupper(int c);`
> Normally returns true if c is an upper case letter.

`int isxdigit(int c);`
> Returns true if c is any hexadecimal digit.

`int tolower(int c);`
> Converts c to lower case.

`int toupper(int c);`
> Converts c to upper case.

D.3   MATHEMATICS (*include* `<math.h>`)

(For all parameters of type **double**, a **float** may be supplied.)

`double acos(double x);`
> Returns the principal value of the arccos of x.

`double asin(double x);`
> Returns the principal value of the arcsin of x.

`double atan(double x);`
> Returns the principal value of the arctan of x.

`double atan2(double y, double x);`
> Returns the principal value of the arctan of y/x.

`double ceil(double x);`
> Returns the smallest integral value not less than x.

`double cos(double x);`
> Returns the cosine of x.

```
double cosh(double x);
```
Returns the hyperbolic cosine of x.

```
double exp(double x);
```
Returns the exponential function of x (i.e. e^x).

```
double fabs(double x);
```
Returns the absolute value of x.

```
double floor(double x);
```
Returns the largest integral value not greater than x.

```
double fmod(double x, double y);
```
Returns the floating point remainder of x divided by y.

```
double frexp(double value, int *exp);
```
Breaks value into a normalized fraction and an integral power of 2. Returns the fraction and assigns the power to *exp.

```
double ldexp(double value, int exp);
```
Multiplies a number by an integral power of 2. Returns value times 2 raised to the power exp.

```
double log(double x);
```
Returns the natural logarithm of x (i.e. $\log_e x$).

```
double log10(double x);
```
Returns the base-ten logarithm of x (i.e. $\log_{10} x$).

```
double modf(double value, double *iptr);
```
Returns the fractional part of value, and assigns the integral part of value to *iptr. Both parts have the same sign as value.

```
double pow(double x, double y);
```
Returns x raised to the power y.

```
double sin(double x);
```
Returns the sine of x.

```
double sinh(double x);
```
Returns the hyperbolic sine of x.

```
double sqrt(double x);
```
Returns the square root of x.

```
double tan(double x);
```
Returns the tangent of x.

```
double tanh(double x);
```
Returns the hyperbolic tangent of x.

D.4 NONLOCAL JUMPS (*include* `<setjmp.h>`)

These functions provide the equivalent of a `goto` statement capable of jumping out of a function to a predetermined place in one of that function's calling functions. A variable of the type `jmp_buf` is required.

`int setjmp(jmp_buf env);`

Called to mark a position in the program to which a later call to `longjmp` can transfer control. Thus statements after the `setjmp` call can be executed in two circumstances: (1) as a result of the normal return from the `setjmp` call, or (2) as a result of transfer of control to the marked place due to a call to `longjmp` at a later time. To allow the program to distinguish these two circumstances, the return value of `setjmp` in case (1) is always 0, and in case (2) is the value of the `val` parameter to `longjmp`. `setjmp` is usually called inside an `if` test, where the 'true' option of the `if` is executed upon transfer from a `longjmp` call.

`void longjmp(jmp_buf env, int val);`

Causes execution to transfer to the return point of the `setjmp` call that had `env` as its parameter. `val` provides the return value for that `setjmp` call. `longjmp` cannot be used to jump **into** a function that has terminated execution since the call to `setjmp`; it can only transfer **out of** a function.

These functions are usually used only when a nested function discovers an error that requires termination of a section of the processing; the `longjmp` can transfer execution out of the offending function to a stable place where the program can recover from the error.

D.5 VARIABLE ARGUMENTS (*include* `<stdarg.h>`)

All the macros in this category are described elsewhere in the text.

```
void va_start(va_list ap, parmN);
type va_arg(va_list ap, type);
void va_end(va_list ap);
```

D.6 INPUT/OUTPUT (*include* `<stdio.h>`)

`void clearerr(FILE *stream);`

Clears the EOF and error indicators for `stream`.

`EOF`

Macro value returned by some functions to indicate end of file.

`int fclose(FILE *stream);`

Closes the file opened on `stream`; returns 0 for success, EOF otherwise.

`int feof(FILE *stream);`

Returns true if the EOF indicator is set for `stream`.

`int ferror(FILE *stream);`

Returns nonzero if and only if the error indicator is set for the `stream`.

`int fflush(FILE *stream);`

For output files, transmits any unwritten data waiting in output buffers for the `stream`. If `stream` is NULL, flushes all output files.

`int fgetc(FILE *stream);`

Returns the next character from the input `stream`, as an `unsigned char` converted to an `int`. Returns EOF on end of file or error.

`int fgetpos(FILE *stream, fpos_t *pos);`

Stores information for the current file position in `*pos`; returns non-zero upon failure.

`char *fgets(char *s, int n, FILE *stream);`

Reads up to $n-1$ chars from `stream` to memory at `*s`, stopping earlier if end of line encountered. Adds a nul character at the end. Returns `s` on success, NULL on failure.

FILENAME_MAX

Macro equal to the size needed for a `char` array able to hold the longest possible filename string.

`FILE *fopen(const char *filename, const char *mode);`

Opens the file named `filename`; returns the address of a stream on success, NULL on failure. modes: `r` read, `w` write, `a` append, `r+` update existing file (reading and writing), `w+` update a new file or truncate an old one to zero length, `a+` update, writing at end of file. Add `b` to any mode to specify a binary file.

FOPEN_MAX

Macro equal to the minimum number of files a program is guaranteed to be able to open simultaneously.

`int fprintf(FILE *stream, const char *format, ...);`

Writes the `format` string to the `stream`, substituting for any format sequences encountered; further arguments are written if requested by a `%` format sequence. For the common formats, see the sections referred to under the `printf` library function entry in the Index by Language Feature. Additional formats: `%i` is the same as `%d`; `%p` prints a pointer (address); `%n`, which requires an `int *` argument, assigns to the indicated `int` the number of characters written so far by this call to `fprintf` — `%n` does not output any data. Returns the number of characters output, or a negative value upon error.

`int fputc(int c, FILE *stream);`

Writes the character c to the stream `stream`. Returns the character written, or EOF on failure.

```
int fputs(const char *s, FILE *stream);
```
Writes the string s to stream. Returns nonnegative for success, EOF for failure.

```
size_t fread(void *ptr, size_t size, size_t num, FILE *stream);
```
Reads up to num elements, each of size size, from stream into the buffer at *ptr. Returns the number of elements successfully read.

```
int fscanf(FILE *stream, const char *format, ...);
```
Reads from the stream under the control of the format string, assigning data to the variables pointed to by the third and subsequent arguments. Whitespace in the format causes fscanf to read up to the first non-whitespace input character. For the common % formats, see the sections referred to under the scanf library function entry in the Index by Language Feature. Additional % specifiers: %p inputs a pointer (not recommended for high-level programming); %n, which requires an int* argument, assigns to the int the number of characters read by this fscanf call so far; %% matches a single % in the input. Any characters in the format that are **not** % format specifier sequences cause fscanf to check for an exact match in the input data (i.e. if the input data differs from the format, the fscanf input fails at that point, and the function terminates).

```
int fseek(FILE *stream, long int offset, int whence);
```
Clears the end-of-file indicator and sets the position of the stream to offset bytes from the position whence. whence can be: SEEK_SET (beginning of file), SEEK_CUR (the current position), SEEK_END (end of file). Binary streams might not support SEEK_END. Returns nonzero for failure.

```
int fsetpos(FILE *stream, const fpos_t *pos);
```
Sets the position of the stream to position *pos, obtained from a previous call to fgetpos. Returns nonzero on failure.

```
long int ftell(FILE *stream);
```
Returns the current position in the stream. For binary files, this is the number of characters from the beginning of the file. Returns −1L on failure.

```
size_t fwrite(const void *ptr, size_t size, size_t num, FILE *stream);
```
Writes from the buffer at *ptr, num elements each of size size to the stream. Returns the number of elements successfully written.

```
int getc(FILE *stream);
```
Like fgetc, but it might be a macro, not a genuine function.

```
int getchar(void);
```
getchar() is equivalent to getc(stdin).

```
char *gets(char *s);
```
Reads characters from stdin into the buffer at *s, until end of file or end of line. The newline is discarded, and a nul character added. Returns s on success, or NULL on failure.

`void perror(const char *s);`
> Writes to `stderr` an error message explaining the latest error; this includes the string `s` (if non-empty) for identification.

`int printf(const char *format, ...);`
> `printf(format,args)` is equivalent to `fprintf(stdout,format,args)`.

`int putc(int c, FILE *stream);`
> Like `fputc`, but it might be a macro, not a genuine function.

`int putchar(int c);`
> `putchar(c)` is equivalent to `putc(c,stdout)`.

`int puts(const char *s);`
> Writes the string `s` to `stdout`, and appends a newline. Returns nonnegative for success, `EOF` for failure.

`int remove(const char *filename);`
> Deletes the file whose name is in the string `filename`. Returns zero on success, nonzero on failure.

`int rename(const char *oldname, const char *newname);`
> Renames `oldname` to `newname`. On some computers, any existing file `newname` will be overwritten; on others an existing `newname` file prevents the renaming operation from occurring, and `oldname` is not renamed. Returns zero on success, nonzero on failure.

`void rewind(FILE *stream);`
> Resets the file position indicator for `stream` to the beginning of the file. The error indicator is cleared.

`int scanf(const char *format, ...);`
> `scanf(format,args)` is equivalent to `fscanf(stdin,format,args)`.

`int setvbuf(FILE *stream, char *buf, int mode, size_t size);`
> Specifies the manner in which buffers are allocated for a stream. Must be called after `fopen` and before any other function on the stream. If `buf` is not `NULL`, it should point to the space to be used as the buffer, otherwise the system allocates the buffer. `size` specifies the size of the buffer. `mode` is the type of buffering: if equal to the macro `_IOFBF`, the stream is fully buffered, if `_IOLBF`, it is line-buffered (i.e. data transferred at the end of each line, as with terminals), and if `_IONBF`, the stream is unbuffered. Returns zero on success, nonzero on failure.

`int sprintf(char *s, const char *format, ...);`
> Similar to `fprintf`, except that `s` is an array that receives the 'output', instead of its going to a file. The output is ended with a nul character. Returns the length of the string, not counting the nul.

`int sscanf(const char *s, const char *format, ...);`
> Similar to `fscanf`, except that `s` is an array containing a string that supplies the 'input', instead of its coming from a file.

```
FILE *tmpfile(void);
```
Creates an open, temporary binary file in mode wb+ (see fopen) that is automatically removed when it is closed. Returns a pointer to the stream, or NULL on failure.

```
char *tmpnam(char *s);
```
Returns a string that is a valid filename, and not the same as any existing file. If s is **not** NULL, it stores this name in memory at *s (which must be at least L_tmpnam characters long); otherwise, it stores the name in an internal static array, which might be reused by future tmpnam calls. At least 25 different names can be generated — the macro TMP_MAX tells the exact number for your compiler.

```
int ungetc(int c, FILE *stream);
```
Pushes the character c back into the input stream; that is, c will be the next character obtained by reading from the stream. One character of pushback is guaranteed. Returns EOF on failure, or the character pushed back on success.

D.7   STRING CONVERSION FUNCTIONS (*include* <stdlib.h>)

```
double atof(const char *nptr);
```
Returns the double whose value is represented in character form at the beginning of the string nptr; on error, its behavior is undefined.

```
int atoi(const char *nptr);
```
Returns the int whose value is represented in character form at the beginning of the string nptr; on error, its behavior is undefined.

```
long int atol(const char *nptr);
```
Returns the long int whose value is represented in character form at the beginning of the string nptr; on error, its behavior is undefined.

```
double strtod(const char *nptr, char **endptr);
```
Skips whitespace, then converts and returns the next part of the string nptr as a double. If endptr is not NULL, assigns to *endptr, a pointer to the char following the converted section of nptr.

```
long int strtol(const char *nptr, char **endptr, int base);
```
Similar to strtod, but for long ints. base specifies the expected base of the number, 10 for normal signed decimals, between 2 and 36 for other bases. If base is zero, the string specifies the base: numbers commencing with 0X or 0x are hexadecimal, those commencing with 0 are octal, and others are decimal.

```
unsigned long int strtoul(const char *nptr, char **endptr, int base);
```
Similar to strtol, but for unsigned long ints.

D.8 RANDOM NUMBER FUNCTIONS (*include* `<stdlib.h>`)

`int rand(void);`

Returns a pseudo-random number in the range 0 to `RAND_MAX`, which is at least 32767.

`void srand(unsigned int seed);`

Sets the starting value for the computation of random numbers by `rand`. For a given `seed`, the same sequence of random numbers will be produced by `rand`. To produce an unpredictable sequence, initialize `seed` with a value derived in an unreproducible manner, for example, from the time of day.

For critical mathematical work involving random numbers, the characteristics of the algorithm producing the numbers are important, and some implementations of `rand` have statistical defects. Therefore in such work, verify whether `rand` on your computer produces suitable random sequences before relying on it. A good starting point is the article by Park and Miller mentioned in the bibliography.

D.9 MEMORY ALLOCATION FUNCTIONS (*include* `<stdlib.h>`)

`void *calloc(size_t nmemb, size_t size);`

A `malloc`-like function; allocates space for nmemb objects, each of size `size`. Also, initializes the space to all-zeros. Returns the address of the allocated zeroed space, or `NULL` on failure.

`void free(void *ptr);`

Returns the memory block addressed by `ptr` to free storage so it may be allocated again. `ptr` must be `NULL` (in which case the function does nothing) or a value obtained from `malloc`, `calloc`, or `realloc` (this last not described here), and should not be `freed` twice.

`void *malloc(size_t size);`

Allocates space for an object of size `size`. Returns the address of the allocated space, or `NULL` for failure.

D.10 COMMUNICATION WITH THE ENVIRONMENT (*include* `<stdlib.h>`)

`void abort(void);`

Stops the program, but unlike `exit`, is regarded as a 'failure' termination. The program returns an *unsuccessful termination* message to the operating system. The use to which this is put by the operating system is outside the C language definition.

`int atexit(void (*func)(void));`

Specifies the name of a parameterless function that should be called when the program terminates. Returns zero for success, nonzero for failure.

```
void exit(int status);
```
Terminates the program. First, functions registered by atexit are called in reverse order to their registration, then all files are flushed and closed, temporary files are removed, and the program terminates, returning status as the success status of the program (zero for success, EXIT_FAILURE for failure).

```
char *getenv(const char *name);
```
Many operating systems allow the user to assign strings to names; the list of names and their attached strings is called the *environment*. getenv searches the environment for a name matching the string name, and if found, returns the attached string; this should be copied or used before a subsequent call to getenv. Returns NULL on failure.

```
int system(const char *string);
```
Allows a C program to execute an operating system command. If string is NULL, the function returns nonzero if and only if a command processor is available for executing commands. Otherwise string should point to a buffer containing an operating system command string; in this case, the return value depends on the operating system.

D.11 SEARCHING AND SORTING UTILITIES (*include* <stdlib.h>)

The functions in this category are described elsewhere in the text.

```
void *bsearch(
    const void *key, const void *base, size_t nmemb,
    size_t size, int (*compar)(const void *, const void *)
);
void qsort(
    void *base, size_t nmemb, size_t size,
    int (*compar)(const void *, const void *)
);
```

D.12 INTEGER ARITHMETIC FUNCTIONS (*include* <stdlib.h>)

```
int abs(int j);
```
Returns the absolute value of j.

```
div_t div(int numer, int denom);
```
Computes and returns the quotient and remainder from dividing numer by denom. Returned as a structure of type ldiv_t, containing two int fields, quot and rem.

```
long int labs(long int j);
```
Returns the absolute value of j.

```
ldiv_t ldiv(long int numer, long int denom);
```
Computes and returns the quotient and remainder from dividing numer by denom. Returned as a structure of type ldiv_t, containing two long int fields, quot and rem.

D.13 STRING HANDLING (*include* `<string.h>`)

Most functions here accept `char*` or `void*` arguments, which will in the function call be array names or pointers to a region of memory used as an array. For brevity, in the descriptions that follow, the arrays pointed to by these arguments are referred to simply by the argument name. For example, `memcpy` copies "characters from s2", meaning that the characters are copied from the array or buffer which the actual parameter in the s2 position is the array name of, or is a pointer to.

`void *memchr(const void *s, int c, size_t n);`

Returns the address of the first occurrence of c in the first n characters of s, or NULL if not found.

`int memcmp(const void *s1, const void *s2, size_t n);`

Compares the first n characters of s2 with the first n characters in s1. Returns an integer less than, equal to, or greater than zero depending on the result of the comparison.

`void *memcpy(void *s1, const void *s2, size_t n);`

Copies n characters from s2 to s1; these arrays should not overlap.

`void *memmove(void *s1, const void *s2, size_t n);`

Like `memcpy`, but works correctly even if s1 and s2 overlap.

`void *memset(void *s, int c, size_t n);`

Fills the first n characters of s with the unsigned char value c. Returns s.

`char *strcat(char *s1, const char *s2);`

Concatenates a copy of string s2 onto the string in s1; these arrays should not overlap.

`char *strncat(char *s1, const char *s2, size_t n);`

Concatenates a copy of up to n characters from string s2 onto the string in s1; these arrays should not overlap. A nul character is always appended.

`char *strcpy(char *s1, const char *s2);`

Copies a string from s2 to s1; these arrays should not overlap.

`char *strncpy(char *s1, const char *s2, size_t n);`

Copies a string of up to n characters from s2 to s1; these arrays should not overlap. If the string s2 is n characters or longer, a nul character will **not** be appended to s1. If the string s2 is shorter than n characters, then after copying s2 to s1, sufficient nuls will be added to the end of s1 to fill the entire n characters.

`int strcmp(const char *s1, const char *s2);`

Compares the string s2 with the string s1. Returns an integer less than, equal to, or greater than zero depending on the result of the comparison.

`int strncmp(const char *s1, const char *s2, size_t n);`
Compares up to n characters of the string s2 with the string s1. Returns an integer less than, equal to, or greater than zero depending on the result of the comparison.

`char *strchr(const char *s, int c);`
Returns the address of the first occurrence of c in the string s, or NULL if not found.

`size_t strcspn(const char *s1, const char *s2);`
Returns the length of the longest initial segment of the string s1 which contains no characters from the string s2. That is, the result is the index of the first character in s1 that is also in s2, or the index of the terminating nul if none is found.

`char *strerror(int errnum);`
Returns an error message appropriate to error number errnum. These are the same messages printed by perror. Various library functions place error numbers in errno, which can be accessed by including <errno.h>.

`char *strpbrk(const char *s1, const char *s2);`
Returns a pointer to the first character in s1 which is also in s2, or NULL if none is found.

`char *strrchr(const char *s, int c);`
Returns the address of the last occurrence of c in the string s, or NULL if not found.

`size_t strspn(const char *s1, const char *s2);`
Returns the length of the longest initial segment of the string s1 which consists entirely of characters from the string s2.

`char *strstr(const char *s1, const char *s2);`
Returns the address of the first occurrence in s1 of the string s2, or NULL if none is found.

`size_t strlen(const char *s);`
Returns the length of the string s, not counting the terminating nul.

D.14 DATE AND TIME (*include* <time.h>)

Some functions use the types clock_t, which stores clock ticks, and time_t, which contains a calendar time (i.e. a date and time). Type time_t is meant to be used to store time values in an efficient arithmetic format; we do not need to know how this is done (although it is probably the number of seconds since some fixed starting time, such as midnight on 1 January 1970) because we should use standard functions to convert dates to or from time_t format. The structure type, struct tm, is used to manipulate times in a comprehensible format; it contains the following fields in any order:

```
int tm_sec;     /* seconds after the minute (0..61) */
int tm_min;     /* minutes after the hour (0..59) */
int tm_hour;    /* hours since midnight (0..23) */
int tm_mday;    /* day of the month (1..31) */
int tm_mon;     /* months since January (0..11) */
int tm_year;    /* years since 1900 */
int tm_wday;    /* days since Sunday (0..6) */
int tm_yday;    /* days since January 1 (0..365) */
int tm_isdst;   /* daylight saving flag (greater than zero if daylight
                   saving is in effect, zero if not, less than zero if
                   no information available. */
```

The above types are defined in `<time.h>`.

`clock_t clock(void);`

Returns the amount of processor time (in clock ticks) used by the program since it started; returns –1 if processor time is not available. Divide by the macro `CLOCKS_PER_SEC` to obtain the time in seconds.

`double difftime(time_t time1, time_t time0);`

Returns the difference in seconds between the two times; if `time1` is later than `time0`, the difference is positive.

`time_t mktime(struct tm *timeptr);`

Converts a `struct tm` into a `time_t` value, and also 'fixes up' the `struct tm`. `timeptr` should be the address of a program variable containing a date/time. The first six fields (`tm_sec` to `tm_year`) should be set (but need not be within the ranges shown above), and the function re-scales them to fit the standard ranges, and also fills in the `tm_wday` and `tm_yday` fields. The return value is the equivalent date/time in `time_t` format. Returns –1 if the date/time cannot be represented as a `time_t`. Uses the value of the daylight saving flag, `tm_isdst`; if this is negative, `mktime` attempts to find out whether daylight saving is in effect.

`time_t time(time_t *timer);`

Returns the current calendar time as per the computer's clock; if `timer` is not NULL, this is also assigned to `*timer`. Returns –1 if time is not available.

`size_t strftime(`
`    char *s, size_t maxsize, const char *format, const struct tm *timeptr`
`);`

This is a conversion function designed to create a readable string containing a date/time. Like `printf`, it uses a special format string, but `strftime`'s formats are tailored for representing time values. The variable to which `timeptr` points should contain a date/time, `s` should be the address of a buffer where the readable time is to be placed, and `maxsize` should be the length of `s`, including a character for the trailing nul. `format` should be a format string; ordinary characters in the format are copied unaltered into `s`, but `%` format commands are interpreted as described in the following table. Returns the length of the resulting string or 0 if the string will not fit in `s`.

Meanings of `strftime` format strings

`%a`	abbreviated weekday name	`%p`	AM/PM designation
`%A`	full weekday name	`%S`	the second, 00–61
`%b`	abbreviated month name	`%U`	the week number, see below, 00–53
`%B`	full month name	`%w`	weekday as number, 0–6
`%c`	appropriate date and time representation	`%W`	the week number, see below, 00–53
`%d`	day of the month as a number, 01–31	`%x`	appropriate date representation
`%H`	the hour, 00–23	`%X`	appropriate time representation
`%I`	the hour, 01–12	`%y`	year without century, 00–99
`%j`	day of the year, 001–366	`%Y`	year with century
`%m`	month as a number, 01–12	`%Z`	time zone abbreviation
`%M`	the minute, 00–59	`%%`	a `%` character

Notes: the week number referred to above is the number of the week in the year (00–53); `%U` interprets the first Sunday as the first day of week 1, while `%W` uses Monday as the first day. `%w` (weekday as number) uses Sunday as day 0. Seconds in the minute can go from 0 to 61 because there can be up to two leap seconds in a minute. Finally, the effects of `%a` through `%c`, `%p`, `%x` and `%X` may differ from country to country.

The remaining functions return their results in static buffers, which may be altered by further calls to the same or a different function; after calling a function in the following group, use the results or make a copy before making another call to one of these functions.

`char *asctime(const struct tm *timeptr);`

    `*timeptr` should contain a date/time; returns the address of a standard representation of that date/time, in the following format:

        `Sun Sep 16 01:03:52 1973\n\0`

`char *ctime(const time_t *timer);`

    This function converts the calendar time pointed to by `timer` to a local time string; it is equivalent to:

        `asctime(localtime(timer))`

`struct tm *gmtime(const time_t *timer);`

    Returns a broken-down time representing the calendar time in `*timer`, in Coordinated Universal Time (UTC), or `NULL` if universal time is not available. (The name, `gmtime`, is derived from UTC's predecessor, Greenwich Mean Time.)

`struct tm *localtime(const time_t *timer);`

    Returns a broken-down time representing the calendar time in `*timer`, expressed as local time.

D.15 DIAGNOSTICS (*include* `<assert.h>`)

This facility allows a program to state assertions, such as preconditions, postconditions, and invariants, and have them tested by the system. These assertions are written as logical tests (as in loops and conditionals). The testing is controlled by the macro NDEBUG, which the programmer may choose to define, or not define, prior to including `<assert.h>`.

void assert(int assertion);

If NDEBUG was **not** defined where `<assert.h>` was included, and the `assertion` is false (zero), `assert` writes an informative error message to `stderr`, and then terminates the program by calling `abort`. Otherwise, `assert` has no effect.

Program layout rules used in example programs

Experts differ over the 'best' way to set out program text, comments, etc. The layout style used here was adapted from one designed by A H Sale for the Pascal language (see the bibliography). It has the advantage of conserving both vertical space (fewer lines with little information, such as a line with only a {), and horizontal space (fewer nested indentations), leaving more room for creative use of space (for example, leaving blank lines where appropriate for readability). More importantly, it provides an easy way to check for block-structuring errors without having to switch attention back-and-forth between different sections of the program. Further, all statements that extend over multiple lines are treated consistently, so the reader will know what to expect.

The rules are as follows, with interspersed examples:

1 All objects declared at the outermost (global) level commence in column one.
2 All declarations or statements that start a nested syntax level (functions, if, while etc.) are written with the symbol that introduces the nested level at the **end** of a line; lines are not split before this symbol.
   – The symbol starting the nested level is never omitted, whether this is permitted by the language or not, with the single exception of an if that follows an else.
3 The text forming the nested syntax level is indented four spaces.
4 At the end of the nested syntax level mentioned in (2), the symbol that terminates the nested level is placed at the **beginning** of a line, directly underneath the first symbol of the original declaration or statement mentioned in (2).

Examples

```
int i;                                          Start global declaration at left
                                                margin.
float func1(int c, double d) {                  Ditto, and { starts a nested level.
    return d*c;                                 Nested text indented four spaces.
}                                               End nested text at original
                                                indentation level.
float func2(                                    Here the parameters will not fit
    unsigned long int longparameter[],          on one line, so the ( introduces
    unsigned int anotherone,                    the nested level, which is
    long double andyetanotherone                indented as usual.
) {                                             ) ends the first nested level,
                                                and { starts another one.

    i = anotherone + 2;
    return longparameter[5] / 2;
}                                               Return to original indentation.
```

5   `switch` statements present a problem, due to their irregular syntax. `case` and `default` options are written directly under the word `switch`. The statements making up each case start a fresh line indented four spaces. The final } of the switch is lined up underneath the word `switch`.

These rules mean that program indentation always occurs in steps of four columns. We can therefore check, for example, whether we have omitted a brace, just by making sure that the indentation changes appropriately by exactly four when, and only when, an appropriate level-changing symbol occurs:

```
blahblahblah;
do {
    blahblahblah;   ◄───── Change by 4, correct.
    ...
    if (
        whatever   ◄───── Change by 4, correct.
        ...
    ) {   ◄──────────────── Change by 4, correct.
        moreblahblah;   ◄─ Change by 4, correct.
        evenmoreblah;
} while (something);   ◄── Change by 8, INcorrect!
etcetcetc;
    morestuff;   ◄──────── INcorrect, extra indentation without
                            a { or ( ending the preceding line.
```

Note in the above example, we can spot the errors by looking at the lines two at a time without looking back up through the program; for example:

```
        evenmoreblah;
} while (something);   ◄── Change by 8, INcorrect!
```

6   Each function is preceded by a comment stating (1) the task performed, as a brief remark, (2) the precondition (On entry), and (3) the postcondition (On exit). The *method* used is not described in the heading comment; it is written later, if necessary.

7   Where the method used to program a function (or any other piece of code) is not obvious, explanatory comments are introduced. Comments should never merely translate C into equally opaque English, and they should be omitted unless they tell us something that is not obvious. The briefer, while still being coherent, informative, and grammatically correct, the better.

8   Comments should either be to the right of the statements they explain, or in-line, indented the same amount as the normal statements (to avoid obscuring the indentation).

9   Compound statements should be remembered as line-oriented patterns; see Chapter 4 for layout of looping statements, and Chapter 6 for layout of conditional statements.

10 Operators, except for unary operators and ->, ., [,], (, and) are surrounded by spaces; comma and semicolon are followed by a space, but not preceded by one.

11 If you must write an `if` or other structured statement all on one line, still include the braces; that is, write

```
if (found) { printf("Found\n"); }
```

Do not write:

```
if (found) printf("Found\n");     /* poor */
```

Why? Suppose we decide to also add 1 to k if `found`. A quick edit of each is likely to produce:

```
if (found) { printf("Found\n"); k++; }
```

and:

```
if (found) printf("Found\n"); k++;     /* WRONG!!! */
```

In other words, in the second case we are at risk of making an error unless we think carefully; in the first case, we just make the obvious change. Since the entire game is avoiding complexity, it is clearly better to invest in typing two extra characters ('{' and '}'), in order to have a simpler program.

APPENDIX F
C syntax summary

This is an informal summary of the syntax of the C language. In order to make it as intelligible as possible, it is presented in a different format from that of the official syntax in the ANSI/ISO C language definition. Also, many obvious definitions are omitted. If an authoritative verdict on any aspect of C syntax is required, the official syntax of the C standard should be consulted.

In the following, words or symbols that should appear as-written are shown in **bold**, names of syntactic categories (nonterminals) are shown in *italics*, while items described in English are shown in normal text. If a syntactic category is followed by a superscript bold plus ($^+$), it may occur one or more times. If a syntactic category is followed by a superscript bold asterisk (*), it may occur zero or more times. A syntactic category followed by a superscript bold question mark ($^?$) is optional. Finally, hints and comments about the meaning of the syntax are shown in *sans serif*. Some syntactic categories have alternative forms; a line starting with bold-italic *or:* introduces the next alternative; if *or* separates two items on the same line, the two items on either side are alternatives.

F.1 LEXICAL GRAMMAR ('BUILDING BLOCKS' OF THE LANGUAGE)

F.1.1 Keywords

keyword: One of the following:

auto	default	float	register	struct	volatile
break	do	for	return	switch	while
case	double	goto	short	typedef	
char	else	if	signed	union	
const	enum	int	sizeof	unsigned	
continue	extern	long	static	void	

(C++ only) *or* one of the following:

asm	delete	inline	operator	public	virtual
class	friend	new	overload	this	

F.1.2 Identifiers

identifier:
>   *nondigit*
>
> *or:*   *identifier nondigit*
>
> *or:*   *identifier digit*
>
> The identifier must not spell out a keyword.

nondigit:
>   An underscore (_) or a lower or upper case English letter.

digit: one of: **0 1 2 3 4 5 6 7 8 9**

F.1.3 Constants

constant:
>   *floating-constant*
>   *integer-constant*
>   *enumeration-constant*
>   *character-constant*

floating-constant:
>   *fractional-constant exponent-part$^?$ floating-suffix$^?$*
>
> *or:*   *digit$^+$ exponent-part floating-suffix$^?$*

fractional-constant:
>   *digit*. digit$^+$*
>
> *or:*   *digit$^+$.*

exponent-part: **e** *or* **E** *sign$^?$ digit$^+$*

sign: one of: **+ −**

floating-suffix: one of: **f l F L**

integer-constant:
>   *decimal-constant integer-suffix$^?$*
>
> *or:*   *octal-constant integer-suffix$^?$*
>
> *or:*   *hexadecimal-constant integer-suffix$^?$*

decimal-constant: *non-zero-digit digit**

octal-constant: **0** *octal-digit**

hexadecimal-constant: **0x** *or* **0X** *hexadecimal-digit$^+$*

non-zero-digit: one of: **1 2 3 4 5 6 7 8 9**

octal-digit: one of: **0 1 2 3 4 5 6 7**

hexadecimal-digit: one of: **0 1 2 3 4 5 6 7 8 9 a b c d e f A B C D E F**

integer-suffix:
> *unsigned-suffix long-suffix?*
> *long-suffix unsigned-suffix?*

unsigned suffix: one of: **u U**

long-suffix: one of: **l L**

enumeration-constant: *identifier* (*These are 'enum' constant names.*)

character-constant:
> ' *c-char*⁺ '

or: **L** ' *c-char*⁺ '   (*Used only for wide characters*)

c-char:
> any character except single-quote ', backslash \ or new-line

or: *escape-sequence*

escape-sequence:
> one of: \' \'' \? \\ \a \b \f \n \r \t \v

or: \ followed by up to three *octal-digit*⁺

or: \x *hexadecimal-digit*⁺

F.1.4 String literals

string-literal:
> '' *s-char*⁺ ''

or: **L** '' *s-char*⁺ ''   (*Used only for wide characters*)

s-char:
> any character except double-quote '', backslash \, or new-line

or: *escape-sequence*

F.1.5 Operators

operator: one of:
> [ ] ( ) . ->
> ++ -- & * + - ~ ! **sizeof**
> *binary-operator*
> ? :
> *assignment-operator*
> , # ##

F.1.6 Punctuators

punctuator: one of:
> [ ] ( ) { } * , : = ; ... #

F.1.7 Header names

> *header-name:*
>> Angle brackets <> around any characters except *new-line* and >
>
> or: Double quotes around any characters except *new-line* and "

F.2   PHRASE STRUCTURE GRAMMAR

F.2.1 Expressions

> *expression:*
>> *assignment-expression*
>
> *or:*   *expression , assignment-expression*

> *constant-expression:*
>> *binary-expression*   (involving only constants)

> *assignment-expression:*
>> *conditional-expression*
>
> *or:*   *unary-expression assignment-operator assignment-expression*

> *conditional-expression:*
>> *binary-expression*
>
> *or:*   *binary-expression ? expression : conditional-expression*

> *binary-expression:*
>> *cast-expression*
>
> *or:*   *binary-expression binary-operator binary-expression* (where the precedence
>> of operators is decided according to the table in Appendix C.3.3)

> *cast-expression:*
>> *unary-expression*
>
> *or:*   *(type-name) cast-expression*

> *unary-expression:*
>> *postfix-expression*
>
> *or:*   *++ unary-expression*
>
> *or:*   *−− unary-expression*
>
> *or:*   *unary-operator cast-expression*
>
> *or:*   **sizeof** *unary-expression*
>
> *or:*   **sizeof** *(type-name)*

> *unary-operator:*   one of **&** * + − ~ !

postfix-expression:
    primary-expression
or: *postfix-expression* [*expression*]
or: *postfix-expression* (*argument-expression-list*?)
or: *postfix-expression* . *identifier*
or: *postfix-expression* –> *identifier*
or: *postfix-expression* ++
or: *postfix-expression* – –

primary-expression:
    identifier
    constant
    string-literal
    (*expression*)

argument-expression-list:
    assignment-expression+ separated by commas (,)

F.2.2 Declarations

declaration:
    declaration-specifiers init-declarator-list? ;

declaration-specifiers:
    storage-class-specifier declaration-specifiers?
or: *type-specifier declaration-specifiers*?
or: *type-qualifier declaration-specifiers*?

init-declarator-list:
    init-declarator+ separated by commas (,)

init-declarator:
    declarator
or: *declarator* = *initializer*

storage-class-specifier: one of:
    typedef extern static auto register

type-specifier: one of:
    void char short int long float double signed unsigned
    struct-or-union-specifier enum-specifier typedef-name

struct-or-union-specifier:
    struct *or* **union** *identifier*? { *struct-declaration*+}
    struct *or* **union** *identifier*

struct-declaration: *specifier-qualifier-list struct-declarator-list* ;

specifier-qualifier-list:
    type-specifier *specifier-qualifier-list$^?$*
    type-qualifier *specifier-qualifier-list$^?$*

struct-declarator-list:
    struct-declarator$^+$ separated by commas (,)

struct-declarator:
    declarator   *(the usual case)*
or: *declarator$^?$* : *constant-expression* *(bit-fields)*

enum-specifier:
    enum *identifier$^?$* { *enumerator-list* }
or: **enum** *identifier*

enumerator-list: *enumerator$^+$* separated by commas (,)

enumerator:
    enumeration-constant
or: *enumeration-constant* = *constant-expression*

type-qualifier: one of: **const** **volatile**

declarator: *pointer$^?$* *direct-declarator*

direct-declarator:
    identifier
or: (*declarator*)
or: *direct-declarator* [*constant-expression$^?$*]
or: *direct-declarator* (*parameter-type-list*)
or: *direct-declarator* (*identifier-list$^?$*)

pointer: * *type-qualifier* pointer$^?$*

parameter-type-list:
    parameter-list
or: *parameter-list* , **...**

parameter-list: *parameter-declaration$^?$* separated by commas (,)

parameter-declaration:
    declaration-specifiers *declarator*
or: *declaration-specifiers* *abstract-declarator$^?$*

identifier-list: *identifier$^+$* separated by commas (,)

type-name: *specifier-qualifier-list* *abstract-declarator$^?$*

abstract-declarator:
    pointer
or: *pointer$^?$* *direct-abstract-declarator*

direct-abstract-declarator:
>(*abstract-declarator*)

or: *direct-abstract-declarator*? [*constant-expression*?]

or: *direct-abstract-declarator*? (*parameter-type-list*?)

typedef-name: *identifier*

initializer:
>*assignment-expression*

or: { *initializer-list* ,? }

initializer-list: *initializer*+ separated by commas (,)

F.2.3 Statements

statement: one of:
>*labelled-statement* *compound-statement* *expression-statement*
>*selection-statement* *iteration-statement* *jump-statement*

labelled-statement:
>*identifier* : *statement*

or: **case** *constant-expression* : *statement*

or: **default** : *statement*

compound-statement: { *declaration** *statement** }

expression-statement: *expression*? ;

selection-statement:
>**if** (*expression*) *statement*

or: **if** (*expression*) *statement* **else** *statement*

or: **switch** (*expression*) *statement*

iteration-statement:
>**while** (*expression*) *statement*

or: **do** *statement* **while** (*expression*) ;

or: **for** (*expression*? ; *expression*? ; *expression*?) *statement*

jump-statement:
>**goto** *identifier* ;

or: **continue** ;

or: **break** ;

or: **return** *expression*? ;

F.2.4 External definitions

translation-unit: *external-declaration*+
>*This is the fundamental syntactic category defining a valid C source file.*

external-declaration:
>   *function-definition*
>
> *or:*   *declaration*

function-definition:
>   *declaration-specifiers*? *declarator* *compound-statement*
>
> *or:*   *declaration-specifiers*? *declarator* *declaration*+ *compound-statement*
>   The second alternative applies only to old-style function definitions.

F.3   PREPROCESSING DIRECTIVES

(The syntactic categories *if-section*, *if-group*, *elif-group*, *else-group*, *endif-line*, and *control-line* must all commence on a fresh line.)

group-part:
>   *preprocessing-token** *new-line*
>
> *or:*   *if-section*
>
> *or:*   *control-line*

if-section: *if-group elif-group** *else-group*? *endif-line*

if-group:
>   **# if**   *constant-expression new-line group-part**
>
> *or:*   **# ifdef**   *identifier new-line group-part**
>
> *or:*   **# ifndef** *identifier new-line group-part**

elif-group: **# elif**   *constant-expression new-line group-part**

else-group: **# else**   *new-line group-part**

endif-line: **# endif**   *new-line*

control-line:
>   **# include** *preprocessing-token*+ *new-line*
>
> *or:*   **# define** *identifier replacement-list new-line*
>
> *or:*   **# define** *identifier lparen identifier**) *replacement-list new-line*
>
> *or:*   **# undef**   *identifier new-line*
>
> *or:*   **# line**   *preprocessing-token*+ *new-line*
>
> *or:*   **# error**   *preprocessing-token** *new-line*
>
> *or:*   **# pragma** *preprocessing-token** *new-line*
>
> *or:*   **#**   *new-line*

lparen: the left-parenthesis (with no preceding whitespace

replacement-list: *preprocessing-token**

new-line: the newline character

preprocessing-token: one of:
    header-name identifier pp-number character-constant string-literal
    operator punctuator
        or any non-whitespace character that cannot be one of the above

pp-number: a sequence of characters that looks like a numeric constant

APPENDIX G
ASCII CODES

The following tables show the character codes for ASCII, the coding system used on most computers. The first 32 codes represent non-printable characters; the table shows their control code (the control-key combination used to type them) and also their official name. Of interest are the following, which are often used for certain C escape characters: NUL (`'\0'`), BEL (`'\a'`), BS (`'\b'`), HT (`'\t'`), LF (`'\n'`), VT (`'\v'`), FF (`'\f'`), and CR (`'\r'`).

Dec	Hex	Ctrl	Name	Dec	Hex	Ctrl	Name
0	00	^@	NUL	16	10	^P	DLE
1	01	^A	SOH	17	11	^Q	DC1
2	02	^B	STX	18	12	^R	DC2
3	03	^C	ETX	19	13	^S	DC3
4	04	^D	EOT	20	14	^T	DC4
5	05	^E	ENQ	21	15	^U	NAK
6	06	^F	ACK	22	16	^V	SYN
7	07	^G	BEL	23	17	^W	ETB
8	08	^H	BS	24	18	^X	CAN
9	09	^I	HT	25	19	^Y	EM
10	0A	^J	LF	26	1A	^Z	SUB
11	0B	^K	VT	27	1B	^[	ESC
12	0C	^L	FF	28	1C	^\	FS
13	0D	^M	CR	29	1D	^]	GS
14	0E	^N	SO	30	1E	^^	RS
15	0F	^O	SI	31	1F	^_	US

Dec	Hex	Chr	Dec	Hex	Chr	Dec	Hex	Chr	Dec	Hex	Chr	Dec	Hex	Chr	Dec	Hex	Chr
32	20		48	30	0	64	40	@	80	50	P	96	60	`	112	70	p
33	21	!	49	31	1	65	41	A	81	51	Q	97	61	a	113	71	q
34	22	"	50	32	2	66	42	B	82	52	R	98	62	b	114	72	r
35	23	#	51	33	3	67	43	C	83	53	S	99	63	c	115	73	s
36	24	$	52	34	4	68	44	D	84	54	T	100	64	d	116	74	t
37	25	%	53	35	5	69	45	E	85	55	U	101	65	e	117	75	u
38	26	&	54	36	6	70	46	F	86	56	V	102	66	f	118	76	v
39	27	'	55	37	7	71	47	G	87	57	W	103	67	g	119	77	w
40	28	(	56	38	8	72	48	H	88	58	X	104	68	h	120	78	x
41	29	)	57	39	9	73	49	I	89	59	Y	105	69	i	121	79	y
42	2A	*	58	3A	:	74	4A	J	90	5A	Z	106	6A	j	122	7A	z
43	2B	+	59	3B	;	75	4B	K	91	5B	[	107	6B	k	123	7B	{
44	2C	,	60	3C	<	76	4C	L	92	5C	\	108	6C	l	124	7C		
45	2D	–	61	3D	=	77	4D	M	93	5D	]	109	6D	m	125	7D	}
46	2E	.	62	3E	>	78	4E	N	94	5E	^	110	6E	n	126	7E	~
47	2F	/	63	3F	?	79	4F	O	95	5F	_	111	6F	o	127	7F	DEL

The above codes use only seven bits of an eight-bit byte. Therefore most systems allocate characters to the next 128 codes; these are used for graphic, scientific, and non-English language characters. Unfortunately, the symbols allocated to these non-ASCII codes are not standard. (In fact, even a few of the ASCII codes are allocated to different symbols in different countries; code 35 (hex 23), for example, is often the pound sign in England.) Preparations are being made for a standard coding system capable of representing all characters from the world's languages. Such a system would require the wide-character features of C.

Glossary

This glossary provides short explanations of the various terms used throughout this text, as well as some others that the student will commonly encounter. The explanations should not be taken as precise definitions.

abstract data type: A data type defined only by the properties of the operations and functions that can be performed on the data.

address: The number used, like a street address, to locate a particular memory location. Some computers assign addresses to words, some to bytes. Computers that address bytes still have addresses for words, namely the address of the first byte in each word. In a program, an address is often called a pointer.

algorithm: A finite, precise list of instructions for performing a given task in a finite number of steps.

analyst (systems): See *systems analyst*.

append to a file: Add data to the end of an existing file.

arguments: See *parameters, actual*.

array: A region of memory reserved for holding multiple values of a given datatype. In C, the name of an array stands for the address of the first element of the array.

ASCII: American Standard Code for Information Interchange; the character codes used on most computers.

assignment: A statement that assigns a value to a variable.

assembly language, or assembler: A language corresponding closely with machine language, but where numeric instruction codes are replaced with alphabetic mnemonics, and other elementary aids to programming are provided.

assertion: A claim, such as a precondition, postcondition, or invariant, that must be true at some point in the program text.

associativity: Whether a series of operators of equal precedence are performed in a left-to-right, or right-to-left order.

beauty: Delight to the eye; beauty is a desirable property in a program.

binary numbers: Numbers written with two symbols, 0 and 1. Each place to the left increases a value by two: for example, 10 is twice 1.

binary operator: An operator taking two operands, one written before, and one after, the operator. Sometimes called a dyadic operator.

bit: A single binary digit (0 or 1) stored in memory or some other device.

Boolean: Logical. Boolean operators are those evaluating logical conditions, resulting in a truth value (true or false). In C, Boolean values are represented numerically: zero for false, nonzero for true.

bottom-up design: The process of designing programs by considering the basic functions to be performed, writing functions to perform them, and then composing them into larger units. Not usually a good method for writing an entire program, but often used when designing libraries.

bound function: A mathematical function expressing an integral value that decreases with each iteration through a loop.

buffer: A region of memory used during input-output to hold data, either intended for output but not yet output, or input but not yet used by the processor.

bug: An error in the logic of a program that prevents it from conforming to its specifications under some circumstances. A program can operate correctly and still contain a bug, as some combinations of input might not activate the code containing the bug.

byte: A group of memory *bits*, intended to hold small numbers or character codes; usually but not always, bytes have eight bits.

C++: A language which is almost a superset of C, including object-oriented extensions.

cast: A means of forcing the value of an expression to have a certain type.

close a file: Terminate a program's access to a file; see also *open a file*.

code: A value that stands for something else; for example, a character code is a number that stands for a certain character. Also, 'code' is often used as a slang term for executable programs, or sections thereof, e.g. "There is a bug in your code."

comment: A remark in a program source file intended as explanation for human readers. They are marked in some way so that the compiler will ignore them; in C this is done by surrounding them with / * . . . * /.

compilation: The process of translation from high-level language into machine code, as performed by a compiler. Often used to refer to the combined processes of compilation and *linkage*.

compile time: The time during which a program is being compiled.

compiler: A program designed to automatically translate a specific high-level language into machine code for a particular computer.

conditional compilation: The ability of the preprocessor to include in, or exclude from, the compilation certain sections of source file.

conditional statement: Statement providing alternative execution paths, one of which is chosen at run time depending on the result of a test.

constant: A fixed value written in a program source text, e.g. 34.67.

constant expression: An expression with a fixed value computable by the compiler during compilation; it may not involve variables.

control character: A character code that, instead of standing for a visible character, stands for some special function, for example, form-feed, bell, backspace, etc.

correctness: The ability of a program to act according to its specifications for all legitimate combinations of input data.

corruption, memory: Placing data in memory that has not been allocated for the purpose; usually causes obscure errors.

crash (hardware): The failure of a computer to continue to function because of hardware failure. Colloquial.

crash (software): The failure of a program to continue to operate because of a bug or invalid input. Colloquial.

dangling pointer: A pointer pointing at memory that is not correctly allocated for use; e.g. a pointer that has been freed, or a pointer pointing at a local variable whose function has been exited.

data: Information represented in some manner, for example, printed words on a page, or a file on a computer disk.

data structure: An organized collection of data values.

data type: In C, a particular way to store a particular kind of information, e.g. `int` stores integral values in binary.

database: A special file or series of files containing data, together with a system for accessing the data without needing to know the layout of the data in the files.

De Morgan's laws: Certain rules for manipulation of logical expressions.

decimal numbers: Numbers written in the usual way with ten symbols, 0 to 9. Each place to the left increases a value tenfold: for example, 20 is ten times 2.

declaration: A part of a C program that defines the meaning of one or more identifiers.

definition, function: The full source text of a function.

dereference: Access the object that a pointer points to.

direct file access: See *random file access*.

documentation, internal: documentation intended for the programmer or future maintainers of a program, explaining what portions of the program (e.g. functions) do, how they interrelate, algorithms used, etc.

documentation, user: A document or computer file containing instructions for the users of a program.

documentation, system: See *documentation, internal*.

device: Anything connected to a computer and capable of sending or receiving data to or from the processor, with the exception of main memory.

editor: A program allowing one to enter or modify a source program or other readable data file.

EOF: A macro denoting the value returned by some library functions upon encountering end of file.

escape sequence: A short sequence of characters, introduced by a backslash (\), which denotes a single character that usually cannot otherwise be inserted in program text.

exception: A runtime error caused by an unpredictable event, such as bad input data, and for which the normal order of processing must be interrupted.

executable: Used as a noun, refers to an executable machine-language program file.

execute: To run a program in a computer.

exit status: See *termination status*.

exponent: The 'power' part of a floating point number; e.g. in `0.527E28`, 28 is the exponent.

expression: A rule for computing a value, written in a mathematics-like notation, e.g.: `12 + sin(pi/2.8)`.

field: A component of a structure.

file: A named unit of data on a computer disk. In C, all input-output is treated as accessing a file, even though some input-output does not involve true files (such as output to a terminal).

file, binary: A file intended to hold data in the computer's internal data formats; it may contain readable text.

file, text: A file intended to store data in readable character format only.

flag: A variable intended to indicate whether a particular event has occurred.

floating point notation: A version of the normal scientific notation for writing numbers, e.g. `1.357E20`

floating point storage method: A method of storing numbers in a binary version of floating point notation. The sign, significand, and binary exponent are each stored in binary.

flow: The path through the program followed during execution.

flush input: Read input to advance through a file, but do nothing with the data thus read.

flush a line: Flush input up to, and including, the next newline character.

flush output: Force the system to physically write buffered output data to a file (or other device).

format sequence: A special character sequence used in the format string of `printf` and `scanf`, requesting special action from the function. They commence with `%`.

function (C): A structural unit of the C language for performing a task; may be called anywhere that task must be done.

function call: A statement or factor in an expression, that executes a function.

global variable: A variable declared outside a function.

hardware: Physical machinery: computers, printers, etc.

header file: A C file containing declarations, included in a program file with a `#include` statement.

heap: A region of memory used to satisfy memory requests; in C, `malloc` and `calloc` allocate memory from a heap.

hexadecimal numbers: Numbers written with sixteen symbols, 0 to 9 and A to F (where A is ten, B eleven, etc.). Each place to the left increases a value by sixteen: for example, 20 hex is sixteen times 2, or 32 decimal. In C, written with a leading '0x', e.g. `0x20`.

high-level languages: Programming languages that provide features designed to match as closely as possible human ways of thinking: for example, `if` statements, expressions. See also *low-level languages*.

identifier: A 'word' to which a meaning can be assigned; in C, they consist of any characters A...Z, a...z, 0...9, or underscore (_), but may not start with a digit. Also, they may not spell out a keyword.

i-o: Common abbreviation for input-output.

incomplete type: A `struct` declaration that does not define the fields that make up the structure.

index: See *subscript*.

indirection operator: The character * when used as a prefix operator to find the variable to which a pointer points.

infinite loop: A loop that never terminates, usually due to a program bug.

information: The meaning that data possesses when correctly interpreted. For example, the data item 12, interpreted as a decimal number, means this many items: # # # # # # # # # # # #.

inheritance: A feature of object-oriented programming implementing the 'is a' relation; for example, a dog is a pet, so in a database of pets, all features of a pet (such as name, owner) will be available for dogs, plus 'dog-only' features, such as whether it has had distemper shots.

initialization: Setting a variable to its first value following declaration. C allows initialization as part of the declaration step.

input: The action by a computer of obtaining data from an outside source, such as a terminal or disk, and storing it in main memory. Sometimes the data is converted from one form to another as it is input. Can be used as a noun to refer to the data that is input.

interactive: Adjective applied to devices, files, or programs that communicate directly with a human user, for example, a terminal.

interface: A public definition of the observable behavior of a software or hardware component, for example, the preconditions and postconditions of a function.

interpreter: Like a compiler, an interpreter allows a high-level language program to run on a computer, but instead of translating the program into machine language so the machine code can run independently, an interpreter figures out what the program is intended to do, and does it itself. Therefore interpreters never produce an executable program file.

invariant: An assertion within a loop which must be true for every iteration of the loop.

iteration: The process of executing a loop; thus, iterative methods are methods containing a loop.

keyword: An identifier to which a special meaning is assigned in C.

library: A collection of functions providing certain facilities, and intended for use in various programs. Example: the standard C library.

linkage: The process of combining separately compiled program modules to produce the final executable program. Usually, libraries such as the standard C library (in compiled form) must be scanned to obtain functions used by a program.

linked list: A data structure composed of a list of nodes, where pointers are used to indicate the order of the nodes.

literal, string: See *string literal.*

local variable: Variable declared inside a function; its name may only be used within that function.

logical: See *Boolean.*

loop: A language construction requesting that the program execute some given instructions repeatedly. The instructions to be repeated are the *loop body*, and the test for continuation is the *loop test.*

low-level languages: Programming languages designed to provide features that match the facilities available on a particular computer; machine language is the ultimate low-level language, followed by assembly language.

machine code: A program or section of program in machine language.

machine language: The language used by the computer processor; usually a language of binary numbers.

macro: A preprocessor identifier (given a value, e.g. in a `#define` statement).

main memory, main storage: See *memory.*

maintenance: Modifying or extending software to fix errors detected while the software is in operation, or to keep it relevant to changing user needs. Since software cannot literally break or wear out, but hardware can, software maintenance and hardware maintenance are not the same thing.

memory: The second essential component of a computer, apart from the *processor.* Memory holds instructions and data for access by the processor. It consists of *bytes* arranged in *words*, and these have *addresses.* All memory locations can be accessed equally rapidly.

merge files: Combine two sorted files into a single larger sorted file.

newline: The indicator for the end of a text line. Most printers, terminals, etc., require two codes, return, to reset output to the left margin, and line-feed, to advance down one line. C pretends this is done by a single 'newline' character, `'\n'` (which is usually the code for line-feed); the system should take care of inserting returns on output, or removing them on input, provided the file concerned is not opened in binary mode.

node: One data element in a data structure.

nul: The character with code 0, written `'\0'`.

null: The C language pointer value denoting a pointer that points nowhere.

object file, object code: The output of a compiler, prior to linkage to form the final executable program. Cannot be executed, as required functions such as standard library functions are missing.

object oriented programming: A programming style encouraging focusing on the real-world objects involved in the problem, and the relationships between them. In the program, this results in focusing on the data rather than the processes being performed. Ideally, it works best with an object-oriented language such as C++.

octal numbers: Numbers written with eight symbols, 0 to 7. Each place to the left increases a value by eight: for example, 20 octal is eight times 2, or 16 decimal. In C, written with a leading zero, e.g. 020.

open a file: Prepare for accessing a file with a program. See also *close a file*.

operand: A value operated on by an operator.

operating system: The master program that controls a computer; it organizes the execution of other programs, and provides facilities such as the disk file system.

operator: In C, one of a fixed list of symbols denoting certain operations to be performed on data, e.g. in a+b, + is the operator. See also *unary*, *prefix*, *postfix*, and *binary* operators.

output: The action by a computer of transmitting data from main memory to an exterior device, such as a screen or disk. Sometimes the data is converted from one form to another as it is output. Can be used as a noun to refer to the data that is output.

overflow: Production in a calculation of a result larger than the largest representable value for the numeric type concerned.

parameters, actual: Values written in parentheses after a function name in a function call; the values are assigned to the corresponding formal parameters. Also called arguments.

parameters, formal: Variable declarations in parentheses in a function heading; they are assigned values obtained from the actual parameters. Also called dummy arguments.

pointer: See *address*.

portability: The ability of a program to run on different types and models of computer. Usually, the program must be recompiled for each computer type, but a program requiring no other changes than recompilation would be considered very portable. C allows one to write both portable and non-portable programs.

postcondition: A statement describing the state of affairs after the execution of a function or other piece of code for which the precondition was met.

postfix operator: A unary operator written after its operand.

posttest loop: A loop in which the first step is execution of the loop body before the first execution of the loop test.

precedence: The order in which the various operators are performed by the compiler. May be overridden by parentheses.

precondition: A statement at the start of a function or section of code, describing the conditions under which that code will execute correctly.

prefix operator: A unary operator written before its operand.

preprocessor: A utility that transforms a C source program prior to its compilation by the compiler proper.

pretest loop: A loop in which the first step is execution of the loop test before the first execution of the loop body.

priority: See *precedence*.

processing: Manipulation of data by a computer, for example, arithmetic operations, logical tests, etc.

processor: The component of the computer that performs processing.

program: A complete list of machine instructions for performing a particular job. A program is usually stored in a single file on disk. The word is sometimes used loosely to refer to program *source* file(s).

prompt: A message printed just before the computer attempts to input data from a terminal; informs the user what input the computer expects.

reading: The action of performing input.

random file access: Data input-output at any required position in a file, as determined by the program.

record: Can be another name for a *structure*; also used to refer to a structure stored on a file, or to a line in a file.

recursion: A programming style in which a function directly or indirectly calls itself. In direct recursion, a function calls itself directly; in indirect recursion, it calls itself via another function.

redirection, input/output: A facility provided by some operating systems for redirecting the normal program input/output from/to a file or device.

reference: An address, or pointer.

result: A value returned by a function to the expression in which the function call occurred.

robustness: The ability of software to respond sensibly, without crashing, when input data does not abide by the rules laid down in the software specifications. This is a subjective property.

rounding: Converting a real number to an integer by selecting the closest integer to the given real value.

run time: The time at which a program's instructions are being executed.

scope of an identifier: The region of a program in which the identifier may be used.

searching: Locating a particular value in a collection such as an array.

selection statement: See *conditional statement*.

sequence, statement: A sequence of statements written one after the other, to be executed in the order they appear in the program text.

sequential file access: Data input-output in sequence, from start to finish.

short-circuit operators: The C operators, `&&` and `||`, which under some circumstances, can skip the evaluation of their second operand.

side-effect: A change additional to the most obvious effect of a statement, e.g. a function that modifies a global variable has a side effect.

significand: The 'value' part of a floating point number, e.g. in `.527E27`, `.527` is the significand. Usually used, however, to denote the binary significand in a binary floating point number.

software: Any program or collection of programs (and perhaps associated data files).

software package: Software marketed or distributed as a single unit.

sorting: Rearranging a sequence of values according to an ordering function, such as alphabetic order for strings, or numeric order for numbers.

source, source code, source files: The high-level language files that are compiled to produce a program.

stack: A data structure where the first item to be removed is always the last item that was previously inserted.

statement: A single 'sentence' in a programming language.

stream: A term used in C for the connection to a file via a `FILE*`; the phrase "writing to (reading from) a stream" means to use a particular `FILE*` to access the file to which it was connected by an `fopen` call.

string: A sequence of `char`s terminating with a nul. Can be stored in a `char` array or a string literal.

string literal: A character string written in the program text, for example `"Hi there"`.

structure: A data object composed of a number of simpler data objects, called the *fields* of the structure.

structured programming: Writing programs using no flow-control statements other than loops, conditionals, and sequences.

stub function: A short, non-operational function to act as a 'placeholder' in a program during development, until the full function is written.

subscript: A value written in brackets after the address of an array to select one of the array elements.

syntax: The rules governing the form of a program in a given language.

syntax error: A departure from correct syntax in a source program. The message displayed by a compiler as it finds one is often colloquially called a syntax error.

systems analyst: One who analyzes the operations of a company, etc., and proposes a system (usually including a computer system) to solve the problems under consideration.

termination status: The indication of success or failure returned by a program to the calling environment after program completion.

top-down design: The process of designing programs by considering the overall task to be performed, expressing it in a number of simpler steps, and then repeating that process on those simpler steps, etc., until the steps needed are so simple they can be programmed directly in the programming language.

tracing: Attempting to understand the behavior of a program by 'executing' it manually (i.e. on paper, without a computer).

truncation: Conversion of a real number to integer by discarding the fractional part.

twos complement: A system for storing binary integer values whereby a negative value is formed by complementing all the bits of the corresponding positive number, and adding one.

type: See *data type*.

type promotion: Conversion of a value of (usually) an arithmetic type to another with greater accuracy or range, e.g. `int` to `float`.

unary operator: An operator which takes only one operand, such as '−' in −5. Sometimes called a monadic operator.

underflow: The production in a floating point calculation of a nonzero value too close to zero to be represented as other than zero.

variable: A memory location or locations assigned to store a value of a given type. Named variables are declared in a declaration, and the name stands for the variable in the program text.

verification, program: Strictly, the process of devising a proof that a program is correct; this proof will usually be mathematical.

void function: A function returning no result.

whitespace: In C, any sequence of non-printing characters, such as spaces, tabs, and form-feeds.

wildcard: A character used in a pattern to stand for any character from some set; for example, $\ast$ is often used as a wildcard in filename search patterns to indicate any sequence of characters.

word: The most efficient storage unit in memory; usually a collection of two, four, or more bytes.

wordsize: The number of bits in a given computer's word.

writing: The action of performing output.

Bibliography

Here are a few books I have found enlightening, along with my personal opinions —
you might disagree.

American National Standard for Information Systems — Programming Language — C.
ANSI X3.159-1989.
> The official definition of C. Not recommended as a means of learning C, but useful
> for the correct answer on specific issues. This edition has a nice rationale section
> that explains the thinking behind the official standard. Unfortunately, this has been
> dropped from the current edition, which is *ISO/IEC 9899;1990*. The Australian
> edition is *AS 3955-1991*. There is no difference in substance among these three
> editions apart from the numbering of sections.

Gries, David: *The Science of Programming*. Springer-Verlag, 1981.
> A book on program verification, using the precondition-postcondition methods
> sketched out this text. Uses full mathematical techniques, but well-written and by
> no means impenetrable to a reader with average mathematical skills.

Hoffman, Joe D: *Numerical Methods for Engineers and Scientists*. McGraw Hill,
1992.
> Presents numerical methods for finding solutions to the kinds of equations that arise
> in science and engineering. Does not include programs.

Meyer, Bertrand: *Object-oriented Software Construction*. Prentice Hall, 1988.
> A book with much thoughtful material for anyone interested in pursuing object-
> oriented programming. Uses Meyer's own language, Eiffel, but the sections on the
> philosophy and principles of object-oriented programming are still very useful to
> non-Eiffel programmers.

Park, Stephen K & Miller, Keith W: 'Random number generators: good ones are hard
to find', *Communications of the ACM*, vol 31, no 10, October 1988.
> Advised reading for anyone doing serious work with random numbers.

Press, William H, Flannery, Brian P, Teukolsky, Saul A, and Vetterling, William T:
Numerical Recipes in C: The Art of Scientific Computing. Cambridge University
Press, 1988.
> Another text about numerical computation techniques. Presents algorithms in C.

Saint-Exupéry, Antoine de: *The Little Prince*. Pan Books, 1982.
> When you tire of staring at the computer screen, try this wonderful philosophy book
> disguised as a children's fairy story.

Sale, A H: 'Stylistics in Languages with Compound Statements', *The Australian
Computer Journal*, vol 10, no 2, May 1978.
> The program layout rules used in this text are based on ones proposed by Sale in
> this article.

Strunk, William Jr & White, E B *The Elements of Style*. 3rd edition. Macmillan, NY, 1979.

A slim volume on writing well in English; it is both enjoyable and enlightening. Good English expression is essential for a programmer, if for no other reason than that it encourages precision of thought.

For electronic reading matter, try to get access to the Internet (called AARNet in Australia). This network connects most universities and many commercial enterprises throughout the world. It is possible to read and post news on this network in things called newsgroups. There are two newsgroups concerned with C: comp.lang.c and comp.std.c. The former is for asking and answering questions about C. The latter is for discussing the design of the C language.

Index by topic and language feature

This index lists the sections where each topic or C language feature is discussed. Section numbers in bold refer to sections primarily devoted to the particular topic or feature.

Topic or language feature	Sections
General programming facts and concepts	
abstract data types	**15**, 17.3
addresses (pointers)	**3.2.1**, 5.2.4
algorithms	**1.3**
ASCII	**3.2.1**, 3.2.2, 6.5, **G**
assignment	**3.3**
data — concepts	**3.1**
data representation	**3.1**
data structures	**13.2**, **15**
debugging	8.6
efficiency	**19.2**
files	**10**, **17**
end of file	**10.4.1**
functions	**2.2**, 2.2.6, **3.6.2**, **7**
calling functions	**2.2.2**, **3.6.2**
results	**3.6.2**, **7.5**, **7.6**
result of `main`	**7.6.1**
hierarchies	**2.1**
high-level languages	**1.2.3**
input	1.1, **5** **5.1**
input-output redirection	**5.5**
libraries	**7.8**
standard C library	**2.2.3**
loops	**4**
pretest	**4.2**
posttest	**4.2**
using a counter	**4.3.1**
correctness	**4.7**
calculating products and sums	**4.5**
skipping incorrect input	**5.4.3**
looping until a certain event happens	**5.4.2**

memory	1.2, **3.2.1**
dynamic allocation	**13, 13.1**
object-oriented programming	**8.5**
output	1.1
processing	1.1
program development	**1.4, 8, 8.2**
random-access and binary input-output	**17, 17.2, 17.3**
recursion	**14**
searching and sorting	**9.4, 19**
string representation	3.2.2, **3.3**
structured programming	**6.6**
top-down programming	**8.1**
variables	**3.2, 3.3**
local	**3.2**, 5.4.5
global	**3.2**, 7.2, 7.9
verification	**4.7**, 8.3
preconditions and postconditions	2.3.1, **4.7**, 6.6
Documentation principles	
comments	1.5, **2.3**, 3.5, 5.4.2
documenting functions	2.2.6, **2.3.1**
functional specifications	15.3
preconditions and postconditions	**2.3.1, 4.7**
user documentation	**1.5**
Program structure	
the `main` function	**2.2.1**
`main` called to start program	**2.2**
`main` parameters	**13.3**
global variables	**3.2, 18.2**
local variables	**3.2**
scopes of identifiers:	**18.2**
variables	3.2
functions	**18.2**
macro names	4.6
pointers	**18.2**
tags: `structs, unions`	**11.3**
scopes of identifiers (multiple files)	**18.2, 18.3**
storage duration, linkage:	**3.1, 18.4**
static	**18.3, 18.4**
automatic	**3.1, 18.4, C.2.1**

C language elements
    comments   **2.3**
    constants   **3.2**, 3.2.2
    escape sequences   3.2.1, **F.1.3**
    identifiers   **2.6, F.1.1**
    keywords   **2.6, F.1.1**
    multibyte characters   **C.4.1**
    numerical representation of characters   **3.2.2**
    string literal   **3.2.1**
    trigraphs   **C.4.2**

Types
    `char` types   **3.3**
    integer types   **3.3, 3.7.2, 16.2**, 16.2.1
      range of `ints`   **3.3**, 3.7.2, **16.2**
      `<limits.h>`   **16.2**
    floating point   **3.7.1, 16.3**, 16.7
      accuracy and range   **16.3, 16.6**
      overflow, underflow   **16.6**
      `<float.h>`   **16.3**
    enumeration types   **C.2.4**
    arrays   **3.3**, 7.3, **9, 9.1, 9.2**, 9.3, **9.5**
    `structs`   **11.3, 12.4**
      incomplete types   **15.2**
    unions   **C.2.2**
    pointers   **12, 12.1, 12.3, 12.4**
    functions   **7.5**
    qualified types (`const` and/or `volatile`)   **18.6, C.2.5**

Constants:
    floating   **3.7.1, 16.3.1, F.1.1**
    character   **3.2.2, F.1.1**
    integer   **3.2.2, 16.2.2, F.1.1**
    enumeration   **F.1.1**
    string literals   **3.2.1, F.1.4**

Conversions
    arithmetic   **16.5**
      floating point to integer   3.7.1
    pointer to `void`   **13.1**

Declarations	F.2.2
position of declarations	2.4, 2.5, **3.2**
simple variable declarations	**3.2**
structured declarations	**13.5**
pointers	**12, 12.1, 12.3, 13.4**, C.5
arrays	**3.3**, 7.3, **9, 9.1, 9.2**, 9.3, **9.5, 12.3,** C.5
`structs`	**11.3**
bit-fields	C.2.3
`unions`	C.2.2
multidimensional arrays	**9.5**
enumeration types	C.2.4
storage class	
`auto`	C.2.1
`extern`	**18.3**
`register`	C.2.1
`static`	**18.3**, C.2.1
type definitions and type equivalence (`typedef`)	**11.2**
type qualifiers	
`const`	**18.6**
`volatile`	C.2.5
function declarations	**2.4, 13.4**
`void` functions	**2.2.4**, 7.5
specifying parameters (arguments)	**7.2, 7.3**
specifying return type	**7.5**
specifying old style arguments	**7.7**
variable number of arguments	C.2.6
function definitions	**2.4, 7.2**, 7.3, **7.5**
specifying return value	**7.5, 7.6**
initialization	
simple variables	**9.5.1**
arrays	**9.5.1**
`structs`	**11.3**
`unions`	C.2.2
multidimensional arrays	**9.5.1**
Expressions	**3.2, F.2.1**
binary operators	**3.6.1**
postfix, prefix operators	**3.6.1**
maths operators	**3.6.1**
comparison operators	**4.4.1**
logical operators	**6.3.1**

other operators

    address-of   5.2.1, 5.2.4, 5.3.1, 12.1, 13.1

    array subscripts   **9.1**

    function calls   3.6.2

    casts   **13.1**

    .   **11.3**

    indirection (`*`) and ->   **12.1**, 12.2, **12.4**

    `sizeof`   **13.1**, 19.4.2, C.5

    assignment   **3.3**, 3.6.1, **10.4.1**

    combined math/assignment   **3.6.1**

    bitwise shift and logical operators   **C.3.1**

    comma   9.5, **10.4.1**

  constant expressions   3.3

  function results   **3.6.2**

  pointer arithmetic   **12.3**, **12.3.1**, 12.3.2

  precedence rules   **3.6.1**, **4.4.2**, **C.3.3**

  sequence points   **C.3.3**

  arithmetic conversions and promotions   **16.5**

  lvalues and rvalues   **C.5**

Statements   **F.2.3**

  labelled statements   **C.1.1**

  compound statements   **F.2.3**

  expression (assignment) and null statements   **3.3**, **C.1.4**

  jump statements

    `goto`   **C.1.1**

    `continue`   **C.1.3**

    `break`   **6.4**, **C.1.2**

    `return`   **7.5**, **7.6**

  conditional statements   **6**

    `if`   **6.2**, **6.2.1**, **6.2.3**

    `switch` and `case`   **6.4**

  loops   **4**

    `while`   **4.3.1**

    `for`   **4.3.2**

    `do`   **4.3.3**

Preprocessor   **4.6**, **F.3**

  `#define`   **4.6**, **18.5.3**

    multi-line   **11.1**

  `#undef`   **C.4.3**

  `#if`   **18.5.1**

  `#ifdef`   **18.5.1**

`#ifndef`	**18.5.1**
`#include`	**2.2.3**
library headers	2.2.3, 18.5.2
`#line`	**C.4.3**
`#error`	**C.4.3**
`#pragma`	**C.4.3**
`# and ##`	**C.4.3**
predefined macro names	C.4.3
`<limits.h>`	**16.2**
`<float.h>`	**16.3**

General library functions
`gets`	**5.3.2**
mathematical	**3.7.1**
`printf`	3.2.2, **3.4**
% formats s, c, d, f, c, e, g, x	3.2.2, 3.4, **3.7.1**, **16.4**
width, precision	3.4, 3.7.1
other % formats	**16.4**
flags −, +, <space>, 0, and #	**16.4**
`scanf`	5.2, **5.2.1**, **5.2.2**, **5.2.3**, **5.3**, 10.4.1
% formats d, c, s, f	**5.2.1**, **5.2.2**, **5.2.3**, 5.3.1, 16.4
% formats [, x, p, n, %	**10.4.1**
other % formats	**16.4**
exact match, whitespace	**5.2.3**
function return value	5.4.4
assignment suppression (%*)	**7.4**
string functions	**3.5**, **6.5**, **12.3.2**
`malloc`, `free` etc.	**13.1**

Index

. operator 277, 504
.h 21, 161, 173
, *see* comma operator
! operator 137, 139, 504
!= operator 75, 504
?: operator 503, 504
() function call operator 504
() casts *see* Casts
[] 504
{} 19
+ operator 45, 58, 504
++ operator 56, 504
+= operator 56
- operator 42, 58, 504
− operator 56, 504
-> operator 504
* indirection operator 241, 301, 479, 504
* multiplication operator 58, 504
*/ 27
/ operator 58, 504
/* 27
^ operator 503, 504
< operator 75, 504
<< operator 503, 504
<= operator 75, 504
<assert.h> 523
<ctype.h> 509
<float.h> 403
<limits.h> 399
<malloc.h> 324
<math.h> 59, 510
<setjmp.h> 512
<stdarg.h> 512
<stddef.h> 509
<stdio.h> 19, 21, 423, 431, 512
<stdlib.h> 324, 516– 518
<string.h> 147, 519
<time.h> 520
= in mathematics 52
= operator 47, 48, 256, 504
== operator 75, 504
> operator 75, 504
>= operator 75, 504
>> operator 503, 504
% operator 55, 58, 504
#
  in macros 459
  preprocessor directives 21, 536
preprocessor operator 507
preprocessor operator 507
#define 79, 450, 454, 501, 507, 536
#elif 536
#else 536
#endif 450, 536
#error 506, 536
#if 450, 536

#ifdef 450, 536
#ifndef 450, 455, 536
#include 19, 21, 41, 81, 174, 450, 536
#line 506, 536
#pragma 507, 536
#undef 506, 536
& operator 99, 103, 324, 503, 504
&& operator 137, 504
\ 46
\" 43
\0 44
\n 20, 43, 45, 46
__DATE__ 507
__FILE__ 507
__LINE__ 507
__STDC__ 507
__TIME__ 507
! operator 503, 504
|| operator 137, 504
~ operator 503, 504

A

abort 171, 517
abs 60, 518
Abstract data type 384– 394
Accuracy 408
Ackermann's function 380
acos 60, 510
Actual parameters 160
Addition 55
Address 44, 301
  and scanf 99
  memory 5
  of string 43
Address-of operator 99, 103–105, 300, 324
Addresses 41, 45, 99, 103, 299
Adjacent string literals 459
ADT *see* Abstract data type
Algorithm efficiency 466
Algorithms 1, 7, 8, 10, 82, 130, 460
and operator 137
ANSI 161
ANSI/IEEE 754–1985, 403
Area of a triangle 152
argc 342
Arguments 20, 156, 170, 172–173
  command-line 341, 350
  dummy 160
  modifying 302
  simple 156
  to printf 49
  to scanf 99
argv 342

Arithmetic 3
floating point standard 403
pointer 305, 306
Arithmetic expressions 136
Arithmetic operators 47
Array 47, 48, 104
  contents 217
  filling with data 216
  overflow 214
  parameters 163–165
  subscripts 213, 217
Array Arguments 162
Array indexes
  storing in files 420
Arrays 212, 305
  and pointers 305, 507
  and scanf 104
  char 47, 174
  deciding length of 217
  expressions with fewer subscripts 227
  initialization 224
  multi-dimensional 224
  omitting size 226
  storing Numeric Data 213
  to represent categories 217
  to store any kind of data 212
  to store chars 212
  unused elements 215
  when to use 216
ASCII 44–46, 240, 539
asctime 522
asin 60, 510
asm 34, 529
Assemblers 5
assert 523
assert.h 523
Assertion
  in loop test 70
Assertions 83
Assigning floats to ints 58
Assigning ints to floats 58
Assignment 55
  within expression 256
Assignment operator 47, 75, 256
Associativity 505
Asterisk in scanf format 167
atan 60, 510
atan2 510
atexit 518
atof 516
atoi 516
atol 516
Australia 44
auto 33, 499, 529
Automata 238
Automatic storage duration 449
Automatic variables 42
Average 213
Avogadro's number 58

B

Backslash 43, 44, 46
Baker's dozens 124
Base class 394
BASIC programmers
 warning for 99
Becomes 47
Behaviours
 of objects 203
Bentley, Jon 468
Big-O notation 466
Binary 4, 40, 45, 46
 code 5
 digit 5
 file access 416
 files 240, 419
 fopen mode 418
 input-output 416
 operators 56
 search 466, 468, 470
Bit 5
Bit fields 500
Bitwise operators 503
Black-box testing 205
Blank padding 49
Block 444
 entry 499
 exit 499
 scope 444, 446
Body, loop 68
Boolean 70
Bottom-up debugging 204
Bottom-up programming 184
Bound function 82, 83
Brace 22
Braces 19, 133
 in macros 457
break 33, 141, 148, 497, 529,
 535
Britain 44
bsearch 470, 471, 518
 programming 473
Bubble sort 222, 232, 475
Buffer 438
Buffering 98, 437, 438
Buffers 98
Bugs 1, 9
Business 2
Byte 5, 43–45

C

C 6, 7
C compiler 6
C library 19
C program 6
C++ 34, 529
 and old-style arguments 173
Calculation 45
Call, function 18, 19
calloc 327, 517

case 33, 140, 148, 529, 535
Casts 325, 407, 471, 472, 474,
 532
 priority 504
ceil 510
Cellular automata 238
Celsius 122
char 33, 47, 398, 400, 529
 storage 47
char arrays 47, 162, 174
 length of 48
Character code 47
Character constants 46, 81
Character sequences 43
Characters 45
 multibyte 505
chars and scanf 101
Check, compiler 460
Chess 179, 296, 377
Circuits, processor 5
Circular lists 332
Clarity 8
class 34, 529
clearerr 512
clock 521
clock_t 520
Closing files 240
Code 40
 character 44, 45
Codes 4
Coding methods 44
Coins 124
Collisions, hash table 467
Combinations 179
Comma operator 221, 225, 255,
 256, 504
Command line 422
 arguments 341, 350
Comments 1, 10, 27, 81, 109,
 110, 356
Comparison Operators 75
Compilation 7
 conditional 450
Compiler 6, 7, 10, 41, 46
Compiler check 460
Completeness 8
Complex systems 16
Complexity 480
Computation 42
 numeric 398
Computer
 behaviour 48
 operations 1, 2
Computer languages
 other 161
Computer memory 44
Computers
 speed of 68
 timesharing 98
Condition 131
Conditional 130
Conditional compilation 450,
 454

Conditional operator 503
const 33, 460, 461, 529
Constant 49
Constant expression 48, 140
Constants 41, 42, 45, 46, 530
 base 401
 character 46, 402
 floating point 88
 Floating-Point 404
 giving names to 79
 integral 401
 long 60
 signed 401
 unsigned 401
Contents 45, 300
 array 212
 memory 5
continue 33, 498, 529, 535
Conway's Life see Life
Correctness 3, 8
 loop 82
cos 59, 510
cosh 60, 511
Counter, loop 70
Counting 58
cp Unix command 420
ctime 522
clock_t 520
ctype.h 509

D

Data 2, 5, 40, 41
 binary 416
 binary storage 4
 conversion functions 265
 hiding 394
 input 98
 representation accuracy 417
Data base 422
Data structures 384
 linked 331
Data types 40, 57, 274
 abstract 384
 choosing correct 58
 floating 402
 integral 398
 storage ranges 47
Dates 156, 520
Daylight saving 521
De Morgan's laws 139
Debugging 109, 203
 bottom-up 204
 top-down 204
Decay
 radioactive 87
Decimal notation 45
Decimal number 40
Declaration 41
 function 160
 struct 274
Declarations 499, 533
 complicated 346

function 29
  scope of 446
  variable 47
default 33, 140, 141, 529, 535
Definition, function 22, 160
Degrees 60, 122
delete 34, 529
Demotion, type 408
Derivative 153
Designing programs 16
Development process, program 8
Devices 98
Diagrams 10
difftime 521
Digits 33
  significant 403
Direct access 422
Direct recursion 358
Directives 21
Disks 7, 98
div 518
Division 55
do 33, 529, 535
do...while 69, 73, 74
Documentation 1, 9, 27
  internal 9, 10
  user 9
Documenting functions 28
DOS 346, 420
  sample session 493
Dot operator *see* . operator
double 33, 57, 58, 88, 402, 404, 529
  output 59
  scanf input 101
Double quotes 46
Doubly linked list 331
Dummy arguments 160
Dyadic operators 56
Dynamic memory allocation 324

E

e *see* Natural logarithms
Easter 151
Editor 7
Education 2
Efficiency 8, 466
  program 499
  sorting 475
Eiffel 203
Electronic components 4
Elements
  array 212
else 33, 529, 535
Empty statements 498
End of file 250
enum 33, 500, 529
Environment, integrated 495

EOF 250, 252, 512
Equal operator 75
Equals 47
  in mathematics 52
Eratosthenes, sieve of 236
errno 266
Error, logic 33
Errors 1
  syntax 9
Escape codes 46
Escape sequences 43, 44, 46, 210
Exclusive-or 150
Executables 5
Execution
  program 5
exit 518
Exit Status 172
EXIT_FAILURE 172
exp 60, 511
Exponent 402
  of floating number 58
Exponential 57
Expression evaluation 505
Expression, constant 48
Expressions 41, 42, 55, 532
  arithmetic 136
  logical 136
  mixing types in 406
extern 33, 529
External definitions 535
External linkage 447

F

fabs 60, 511
Factorial 94
Factorials 77
Fahrenheit 122
fclose 240, 258, 512
feof 513
ferror 513
fflush 436, 438, 513
fgetc 513
fgetpos 422, 423, 513
fgets 107, 249, 257, 513
  end of file 253
Fibonacci sequence 92, 123
  and recursion 369
Field selection operator 277
Field selection priority 504
Fields 276, 279
FILE 240, 243–245, 249, 384, 418, 436
File input 245
File merge 258
File output 241
File processing 240
File scope 444
FILENAME_MAX 431, 513
Files 7

binary 240
binary access 416
  end of 250
  random access 416, 422
  storing pointers in 420
  Text 240
Financial planning 2
float 33, 41, 57, 58, 402, 529
  output 59
  scanf input 101
float.h 403
Floating point 41
  data 57
  data types 402
  inaccuracy 88, 116
Floating point standard 403
Floating point constants 404
floor 411, 511
fmod 58, 511
fopen 240, 243, 244, 247, 258, 266, 436, 513
  binary mode 418
  mode 244
  update mode 436
FOPEN_MAX 513
for 33, 69, 72, 529, 535
Formal parameter 161
Formal parameters 160
Format sequences 45, 46
fpos_t 423, 440
fprintf 244, 249, 405, 513
  see also printf
fputc 513
fputs 245, 514
Fractional numbers 41
France 44
fread 418, 422, 436, 514
free 324, 327, 517
freopen 509
frexp 511
friend 34, 529
fscanf 249, 252, 406, 514
fscanf's result 250
fseek 436, 514
fsetpos 422, 436, 514
ftell 436, 514
Function 42
  arguments 170
  array arguments 162
  call 18
  declarations 29, 160
  definitions 22, 160
  documentation 28
  libraries 7, 173, 509
  names 26, 33
  old-style definitions 172
  result 42, 57, 170
  scanf result 115
  scope 444
  side-effects 167
Function-prototype scope 444
Functional specification 393

Functions 4, 18, 41
  for structuring programs 26
  hash 467
  linkage of 447
  mathematical 59
  recursive 24
  returning results 167
  String 146
  variable number of
    parameters 501
  void 22, 168, 169, 172
fwrite 418, 422, 436, 514

G

Games 2
Gas, ideal 125
GCD 152, 180
Geometric sequence 126
German 40
getc 252, 514
getchar 99, 103, 514
getenv 518
gets 99, 104, 106, 167, 249,
  257, 514
Global 42, 162
Global variables 41, 156, 167,
  447
  and recursion 364, 371
gmtime 522
goto 33, 148, 497, 512, 529,
  535
Graphics 331
Greatest common denominator
  152, 180
Gries, David 85, 553

H

Hashing 467
Header 161
  multiple inclusion 454
  names 532
  standard library 21
Header files
  writing reliable 454
Heap 324
Hexadecimal 40, 404
Hierarchies 16, 184
High-level languages 6, 7
Human user 98
Hypotenuse 42

I

Ideal gas 125
Identifier, length of 33
Identifiers 33, 446, 530
IEEE arithmetic 403, 411

if statements 33, 131, 135,
  136, 445, 452, 529, 535
  multiple-test 134
Implies 177
Incrementing variables 52
Indentation in listings 72
Index
  array 212
  permuted 352
Indirect recursion 358
Indirection 241, 300, 301
Indirection operator 241
Inefficiency 8
Information 40
Inheritance 394
Initialization 224, 226
Initializing loops 70
inline 34, 529
Input 1, 2, 98, 99
  and loops 109
  and program structure 186
  buffered 437
  deciding array subscript 218
  devices 98
  File 245
  incorrect 3, 112
  redirection 120
  Strings 104
Input-output 240, 512
  binary 416
  Unix 266
Insertion sort 235
Instructions 5, 18
  mnemonic 5
  speed of 98
int 33, 47, 398, 400, 529
  and scanf 99
  storage 47
Integers 41, 45
Integral constants 401
Integral data types 398
Integral type
  choosing 400
Integrated environment 495
Integration 208
Interface 384
Internal documentation 9, 10,
  27
Internal linkage 447
Interpretation of data as
information 40
Interpreters 6
Introductory comment 110
Invariant 83, 84
isalnum 509
isalpha 509
iscntrl 509
isdigit 510
isgraph 510
islower 510
isprint 510
ispunct 510
isspace 510

isupper 510
isxdigit 510
Iteration 68, 130

J

jmp_buf 512
Justification 49

K

Keyboards 98
Keystroke 98
Keywords 33

L

Labels 497
labs 60, 518
Language, machine 1, 41
Language designers 40
Languages
  computer 40
  high-level 6, 7
  low-level 5
  programming 1
Layout 119
  program 72
Layout rules 133, 525
ldexp 511
ldiv 518
Libraries, function 173
Library 171, 184
  input functions 99
  memory functions 308
  standard 7, 19, 156, 509
  string functions 308
Library functions
  string comparison 146
Life 238, 321, 441
limits.h 399
Linear search 475
Linkage 444, 447
Linked data structures 331
Linked list 331
  and stacks 391
Linking 7
Literals
  adjacent 459
  string 41, 43, 44, 531
Local variables 41, 42, 444
  and recursion 364
localeconv 509
localtime 522
Locations, memory 4, 41
log 60, 511
log10 511
Logic 40
Logic error 33

Logical 70
  operators 137
Logical expressions 136
  manipulation 138
`long` 33, 60, 398, 400, 529
  `scanf` input 101
  size range 60
`long double` 402, 404
`longjmp` 512
Loop
  body 68
  correctness 82, 259
  counter 70
  indentation 72
  invariant 83
  postcondition 83
  test 68, 70
Looping 130
Loops 68, 136, 497, 498
  and break 141
Lorentz contraction 86
Low-level languages 5
Lvalues 507

M

Machine 2
Machine language 1, 41
Machine language programs 4, 5
Macro parameters 456, 459
Macros 81, 82, 214, 454
  # 459
  `__DATE__` 507
  `__FILE__` 507
  `__LINE__` 507
  `__STDC__` 507
  `__TIME__` 507
  EOF 250
  NULL 244, 301
  parameterized 450, 455, 460
  predefined 507
  `ptrdiff_t` 307
  `size_t` 308
`main` 18, 19, 184
  executed first 24
  return inside 172
Main memory 3, 7
Maintainability 3, 8
`malloc` 324, 327, 333, 517
`malloc.h` 324
Manipulating logical expressions 138
Manufacturing 2
`math.h` 59, 510
Mathematical expressions 47
Mathematical functions 59
Matrix 224
Matrix manipulation 316, 318
Matrix multiplication 228
`mblen` 509
`mbstowcs` 509
`mbtowc` 509
Mean 213

Measuring 58
`memchr` 519
`memcmp` 519
`memcpy` 308, 309, 519
`memmove` 308, 519
Memory 3, 44, 47, 58, 99
  addresses 299
  computer 43
  corruption 107
  dynamic allocation 324
  functions 308
  locations 41
`memset` 519
Merge sort 475
Merging files 258
Methods 203
  programming 4
Meyer, Bertrand 203
Mice 98
Minus *see* - operator
Mixing types in expressions 406
`mktime` 521
Mnemonic instructions 5
Mnemonics 5
Modems 98
`modf` 511
Money 411
MS-DOS 120, 266
Multi-dimensional Arrays 224
Multibyte Characters 505
Multiplication 42, 55

N

Names 5
  of functions 26
  of variables 47, 110
  symbolic 41
  variable 110
Natural logarithms 93, 209
Negation 55
new 34, 529
Newline 20, 43
Newton's method 153
Not operator 137, 139
Nul 44, 46, 48, 212
NULL 244, 253, 301, 309, 324, 332, 438, 509
Numbers 5
Numeric computation 398
Numeric data in arrays 213
Numerical integration 208

O

O(n) 466
Object-oriented programming 203, 394
Objective C 203
Objects 203, 507
Octal 40, 404

offsetof 509
Old style function definitions 172
Opening files 240
Operands 56
Operating systems 98
Operator 34, 529
  . 277
  ! 137, 139
  != 75
  ?: 503
  ++ 56
  += 56
  − 56
  * 241, 300, 301
  < 75
  <= 75
  = 256
  == 75
  > 75
  >= 75
  & 99, 103, 300, 324
  && 137
  || 137
  address-of 99
  comma 225
  conditional 503
  plus 45
  precedence 55, 75
  priority 504
  results 256
  `sizeof` 325, 479
Operators 42, 47, 55, 531
  binary 56
  bitwise 503
  comparison 75
  dyadic 56
  logical 137
  monadic 56
  shortcut 56
  unary 56
Organization, program 4
Outdated documents 10
Output 1, 2, 98
  and program structure 186
  buffered 437
  decimal integers 45
  file 241
  string 45
  strings 104
Outputting `floats` and `doubles` 59
Overflow 408
  array 106, 214
Overload 34, 529

P

Palindromes 92, 270
Parameterized macros 450, 455
Parameters 156, 165, 174, 460, 508
  actual 160
  array 165

formal 160
macro 455, 459
variable number of 501
Parentheses 23
function calls 20
Pascal 6, 136, 161, 165, 525
Pascal's triangle 234
Performance 437
Peripheral devices 210
Permuted index 352
perror 247, 265, 515
Planets 296
Plus 42, 45
Pointer
arithmetic 305, 306
dangling 450
FILE 240
variables 241
Pointers 43, 99, 300, 305
and arrays 305, 507
and const 461
and storage duration 449
and structures 312
and subscripts 308
storing in files 420
to functions 343
void 325
Polar coordinates 94
Polynomial 153
Portability 6
Postconditions 28, 83, 117, 247
loop 83
Postfix operators 56
pow 60, 511
Precedence 505
operator 55, 75
Precision 58
Preconditions 28, 83, 117, 247
Predefined FILE pointer names
257
Prefix operators 56
Preprocessing directives 536
Preprocessor 21, 79, 444, 450,
455, 456, 459, 506
#define 79, 450, 454, 501,
507, 536
#elif 536
#else 536
#endif 450, 536
#error 506, 536
#if 450, 536
#ifdef 450, 536
#ifndef 450, 455, 536
#include 19, 21, 41, 81,
174, 450, 536
#line 506, 536
#pragma 507, 536
#undef 506, 536
Pretty printer 271
Primary store 7
Printers 43

printf 19, 20, 43, 45, 49,
162, 249, 405, 416, 501, 515
% 46
%*s 249
%% 50
%c 45
%d 45, 46, 404
%e 59, 404
%f 59, 404
%g 59, 404
%i 404
%ld 60, 405
%lo 405
%lu 405
%lx 405
%lX 405
%o 404
%s 45, 49, 50
%u 404
%x 404
argument list 45
first argument 49
flags 405
format sequences 45, 46
formats 49, 50, 404
in standard library 21
integer output 50
long values 60
outputting numeric values 45
precision 50, 59
printing % sign 50
variable width or precision
50
width 49, 50, 59
Priorities
&& and || 138
Priority, operator 504
Processing 1, 2
Processor 3
instructions 5
speed 98
Products 76
Professional software 98
Program 3, 6–8, 18
behaviour 10
correctness 3
debugging 203
development process 8
efficiency 499
execution 5
exit Status 172
layout 72
linking 7
organization 4
specifications 10
structure 41, 185, 219
structuring 17
verification 28, 82
Programmers 10
Programming 3, 185
bottom-up 184
methods 4

object-oriented 203, 394
top-down 184
Programming languages 1, 5,
46
Programs 1, 18
compiling 7
designing 16
keeping simple 480
machine language 4
portable 6
structuring 16
Promotion, type 406
Prompt 98
ptrdiff_t 307, 509
public 34, 529
Punctuators 531
putc 515
putchar 244, 515
puts 515

Q

qsort 478, 518
Qualifiers
const 460
volatile 461, 501
Quality programs 79
Quick sort 222, 476
Quotes
double 43, 46
in #include directive 174
in string literals 43
left and right 43
single 46

R

Radians 60
Radioactive decay 87
Radix 402
raise 509
rand 517
Random file access 416, 422
Reading 98
realloc 509
Rearranging data 220
Records 276
Recursion 24, 356
check for correct 365
direct 358
efficiency 369
indirect 358
pitfalls 368
Recursive algorithms
designing 359, 364
Redirection
input 120
register 33, 499, 529
Register variables 499
Relativity, Theory of 86

Reliability 3, 8
Remainder 55
floating point 58
Remarks 27
remove 515
rename 21, 515
Repeating statements 68
Representation 45
Representation, data 40
Resistors 180
Result 170
    function 42
    of operators 256
Results 173
    function 57, 156, 167
return 33, 168, 171, 172,
    529, 535
    inside main 172
Return address 369
Return value 156
    function 57
rewind 436, 515
Robots 2
Robustness 3, 8
Roman numerals 40, 152, 180
Rounding 58
Runtime 447
Rvalues 507

S

Sale, A H   525
scanf 99, 101, 104, 115, 243,
    249, 252, 300, 406, 416, 501,
    515
    %*c 167
    %c 101
    %d 100, 167, 406
    %e 406
    %f 101, 406
    %g 101, 406
    %hd 406
    %ho 406
    %hu 406
    %hx 406
    %i 406
    %ld 101, 406
    %le 101, 406
    %lf 101, 406
    %lg 101, 406
    %lo 406
    %lu 406
    %lx 406
    %o 406
    %s 104
    %u 406
    %x 406
    %[256
    arguments 99
    asterisk in format 167
    chars 101
    discarding result 169
    format string 99

formats 101, 404, 405
function return 113
int 99, 100
numeric data 101
variable widths 101
whitespace 101
width 101, 106
Science 2
Scope 444
    block 444, 446
    file 444
    function 444
    function prototype 444
Scope rules
    static 446
Scoping rules 444
Search
    binary 466
    efficiency 467
    linear 475
    sequential 220
Searching 220, 466
Secondary storage 7
SEEK_CUR 437
SEEK_END 437
SEEK_SET 437
Selection 130
Selection sort 222
Semicolon 498
Sequence, geometric 126
Sequence points 504, 505
Sequencing 130
setbuf 509
setjmp 512
setjmp.h 512
setlocale 509
setvbuf 438, 515
Shell sort 222, 481
short 33, 398, 400, 529
Short-circuit operators 138
Shortcut operators 56
Shuffling cards 238
Side-effects 167
signal 509
signed 33, 398, 529
Significand 402
Significant characters 33
Significant digits 403
sin 59, 127, 167, 511
Sine 152
Single quotes 46
sinh 60, 511
Size of long values 60
size_t 308, 473, 509
sizeof 33, 325, 479, 504,
    529
Smalltalk 203
Software 3
    maintenance 109
    packages 3
    professional 3, 98
    quality 3
Sort
    bubble 222, 232, 475

insertion 235
merge 475
quick 222, 476
selection 222
Shell 222, 481
Sorting 212, 220, 280, 475
    using arrays for 212
Source 8, 455
Source code 8
Source file 447
Spaghetti code 148
Specification, functional 393
Specifications 10
Speed 8
sprintf 265, 266, 405, 515
    see also printf
sqrt 42, 57, 60, 167, 511
Square root function 57
srand 517
sscanf 265, 406, 515 see also
    scanf
Stack 384, 389, 391
    as ADT 385
Standard C function library 21
Standard library 19, 171
Standard library functions 509
Statements 19, 535
static 33, 447, 449, 529
Static duration 226
Static scope rules 446
Static storage 499
Static storage duration 449
stdarg.h 512
stddef.h 509
stderr 258
stdin 192, 257, 258
stdio.h 19, 21, 423, 431,
    512
stdlib.h 324, 516–518
stdout 257, 258
Stirling's formula 94
Storage
    auto 499
    binary 4
    secondary 7
    string 47
Storage class specifiers 499
Storage duration 449
Storage ranges 47
Storing data in files 240
strcat 269, 519
strchr 308, 520
strcmp 146, 460, 479, 519
strcoll 509
strcpy 48, 52, 163, 460, 519
strcspn 520
Streams 240
    predefined 257
strerror 520
strftime 521
String
    comparison functions 146
    functions 308

literals 41, 43, 44, 48, 531
  storage 47
string.h 147, 519
Strings 81, 162
  adjacent 459
  in macros 459
  input-output 104
  over multiple lines 43
strlen 520
strncat 269, 519
strncmp 147, 520
strncpy 519
strpbrk 308, 520
strrchr 308, 520
strspn 520
strstr 308, 309, 520
strtod 516
strtok 509
strtol 516
strtoul 516
struct 33, 274, 276, 331,
  332, 384, 500, 529
Structure 508
  of programs 16
  program 41, 185
Structured programming 148
Structured statements 133
Structures 279, 280, 285
  and pointers 312
  creating 276
Structuring data 274
Structuring the program 26
strxfrm 509
Stub functions 204
Subscript 212
Subscripting 212
Subscripts
  and pointers 308
  priority 504
Subtraction 55
Sums 76
switch 33, 140, 141, 148,
  529, 535
Syntax 33, 529
Syntax errors 9, 456
system 518
Systems analysis 4

T

Table 224
  hash 467
tan 59, 511
tanh 60, 511
Techniques, programming 4,
  148, 184, 204 *see also*
  Programming
Telescopes 2
Termination status 172

Test, loop 68
Testing 109
Tests 130
Text, printable 43
Text editor 7
Text files 240
Theory of Relativity 86
this 34, 529
Time 520, 521
time.h 520
time_t 520
tm, struct 520
tm_hour 521
tm_isdst 521
tm_mday 521
tm_min 521
tm_mon 521
tm_sec 521
tm_wday 521
tm_yday 521
tm_year 521
tmpfile 516
tmpnam 516
Token substitution 456
tolower 510
Top-down debugging 204
Top-down design 17
Top-down programming 184
Totals 76
toupper 510
Towers of Hanoi 38, 379
Tracing 72
Triangle
  area of 152
Trigonometric functions 57
Trigraphs 506
Truncation 58
Type 40
  data 40
Type demotion 408
Type promotion 406
typedef 33, 274, 275, 529
Types 275, 280
Types of loops 68

U

Underflow 408
ungetc 192, 516
union 33, 500, 508, 529
Universities 2
Unix 120, 266, 420
  sample session 491
Unix input-output 266
unsigned 33, 398, 400, 529
Unterminated comment 27
Update mode of fopen 436
User documentation 9
Users 9

V

va_arg 512
va_end 512
va_start 512
Value 41
  stored in a variable 47
Values 47, 507
Variable names 47
Variables 41, 42, 47–49, 81,
  82, 275
  automatic 42
  char 47
  global 41, 42
  incrementing 52
  int 47
  local 41, 42
  long 60
  pointer 241
  register 499
  simple 48
Vector 410
Vectors 285
Verification
  of program correctness 28
vfprintf 509
virtual 34, 529
void 33, 158, 529
void function names 26
void functions 22, 168, 169,
  172
void pointer 325
volatile 33, 501, 529
vprintf 509
vsprintf 509

W

wcstombs 509
wctomb 509
while 33, 69, 529, 535
Whitespace 19
  in macros 456
  scanf 101
Width
  in printf format 49
  in scanf formats 101, 106
Word 5
Word processing 2
Writing 98
Writing loops in C 69

Z

Zero of a function
  finding 153